Habsburg England

Studies in Medieval and Reformation Traditions

VOLUME 238

The titles published in this series are listed at *brill.com/smrt*

Habsburg England

Politics and Religion in the Reign of Philip I (1554–1558)

By

Gonzalo Velasco Berenguer

TUTA SUB AEGIDE PALLAS · 1683 ·

BRILL

LEIDEN | BOSTON

Cover illustration: Philip, king of England. Gold seal obverse. Archivio Apostolico Vaticano A. A., Arm. I–XVIII 522. This gold seal, showing King Philip enthroned as king of England, France, Naples and Jerusalem, was part of an official letter the monarch sent to Pope Paul IV in 1555 requesting the recognition of his sovereignty over the kingdoms of Naples and Jerusalem. Reproduced by courtesy of the Archivio Apostolico Vaticano.

Library of Congress Cataloging-in-Publication Data

Names: Velasco Berenguer, Gonzalo, author.
Title: Habsburg England : politics and religion in the reign of Philip I (1554-1558) / by Gonzalo Velasco Berenguer.
Description: Leiden ; Boston : Brill, [2023] | Series: Studies in medieval and Reformation traditions, 1573-4188 ; volume 238 | Note about subtitle: author uses Philip I (instead of Philip II) to show Philip as full king of England and not just a consort to Mary. | Includes bibliographical references and index.
Identifiers: LCCN 2022061077 (print) | LCCN 2022061078 (ebook) | ISBN 9789004421967 (hardback) | ISBN 9789004536210 (ebook)
Subjects: LCSH: Philip II, King of Spain, 1527-1598. | Philip II, King of Spain, 1527-1598—Marriage. | Mary I, Queen of England, 1516-1558. | Spain—History—Philip II, 1556-1598. | Great Britain—History—Mary I, 1553-1558. | Spain—Relations—Great Britain. | Great Britain—Relations—Spain.
Classification: LCC DP178 .V45 2023 (print) | LCC DP178 (ebook) | DDC 946/.043--dc23/eng/20230103
LC record available at https://lccn.loc.gov/2022061077
LC ebook record available at https://lccn.loc.gov/2022061078

Typeface for the Latin, Greek, and Cyrillic scripts: “Brill”. See and download: brill.com/brill-typeface.

ISSN 1573-4188
ISBN 978-90-04-42196-7 (hardback)
ISBN 978-90-04-53621-0 (e-book)

This book is printed on acid-free paper and produced in a sustainable manner.

Printed by Printforce, United Kingdom

To Colin, and to the success of Anglo-Spanish unions

Contents

Acknowledgements

There are many people to whom I am indebted for their unfaltering support throughout the years and for their encouragement to see me turn my Ph.D. dissertation into a monograph. The first of my many debts is owed to Madeleine Quinn, my history teacher at school, who first instilled the love for history in me with her inspirational lessons. It was during one of those lessons that I first came across the reign of Philip and Mary, and the topic has captivated me ever since. The fact that a king of Spain had also been a king of England seemed unfathomable (it is not, as the pages that follow will show) and this book is the eventual product of that initial early teenager curiosity. For opening that first door, I will always be grateful to her, as well as to my other history teachers at school, Marta Argüelles de Andrés and Rafael Rodrigo Fernández, who sustained and encouraged my passion.

The British-Spanish Society, together with Santander Universities, provided me with much-needed funds for my research. Special thanks go to Albert Jones, Luis Juste and Gloria, Baroness Hooper, the latter of whom took a particular interest in my project and kindly invited me to spend the day with her at the House of Lords in the autumn of 2013 – an experience I shall never forget. I would also like to thank the Mytton Scholarship scheme, the School of Humanities, and the Alumni Foundation at the University of Bristol, as well as the Catholic Record Society, all of which have also furnished me with valuable financial assistance to carry out my research at different stages. This book would have been impossible to write were it not for the indispensable assistance provided by the staff at the various archives and libraries that I have visited throughout the years. Special mention is owed to the always kind and effective help that Isabel Aguirre Landa, from the Archivo General de Simancas, never failed to offer, and to Tim Kirtley from Wadham College, Oxford, who, several years ago, generously made room in his office for me to read Pedro de Soto's *Defensio catholicae confessionis*. I am also indebted to everyone involved in getting the images for the monograph ready, especially to David Mason (The Royal Mint Museum), Nuria Moreu Toloba and her team (Museo de Artes Decorativas de Madrid) and Jorge San Juan Breña (Real Casa de la Moneda), who went out of their way to assist me, and to Dr Gabrielle Storey, who helped with the King's Bench illustrations.

My foremost academic debt is owed to Dr Fernando Cervantes, whom I had the immense privilege of having as my Ph.D. supervisor and who has always very generously assisted me with his knowledge, readily offering his inestimable guidance with no caveats, including – and especially – at the most difficult of times. Not only has he been my academic mentor before, during, and after my doctoral studies, but he has also become a very close friend, too. *La deuda y el afecto contraídos son inconmensurables*. Similarly, I would not have been able to bring this book to light without the brilliance and support of Professor Ronald Hutton who, with characteristic bonhomie, has always provided great advice, first as my second supervisor and later as my colleague, and has always made me question things from angles which I had not previously considered.

Professor Eamon Duffy and Professor Kenneth Austin both gave me invaluable guidance to develop my doctoral thesis into this monograph, and my knowledge and understanding of Philip and Mary's reign would have been much poorer without the warm recommendations, enthusiasm and encouragement of Dr John Edwards and Dr Alexander Samson, both of whom believed in my research from the beginning and generously put their expertise at my disposal, providing indispensable suggestions to the first draft. This gratefulness extends to Professor Suzannah Lipscomb, who also read the first version of the manuscript and provided vital observations and corrections, enriching the final result in the process. I would also like to thank Brill, and especially Ivo Romein, Gera van Bedaf and Arjan van Dijk, for their support and counsel and, especially, for their patience. And thanks, Ivo, because you always seemed to have the most pragmatic of solutions at hand whenever I started fretting. The comments made by the anonymous reviewer of the first manuscript version of this book were very positive and insightful and Professor Christopher Ocker, editor of the Studies in Medieval and Reformation Traditions series, showed me great support and encouragement. I am extremely grateful to both.

Many others have spurred me on my journey or have contributed with their insights, advice, proofreading, support or friendship to the completion of this book: Dr Hélder Carvalhal, Dr Anna Demoux, Dr Emily Derbyshire, the late Professor Sir John H. Elliott, Dr Elizabeth Evenden-Kenyon, Dr Steven M. Foster, Professor Enrique García Hernán, Claudia Gumm, Dr Andrew Hegarty, Dr Catherine Hunt, Dr Evan Jones, Dr Pamela Lock, Professor Giuseppe Marcocci, Professor José Antonio Martínez Torres, Dr Giuseppe Mrozek Eliszezynski, Dr Fernando J. Padilla Angulo, Dr Glyn Redworth, Dr John Reeks, Professor Ana Sáez-Hidalgo, Daniel Smith Ramos, Dr Richard Stone, Dr Nasim Tadghighi, Dr Alberto Viso Outeiriño, and many, many others. To all of them I am very grateful. I would also like to thank my fantastic colleagues at the Department of History in Bristol for being so welcoming, friendly, and inspirational – I am always in awe of all of you! I could not close this section without showing gratitude to my students, thanks to whom my job is a very enjoyable one and whose insights are often very valuable and stimulating.

Thanks are due, for bearing with me, to all my friends in Madrid and Bristol and to those scattered around the globe. Many of them have always known, even, perhaps, before I did, that history was my calling, and they did not cease to repeat it until I finally listened. Over the years they have put up with their friend always being very busy and they have done so with grace – I hope I am now making up for time lost.

I would like to conclude by thanking my family for their steadfast support and understanding. I want to pay tribute to my four grandparents, Gonzalo, Pilar, Manuel, and Teresa, all now sadly departed, for the fantastic examples they have all furnished me with. I cherish all the gifts that their generation bestowed upon mine and I will always miss them. Special thanks go to my parents, Gonzalo and Ana, for their unflinching support and encouragement throughout my entire life and for being the best role-models I could ever have hoped for. My sister Patricia is the epitome of strength and constancy and I am grateful for everything that she has taught me and for how loudly and hysterically she makes me laugh. *Os quiero muchísimo*. I would also like to thank my numerous aunts, uncles, and cousins for always being there for me. My beautiful English family welcomed me with open arms and has always made me feel at home. Thank you very much Karen, Verity, and Michael. Special tribute is owed to the children in the family, as they never fail to bring joy and happiness. Heartfelt thanks, therefore, go to my nieces and nephews, Isla, Mikey, Valentina, and Freddie, because they bring light to my days. Henry the Cocker Spaniel also deserves to be mentioned, for he has been the most faithful and reliable of research assistants (if not, perhaps, the most productive) and has often slept and snored by my side as I typed away.

Finally, my greatest debt of gratitude goes to my husband, Colin, who has believed in me since we first met and has never since wavered. He has generously accepted Philip and Mary as part of his life for the last few years and has managed to make room for them (at one point, quite literally, in the dining room, which I hijacked with my books and papers for years). To this most loyal, kind, and constant of men I dedicate this book (despite his entrenched refusal to watch *Becoming Elizabeth* with me). *Te quiero; siempre.*

Bristol, 18 August 2022

Figures and Tables

Figures

Tables

Abbreviations

AAV Archivio Apostolico Vaticano
AGS Archivo General de Simancas
APC *Acts of the Privy Council of England*, vols 4–6. Edited by John Roche Dasent. London: Her Majesty's Stationery Office, 1892–1893.
BAV Biblioteca Apostolica Vaticana
BL British Library
Carew Manuscripts *Calendar of the Carew Manuscripts, Preserved in the Archiepiscopal Library at Lambeth, 1515–1574*. Edited by J. S. Brewer and William Bullen. London: Public Record Office, 1867.
Chronicle of Jane and Mary *The Chronicle of Queen Jane, Two Years of Queen Mary, and Especially of the Rebellion of Sir Thomas Wyatt. By a Resident in the Tower of London*. Edited by John Gough Nichols. London: The Camden Society, 1850.
CODOIN *Colección de documentos inéditos para la Historia de España*, vol. 1 and 3. Edited by Martín Fernández Navarrete, Miguel Salvá and Pedro Sáinz de Baranda. Madrid: Viuda de Calero, 1842–3.
Correspondence Pole *The Correspondence of Reginald Pole*, 3 vols. Edited by Thomas F. Mayer. London and New York: Routledge: Taylor & Francis Group, 2003.
CPR *Calendar of the Patent Rolls Preserved in the Public Record Office. Prepared under the Superintendence of the Deputy Keeper of the Records. Philip and Mary*, 2 vols. Edited by M. S. Giuseppi. London: Public Record Office, 1936.
CSP Domestic *Calendar of State Papers, Domestic Series of the reign of Mary I, 1553–1558*. Edited by C. S. Knighton. London: Public Record Office, 1998.
CSP Spain *Calendar of Letters, Despatches and State Papers Relating to the Negotiations Between England and Spain Preserved in the Archives at Vienna, Simancas, Besançon, Brussels, Madrid and Lille* (vols. 10, 12 and 13). Edited by Royall Tyler. London: Her Majesty's Stationery Office, 1914–54.
CSP Venice *Calendar of State Papers and Manuscripts Existing in the Archives and Collections of Venice, and in Other Libraries of Northern Italy*, (vols. 5 and 6). Edited by Rawdon Brown. London: Her Majesty's Stationery Office, 1873–77.
HHL Hatfield House Library
ODNB Oxford Dictionary of National Biography

Papers of George Wyatt *The Papers of George Wyatt, Esquire of Boxley Abbey in the County of Kent, Son and Heir of Sir Thomas Wyatt the Younger. Camden Fourth Series, vol. 5. Edited by D. M. Loades. London: Royal Historical Society, 1968.*

RBME Real Biblioteca del Monasterio de El Escorial

RBPRM Real Biblioteca del Palacio Real de Madrid

Relations politiques *Relations politiques des Pays-Bas et de l'Angleterre, sous le règne de Philippe II*, vol. 1. Edited by Joseph, Baron Kervyn de Lettenhove. Brussels: F. Hayez/Académie Royale de Belgique, 1882.

TNA The National Archives

TPR *Tudor Royal Proclamations*, vol. 2, The Later Tudors, 1553–1587. Edited by Paul L. Hughes and James F. Larkin, eds. New Haven: Yale University Press, 1969.

Tudor Constitution *The Tudor Constitution: Documents and Commentary.* Edited by G. R. Elton. Cambridge: Cambridge University Press, 1965.

Note on the Text

Whenever possible, I have explored the primary material in its original form and language and have privileged printed volumes of letters and state papers edited in their original languages over translations in order to ensure as much accuracy as possible. Unless otherwise stated, therefore, all translations are my own. For the sake of clarity and transparency, and to provide further context, crucial and short passages translated into English in the main body of text have been added in their original forms as part of a footnote. Grammar and spelling have been left untouched except for modern accent marks in Spanish, French and Italian, which have been added to enhance readability. With regards to terminology, 'Spain' has been used at times as an umbrella term to designate the entire political entity (the composite monarchy) over which King Philip ruled but also to describe the geographical area that delimits the actual Spanish territory in a way that can be discerned from the context. Terms which convey the full extent and intent of the Spanish monarchical project, such as 'Spanish Monarchy' (*Monarquía Hispánica*) or 'Catholic Monarchy' (*Monarquía Católica*) have been used throughout, too. The term 'Spanish Empire' (*Imperio español*) has been generally avoided, as it does not fully convey the system of independent and interdependent states under a single monarch which defined the Spanish Monarchy and was not in use in the sixteenth century. With coherence and simplicity in mind, the terms used to describe those in each side of the religious divide have mostly been 'Catholic' and 'Protestant'. The myriad currents of thought and theological interpretations co-existing on both sides – as well as the different Protestant Churches – are fully acknowledged, but in the years leading up to and in the aftermath of the Peace of Augsburg of 1555, the term 'Protestant' had already begun to be appropriated by those reformers who had embraced an infrangible break with papal primacy.

Family Trees

1 The Habsburg-Trastámara Family

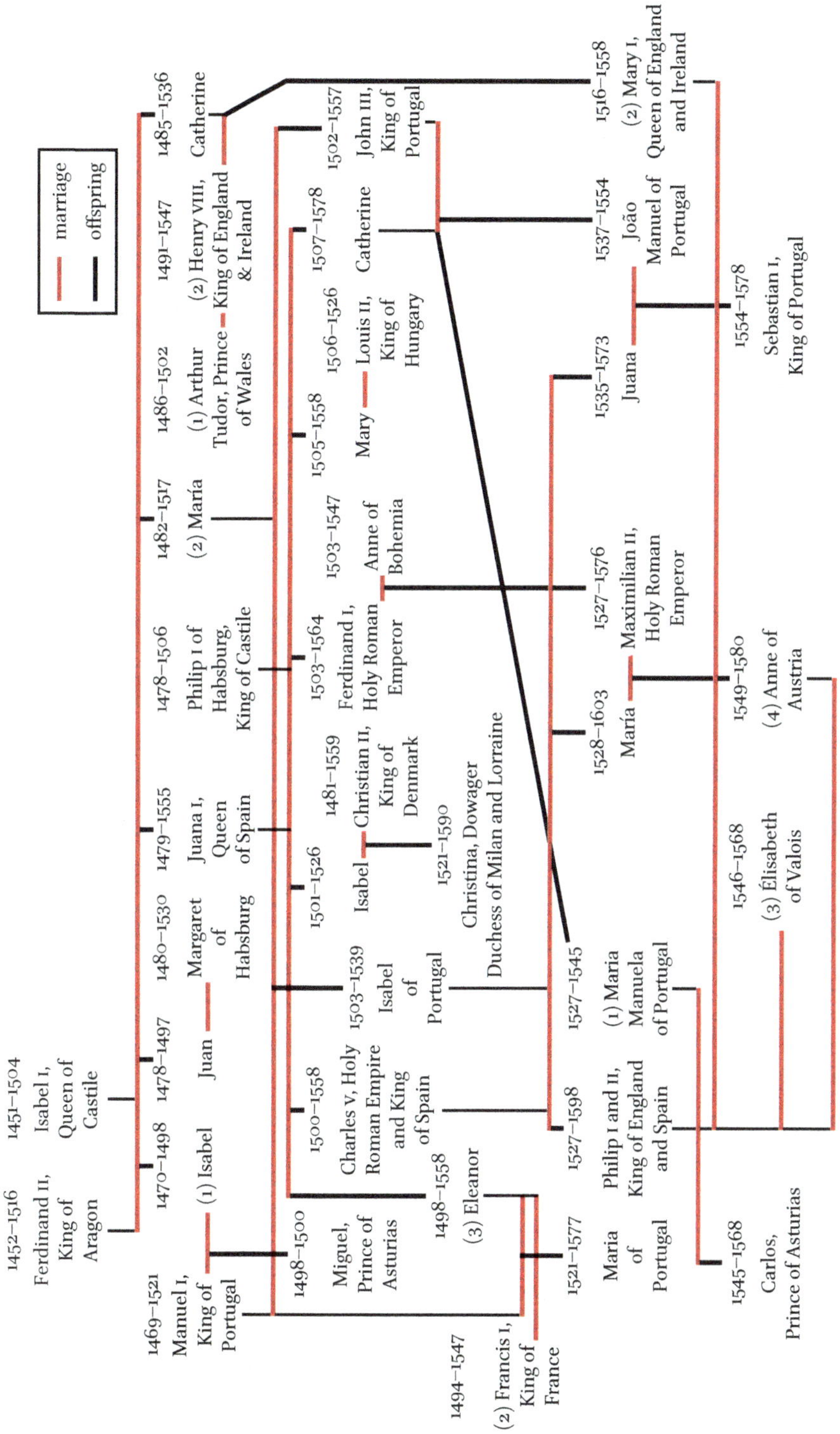

2 The Tudor Family

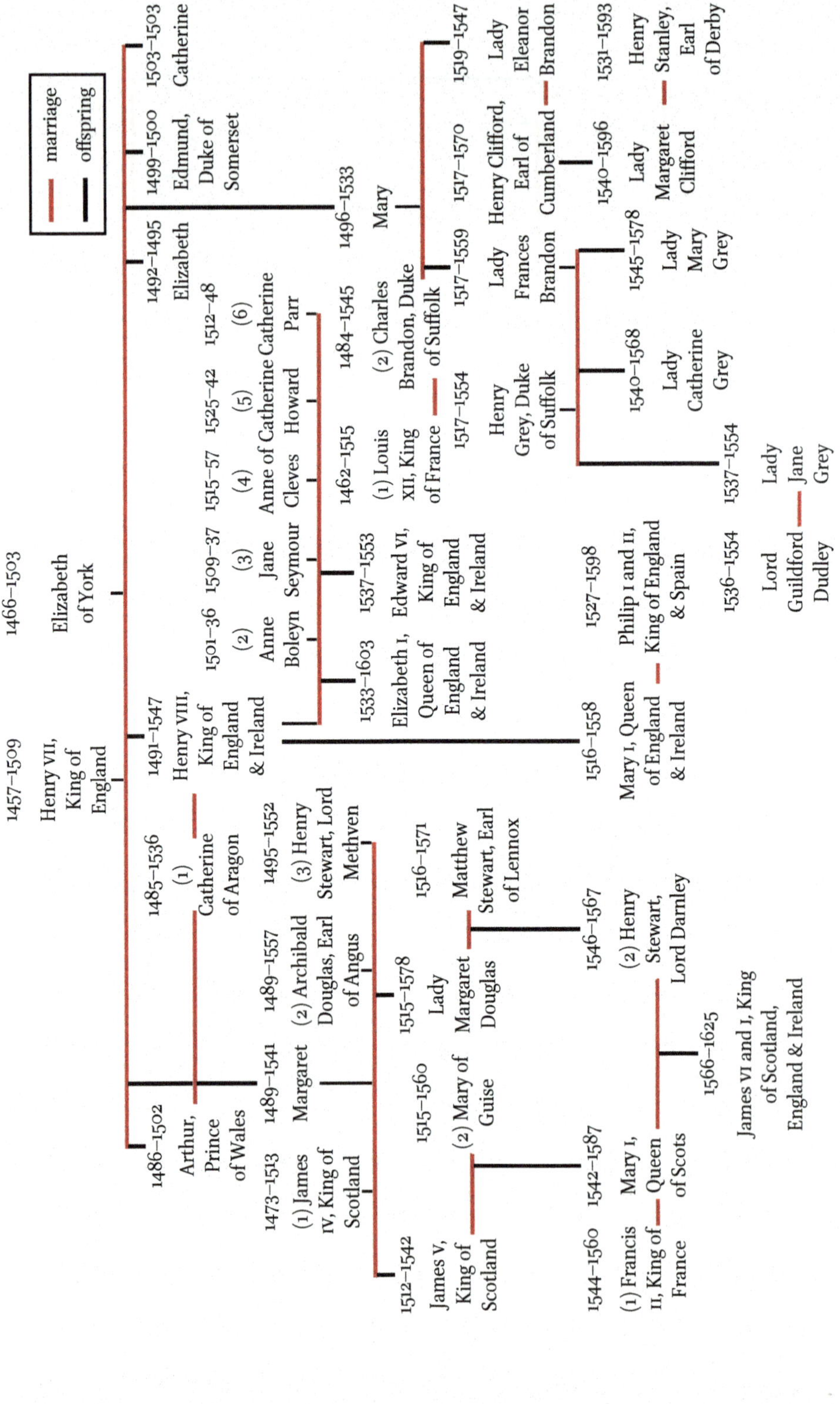

Introduction: A Reasonable Regret?

An analysis of the extensive literature available on the reign of Philip and Mary (1554–1558) will show that the historiography has been, until recently, consistently characterised by opposition. Either Mary and her reign were put in opposition against her sister and successor, Elizabeth I (r. 1558–1603), or they were put in opposition against her husband, Philip. In the first case, the achievements and successes of Elizabeth's reign are contrasted to the alleged failures and disappointments of Mary's.[1] Both sisters were eventually childless, but only to Mary does it correspond to carry the dubious (and uncharitable) honour of being branded a 'sterile' interlude in her country's history, a description engendered by A. F. Pollard (1869–1948) which has proven extremely resilient.[2] In similar vein, when historians sought to rehabilitate Mary's figure or bring balance to the study of her reign, this was often done at the expense of Philip's role as king of England. In this narrative, Philip was intensely disliked by Mary's court and by Mary's people, a dislike the Spanish king reciprocated. Unimpressed by a cold reception and his demotion as a mere king consort, we are told, he abandoned his wife and his new kingdom as soon as he could and only returned to plunge England into a disastrous war which cost the English Calais, their last Continental stronghold.[3]

Perhaps the scholar who most contributed to the blackening of the reign's reputation in modern times was James Anthony Froude (1818–1894), who thought that the queen had suffered from 'hysterical derangement'. Although initially kind and leading a frugal and respectful life, the treatment she suffered at the hands of her husband and her inability to conceive a child, among other failures of her life and reign, led Mary to insanity, and her 'madness was of a kind which placed her absolutely under her spiritual directors'. Froude targeted Stephen Gardiner, bishop of Winchester, and Cardinal Reginald Pole as the main perpetrators of Mary's cruel persecutions, but she, as queen, was to blame too. In Froude's view, therefore, Queen Mary became, simultaneously, a cruel persecutor and a hysterical woman who had no actual agency, for this corresponded to the men around her. Erroneously dating the infamous sobriquet with which she has been known, Bloody Mary, to her lifetime, Froude

1 Typical of this trend is G. R. Elton, *Reform and Reformation: England, 1509–1558* (London: Edward Arnold, 1977), 376–96.

2 A. F. Pollard, *The History of England from the accession of Edward VI to the death of Elizabeth* (London: Longmans/Greens, 1910), 172.

3 This perspective was strongly put forward by D. M. Loades, *The Reign of Mary Tudor: Politics, Government, and Religion in England, 1553–1558* (London: Ernest Benn, 1979), 138, 215, 243.

 | DOI:10.1163/9789004536210_002

explained that in five years 'she had swathed her name in the horrid epithet which will cling to it for ever' and that with her death and that of Pole the same day, 'the reign of the Pope in England, and the reign of terror, closed together'. Mary's great mistake was that she could not grasp the superiority of Protestantism over Catholicism and the innate moderation of the English character, for,

> Had Mary been content with mild repression, had she left the Pope to those who loved him, and married, instead of Philip, some English lord, the mass would have retained its place, the clergy in moderate form would have resumed their old authority, and the Reformation would have waited for a century.[4]

What this mild repression would have consisted of, who from among her own subjects should the queen have married or why the (Protestant) Reformation, so obvious a necessity in Froude's account, should have had to wait for another century are questions left unexplained, but his account became a blueprint for English-speaking historians of the reign for the rest of the nineteenth century and for most of the twentieth. If for Pollard the reign had been a 'sterile interlude', for S. T. Bindoff (1908–1980) it had been so disastrous at all levels – political, spiritual, economic, and intellectual – that all Marian England could do was to await 'the day of its deliverance'.[5] Even historians who sought to bring more balance to the study of Mary, like H. F. M. Prescott (1896–1972), whose biography of the queen was largely more sympathetic, concluded that, for all her achievements and failures, the queen remained a 'practical, housewifely little woman' whose 'mind was narrow and by no means acute'.[6] This stereotype has been picked up by many historians after her, most notably by G. R. Elton (1921–1994), who stated in what has become a famous remark, that Mary was 'arrogant, assertive, bigoted, stubborn, suspicious, and (not to put too fine a point on it) rather stupid'.[7] The fact that some of those very same

4 James Anthony Froude, *History of England: From the Fall of Wolsey to the Death of Elizabeth*, vol. 6 (New York: Scribner, Armstrong, and Co., 1875), 488–95.

5 S. T. Bindoff, *Tudor England* (London: Penguin, 1950), 182.

6 H. F. M. Prescott, *Mary Tudor: The Spanish Tudor* [1940] (London: Phoenix, 2003), 125.

7 G. R. Elton, *Reform and Reformation: England, 1509–1558* (London: Edward Arnold, 1977), 376. Elton's comment was remarkably similar to that made by the nineteenth-century Spanish liberal politician Fernando Garrido Tortosa (1821–1883), who claimed that Mary had been 'stubborn, superstitious, violent, cruel, fanatical, vengeful, despotic; all her actions bore the imprint of her natural instincts and those of her husband, each being worthy of the other'. ('Testaruda, supersticiosa, violenta, cruel, fanática, vengativa, despótica, todas sus acciones llevaron el sello de sus naturales instintos y de los de su esposo, dignos el uno del otro'). A

attitudes – assertiveness, stubbornness, and suspicion – are praised when it comes to assess Elizabeth's reign, bears witness to the one-sided scope of some of these works.[8]

It appears that, in this view, half of Mary's blood was the wrong blood, she married the wrong man, she restored the wrong religion, she chose the wrong war, and she wrongly murdered her own people. Little did it matter that Elizabeth similarly failed to secure the succession, that her own establishment of what she conceived as the right religion brought new divisions, tensions and persecutions within English society; that she involved herself in foreign wars which depleted her treasury and could have cost her dearly or that, like her sister Mary – and all other rulers of their time – she had a tendency to execute those subjects who conspired or rebelled against her.[9] Mary was a tragic, sad, abandoned and misguided woman, or a cruel and bloodthirsty tyrant who tried to avoid the inevitable by establishing a backward reaction and releasing her kingdom into the hands of the greedy and tyrannical Spaniards. Often, these two views are made to coincide. The queen's attempts to forestall the English Reformation have been interpreted as a mere interruption in Britain's glorious path to Protestantism; they failed due to their medieval impetus, their clumsy cruelty, and their pathetic emptiness. Most traditional historiographical approaches to Philip and Mary's reign saw it, therefore, as a glitch in England's history. It was perceived as an unmitigated and un-English disaster

fierce opponent of any ecclesiastical intervention in state affairs, it is noteworthy that Garrido Tortosa, when treating Thomas Cranmer's death, described the archbishop of Canterbury as a great persecutor himself, dismissing his gesture of burning the hand with which he had signed his recantation as mere hypocrisy. See Alfonso Torres de Castilla (pseudonym of Fernando Garrido Tortosa), *Historia de las persecuciones políticas y religiosas, ocurridas en Europa desde la Edad Media hasta nuestros días*, vol. 4 (Barcelona: Salvador Manero, 1865), 285–90, 297.

8 Many historians have made the assumption that Mary was intent on forcing her subjects to accept Spanish rule and Catholicism despite their patriotic resistance, which could only bring about the failure that the regime turned out to be. See, for instance, A. G. Dickens, *The English Reformation* [1964] (London and Glasgow: Collins/Fontana, 1972), 355–85; Loades, *Reign of Mary*, 458–72.

9 In the aftermath of the Northern Rebellion of 1569 alone, Elizabeth I ordered the execution by hanging, drawing, and quartering of 450 to 600 people (accounts differ on the numbers), the smaller figure being considerably larger than the number of people executed under Philip and Mary's heresy laws (284). See K. J. Kesselring, *The Northern Rebellion of 1569: Faith, Politics, and Protest in Elizabethan England* (Basingstoke and New York: Palgrave Macmillan 2007), 119–43. To those figures should be added the persecution of Catholics through fines, imprisonment, and death throughout the reign. The persecution and punishment of dissent was a common feature of early modern rulership, not a Marian peculiarity.

by those who understood the English Reformation as 'a movement of national liberation', to use Alexander Samson's apt expression.[10]

Apart from their apparent misogyny, these negative views were steeped in a long tradition which attacked the reign through the lenses of a growing Protestant national sentiment that saw Mary's life and reign as inimical to true English political, religious, and social values. The roots of this perception stemmed from contemporary understandings of the reign as propounded by Protestant critics. The Scottish clergyman John Knox, (*c.*1514–1572), who was busy destabilising the regime of Mary, Queen of Scots and her mother, Mary of Guise, published a treatise in 1558, his famous *The First Blast of the Trumpet against the Monstrous Regiment of Women*, which sought to prove that female rule was against God's laws. Although he did not shy away from criticising his own sovereign and her mother and regent, the main target of his work was Queen Mary of England. Knox explained that 'it is a thing moste repugnant to nature, to Goddes will and apointed ordinance, […] that a woman should be promoted to dominion or empire to reigne ouer man, be it in realme, natio[n], prouince or citie'. Female rule, he concluded, was 'a thing plainlie repugnant to good ordre, yea it is the subuersion of the same'.[11] There could be no better proof of this than Queen Mary, the 'cursed Iesabel of Engla[n]d', a 'horrible monstre' who had usurped authority in England against God's Word and had delivered her kingdom and people to 'proude ministres, pestilent papistes' and England's 'mortall enemie the spaniard'.[12]

John Foxe (1516–1587), the famous English martyrologist, published the first English edition of his *Acts and Monuments* (popularly known as the *Book of Martyrs*) in 1563, five years after Mary's death and Elizabeth's accession. His work would undergo four more editions between then and 1583, when the last version to be released in Foxe's lifetime was published. Foxe was not fiercely misogynistic in the way that Knox had been, because, unlike Mary, Queen of Scots, Queen Mary of England had a suitable Protestant replacement in the person of her sister Elizabeth, who was also, of course, a woman. Foxe was also careful not to be too critical of Mary herself, as this would have a negative impact on the crown which Elizabeth now incarnated and could bring negative attention to himself from the new queen too. By his 1570 edition, however, he had begun to include a reassessment of the reign with a description

10 Alexander Samson, *Mary and Philip: The Marriage of Tudor England and Habsburg Spain* (Manchester: Manchester University Press, 2020), 222.

11 John Knox, *The First Blast of the Trumpet Against the Monstrvovs Regiment of Women* (1558), f. 26^{r-v}.

12 Knox, *First Blast*, ff. 32^r, 55^r, 56^r.

of Mary's last days and death which have coloured all subsequent approaches to the reign. First, the chapter's title promised to recount to the reader 'the vnprosperous successe of thinges vnder Queene Mary' and proceeded to explain the 'great afflictions' which had befallen the realm during her reign, 'wherin so many me[n], women, and children were burned, many imprisoned and in prisons starued, diuers exiled, some spoyled of goods and possessions'.[13] In Mary's time, he added, children were made fatherless and fathers were deprived of their wives and children. England, however, had been delivered of this 'bloudy persecution' when Mary died on 17 November 1558. Foxe's description of Mary's last hours is full of some of the tropes that have formed the basis of Mary's reputation as a sad and tragic figure. Many thought that 'she dyed of thought and sorow' and, when asked by her close confidants if her sadness was due to Philip's abandonment, she retorted that 'Not that onely [...] but when I am dead & opened, you shall find Calyce [Calais] lying in my hart'.[14] Foxe claimed that the exchange had taken place between the queen and her trusted servants and friends David ap Rhys and Susan Clarencieux, and that he had heard it first-hand from someone who had in turn heard it first-hand from Ap Rhys. This dramatic anecdote is no more than courtly gossip conveyed eleven years later by an author who was ostensibly hostile to Mary and her regime and is far from being historical fact, yet it has come to represent the accepted version of Mary's reign – tragic, futile, sad. However, Foxe's boldest statement was reserved for his conclusion on Mary's 'vnprosperous' reign:

> Of which Queene this truly may be affirmed and left in story for a perpetuall memoriall or epitaph, for all Kinges and Queenes that shall succede her to be noted, that before her neuer was read in story of any Kyng or Queene in England since the tyme of kyng Lucius, vnder whom in tyme of peace, by hangyng, headyng, burnyng, and prisoning, so much Christian bloud, so many Englishmens liues were spilled within this Realme, as vnder the sayd Queene Mary for the space of foure yeares was to be seene, and I besech the Lord neuer may be seene hereafter.[15]

Mary was a negative mirror image in which her sister, and all future English monarchs, could reflect themselves. To do the contrary of what Mary had done

13 John Foxe, *The First Volume of the Ecclesiasticall history contaynyng the Actes and Monumentes of thynges passed in eyery kynges tyme in this Realme, especially in the Church of England principally to be noted* (...) (London: John Day, 1570) [henceforth A&M, 1570], 2336.

14 A&M, 1570, 2336–7.

15 A&M, 1570, 2337.

was a recipe for success. It did not matter that Philip and Mary's regime did not see Protestantism as a peaceful endeavour, but as a heretical rebellion which brought dissension to the realm (as we shall see), nor that a quick glance at the numbers of those executed during or in the aftermaths of the Pilgrimage of Grace under Henry VIII (216), the Prayer Book rebellion under Edward VI (more than 4,000), or the Rising of the North under Elizabeth I (450 to 650) – to give but a few examples in which religion was unmistakably a factor – were either similar or greatly surpassed the number of victims of Philip and Mary's campaign against heresy (284).[16]

This coupling of Mary and Philip to a 'bloody' reputation was not immediately taken for granted, however. In fact, the first instance of the term Bloody Mary does not appear until 1658, in a work titled *The Infancy of the World* by the Presbyterian minister Nicholas Billingsley (1633–1709). In his poem, 'The Praise of Nothing', Billingsley pondered about the futility of some of humankind's undertakings and, after wondering what had become of William the Conqueror's feats, he asked himself 'Where's bloody *Mary*, and *Elizabeth*, / Of blessed memory, but kil'd by death'.[17] The efforts of great princes may be futile in the face of death and the passing of time, but whereas Elizabeth's legacy was one 'of blessed memory' Mary's was 'bloody'. In 1681 the cleric Gilbert Burnet (1641–1715) would claim that her reign had opened the eyes of the English to the cruelty of 'popery' and the 'uneasie Yoak of Spanish Government'. He continued:

> The *Genius* of the *English* leads them to hate Cruelty and Tyranny; and when they saw these were the necessary Concomitants of Popery, no wonder it was thrown with so general an agreement, that there was scarce any considerable Opposition made to it, except by some few of their Clergy.[18]

---

16 Madeleine Hope Dodds and Ruth Dodds, *The Pilgrimage of Grace, 1536–1537 and the Exeter Conspiracy, 1538*, vol. II (Cambridge: Cambridge University Press, 1915), 226; Anthony Fletcher and Diarmaid MacCulloch, *Tudor Rebellions* [1968] (Abingdon and New York: Routledge, 2016), 59–60, 107–8; Kesselring, *Northern Rebellion*, 119–43.

17 Nicholas Billingsley, *Kosmobrephia, or the Infancy of the World: With and Appendix of Gods Resting Day, Eden Garden; Mans Happiness Before, Misery After, his Fall* (London: Robert Crofts, 1658), 76. Thomas S. Freeman, who identified Billingsley's work as containing the first mention of the sobriquet in print, has reconstructed perceptions of Mary from the second half of the seventeenth century. See his 'Inventing Bloody Mary: Perceptions of Mary Tudor from the Restoration to the Twentieth Century', in Susan Doran and Thomas S. Freeman, eds., *Mary Tudor: Old and New Perspectives* (New York: Palgrave Macmillan, 2011), 78–100.

18 Gilbert Burnet, *The History of the Reformation of the Church of England. In Two Parts*, part II (London: T. H. for Richard Chiswell, 1683), preface and 370–71.

The inherent cruelty of the Catholic religion, of the primacy of Rome and of Spanish rule were, therefore, elements of Philip and Mary's reign which went against the very nature of the English. This, in turn, explained why, from Burnet's perspective, they had not survived. The English had a particular sixth sense, a 'genius' that allowed them to discern good government, which other peoples did not possess. The trend continued unabated and, by the early nineteenth century, this version was so widespread that it was used as ammunition in polemics against Catholic Emancipation in 1826.[19] In 1851, the English nonconformist Edwin Paxton Hood (1820–1885) wrote a scathing biography of the queen, ominously titled *The Dark Days of Queen Mary*, in which he stated that anyone who found 'any redeeming points' in Mary's character 'must have sharp eyes, or a moral squint'.[20] As Isabel of Castile's granddaughter, Catherine of Aragon's daughter, and Charles V's cousin, it was no wonder that Mary had always turned to Spain. She was, Hood contended, 'by temperament and character more truly Spanish than English'.[21] Philip and Mary had been a perfect match in their 'cruel and most unscrupulous advancement of the Roman Catholic Cause' and in their 'gloomy, morose, ascetic' characters.[22] The unnatural connection established by Mary with the land of her maternal ancestors had made the queen as unpopular as her 'Smithfield fires' and 'extortion and knavery were the leading principles of her political, as persecution and Popery were of her religious policy'. These negative characteristics often went together and Spanish history, Hood claimed, 'most abundantly illustrates this'.[23]

Not all assessments of Mary and her reign were entirely negative, however, and scholars like Patrick Fraser Tytler (1791–1849), the Strickland sisters, Agnes (1796–1874) and Elizabeth (1794–1875), or Sir Frederick Madden (1801–73), all provided positive accounts of the queen's character and reign, even if they condemned the persecution or her marriage to Philip.[24] The works by J. M. Stone

---

19 See, for instance, the anonymous pamphlet *An Address to Electors, on Their Duty as Englishmen, or the Triumph of British Right over Infidel & Papal Tyranny* (Whitby: R. Rodgers, 1826), 3.

20 Edwin Paxton Hood, *The Dark Days of Queen Mary* (London: Partridge & Oakey, 1851), 209.

21 Hood, *Dark Days*, 87.

22 Hood, *Dark Days*, 108–9.

23 Hood, *Dark Days*, 117–8.

24 Patrick Fraser Tytler, *England under the Reigns of Edward VI, and Mary, with the Contemporary History of Europe, Illustrated in a Series of Original Letters Never Before Printed. With Historical Introductions and Biographical and Critical Notes*, vol. 1 (London: Richard Bentley, 1839), 49–50; Frederick Madden, *Privy Purse Expenses of the Princess Mary, Daughter of King Henry the Eighth, Afterwards Queen Mary: with a Memoir of the Princess, and Notes* (London: William Pickering, 1831), 15–16, 170; Agnes Strickland, *Lives of the Queens of England, from the Norman Conquest; with Anecdotes of Their Courts, Now First Published from Official Records and other Authentic Documents, Private as Well as Public,*

(1854–1908), *Mary I, Queen of England* (1901) and Beatrice White (1902–1986), *Mary Tudor* (1935), also went in this direction, even if they still viewed Mary as a practical housewife who suffered, in White's words, from 'a fatal lack of that subtle appeal that awakens popular sympathies'.[25] In 1940, Prescott published her *Spanish Tudor*, already mentioned above, which also portrayed a more sympathetic picture of Mary and her reign, and this direction crystallised in the second half of the twentieth century – especially after the 1970s – in the contributions of some historians who were looking at the reign through a more balanced lens. Explaining away the reign in Whiggish teleological terms as an 'interlude' before the arrival of true Protestant English values would simply not do anymore.

D. M. Loades (1934–2016) began his lifelong work on the queen and her reign with the publication, in 1965, of his study of the Wyatt rebellion and the Dudley conspiracy, in which he claimed that although Mary had many good qualities and, indeed, good policies, her decision to marry Philip gave ground to widespread opposition which the regime never managed to dilute. It was the first of a series of wrong decisions which undid what had started as a promising reign.[26] Loades' next major contribution was his *The Reign of Mary Tudor* (1979), which provided a comprehensive account of the reign with an outstanding use of domestic and foreign primary material. His conclusions, however, were still coloured by the traditional historiographical assumption that the marriage to Philip and the persecution were disastrous policies which cost the queen her popularity, a thesis that Loades always maintained with little variation.[27] Other significant contributions were made, among many others, by Jennifer Loach (1945–1995) and Robert Tittler, who argued for Mary's capability in managing parliament, council and court, and Eamon Duffy, John Edwards, Christopher Haigh, Peter Marshall, Rex Pogson, and William Wizeman

---

vol. 5 (London: Henry Colburn, 1842), 382, 420–22. Although in need of updating, the best assessment on the existing historiography on Mary up to the 1980s in the English language is to be found in David Loades, 'The Reign of Mary Tudor: Historiography and Research', *Albion: A Quarterly Journal Concerned with British Studies* 21, no. 4 (1989), 547–58. The latest reappraisal of Marian historiography can be found in Alberto Viso, 'Historiografía reciente sobre el reinado de María Tudor', *Espacio, Tiempo y Forma* 27 (2014), 327–51.

25 J. M. Stone, *Mary I, Queen of England. As Found in the Public Records, Despatches of Ambassadors in Original Private Letters, and Other Contemporary Documents* (London: Sands & Co., 1901), 476–92; Beatrice White, *Mary Tudor* (London: Macmillan, 1935), vii.

26 D. M. Loades, *Two Tudor Conspiracies* (Cambridge: Cambridge University Press, 1965).

27 Loades, *Reign of Mary*, 458–72; David Loades, *The Religious Culture of Marian England* (London: Pickering & Chatto, 2010), 155; David Loades, *Mary Tudor* (The Hill, Stroud: Amberley, 2011), 258–71.

(1964–2010), who have generally argued for a successful and vibrant – even if not always unproblematic – revival of Catholicism under Philip and Mary.[28]

This renewed interest has brought new vistas to the fore. Among them, for example, is the realisation that Elizabeth's language of power and conceptualisation of her authority owed more to Mary than has been hitherto recognised. Many of the symbols, imagery, gestures, and words chosen by Elizabeth were greatly influenced by her elder sister's experience.[29] In these new explorations of Mary's life and reign, the sad, abandoned housewife or the cruel, murderous tyrant of previous centuries disappeared, and a new Mary emerged. England's first queen regnant had received a careful humanist education and from a very young age she had been exposed to the intricacies of power and court intrigue, especially after Henry VIII's repudiation of Catherine of Aragon. She had fiercely defended her right to hear the Latin Mass and eventually became the visible head of opposition against the regime of John Dudley, duke of Northumberland, during the reign of her brother, Edward VI.[30] She harboured Catholics and conservative malcontents and, after an aborted attempt to flee to the safety of the Spanish Netherlands in 1551, she weaved an important Catholic network that would aid her when, in 1553, Northumberland tried to seize the throne for his daughter-in-law, Lady Jane Grey, Mary's cousin, after Edward's death on 6 July. In those crucial days, Mary, with help from her

28 Jennifer Loach and Robert Tittler, eds., *The Mid-Tudor Polity, c. 1540–1560* (London: Macmillan, 1980); Robert Tittler, *The Reign of Mary I* (London: Longman, 1983); Jennifer Loach, *Parliament and the Crown in the Reign of Mary Tudor* (Oxford: Oxford University Press, 1986); Rex Pogson, 'Revival and reform in Mary Tudor's church: A question of money', *Journal of Ecclesiastical History*, vol. 25 (1974), 249–65, Eamon Duffy, *The Stripping of the Altars: Traditional Religion in England, c.1400–c.1580* (New Haven and London: Yale University Press, 1992), 524–64; Christopher Haigh, *English Reformations: Religion, Politics and Society under the Tudors* (Oxford: Oxford University Press, 1993), 203–34; Peter Marshall, *Reformation England, 1480–1642* [2003] (London: Bloomsbury Academic, 2012), 93–120; William Wizeman, SJ, *The Theology and Spirituality of Mary Tudor's Church* (Aldershot and Burlington: Ashgate, 2006); William Wizeman, SJ, 'The Religious Policy of Mary I', in Doran and Freeman, *Old and New Perspectives*, 153–70. John Edwards has treated Marian religiosity throughout his works (as will be surveyed below), but it is especially prominent in his *Archbishop Pole* (Farnham: Ashgate, 2014).

29 Paulina Kewes, 'Two Queens, One Inventory: The Lives of Mary and Elizabeth Tudor' in Kevin Sharpe and Steven Zwicker, eds., *Writing Lives: Biography and Textuality, Identity and Representation in Early Modern England* (Oxford: Oxford University Press, 2008), 187–207; Judith Richards, 'Examples and Admonitions: What Mary Demonstrated for Elizabeth' and Paulina Kewes, 'Godly Queens: The Royal Iconographies of Mary and Elizabeth' in Alice Hunt and Anna Whitelock, eds., *Tudor Queenship: The Reigns of Mary and Elizabeth* (New York: Palgrave Macmillan, 2010), 31–45, 47–62.

30 John Edwards, *Mary I: England's Catholic Queen* (New Haven and London: Yale University Press, 2011), 1–17; 38–55.

networks, organised resistance to the Grey coup and recruited an army to which Northumberland's troops soon defected. Proclaimed queen on 19 July 1553, she triumphantly entered London on 3 August.[31] This was not the meek little housewife of popular imagery, but a courageous woman and a shrewd politician who opened the path of female sovereignty in England even if that path had been full of obstacles.[32] The culmination of this trend was the publication, in 2011, of *Mary I: England's Catholic Queen*, John Edwards' biography of the queen, the most comprehensive reassessment of Mary's life to date. Philip's figure as king of England and the insertion of England within the structure of the Spanish Monarchy remain, however, grossly underexplored.

For centuries, Philip's reign in England has been widely ignored in the historiographical debate. Although Martin A. S. Hume (1847–1910) published an article on Philip's stay in England in 1892, the subject remained largely unknown throughout most of the twentieth century.[33] When the king's figure attracted the attention of historians, it was usually to point out his inadequacy as a partner for Mary and his unworthiness to sit on the throne of England. In general, historians have tended to see the Spanish marriage as a great mistake for the Marian regime, a view epitomised in Owen Chadwick's (1916–2015) conclusion that it was 'the most disastrous act of the reign'.[34] Henry Kamen, in his 1997 work *Philip of Spain*, claimed that Philip was largely uninterested in English domestic affairs and that during his first stay in England he 'devoted himself closely to the politics of Spain, Italy and America'.[35] For all its richness in primary sources, the late Manuel Fernández Álvarez's (1921–2010) 1998

31 Edwards, *Mary I*, 87–122; Loades, *Reign of Mary*, 70–4; insight into the same events from the point of view of Lady Jane Grey is provided in Eric Ives, *Lady Jane Grey: A Tudor Mystery* (Oxford: Wiley-Blackwell, 2009), 248–78 and Leanda de Lisle, *The Sisters Who Would Be Queen: The Tragedy of Mary, Katherine and Lady Jane Grey* (London: Harper Press 2008), 112–24.

32 Two of the most recent biographies of the queen, which seek to bring balance into the debate are those by Linda Porter, *The First Queen of England: The Myth of "Bloody Mary"* (Great Britain: Portrait, 2007), re-edited as *Mary Tudor: The First Queen* (London: Piaktus, 2009), and Anna Whitelock, *Mary Tudor: England's First Queen* (London: Bloomsbury, 2009). A recent reassessment of the queen's life and reign is that by the French scholar Isabelle Fernandes, who has also stressed Mary's courage and the effect of Protestant propaganda in the blackening of her name. See Isabelle Fernandes, *Marie Tudor. La souffrance du pouvoir* (Paris: Tallandier, 2012). John Edwards has also published a short biography of the queen in recent years. See his *Mary I: The Daughter of Time* (London: Allen Lane, 2016).

33 Martin A. S. Hume, 'The Visit of Philip II', *The English Historical Review*, vol. 7, no. 26 (1892), 253–80.

34 Owen Chadwick, *The Reformation* [1964] (London: Penguin Books, 1990), 123.

35 Henry Kamen, *Philip of Spain* (New Haven and London: Yale University Press, 1997), 59.

Felipe II y su tiempo fails to grasp the importance of the event, providing us with a very superficial account of the period, even though he devotes a whole chapter to the marriage.[36] In María Jesús Pérez Martín's (1931–2006) posthumous work, *María Tudor. La gran reina desconocida* (2008), a rather conventional account of the Anglo-Spanish marriage was presented which added little to the historiographical debate; it portrays Philip as the indifferent husband who unscrupulously abandoned his ailing wife.[37] Sarah Duncan has brilliantly reconstructed the world, the court, and the gendered spaces inhabited, negotiated and manipulated by Mary, but her conclusions on Philip's alleged limited role owe much to previous assumptions that the measures designed to curtail his power in 1554 were still in place at the end of the reign in 1558.[38] In similar vein, and despite his incisive exploration of the complexities of the reign, David Loades considered that Philip, as king of England, had been a 'failure'.[39]

An attempt has recently been made by Harry Kelsey to bring Philip back to the limelight in the English context. His 2012 work, *Philip of Spain, King of England: The Forgotten Sovereign* deserves praise for the pains taken to go back to the Spanish original manuscripts, avoiding too heavy a reliance on the translations of the Calendars. His conclusions, however, are disappointing, as he claimed that Philip's role as king of England was not as successful as it could have been because he 'could not bring himself to accept a secondary role' and because his training had not taught him 'that a king should love his wife'.[40] Royal marriages in the early modern period were not made in the pursuit of personal happiness and romantic love as understood in the twenty-first century, but with the aim of obtaining diplomatic, political, financial, and dynastic advantages. This was perfectly understood by Philip. The king's confidant, Ruy Gómez de Silva, explained unchivalrously in a letter to Francisco de Eraso, Charles V's secretary, that Queen Mary was old and thin and, to add to his caddish remarks, he lamented that 'much help from God will be needed to swallow this cup'. However, after this salacious comment about his master's sexual life, he felt compelled to explain that, fortunately, 'the king sees and understands

36 Manuel Fernández Álvarez, *Felipe II y su tiempo* [1998] (Pozuelo de Alarcón: Espasa, 2006), 741–59.

37 María Jesús Pérez Martín, *María Tudor. La gran reina desconocida* (Madrid: Rialp, 2008), 679–82, 783, 835.

38 Sarah Duncan, *Mary I: Gender, Power, and Ceremony in the Reign of England's First Queen* (New York: Palgrave Macmillan, 2012), *passim* but especially 98–101.

39 David Loades, 'Philip II and the government of England', in Claire Cross, David Loades and J. J. Scarisbrick, eds., *Law and Government under the Tudors: Essays Presented to Sir Geoffrey Elton on his retirement* (Cambridge: Cambridge University Press, 1988), 177–94.

40 Harry Kelsey, *Philip of Spain, King of England: The Forgotten Sovereign* (London and New York: I. B. Tauris, 2012), 152.

that it was not for the flesh that this marriage was made, but for the remedy of this kingdom [England] and for the conservation of those estates [the Low Countries]'.[41]

The narratives accusing Philip of being uninterested in English affairs and of ignoring and abandoning his English wife, now so ingrained in the historiography, can be shown to derive from inaccurate translations in the Calendars. The epitome of this perceived slackness on Philip's part is an often-quoted passage that he wrote to his sister Juana, dowager princess of Portugal and regent of Spain, on 4 December 1558, after he received the news of Mary's death. These lines were translated by Royall Tyler (1884–1953) as follows:

> The Calais question cannot be settled so soon, now that the Queen, my wife, is dead. May God have received her in His glory! I felt a reasonable regret for her death. I shall miss her, even on this account. I have given my agreement to the prolongation of the truce, in order not to break off with the French.[42]

This quotation, with special emphasis on the words 'reasonable regret for her death', has been repeatedly inserted in works dealing with Philip and Mary's reign – both academic and popular – and has become the point of reference to assess their marriage, relationship, and joint rule.[43] In many ways, it has come to be a metaphor for the reign, often used as one of the closing statements in works surveying the topic to stress, in Foxe-like fashion, the alleged failure of Mary's undertakings. She had fought against her councillors and her people and had faced a dangerous rebellion to marry a man who not only

41 AGS, Estado 808, leg. 143. Ruy Gómez de Silva to Francisco de Eraso, Winchester, 29 July 1554: 'La princesa de portugal enbió vn gran presente a la rreyna de vestidos y tocados y la rreyna los estuuo mjrando y olgándose con ellos de manera q[ue] agora no a acabado paréçeme q[ue] si vsase n[uest]ros vestidos y tocados q[ue] se le pareçería menos la vegez y la flaq[ue]za para hablar verdad con v[uestra] m[erced] mucho dios es menester para tragar este cáliz y así tengo hechas grandes preparaçiones de mj parte y lo mejor del negoçio es q[ue] el rey lo ve y entiende q[ue] no por la carne se hizo este casamy[en]to sino por el rremiedio deste rreyno y conservaçión desos estados [...]'.

42 CSP Spain, vol. 13, 440.

43 See, for instance, Carolly Erickson, *Bloody Mary* (Garden City, N.Y.: Doubleday, 1978), 483; David Loades, *Mary Tudor: A Life* (Oxford: Oxford University Press, 1989), 311; Elizabeth Longford, *The Oxford Book of Royal Anecdotes* (Oxford: Oxford University Press, 1989), 231; Alison Weir, *Children of England: The Heirs of King Henry VIII, 1547–1558* (London: Jonathan Cape, 1996), 364; Maureen Waller, *Sovereign Ladies: The Six Reigning Queens of England* (New York: John Murray, 2006), 109; Whitelock, *Mary Tudor*, 303; Margaret Scard, *Tudor Survivor: The Life and Times of William Paulet* (Stroud: The History Press, 2011), 195, to name but a few.

abandoned her in her time of need, but who also displayed such a nonchalant, even callous, attitude at the news of her death. The whole affair, some of these works seem to tell us, can only be seen as an episode that we should reasonably regret. This dramatic quotation, which has proven so popular is, in fact, a mistranslation. Tyler took the Spanish expression *quanto es razón*, which conveys a meaning of justice or righteousness, to mean 'reasonable', and he mistook the transitive construction *hará falta* (to need someone or something) for the transitive locution *echar en falta* (to notice the absence of someone or something, to miss). A more accurate rendition of Philip's remarks would be:

> The question of Calais could not be negotiated quickly, especially now that the most serene queen, my wife, is dead. May she be in God's glory, for I have felt it as much as is to be expected and even in this matter I would have much needed her. I therefore resolved to agree in the said suspension in order not to break the talks, leaving them thus pending.[44]

It may not be an outpouring of emotion on the death of a spouse, but Philip's letters seldom were. Furthermore, the letter does not only indicate the king's commitment to the retrieval of Calais (a commitment not reciprocated by the privy council or, as it would turn out, by Queen Elizabeth herself) but also that he had been saddened by Mary's death and, crucially, that in the negotiations with the French which would eventually lead to the peace of Cateau-Cambrésis in 1559, he 'would have much needed her'. This suggests that the couple had enjoyed a good political partnership and that their co-monarchy had been a success. In fact, throughout their marriage, there was only one irreconcilable disagreement between the two when Philip insistently sought to marry off Elizabeth to his cousin, Duke Emmanuel Philibert of Savoy and Mary, surprisingly, sided with her sister and prevented the wedding from happening.[45]

---

44 AGS, Estado 516, leg. 86; King Philip to Juana of Austria, Monastery of Grunendal, 4 December 1558: '[…] Visto que lo de calés no se podía negoçiar tan presto espeçialmente con ser Muerta la ser[enísi]ma reyna mi muger que aya gloria que lo he sentido quanto es razón que aun para esto me hará mucha falta, me ha paresçido de venir en lo de la dicha suspensión por no romper la plática y que quede todavía pendiente […]'.

45 It is unclear why Mary refused to contemplate Elizabeth's marriage. In a heartfelt letter, Mary explained to her husband that she had been against a marriage for Elizabeth ever since her sister had been born and that she did not understand Philip's insistence, although she did not provide further details as to why she would not contemplate it. When Philip returned to England in 1557, he tried again in person and also through his sister Margaret of Parma and his cousin Christina of Denmark, but Mary's opposition and Elizabeth's strong refusal made him desist. Whether Mary could not contemplate the daughter of Anne Boleyn bearing the children that she had been unable to conceive,

Perhaps Philip and Mary's marriage had not been the love match of the century, but in sixteenth-century high politics that was hardly a concern. What mattered was what Philip's words suggest; that is, that the brief union of the English and Spanish crowns had been successful.

Besides, there is no reason to believe that they did not enjoy a good personal relationship. Despite the age difference – Mary was eleven years Philip's senior – and Ruy Gómez de Silva's and others' uncharitable comments about Mary's looks, there is no indication in Philip's correspondence that he was displeased by her, and we know that she was very happy with him.[46] After the wedding it was reported that the king was most solicitous to his new wife and they were seen being affectionate and warm towards each other in public. It is again Silva, and again not very tastefully, who reports on this, as he claimed that the king,

> entertains the queen very well and he knows how to ignore that which is not very good in her for the senses of the flesh. He keeps her so happy that the other day, them being alone, she uttered love words to him, and he corresponded in like fashion.[47]

Stories have circulated about Philip's alleged indiscretions. One such account is Philip's attempt to reach Lady Magdalen Dacre with his hand through a window whilst she was washing, an advance that Lady Dacre would have rejected

---

or whether she was trying to find ways to disinherit her sister is difficult to know, but the disagreement caused a great deal of tension between the spouses. By refusing to force Elizabeth into the marriage with the duke of Savoy, Mary lost her last chance to ensure that England would remain within the Catholic and Spanish spheres of influence. Edwards, *Mary I*, 323–4; Samson, *Mary and Philip*, 174–5.

46 Philip seems never to have made his thoughts known on the matter, one way or the other. Ruy Gómez de Silva clearly found Mary irredeemably unattractive, but others did not agree. In 1557, when she was forty-one, the Venetian ambassador, Giovanni Michieli, wrote that '[h]er face is well formed, as shown by her features and lineaments, and as seen by her portraits. When younger she was considered, not merely tolerably handsome, but of beauty exceeding mediocrity. At present, with the exception of some wrinkles, caused more by anxieties than by age, which makes her appear some years older, her aspect, for the rest, is very grave'. See CSP Venice, vol. 6, 1054. In any case, the physical attributes of either wife or husband, which are subjective anyway, would not have precluded them from having a good marital relationship.

47 AGS, Estado 808, leg. 143; Ruy Gómez de Silva to Francisco de Eraso, Richmond, 12 August 1554: 'el rrey […] entretiene muy bien a la rreyna y sabe muy bien pasar lo q[ue] no es bueno en ella para la sensualidad de la carne y tiénela tan contenta q[ue] çierto estando el otro día ellos dos a solas casi le dezía ella amores y él rrespondía por los consonantes'.

by striking him with a stick.[48] We are also told that in 1557, in a fit of jealousy for the deference and affection that Philip showed his cousin Christina of Denmark, dowager duchess of Lorraine, who was then visiting in London, Queen Mary tore one of his portraits to pieces with her own hands.[49] Neither of these stories are, however, contemporary to the events they refer to. The anecdote that involves Philip and Lady Dacre only surfaced for the first time in the 1609 biography of the latter, who was to become Viscountess Montague, written by Richard Smith (1568–1655), titular bishop of Chalcedon. Not only had Smith been born fourteen years after the event he alleged had taken place between King Philip and Lady Dacre but, also, both Philip and the lady in question were dead by the time the biography was published. With regards to the episode of Mary's alleged destruction of Philip's portrait in a fit of jealousy, it was recounted by the Strickland sisters in 1842, who in turn quoted James Granger's (1723–1776) *A Biographical History of England*.[50] Granger recounts the anecdote as coming from *The Life of Sir Thomas Pope* (1772) by Thomas Warton (1728–1790) but, although Warton does mention Mary's jealousy towards Philip's relationship with Christina of Denmark, he does not mention the portrait episode.[51] Even if we allowed for the veracity of these two anecdotes, and to take them at face value would be a stretch of the historian's endeavour, given their problematic origins, this would still not necessarily mean that Philip and Mary did not enjoy a fulfilling personal relationship as husband and wife. Not only did they share a common Spanish heritage, but they were also both very devout Catholics and had a keen interest in religion and theology. The pair had received careful humanist educations and were enthusiastic patrons of the arts. There is also plenty of evidence that they revelled in dances, parties and other court ceremonies and they both had a very strong sense of duty which translated in an indefatigable work ethic – the two of them sat at their desks to transact business for hours every day, sometimes working into the early hours of the morning.[52]

48 Richard Smith, *The Life of the Most Honovrable and Vertvovs Lady the Lady Magdalen Viscovntesse Montagve*, trans. By C. F. [1609] (Saint-Omer: English College Press, 1627), 19–20.

49 Strickland, *Lives of the Queens of England*, v, 436–7.

50 James Granger, *A Biographical History of England, from Egbert the Great to the Revolution*, vol. 1 [1769] (London: William Baynes and Son, 1824), 213.

51 Thomas Warton, *The Life of Sir Thomas Pope, Founder of Trinity College Oxford* [1772] (London: Thomas Cadell, 1780), 105–8.

52 On their work ethic see, for Philip, Geoffrey Parker, *Imprudent King: A New Life of Philip II* (New Haven and London: Yale University Press, 2014), xvii, 113–17 and CSP Venice, vol. 5, 533 for Mary, where Giacomo Soranzo, the Venetian ambassador, says of the queen that 'she rises at daybreak, when, after saying her prayers and hearing mass in private, she

In any case, their marriage meant much more than whatever their relationship as a couple amounted to. This was no mere royal marriage, but a true union of the Spanish and English crowns. It is time to eschew the title of 'king consort' which the literature usually ascribes to Philip, for it represents a concept that did not exist, as their rulership was conceived and enacted as a joint-monarchy. This was acknowledged by contemporaries, as we shall see, and reflected in parliamentary acts, which included both monarchs' names together with their respective regnal years.[53] This was the case because Philip was not a 'prince consort' in the way that husbands of regnant queens have been in the United Kingdom since the reign of Queen Anne (r. 1702–1714), mainly carrying out ceremonial and supportive roles. Nor was he a 'king consort' (*rey consorte*) like Francisco de Asís de Borbón (1822–1902) was to Queen Isabel II of Spain (r. 1833–1868) in the nineteenth century, a courtesy title for the queen's husband who, besides some ceremonial and patronage duties, had little else to do in an official capacity.[54]

It is important to remember that, at the time of Philip's accession to the throne of Spain in 1556, when he was already married to Mary, theirs was the fifth consecutive co-monarchy in the Spanish kingdoms. Mary's grandparents and Philip's great-grandparents, Ferdinand and Isabel (r. 1474–1504), were followed by Philip I and Juana I (r. 1504–1506), then by Juana and Ferdinand (r. 1506–1516) and, finally, by Juana and Charles (r. 1516–1555). Even if the latter two associations had been legally dubious and formed by a father and daughter and mother and son respectively, rather than by husband and wife like the first two, it is telling that Philip and Mary's marriage was conceived in the way that it was and at the time that it was. Mary's childless death in 1558 ended the trend, and theirs was Spain's last co-monarchy. Not so, however, in England, where the last was formed by William III and Mary II (r. 1689–1694). Although this second joint rulership was engendered in very different circumstances

---

transacts business incessantly, until after midnight, when she retires to rest; for she chooses to give audience not only to all the members of her Privy Council, and to hear from them every detail of public business, but also to all other persons who ask it of her'.

53 That it was conceived in this way is borne out by the existence of King Philip's portrait which adorns the Prince's Chamber in the House of Lords, occupying the place that corresponds him in the gallery of portraits of Tudor monarchs between Mary and Elizabeth. The decoration of the Prince's Chamber was undertaken in 1854 by the students of the Royal School of Art, under the direction of Richard Burchett. I am grateful to the Baroness Hooper, who pointed out to me the existence of this portrait and kindly invited me to visit the House of Lords to see it for myself in October 2013.

54 On the role of Spain's only king consort, Francisco de Asís de Borbón, see Isabel Burdiel, *Isabel II. Una biografía* (Madrid: Taurus, 2010), *passim* but especially 203–7, 223–30, 429–46, 749–55.

and had very different aims, it is nevertheless noteworthy that the only two co-monarchies that England has ever had have both been with rulers of the Low Countries. This fact is crucial to understand the motivations for Philip and Mary's marriage. Indeed, the link to the Low Countries was very attractive for both parties. For Spain, a firm alliance with England ensured that the Netherlandish inheritance would remain in Spanish hands. For England, the cultural and commercial ties with their neighbours from across the Channel would be strengthened and, if children were born of the marriage, they would be poised to inherit England, Ireland, and the Low Countries (and if Philip's son, the Infante Carlos, died, the whole Spanish inheritance, too).

The marriage was also crucial to Spain because the acquisition of England and Ireland added new territories to the Habsburgs' expansive monarchy. In this sense, perhaps the most incisive of early modern Protestant criticisms of the marriage came amidst the debates surrounding another – ultimately failed – Anglo-Spanish match, that between Charles Stuart, prince of Wales, heir to James VI and I (r. 1603–1625) and the Infanta María Ana of Spain, sister to Philip IV of Spain (r. 1621–1665). In John Reynolds' (*c.*1588–*c.*1625) *Vox Cœli, or Newes from Heaven* (1624), an imaginary party composed of Henry VIII, Edward VI, Henry Stuart, prince of Wales, Queen Mary, Queen Elizabeth, and Anne of Denmark get together in heaven to discuss the convenience of the Spanish match of 1623. Reynolds' fictional Mary is alone in promoting it, epitomising what was to become the predominant view in England about Spanish imperialistic designs. Here is her reply to Edward VI's complaints about the Castilian taking of Navarre in 1512:

> O but Nauarre lay fit and commodious for the Prouinces of old Castile, Biscay, and Galicia, besides, the Kings of Spaine are the Catholique Kings, and therefore it is both proper and naturall for them to be Vniuersall.[55]

Moving on to different subjects, Mary closes one of the discussions by stating that, had she become a mother, 'England had beene long since a Prouince of Spaine'.[56] The implications of this statement are clear and, although written decades after the marriage, no one in the 1550s would have doubted that, had Mary had any children by Philip, the Tudor dynasty would have come to an

55 John Reynolds, *Vox Cœli, or Newes from Heaven, of a consvltation there held by the high and mighty Princes King Hen.8. King Edw.6. Prince Henry. Queene Mary. Queene Elizabeth, and Queene Anne; wherein Spaines ambition and treacheries to most Kingdomes and free Estates of Evrope, are vnmask'd and truly represented* [...] (London: William Jones, 1624), 4.

56 Reynolds, *Vox Cœli*, E.6.

end, to be replaced by the Habsburgs. These points are crucial to the understanding of early modern anxieties over emerging nationalities and the concept of *monarchia universalis* or universal monarchy to which the Habsburgs aspired. With these remarks, Reynolds did something which a great deal of the subsequent historiography on the matter has not done; he looked at the motivations of the marriage from the Spanish point of view.

Moving away from the Anglocentric views which have characterised most approaches to the topic, this book seeks to redress the imbalance enunciated in the preceding pages. There have been recent works which have looked at the reign from more positive and stimulating angles, on which this book will expand. In John Edwards' biography of Mary, Philip is not the reluctant and helpless king consort anymore, but a young humanist prince who was active in his role as king of England. Edwards has really brought to the fore, not only that Philip was not the gloomy ogre of Protestant imagery but, also, that together with Mary he brought England back to the limelight of European politics in what he has called England's attempt at 'European integration'.[57] Similarly, Alexander Samson has rediscovered a king who was earnestly involved in the government of England and that the reign fostered a period of creative cultural exchange between both kingdoms which would outlive the regime. England and Spain were not, Samson found, the caricature-like antagonistic enemies of old, but two countries which admired each other and exerted considerable cultural and economic influence on a mutual basis.[58]

Drawing from these new perspectives, the present work is the first fully to explore England's position as an integral part of the Spanish Monarchy (commonly known as the Spanish Empire) during the reign of Philip I of England and II of Spain. The book is divided into two thematic sections, each consisting of three chapters. The first three chapters look at the conceptualisation of the Anglo-Spanish co-monarchy from the Spanish point of view and how this framing translated into different attitudes and expressions of power. This first section, therefore, pays full attention to the Spanish idea of empire, a 'composite monarchy' founded upon the concept of *monarchia universalis* (universal monarchy), and the way England was envisaged to fit within this structure. Contemporary critics of the marriage were concerned that a foreign prince would alter the laws and customs of the realm, yet the Habsburgs were very

57 Edwards, *Mary I*, *passim* but especially 159–225.

58 Samson, *Mary and Philip*, *passim*. Other relevant reassessments of the joint reign that have looked at it in the wider European context are to be found in, for instance, M. J. Rodríguez-Salgado, *The Changing Face of Empire: Charles V, Philip II and Habsburg Authority, 1551–1559* (Cambridge: Cambridge University Press, 1988), 79–94, 183–5, 305–25 and Parker, *Imprudent King*, 41–58.

aware of national sensibilities and the need to preserve local laws to ensure the correct functioning of the Monarchy by avoiding dissent and rebellion. This realisation stemmed, in part, from the anxieties born out of the Comunero revolt that Charles V had faced in 1520–1521 but, also, from the ideological foundations of the Habsburg conceptualisation of the Spanish Monarchy, which recognised in the king of Spain the best candidate for universal monarchy. This concept and the notions of community which influenced it are given full attention in the first chapter.

In February 1554, Mary faced a rebellion which was ostensibly aimed at preventing her marriage to Philip. Commonly known as the Wyatt rebellion after one of its main leaders, Sir Thomas Wyatt, it actually involved four different rebellions in the south of England which ultimately failed. The rebels always claimed that they had risen against the idea of having a foreign king because they understood it as an invasion and an alteration of England's laws and customs. The rebels' Protestant credentials, however, have not received the attention they deserve but they have been fully addressed in the second chapter. There also exists a myth that the coexistence between the Spanish and the English once the marriage took place in July 1554, was marred by constant conflict and violence. The two nations were, in this view, simply not destined to understand each other. Although it is undeniable that there were clashes between both nations, there was also plenty of room for friendship and collaboration too and this topic is explored thoroughly in the same chapter, including a survey of the Anglo-Spanish commission of justice that was set up to quell discord. Finally, in the third chapter, the Anglo-Spanish court that emerged from the marriage is given full attention. Representations of Philip are studied to show how he was depicted and imagined as king of England. There is a persisting view that Philip's capacity to exert patronage had been seriously curtailed in the marriage treaty and that, therefore, he was somewhat isolated from his English courtiers. In this chapter this view is challenged to show that he not only exerted patronage, but, also, that this patronage extended into Elizabeth I's reign. Other topics which are also investigated in this section include diplomatic relations and the place of England in Spanish diplomacy, the campaign to win over those who had originally been against the Spanish marriage and the creation of the select council.

The second thematic section of the book looks at the religious aspects of the reign. The secular aspiration to universal monarchy of the Habsburgs was underpinned by the association of Spain to the Catholic Church, the *ecclesia universalis* (universal Church). The most important task faced by Philip as king of England was to reconcile the kingdom to Rome. England had been in schism since Henry VIII had first defied the papacy in the 1530s and bringing her back to the Catholic fold was Philip and Mary's most pressing matter, a challenge they surmounted in an emotional ceremony of reconciliation in parliament on 30 November 1554. In 1561, three years after Mary's death and the end of his reign in England, Philip reminisced that it had been thanks to his actions as king that God had granted the great gift of opening the eyes of the English 'and thus subduing that kingdom, in our time and through our hand, to the true path and to obedience and union with the Holy Roman Church'.[59] A few years later, in 1570, in the context of Elizabeth I's excommunication by Pope Pius V (r. 1566–72), and displeased that the pope had kept him in the dark about the process, Philip would repeat the claim. In an incensed letter to the duke of Alba he explained his frustration at the bull's narrative:

> When referring to how that kingdom was subdued and the subsequent obedience it gave to the Apostolic See in times of Queen Mary, my wife (may she be in glory), he only mentions her, without mentioning me when, as you know, I was the head and main instrument in that affair.[60]

These assertions by King Philip will be put to the test in the fourth chapter of the book, with an extensive exploration of his role and agency in the process of reconciliation with Rome. If A. G. Dickens claimed that Mary 'failed to discover the Counter-Reformation' and Eamon Duffy that her regime, in a sense, 'invented' it, this book will argue that the reforming and vibrant impetus of Marian Catholicism owed much to the Spanish element present within it.[61] Although the religious aspects of the reign were absolutely central to the

---

59 François Mignet, *Histoire de Marie Stuart*, vol. 1 (Paris: Bonaventure et Ducessois, 1852), 444: '[...] lo qual dimos por bien empleado con la merced que Dios nos havía hecho en abrir los ojos a los de aquel reino y haverse reducido, en nuestro tiempo y por nyestro medio, al verdadero camino y a la obediencia y gremio de la Santa Iglesia Romana [...]'.

60 AGS, Estado 544, leg. 21, King Philip to Fernando Álvarez de Toledo, duke of Alba, El Escorial, 30 June 1570: 'Y no menos ay bien que mirar en la forma del Breue de la priuación de la Reyna, señaladamente en la narrativa, que tratando de la redutión que se hizo de aquel Reyno y la obediencia que dio a la sede Ap[ostóli]ca en tiempo de la Reyna María, mi mujer que aya Gloria, hace mención della solam[en]te y ninguna de mí, hauiendo sido yo la cabeça y el principal Instrumento (como sabéis) [...]'. For the excommunication process and Philip's reaction to it see Gonzalo Velasco Berenguer, 'Reigning in the Highest Places: The Excommunication of Queen Elizabeth I in Its Roman and Spanish Contexts', *Sixteenth Century Journal*, 51, no. 3 (2020), 763–90. The most comprehensive analysis of the excommunication and its implications in England is the to be found in Aislinn Muller, *The Excommunication of Elizabeth I: Faith, Politics, and Resistance in Post-Reformation England, 1570–1603* (Leiden: Brill, 2020).

61 Dickens, *English Reformation*, 384; Eamon Duffy, *Fires of Faith: Catholic England under Mary Tudor* (New Haven and London: Yale University Press, 2009), 207.

monarchical project of Philip and Mary, their study has also suffered from the Anglocentric lens that has been used to study the secular aspects of the reign. Paradoxically, even though the presence of Spanish theologians in England has generally been acknowledged, their roles have been strangely neglected. The study of Marian religiosity has been characterised by its focus on a supposed insularity of the Catholicism revitalised by Mary and it has even been claimed that it imported no foreign ideas.[62]

Some works, however, have strongly questioned these views. José Ignacio Tellechea Idígoras (1928–2008) dedicated his life to the research of Bartolomé de Carranza (1503–1576), the famous archbishop of Toledo who would be embroiled in a decades-long inquisitorial process and was a key figure in the revitalisation of Catholicism under Philip and Mary. John Edwards has expanded on this topic and, from their research, Carranza's centrality in religious matters during the reign has been firmly established.[63] However, very little is known of the other Spanish men who were in England and, in one way or another, contributed to Marian Catholicism – men like the Franciscan Alfonso de Castro (1495–1558), who wrote two of the most utilised contemporary manuals against heresy, and the Dominicans Pedro de Soto (1493–1563) and Juan de Villagarcía (1529–1564), both lecturers at Oxford. Full attention is given to the theology that these men brought to England and its links and similarities with the theology of their English counterparts in the fifth chapter.

Finally, the book deals with the approaches taken by Philip and Mary's regime to tackle the problem of heresy. The persecution of Protestants has been central to most assessments of the reign and it will be, therefore, crucial, to explore the full extent of Spanish influence and involvement in it and the ramifications of such an involvement. As is well known, and as dramatically recounted by John

62 Ellen A. Macek, *The Loyal Opposition: Tudor Traditionalist Polemics, 1535–1558* (New York: Peter Lang, 1996), 163–84; Lucy E. C. Wooding, *Rethinking Catholicism in Reformation England* (Oxford: Oxford University Press, 2000), 150–1, 179–80.

63 Among Tellechea's many findings was the fact that Carranza was not only active in the restoration, but he also influenced and was in turn influenced by the religiosity of Marian England. His blueprint for a visitation of the diocese of Toledo, for instance, was extremely similar to the visitation process envisaged by the English Synod of 1556 and this, in turn, had been heavily influenced by Tridentine guidelines. See José Ignacio Tellechea Idígoras, *Fray Bartolomé Carranza y el Cardenal Pole. Un navarro en la restauración católica de Inglaterra (1554–1558)* (Pamplona: Diputación Foral de Navarra/Institución Príncipe de Viana/Consejo Superior de Investigaciones Científicas, 1977), 303–51. John Edwards has surveyed Carranza's reformed Catholicism and his plans for England in the context of its revitalisation. See John Edwards, 'Fray Bartolomé Carranza's Blueprint for a Reformed Catholic Church in England', in Thomas F. Mayer, ed., *Reforming Reformation* (Farnham: Ashgate, 2012), 141–60.

Foxe in his *Acts and Monuments*, during the reign 284 men and women were sent to the flames, accused of holding heretical beliefs. Traditionally, this has been interpreted as having been as big a mistake for Mary as the Spanish marriage was and one which cost the queen and Catholicism any popularity they had left in England. Eamon Duffy argued in 2009 that, on the contrary, the persecution of religious dissent was a tested means to eradicate what was seen as a destabilising element within the community. Staying aloof from twenty-first century sensibilities, Duffy contended that, far from being a disastrous decision, the persecution worked well and was largely winning the battle against Protestantism in England by the end of Philip and Mary's reign.[64] This book expands on this topic by looking at Anglo-Spanish notions of what constituted heresy and how heretics were equated to rebels against God and prince. It is seldom noticed that, at the same time as the Marian persecution was taking place, the regency government in Spain launched its own campaign against pockets of Protestants in Valladolid and Seville.[65] The persecution in Spain is, therefore, given full attention in the sixth and last chapter, for its contemporaneity to the English campaign against heresy was no mere coincidence.

The reader will find no detailed assessments of the war with France and the papacy, the fall of Calais, the Dudley conspiracy, or the relationship between Philip, the Spanish, and reformed Catholicism with Ireland. The first three topics have been left out because they have already been explored elsewhere and this book had different priorities.[66] The latter subject, because, unfortunately, it is beyond the scope of this study, but it is undoubtedly one of the least

64 Duffy, *Fires of Faith*, 171–87.

65 An exception to this neglect is John Edwards, who has written an article on the links between the persecution of heresy in England and in Valladolid in which he reveals, among other things, Carranza's influence in the burning of the bones of heretics at the English universities. See John Edwards, 'The Spanish Inquisition Refashioned: The Experience of Mary I's England and the Valladolid Tribunal, 1559', *Hispanic Research Journal*, 13, no. 1, 41–54.

66 The most incisive account of the war with France and the papacy is still that by C. S. L. Davies, 'England and the French War, 1557–1559', in Loach and Tittler, *Mid-Tudor Polity*, 159–85. Glyn Redworth has recently challenged previous claims that the participation of the English in the war was negligible in 'Where Were the English? Antoon van den Wijngaerde, the Evidence of Visual Culture, and the 1557 Siege of Saint-Quentin', in Ana Sáez-Hidalgo and Berta Cano-Echevarría, eds., *Exile, Diplomacy and Texts: Exchanges between Iberia and the British Isles, 1500–1767* (Leiden: Brill, 2021), 15–31. See also Loades, *Reign of Mary*, 365–427; Rodríguez-Salgado, *Changing Face of Empire*, 137–252; Parker, *Felipe II*, 143–54; Edwards, *Mary I*, 266–322. For Sir Henry Dudley's conspiracy of 1556, although there is probably justification for a future reappraisal of the subject, see Loades, *Two Tudor Conspiracies*, 176–237; Loades, *Reign of Mary*, 234–6, 241, 245, 249, 265–6, 278, 281–2.

explored of Philip and Mary's reign; an absence in the historiography which deserves future redress.[67]

Ultimately, this book seeks to bring some much-needed balance to the historiographical debate surrounding Philip of Spain's rule as king of England and to correct some of the misunderstandings that have marred previous interpretations of the reign. By placing England within the orbit of the Habsburgs as an integral part of the Spanish Monarchy and not as an unwilling and unnatural partner, I seek to understand the precise ideological, political, religious, and social mechanisms that the marriage set in motion. For four brief years, England and Ireland were two more of the many territories integrating the empire of the Spanish Habsburgs, and it is imperative that the reign is finally explored from this angle. This is, primarily, what this book aims to do. This work is, therefore, an historical assessment of Philip's role as king of England and Catholic monarch and of how the crown he briefly acquired through his marriage to Mary I fitted into the wider world of the Spanish Monarchy and the Catholic Reformation.

67 Some work has been done on the relationship between Catholicism and the English and Irish crowns, although the subject is still in need of further exploration and the link with Spain is still to be studied. See James Murray, *Enforcing the English Reformation in Ireland: Clerical Resistance and Political Conflict in the Diocese of Dublin* (Cambridge: Cambridge University Press, 2009), 204–41; Steven G. Ellis, *Tudor Ireland: Crown, Community and the Conflict of Cultures, 1470–1603* (London and New York: Longman, 1985), 209–10. For the relationship of Philip II with Ireland after his time as king (a brief exploration of his tenure is offered in the first chapter), see Enrique García Hernán, *Irlanda y el Rey Prudente* (Madrid: Ediciones del Laberinto, 2000).

CHAPTER 1

Monarchia universalis: England and Spanish Imperial Ideology

Until recently, approaches to the reign of Mary I and her marriage to King Philip had reached a consensus that has certain resonance with a letter sent by Ruy Gómez de Silva to Francisco de Eraso from London on 23 August 1554, barely a month after the wedding:

> They [the members of the privy council] are divided, as I believe I have already told your worship. Some of them follow the king's party and others follow the queen's, but the king conducts himself so well towards all of them that they are all happy with him. The emperor has always written to his son encouraging him to uphold this business, for [...] the queen is a very able woman but not as much as we had been told in terms of government. The ambassador [Simon Renard] does not only leave business unsolved, but he also obstructs it. We should be enlightened by him and yet he leaves us in the dark. However, I do not blame him, but whoever sent a man of his quality to such an event as the arrangement of so important a marriage without including a Spaniard in the business.[1]

The picture painted by Philip's Portuguese-born confidant and councillor has coloured subsequent interpretations of the marriage and the reign of Philip and Mary. According to this view the Spaniards were stuck in a country ridden with factions and mismanagement due to Mary's lack of experience and good judgement and they had to deal with an inefficient and troublesome Flemish ambassador who had constantly meddled in Spanish affairs. Gómez de Silva's

1 AGS, Estado 808, no. 141. Ruy Gómez de Silva to Francisco de Eraso; London, 23 August 1554: '[...] ellos se an partido como creo q[ue] tengo escrito a v[uestra] m[erced] los vnos quieren la banda del rey y los otros la de la reyna mas el rey se a también con todos q[ue] a cada vno tiene contento. Siempre escriuía el enperador a su hijo esforçándole a la sustentación deste negoçio porq[ue] como tengo escrito la reyna es muy buena cosa mas no p[ar]a tanto como nos dezían digo en quanto a gobierno y el enbaxador no resuelue negoçio ninguno antes mete confusión en algunos y siendo él del q[ue] nos tendríamos de alumbrar podría dezir q[ue] nos trae a escuras mas no le pongo culpa a él sino a quien enbió a vna cosa tan grande como a concertar vn matrimonio como este a vn onbre de su calidad sin meter en este negoçio vn poco de vn español'.

 | DOI:10.1163/9789004536210_003

comment about the lack of Spanish influence in the marriage negotiations has had a profound impact in the way historians have interpreted the period, with a tendency to view the whole affair in strictly Anglo-Burgundian terms. From this perspective, the negotiations were carried out entirely by Charles v and Mary, with a reluctant Philip acquiescing when the marriage was presented as a *fait accompli*, an attitude which set the tone for his future disregard for England and his English queen.[2] The only thing that interested the English was, therefore, the links to Flanders and its commerce and the centuries-old relationship between the English crown and the House of Burgundy. Alexander Samson has recently shown this supposed marginalisation of Philip and the Spanish to be untrue. Philip's *mayordomo*, Diego de Acevedo, had been in England since the late spring of 1553 and had witnessed Mary's accession and coronation, even writing an incisive narrative of the events to his wife. In addition, Philip had sent one of his favourites, Íñigo de Mendoza y Mendoza, to congratulate Mary on her accession and to establish independent communications with her in the summer of 1553. The prince was certainly not unaware of the negotiations or their evolution.[3] When Mary died in 1558, Philip instructed Gómez Suárez de Figueroa, count of Feria, who was then representing him in London, to burn all his private correspondence with the deceased queen, so it is plausible that their communications during this period were more regular than previously thought.[4] A closer scrutiny also reveals a stronger Spanish influence, as we shall see. Indeed, the anxiety experienced by the English was very similar to that experienced by Castilians when Ferdinand and Isabel married in 1469, or when Charles of Ghent arrived in Spain as her king in 1517, bringing with him a large retinue of Flemings whom he quickly placed in some of the highest offices of the realm. There is therefore a glaring need to explore the extent to which recent Spanish history might have influenced the drawing up of the marriage treaty and how the Spanish idea of empire, the 'composite monarchy', could accommodate to English sensibilities. Unless conquered in war (and even then, the notion could be qualified), it was usually the assumption of Spanish monarchs that the union of territories was an association based on

2 See, for instance, G. R. Elton, *England under the Tudors* [1955] (London: Methuen, 1974), 215–18; D. M. Loades, *The Reign of Mary Tudor: Politics, Government, and Religion in England, 1553–1558* (London: Ernest Benn, 1979), 111–12, 128–39.

3 Alexander Samson, *Mary and Philip: The Marriage of Tudor England and Habsburg Spain* (Manchester: Manchester University Press, 2020), 34, 61–3.

4 In fact, the burning of private correspondence was common practice for Philip after the death of a spouse – only two personal letters from any of his four wives survive. Both are draft letters of delicate topics written by Queen Mary. See Geoffrey Parker, *Imprudent King: A New Life of Philip II* (New Haven and London: Yale University Press: 2014), 382.

the principle of *aeque principaliter* (equally important), for the sustenance of which the observance of native laws and respect for native institutions was crucial and it was in this context that Philip and Mary's marriage, and the union of their crowns, took place.[5]

1.1 Mary's Accession and the Centrality of Community

Different historians have agreed that Mary's accession saw an explosion of joy among the population of England.[6] John Seton (*c.*1498–1567), a Catholic priest who would end his days in Rome, wrote a treatise to thank God for Mary's victory in which he compared her to the Virgin Mary, and which included a poem to celebrate Christ's real presence in the Eucharist. This was one among several other publications to commemorate the event.[7] Even Protestants, such as Richard Taverner (1505–1575) and Richard Beeard († after 1574), congratulated the queen, the latter even encouraging her to continue to 'buyld the house, and fortresse vp / Of trewe religion'.[8] In the Spanish world, the news of her victory was widely celebrated, and imperial propaganda soon set out to publish works

5 The term 'composite monarchy' was coined by H. G. Koenigsberger in 1975 and has been amply studied by the late John H. Elliott, who has been its most convincing supporter. See H. G. Koenigsberger, *Politicians and Virtuosi: Essays in Early Modern History* (London: A & C Black, 1986), 1–26; John H. Elliott, 'A Europe of Composite Monarchies' in his *Spain, Europe & the Wider World, 1500–1800* (New Haven and London: Yale University Press, 2009), 3–24.

6 On the accession of Mary and her popularity see, for example, John Edwards, *Mary I: England's Catholic Queen* (New Haven and London: Yale University Press, 2011), 98–100; Peter Marshall, *Heretics and Believers: A History of the English Reformation* (New Haven and London: Yale University Press, 2017), 359; Loades, *Reign of Mary*, 63–4; María Jesús Pérez Martín, *María Tudor. La gran reina desconocida* (Madrid: Ediciones Rialp, 2008), 486–7, 496–7; H. F. M. Prescott, *Mary Tudor: The Spanish Tudor* [1940] (London: Phoenix, 2003), 224–5; Anna Whitelock, *Mary Tudor: England's First Queen* (London: Bloomsbury, 2009), 177–83.

7 John Seton, *Panegyrici in victoriam illvstrissimae D. Mariae, Angliae, Franciae, & Hiberniae Reginae, &c. Item In Coronationem eiusdem Serenis. Reginae, congratulation. Ad haec De sacrosanta Eucharistia Carmen* (London: Reginald Wolfe, 1553). See also Leonard Stopes, *An Ave Maria in commendation of our most virtuous queene* (London: Richard Lant, 1553) and John Gwynneth, *A briefe declaration of the notable victory given of God to our Soveraygne Ladye Quene Marye made in the church of Luton the 23 July in the first yere of her gracious reign* (London: John Cawood, 1553).

8 Richard Taverner, *An oration gratulatory made upon the joyfull proclayming of the moste noble princes Quene Mary Quene of Englande* (London: John Day, 1553); Richard Beeard, *A godly psalme of Marye Queene which brought us comfort al, through God, whom wee of dewtye prayse, that gives her foes a fal* (London: John Kingston for William Griffith, 1553), sig. A5^{r}.

to rejoice with the English in an event that was seen by many as a new era and a golden opportunity to strengthen the traditional links between the two kingdoms.[9] One of these works was the Spanish merchant Antonio de Guaras' (1520–1584) newsletter to Beltrán de la Cueva y Toledo, duke of Alburquerque and viceroy of Navarre.[10] Written on 1 September 1553 and published later the same year, Guaras' lengthy account covered the reign of Edward VI, Mary's accession, and the duke of Northumberland's execution.[11] In it, the Spanish merchant considered that all the 'calamities' which had befallen England had been caused by the ambition and godlessness of the dukes of Somerset and Northumberland, who had

> [...] allowed that all heretics from other lands would be admitted here. So many have come, and they have preached so confusedly regarding ceremonies and everything else, that every parish was being managed differently, even if most English people were contrary to this; them being Catholics.[12]

---

9 For further information on the propagandistic efforts to celebrate Mary's accession as a Catholic triumph on the Continent see María José Bertoméu Masiá, 'Relaciones de sucesos italianas sobre la boda de Felipe II con María Tudor', *Cartaphilus*, 5 (2009), 6–17 and, especially, the illustrative piece by Corinna Streckfuss, '"Spes maxima nostra": European Propaganda and the Spanish Match' in Alice Hunt and Anna Whitelock, eds., *Tudor Queenship: The Reigns of Mary and Elizabeth* (New York: Palgrave Macmillan, 2010), 145–57.

10 Guaras, whose stay in London can be traced back to at least 1544, was a wool merchant from Tarazona, in Aragon, who would be a prominent Spanish agent for the Habsburgs even after Mary I's death in 1558. Not always at odds with Queen Elizabeth, Antonio de Guaras became the unofficial ambassador of Spain after Guerau de Espés was expelled following his involvement in the Ridolfi plot in 1571. Guaras coordinated the negotiations for the Treaty of Bristol of 1574, which put a temporary end to Anglo-Spanish tensions over commerce in the Low Countries and English sequestering of Spanish ships. Involved in Don John of Austria's schemes to marry Mary Stuart in 1577, Guaras was imprisoned in the Tower of London, where he would remain until 1579, when he was released and ordered to return to Spain, never to set foot in England again. See Jesús Criado Mainar, *El palacio de la familia Guaras en Tarazona* (Tarazona: Centro de Estudios Turiasonenses and Fundación Tarazona Monumental, 2009), 29–106.

11 More information on the different contemporary editions of Guaras's work can be found in José Solís de los Santos, 'Relaciones de sucesos de Inglaterra en el reinado de Carlos V', in Manuel F. Fernández, Carlos Alberto González and Natalia Maillard, eds., *Testigo del tiempo, memoria del unvierso. Cultura escrita y sociedad en el mundo ibérico* (*siglos XV–XVIII*) (Málaga: Ediciones Rubeo, 2009), 640–98.

12 Antonio de Guaras, *Carta de nueuas de Antonio de Guaras criado de la Serenissima y Cathólica Reyna de Inglaterra, al Ilustre S*[*eñor*] *Duque de Alburquerque: Visorrey y Capitán*

Guaras was describing the Edwardian religious establishment as chaotic and lacking in uniformity. By the mid-sixteenth century, to accuse Protestants of being orderless and inconsistent had become a common trope among Catholics. To this contributed, among other things, the failure of the Colloquy of Marburg in 1529, which aimed to reconcile the views of Martin Luther (1483–1546) and Huldrych Zwingli (1484–1531), and the different strands of Protestantism being born and developed in Europe, especially the very distinctive form established by John Calvin (1509–1564).[13] In this case, Guaras referred to the many changes in religion which had taken place in England after the break with Rome in the 1530s, but especially after Henry VIII's death. Following Charles V's victory against the German Protestant princes in April 1547 at the battle of Mülhberg, Edward VI's England began to be seen as one of the safest refuges for Protestants in Europe.[14] Soon afterwards, the Edwardian regime set out to recruit some of the most prominent evangelical theologians from the Continent. The first two to arrive, in December 1547, were the Italians Peter Martyr Vermigli (1499–1562) and Bernardino Ochino (1487–1564), soon to be joined by the German Martin Bucer (1491–1551) and the Pole Jan Łaski (1499–1560). The connections established with Strasbourg and Geneva were intended to cement a Protestant alliance between England and the Continent, taking advantage of the fact that King Edward was one of the few sovereigns who could freely support the new religion.[15]

---

general del Reyno de Nauarra etc. En la qual se trata en qué miserias y calamidades ha estado el Reyno tantos años ha: y de las passiones y muertes que ha huuido. Cómo Doña María fue proclamada por Reyna: y de todos obedescida. Un Razonamiento que hizo el Duque de Northu[m]berland antes de morir: amonestando al pueblo que dexassen la secta en que viuían: y se abraçassen con la Sancta Fe Cathólica: y que en todo obedesciessen a la Magestad de la Reyna María (1553), f. 420^{v}: 'permitiendo que todos los hereges de otras tierras se acogiessen aquí. E han venido tantos: [y] han predicado tan confusamente: assí en las ceremonias como en todo lo de más: que en cada perrochia administrauan differentemente: aunque la mayor parte de los Ingleses era de co[n]trario parescer por ser cathólicos'. (Real Biblioteca del Monasterio de San Lorenzo de El Escorial, MS V-II-4). For an alternative English translation see C. V. Malfatti, ed., *The Accession, Coronation and Marriage of Mary Tudor as Related by Four Manuscripts of the Escorial* (Barcelona: Sociedad Alianza de Artes Gráficas and Ricardo Fontá, 1956).

13 Diarmaid MacCulloch, *Reformation: Europe's House Divided, 1490–1700* (London: Penguin Books, 2004), 172–5; 270–313. This view ignored, of course, the internal divisions among Catholicism itself but it served to point out the Catholic perspective that, whereas Catholics quelled their disagreements through Scripture, the authority of the Church and tradition, Protestants' disagreements only produced further "sects".

14 Diarmaid MacCulloch, *Thomas Cranmer: A Life* (New Haven and London: Yale University Press, 1996), 180.

15 MacCulloch, *Thomas Cranmer*, 180–3.

From a Catholic perspective, the Protestant Reformation attacked the very foundations of the concept of *ecclesia universalis* or 'universal church' which Rome had traditionally claimed to be. According to Guaras, the greed, divisions and plots of Edward VI's reign were indicative of England's abandonment of God's plan. In this line, the Spanish merchant criticised Northumberland for having surreptitiously worked on king and council in order to win a crown for his son Guildford Dudley, Lady Jane Grey's husband, and 'shamelessly' proclaiming Mary a 'bastard' because she was, 'as they said, a papist, which is the name by which they now call the Catholics'. 'And', he added, 'because she wanted to marry a foreign prince, it seemed reasonable to them to disinherit her'.[16] Guaras had indeed identified the fears of those opposed to Mary's accession, as it is made clear in King Edward's 'Letters patent for the limitation of the crown', where the young king had stated that Mary and Elizabeth were not only being barred from the succession on the grounds of illegitimacy, but also because if they,

> should then happen to marry with any stranger, borne out of this realme, that then the same stranger, having the governmente and the imperiall crowne in his hands, would rather adhere and practice to have the lawes and customes of his or their own native countrey or countreyes.

Lady Jane's proclamation as heir against Henry VIII's will and, more importantly, parliamentary legality, may have owed much to Edward's religious preferences and Northumberland's ambitions for his son, but the fear of foreign domination through an "unnatural" overlordship was very real. If Edward were to die without issue, the document stressed, the crown would then pass to the Grey line, represented by Jane and her sisters Catherine and Mary – mysteriously bypassing their mother, Lady Frances Brandon – or – their line failing – to their cousin Lady Margaret Clifford. According to the conscientious young king, these ladies were better suited to succeed him than his own sisters on the grounds that they were 'naturall-borne here within the realme, and have ben also very honorably brought upe and exercised in good and godly

16 Guaras, *Carta de nueuas*, fols 422ᵛ–423ʳ: 'E hizo tanto el dicho de Nortumberland con el Rey y con los grandes: que se desuergonçaron a declarar públicamente que su Alteza era bastarda. E assí por esto como porque era como ellos dezían Papista el qual nombre han puesto a los cathólicos: porque se quería casar con Príncipe estrangero: que era cosa razonable que fuesse desheredada. Y como estaua cierto de la muerte del Rey: hizo que casasse doña Joanna hija mayor del dicho duque de Sofolc y de la dicha doña Francisca: con el tercer hijo suyo del dicho de Northumberland para efecto que por parte de la muger viniesse su hijo que se dize Milard Guilbert a ser Rey'.

learninge, and other noble vertues', which made them, 'very well inclined to the advancement and setting forth of our common welth'.[17]

The emphasis in this passage was on the nativeness ('naturall-borne') and right kind of religiosity ('good and godly learninge') which adorned the English ladies proposed to succeed King Edward in detriment of the monarch's own sisters, which in the young king's perspective was a necessary step to safeguard the 'common welth' as he and his regime conceived it. Pains have been taken by historians of the political and religious upheavals of the mid-Tudor period to disassociate the surprising flow of support for Mary's case during the Grey coup from any Catholic implications'.[18] However, Mary was a shrewd politician who had survived two dangerous regimes while being the visible head of opposition – especially during Northumberland's government – and she had exploited every opportunity to flaunt very publicly where her religious sympathies lay. At one point, during one of her visits to King Edward, Mary and her household had even paraded through the streets of London with their rosaries ostensibly displayed, to the dismay of her brother and his government.[19] As has been shown by Anna Whitelock and Diarmaid MacCulloch, during Edward's reign Mary had also cultivated strategic and crucial relationships with Catholic magnates and had exploited the revenues granted to her by her father and her brother's government to create an affinity group which rapidly came to her aid in the summer of 1553.[20] The stability represented by the continuity of the royal bloodline and respect for parliamentary acts and legality – although essential – cannot entirely explain Mary's success against Northumberland and Lady Jane Grey.[21] The common people were delighted at her accession, and Guaras attributed this to their Catholicism. He dumbfoundedly describes how everyone was throwing off their bonnets in the air and giving their money away to the poor. Old men and people of authority lost their clothes while jumping and dancing around, 'as if they were out of their minds'. Some were scared at first, because Northumberland had declared that crying out for Mary would be punishable by death, but soon everyone had joined in the general joy, shouting 'Long live Queen Mary!', lighting up bonfires, and dining in the streets merrily while music played. Guaras tells us that:

---

17 *Chronicle of Jane and Mary*, 93–4.

18 See, for instance, Loades, *Reign of Mary*, 63–4.

19 Loades, *Reign of Mary*, 30.

20 Anna Whitelock and Diarmaid MacCulloch, 'Princess Mary's Household and the Succession Crisis, July 1553', *The Historical Journal*, 50, no. 2 (2007), 265–87.

21 This point has also recently been made by Samson, *Mary and Philip*, 32–3 and had originally been suggested in 1986 by Jennifer Loach, *Parliament and Crown in the Reign of Mary Tudor* (Oxford: Clarendon Press, 1986), 6–9.

> It is a marvel to see the love that the people bear to this lady. It could even be argued that they offend our Lord, because more than loving her, they adore her. [...] [S]he has been very patient in her many and difficult travails, and she has taken them as devised by God's hand. Her life is so exemplary, and she is such a good Catholic, that it is no wonder the regard and natural love that her people have for her.[22]

In short, when Mary came to the throne, her Catholicism was no secret. Popular support for Mary is evident in an anonymous short Spanish treatise narrating Mary's coronation, which took place in Westminster Abbey on 1 October 1553. The treatise describes how, before the ceremony, Stephen Gardiner, bishop of Winchester led the queen to a platform so that 'all the people could see her'. And then,

> the said bishop asked in a loud voice, so that it could be heard by everyone: 'Is this the true heiress of this kingdom?' And the people answered loudly and happily: 'Yes! Yes!' He replied: 'Are you happy to receive her for your queen and lady?' And they all replied: 'Yes! Yes!' This done, her Majesty went to the altar to listen to the sermon.[23]

---

22 Guaras, *Carta de nueuas*, fols 426^{v}–427^{r}: 'Fue tanto el contentamiento [y] alegría de todos: que arrojauan quasi todos los bonetes al ayre perdidos: y todos los que tenían dineros en sus bolsas: los arrojauan al pueblo. Otros siendo hombres de autoridad y viejos: no se podían contener echando de sí sus ropas: saltando y baylando como si estuuieran fuera de seso. Otros yuan corriendo por las calles en donde no hauía houido noticia destata[n] gra[n]de nouedad: gritando. Viva la Reyna María. Y los q[ue] lo oÿan quedauan atónitos: que no osauan alegrarse: porque era peligro de muerte hablar en fauor della. Y luego que por todo se supo: se hizieron tantos fuegos: que era mucho de ver: y cenó aquella noche la gente en las calles: con grande alegría y músicas. [...] E es de marauillar el amor que este pueblo tiene a esta Señora: que cierto offenden a nuestro Señor en ello: porque la dexan de querer: y la adora[n]. Pero como está V[uestra] S[eñoría] informado: en sus muchos y largos trabajos: ha seÿdo tan paciente: tomando los todos como embiados de la mano de Dios: y su vida de tal exemplo y tan cathólica: quel natural amor deste su pueblo: [y] estas co[n]sideraciones son causa dello'. Robert Wingfield, in his chronicle, also expressed the view that the English adored her in an exaggerated fashion, verging almost on the blasphemous. See Diarmaid MacCulloch, ed., 'The "Vita Mariae Angliae Reginae" of Robert Wingfield', in *Camden Miscellany* 28 (London: Royal Historical Society, 1984), 251.

23 Anon., *La coronaçión de la ínclita y sereníssima reyna doña María de Inglaterra que oy reyna bienauenturadamente en aquel reyno con todos los autos solenidades y cerimonias que se hizieron el día de su coronación: y la manera como fue jurada y alçada por reyna en primero de octubre: Año de mil y quinientos y cinquenta y tres Años* (1553) – 'Y luego leuantándose y la lleuó de braço el obispo de Vincestregra[n] chanciller por todas quatro partes del cadabalso para que todo el pueblo la viesse: el qual obispo dezía en alta boz q[ue] se pudiesseoÿr. Es esta la verdadera heredera deste Reyno: y todo el pueblo respondía a

Popularity and devotion were thus intertwined in the regime's outward language of power. The ritualised acceptance of the queen in front of the church, moments before she partakes in the sermon and Mass, and, therefore, in the Body of Christ, knit together Mary's religious preferences with the public assent of the community to receive her as their lawful queen. The text might have been a standard piece of propaganda, personalising the people and making them a single body with a single voice, but these examples point out that from the very beginning it had been obvious that Mary would turn towards Catholicism. In her proclamation on religion issued at Richmond on 18 August 1553, the queen had expressed her concern for the 'great inconveniences and dangers' which had arisen in the realm 'through the diversity of opinions in questions of religion'. After openly stating her Catholic faith, Mary affirmed that she 'mindeth not to compel any her said subjects thereunto unto such time as further order by common assent may be taken therein'.[24] John Edwards has convincingly argued that the proclamation should not be understood as a call for religious tolerance, but that it should instead be understood in the light of the Protestant riots and attacks on Catholic priests which had taken place in London.[25] The queen, at a time when she was still lawfully the supreme head of the English Church, wanted caution. However, her intentions were clear and, indeed, Antonio de Guaras recounted that the same proclamation had caused fear among the Protestants who 'do not dare to mutter or say a word'. He affirmed that the 'heretics are astonished to see what is happening', and added that 'the good ones', by contrast, who were 'many, many more', were very happy and kept praying that God would guard the queen, because 'on her life depends all the good or evil that could befall this kingdom'. Furthermore:

> We have great hopes in our Lord that matters spiritual and temporal will be reformed little by little. Your lordship can be sure about this, because I know it on good authority, that if it pleases God, everything here will be as it is there [in Spain] regarding the obedience due to the pope as well as in everything else. And even if the heretics are very obstinate in what touches the pontiff, the queen is so good a Catholic, that it is held for certain that her Highness will have no respect for heretical knaves, but only for her conscience, which is the truth.[26]

---

bozes y con alegría sí. Replicaua soys contentos de recebilla por reyna y señora: respondieron sí. Lo qual acabó su magestad se fue al altar a oýr el sermón'. (Real Biblioteca del Monasterio de El Escorial, MS V-II-4).

24 TPR, vol. 2, 5–8.

25 Edwards, *Mary I*, 119–2; TPR, vol. 2, n. 390.

26 Guaras, *Carta de nueuas*, fols 433^r–433^v: 'Ha puesto tanto temor esto en el pueblo: q[ue] ni osan murmurar: ni hablar palabra: [y] está[n] como atónitos los hereges de ver lo que

This passage is crucial, as it encapsulates the early modern understanding of matters temporal and spiritual as being inextricably linked. The poignant comparison between what happened in England (*aquí*) – and what happened in Spain (*aý*) and the hope that things in the former would be the same as in the latter is a most significant one which relates directly to the universality claimed by Catholicism. Political and religious issues in the early modern period were inseparable and we see further evidence of this in a letter written by Philip to the viceroys of the territories of the Spanish Monarchy announcing his impending marriage in May 1554. In this letter, Philip explained that the emperor had arranged for him to marry his 'most beloved aunt' considering that this was 'a thing much needed for the preservation and augmentation of his Majesty's estates and the universal peace of Christendom'. Philip added that this marriage was also crucial for the 'quietude and calm' that would ensue from the union of the Catholic Monarchy and the English crown.[27] The restoration of Catholicism in England was of major importance for the hegemonic strategy of the Spanish Habsburgs, but there were deeper implications in relation to the traditional concept of *ecclesia universalis* (universal Church) and its relationship to the *monarchia universalis* (universal monarchy) – the Spanish idea of empire.

passa: y que veen lo q[ue] ha de ser: y que los buenos q[ue] son muy muchos más: están tan alegres que no saben de sí: rogando a nuestro señor guarde a la Reyna: en la vida de la qual está todo el bien o mal deste Reyno [...]. Tenemos mucha sperança en nuestro señor: que lo spiritual y temporal se reformará poco a poco; y puede V[uestra] S[eñoría] creer esto: porque lo sé yo de buena parte: que plazendo a Dios será aquí como aý: assí en la obediencia del Papa: como en lo de más. E aun que en esto del Pontífice están los hereges muy obstinados: es la Reyna tan cathólica: que se tiene por cierto: que no terná su Alteza respecto a bellacos hereges: sino a su consciencia que es la verdad'.

27 AGS, Estado 808, leg. 24; Philip to Diego Hurtado de Mendoza, Count of Mélito and Viceroy of Aragon, Valladolid, 11 May 1554: 'Conde Primo ya deuéys sauer como por fallecimiento de / Eduardo / rey de Inglaterra ha sucedido en aquel reyno la ser[ení]s[i]ma reyna doña maría n[uest]ra muy cara y muy amada tía con la qual su m[ajesta]d ha tratado y conçertado de casarme pareçiéndole ser cosa muy neçesaria para la conseruaçión y aumento de los Estados de su m[ajesta]d y la Vniversal paz de la [Crist]iandad y principalmente por lo mucho q[ue] conuiene destos reynos la Vnión de aquel reyno con ellos para su quietud y sosiego [...]'. The word used to describe Mary is *tía*, which means 'aunt' in Spanish, in accordance with the generational system used for family relations in Spanish. Since Mary belonged to Charles's generation, them being first cousins, to Philip she would have been his 'second aunt', rather than his first cousin once removed. Identical letters as the one sent to Mélito were also sent to Luis de Velasco, Viceroy of New Spain; Melchor Bravo de Saravia, Viceroy of Peru, and others. They can be found in AGI, Indiferente, 427, leg. 30, fols 69^r–70^r.

1.2 *Monarchia universalis* in the Spanish Context

In 1970, Joseph Strayer (1904–1987) wrote that the 'universal empire had never been anything but a dream' and that the Church had been forced to admit that the strongest loyalties were directed at the individual state rather than the Christian commonwealth.[28] This theme, imbued as it was by ideas shaped by the existence of nation-states, which of course did not exist in the early modern period, would figure prominently in numerous historical works of the nineteenth and twentieth centuries, and the historiography reached the conclusion that all attempts to unite Europe through a 'universal empire' or a 'universal Church' had failed.[29] In this respect, Spanish universalist aspirations have been understood, at best, as chimerical and, at worst, as fuelled solely by greed or ambition.[30] Despite these views, it would be difficult to deny that Charles v appeared to most Europeans as a more than likely candidate to universal empire. He was providentially endowed with the title of Holy Roman Emperor; he had inherited territories whose composition was reminiscent of the Roman Empire; and he was the ruler of a New World in need of Christian evangelisation.[31] It was no surprise, then, and especially after the conquests of Mexico in 1521 and Peru in 1533, that many Europeans believed that Spain could soon rule the whole world.[32] The fact that Charles's cousin Mary came to the throne in 1553, after the defeat of Lady Jane Grey and her supporters, was indeed seen as providential and it tied in nicely with the expansionist and universalist approach of the Spanish Monarchy. To conceive the episode of Philip and Mary's marriage in these terms is critical because it has been studied, like the topic of universal empire, through lenses benefitting from hindsight.

---

28 Joseph Strayer, *On the Medieval Origins of the Modern State* (Princeton: Princeton Univerisy Press, 1970), 57.

29 J. H. Elliott, 'A Europe of Composite Monarchies', 3.

30 The focus on the excesses of Spanish conquests in the New World and of Spanish repression during the Dutch revolt has at times prevented a more balanced approach to our understanding of the ideological, intellectual, and religious motivations of the people in charge of the Spanish Monarchy. The proponents of this reductionist approach to the history of Spain, have seen in it, as Fernando Cervantes has aptly put it, 'nothing but a record of cruelty and exploitation at the service of political reaction and religious obscurantism and intolerance'. See Fernando Cervantes, *The Hispanic World in the Historical Imagination: The John Coffin Memorial Lecture in the History of Ideas (28 January 2005)* (London: Institute for the Study of the Americas, 2006).

31 Frances A. Yates, *Astraea: The Imperial Theme in the Sixteenth Century* (London and Boston: Routledge and Kegan Paul, 1975), 25.

32 Anthony Pagden, *Lords of all the World: Ideologies of Empire in Spain, Britain and France, c. 1500–c. 1800* (New Haven and London: Yale University Press, 1995), 45.

However, that things did not happen does not mean that they were bound not to happen or, indeed, that those involved did not believe them possible. To understand the motivations for the marriage, it will be imperative to survey the concept of *monarchia universalis* and its application to the conception of the Anglo-Spanish union.

The comparison made by Guaras between *aquí* and *aý* was rooted in the Augustinian metaphor of the city. In *De civitate Dei*, St Augustine (354–430) had written about the distinction between the *civitas Dei*, or the City of God, represented by Christianity; and the *civitas terrena*, the earthly city, which were to be mixed and confused until the end of times. Augustine explained that the difference between the earthly city and the City of God, the Heavenly City, is that '[t]he former looks for glory from men, the latter finds its highest glory in God'. Princes of the earthly city and their subjects were lorded over by 'the lust for domination' and their greed for worldly honours and material gain whereas the rulers and subjects of the City of God 'serve one another in love, the rulers by their counsel, the subjects by obedience' and focused that love in God and His strength.[33] This opposition between what happened in England and what happened in Spain was an open criticism of previous English regimes which, concerned with worldly matters, had abandoned godly purposes and plunged the kingdom into the abandonment of its former Christian outlook. England had become the earthly city; it had abandoned the practices and beliefs which joined her to Spain and to the rest of Christendom, but now that a pious ruler had ascended the throne, England could aspire to be a part of Christianity again. Guaras's comparison also linked the notion of *ecclesia universalis* to that of *monarchia universalis*, which derived from the concept of *translatio imperii* of the Book of Daniel (2:44) in which a kingdom would be favoured by God to replace the rest and stand forever as a prelude to the Last Judgement.[34] The interpretation of this biblical passage in which Nabuchadnezzar dreams of a succession of empires gave rise to the identification of these polities as the empires or monarchies of the Assyrians, Persians, Greeks and Romans, and a widely distributed understanding that the Fifth Monarchy was to be the last, a

33 See especially Book XIV, chapter 28 and Book XIX, chapter 17. I have used St Augustine, *Concerning the City of God against the Pagans*, trans. Henry Bettenson (London: Penguin Books, 2003), 593–4, 877–8. For further background and the concepts' application in other contexts see Pagden, *Lords of all the World*, 2–3; Quentin Skinner, *The Foundations of Modern Political Thought*, vol. 1 (Cambridge: Cambridge University Press, 1978), 50.

34 Daniel 2:44: 'in diebus autem regnorum illorum suscitabit Deus caeli regnum quod in aeternum non dissipabitur et regnum eius populo alteri non tradetur comminuet et consumet universa regna haec et ipsum stabit in aeternum'.

notion which had deep ramifications for Spanish understandings of empire.[35] The conviction that England could reform itself as a mirror image of Spain had weighty implications in relation to the universal conceptualisation of imperial and monarchical power in Spain.

By the sixteenth century there were two widely disseminated traditional theories on supremacy. One of them stemmed directly from Roman legal language, and it placed the imperial sovereign in a position in which he was the holder of the *imperium* or *regimen mundi*; that is, the emperor was the *dominus* or *moderator* of the world. In this capacity, the emperor became the recipient of dominion over God's people. Another approach related to the concept of 'universal Church', the universal monarch being its political head and a 'prince of princes'.[36] For centuries, this moderator had been identified with the Holy Roman Emperor, and when Charles v became emperor after obtaining the Spanish crown, this equivalence figured prominently in Spanish political and historical treatises. The kingdoms of Spain were perceived to have been miraculously recovered from the decadence that the Muslim conquest and the fall of the Visigothic kingdom had plunged them into. This had been achieved through God's immeasurable favour and the efforts of a long line of pious monarchs which had culminated in Ferdinand and Isabel's conquest of Granada, the expulsion of the Jews, and the discovery of America, all three events having taken place in 1492. In the same year, the humanist and grammarian Antonio de Nebrija (1444–1522) explained that through 'divine providence' and Isabel's 'industry, labour and diligence', the scattered 'members and pieces of Spain' had been brought together 'into one body and the unity of one kingdom' in such a way that neither time nor injury would be able 'to break or untie' such a union. Moreover, the 'newly cleansed' Christian religion meant that Spaniards were now 'friends with God or have reconciled with Him'.[37]

---

35 Pagden, *Lords of all the World*, 42–3; Eva Botella-Ordinas, '"Exempt from Time and from its Fatal Change": Spanish Imperial Ideology, 1450–1700', *Renaissance Studies*, 26, no. 4 (2012), 580–604.

36 Franz Bosbach, *Monarchia universalis: Storia di un concetto cardine della politica europea (secoli XVI–XVIII)*, tr. Cesare De Marchi [1988] (Milan: Vita e Pensiero, 1998), 44–5.

37 Antonio de Nebrija, *Arte de la lengua castellana* (Salamanca, 1492), sig. a3^{r-v}: 'Y assí creció hasta la monarchía & paz de que gozamos primera mente por la bondad & prouidencia diuina: después por la industria trabajo y diligencia de vuestra real majestad. En la fortuna & buena dicha dela cual los miembros & pedaços de españa que estauan por muchas partes derramados: se reduxeron & aiuntaro[n] en un cuerpo & unidad de reino. La forma & travazó[n] del cual assí está ordenada q[ue] muchos siglos iniuria & tie[m]pos no la podrá[n] ro[m]per ni desatar. Assí que después de repurgada la cristiana religión: por la cual somos amigos de dios o reco[n]ciliados co[n] él'.

Charles's accession to the Empire in 1519, only three years after acceding to the Spanish thrones was understood in a providential way, too. In 1524, the historian and astrologer Álvaro Gutiérrez de Torres, for instance, commented on the happy event of Charles's election in relation to the ultimately unsuccessful attempt, three centuries before, of his Spanish forebear, Alfonso X the Wise, king of Castile and León (r. 1252–1284) to be 'emperor of the world'.[38] The notion of a Spanish emperor was, therefore, not a new one. Furthermore, his position as king of Spain and Holy Roman emperor did not contravene any of the laws of the *Siete Partidas* which ruled the kingdom of Castile, nor the laws of the Empire. This understanding, whilst recognising the excellency of 'the great Empire and Roman lordship', placed the authority of the monarch of Spain alongside it, rather than as a subordinate.[39] The propitious chain of events which had elevated Charles to the Empire was compounded by the election of Adrian of Utrecht, Charles's tutor, as Pope Adrian VI (r. 1522–1523) in 1522, whilst he was the governor of Spain, an event which signalled the latter kingdom as the epicentre of the temporal and spiritual lights (*lumbrera*) of the world. That the emperor and the pope had been elected to the Holy Roman Empire and to the pontifical throne whilst in Spain was a coincidence which had never before taken place in any other kingdom.[40]

Although not all thinkers agreed that universal empire was feasible or, indeed, desirable, many Spanish authors tended to make a strong connection

38 Álvaro Gutiérrez de Torres, *El sumario de las marauillosas: y espantables cosas que en el mundo han acontescido* (Toledo: Ramón de Petras, 1524), sig. L6^{v}–7^{r}: 'De la elección del qual [Charles] para el romano imperio breuemente hablando: digo que assý como en los tiempos passados la fama de las grandes y muy crecidas virtudes del sapientíssimo rey don Alonso el décimo que estaua en españa mouió a los electores del imperio esta[n]do en alemaña para q[ue] por ellos emp[er]ador del mundo fuesse elegido: assí agora en n[uest]ros días con justa razó[n] fuero[n] mouidos los electores para elegir & llamar al mismo ymperio & señorío romano a n[uest]ro señor el rey don Karlos […]'.

39 Gutiérrez de Torres, *Sumario de las marauillosas y espantables cosas*, sig. L8^{r}: 'Teniendo por cierto el grauíssimo & muy alto consejo de la yllustríssima nobleza & cauallería de España: y el de los príncipes y electores del ymperio non ser hecha violación de alfonsíes: ni ymperiales leyes por dar la obediencia de España: y el señorío y gouernación del ymperio a aquel que doctado de nobilíssima naturaleza [sic: missing verb]'. The explicit mention to the *Siete Partidas* is poignant, for they had been influenced by the notion of *rex in regno suo imperator est* (the king is an emperor in his kingdom). See Daniel Panateri, 'Las Siete Partidas: entropía, control y variación. Un itinerario histórico-político de su existencia', *Conceptos Históricos*, vol. 2 (2016), 154–87.

40 Gutiérrez de Torres, *Sumario de las marauillosas y espantables cosas*, sig. L8^{v}: 'El papa Adriano sesto que es la vna [lumbrera] en lo espiritual: y el emperador do[n] Karlos q[ue] es la otra en lo te[m]poral. Lo q[ua]l en vn mismo tie[m]po como agora en reyno ningu[n]o auer acontecido se halla'.

between the office of emperor and the *regimen mundi*, but this link was often made with reference to Spain.[41] The Navarrese Miguel de Ulzurrun explained in his dedication to the emperor of his *Catholicum opus imperiale* (1525), that with Charles's Spanish inheritance, his rule over other 'nations' in Europe and Africa and after his election as emperor, he had become the '*regem regum*' and '*principem principum*', the 'king of kings' and 'prince of princes' to rule over the whole world and to lead humans as God's immediate secular representative.[42] Ulzurrun claimed that temporal matters were not within the pope's remit just as spiritual matters were not within the emperor's, and that the latter derived his power from God in order to tend to human happiness and tranquillity. The pope's spiritual jurisdiction applied only to the Christian faithful, but the emperor's jurisdiction allowed him to exert *imperium* over all, including Christians as well as infidels under his dominion.[43] The emperor was, in sum, the 'lord of the whole world' and the 'head of all human society'.[44] In similar vein, Gonzalo de Arredondo y Alvarado († *c.*1528), prior of Bóveda, called the

41 Among those against the concept itself or its feasibility were Erasmus and Domingo de Soto, OP. Typical criticisms of *monarchia universalis* included the geographical impossibility of its existence, for it was deemed impossible by these critics that a sole ruler could be in charge of such a vast number of lands and peoples; the unfeasibility of an assembly of all humankind to assent to and consolidate the *potestas* of such a ruler, and the historical fiction upon which they considered the concept rested, for the Roman emperors had never held their rule over the whole world. For Domingo de Soto's views, widely – although not universally – held in the School of Salamanca see *De iustitia e iure* (Salamanca: Andrea de Portonaris, 1553), 300–306. See also Bosbach, *Monarchia universalis*, 47–53.

42 Miguel de Ulzurrun, *Catholicum opus imperiale regiminis mundi* (Zaragoza: Jorge Coci, 1525), *prefatio* (unnumbered): '[…] videlicet te Carolu[m] quintu[m] inuenie[n]s: (que[m] ante p[er] successione[m] totius Hispanię / vtriusq[ue] Sicilię: pluriu[m]q[ue] aliaru[m] nationu[m] in Europa / ac etia[m] Affrica / regem & dominu[m] co[n]stituit:) mirabiliter per vniforme[m] electione[m] eoruz: qui vices omniu[m] gerunt: et vltimus finibus Hispanię vniuersi orbis Regem regum / principem principum / vicarium suum immediatum [God's] / vt humanis presideas: assumeret'.

43 Ulzurrun, *Catholicum opus*, f. 25^r^: 'Dico igit[ur] q[ue] pontifex maximus non secularib[us] negociis se implicat: et vicissim nec imp[er]ator spiritualib[us] presidere potest. Et per hoc co[n]cluditur cum petrus fuit co[n]stitutus caput du[n]taxat ecclesie militantis: hoc est vniuersitatis fidelium: non potest dici caput infidelium: et per consequens non fuit data sibi potestas i[m]perij te[m]p[or]alis: q[uo]d est ad fine[m] felicitates societatis hu[m]ane. […] Ideo de necessitate est dicendu[m]: q[uod] imperator qui potest preesse fidelibus & infidelibus ad hu[n] finem: habet potestatem temporale[m] a deo i[m]mediate / & suprema[m] ad tra[n]quilitate[m] humana[m]: cuius imperium est animaduersio in facinorosos homines quposcu[m]q[ue] fideles & infideles'.

44 Ulzurrun, *Catholicum opus*, f. 47^r^: '[…] imperatore[m] esse dominu[m] totius orbis: et q[uo]d nullus potest esse exemptus in te[m]poralibus ab eo: et sic est capus totius societatis humane: sicut papa est in sp[irit]ualib[us] […]'.

emperor 'father of the fatherland' (*padre de la patria*), possessor of 'true friendship' (*vera amicicia*), the 'life of the law' (*ánima de las leyes*), 'lord and prince of the globe in temporal matters' (*señor y príncipe del orbe en lo temporal*) and 'universal monarch' (*vniuersal monarcha*).[45] The humanist Francisco de Támara († after 1556), who in 1553 translated, edited and expanded the famous Latin *Chronica* published by the German Johann Carion (1499–1537) in 1533, explained that the Empire or German Monarchy was, according to Carion, the Fifth Monarchy of Daniel's prophecy. In Támara's own words in the introduction, Charles v happily reigned 'in our orb and Christian world' but, he cautioned, should this 'administration and government, which is today the head of the whole world' be destroyed or perverted, it would signal the alteration of Christendom and it would herald the Last Judgement unless God willed otherwise. The end of the Empire, of the Fifth Monarchy, would mean the end of the world.[46]

This association of the Holy Roman Empire with universal monarchy in the Spanish context worked well whilst Charles v was also the king of Spain, but it had the potential to become problematic once it started to become apparent that the imperial throne was to pass to the line of Charles's brother, Ferdinand, rather than to Philip.[47] Nonetheless, even though there was a strong tendency in Spanish political thought to recognise the excellence of imperial authority, authors also presented the Spanish Monarchy as exempt

45 Gonzalo de Arredondo y Alvarado, *Castillo inexpugnable defensorio d[e] la fee y concionatorio admirable para vencer a todos enemigos espirituales y corporales, y verdadera relació[n] de las cosas marauillosas antiguas y modernas, y exortación para yr contra el turco y le vencer y anichilar la seta de mahoma y toda infidelidad y ganar la tierra sancta con famoso y bienauenturado triumpho* (Burgos: Juan de Junta, 1528), ff. 2^r, 6^v.

46 Johann Carion and Francisco de Támara, *Suma y compendio de todas las chrónicas del mundo, desde su principio hasta el año presente, traduzida por el bachiller Fra[n]cisco Thámara, Cathedrático en Cádiz. Es la Chrónica de Iuan Carion, con diligencia del traductor quitado todo lo superfluo, y añadidas muchas cosas notables de España* (Medina del Campo: Guillermo de Millis, 1553), ff. 4^v–5^r: '[…] nuestro inuictíssimo y fortunatíssimo emperador Carlos Máximo, quinto deste nombre, que al presente impera y reyna en nuestro orbe y mundo Christiano' and ff. 8^r–9^r: 'Y assí se puede creer q[ue] quando esta administración y gouernación, que es oy cabeça de todo el mundo, fuere destruyda, o p[er]uertida, sin duda no puede ser sino que todas las otras cosas se perturbarán y alterarán en toda la religión Christiana, y en todo el mundo, y que grandes calamidades y desuenturas vendrán, si Dios no las ataja y anticipa co[n] su venida del juyzio final. Y assí nos consuelan las letras sagradas, dando nos auiso muy a la clara, que quando este imperio presente fenesciere, luego el día postrimero y final juyzio será, y el mundo se acabará'.

47 For the bitter family feud which followed Charles and Ferdinand's disagreement over who should succeed the former in the Empire see Geoffrey Parker, *Emperor: A New Life of Charles v* (New Haven and London: Yale University Press, 2019), 420–4.

from being subordinated to it. Indeed, Spain claimed its own imperial tradition, derived directly from the Roman Empire, the Visigothic kingdom and the Christian Reconquista, which meant that when Ferdinand of Austria became emperor in 1556, the separation of the formal *imperium* from the *monarchia* did not diminish Spanish claims to *monarchia universalis*. From a historical perspective, Alfonso VI of Castile (r. 1077–1109) exhibited the title of *imperator constitutos super omnes Ispanae nationes* in 1077, while his daughter, Urraca I (r. 1109–1126), was declared *totius Hispaniae imperatrix* in 1114 and her son and successor, Alfonso VII (r. 1126–1157), was crowned as *Hispaniae imperator* in 1135.[48] There was also the precedent of Alfonso X's ultimately failed attempt to be elected Holy Roman emperor in the mid-thirteenth century through his mother, Beatrice of Swabia's Hohenstaufen blood.[49] The concept of an emperor of 'all the nations of Spain' was given new impulse by Ferdinand and Isabel's marriage in 1469 and their conquest of the kingdom of Granada in 1492 and that of Navarre, after Isabel's death, in 1512. The concept gained new vitality with the incorporations of the kingdoms of Naples and Sicily and the duchy of Milan. With the Flemish inheritance, the territories acquired in the New World and the association to the Holy Roman Empire, the Spanish Monarchy had become the head of an *imperium* which was ready to fight the threat posed by the Turks externally and by the Protestants from within and to expand Christendom in the New World.

The defence of universal monarchy as embodied by Charles V was, therefore, often made with reference to Spain. The Spanish people, according to the chronicler Florián de Ocampo (1499–1558), had been blessed by the noble lineage provided by their common ancestor, Tubal, Noah's grandson, 'a man full of virtue and great ability' considered to have been the first settler of the Iberian peninsula, which his grandfather had ordered him to populate.[50] In contrast to the Empire, which had no consistent lineage as a result of the nature of its elective system, the kings of Castile could boast a direct descent not only from Tubal and the natural inhabitants of Spain, his descendants, but also from the Visigoths. The humanist historian from Seville, Pedro Mejía (1497–1551), explained in his popular 1545 *Historia imperial y cesárea* that the nobility of

48 Pagden, *Lords of all the World*, 91; María del Carmen Pallarés Méndez and Ermelindo Portela Silva, *La reina Urraca* (San Sebastián: Editorial Nerea 2006), 106–7.

49 An episode which came to be known as the *Fecho del Imperio* (roughly the 'feat of the Empire'). See Julio Valdeón Baruque, 'Alfonso X y el Imperio', *Alcanate: Revista de estudios Alfonsíes*, 4 (2004–5), 243–55.

50 Florián de Ocampo, *Los cinco libros primeros de la Crónica general de España, que recopila el maestro Florián de Ocampo, Cronista del Rey nuestro señor, por mandado de su Magestad, en Çamora* (Medina del Campo: Guillermo de Millis, 1553), f. 7v.

Spain ought to be preferred to any other, as it alone was directly descended from the blood of the Goths, that bravest of nations who had managed to subdue and exert dominion over the Romans, 'the people and empire who had subdued all other peoples'. When the Visigoths retreated to the north after 'Spain was lost' to the Muslims, they had mixed with the noble native blood of the kingdom and that of the Romans who, established in the peninsula, had become natives of Spain.[51] To this wondrous inheritance, Mejía added a further boast:

> It cannot be denied that the blood and lineage of the kings of Spain, and that of the emperor and king our lord who now reigns over her, descends from the most high and noble kings of the Goths, nor that for 1,100 years, the House of Castile has not once broken the thread that goes from father to son or daughter, or brother, or nephew, or cousin, neither has it ever changed the lineage and royal line of the Goth kings whence it came, nor has it passed on the royal sceptre to a different lineage. This is so because the Infante Pelagius, who reigned after the destruction of Spain, belonged to the same, and he was even, according to some, the brother of King Roderic.[52] There is no other kingdom, either of Christians or Moors, with such a durable lineage.[53]

51 Pedro Mejía, *Historia Imperial y Cesárea, en la qval en svmma se contienen las vidas y hechos de todos los césares Emperadores de Roma, desde Iulio César hasta el Emperador Maximiliano: la qual compuso el Magnífico Cauallero Pero Mexía, vezino de Seuilla. Agora nueuamente impressa con tres tablas muy copiosas* [1545] (Antwerp: Martín Nucio, 1552), f. 152^{r}: 'Y por esto la nobleza de España se deue anteponer y preferir a todas las del mundo en este caso, pues ciertamente descienden desta ta[n] Antigua y tan valerosa sangre de los Godos, q[ue] escaparon de las batallas, qua[n]do España se perdió y se retruxero[n] a las mo[n]tañas, y de los antiguos nobles Españoles naturales dela tierra de antes q[ue] ellos viniesen. Y si algu[n]a mezcla puede auer sería de los Romanos q[ue] primero se aurían ya hecho naturales de España'.

52 King Roderic (r. 710–711) was the last of the kings of Visigothic Spain, who lost the kingdom at the battle of Guadalete.

53 Mejía, *Historia imperial y cesárea*, f. 152^{r}: 'Pues la sangre y línea de los Reyes de España, y del Emperador y rey nuestro señor q[ue] en ella oy reyna, no se puede negar q[ue] no descie[n]de delos más altos y nobles Reyes delos Godos, y que de mil y cient años a esta parte, la casa de Castilla nu[n]ca ha q[ue]brado el hilo vinie[n]do de padre a hijo o hija, o hermano, o sobrino, o primo, sin salir del linaje y línea real de los Reyes Godos de do començó, ni pasar el ceptro real a otro linaje. Por[ue] el infante do[n] Pelayo q[ue] reynó después de la destruyció[n] de España, del mismo era, y aun segú[n] algunos hermano del rey do[n] Rodrigo. Lo qual no ay reyno en Christianos, ni Moros q[ue] tal aya durado, porq[ue] en todos ha auido mudanças muy notables, y passados los Reynos a otros linajes, o ge[n]tes, o ha[n] sido co[n]quistados por otros'.

Mejía's linking of the royal blood of Castile to King Pelagius of Asturias (r. 718–737), whose historical feats were – then as now – inseparable from legend, and to the Visigoths, established a direct claim to the Roman Empire for the Spanish Monarchy. Dynasties might change, but thanks to hereditary and female succession (*de padre a hijo o hija*) the crown's authority remained in the same venerable blood; the oldest lineage in the world. The Holy Roman Empire, with its elective succession, could never make the same claim. In addition to this political utilisation of history, Mejía also emphasised that the Roman Empire had never been better governed than when it had been under the Spanish emperors Trajan (r. 98–117) and Theodosius I (r. 379–395) and cautioned that if people would not believe what books said, they should at least believe their own eyes and consider the state of the Holy Roman Empire in the last 200 years and acknowledge that there had never been the same 'authority, valour and command that it has now that the emperor is the king of Spain, our lord Charles, the fifth emperor of his name'.[54]

The connection to Rome's grandeur was also remarked upon in 1551 by the Valencian theologian and historian of German origin Pere Antoni Beuter (1490–1554) in his historical study of Aragon, Catalonia and Valencia, where he claimed that Spain had always been praised 'by all the nations of the world' as 'strong and heroic' and that it was notorious that 'the Romans only conquered the world when the Spaniards walked among them'.[55] Moreover, the insistence in the Roman and Visigothic connection and its association of Spain to its own *imperium* was also commented upon by Támara in his expansion of Carion's *Chronica*, in which he explained that King Athaulf (r. 411–415), who had respected Rome due to his marriage to Galla Placidia, Emperor Honorius's

54 Mejía, *Historia imperial y cesárea*, f. 152v: 'De manera que es cierto, que nunca el Imperio estuuo más honrrado ni mejor defendido, que el tiempo en que imperaron Españoles en él. Y si alos libros no quisieren dar fe los hombres, por vista de ojos ven oy día, que en lo que es el estado del imperio, de dozientos años acá nunca ha llegado la autoridad, y valor, y mando que oy día tiene, imperando en él el Rey de España, nuestro señor, do[n] Carlos quinto Emperador deste nombre'.

55 Pere Antoni Beuter, *Segunda parte De la Corónica general de España, y especialmente de Aragón, Cathaluña y Valencia. Donde se tratan las cobranças destas tierras de poder de Moros: por los ínclytos Reyes de Aragón, y Condes de Barcelona. Y pónese en particular la conquista de la ciudad y reyno de Valencia, y Murcia, con las yslas Mallorca, Menorca, Euiça, y las otras: con muchas cosas de notar, como por las tablas se podrá ver* (Valencia: Joan de Mey, 1551), *epístola*, unnumbered: 'Ca cómo puede ser que en general haya sido siempre alabada la España por todas las naciones del mundo, y sobre todas ellas, de fuerte y hazañosa, sin q[ue] toda ella aya tenido muy muchos nobles y hazañosos Varones? De lo que vno y otro y muchos y muy muchos hazen, viene la loa a la prouincia. Sabemos que los Romanos no conquistaron el mundo sin que el Español anduuiesse entre ellos'.

sister, had settled in Spain with his Goths, and that from this people descended the kings of Spain and, among them, 'our undefeated and most illustrious emperor, Charles v'.[56] This theme, and the descent from Pelagius, would also be treated by the influential humanist Juan Ginés de Sepúlveda (1490–1557), who extolled the virtues of hereditary monarchy over the tendency of elective monarchies to be corrupt and to betray the community, praising the unique continuous succession of forty-four monarchs since Pelagius, of Visigothic origin, started the recovery of Spain, occupied 840 years before by 'Mohammedan barbarians from Africa and Arabia'.[57]

The emphasis on the timelessness of Spanish royal blood and its links to Christianity was a means to safeguard Spanish claims to universal monarchy. The understanding that the emperor's authority was global was compounded by the coincidence that the emperor also happened to be the king of Spain. This notion was already clear in Ulzurrun's 1525 work. When praising Charles v's patrilineal lineage, the Navarrese explained that even if Charles's' paternal grandfather, Maximilian i (r. 1493–1519), had been emperor, it was his maternal grandparents, Ferdinand (r. 1479–1516) and Isabel (r. 1474–1504), who had received the title of Catholic Monarchs (*catholicorum regum*) – which, of course, meant universal – from Pope Alexander vi (r. 1492–1503). They had deserved this title for their good government of Spain, the Two Sicilies and other territories, their subduing of 'many infidel islands and kingdoms', their

---

56 Támara and Carion, *Suma y compendio*, f. 104r: 'Después déste [King Alaric i] fue rey de los Godos Adolpho [Athaulf], éste boluió, sobre Roma, y por[ue] tomó por muger a Placidia hermana d[e] Honorio, no quiso hazer daño alguno en Roma, mas antes se fue a Francia, y de aý en España. Donde se quedaron los Godos, y tuuieron el reyno de España de aý adelante. Destos Godos procede[n] los reyes de España, y de la generació[n] dellos trae su origen nuestro inuictíssimo y claríssimo emperador don Carlos quinto'.

57 Juan Ginés de Sepúlveda, *De regno et regis oficio* [1571] in Real Academia de la Historia, ed., *Joannis Genesii Sepulvedæ cordubensis. Opera, cum edita, cum inedita*, vol. 4 (Madrid: Tipografía regia de la Gaceta, 1780), 109: 'Confer nunc regum horum suffragio populi delectorum statum cum Hispaniorum, qui jure hereditario ex eadem Pelagidarum familia in regnum succedunt, conditione, fortasse nihil præterea ad hanc causam dijudicandam desiderabis. Octigenti quadraginta circiter anni sunt, cum rege Roderico ex Gotthorum gente prælio devicto atque necato, et a barbaris Mahumetanis ex Africa et Arabia Hispaniæ máxima parte scelere et auxilio quorumdam nostrorum occupata, regnum majores nostri, qui se in Asturias Cantabriamque receperant, Pelagio Favilæ Cantabriæ ducis filio detulerunt, eoque ductore amissam Hispaniam recipere cœperunt: ab eo prorsus, qui cum multis aliis regnis nunc rerum Hispaniarum potitur, perpetua ejusdem familiæ successione quadragesimus quartus numeratur [...]'. Sepúlveda's work was not printed until 1571, but he was one of the most influential Spanish thinkers of the mid-sixteenth century and he had begun to write his tract around 1545. On Sepúlveda's *De regno* and its centrality to understand his thought see José Manuel Pérez-Prendes Muñoz-Arraco, '*De regno*: Introducción jurídica', *Interpretatio: revista de historia del derecho*, 10 (2004), 497–508.

destruction of all heretics, and the expulsion of the Jews, whereby their subjects had been brought under 'the yoke of tranquillity and justice' provided by their 'animated laws' (*animate legi*).[58] The association of *monarchia universalis* with Spain became stronger when the transfer of power from Charles to Philip began. During Philip's European tour of 1548–1551 to be sworn as heir across Charles's patrimonial estates, many of the cities where he passed set up pageants which stressed his place as inheritor of Charles's universal aspirations. In the account of the chronicler Juan Cristóbal Calvete de Estrella (*c*.1520–1593) we are told that Genoa, which was not under Spanish rule but had close financial relations with Spain, welcomed Philip with an arch stating: 'He who loves weapons and justice shall govern the world'.[59] In Pavia, nominally under Philip's authority as duke of Milan since 1540, the 'fortunate prince' was invited to enter the city as him who had God's 'special care' and was destined to ensure that there would be 'a single shepherd and a single sheepfold'.[60] The city of Milan installed an imposing arch presided over by an imperial eagle and displaying figures which represented Charles V, Maximilian I, Philip I (r. 1505–1506) and Ferdinand, king of the Romans on one side, and Albert V of Austria, king of Germany (r. 1438–1439), emperor Frederick III (r. 1452–1493), Prince Philip and his cousin Maximilian, Ferdinand's son, on the other. The arch celebrated the House of Habsburg and Philip's belonging to the 'most happy lineage of the Caesars' and singled him out as him who 'will extend the limits of the Christian

58 Ulzurrun, *Catholicum opus imperiale*, f. 47ᵛ: 'Sed ei[us] au[us] maximilianus quondam[m] Romanoru[m] rex erat: cui etiam in dignitate imperiali succedit. Ex alia vero parte Fedina[n]d[us] eius auus / & Helisabeth auia primu[m] nome[n] catholicorum regu[m] merito obtinueru[n]t: tota[m] Hispaniam cum vtraq[ue] Sicilia ditioni sue iure subiugarunt: et multas insulas / & regna infideliu[m] victoriose sibi subijcie[n]tes: nunq[uam] de acquisitis quicq[uam] perdideru[n]t. Hereses omnes destruentes / iudeos om[n]es a suis dominijs expulerunt: et fidem in om[n]ibus seruaueru[n]t: aci tranq[ui]llitat[em] & iusticie iugu[m] omnes sibi subditos reduxeru[n]t. Non immerito igitur a natione eidem animate legi iusticia est sociata'.

59 Juan Cristóbal Calvete de Estrella, *El felicíssimo viaie del mvy alto y mvy Poderoso Príncipe Don Phelippe, Hijo d'el Emperador Don Carlos Quinto Máximo, desde España a sus tierras dela baxa Alemaña: con la descripción de todos los Estados de Brabante y Flandes* (Antwerp: Martín Nucio, 1552), f. 12ʳ: 'EQVORVM AMATOR ET AEQVI SIC MODERABITVR ORBI / Gouernará el mundo el amador delas armas, y dela justicia'. *Equorum* literally means "horses". Calvete has taken it to mean "charger horses" and has quite freely translated it to "weapons" to ensure the translation makes sense in the context in which it is inserted.

60 Calvete de Estrella, *El felicíssimo viaie*, f. 20ʳ: 'INGREDERE HVC FELIX O MAXIMA CVRA TONANTIS, QVOD SIS PASTOREM, ATQVE VNVM FACTVRVS OVILE / Entrad en esta ciudad Príncipe venturoso, de quien Dios tiene tan gran cuidado, que vos auéys de hazer que aya vn solo pastor y vn solo aprisco'.

empire to the far corners of the Earth'.[61] The task to extend Christendom, to be the backbone of the *ecclesia universalis*, was ascribed to Philip, rather than to Ferdinand or his son Maximilian, and this had profound implications for the prince of Spain's role as heir to the New World. These themes were echoed at the pageants in Marignano, where a triumphal arch was installed which explained that 'Philip, prince of the Spains' was 'heir to the roundness of the Earth'.[62]

Similar treatment was given to Philip's figure in a treatise ascribed to Stephen Gardiner, bishop of Winchester and lord chancellor, extant in manuscript form in Italian and written at some point after Philip and Mary's marriage. In the preface, George Rainsford referred to him as 'the most potent Philip, Defender of the Faith, and most clement king and father to so many different peoples'. Through divine providence, Philip had been exalted, Rainsford continued, to 'dominion' (*imperio*) of many powerful kingdoms 'for the benefit of the true faith, for the concord of the Christian flock, and for the ancient glory of Britain'.[63] At the end of the treatise, written in the form of a dialogue between Stephano and Alphonso, the former refers to Philip's accession to the throne of England not as 'change or alteration of the kingdom, but as legitimate succession, confirmed by all orders, for the restitution of religion, for the kingdom's honour, and for the advantage of the people'.[64] He then launched a panegyric tirade on the Habsburg dynasty, from Emperor Frederick III, through to Maximilian and Charles, leaving out Philip the Fair because of his premature death. They had all worked to increase religion and Charles had been 'emperor

61 Calvete de Estrella, *El felicíssimo viaie*, ff. 23^r–24^r: 'CÆSARVM PROLES FELICISSIMA PATRE TE INTER CÆSARES MAXIMO TE DIGNVM FILIVM HABERE RELIGIO CHRISTIANA LAETATVR, QVI AD EXTREMVM VSQVE TERRARVM ORBEM IPSIUS TERMINOS STATVAS. / Linaje felicíssimo delos Césares la Religión Christiana se alegra en tener os consigo como a hijo digno de tal padre, que es el mayor entre los Césares, y porque vos estenderéys los términos d'el Imperio Christiano hasta lo estremo de las tierras'.

62 Calvete de Estrella, *El felicíssimo viaie*, f. 33^v: 'QVOD PHILIPPVS HISPANIARVM PRINCEPS ORBIS TERRARVM FVTVRVS HAERES TVO DIGNATVR HOSPITIO. / Porque don Phelippe Príncipe delas Españas y heredero que será dela redondez dela tierra no se ha desdeñado de tomarte por su aposento'.

63 Peter Samuel Donaldson, ed., *A Machiavellian Treatise by Stephen Gardiner* (Cambridge: Cambridge University Press, 1975), 44: '[…] con chi sopranomi potron hora gli cristiani salutare il felice nome di Philippo potentissimo, defensore della fede, et re et padre di tanti varii popoli clementissimo? […] Imperò, per la somma providentia divina, al imperio di si ampli et potenti regni essaltato p'el beneficio della fede vera, per la concordia della grege cristiana, et per l'antica gloria di Britannia'. The editor's English translation in 102.

64 *Machiavellian Treatise*, 97: 'Questo io non chiamo mutatione, ne alteratione del regno ma successione legitima, confirmata per tutti gli ordini, alla restitutione della religione, honore del regno, et utile delli popoli'. Translated in 149.

and monarch of the world' (*imperadore et monarcha del mondo*). From this righteous blood, one could only expect goodness from Philip. Indeed, the king held 'the sword of so many great kingdoms in his right hand' and, through his marriage, he had now come to 'rule (as a most pious father) the powerful kingdom of England' and had become the 'arbiter of all peace and war in Christendom'.[65] There was no explicit reference to Spain (which is consistent with Gardiner's reluctance for the Spanish marriage), but her heir was still seen as restorer of the universal Church and arbiter of Christendom.

In 1553, Támara recounted several prophecies relating to imperial authority and its connection to the Fifth Monarchy, which Carion had identified with the Empire, but he ended with one which made direct reference to the Spanish Monarchy:

> Another great astrologer told King Ferdinand the Catholic, grandfather of our emperor, that the empire of the Turks was to be subdued and destroyed by a king of Spain, and the Catholic King replied that the prophecy should not be understood as a reference to himself, but to one of his heirs and successors. May our Lord God, Father of mercy, grant such grace and victory to our princes, that through them such a conquest shall come to pass and that in our times we shall see all the lordships of the world in firm union and conformity under the true union of Christ our Lord. And thus all of us shall be but of one pen and of one shepherd and the Kingdom which we await and always hope for shall come. Amen.[66]

The Spanish Monarchy was thus seen as the catalyst of eschatological understandings of the end of the world and the Fifth Monarchy and as the bulwark of Christianity and the Church's instrument to bring about global conversion. Embodied in its prince – whether emperor or king – the Catholic Monarchy had the potential and, indeed, the mission, to unify the *monarchia universalis* and the *ecclesia universalis*. It is within this intellectual ferment that the marriage of Philip and Mary, and the union of their crowns, was conceived.

---

65 *Machiavellian Treatise*, 98–9 and translated in 150–51.

66 Támara, *Suma y compendio*, ff. 183^{r-v}: 'Otro gra[n]de Astrólogo dixo al rey don Fernando el Cathólico, abuelo de nuestro emperador, q[ue] el imperio de los Turcos auía de ser sojuzgado y destruydo por vn rey de España, y el rey Cathólico respo[n]dio, q[ue] aquella prophecía no se entendía por él, mas por alguno d[e] sus herederos, y successores. Dios nuestro señor padre d[e] misericordia tenga por bien de dar tal gracia y victoria a nuestros príncipes, que por ellos se haga y effectúe tan gran conquista, y que en nuestro tiempo veamos todos los señoríos del mu[n]do en cierta vnió[n] y conformidad, y debaxo de la v[erd]adera [unión] de Christo nuestro señor, para que se haga de todos vn corral y vn pastor, y ve[n]ga nuestro reyno, el qual esperamos, y por el qual siempre rogamos. Amén'.

1.3 England, the Community, and Their Place in the Spanish Monarchy

The implication in Guaras's statements was that the unification of the *monarchia universalis* and the *ecclesia universalis* was at hand, and it would be embodied by Philip if he married Queen Mary. The perceptive merchant envisaged a union of both monarchies through the marriage and thought that it was an opportunity not to be missed by the emperor and his son,

> because it is to be believed, that being so closely related, and being – thanks be unto God – so well suited in religion, and not too unequal in their power, something could be envisaged to happen if the business with Portugal has not been yet concluded. If only our Lord would let us see such a glorious day! What great benefits it could bring to our Spain! Should these kingdoms and those belonging to his Majesty become one, we would be able to stop the French. Even if only for the preservation of the states of Flanders, his Majesty and his son should desire it wholeheartedly.[67]

The inference in this passage is that the Spanish and English kingdoms were to be united in the sort of personal union which had characterised Ferdinand and Isabel's marriage rather than as a simple partnership or alliance, as the historiography has often claimed. Guaras was clearly aware that marriage negotiations were under way and he was more enthusiastic about the English match than the Portuguese one which Philip was about to conclude to marry his aunt and cousin, the Infanta Maria of Portugal (1521–1577).[68] This match was so advanced that letters announcing it had already been produced and it was in

---

67 Guaras, *Carta de nueuas*, fol. 434r: 'Paresce que no lo errarán el Emperador y su hijo si se aprouechan desta tan grande co[m]modidad: pues es de creer que atrauessando tanto deudo: y siendo a Dios gracias tan conformes en la religión: y no muy desiguales en la potencia: q[ue] mouiendo lo alguno que podría venir en effecto: si el negocio de Portugal no está concluydo. Y si este día de tanta gloria nos dexasse nuestro Señor dios ver: que beneficio tan grande succedería a nuestra España: en detener al Francés: co[n] estar estos Reynos y los de su Magestad vnos: [y] aun que no fuesse por más: de por conseruar los estados de Flandes: lo hauían más de dessear su Magestad y su hijo [...]'.

68 Maria was the daughter of King Manuel I of Portugal (r. 1495–1521) and his third wife, Eleanor of Austria. Since Manuel was Philip's maternal grandfather and Eleanor was Charles's elder sister, Maria was at the same time her prospective groom's aunt and first cousin. After the negotiations for their marriage failed, she remained unmarried and became a wealthy patroness of the arts. On the failed marriage negotiations see Félix de Llanos y Torriglia, *María I de Inglaterra ¿la Sanguinaria?, reina de España* (Madrid: Espasa-Calpe, 1945), 273–80; M. J. Rodríguez-Salgado, *The Changing Face of Empire: Charles V, Philip II and Habsburg Authority, 1551–1559* (Cambridge: Cambridge University Press, 1988), 77–9.

line with the traditional Trastamaran policy of growing closer to the Portuguese, which had been constant for more than a century and which had been sealed through several marriages, including that of Charles v to Philip's mother, Isabel (1503–1539), and Philip's first union to Maria Manuela of Portugal (1527–1545) in 1543. The advantages of Philip and Mary's marriage were not only in concordance with Spanish notions of universal power, but they also fitted perfectly with the traditional commercial and political alliance formed by the triangle England-Flanders-Castile which had become increasingly important in the fifteenth and early sixteenth centuries.[69] The benefits of the union were not one-sided. From Guaras's perspective, England had lost much of its international reputation since the reign of Henry VIII so it would be advantageous to associate herself with the most powerful monarchy in Christendom, which also happened to be a deadly enemy of England's traditional foes, the French. Moreover, and intriguingly, Guaras was careful to point out that should the Infante Carlos (1545–1568), Philip's son, die, the child born 'here' – that is, in England – would one day become the lord of everything, which would be 'most welcome to the English'. The English would naturally prefer a native-born king, but the aforementioned reasons and the defence that Spain could provide against Scotland and France meant that the union 'would seem like gold to them', especially if Philip resided alternatively in England and Flanders, leaving Carlos in Spain. In the event that the union did take place, he continued,

> Catholics would raise their hands to God, because they bear a natural love to their kingdom and they also bear a natural love to his Majesty [Charles v] and to Spain, especially for the love they felt towards the good Catholic queen [Catherine of Aragon]. And there are so many of the good ones, that for every four heretics, there are a hundred Catholics.[70]

---

69 See Enrique García Hernán, *Vives y Moro. La amistad en tiempos difíciles* (Madrid: Cátedra, 2016), *passim*, and Alexander Samson, *Mary and Philip*, 19–23.

70 Guaras, *Carta de nueuas*, fol. 434[r]: 'También para esta tierra vernía más que a propósito: porque en caso que muriesse el hijo del Príncipe: a quien Dios guarde: sería el hijo nascido aquí señor de todo: [y] a la verdad a los Ingleses estaría co[m]modíssimo. E aun que ellos naturalmente dessean q[ue] sea su Rey nascido aquí: consideradas todas estas cosas [y] otras: y que el Francés se les ha de entrar algún día por Escocia: a ellos les es oro todo: y specialmente hauiendo de venir a viuir aquí el Príncipe [y] en Flandes: y dexando allá vn hijo sería bien a propósito. Y de vna cosa este V[uestra] S[eñoría] certificado: que todos los cathólicos alçarían las manos a dios: porque assí naturalmente quiere[n] bien a su Reyno: y naturalmente tienen amor a su Magestad [y] a España: specialmente por el amor que tuuieron a la buena Reyna Cathólica: y son tantos los buenos: que para quatro hereges ay cient cathólicos'.

The union of England and Spain was, therefore, a positive outcome for the communities of both crowns and it would be sanctioned by the English population, who were overwhelmingly Catholic. This argument resonated with an anonymous report sent to Philip – who was then acting as regent in Spain – in the summer of 1553 to describe Mary's accession and the implications it had for the community of England:

> The king of England died from poisoning, and the [...] duke of Northumberland seized the treasury and the ships that were docked in the ports. He had already seized many lands and castles and had conspired with many of the leading noblemen of the kingdom. He made them swear for their queen one of the daughters that King Henry had had with one of his subsequent wives. Because of this, some other leading noblemen of the realm were inspired by God to favour the party of Princess Mary, eldest daughter to King Henry. She had the support of these men and of the greater part of the community. [...] Thus [...], the princess rose in arms together with twenty-five thousand men and she proclaimed herself queen. She was sworn as such by the council of London, and by many leading noblemen, private persons, and the community. All of this is God's work, and with His favour she currently reigns peacefully in England.[71]

71 RBME, MS V-II-4: 'Relació[n] de lo q[ue] se entiende del exército q[ue] su magestad tiene en francia y de las cosas de alemaña e inglaterra', fols 414^{v}–415^{r}: 'El rey de Inglaterra murió atosigado y a[que]l conde de Varevichi q[ue] después se llamó duq[ue] de noçonaldola se apoderó de todo el tesoro y navíos q[ue] estaua[n] en los puertos. Y estaua apoderado de muchas tierras y castillos. tenía hecha co[n]juraçión co[n] muchos prinçipales del reyno a los quales hizo jurar por reyna vna hija del rey Enrrico avida en vna de las segu[n]das mugeres. esto hecho enspiró dios en algunos otros prinçipales del reyno y fauoresiero[n] al partido de la princesa doña María primera hija del rey enrrico la qual co[n] fauor destos y de la mayor parte de la comunidad y aunq[ue] en el consejo real tuuo mucho fauor entendiendo su justicia y q[ue] vno del consejo hombre prinçipal la fauoresció le avisó de lo q[ue] deuía fazer porq[ue] la princesa se yua amilana[n]do y estrayendo por ver la mucha gente que de la otra parte estaua puesta contra ella en armas. y así por los medios q[ue] he dicho la princesa se puso en armas y en compañía co[n] venite y cinco myll ho[m]bres y se llamó reyna. Y así la juraro[n] por tal en el consejo de londres y muchas personas principales y particulares y la comunidad lo qual ha hecho dios. con todo fauor suyo q[ue] está paçífica reynando inglaterra y tuuo presos a este tirano co[n]de enrriq[ue] y sus hijos y yernos y a otros muchos de la conjuración'. There were rumours following Edward VI's death that he had been poisoned by the duke of Northumberland in order to have Lady Jane Grey and his son Guildford crowned. This would have made little sense, given the urgency with which both king and duke tried to implement the succession change in Lady Jane's favour before the young king's death, with ostensibly unsuccessful results. On the death of the young king and its possible causes see Jennifer Loach,

Although the author was clearly not very well informed about Lady Jane Grey, whom he seemed to confuse with Elizabeth, two main concepts in the account need to be highlighted. First, Mary was seen as a God-sent monarch, and the support she received had been divinely inspired. Second, the author underlines that everyone had understood the justice of her cause, especially the *community*. Although the term 'community' (*comunidad*) in the early modern period can bring together concepts as different as 'the people' or 'autonomous cities', the sense in this account can be likened to the term used during the Comunero revolt of Castile in 1520–1521.[72] The community is seen by the anonymous author as not only that unknown entity called 'the people', but also as a quasi-independent organism that knows what is best for the commonwealth.[73] The anonymous reporter states that prominent members of society had backed Mary's bid for the throne, but that she had also been supported by the community. This autonomous entity was conceived in the same way as the one which had rebelled against Charles's foreign advisers in 1520. The Comunero revolt had been backed in most Castilian cities by

---

Edward VI (New Haven and London: Yale University Press, 1999), 161–2. The account of Mary's accession kept at El Escorial is very similar to the one sent from London by Philip's confidant, Diego de Acevedo, to his wife, which again highlights the fact that Philip was, even at this early stage in the negotiations, quite aware of English affairs. See Samson, *Mary and Philip*, 34. The manuscript containing Acevedo's account can be found in Biblioteca Nacional de España, MS 9937, ff. 97^r–99^r.

72 On Spanish and Engish notions of the term 'commonwealth', see Alexander Winton Seton Samson, 'The Marriage of Philip of Habsburg and Mary Tudor and Anti-Spanish Sentiment in England: Political Economies and Culture, 1553–1557' (PhD thesis, Queen Mary and Westfield College, unpublished, 1999), 138–60.

73 For an assessment of the implications of this view in the Comunero revolt see the still relevant work by Stephen Haliczer, *The Comuneros of Castile: The Forging of a Revolution, 1475–1521* (Madison, Wisconsin; Univeristy of Wisconsin Press, 1981), 3. Other classic works on this revolt, which was one of the most dangerous threats ever encountered by Charles V, are those by Manuel Danvila y Collado, *Historia crítica y documentada de las Comunidades de Castilla* 6 vols. (Madrid: Viuda e hijos de M. Tello, 1897–1900) and José Antonio Maravall, *Las comunidades de Castilla: Una primera revolución moderna* (Madrid: Revista de Occidente, 1963). More recent interpretations of the revolt and its impact can be found in Joseph Pérez, *Los comuneros* (Madrid: La Esfera de los Libros, 2001) and his extensive and detailed *La revolución de las Comunidades de Castilla (1520–1521)*, trans. by Juan José Faci Lacasta (Barcelona: Siglo XXI de España, 2005) and José Joaquín Jerez, *Pensamiento político y reforma constitucional durante la guerra de las Comunidades de Castilla (1520–1521)* (Madrid, Barcelona, and Buenos Aires: Marcial Pons, 2007). The latest reassessment is the suggestive study by Miguel Martínez, *Comuneros. El rayo y la semilla (1520–1521)* (Gijón: Hoja de Lata, 2021), an innovative work in which he proposes new ways of interpreting and understanding the place of the revolt in the history of Spain.

their city councils, clergy, and common people. In Salamanca, for instance, representatives of the three mendicant orders had collaborated with the city council in issuing a reply to the regency government's orders to halt the disorders. In their reply, they requested Charles not to leave the kingdom until he had married and secured the succession or at least until he had recalled his brother Ferdinand from Austria and installed him as his regent. Failing this, they threatened, 'the comunidad of Castile would be able to take matters into its own hands in order to protect the kingdom's resources from exploitation'.[74] The demands of the Salamanca representatives as well as the role ascribed to the community in Mary's accession both echo the Thomist theory of the *civitas* as being the *communitas perfecta*, which is not only a politically autonomous society, but also one which provides what is best for itself, an idea which was directly linked to Aristotelian notions of *autarkeia*, or 'self-sufficiency'. The community was able to determine that which was 'necessary for life' (*necessarium ad vitam*) in a natural, as well as in a political sense.[75]

In relation to Mary's intended restoration of Catholicism – which was certainly no secret, at least not to the Spanish commentators here explored – the support she had received from the community was a result of the same community's desire to protect its commonwealth. She had not been imposed on the throne of England by foreign intervention or by the pope, but by her own people, who knew what was best for them, in agreement with Francisco de Vitoria's (1483–1546) statements that popes did not possess temporal authority over princes and their territories.[76] The pontiff could only intervene, Vitoria claimed, if a prince acted against 'the salvation of souls and religion'. Otherwise, his 'office ceases'.[77] Mary's accession had been an act of God

74 Haliczer, *Comuneros of Castile*, 159.

75 St Thomas Aquinas, *Commentary on Aristotle's* Politics (*In libros Politicorum expositio*), I, l. 1n23. Further on these concepts in Pagden, *Lords of all the World*, 18; Christoph Philipp Haar, *Natural and Political Conceptions of Community: The Role of the Household in Early Modern Jesuit Thought, c. 1590–1650* (Leiden and Boston: Brill, 2019), 92–4.

76 Quentin Skinner, *The Foundations of Modern Political Thought*, vol. 2 (Cambridge: Cambridge University Press, 1978), 175–6.

77 This could be interpreted, of course, as being the case in Edward VI's reign from a Catholic perspective, but the King's minority warranted a policy of waiting to see what would happen, as religious developments under the young King could be easily blamed on 'evil counsellors'. For Vitoria's statements see Francisco de Vitoria, OP, *Reverendis patri F. Francisci de Victoria, ordinis Praedicatoru[m], sacrae Theologiae in Salmanticensi Academia quondam primarij Professoris, Relectiones Theologicae XII in duos Tomos diuisae*, vol. I (Lyon: Jacques Boyer, 1557), 86–7: 'Eo enim ipso quod hoc non sit contrarium saluti animarum, & religioni, cessat officium papae. Sed si papa dicat talem administrationem

performed through the agency of the community. The concepts of divine protection and the welfare of the community are constantly intertwined, and they figure prominently in the history of Philip and Mary's joint monarchy.

More prosaic interventions came into play in order to safeguard the welfare of the community. In the case of England and the impending marriage of Philip and Mary, concerns were raised about what would effectively be a change of dynasty. Charles v had learnt the hard way about the dangers of such an eventuality during the Comunero revolt already alluded to. To make matters worse, a queen regnant was a novelty in England, and one bound to stir up sensibilities easily. There was a virulent opposition to female rule which manifested itself mainly through the works of Protestant authors, but concerns about the subversion of expected gender roles were not confined to religious objections to Mary's accession.[78] The short-lived co-monarchy of Charles's parents, Philip I and Juana I between 1504 and 1506 was a convenient reminder of the perceived troubles of female succession. Their reign, in stark contrast with that of Ferdinand and Isabel, whose disagreements were usually solved successfully, had been marred by aggressive power struggles between Ferdinand, Philip, and Juana, the rumours of Juana's inability to govern due to her alleged mental instability, and Philip's blatant disregard for Castilian law and his appointment of Flemish advisors to Castilian offices. Following Philip's sudden death, Juana was eventually interned in the castle of Tordesillas and Ferdinand assumed the role of governor of Castile until his death in 1516 to be succeeded, in a more than irregular way, by the fourth successive co-monarchy of Spain – that of Charles and his mother Juana, which would endure until the latter's death in 1555.[79] Situations like these were perceived as a threat to the 'community' with the potential to damage the entire body politic. In this context, the English sought to protect their laws and customs through the

cedere in detrime[n]tum salutis spiritualis, ut quod talis lex seruari no[n] posset sine peccato mortali, aut esse contra ius diuinum, aut esse fomentum peccatorum, standum esset iudicio Pontificis, quia Rex non habet iudicare de rebus spiritualibus, ut supra dictum est'.

78 There were active calls by Protestant authors to resist 'female tyranny', with the common representation of Mary as a cruel Jezebel (1 Kings 16:31) or Athaliah (2 Kings 8:16, 11:16 and 2 Chronicles 22:10, 23:15). See Sarah Duncan, *Mary I: Gender, Power, and Ceremony in the Reign of England's First Queen* (New York: Palgrave Macmillan, 2012), 111–133 and Samson, *Mary and Philip*, 87–90.

79 Consensus seems to be growing around the accession of Charles in 1516 having been against strict legality, given that his mother, the proprietary queen of Castile and Aragon, was still alive. The latest and most incisive reassessment of Juana's life and reign is to be found in Gillian B. Fleming, *Juana I: Legitimacy and Conflict in Sixteenth-Century Castile* (London: Palgrave Macmillan, 2018).

passing in parliament in the spring of 1554 of a marriage treaty (made public in January) which stressed Mary's position as queen regnant. Parliament also passed the Act for the Queen's Regal Power, which confirmed that regal authority and power resided in Mary 'as fully and absolutely as ever it was in any of her most noble progenitors kings of this realm'. These measures, and the courtly and public representations of queen and monarchy that they elicited cast Mary as queen and king at the same time, displaying traditional female and male attributes, as well as motherly and virginal characteristics as determined by context.[80]

Alexander Samson has been the first to point out that the treaty that sealed Philip and Mary's marriage was modelled after that which had sealed Ferdinand and Isabel's.[81] Indeed, despite the insistence on the Anglo-Burgundian character of the marriage, we merely need to remember that, after the preliminary negotiations for Ferdinand and Isabel's marriage had been signed in February 1469, Isabel had given a note written in her own hand to Ferdinand's envoys in which she told him: 'command me what you want me to do now, for I am bound to do it'.[82] Wives were subject to their husbands' wishes, and Isabel's words were the expected reflection of this notion. Yet, the degree of independence she showed by allowing herself to be proclaimed queen of Castile in Ferdinand's absence in January 1475 provoked her husband's fury.[83] This independence of character would also be displayed, in a similar context, by her granddaughter Mary. During the marriage negotiations, Mary made a similar demonstration of the resulting hybrid between wifely humility and power-awareness that female rule could entail. She told ambassador Renard that, in accepting Philip as her husband, she,

> would perfectly love and obey him to whom she was destined, following the divine commandment, and would do nothing without him so wishing. But if he wished to assail the government of the kingdom, she would

80 For more information on the Act and the gendering of Mary's monarchy in general see J. D. Alsop, 'The Act for the Queen's Regal Power, 1554', *Parliamentary History*, 13, no. 3 (1994), 261–76; Charles Beem, *The Lioness Roared: The Problems of Female Rule in English History* (New York: Palgrave Macmillan, 2006), 63–99; Duncan, *Mary I*, *passim* and especially 58–9; Samson, *Mary and Philip*, *passim* and especially 91–8.

81 Alexander Samson, 'Power Sharing: The Co-Monarchy of Philip and Mary' in Alice Hunt and Anna Whitelock, eds., *Tudor Queenship: The Reigns of Mary and Elizabeth* (New York, 2010), 159–72.

82 Luis Suárez, *Isabel I, Reina* (Barcelona: Ariel, 2010), 64–5.

83 Samson, 'Power Sharing', 160–1.

> not be able to suffer it, much less so to place strangers in offices and posts of the same, and the kingdom would not suffer it either.[84]

This was, of course, easier said than done, but at this stage Mary saw no contradiction in being a dutiful wife and a female sovereign, even if her husband's desires were to be at odds with what was best for the kingdom; and neither had Isabel. In order to placate Ferdinand after her proclamation, Isabel reached a similar agreement with him on the order of their joint titles as Philip and Mary would reach later on: Castile would be the first title mentioned, but Ferdinand's name would come first.[85] Isabel further confirmed this by granting her husband more political independence to govern in Castile in her absences, making good the Machiavellian motto chosen by Ferdinand that made reference to the Gordian knot, *tanto monta cortar como desatar* (it amounts to the same, cutting as untying). The motto would come to be associated with both monarchs and their initials, 'F' and 'Y', making them equal sovereigns through the popular saying derived from the original motto, *tanto monta, monta tanto/ Isabel como Fernando* (Ferdinand and Isabel amount to the same).[86] Philip and Mary's marriage treaty had much to do with Ferdinand and Isabel's *capitulaciones matrimoniales*. The political concerns which made possible such an advantageous contract for the English stemmed from an implicit fear of foreign domination through marriage. To prevent this from happening, they had produced a series of negotiating points which aimed to curtail Prince Philip's potential manoeuvring in the government of England.[87] English fears of foreign domination were understandable, but the Habsburgs were, after the Comunero revolt, punctiliously careful when it came to the 'laws and customs' of the different dominions belonging to their crown. Above all, as we shall see,

84 Österreichisches Staatsarchiv, Haus-, Hof- und Staatsarchiv, Staatenabteilungen, Großbritannien Diplomatische Korrespondenz 15, Konv. 1553: Simon Renard to Charles V, London, 25 October 1553: '[…] quelle aymera / et obeira p[ar]faictement celluy à cuy elle sera dedié / suyvant le co[m]mandement diuin / et ne fera rien sans son vouloir / Que sil vouloit attempter au gouuernement du royaulme, elle ne le pouroit comporter / moins entremectre en office[e]s et charges dicelluy estrangiers / co[m]me aussy le royaulme ne le comporteroit / […]'.

85 Ana Belén Sánchez Prieto, 'La intitulación diplomática de los Reyes Católicos: un programa político y una lección de historia', in Juan Carlos Galende Díaz, ed., *III Jornadas Científicas sobre Documentación de la época de los Reyes Católicos* (Madrid: Universidad Complutense de Madrid, 2004), 273–301.

86 Samson, 'Power Sharing', 161; Henry Kamen, *Spain, 1469–1714: A Society of Conflict* (Harlow: Longman, 2005; 1983), 10.

87 Samson, *Mary and Philip*, 60–74.

Philip was aware that the observance of legality – at least outwardly – was absolutely fundamental.

This can be further illustrated by the treatment given to the territories composing the Catholic Monarchy. Considering the origins of those appointed as governors, lieutenants or viceroys, it stands out that those territories which had previously been independent but had for a long time been associated with the crowns of Castile and Aragon, or had been incorporated through conquest, such as Catalonia, Valencia, Navarre, and Naples, were often granted governors who were not necessarily natives. On the other hand, however, Charles and Philip were much more punctilious when it came to appointing governors to stronger independent political entities, as were Castile, Aragon, Sicily, or Flanders.[88] This had become acutely necessary after the Comunero revolt, since one of the rebels' demands was that any governors appointed during the absence of the monarch would have to be natural-born subjects of Castile. This was seen as a favourable 'quality' that would incline them to 'procure the benefit of the kingdom', a clear reaction to Adrian of Utrecht's appointment as regent when Charles left Spain in 1520.[89] Isabel of Portugal, Charles's wife, and herself a granddaughter of Ferdinand and Isabel, acted as regent of Castile and the kingdoms of Spain during Charles's absences and after her death the task fell to Philip, who was officially appointed regent in 1543. When Philip left Spain for his European tour between 1548 and 1551, he appointed his sister María and her husband, their cousin Maximilian of Austria, to fill in his post. Similarly, when he left for England in 1554, he made sure that his youngest sister, Juana, recently widowed in Portugal, would go to Spain to take his place as regent. In the case of the kingdom of Aragon, after the death in 1520 of the lieutenant general Alonso de Aragón, archbishop of Saragossa and an illegitimate son of Ferdinand the Catholic, Charles V appointed the Aragonese Juan de Lanuza (1520–1535). The next two lieutenants would be Beltrán de la Cueva y Toledo, duke of Alburquerque (1535–1539), himself a Castilian but married

88 One of the most recent and complete reassessments of the viceregal system of the Spanish Monarchy can be found in Pedro Cardim and Joan-Lluís Palos, eds., *El mundo de los virreyes en las monarquías de España y Portugal* (Madrid and Frankfurt am Main: Iberoamericana-Vervuert, 2012).

89 AGS, Patronato Real, leg. 3, 137, 'Capítulos que pidieron los Comuneros al Emperador', no. 8: 'Yten queda que adelante el t[iem]po que su mag[es]t[ad] estuuiere avsente destos rey[n]os por cuya causa aya nesçesidad de poner gouernadores en ellos que tal gouernador o gouernadores sean naturales por origen destos reynos de castilla y delas personas aprobadas en quien concurra esta calidad de naturaleza de origen e las otras qualidades que para tan gran cargo se requieren para que mire[n] e procure[n] el bien del Reyno'.

to the Aragonese Juana de Aragón y Gurrea, daughter to the late archbishop of Saragossa, and the Aragonese Pedro Martínez de Luna, count of Morata de Jalón (1539–1554). Philip would then confirm the latter's designation in 1543. Philip's appointment of Diego Hurtado de Mendoza, count of Mélito, in 1554, incurring in a *desafuero* (a violation of the laws or *fueros* of the kingdom of Aragon), proved to be disastrous, as Mélito, Ruy Gómez's cantankerous father-in-law, repeatedly created problems in the kingdom. Mélito's mother had been an Aragonese, but this had not proven to be enough, and Philip learnt the lesson well: he would not appoint a non-Aragonese for over thirty years, and that appointment would again lead to conflict.[90]

Much of the historiography has stressed – not without reason – that the marriage treaty between Philip and Mary could be interpreted as disadvantageous to the prince of Spain. Although the treaty provided for him to 'be allowed to have and enjoy the style, honor, and kingly name of the realms and dominions unto the said most noble queen appertaining', it was clear that this would be 'for so long as the matrimony endureth' and that the king's task would be to 'aid' her 'in the prosperous administration of her realms and dominions'. Philip was not entitled to meddle with 'the benefits and offices, lands, revenues, and fruits' of the realm, which were to be disposed of by Mary and distributed 'to such as be naturally born in the same'. Furthermore, all matters of state were to be treated in English.[91] These dispositions were clarified as soon as the marriage had taken place; and they were clarified in Philip's favour. On 27 July 1554, when the privy council sat for the first time in Winchester under Philip and Mary's joint reign, it was decided that a copy of matters of state discussed would be produced in Latin or Spanish and be delivered to the King, that all matters requiring a royal signature would need to 'be signed with both thier [sic] hands', and that a royal stamp bearing both their names would be created for 'suche matiers as shuld be requisite'.[92]

90 Manuel Rivero Rodríguez, *La edad de oro de los virreyes. El virreinato en la Monarquía Hispánica durante los siglos XVI y XVII* (Madrid: Akal, 2011), 59–64. See also Pere Molas i Ribalta, 'La administración real en la Corona de Aragón', *Chronica nova: Revista de historia moderna de la Universidad de Granada*, 21 (1993–1994), 427–40. Philip would, however, appoint Mélito as viceroy of Catalonia, where rules about the lieutenancy were more lax, in 1564. The king's appointment for the lieutenancy of the Castilian Íñigo López de Mendoza, marquis of Almenara, in 1587 was rejected by the Aragonese and this, coupled with the presence of the fugitive royal secretary, Antonio Pérez, and Almenara's attempts to have him processed by the Inquisition were seen as a violation of the kingdom's *fueros*, which led to revolt. See Parker, *Imprudent King*, 333–40.

91 TRP, vol. 2, 21–6.

92 APC, vol. 5, 53.

Hernando del Pulgar (*c.*1436–*c.*1493), who had been Ferdinand and Isabel's official chronicler from 1482 described in his *Chrónica de los* [...] *Reyes Cathólicos don Fernando y doña Ysabel*, first printed in 1565, the dispositions agreed by the Catholic Monarchs in Segovia in 1475, whichwere very similar to those devised for Philip and Mary:

> They agreed that both their names would appear in any letters patent that they should issue; and that their seal would be one, with the arms of both Castile and Aragon. Likewise, the coinage that they ordered to be minted showed the figures of both him and her, as well as both their names.[93]

This, and the fact that in Ferdinand and Isabel's marriage contract their representatives had stressed – twice – the commitment to admit only natives of Castile and not any foreigners into the kingdom's offices, gives credence to the view that Philip and Mary's treaty, even if drawn up by Flemings and Englishmen, had a distinctive Spanish flavour.[94] Their coinage, like that of Ferdinand and Isabel, also represented them facing each other with their quartered arms in the reverse (see Figures 1.1, 1.2, 1.3, 1.4). There were differences, such as Ferdinand and Isabel wearing their own individual crowns and Philip and Mary being represented under a single floating one, but their joint representation signified their joint sovereignty.[95] Consorts were not represented in coinage, only regnant monarchs, which establishes Philip and Mary's status as co-rulers.

---

93 Hernando del Pulgar, *Chrónica. De los muy altos y esclarecidos reyes Cathólicos don Fernando y doña Ysabel de gloriosa memoria. Dirigida a la Cathólica Real Magestad del Rey don Philipe nuestro Señor* (Valladolid: Sebastián Martínez, 1565), fol. 26v: '[...] y dende en adelante él y ella mandaron, que no se hablasse más en esta materia: y acordaron que en todas las cartas que diessen, fuessen nombrados él y ella: y que el sello vno fuesse con las armas de Castilla y Aragón. Assí mesmo en la moneda que mandaron labrar, estouiessen puestas las figuras dél y della, y los nombres de ambos'. Although written in the early 1490s in Latin, the text would not see the light in print until 1565, when it was mistakenly attributed to Antonio de Nebrija.

94 'Capitulaciones del matrimonio entre la princesa Doña Isabel y D. Fernando, Rei de Sicilia, ajustadas en Cervera a 7 de enero de 1469, y confirmadas por el Rei D. Juan de Aragón en Zaragoza a 12 del mismo mes y año', in Diego Clemencín, *Elogio de la reina Católica doña Isabel, al que siguen varias ilustraciones sobre su reinado* (Madrid: J. Sancha for Academia de la Historia, 1821), 578; Samson, 'Power Sharing', 161–2.

95 See further information of Philip's coinage as king of England in José María de Francisco Olmos, 'Las primeras acuñaciones del príncipe Felipe de España (1554–1556): Soberano de Milán, Nápoles e Inglaterra', *Documenta & Instrumenta*, vol. 3 (2005), 155–86.

FIGURE 1.1
Ferdinand and Isabel Doble Excelente obverse
MUSEO CASA DE LA MONEDA, 11140

FIGURE 1.2
Ferdinand and Isabel Doble Excelente reverse
MUSEO CASA DE LA MONEDA, 11140

FIGURE 1.3
Philip and Mary Shilling obverse
THE ROYAL MINT MUSEUM

FIGURE 1.4
Philip and Mary Shilling reverse
THE ROYAL MINT MUSEUM

Contrasting heavily with the lack of English patrimony assigned to Philip in the treaty, Mary was to 'be admitted into the society of the realms and dominions of the said noble Prince, as well such as he now hath presently as also such other as during the same matrimony may come hereafter unto him'.[96]

96 TPR, vol. 2 22.

That Mary was thus included in the prince's 'society' speaks not only of the indissolubility of marriage and the status of the parties as a *same person/conjunta persona*, but also of the contractual and business-oriented character of royal marriages. The dowry envisaged for Mary assigned to her '£60,000 at 40 Flemish groats the £20,000 from the realms of the emperor, £40,000 from Spain, Castile and Aragon and their appurtenances – Brabant, Flanders, Hainault, Holland'. These four provinces – which were not dependencies of Spain but were the emperor's patrimonial estates – had been assigned as revenue sources for Margaret of York, widow of Charles the Bold, duke of Burgundy, Philip's great-great-grandfather, and to be used by her in right of usufruct and the same was agreed for Mary.[97] The inclusion of the terms and specific mention of Margaret of York's appanage certainly speaks in favour of the revival of the Anglo-Burgundian alliance. However, the fact that Mary was to receive £40,000 from Spain – with allusion to the kingdoms of Castile and Aragon – and its dominions or 'appurtenances', in which the Low Countries were unmistakably included, manifests that the treaty was indeed being signed with the Spanish Monarchy, and not solely with the king of Spain as heir to the dukes of Burgundy, despite Ruy Gómez's complaints already alluded to and the perceptions of the Grey Friars chronicler, who had described Charles V's envoys as 'imbassators in the name of the hole howse of Bowrgone'.[98] Philip had not yet received his inheritance, which is the reason behind the treaty's allusion to 'the principal dominions of the [...] most virtuous Lord the Emperor his father'. In the same manner, when Ferdinand had signed his marriage treaty in Cervera on 7 March 1469, his father, King John II of Aragon (r. 1458–1479), had abdicated the throne of Sicily in his favour – as Charles V was to do upon Philip with the kingdom of Naples just before the Prince's marriage – so that whenever Isabel ascended the Castilian throne, they would be equals. Furthermore, the treaty had provided Isabel with the lordships of Borja, Magallón, Crevillente, Siracusa, and Catania. The fact that only the latter two already belonged to Ferdinand when the treaty was signed, points at more similarities between the two marriage treaties.[99]

That the marriage was not conceived as a regular royal marriage but as an augmentation of each monarch's crowns is undeniable. Ana de Aragón y Gurrea, duchess of Medina Sidonia, in her congratulatory letter to Queen Mary after the proxy marriage had taken place, wrote that since God had seen fit that Philip should go 'to that kingdom for such a blessed business', she hoped that

97 TRP, vol. 2, 22; CSP Domestic, 13–5.

98 For the Grey Friars citation see Samson, 'Power Sharing', 86.

99 Suárez, *Isabel I*, 64–5.

the queen and her husband would enjoy many years of happiness. The duchess was also hopeful that they should soon witness the 'fruit and effects' that all of Mary's subjects – in which the duchess included herself – longed for, 'for the sake of Christianity and of our honour'. She closed the letter by expressing her desire that God would 'prosper and exalt' Mary with the acquisition of 'more kingdoms and fiefdoms'.[100] Through her marriage, Mary was acquiring more territories that she would then be able to transmit to her descendants. The inclusion of England and Ireland within Spain's composite monarchy is also made apparent in a letter sent by Nicholas Wotton, the English ambassador in France, to master secretary sir William Petre after the marriage had taken place. In it, Wotton wrote that 'by most mennes Judgemente' on the marriage depended not only 'the weale and conseruation' of England, 'but also the greate comodite of all Christendome'. However, he also expressed concern about the way in which Philip's new title of king of Naples (granted by Charles v before the marriage) had been proclaimed:

> [...] yn one of yowr l[ett]res yow wryte that thenp[er]o[ur] hath made cession to the kings highnesse, of the Realmes of Naples and Sicily and yn yowr other l[ett]re yow saye that it is of Naples and Hier[usa]l[e]m, and not of Sicily [...] I remember to haue redde, although yn co[m]mon speeche and talke so[m]me men vse to saye the Realme of Naples: yet yn all gifts and cessions and such other lyke wrytinge [...] it is not so callid but by theese words, Regnu[m] or Regna vtrisq[ue] Sicilie cis et trans phary. So that cis pharu[m] conteynith all that Realme [...] callid Naples, and trans pharu[m] the verye sicilye.

Wotton wondered why the emperor would have used these 'vnaccoustummid wourdes' rather than 'the words of all tymes vsid'. As papal fiefs, Wotton added, both realms should always go together, and the ambassador considered that it would have been better had Charles used both titles instead of

100 TNA, SP, 69/4, no. 189. Ana de Aragón y Gurrea, Duchess of Medina Sidonia to Queen Mary, Sanlúcar de Barrameda, 20 April 1554: '[...] pues dios a tenido por bien que el príncipe y R[e]y n[uest]ro Señor vaya a ése R[e]yno a negoçio tan bienauenturado plega a dios que con él goze v[uestra] m[ajes]t[ad] muchos años y que presto veamos fruto y efectos señalados desta conformidad que así lo esperamos sus vasallos / para bien de la christiandad y Honrra n[uest]ra y [...] no digo más aquí sino que n[uest]ro s[eño]r la R[e]al p[er]sona de v[uestra] s[acra] m[ajes]t[ad] prosp[er]e y ensalçe bien auenturadamente con acresçentamiento de más R[e]ynos y Señoríos'. Curiously, Ana de Aragón was Mary's first cousin, as she was the youngest daughter of Alonso of Aragon, archbishop of Saragossa, who was anillegitimate son of Ferdinand the Catholic, which made him a half-brother to Catherine of Aragon.

making 'a Donac[i]on yn doubtfull words. wherof maye ryse contenc[i]on'.[101] The English ambassador in France was already thinking ahead and imagining scenarios in which the king of England's rights to the Two Sicilies might be contested, showing a full understanding of England's new place as a member of the Spanish Monarchy and an acute awareness of the traditional French claims over the kingdoms.[102] Wotton's and Ana de Aragón's statements clearly show that the marriage was understood as an effectual union of both crowns, rather than as a mere royal marriage. To insist in the portrayal of either Philip or Mary as mere consorts, the word understood in its most common acceptation of a royal spouse who is subordinate to the other party but enjoyed certain privileges and power by association, is wrong and it disregards Spanish understandings of co-monarchy. This is not to say that there was not a distinction to be made between the source of sovereignty and authority that each of the monarchs' enjoyed in their respective kingdoms and territories. Indeed, Philip was acutely aware of the difference between kingdoms received through inheritance and kingdoms received through marriage. Years later, in a revealing letter that he would send from Brussels in May 1558 to the count of Feria, who was then in London, Philip made clear how he understood this distinction and how he viewed himself as king of England. 'I wish for the welfare of that kingdom', he stated, 'and I have to procure it by all possible means; no less than I wish and procure the welfare of the rest, which came to me through inheritance'.[103] In this remark, Philip was displaying that punctilious observance with regard to legality which the Habsburgs were so insistent upon whilst, at the same time, he was claiming to be king of England as fully as he was king of his other territories. This point should also be put in relation to one of the most pivotal aspects of the marriage treaty, which was the question of the succession.

---

101 TNA, SP 69/5, no. 251; Nicholas Wotton to Sir William Petre, Compiègne, 10 August 1554.

102 There was, indeed, some contention about the legality of Emperor Charles's cession of the kingdom of Naples, not least because his mother, Queen Juana, was still alive in July 1554. Charles's brother, Ferdinand, and King Henry II of France were already devising ways to contest Philip's position, but the king took decisive action to exert his rights and then Juana died in April 1555. Her death, as M. J. Rodríguez-Salgado has argued, was 'almost providential' but it did not prevent several years of legal disputations to assert the kingdom's exemption from papal jurisdiction. See M. J. Rodríguez-Salgado, *The Changing Face of Empire: Charles V, Philip II and Habsburg Authority, 1551–1559* (Cambridge: Cambridge University Press, 1988), 108–10.

103 AGS, Estado 811, leg. 56. Philip to Gómez Suárez de Figueroa, count of Feria, Brussels, 27 May 1558: '[…]y es que assí como desseo el bien desse reyno, y lo tengo de procurar por todas las vías que pudiere, no menos que el de los otros, que me vienen de herencia, así holgaría mucho por lo que toca al bien dél, que se conseruasse el amistad y comercio que tienen con los de la dicha Ansa Theutónica'.

The succession was a delicate matter not only due to English fears of foreign domination – which were allayed by the inclusion of a clause denying Philip any rights to the throne after Mary's death – but also because Philip already had a son, Carlos, born to his first wife, Maria Manuela of Portugal, in 1545. Carlos's rights to Spain, the Italian territories and the New World were safeguarded, but the contract envisaged the separation of the Low Countries from the Spanish inheritance. The Netherlandish territories would be left, together with England and Ireland, to any child born to Philip and Mary, with the caveat that should this child be a girl, she would need Carlos's permission to marry outside of her kingdoms. The only scenario in which Philip and Mary's descendants would inherit everything was if Carlos's line became extinct (as we now know it did, but would have been impossible to predict in 1554).[104] Charles v had for long toyed with the idea of separating the Low Countries from the Spanish inheritance, as shown by his plans to marry off his daughter María first to one of Ferdinand's sons and then to a French prince in the 1540s and bestowing the Netherlands on them, although neither project ever came to term.[105] This was a contentious decision, even if an advantageous clause for the English, because it could mean the dismemberment of the Spanish Monarchy. Philip's often quoted *ad cautelam* document should be understood in this light.[106] Signed in Valladolid on 4 January 1554, it was witnessed by Philip's advisers: Fernando Álvarez de Toledo, duke of Alba, Ruy Gómez de Silva and Francisco de Menchaca, a trusted jurist from Philip's inner circle of confidants. In it, Philip explained that the Emperor had sent Lamoral, count of Egmont, Charles, count of Lalaing, Jean de Montmorency, lord of Courrières and Philippe Negri, chancellor of the Order of the Golden Fleece to negotiate his marriage together with Renard and the queen's council, 'so that on his behalf and in his name, they could ratify, swear, and approve the said articles'. 'However', the declaration went on,

> because before these articles were made and granted by his Majesty [Charles v], he [Philip] had not been informed about their contents, he will indeed grant the said proxy authority, and he will approve, grant, and swear the same articles in order for his marriage to the most serene queen of England to take place; but not to be bound or liable in any manner, nor

104 TRP, vol. 2, 23.

105 Manuel Fernández Álvarez, *Carlos V. El César y el hombre* [1999] (Barcelona: Planeta DeAsgostini, 2007), 597; Parker, *Emperor*, 263–7.

106 See some recent interpretations of Philip's *ad cautelam* document in Samson, *Mary and Philip*, 63–4 and "Power Sharing", 164–5; Edwards, *Mary I*, 157–8.

> his goods, nor his heirs and successors, to the keeping and observance of the same articles, especially those that may trouble his conscience.[107]

It is clear that Philip was willing for his marriage to Mary to be concluded, and he expressly mentioned that he granted the proxy power to that effect. The articles that could 'trouble his conscience', as he describes them, can only make reference to the articles touching the succession to his inheritance. Hence the reference not only to his own person, but also to his 'goods' and 'heirs and successors'. It seems that Philip was not ready to contemplate the Low Countries being severed from the Spanish Monarchy, as he had a responsibility to keep such inheritance, given to him by God, intact. As Rodríguez-Salgado discovered, in 1559 Philip would consider marrying Queen Elizabeth I only if two points were agreed first: that England would remain Catholic, and that the Low Countries would remain part of Carlos's inheritance, which confirms that his protestations in 1554 went in this direction.[108]

1.4 The Offices of the Realm, Foreigners and the Spanish Historical Experience

Potential attacks on the laws and customs of the realm were the epitome of English fears of foreign domination. The fact that a stranger should come to reign over them was perceived as an unnatural subversion of the established

107 AGS, Patronato, leg. 55, no. 32; Testimonio del poder que da el Príncipe Felipe de España para concertar su matrimonio con María Tudor, Reina de Inglaterra y revocación de algunos artículos ya asentados que el Príncipe jura pero no acepta, Valladolid, 4 January 1554: '[…] a de otorgar poder en forma al p[rí]ncipe de gavere y al c[on]de lalaing, caballeros del tusón doro y a Jvan de memoranci señor de currier[e]s y a felipo nygro chanciller de la d[ic]ha horde[n] del tusón y a simón rreynart, enbaxador de su mag[es]t[ad] en Ingalat[e]rra – todos del su consejo y a los dos o qualq[ui]er dellos p[ar]a q[ue] por él y en su nombre rratifiq[ue]n jure[n] y aprueben los d[ic]hos artículos y él se obligare de los rratificar y otorgar + aprovare y jurar en forma como se conterná en el poder […] porq[ue] antes q[ue] se hiziesen [y] por su mag[es]t[ad] se otorgasen los d[ic]hos artículos no supo dellos + otorgará el d[ic]ho poder y él aprouará y otorgará y jurará los d[ic]hos artículos a fin q[ue] el d[ic]ho su casamye[n]to con la d[ic]ha s[erenísi]ma Reyna de Ingalat[e]rra aya efecto y no para q[ue]dar y estar obligado él ny sus bienes ny sus herederos y sucesor[e]s a la guarda y op[ser]uado de los d[ic]hos artículos ny de alguno dellos en especial de los en q[ue] encargare su conciencia'.

108 Rodríguez-Salgado, *Changing Face of Empire*, 320. Philip explained that what had been agreed for his marriage with Mary to take place had been unwise and it would be even more so in 1559, as Carlos, at the age of fourteen, had now grown up. 'Under no circumstances will I agree to it', he claimed. See Parker, *Imprudent King*, 123–4.

order. In the opening lines of the 1555 work *A Supplicachon to the queens maiestie*, its anonymous author wrote that they,

> [I]n moste humble wise co[m]playnyth vnto your highnes / that wheras this noble realm off England / hath of long tyme out of mynd bene the most fre contre in all Christe[n]dome Now is like to be brought into bo[n]dag and slauery of such a nacyon as all the world both hatyth and abhoryth.[109]

Similarly, after the first news of the Wyatt rebellion had arrived in Mary's court, Renard anxiously reported to Charles V:

> Wyatt, Harper, Isley, Culpepper, and many others have risen in revolt and have declared that they did not want to consent on any marriage with a stranger. They have published that him who is a good Englishman must join them in their fight against the Spaniards.[110]

Later in the same letter, Renard tried to play down the xenophobic motives adduced by the rebels by assigning their motivations to religious dissent.[111] However, both examples give proof of the fear that a foreign king and a change of dynasty entailed, with terms as ideologically charged as 'bondage' or 'slavery' being used in the *Supplicachon*. The marriage treaty made provisions against this possibility too. Regardless of who succeeded Philip and Mary, 'he or she' was bound by the treaty to leave to all the kingdoms coming from both the king and the queen, 'whole and entire their privileges, rights, and customs'. Apart from this, their successor would have to make sure that these realms were 'administered by the natural born of the same realms'.[112] These points of the treaty have always been interpreted as an English reaction to Habsburg marital expansion, and it is certainly true that the English were anxious to lay down from the beginning that the prince of Spain would not be able to alter the constitutional basis of English laws. However, a close scrutiny of the language used in the marriage treaty reveals that Spanish influence played a hitherto

109 Anon., *A Supplicachon to the quenes maiestie* (1555), fol. 1^{v}.

110 AGS, Estado 808, leg. 7. Simon Renard to Charles V. London, 27 January 1554: 'vietz / arper / als / colpeper et plusieurs autres se sont rreuoltez et déclairez quilz ne voulouent consentir mariage estrangier faisans publier que gui stroit bon anglois il se deust joindre pour combatre les espagnolz'.

111 The relationship between anti-Spanish and anti-Catholic sentiments will be explored in Chapter 2.

112 TRP, vol. 2, 24; CSP Domestic, 13–5.

unrecognised but crucial role. Indeed, the whole style is unmistakably reminiscent of the arrangements between Ferdinand and Isabel and the demands made to Charles V by the Comuneros, as we shall see.

The marriage treaty also envisaged several additional clauses that would have to be solemnly sworn by Philip. First, the new king was not to 'promote, admit, or receive to any office, administration or benefice [...] any stranger or person' who had not been born a subject of Queen Mary. The first clause also made clear that Philip was to admit to his household English gentlemen and yeomen in convenient number. This clause was intended to grant English access to Philip's presence whilst it proclaimed Philip's undeniable new status as king of England, clearly stating that these new English servants, 'as his proper subjects shall esteem, entertain, and nourish'.[113] The phrasing of the second demand of this clause is echoed in a letter written by Philip to Simon Renard in early February 1554:

> Once there I will take in the natural-born of the realm, so that they understand that I will have them serve me, and that I will trust them and favour them, as if I were their natural-born lord. They will understand this by seeing the trust that I have in them, coming into their kingdom and into their power [...]. I am also determined not to take with me more people than those already in my household because the fewer they are, the better it will be for my household's management and for our adaptation to the customs of the natives; whom myself and those who will come with me will treat as if they were our own fellow countrymen.[114]

These comments, even if the promise not to bring many retainers was unfulfilled, give proof of Philip's goodwill and his commitment to the marriage and to those who were to become his subjects and his 'own fellow countrymen'. Anxiety over the offices of the realm being granted to foreigners was understandable from the English point of view. The author of the *Supplicachon*, in their warning to the English noblemen, blamed the Marian clergy for trying to have Philip crowned. For as long as they were allowed to ruin the country

113 TRP, vol. 2, 24–25.

114 AGS, Estado 808, leg. 15; Philip to Simon Renard, Valladolid, 3 February 1554: '[...]allá tomaré de los naturales de aq[ue]l reyno p[ar]a q[ue] entiendan q[ue] me e de seruir y confiar de ellos y hazelles m[erce]d como si fuera nasçido su natural / y q[ue] podrán [por] la confianza q[ue] yo tengo dellos en irme a meter en el reyno y en su poder sin más compañía q[ue] la dicha / y q[ue] también me muebe a no llebar más gente q[ue] la de my casa porq[ue] siendo poca tanto mejor se podrá gov[er]nar y acomodar a la costumbre de los naturales / los cuales yo y los q[ue] fueren emos de tener por propios'.

through persecution and corruption in order to enrich themselves, the author argued, the bishops and clergymen would help Philip and 'gratefie hym by whom they may as they thinke / sauely enioye again ther god the pope / wyth all ther spitefull ecclesiasticall Jurisdiccio[n]s'. The author then elaborated on this:

> As in helping hym to haue placide [i.e. placed] / and machyd [i.e. matched] in offices some of hys spanierds / wyth men of our own Englishe nacyon / And that not in the worst romes nether / but euen no lesse then in the romes of lord chamberlaine and wyth the mayster of the horse / and wyth the knight marschall / et. And this is the beginning to shewe ther good wyll to hym / against our natiue cou[n]tre.[115]

The fact that Philip, once in England, was employing Spaniards in his household was seen as evidence that the dreaded subversion of the laws and customs of the realm was already afoot, manoeuvred by Philip, who was being aided and abetted by obliging and ambitious bishops who saw in this practice a means by which they could benefit themselves. These accusations were not in tune with the intentions declared by Philip in his quoted letter to Renard. Ruy Gómez de Silva also commented on this issue in a letter sent from Winchester only two days after the wedding had taken place. He explained that a 'great inconvenience' had emerged because the queen had already prepared an English household for Philip 'with all its officials, high and low', even with a master of the horse, a lord chamberlain, gentlemen of the privy chamber and one hundred archers. He blamed the confusion not only on Renard, whom he obviously disliked, but also on the Spaniards, whom he judged had not paid enough attention. The officials appointed by the queen and the council, he continued, were doing their jobs, but they would not allow any Spaniard to serve, and they were 'taking it badly', if any of the Spaniards tried to do so. Complaining too about how the English expected Philip to pay both households from his own expenses, Ruy Gómez made clear that Philip was indeed willing to comply in order to satisfy Mary, the council, and his new subjects.

> His highness plans to remedy this by making them mingle and serve together. Concerning the costs, which are increasing, he will not cease to pay, because it would be a greater inconvenience not to put up with what the queen and the council have ordered than to search for a supply to cover the expenses; and that is what his highness will do [...]. I have

115 *A Supplicachon*, fol. 18^{r}.

> hopes that everything will be solved, for they show great contentment with us, and all of us that came here try to please them by all means.[116]

What was deemed by Philip and his courtiers as a fair and sensible solution, had nevertheless been resented by critics of the regime, like the author of the *Supplicachon*. However, the Spanish response to the problem of the double household should be seen in the light of Philip's willingness to be accepted by his new subjects. It should be linked to that desire, so enthusiastically expressed by Antonio de Guaras in his letter to the viceroy of Navarre, that the kingdom of England and the emperor's realms should 'become one'.[117]

The perception that protecting the offices from the hands of aliens who were not 'natural born of the realm' was tantamount to protecting the kingdom from foreign interference and dominance was not a new notion. Charles V had faced similar demands from the Junta of Tordesillas during the Comunero revolt. The Junta, which was the most visible political body organised by the rebels, had established itself in Tordesillas in August 1520 in an attempt to bolster the legitimacy of their demands by gaining the approval or acquiescence of the emperor's mother, Queen Juana, who had been interned in the castle of Tordesillas due to her alleged insanity since 1509. Their demands did not only include a petition that all offices relating to 'councils, aldermanships, […], scrivenerships, bailiwicks', and other bureaucratic fields should be granted to people who had been born in the city or village to which the office belonged,

116 AGS, Estado 808, leg. 147. Ruy Gómez de Silva to Francisco de Eraso, Winchester, 27 July 1554: '[…] tanbién se a atravesado otro ynconvinjente grande y es q[ue] antes de llegar su alteza aquí le tenjan aparejada vna casa con todos sus oficiales altos y bajos en q[ue] ay cauallerizo mayor y camarero mayor y gentiles onbres de cámara y de aquí abajo todos los más oficiales y guarda de çien archeros y todo esto entienden ellos q[ue] su alteza lo a de ma[n]dar pagar de su casa sin q[ue] de la parte de la rreyna se ponga ninguna ayuda de costa p[ar]a esto pienso yo q[ue] ansý de la parte del enbaxador q[ue] aquí está como de la n[uest]ra a avido ynadvertençia en esto y ansý los oficiales q[ue] por parte de la rreyna y del consejo están puestos hazen sus ofiçios y los siruen y si de n[uest]ra parte alguno quiere meter mano en algo tóma[n]lo mal y no lo quieren dexar hazer su alteza piensa rremediar esto ma[n]dándolos mezclar y q[ue] sirvan juntos y en cuanto a la costa q[ue] se le rrecreçe no ay q[ue] parar pues sería más ynconvinjente no pasar por lo q[ue] la rreyna y el consejo tienen ordenado q[ue] buscar de dónde cumplir la costa q[ue] esto hará a su alteza. sólo vvo al prinçipio falta en no dalles a entender cómo el príncipe traýa sus oficiales y q[ue] cuando más no pudieran acabar con ellos se vviera de suspender este determjnar esta casa hasta q[ue] su alteza llegara tengo esperança q[ue] todo se hará bien porq[ue] ellos muestran contentamy[ent]o de nosotros y todos los q[ue] aquí venjmos se le damos en lo q[ue] podemos […]'.

117 Guaras, *Carta de nueuas*, fol. 434^r.

but they were also very clear about the rebels' position concerning offices in the royal household.

> Another condition: that the offices in the royal household will be granted to those who have been born and baptised in Castile, and that the king will not be served during the time when he shall be in Castile, but by those who have been born in Castile.

Since Charles had already granted several offices to some of his Flemish courtiers, the Junta made further demands on this respect:

> The king shall revoke and take away all the offices, benefices, dignities, encomiendas, and fortresses which have been granted to those who have not been born and baptised in the kingdom, and give them to those who are natives and natural born and baptised in the kingdom.[118]

Similarly, in the petition presented to Charles v by his special envoy, Friar Francisco de los Ángeles, on behalf of the Comuneros in 1521, two of the dispositions drawn up are identical reflections of English fears of domination. During the monarch's absences, no strangers born outside the Crown of Castile were to be appointed as governors of the realm, and all appointments to bishoprics, archbishoprics, and all other offices 'of any quality' were also to be granted to Castilians.[119]

---

118 Martín Fernández Navarrete, Miguel Salvá and Pedro Sáinz de Baranda, eds., *Colección de documentos inéditos para la Historia de España*, vol. I (Madrid: Viuda de Calero, 1842), 272–284: 'Lo otro a condición que los oficios de regimientos, veinticuatrías, juraderías, escribanías, alguaciladgos e otros oficios se hayan de dar cuando vacaren a los nacidos e bautizados en los mismos logares a donde vacaren los tales oficios o en sus aldeas, e que no se puedan dar a otras personas [...]. Lo otro á condición que los oficios de la casa Real se hayan de dar a personas que sean nascidos é bautizados en Castilla, e quel Rey no pueda servirse durante estuviere en Castilla sino de personas que sean nacidos en Castilla [...]. Quel Rey revoque é quite todos los oficios, é beneficios, é dignidades, y encomiendas, é fortalezas questán dados á las personas que no son nascidos e bautizados en el reino, é las dé á los naturales é nascidos é bautizados en el reino, é las dé a los naturales é nascidos en los reinos, que no dé fortaleza ninguna á ningún gran Señor sino á personas que ellos por sí están en ellas en personas, ni dé capitanías á ninguno que por su persona no la sirviere'. See also Pérez, *Los Comuneros*, 87–94.

119 AGS, Patronato, legajo 3, 137, no. 8 (quoted above) and no. 99: 'Yten que los obispados arçobispados e dinidades calongías e otros qualesquier beneficios eclesiásticos e pensiones en ellos ni en tene[n]çias ni encomiendas ni otros ofiçios algunos de qualquier calidad que sean no se puedan dar ni proueer a estrangeros destos reynos e que solamente se den y prouean a naturales v[e]z[in]os dellos e los questán dados se reboquen'.

Clearly, the marriage treaty and the whole conception of the Anglo-Spanish co-monarchy owed much to the recent history of Spain. In his *Chrónica*, Hernando del Pulgar made a revealing comment on the arrangement reached in similar circumstances by Ferdinand and Isabel:

> This queen worked much in all things touching the government of these kingdoms [of Castile and Aragon], as well as in those touching wars, [...] in the administration of justice, and other things that were then happening. And when it was necessary that the king should go and provide in some places and the queen in others; even if separated they never issued a commandment that would annul the provisions made by the other. Because if necessity set their persons apart, love ensured that their wills remained united.[120]

Even through this blatantly rhetorical use of the language of love, it is apparent that Philip and Mary's co-monarchy was modelled in a very similar way. Charles himself had employed his wife, Isabel of Portugal, as one of his most trusted political advisers and as his regent. In Flanders, his aunt Margaret of Austria governed in his place until her death in 1530, and she was followed by the emperor's sister, Queen Mary of Hungary. In Valencia, Charles appointed Ferdinand the Catholic's widow, Germaine of Foix, as vicereine of the kingdom in 1523 and Philip, as we have seen, appointed his two sisters, María and Juana, as regents of Spain during his absences.[121] Recruiting female relatives as governors and rulers was a natural political tool for the Habsburgs, and it was used repeatedly throughout the sixteenth and seventeenth centuries. Judging

---

120 Pulgar, *Chrónica*, fol. 26^{v}: 'Esta Reyna trabajaua mucho en las cosas de la gouernación destos reynos, assí en lo tocante a las guerras que en ellos acaescieron, como en la administración de la justicia. Y en ellas, y en las otras cosas que ocurrían, y qua[n]do era necessario que el Rey fuesse a proueer en vnas partes y la Reyna a otras, aunque estauan apartados, nunca se halló que el vno diesse mandamiento que derogasse a la prouisión que el otro ouiesse dado. Porque si la necessidad apartaua las personas, el amor tenía juntas las voluntades'.

121 See Miguel Dongil y Sánchez, 'Margarita de Austria (1480–1530): Regente de los Países Bajos y tutora de Carlos I de España', *Iberian*, vol. 2 (2011), 6–17 and especially Jane de Iongh, *Margaret of Austria: Regent of the Netherlands* (New York: W. W. Norton, 1953); Rodríguez-Salgado, *Changing Face of Empire*, 59–60, 63, 66, 71, 73–5, 78, 81, 85, 103, 236; Regina Pinilla Pérez de Tudela, *Valencia y doña Germana: castigo de agermanados y problemas religiosos* (Valencia: Consell Valencià de Cultura, 1994); Juan Carlos Galende Díaz and Manuel Salamanca López, eds., *Epistolario de la emperatriz María de Austria: Textos inéditos del Archivo de la Casa de Alba* (Madrid: Nuevos Escritores, 2004) and Antonio Villacorta Baños, *La jesuita: Juana de Austria* (Barcelona: Ariel, 2005).

from his subsequent behaviour, it is more than plausible that Philip envisaged Mary's role in England to be analogous to that of other female members of his family. Happily, in this case, the female relative also happened to be the proprietary queen. There was no contradiction in the fact that the sovereignty of England and Ireland resided in Mary. As long as she lived, however, he would also be the king, both kingdoms would be his, and he would procure their welfare as much as he procured that of his other kingdoms, which came to him 'through inheritance'.[122]

1.5 Conclusion

That the new marriage had been conceived as a mirror-image of that of Ferdinand and Isabel did not go unnoticed in English circles. Nicholas Wotton, writing to congratulate Philip and Mary on their marriage on 10 August 1554, wrote that many would still be able to remember 'the greate co[m]modite, and benefyte' that had come to the realms of Spain and to all Christendom through

> [...] the mariaige of your both most noble progenitours king Fferdinand and queene Isabell. No lesse, but rather much more I trust wilbe seene of this your mariaige. for neyther ar your zeale and good willes to do good, lesse then theirs. and your powers ar, and god willing shalbe farre greater then theirs.[123]

The comparison, in light of what has been argued in this chapter, is most revealing. Whatever misgivings the English elite may have had about the marriage, once it had been arranged, they seem to have embraced it. Wotton had come to terms with the idea of being ruled by Philip as early as April, when he had written to secretary William Petre asking for advice on how to conduct himself in his future letters since when the prince 'is come, then nouus rex noua lex, as they saye'.[124] There was in this expression ('a new king, a new law') an assumption that when England had her new king, things would be done in a new way. Wotton's remark is very significant, since it linked directly with the theories of *monarchia universalis* upheld by thinkers like Ulzurrun for whom, as we have seen, from the Catholic monarch emanated the *animate legi*, the

---

122 AGS, Estado 811, no. 56.

123 TNA, SP 69/5, no. 249. Nicholas Wotton to Philip and Mary, Compiegne, 10 August 1554.

124 TNA, SP 69/4, no. 197. Nicholas Wotton to Sir William Petre, Paris, 28 April 1554.

'animated laws', which conformed justice.[125] It was in this capacity that Wotton was ready to accept Philip as his new king.

Sir John Mason, English ambassador to the emperor in Brussels, wrote to the queen that the news of the marriage 'hath vniuersally bred here soch a joye as euery man semeth to haue gotten a new kind of cheare in his face'.[126] For all their hyperbole, these despatches suggest that the times were changing and that at least the elites had come to accept the idea of having a foreign king. It still remained to be seen, though, whether the change would be so readily accepted by the English community at large.

---

125 Ulzurrun, *Catholicum opus imperiale*, fol. 47^{v}.

126 TNA, SP 69/5, no. 246. Sir John Mason to Queen Mary, Brussels, 2 August 1554.

CHAPTER 2

Resistance and Reception: Rebellion, Religion, and the Coming of the Spaniards

In 1555, as has been mentioned, the anonymous author of *A Supplicachon to the queens maiestie* stated that England had been, by means of the Spanish marriage, enslaved by a nation which was 'hatyth and abhoryth' by the whole world, a mirror image in the negative of the Spanish conceptualisation of *monarchia universalis*.[1] This had come to pass because the sinfulness of the English had prevented them from acknowledging the great gift conferred upon them by God in the person of Edward VI, their 'vertues king'. Just like the Bible taught it had happened to the Jews, who murdered the prophets that God sent to warn them, the godly king of the English had been replaced by 'a strang king to raygne ouer vs […] who should bring in again / popery / ydolatry / and all abhomynacyons'. The bishops would soon murder God's true gospellers, as the prophets of the Jews had been murdered, and this would be the preamble to England's destruction by imperial hands, just as Jerusalem had been destroyed by Titus and Vespasian.[2] In this analogy, Charles V was equated with the destructive Roman emperors, and with the help of the ambitious and godless English bishops – especially Stephen Gardiner of Winchester and Edmund Bonner of London – he would soon be able to complete his scheme to plant his son Philip in England once the latter's coronation had taken place. This done, Philip would then endeavour to have the crown for himself and his heirs, 'and so contrary to the statutis made in the other perlyame[n]ts / dysinheryte all the reightfull heyres of the Realme', a particularly ironic remark, given that that was precisely what Edward VI's regime had attempted to do in 1553. In this way, Philip would fulfil his promise to his father and enslave England just as Charles had enslaved Naples, Milan, and the Low Countries, where he had decimated the nobility, and placed his new subjects under the yoke of excessive and unaffordable taxes.[3]

The same year saw the clandestine publication of *An Admonicion to all Englishe men* – although it was specifically dedicated to the earls of Arundel, Derby, Shrewsbury, and Pembroke – written by the gentleman John Bradford

1 Anonymous, *A Supplicacho[n] to the quenes maiestie*, (Unknown, 1555), fol. 1^{r}.
2 *A Supplicachon*, fols 1^{v}–3^{r}.
3 *A Supplicachon*, fols 21^{r-v}.

 | DOI:10.1163/9789004536210_004

of Nantwich in Cheshire († 1557). Although Bradford claimed to be a Catholic, which gives his account an interesting edge, he was nonetheless involved in plots against Queen Mary which had eminently Protestant overtones, such as the Dudley conspiracy or Sir Thomas Stafford's fiasco at Scarborough Castle, for which Bradford would be executed at Tyburn in 1557.[4] In his work, Bradford took an even more virulent stand against the Spaniards than the anonymous author of *A Supplicachon*. In Bradford's view, Spaniards were dissembling until such time as they would feel secure enough to show their true nature; that is, after Philip's coronation. Once that had been achieved, Bradford denounced how,

> shall ye perceiue perfectly their puffed pride, with many mischeffes beside, their prowling, and poli[n]g, their bribing and shauing, their most deceitfull dealing, their braging and bosting, their flattering and fayninge, their abominable whore huntynge [...] with al other vilanie, of what kinde soeuer it be: supersticion, suppression, inuocacion, and all abominacion.[5]

This generalised cruelty and deceitfulness of the Spaniards was also a common theme in *A Shorte Treatise of Politike Pouuer* (1556), written by John Ponet (*c.*1514–1556), the deprived bishop of Winchester then exiled in Strasbourg, who advocated active resistance, and even assassination, against ungodly and tyrannous rulers.[6] Ponet affirmed that no people wished to be ruled by 'vnreasonable beasts' and he followed the point with a description of Spanish America. The natives of the Indies had lived a simple life in plentiful lands, not being

4 He is not to be confused with John Bradford (1510–1555), the prebendary of St Paul's, burnt at Smithfield in 1555 (of whom more will be said below in Chapter 6), as D. M. Loades clarified in 1960. See D. M. Loades 'The Authorship and Publication of "The Copye of a Letter Sent by John Bradforth to the Right Honorable Lordes the Erles of Arundel, Darbie, Shrewsbury and Penbroke" (S.T.C. 3480)', *Transactions of the Cambridge Bibliographical Society*, vol. 3 no. 2 (1960), 155–60.

5 John Bradford, *An Admonicion to all Englishe men. To the right honorable lords &c. the erles of Aru[n]dell, Darby, Shreusbury & Pe[n]brok, their true and faythfull seruant wisheth, as to al other of our nobilitie increase of grace in gods fauour, with perfect honor, and the preseruacyon of their most honorable states and country. Thoughe ye reioyce not in readyng my foolyshe reasons, yet geue God thankes, that I haue discouered suche detestable treasons* (1555), sig. $B1^r$–$B1^v$.

6 On Ponet's thought and theology see Barbara Peardon, 'The Politics of Polemic: John Ponet's *Short Treatise of Politic Power* and Contemporary Circumstance, 1553–1556', *Journal of British Studies*, 22, no. 1 (1982), 35–49 and Ryan J. Croft, 'Sanctified Tyrannicide: Tyranny and Theology in John Ponet's *Shorte Treatise of Politike Power* and Edmund Spenser's *The Faerie Queene*', *Studies in Philology*, 108, no. 4 (2011), 538–571.

used to labour and knowing 'of Christ nothing at all, and of God no more than nature taught them'. Through 'flatterie', the Spaniards had managed to get a hold of the land and condemned the inhabitants to such a state of misery and slavery that many had committed suicide, others had refused to marry to avoid leaving offspring behind and pregnant women 'wolde eat a certain herbe to destroie the childe in the wombe'. Only a negligible amount of the original 900,000 inhabitants of New Spain, Ponet claimed, had survived.[7] In line with *A Supplicachon*, God's preachers during the reign of Edward VI, equated in the text to the godly Josiah, king of Judah, had warned the English, but their sinfulness had brought about plague, loss of goods, raping of wives and daughters and 'the subuersion of the policie and state of the Realme: that a straunge king and straunge people (not only in countrey, but also in condiciones and maners in respecte of your owne) should reigne and rule by force ouer you'.[8]

There were contemporary signs of this punishment in the form of monstrous births and wondrous events which highlighted the subversion of England. For instance, a baby born in Oxford in 1552 with two heads and two 'euil shaped bodyes ioyned in one' had signified Edward VI's death and his replacement by 'two headdes, diuerse gouernours, and a towarde diuision of the people', an open criticism of the dual character of Philip and Mary's monarchy. The body politic and the community of England were, according to Ponet, grievously ill and deformed.[9] Not only that but, soon enough, 'shall your king returne to his welbeloued wife, England, with great po[m]pe a[n]d power, and shall co[m]pell you [...] to re[n]dre and deliuer her holly in to his handes'. This violation of the realm, would be complete with a Spanish invasion aided by the merchants of the Hanseatic League, whose privileges Philip was trying to restore, and the transportation of the English to New Spain, where they would be chained, forced to row in the galleys, to dig in the mines and 'to pike vp the golde in the hotte sande', just like the Spaniards had done with the native inhabitants of America. Echoing Bradford's words, only when it was too late

7 John Ponet, *A Shorte Treatise of politike pouuer, and of the true Obedience which subiectes owe to kynges and other ciuile Gouernours, with an Exhortacion to all true naturall Englishe men* (1556), sig. F7$^{r–v}$. To bolster his claims, Ponet claimed to have extracted the figure from the works of Pietro Martire d'Anghiera, Charles V's chronicler in America.

8 Ponet, *Shorte Treatise*, sig. K3$^{r–v}$.

9 Ponet, *Shorte Treatise*, sig. K3^{v}–K5^{v}. A child born in Coventry with no arms or legs in 1555 signified that 'the natural body, that is, the people of Englande' was left defenceless against any attack; a baby born in Fulham in 1556 'with agreat head, euil shaped, the armes with bagges hanging out at the Elbowes and heles, and fete lame' meant that the nobility of England, the chief members of the natural body of England would be 'so clogged with chaynes of golde, and bagges of money, that the hande shall not be hable to drawe out the sweorde, nor the heles to spurre the horse to helpe and defende the body, that is, the commones', etc.

would the English realise the double-dealing of the Spaniards, for there was 'no nacio[n] vnder the cope of Christ, like the[m] in pride, crueltie, vnmercifulnesse, nor so farre fro[m] all humanitie', as the European territories under their authority could attest.[10]

The anonymous author of a pamphlet titled *The Lamentacion of England* (1557) expounded that, despite Edward VI's best efforts to bar his sisters from the throne to prevent the coming of 'a strange king', this had come to pass because Queen Mary, although born in England and having 'to here father a noble a[n]d trewe hartid prince and Englishman [...] she foloweth nothing his steppes in trew zeal to this realm, becawse she toke the most part off here blude and stomake fro[m] her spanish mother'. Mary's Spanishness explained why she had allowed her greedy relatives and putative nation to take away England's 'best comodites'.[11] According to the chronicler Robert Wingfield, the rebels of 1554 claimed to have been 'overwhelmed by a Spanish whore'.[12] One of Mary and Philip's most virulent detractors, the clergyman Christopher Goodman (1520–1603), wrote in 1558 that this 'vngodlie a[n]d vnlawful Gouernesse, wicked Iesabel', whose reign, as a woman, was 'contrarie to nature', had forced her subjects 'to become slaues to a strange and foren nation, the prowde Spaniards'.[13] If Philip were crowned, he cautioned, he would soon replace all councillors with Spaniards and would take away lands, possessions, livings and, perhaps even 'your heads vpo[n] your shulders'.[14] Following the line of the author of *A Supplicachon*, just as Jeremiah had prophesised, the English were now 'to serue a strange kinge, strange lawes, and a stra[n]ge nation'; in sum, they were to 'Serue Nabuchadnezer' like the Jews had, in a new Babylonian captivity.[15] Through the 'Spaynishe plague of adoulterous Philippe', the English had been brought under the yoke of a 'cruell and beastly nation'.[16] The accession of Mary, recast as a new Jezebel or Athaliah, had enabled the arrival of Philip

10 Ponet, *Shorte Treatise*, sig. L3^{v}–L4^{r}.

11 Anon., *The Lamentacion of England* (1557), 4–5. For negative portrayals of Mary as a Spaniard see Sarah Duncan, *Mary I: Gender, Power, and Ceremony in the Reign of England's First Queen* (New York: Palgrave Macmillan, 2012), 115–7.

12 Wingfield, *Vitae Mariae*, 273–4. See also Alexander Samson, *Mary and Philip: The Marriage of Tudor England and Habsburg Spain* (Manchester: Manchester University Press, 2020), 87–90.

13 Christopher Goodman, *How svperior powers oght to be obeyd of their subiects: and wherin they may lawfully by Gods worde be disobeyed and resisted. Wherin also is declared the cause of all this present miserie in England, and the onely way to remedy the same* (Geneva: John Crispin, 1558), 34–5.

14 Goodman, *Superior Powers*, 100–1.

15 Goodman, *Superior Powers*, 133–4. See Jeremiah, chapter 5.

16 Goodman, *Superior Powers*, 134–5.

and his Spaniards and both events were God's just punishment for the sinfulness of the English. Xenophobic attacks like these were commonplace in the early modern period and they would figure prominently in centuries to come in the works of those opposed to Spanish rule across the Spanish Monarchy and abroad – the representatives of what has been termed the Black Legend.[17] Comments like those quoted above, together with the fact that there was a rebellion to prevent the match from taking place and that problems arose as soon as the Spaniards set foot in England, have been used as irrefutable proof that the association with Spain was rejected by the English from its inception, and that this mistrust led to open confrontation and would be the beginning of the Anglo-Spanish tensions which would later evolve into open war in the 1580s.

This perception of the Spaniards as barbaric, violent and dissembling has been accepted by historians as a widespread English reaction to the news of the match. The fact that Protestant polemicists, who were very prolific, were so vehemently disposed against the Spaniards has coloured all subsequent interpretations of the extent and strength of anti-Spanish sentiment in England. This pejorative narrative of attitudes towards Spaniards has helped portray the Spanish marriage as well as Philip and his foreign courtiers as unpopular and mistrusted, their presence in England seen as an unwelcome source of conflict which did not evaporate until Queen Mary's death in November 1558 but whose shadow lingered to threaten the English until 1588 and beyond. Through these works, and the comments made by many about the alleged dislike that English people felt for foreigners, the marriage has been portrayed as overwhelmingly unpopular, a political development rejected by the entire kingdom.[18] Other accounts, whilst more balanced, still take for granted that anti-Spanish sentiment was a widespread phenomenon or that the marriage was at the genesis of the Anglo-Spanish conflicts of the latter part of the century.[19] The theme has most definitely featured prominently in the historiography.[20]

17 Julián Juderías, *La Leyenda Negra de España* [1914] (Madrid: La Esfera de los Libros, 2014), 267–325; W. S. Maltby, *The Black Legend in England: the Development of anti-Spanish Sentiment, 1558–1660* (Durham, North Carolina: Duke University Press, 1971); Mark G. Sanchez, 'Anti-Spanish sentiment in English literary and political writing 1553–1603' (PhD thesis, University of Leeds, unpublished, 2004).

18 D. M. Loades, *Two Tudor Conspiracies* (Cambridge: Cambridge University Press, 1965), 12.

19 See for instance James McDermott, *England and the Spanish Armada: The Necessary Quarrel* (New Haven and London: Yale University Press, 2005), 31–46, es 41–3; Porfirio Sanz Camañes, *Los ecos de la Armada: España, Inglaterra y la estabilidad del Norte (1585–1660)* (Madrid: Sílex, 2012), 24–5; Anna Whitelock, *Mary Tudor: England's First Queen* (London: Bloomsbury, 2009), 243, 246, 280, 289.

20 Traditional interpretations of this allegedly entrenched Anglo-Spanish enmity can be found, for instance, in A. G. Dickens, *The English Reformation* [1964] (London and Glasgow:

Already in 1940, however, H. F. M. Prescott suspected that there may have been more to this initial rejection of the Spaniards in England. She described the situation as tense, but not volatile, with both parties trying to make the best out of it under the circumstances.[21] In 2011 John Edwards cautioned against the earlier assumptions of English-speaking historians that there was a 'natural' enmity between Englishmen and Spaniards and pointed out that tensions between both nations took place mainly during Philip's first months in England.[22] More recently, in 2020, Alexander Samson has traced and explained the source of Spanish unpopularity, which did not so much stem from a deeply rooted anti-Spanish sentiment as from fears of female rule and the potential subversion of the laws and customs of the realm which, some feared, foreign domination would entail. He concluded that most incidents took place within palace precincts, indicating that enmities were mainly confined to higher circles and that popular opposition has been overestimated.[23] The question of the true extension and evolution of anti-Spanish sentiment in England, however, remains. I will address this question, first, through an analysis of the motives that prompted the fourfold rebellion of 1554 – commonly known as the Wyatt rebellion – which sought to prevent the coming of the Spaniards and, second, by considering how the latter and the English coexisted once the marriage had taken place.

2.1 The Fourfold Rebellion of 1554

As soon as Mary I came to the throne in July 1553, almost everyone – with the notable exception of Cardinal Reginald Pole – agreed that the queen should take a husband.[24] By September, the less politically risky candidates for Mary's hand, the Infante Luis of Portugal, Archduke Ferdinand of Austria and even Pole – who, as a deacon could have been dispensed of his vows and orders by Pope Julius III (r. 1550–1555) – had already been displaced by Prince Philip

Collins/Fontana, 1972), 358–9; G. R. Elton, *Reform and Reformation: England, 1509–1558* (London: Edward Arnold, 1977), 381–2; D. M. Loades, *The Reign of Mary Tudor: Politics, Government, and Religion in England, 1553–1558* (London: Ernest Benn, 1979), 115, 119, 122, 126, 127, 211–16 *et passim*; María Jesús Pérez Martín, *María Tudor. La gran reina desconocida* (Madrid: Ediciones Rialp, 2008), 630–7, to cite but a few.

21 H. F. M. Prescott, *Mary Tudor: The Spanish Tudor* [1940] (London: Phoenix, 2003), 355–6.

22 John Edwards, *Mary I: England's Catholic Queen* (New Haven and London: Yale University Press, 2011), 211–3.

23 Samson, *Mary and Philip*, 86–91, 124, 137–64.

24 As late as March 1554, Pole still considered that it was advisable for Mary to remain single instead of jumping into a foreign match. See Thomas F. Mayer, *Reginald Pole: Prince & Prophet* (Cambridge: Cambridge University Press, 2000), 210–2.

of Spain and Edward Courtenay, earl of Devon.[25] When rumours leaked out that Mary and the imperial ambassador, Simon Renard, had discussed Philip's option in private, opposition to the Spanish marriage began to grow within the privy council around Stephen Gardiner, bishop of Winchester and lord chancellor, who was supported by some of Mary's oldest and most trusted friends, the councillors Sir Robert Rochester, Sir Edward Waldegrave and Sir Francis Englefield.[26] Courtenay's candidacy was not without advantages. He was the son of Gertrude Blount, a loyal friend to Mary since the days when she had been in the household of Catherine of Aragon, and of Henry, marquess of Exeter, a first cousin to Henry VIII who had been executed for treason by the latter in 1539.[27] Courtenay was thus an Englishman of the royal blood and he came from a religiously conservative background which had been loyal to Catherine of Aragon. These were qualities which made him a good candidate to Mary's hand, especially in the eyes of Gardiner, who had protected him during their time together as prisoners in the Tower of London during the reign of Edward VI.[28] Around the same time, Gardiner told Renard that he believed that the English would be unwilling to receive a Spaniard as their king because of the qualities of the Spanish nation, which were already stirring opposition in Flanders.[29]

While Renard was gaining support among the councillors with the help of Lord William Paget (who had been enthusiastic about the marriage from the beginning), Gardiner, Waldegrave and Englefield visited the queen in late October 1553 to try to dissuade her from entering the marriage negotiations with Philip. Their meeting with Mary bore no fruits, even if the queen had shown herself inclined to hear all sides. In the meantime, Lord Paget and John Russell, earl of Bedford and lord privy seal, were recruiting supporters of the Spanish match among the privy councillors, soon winning over Rochester, who abandoned his allegiance to Gardiner, Cuthbert Tunstall, bishop of Durham, the earls of Arundel and Shrewsbury, and the lord treasurer, Sir William

25 Edwards, *Mary I*, 148–51.

26 Edwards, *Mary I*, 151–2. On the loyal bonds which united these men to Mary as members of her household as princess see Anna Whitelock and Diarmaid MacCulloch, 'Princess Mary's Household and the Succession Crisis, July 1553', *The Historical Journal*, vol. 50, no. 2 (2007), 265–87. For an account of their careers after Mary's death see Ralph Houlbrooke, 'What Happened to Mary's Councillors?', in Alice Hunt and Anna Whitelock, eds., *Tudor Queenship: The Reigns of Mary and Elizabeth* (New York: Palgrave Macmillan, 2010), 209–24.

27 G. W. Bernard, *The King's Reformation: Henry VIII and the Remaking of the English Church* (New Haven and London: Yale University Press, 2005), 407–432.

28 Loades, *Reign of Mary*, 109–16; Whitelock, *Mary Tudor*, 202–7; Edwards, *Mary I*, 149–56.

29 Edwards, *Mary I*, 154.

Petre.[30] Mary soon made up her mind that she would take Philip as a husband, and a parliamentary petition on 16 November 1553 in favour of her marrying an Englishman led by the speaker, Sir John Pollard, was to no avail. The episode ended with Mary rebuking both Pollard and Gardiner for trying to interfere in a decision which was only hers.[31] Although this was the end of the official opposition to the Spanish match, a greater and more aggressive threat was brewing within the very heart of Mary's court.

The first meeting of the conspirators took place in London on 26 November 1553 and it was attended by Sir Nicholas Arnold, Sir Peter Carew, Sir James Croftes, Sir George Harper, Sir William Pickering, Sir Edward Rogers, William Thomas, Sir Nicholas Throckmorton, Sir Edward Warner, Sir William Winter, and Sir Thomas Wyatt. Before Christmas they were joined by the only two members of the higher nobility who took part in the rebellion: Henry Grey, duke of Suffolk, and the earl of Devon himself.[32] The conspirators agreed that a fourfold rebellion marching towards London should take place on Palm Sunday, 18 March 1554, the day when it was believed that Philip would start his journey from Spain. The duke of Suffolk had the responsibility to lead the rebellion in Leicestershire, Wyatt that of Kent, Croftes that of Herefordshire and Carew and Courtenay that of Devon.[33] At this point, the key person in the insurrection was Courtenay, who would marry Elizabeth and replace Mary in a joint monarchy. Elizabeth was aware that something was afoot through her private communications with Croftes and Antoine de Noailles, the French ambassador, who knew about the conspiracy, but the extent of her involvement was never ascertained, and she would eventually be pardoned by Mary.[34] Although he would later deny it, it is likely that Suffolk entertained the ambition of regaining the throne for his daughter, Lady Jane Grey, still a prisoner in the Tower.

Suspicions were rampant among the members of Mary's government and court early on. On 2 January 1554 Carew, who was by then at Exeter, ignored a

30 Edwards, *Mary I*, 152; Bedford most probably had a personal interest in preventing the Courtenay marriage. Not only had he lands in the same areas as those which had been forfeited by the marquess of Exeter, but, also, after the execution of the latter in 1539, Henry VIII had granted Bedford the position of lord president of the council of the West which had belonged to the executed marquess. See Diane Willen, 'Lord Russell and the Western Counties, 1539–1555', *Journal of British Studies*, 15, no. 1 (1975), 26–45.

31 Edwards, *Mary I*, 154–5; Duncan, *Mary I*, 40, 52, 57; Samson, *Mary and Philip*, 59.

32 TNA, King's Bench 27/1174; TNA KB 8/29; Loades, *Two Tudor Conspiracies*, 13–16.

33 T. B. Howell, ed., *A Complete Collection of State Trials and Proceedings for High Treason and Other Crimes and Misdemeanors from the Earliest Period to the Year 1789*, vol. 1 (London: T. C. Hansard, 1816), 883; Loades, *Two Tudor Conspiracies*, 21.

34 Loades, *Two Tudor Conspiracies*, 221.

summons from the privy council, and on 18 January Renard told Mary that he had discovered through his secret intelligence that something was afoot against her crown.[35] The following day Wyatt and Pickering left London for Kent and, on 21 January, Gardiner had a private interview with Courtenay, who crumbled and revealed the existence of the conspiracy, forcing the rebels into precipitated action.[36] At this point, Mary gave Suffolk one last chance by offering him military command against the rebels on 25 January, but instead the duke fled to his palace at Bradgate Park, in Leicestershire, with his brothers Sir Thomas and Sir John Grey.[37] On 29 January he entered Leicester without resistance but the next day he found the doors of Coventry – which was crucial to the success of the Leicestershire rebellion – shut to him and his 140 horsemen; he fled to Astley Castle in Warwickshire. Suffolk desperately attempted to stir the people by falsely proclaiming that there were 12,000 Spaniards in the west and another 12,000 in Calais waiting for orders to conquer England, but the messenger carrying the proclamation was caught and hanged.[38] Although Suffolk was planning to flee either to Wales or to Scotland, he was finally constrained to hide with his brother John at Astley, where they were eventually arrested on 2 February by Francis Hastings, earl of Huntingdon. The two Greys were taken to the Tower on 10 February and were joined there by their brother Thomas a few days later.[39] Without a single blow, the rebellion in Leicestershire was over. The course of events in Herefordshire was even less fruitful, as the rebellion never materialised. On 24 January Croftes was still seeking French support, but was soon apprehended and taken to the Tower, where he was imprisoned in late February.[40] In the meantime, Carew and his uncle, Sir Gawain Carew, had striven to seize the city of Exeter which was controlled by Sir Thomas Dennys,

35 APC, vol. 4, 382; Loades, *Two Tudor Conspiracies*, 24.

36 Loades, *Two Tudor Conspiracies*, 24.

37 Loades, *Two Tudor Conspiracies*, 25.

38 Martín Fernández Navarrete, Miguel Salvá and Pedro Sáinz de Baranda, eds., *Colección de documentos inéditos para la historia de España*, vol. 3 (Madrid: Viuda de Calero, 1843), 468; Simon Renard to Charles V, London, early February 1554: 'Aquí han hecho tomar y ahorcar un criado del Duque de Sofort, que fue tomado que llevaba un escrito del dicho Duque para le publicar por la tierra, por el cual él decía que había doce mil españoles en Calés y otros tantos de parte de Vesse para conquistar el reino de Inglaterra […]'. Henceforth CODOIN, vol. 3.

39 Eric Ives, *Lady Jane Grey: A Tudor Mistery* (Oxford: Wiley-Blackwell, 2009), 262–5; Loades, *Two Tudor Conspiracies*, 100. For Suffolk's plans to flee into Scotland see CODOIN, vol. 3, 464.

40 Croftes was already in the Tower on 21 February. See Loades, *Two Tudor Conspiracies*, 42; Steven G. Ellis, 'Croft, Sir James (*c*.1518–1590)', *Oxford Dictionary of National Biography*. http://www.oxforddnb.com/view/article/6719 [accessed 14 January 2023].

the traditionalist sheriff of Devon. The latter, however, was loyal to the crown and garrisoned the city against the rebels. Sir Gawain was soon arrested, and Sir Peter established himself at his seat in Mohun's Ottery. On 24 January, he sent to Dartmouth for more supplies, but they never arrived. On the night of 25 January Carew slipped off to Weymouth and from there he fled to the safety of Norman soil.[41]

Of the four proposed rebellions, only Wyatt's in Kent achieved any degree of success. On 19 January Wyatt reached Allington Castle, where he summoned a council of war with some of his sympathetic neighbours.[42] On 25 January he was at Maidstone, where he read out a proclamation written by himself together with Sir George Harper and Sir Henry Isley in which they exhorted the Kentishmen to join the rebellion, falsely stating that the 'Spaniardes be nowe already ariued at Douer, at one passage to the nombre of an hundreth passing vpwarde to London'.[43] While Wyatt moved on to Rochester, word reached the rebels that Henry Neville, Lord Abergavenny, Sir Richard Southwell, high sheriff of Kent and Sir George Clerk were assembling forces to fight them, which prompted Isley and the brothers Anthony and William Knyvett to issue a proclamation in Tonbridge denouncing the queen's men as 'traytours to God, the crowne, and the common wealthe'.[44] Thomas Howard, duke of Norfolk, Thomas Butler, earl of Ormond, and Sir George Howard – Norfolk's nephew and a brother to Henry VIII's ill-fated fifth queen, Catherine – were sent by Mary to meet the rebels. Perhaps due to Norfolk's old age – he was eighty – the royal troops did not act decisively and soon 500 of the Londoners which formed the Whitecoats, led by Alexander Brett, defected to Wyatt's camp after being approached by a Scottish agent sent to them by the French ambassador, Antoine de Noailles.[45] On 30 January Wyatt left Rochester avoiding direct confrontation with Norfolk's army and took his uncle Lord Cobham's seat at Cooling Castle.[46] The following day, Wyatt received Mary's envoys, Sir Edward Hastings and Sir Thomas Cornwallis, at Dartford, but refused to accept her peace terms.[47] On Saturday 3 February, Wyatt and his army entered Southwark

41 Loades, *Two Tudor Conspiracies*, 38–43.

42 Loades, *Two Tudor Conspiracies*, 51.

43 John Proctor, *The historie of wyates rebellion, with the order and maner of resisting the same, wherinto in the ende is added an earnest conference with the degenerate and sedicious rebelles for the serche of the cause of their daily disorder* (London: Robert Caly, 1554), ff. 8^v–9^v.

44 Proctor, *Historie of wyates rebellion*, fol. 13^v.

45 E. Harris Harbison, 'French Intrigue at the Court of Queen Mary', *The American Historical Review*, 40, no. 3 (1940), 533–51, in 548; Loades, *Two Tudor Conspiracies*, 60.

46 Loades, *Two Tudor Conspiracies*, 68.

47 Proctor, *Historie of wyates rebellion*, fols 48^v–51^r.

without resistance but they found the gate that gave access to the city firmly guarded by Lord William Howard, Sir Thomas White, mayor of London, and the citizens.[48] The rebels remained in Southwark until 6 February, when Wyatt and his men moved to Kingston upon Thames. In the meantime, Mary appointed William Herbert, earl of Pembroke and Edward, Lord Clinton, to the defence of the city of London, and it was Clinton who met the rebels heading to St James's Palace after they entered London in the early hours of Wednesday, 7 February. Clinton's attack broke down Wyatt's formation into two, after which the light cavalry 'slewe many, hurte more, and toke moost of them'.[49] Wyatt, however, was still free, and together with the remaining 500 of his men, reached Charing Cross soon afterwards, but there 'diuers of the quenes household seruauntes and others fought with them', killing sixteen of the rebels. Reaching Temple Bar, Wyatt and his men were stopped by the citizens of London, after which Wyatt surrendered to Sir Maurice Berkeley. Following a brief meeting with the privy council at Westminster, he was taken to the Tower later the same day.[50] In less than a fortnight, the fourfold rebellion was over and most of the rebels were under custody.

The first consequence of the rebellion was the execution, on 12 February, of Lady Jane Grey and her husband, Lord Guildford Dudley, who had been found guilty of treason and condemned to death the previous 14 November, but who had temporarily been left alive partly to serve as hostages to secure their families' and friends' good behaviour and partly because Mary had been initially inclined to show mercy on account of their youth.[51] On the same day, which can hardly have been a coincidence, Courtenay was taken to the Tower.[52] On 14 February a total of fifty-eight people were publicly executed in twenty different scaffolds set up throughout London to serve as exemplary punishment.[53] Four days later Brett, the captain of the Whitecoats, was sent together with twenty-two others into Kent to be publicly executed there and on 20 February one more rebel was hanged in London.[54] Two days later, in

48 Proctor, *Historie of wyates rebellion*, fol. 59^{v}. Proctor incorrectly calls the major of London Sir John instead of Sir Thomas.

49 Proctor, *Historie of wyates rebellion*, fol. 69^{v}–70^{r}.

50 Proctor, *Historie of wyates rebellion*, fols 70^{r}–71^{r}; Edwards, *Mary I*, 172–5.

51 Ives, *Lady Jane Grey*, 248–52, 268.

52 *Chronicle of Jane and Mary*, 59.

53 BL, Cotton Vitellius F. v, fol. 28^{v}; which can be accessed online in Richard W. Bailey, Marilyn Miller, and Colette Moore, eds., *A London Provisioner's Chronicle, 1550–1563, by Henry Machyn: Manuscript, Transcription, and Modernization* (University of Michigan) http://quod.lib.umich.edu/m/machyn [accessed 14 January 2023].

54 BL, Cotton Vitellius F. v, fols 28^{v}–29^{r}; *Chronicle of Jane and Mary*, 61.

what was considered a highly unusual act of mercy, Mary publicly offered a general pardon to the rest of the imprisoned rebels who had not played a leading role in the rebellion.[55] Suffolk, who in his trial confirmed that the rebellion aimed at the setting of 'the crowne apon Courtney's hedd', was beheaded on 23 February and the following day his secretary, Thomas Rampton, was executed too.[56] On 28 February the Knyvetts, Henry Isley and others were sent to Kent to be put to death there, and the same fate was awarded in March to Lord Thomas Grey, one of Suffolk's brothers. The other one, Lord John, was miraculously pardoned.[57] Thomas Wyatt was judged on 15 March and beheaded on 11 April and William Thomas, who had unsuccessfully tried to commit suicide after his arrest, also suffered the death penalty on 18 May.[58] The rest of the leading rebels were soon pardoned and the two loose ends of the conspiracy, Courtenay and Elizabeth, imprisoned. Although Wyatt at first incriminated both Courtenay and Elizabeth during his trial, he later retracted his statement at the scaffold.[59] On 19 May, Elizabeth was escorted from the Tower to Woodstock Palace, where she would remain under house arrest until April 1555 when, thanks to Philip's intercession, she was allowed to return to court and was soon afterwards rehabilitated.[60] Courtenay was sent to Brussels to be monitored there by Charles v.[61] He was later granted permission to travel through Italy, dying in Padua at the age of thirty in September 1556. Although Spanish poison was suspected, the English ambassador to Venice, Peter Vannes, who took care of Courtenay during his last days, made it clear in his despatches that the earl of Devon had died of a fever being 'a very good Christen man' who had expressed his desire to recover his health so that he could confront those who were spreading the rumour that 'he was better frenche then Englishe'.[62] Alas, it was not to be.

55 BL, Cotton Vitellius F. v, fol. 29^{r}.

56 *Chronicle of Jane and Mary*, 61.

57 See the *Chronicle of Jane and Mary*, 65–67.

58 *Chronicle of Jane and Mary*, 68, 72; CSP Spain, vol. 12, 130.

59 *Chronicle of Jane and Mary*, 68–70; 72–4; James D. Taylor, *Sir Thomas Wyatt the Younger, c. 1521–1554 and Wyatt's Rebellion* (New York: Algora Publishing, 2013), 131–2.

60 Jasper Ridley, *Elizabeth I* (London: Constable, 1987), 62–5. Elizabeth would later write to Philip: 'I have been fully informed, and am well persuaded of your generous exertions on my behalf, to liberate me from the wearisome woes of an imprisonment, so hard and so tedious'. Quoted in Duncan, *Mary I*, 157.

61 CSP Spain, vol. 12, 151–2, 165–7, 169.

62 TNA SP 69/9, no. 542: Peter Vannes to Mary, Padua, 18 September 1556.

2.2 Rebellion and Religion

The fourfold rebellion was a sudden event which ended as abruptly as it had started. Traditional interpretations of the episode have assumed that there existed an ubiquitous distaste for the marriage, and have emphasised anti-Spanish sentiment and fears of foreign rule as the main motives behind the rebellion. In this view, religion did not play any significant role either in the development of the conspiracy nor in the actual rebellion, as the only conspirator whose attachment to Protestantism was 'uncompromising' was the duke of Suffolk.[63] Since the 1970s, however, new interpretations have qualified and challenged these interpretations. In 1977, Peter Clark demonstrated that local interests and relationships among local magnates had a great impact on the development of the events of January 1554.[64] In 1987 William B. Robison followed Clark's thesis in his study of the political implications of the rebellion in the person of the Surrey magnate Sir Thomas Cawarden of Bledingley.[65] In his doctoral thesis of 1999, Alexander Samson intensified the debate by convincingly arguing that the grievances of the rebels were strikingly similar to those held by the Comuneros of Castile and stemmed from social perceptions of marriage which had identified that of Philip and Mary as a 'feminisation' of the country as a whole – an imagined process in which foreign interference and the 'loss of liberty' were seen as 'economic and sexual violations'.[66]

The religious aspects of the rebellion, however, remain glaringly underexplored, even though there have been several attempts to place them in their right context. In 1924, E. R. Adair (1888–1965) proved that the Welsh conspirator

---

63 Loades, *Two Tudor Conspiracies*, 12, 16, 17, 34. His theses were strongly held and were argued in several of his subsequent works. See *The Oxford Martyrs* (London: R. T. Batsford, 1970), 123–4; *Politics and the Nation, 1450–1660* (Glasgow: Collins/Fontana, 1974), 226–32, 236; *Reign of Mary*, 159–61; *The Religious Culture of Marian England* (London: Pickering & Chatto, 2010), 90–1; *Mary Tudor* (The Hill, Stroud: Amberley, 2011), 143–4. Loades's views, first expounded in 1965, that the rebellion had been 'secular and anti-clerical rather than protestant' and stemmed from 'the threat of Spanish domination' have been the backbone of numerous assessments of the fourfold rebellion. See, for instance, A. G. Dickens, *The English Reformation* [1964] (London and Glasgow: Collins/Fontana, 1972), 356–60 and G. R. Elton, *Reform and Reformation: England, 1509–1558* (London: Edward Arnold, 1977), 380–2.

64 Peter Clark, *English Provincial Society from the Reformation to the Revolution: Religion, Politics, and Society in Kent, 1500–1640* (Hassocks: The Harvester Press, 1977), 87–98.

65 William B. Robison, 'The National and Local Significance of Wyatt's Rebellion in Surrey', *The Historical Journal*, 30, no. 4 (1987), 769–90.

66 Alexander Winton Seton Samson, 'The Marriage of Philip of Habsburg and Mary Tudor and Anti-Spanish Sentiment in England: Political Economies and Culture, 1553–1557' (PhD thesis, Queen Mary and Westfield College, unpublished, 1999), 126–60.

from Llantomas, William Thomas, was a committed Protestant.[67] Thomas was a scholar who in 1552 published *Il Pellegrino Inglese*, a defence of Henry VIII against the 'sycophants of the Antichristian See' in which he presented the king as the herald of godly reform in England.[68] In 1971, Conrad Russell (1937–2004) argued that several others among the conspirators were Protestants too, and that it was therefore impossible to prove that religion was not integral to the rebellion.[69] This was then further explored by Malcolm R. Thorp, who in 1978 concluded that although the rebellion was not a 'religious crusade', religion was still influential in the shaping of the conspiracy and probably of the rebellion itself too.[70] The first to disassociate the rebellion from any religious implications were the rebels themselves, who based their official motives on fear of foreign domination and the legalistic excuse that Mary had forfeited her right to the throne by not following Henry VIII's will. This was a clever strategy designed to attract both Protestant and Catholic opponents of the Spanish marriage which seems to have been successful to a limited extent. James Cottrell, for instance, a yeoman of Bathurst Manor in Sussex, was indicted for his 'malicious' (*maliciose*) and 'seditious' (*sediciose*) claims that 'my lord courtney shall marry my lady Elizabeth, And be kyng', and also that Mary,

> [...] hath broken her ffathers will, for the duke of Norf[ol]k, the lorde Courtney, and the bysshoppe of wynchester should haue remayned in the towre [and] she should not marry any outlandysshe man therfore she ys not worthy to ware the crowne.[71]

This was, of course, not true, for the clause applied only during Edward VI's minority and it did not flatly forbid a foreign marriage as long as it was approved by the majority of Edward's council, but it shows that the rebels' propaganda,

67 E. R. Adair, 'William Thomas: A Forgotten Clerk of the Privy Council', in R. W. Seton-Watson, ed., *Tudor Studies Presented by the Board of Studies in History in the University of London to Albert Frederick Pollard: Being the Work of Twelve of His Colleagues and Pupils* (London: Longmans, Green & Co, 1924), 133–60.

68 William Thomas, *Il pellegrino inglese ne'l quale si difende l'innocente, et la sincera vita de'l pio, et religioso re d'Inghilterra Henrico ottavo, bugiardamente calonniato da Clemente VII et da gl'altri adulatori de la Sedia Antichristiana* (Zürich: Andreas Gessner and Rudolf Wyssenbach, 1552). See Sergio Rossi, 'Un «italianista» nel Cinquecento inglese: William Thomas', *Aevum*, 40 (1966), 281–314.

69 Conrad Russell, *The Crisis of Parliaments: English History, 1509–1660* (London and New York: Oxford University Press, 1971), 139.

70 Malcolm R. Thorp, 'Religion and the Wyatt Rebellion of 1554', *American Society of Church History*, 47, no. 4 (1978), 363–80.

71 TNA KB 9/587, fol. 77^{r}.

devoid of any religious implications, had been widely disseminated in the southeast of England.[72] In any case, the queen, her government, and the imperial ambassadors were convinced from the beginning that the main motivation of the rebels was a religious one. On 22 January, Mary warned several Devonshire knights and MPs of the impending commotion, stating that the conspirators aimed 'against our personne and State royall', and had joined the conspiracy 'to the hinderaunce of the true catholicq religion and diuine service now by the goodnes of god restored'. They intended to rebel, she affirmed, by spreading 'false rumours of the cumming of the high and mighty […] Prince of Spayne and others of that nation'.[73] Mary's letters to the lord presidents and councils of Wales and the North, to the bishops of Exeter and Salisbury, and to the counties, expressed an identical concern.[74] On 27 January, when the rebellion had already started, the imperial ambassadors wrote to their master that they were pondering 'the troubles that grow every day in this kingdom on the points of religion and of the […] marriage'.[75] This became the main argument in the official history of the rebellion; John Proctor's (1521–1558) *The Historie of wyates rebellion*, published in December 1554, in which the author's main concern was to link heresy with sedition.[76] Wyatt's main motive, Proctor concluded, had been 'the inordinate desire to reteine false religion'.[77] Robert Wingfield (*c*.1513–*c*.1561), who had been one of the first to rally to Mary's cause in the first uncertain days of July 1553, followed the same line in his chronicle, stating that 'men of little religion' had used the Spanish marriage, the 'stiff manners of the Spaniards and their insufferable lust for women', as a pretext 'to support their evil religion'.[78]

---

72 For the limitations imposed on Mary's marriage by Henry VIII's will during Edward's minority see Edwards, *Mary I*, 65.

73 TNA SP 11/2, no. 5: Queen Mary to Sir Hugh Pollard, Sir John St Leger, Sir Richard Edgecombe and Sir John Fulford. St James's Palace, 22 January 1554.

74 TNA SP 11/2, no. 6: Queen Mary to the lord presidents (Nicholas Heath, bishop of Worcester and Francis Talbot, earl of Shrewsbury) and councils of Wales and the North and to John Veysey, bishop of Exeter and John Capon, bishop of Salisbury, St James's Palace, 22 January 1554; SP 11/2, no. 8: Queen Mary to the counties, St James's Palace, 22 January 1554.

75 AGS Estado 808, leg. 6:The imperial ambassadors to Charles V. London, 27 and 29 January 1554: '[…] nous pesons leurs Jnterogatz[ions] que plusiers du consel nous font quant partirons / et le trouble que Jour autre se suscite en ce Royaulme pour le point de la Religion / et dud[it] mariage […]'; CODOIN, vol. 3, 454.

76 The theological understandings of the link between heresy and rebellion will be explored in Chapter 6 below.

77 Proctor, *Historie of wyates rebellion*, fol. 88^{v}.

78 Wingfield, *Vita Mariae*, 274; a transcription of the original Latin in 225: 'At nacti harum sub involucro nuptiarum occasionem rebellandi homines religiosuli, causati in primis

All these pieces of evidence have a clear axe to grind.[79] The 'Defence of Sir Thomas Wyatt', which can be found among the papers of the rebel's son, George Wyatt (1553–1624), took pride in Sir Thomas's Protestantism. It also denied that the motives for the rebellion were religious; but since the document aimed at the rehabilitation of Wyatt's reputation, its usefulness as evidence is unreliable.[80] However, there is evidence of Wyatt's anti-Spanish feelings and militant Protestantism in his 1549 'A Treatise on the Militia', in which he attacked the 'supersticious Spayniard' and encouraged Protector Somerset to 'take in hand to set up the Religion Protestantism that he the Emperor pulleth down'.[81] Indeed, it would seem that those involved perceived the conflict as political as well as religious. According to Proctor, when Wyatt refused Mary's offer of a pardon he told her envoys, Hastings and Cornwallis, that he would only yield if he would be granted custody of the Tower and of the queen's person as well as the 'displacing of certen cou[n]sellers' and the placing of others 'as to me shall seeme best', which was of course no yielding at all.[82] Although Proctor had access to state papers, Renard's closeness to power cannot be doubted, and yet his account to Charles V differed from that of Proctor in that not only had Wyatt demanded the Tower, the queen's person and the removal of 'three or four of the council so that they may be punished', but also to 'restore religion as it had been' – presumably in Edward's time.[83] Whether this was true or hearsay, there may be a hint pointing to Wyatt's commitment to Protestantism in another one of Renard's letters to Charles V. According to Renard, Wyatt, already in custody, had

> greatly scandalised the queen at the Easter communion service by taking communion with the other prisoners without having confessed [...] and Wyatt also uttered strange words about religion and the sacraments.[84]

Hispanorum rigidos mores et libidnem in mulierculas non ferendam, aliquo pessimo tumultu (lena quasi Hispanica cooperti) pessimam suam religionem ruinae proximam suffulcire totis viribus tenant'.

79 The partiality of surviving records and accounts relating to the fourfold rebellion has been commented upon by Thorp, 'Religion and the Wyatt Rebellion', 373–4.

80 *Papers of George Wyatt*, 182–2, 192.

81 *Papers of George Wyatt*, 167–8; Samson, 'The Marriage of Philip and Mary', 107.

82 Proctor, *Historie of wyates rebellion*, fol. 50.

83 CODOIN, vol. 3, 462: 'La respuesta del dicho Vietez fue que quería tener la torre de Londres a su mandado y a la dicha Señora para la proveer de mejor consejo que aquel que ella había tomado, para lo cual quería tener en su poder tres ó cuatro del dicho Consejo para castigarlos y reponer la religión como estaba [...]'.

84 CSP Spain, vol. 12, 200.

Goodman, in many ways Proctor's Protestant counterpart as chronicler of the rebellion, claimed that Wyatt had been a man 'of God, of great estimation amongst all goodmen' and accused the nobles and councillors who had allowed his rebellion to fail of permitting Wyatt, 'and with him the whole Churche and common welth of England to fall into the handes of Gods enimies'.[85]

Although for some cases the evidence is scarce, there is enough material to suggest that all but one of the minor conspirators had known Protestant affinities if not outright commitment to the cause. Sir Nicholas Arnold of Churcham in Gloucestershire, a justice of the peace there, had been one of Thomas Cromwell's agents during the dissolution of the monasteries; he had attacked the religiously conservative sheriff of Gloucestershire, Thomas Bell, and had been described in a letter to Hugh Latimer, the Edwardian bishop of Worcester, as a favourer of religious reform.[86] Sir George Harper of Latton, in Essex, had profited from the dissolution of the monasteries. Although this could apply to many other gentlemen and nobles now loyal to Mary, it may be telling of where his sympathies lay that on 4 July 1553 he had been granted a special licence to retain thirty persons beside his household, in all likelihood in the hope that he would use them to support Lady Jane Grey.[87] Sir William Pickering of Valle Crucis, in Wales, who was resident ambassador to Henry II of France between 1551 and 1553, was notorious for his Protestantism and in 1551, Jean Scheyfve, Charles V's ambassador during Edward VI's reign, described him as Northumberland's creature and a man whose 'zeal for the new religion is great'.[88]

Sir Edward Rogers of Langport, in Somerset, sat as an MP for his shire in Edward VI's last parliament in March 1553, and had soon afterwards signed the young king's 'Device for the Succession' which attempted to nominate Lady Jane Grey as his heir, although so had many who had subsequently become part of Mary's privy council. In October 1553, however, Rogers had been re-elected for Somerset together with his associate, Sir Ralph Hopton, to Mary's first Parliament and they had been among those who 'stood for the true religion' by

85 Goodman, *Superior Powers*, 202, 206.

86 Thorp, 'Religion and the Wyatt Rebellion', 371–2.

87 Loades, *Two Tudor Conspiracies*, 79; Thorp, 'Religion and the Wyatt Rebellion', 367; Helen Miller, 'George Harper (1503–1558)' in http://www.historyofparliamentonline.org/volume/1509-1558/member/harper-george-1503-58 [accessed 14 January 2023].

88 Royall Tyler, ed., *Calendar of Letters, Despatches and State Papers Relating to the Negotiations Between England and Spain*, vol. 10, Edward VI, 1550–1552 (London: Her Majesty's Stationery Office, 1914), 218; Advices from Jehan Scheyfve, January 1551.

travailing against the repealing of the Edwardian religious laws.[89] There is further proof that Rogers's motivation when joining the rebellion was religious. In Christopher Mompesson's deposition of January 1554, he stated that one of Hopton's servants revealed to him that Hopton had been in great council with Rogers for three days and that his master, Rogers's closest associate, was much suspected in the county because he 'offtene mete and cunsell togethere' with several men 'off that Relygyon whyche neuer cumytt to masse ress[e]ynge [sic: receiving] jn there howsses Ingelysshe s[er]wysse'.[90]

William Thomas, as we have seen, has been convincingly found to have been a Protestant too. His religious zeal was such that during Edward VI's reign he managed to involve the privy council in his dispute with Nicholas Ridley, bishop of London, over an ecclesiastical appointment.[91] The council finally ruled in favour of Ridley, but the fact that Thomas's candidate did for some time stand against that of the reformist bishop of London is highly revealing of his Protestantism. Sir Nicholas Throckmorton of Coughton Court in Warwickshire became a Protestant while in the household of his cousin, Queen Catherine Parr, and he was also a close associate of William Thomas, whom he suggested should write political tracts for Edward VI. Throckmorton was also outspoken against Catholicism during Mary's reign at least twice; first, during the parliamentary sessions of October 1553 as an MP for Old Sarum, and again during his trial for treason – from which he was surprisingly acquitted – in April 1554, when he expressed the view that Edward VI's death and Philip and Mary's marriage 'was the plague of God justlie come upon us' because since the death of that 'godlie and vertuous' king, most Englishmen were disguising their 'naughtie affections with a pretense of religion'.[92] Sir Edward Warner of Besthorpe, in Norfolk, had married the widowed Elizabeth Brooke in 1542, which made him Wyatt's stepfather. As the lieutenant of the Tower in July 1553, he tried to hold the same for Northumberland. He was unsurprisingly dismissed by Mary on 28 July, and in January 1554, Simon Renard gathered information, which he

---

89 Roger Virgoe, 'Sir Edward Rogers (1498/1502–1568), of Cannington, Som'. http://www.historyofparliamentonline.org/volume/1509-1558/member/rogers-sir-edward-14981502-68 [accessed 14 January 2023].

90 TNA SP 11/2, no. 33: Deposition of Christopher Mompesson concerning Sir Ralph Hopton. January 1554.

91 Nicholas Ridley, *The Works of Nicholas Ridley, Sometime Bishop of London, Martyr, 1555*, H. Christmas, ed., (Cambridge: Parker Society, 1841), 331–2; Thorp, 'Religion and the Wyatt Rebellion', 368–9.

92 Taylor, *Sir Thomas Wyatt*, 183; Stanford Lehmberg, 'Throckmorton, Sir Nicholas (1515/16–1571)', *Oxford Dictionary of National Biography*, Oxford University Press, 2004; online edn, Jan 2008 http://www.oxforddnb.com/view/article/27394 [accessed 14 January 2023]; Thorp, 'Religion and the Wyatt Rebellion', 369.

delivered to Gardiner, about the intrigues of 'ten or twelve heretics' in which Warner was unmistakably included.[93] The religious sympathies of Sir William Winter, a merchant and naval administrator from Bristol, are less easy to determine. He was sailing to Guinea with Thomas Wyndham in July 1553, so his reaction to the attempt to put Lady Jane Grey on the throne was never recorded. The government entrusted him with the task of escorting the imperial envoys to England from Flanders in December 1553, so the regime may not have been suspicious of him at this point.[94] As a merchant, however, Winter would have had much to profit from the Spanish marriage, and his decision to stand against it is difficult to understand without there having been other reasons. Whether these were religious or not is more difficult to ascertain. With the exception of Winter, therefore, all of the minor conspirators had been Protestants who had prospered under Edward VI's governments.

When it comes to the analysis of the religious affiliations of the leaders of the fourfold rebellion, their Protestantism becomes even more apparent with the notable exception of Courtenay, whose personal beliefs are still to this day shadowy, even if Vannes's comments on his death prove that he died a Catholic.[95] As we have seen, however, Wyatt's commitment to the Protestant religion cannot be doubted, and the same can be said of Sir Peter Carew. A native of Mohun's Ottery in Devon, Carew had prospered as an MP for Tavistock in 1545 and for Dartmouth in 1547. He had also held the office of sheriff of Devon between 1546 and 1547. In 1549 he was sent by Edward Seymour to fight against the religiously conservative Prayer Book rebels, who hated him for 'his religion'.[96] In his eagerness to crush the rebellion, Carew sought a direct confrontation with the rebels by burning a barn in Dartmoor against the specific advice of the local justices.[97] In the same year, Sir Peter and his uncle, Sir Gawain Carew, escorted William Alley, dean of Exeter – who in 1560 would replace the deprived Marian bishop of the city, James Turberville – to the pulpit so that he would be protected against the population's displeasure at his reformed preaching.[98] Carew continued to prosper under Edward VI and in May 1553, the enthusiastically Protestant MP for Dartmouth, Nicholas Adams,

---

93 APC, vol. 4, 422; CSP Spain, vol. 12, 42.

94 David Loades, 'Winter, Sir William (*c*.1525–1589)', *Oxford Dictionary of National Biography*, Oxford University Press, 2004; online edn, Oct 2009 http://www.oxforddnb.com/view/article/29769 [accessed 14 January 2023]. I am thankful to Dr Evan Jones, from the University of Bristol, for sharing his views and insights into Winter's figure.

95 Thorp, 'Religion and the Wyatt Rebellion', 367.

96 W. G. Hoskins, *A New Survey of England: Devon* (London: Collins, 1959), 283, 427.

97 Chris Skidmore, *Edward VI: The Lost King of England* (London: Phoenix, 2007), 114–5.

98 Thorp, 'Religion and the Wyatt Rebellion', 370.

recommended him to Sir William Cecil as a chantry commissioner for his 'worship, learning and discretion'.[99] Furthermore, in his 'Life of Sir Peter Carew', written shortly after Carew's death in 1575, John Hooker claimed that when Edward VI died, Carew refused to proclaim Jane and had instead quickly proclaimed Mary in Dartmouth and Newton Bushel, 'albeit he knew very well that there was like to ensue a great alteration in religion [...] and that as he was well affected so she [Mary] utterly did abhor it [...]'.[100]

In addition to this, and in concordance with Rogers's case, Carew's associates were militant Protestants as well – and of the aggressive sort, too. John Prideaux of Upton Pyne, a councillor of the city of Exeter who was close to Devon's sheriff, Sir Thomas Dennys, reported an incident concerning William Gibbs, an associate of Carew's. This Gibbs would later be accused by Sir Gawain Carew in his deposition of being violently outspoken against the coming of the Spaniards and those who did not oppose it including Prideaux and Dennys whose 'throttes shulld be cutte' if they tried to resist the rebellion.[101] Prideaux's report concerned some twelve neighbours or so of Silverton, where Gibbs lived, who had:

> compleyned [...] of a crosse of latten and of an aulter clothe stolen oute of the churche [...] [and] that the crosse was set vp apon a gate or a hedge by the waye where the pyctaure of [Christ] was dressyd w[i]th a paste or suche like tyre [and] the pictaures of o[u]r Ladie [and] St. John tyed by thredes or suche like things to the armes of the crosse like theves.

Prideaux then asked some of them to repair to Dennys and show to him what had happened, while others should go to Silverton to investigate who had been the author of the profanation. However, one of the neighbours, Henry Norton, stated that they had not been able to do as requested 'for fear of Mr Gybbes and his servaunts', who had hurt Norton himself.[102] The episode reflects not only that Carew was associating himself with people of Protestant affinities, but also that these associates were ostensibly desecrating the religious images

99 TNA SP 10/18, no. 19: Nicholas Adams to Sir William Cecil. Dartington, 6 May 1553.

100 John Hooker, 'Life of Sir Peter Carew', lxxxix in J. S. Brewer and William Bullen, eds., *Calendar of the Carew Manuscripts, Preserved in the Archiepiscopal Library at Lambeth, 1515–1574* (*London: Public Record Office, 1867*) lxvii–cxviii. Henceforth *Carew Manuscripts*.

101 TNA SP 11/3, no. 10 (ii): Deposition of Sir Gawain Carew in the presence of Sir John St Leger. 28 January 1554.

102 TNA SP 11/2, no. 15: Report of John Prideaux of Upton Pyne. 24 January 1554.

which had been restored since Mary's accession, or at least they were protecting those who had.

The case of Sir James Croftes of Croft Castle in Herefordshire, as that of Carew, also leaves no doubts as to his Protestantism. Although during Elizabeth's reign he would be known to be a Catholic and to favour the Spanish, this conversion, as we shall see, happened after the events of 1554.[103] Croftes had been an MP for Herefordshire in 1542 and acted as vice-chancellor of the council in the marches in Wales between 1550 and 1551. In May of the same year, Northumberland appointed him as lord deputy of Ireland, and his instructions were very specific on how the Edwardian settlement was to be implemented in the island. The first of his set of instructions was, 'with the advice of the council', to 'set forth God's service, according to our ordinances, in English'.[104] Croftes' Protestant zeal was such that he forced the Catholic archbishop of Armagh, George Dowdall, into exile in Brabant, after which Croftes vehemently requested that the privy council send a religious adviser who could 'direct the blind and obstinate bishops'.[105]

The duke of Suffolk's commitment to Protestantism, although well-established, needs further comment. The fact that his rebellion in Leicestershire was a fiasco and had been conceived with a fatal lack of organisation has rendered Suffolk's motives irrelevant. As the father of an imprisoned usurper and husband to the queen's first cousin, however, he stands out among the other conspirators as the most relevant in terms of connections and potential benefits to be gained from the overthrowing of Mary. Suffolk's rash decision to join the rebellion when he had so recently escaped punishment after the collapse of his daughter's bid for the throne, has been interpreted as a mixture of foolishness, ambition and, according to the duke's own explanation, prompted by 'the small esteem in which the council held him' rather than by any religious motivations.[106] There is, however, an overwhelming amount of evidence which demonstrates, not only that Suffolk was a committed Protestant, but also that his motivations responded to his religious inclinations. During the reign of Edward VI, Suffolk and his wife, Lady Frances Brandon, had entertained Ulrich Zwingli's successor as Protestant leader in Switzerland, Heinrich Bullinger, who admired the duke's Protestant zeal even if he condemned his arrogant

103 Wallace T. MacCaffrey, *The Shaping of the Elizabethan Regime* (Princeton: Princeton University Press, 1968), 445. Croftes conversion from anti-Spanish Protestant to pro-Spanish Catholic will be explored briefly in Chapter 3.

104 *Carew Manuscripts*, 226–7, 231–2.

105 Steven G. Ellis, *Ireland in the Age of the Tudors, 1447–1603: English Expansion and the End of Gaelic Rule* (Harlow: Longman, 1998), 221.

106 Ives, *Lady Jane Grey*, 266.

demeanour. Bullinger would later correspond with Suffolk and his daughter Jane, and he would thank the duke for his financial support by dedicating his fifth *Decade* (1551) to him and describing him as 'a vigorous maintainer of real godliness'. As is well-known, Suffolk had also made sure that Jane received a thoroughly reformist education at the hands of notorious Protestant reformers such as John Aylmer and the Italian Michelangelo Florio.[107] Furthermore, Renard was convinced of the beneficial impact that the execution of the Greys would have in the advancement of the Catholic cause. In an undated letter, which must have been written soon after the collapse of the fourfold rebellion, Renard wrote to Charles V that:

> [Mary] has no further cause for concern in her kingdom, now that the heads of Jane of Suffolk and of her husband, Guildford, are to be cut off. And thus, the whole House of Suffolk will be rendered level and desolate as long as justice is meted out to the three imprisoned brothers [Suffolk and his brothers Thomas and John], who are heretics, and whose execution will bring about the total re-establishment of religion.[108]

Whereas this was undoubtedly an overstatement, it nevertheless proves how crucial Suffolk's role was considered in relation to the advancement of Protestantism. The duke gave further proof of his commitment when he went to the block on 23 February and, like his daughter, as Renard reported, obstinately 'refused to be converted to the old religion'.[109] More important to this point, however, is the evidence left to us of the connections that Suffolk established while trying to win Coventry over to his failed rebellion. When he was in Leicester, Suffolk sent over his secretary, Thomas Rampton, to gather from the councillors of Coventry whether they would join his master against 'the co[m]myng yn of the Straungers'. Two of them, Richard Aslyn and Francis Symcockes, assured Rampton that, with the exception of a few councillors, the whole city would declare for Suffolk's side, although, as we have seen, when the duke reached Coventry he found that the city refused to open its gates to him.

107 Leanda de Lisle, *The Sisters Who Would Be Queen: The Tragedy of Mary, Katherine and Lady Jane Grey* (London: Harper Press, 2008), 35, 70–3, 82; Ives, *Lady Jane Grey*, 51, 65–75; Thorp, 'Religion and the Wyatt Rebellion', 370.

108 CODOIN, vol. 3, 494; Simon Renard to Charles V, [February] 1554: 'Ella queda sin recelo en su reino, habiendo de cortar la cabeza a Joana de Sofoc y a Guillén Ford su marido, que toda la casa de Sofoc será raída y desolada con tal que se haga justicia de los tres hermanos prisioneros que son heréticos, y que siendo ejecutados causará entero restablecimiento de la religión [...]'.

109 CSP Spain, vol. 12, p. 125.

While Rampton, Aslyn and Symcockes discussed the need to secure the castles of Kenilworth and Warwick, news came that William Glover had arrived at Coventry from London, at which news Rampton 'was co[n]tented therw[i]th bycawse my Arraund was chiefly to hym'. Glover then came into the room with one Clerk, and Rampton disclosed his master's predicament to them. Rampton asked Glover whether Suffolk would be received in Coventry and be assisted by the city in 'the defence of his contrey', to which Glover answered:

> my lordes quarrell is right well knowen it is godes quarrell, Let hym com let hym com and make no staye for this towne is his owne [...].
>
> Then sayed clerk no doubt this towne is at my Lordes co[m]mandem[en]t and yf he com hether he cannot be but welcom / And therw[i]t[h] he began to declare how only my lordes grace dyd cleave and styck to godes truth / wherby I noted hyme to be a protestaunt / And dyd co[n]fesse the samme of my lorde.[110]

Rampton had been sent to Coventry with specific instructions from Suffolk to confer with Glover, a notorious Protestant who would later be prosecuted with his brothers, Robert and John, the former of whom would be burnt at Coventry in 1555. Both John and William Glover later died from natural causes and would be refused burial in consecrated grounds, being interred instead in open fields as excommunicates and heretics. Ralph Banes, bishop of Lichfield and Coventry, referred to William Glover shortly after his death in 1558 as 'a rebellion agaynst our holy faith and Religion'.[111]

In Suffolk's case, as in those of Carew, Wyatt and Rogers, it is possible to discern an awareness of the benefits that could arise from bringing in Protestant dissenters like themselves into the rebellion. It is in any case revealing that not one single unequivocal Catholic has ever been identified as taking part in the conspiracy or the rebellion. It appears, therefore, that Mary's government and sympathisers had been right all along. Christopher Goodman, the Protestant clergyman exiled in Geneva, concurred. Wyatt's motivation to undertake his 'dangerous entreprise', he would claim in 1558, had been 'the zeale of Gods trueth and the pitie that he had to his Countrie'. He had been deemed a traitor and executed for defending 'the Gospel and his Countrie from cruel strangers and enemies'.[112] Those who had betrayed him, Goodman contended, were the real traitors, cowards who would 'mayntayne Philipps warres' and 'please Iesabel',

110 TNA SP 11/3, no. 20: Deposition of Thomas Rampton. February 1554.

111 *A&M* (1570), 1930–31.

112 Goodman, *Superior Powers*, 204.

'whiles their brethern be burned at home and their countrie like to be wasted, spoyled, oppressed, possessed, and replenished with vngodly Spanyardes'. 'Is this the loue', Goodman asked them, 'that ye beare to the worde of God?'.[113] The Spanish marriage was irrevocably associated with the re-establishment of Catholicism. Although never expressed in these terms, opponents of the regime and the Spanish marriage fully understood the implications that joining the Spanish Monarchy would have for England. To become part of the *monarchia universalis* would mean to become the supporter of its spiritual counterpart, the *ecclesia universalis*. The union with the Catholic Monarchy changed the political and religious landscape entirely and provided Mary with the strong support she needed to complete her intended return to Rome successfully. The religious motivations of the conspirators were so inextricably linked with their political concerns, that any attempts at separating them would render the interpretation of the events of early 1554 artificial and incomplete. Since the monarch was the head of the body politic of the kingdom, Philip's arrival meant the end of the schism initiated under Henry VIII and of the development of a Protestant Church under Edward VI. The rebels knew that, fought against it, and lost.

The inseparability of the rebellion from matters religious was commented upon not only by Marian and imperial observers at home, and by Protestant commentators in the Genevan exile, but also in Brussels by Cardinal Pole, who wrote that he would congratulate Mary on her victory, which he hoped would be 'a victory of religion'.[114] In relation to this, the absence of popular support for the rebellions, although not a determining factor, may be telling of where popular sympathies lay. Wyatt only managed to gather 3,000 men in a region known for harbouring the greatest numbers of Protestants in the kingdom, and his accomplices fared much worse. These are negligible amounts when compared to the 30,000 to 40,000 involved in the Pilgrimage of Grace between 1536 and 1537, the 6,000 that the popular Prayer Book rebellion of Devon and Cornwall managed to gather in 1549, or the 5,400 involved in the Northern rebellion of 1569 in favour of Mary Stuart and Catholicism.[115]

---

113 Goodman, *Superior Powers*, 207–8.

114 BL Add MS 25425; Cardinal Pole to Pope Julius III, Brussels, 12 February 1554: 'Hora non differirò a mandare un messo con mie l[ette]re alla Reg[in]a [per] congratularmi con S[ua] M[aes]tà di q[uest]a vittoria la q[ua]le io spero che sarà vittoria della Relig[ion]e [...]'.

115 Anthony Fletcher and Diarmaid MacCulloch, *Tudor Rebellions* [1968] (Abingdon and New York: Routledge, 2016), 34, 59–60, 70, 106; Bernard, *King's Reformation*, 368. For the Catholic impetus of the Northern rebellion against Elizabeth I see K. J. Kesserling, *The Northern Rebellion of 1569: Faith, Politics, and Protest in Elizabethan England* (Basingstoke and New York: Palgrave Macmillan 2007).

There is also evidence that the Spanish marriage and its implications were not as unpopular as they have been traditionally portrayed. On 24 January, for example, the escheator for Devon and Cornwall, John Ridgeway, reported to Dennys, the sheriff of Exeter, that the people of Totnes in Devon and its surrounding areas were 'yn good quyett [and] well contente with the co[m]myng of the prynce of spayn (except a fewe p[er]sone) [and] do myche malygne [...] suche gentilmen as wuld the contrary [...]'. Totnes, he continued, was 'well ffurnysshed with harnesse weapons [and] other mvnysyons for warres', and its people were 'trustie subiectes' ready to defend the queen if anybody, 'as pety hyt were they shuld', were to attempt anything against her or Philip.[116] In mid-February, Renard was informed by the privy council that the gentlemen from Wales, the West and the North had 'on their own initiative' gathered to swear 'fidelity and wholesome service' to Philip and Mary, that Plymouth had of its own accord made preparations in case Philip decided to land there, and that, even in London, the people were starting to 'acknowledge and declare' that Philip 'would be welcome as long as he does not bring foreign soldiers'.[117]

Clearly, therefore, to read the events surrounding the fourfold rebellion as detached from their religious implications is an anachronism which places England and Spain as already engaged in an irreconcilable enmity. This tendency has also affected interpretations of Anglo-Spanish relations in England once the marriage had taken place. Friction between the two nations has been considered unavoidable and the joint Anglo-Spanish commission of justice set up in 1554 to have done well as a purely judicial mechanism, but not as a device to quell discord or to tone down hostilities between both nations.[118] However, a close scrutiny of the evidence paints a very different picture.

116 TNA SP 11/2, no. 13; John Ridgeway to Sir Thomas Dennys: Torre Abbey, 24 January 1554.

117 CODOIN, vol. 3, 495–6; Simon Renard to Charles V, London, February 1554: 'El dicho Consejo me ha dicho como los gentiles hombres de Gaula y de Vesse y de Nort se han de su propio motivo ayuntado y jurado fidelidad y servicio entero a S[u] A[lteza] y a la dicha Señora para mantener el casamiento contratado, y los de la parte de Plemúa han escrito a la dicha Señora como ellos han proveído para recibir a S[u] A[lteza] muy honrosa y seguramente, y ya el pueblo de Londres empieza a reconocer y decir que S[u] A[lteza] será el bien venido con tanto que no traiga soldados extranjeros [...]'.

118 This interpretation, which has coloured subsequent analyses of the topic, is exemplified in Loades, *Reign of Mary*, 138, 215, 243 and, more recently, in his *Mary Tudor*, 169, 261–2.

2.3 Anglo-Spanish Conflict and Enmity

On 20 July 1554, Philip finally landed in Southampton. The wedding, which took place in Winchester Cathedral and was officiated by Gardiner, was celebrated on 25 July to honour the feast of St James, patron saint of Spain. According to John Elder's († 1565) chronicle of the event, during the wedding celebrations there was much 'triumphing, bankating, singing, masking, and daunsing, as was neuer in Englande here tofore'. Philip and Mary dined under the cloth of state at Winchester's city hall, and they danced in the chamber of presence. The scene described by Elder is encapsulated in a revealing metaphor of the political expectations of the Anglo-Spanish marriage, as 'the dukes and noble men of Spain dau[n]se with the faire ladyes and moste beutifull nimphes of England'. It was such a spectacle, Elder added, that 'it should seme to him that neuer see suche, to be an other worlde'.[119] On 31 July Philip, Mary and their train moved to Basing, where the next day 'was suche noble Chere prouided for them, and both their nobilities, as I haue not sene the like'.[120] From Basing, the royal entourage moved to Reading on 2 August and the next day to Windsor, where England's new king was installed as head of the Order of the Garter.[121] After staying at Richmond and then in one of Suffolk's forfeited properties, the king and queen made their official entry to London on 18 August.[122] The royal court paraded through the streets of the capital while the people awarded them a cheerful welcome and an impressive display of pageantry in which Philip was described as 'O noble Prince sole hope of Ceasars side / By god apointed all the world to gyde', a wish which provided a direct link to the Habsburg notion of *monarchia universalis*. The king was compared to King Philip II of Macedon (r. 359–336 BC), the Roman Emperor Philip the Arab (r. 244–249), and to his own ancestors, the dukes of Burgundy Philip the Bold (r. 1363–1404) and Philip the Good (r. 1419–1467). The pageant at the west end of Cheapside went so far as to represent Philip as an Englishman himself by presenting a

---

119 John Elder, *Copie of a letter sent into Scotlande, of the ariuall and landynge, and moste noble marryage of the moste Illustre Prynce Philippe, Prynce of Spaine, to the most excellente Princes Marye Quene of England, solemnisated in the Citie of Winchester: and howe he was receyued and installed at Windsore, and of his triumphyng entries in the noble Citie of London.* (…) (London: John Wayland, 1555), sig. B1ʳ.

120 Elder, *Copie of a letter*, sig. B3ʳ.

121 On Philip's appointment as master of the Garter and the gendered dilemmas it posed both for him and Mary see Duncan, *Mary I*, 69, 99–102.

122 CSP Spain, vol. 13, 443. The most comprehensive accounts of the royal entry can be found in Edwards, *Mary I*, 197–9; Duncan, *Mary I*, 86–8; Samson, *Mary and Philip*, 122–36.

family tree showing Philip and Mary's lines of descent from King Edward III (r. 1327–1377).[123] Indeed, Philip descended directly from Edward III's son, John of Gaunt, through the latter's daughters Philippa, wife of John I of Portugal (r. 1385–1433) and Catherine, wife of Henry III of Castile (r. 1390–1406). Philip was represented as a homecoming king and an Englishman himself, and the verses below the family tree celebrated the reunion of the two branches of the English royal family embodied in Philip and Mary's marriage: 'both descended of one auncient lyne / it hath pleased God by mariage to combyne'.[124] In early September, already in Hampton Court to spend the rest of the summer, Philip himself reported to his sister Juana that in London he had been received 'with many good demonstrations of love and contentment from everyone'.[125]

Despite these good omens, it soon became apparent that the Anglo-Spanish honeymoon was not to be without its thorns. An anonymous Spanish observer complained around the same time that he had heard that 'among the rabble in London it has been shamelessly said that one day they would have us all killed'. The English, he concluded, were 'the roughest people that were ever seen'.[126] The Spanish gentleman Juan de Baraona wrote back home that not only was he ailing due to the corrupted water of England, which caused 'putrefaction of the body', but he was also wary of the English whom, he warned, were 'great scoundrels'.[127] There were dead and stabbed men on both sides every day, although Baraona put the blame on the English, accusing them of provoking

---

123 An analysis of the display of Philip and Mary's genealogy is to be found in Samson, *Mary and Philip*, 130.

124 Elder, *Copie of a letter*, sigs B5^v–C3^r. Accounts of the marriage and royal entry in London can be found in Edwards, *Mary I*, 183–99; Duncan, *Mary I*, 75–88; Samson, *Mary and Philip*, 104–36.

125 AGS, Estado 808, leg. 38/1; King Philip to Princess Juana, Hampton Court, 2 September 1554: '[…] después [of the marriage] venimos a londres donde fui reçibido con toda buena demostraçión de amor y contentamy[en]to de todos y hauiendo estado en aquella çiudad seis o siete días venimos a passar lo que queda del verano en esta casa'.

126 AGS, Estado 808, leg. 174; Anonymous report [summer 1554]: '[…] a mí me han dicho que la Canalla de Londres dezía muy desuergonçadamente q[ue] vn día nos hauía[n] de matar a todos como en otro t[iem]po hizieron a los franceses ellos son la más cruda gente q[ue] nunca se vio […]'.

127 RBME, MS V-II-4; Juan de Baraona to Antonio de Baraona, London, 25 October 1554, fol. 450^r: '[…] agora me prueba la tierra muy fuerte mente que estoi lleno de hibiesos y d[e] sarna y esto me an dicho los médicos que causa la agoa desta tierra porque yo no bebo çerueza / y bebo agora agoa cozida con canela porque las aogas [sic] d[e]sta tierra son muy malas que se haze podre en el cuerpo […] ellos son tan grandes vellacos y que todos tienen el hern[an]do en el cuerpo que no nos marauillamos que agan qual q[ui]er vellaquería por que lo vemos cada día mill cosas d[e]llos que es para tomar grama el hombre […]'.

the attacks. He also described the gruesome assaults suffered by two Spanish gentlemen at the hands of the English. One of them had been beaten up and robbed by eight Englishmen who had then tied him up and abandoned him in the woods, where a girl herding cattle found him more than six hours later. The other gentleman had been assaulted twenty leagues away from London, and he had had to make his journey to the capital in his breeches and doublet because he had been robbed of everything else, and arrived 'half-dead from famine and misfortune'.[128] An anonymous report sent to Spain about the English expressed concern at 'how roughly they treat strangers', as they robbed all of them 'at all hours [...] without sparing anybody'. The same commentator stated that the Spaniards, especially those who had brought their wives with them, were already regretting their coming to England and he predicted that, if things did not change, there would be no Spaniards left in the kingdom in a year's time, as some were already passing over to Flanders.[129]

Closer to the court, reports were alarming too. Andrés Muñoz, servant to Philip's son, the Infante Carlos, explained in his 1554 work, *Svmaria y verdadera relación*, that the Spaniards did not find themselves as well in England as in Castile. He then added that some of them 'would rather be among the stubble of the kingdom of Toledo, than in the greenwoods of Amadís'; an allusion to

128 RBME, V-II-4, fols 450^{v}–451^{r}: 'No ay día ninguno que no aya muertos o cuchillados entre los españoles yngleses [sic] porque avnque no queramos nos hacen ellos rrenir porque ellos vienen d[e]rechos a nos otros para dar nos el encontronaço que d[e]rriban al hombre / y con todo esto se nos ponen d[e]lante a hazer nos cocos [...] avn agora es medio mal por que luego quando venimos así amos como criados yendo por las calles nos tiraban d[e] petacos y pedradas y pasábamos n[uest]ro camino ad[e]lante y an echo muy grandes rrobos que lo que nos a cauido en parte quiero lo dezir / cuebas vino ad[e]lante por posada a Londres y en el camino le salieron hasta ocho yngleses dos d[e] a cauallo y los otros de a pie y le dieron con vn palo y le aturdieron y le asieron luego y lle llebaron a meter en vn monte porque toda esta tierra es montaña y allí le dieron muchos palos y le q[ui]taron tod[o] lo que llebaba que no le d[e]xaron sino en calças y jubón y sin sonbrero y lo d[e]xaron atado en el monte los pies y las manos asta que le llebaron la silla y el freno d[e]l cauallo y estuvo más de seis oras así atado asta que pasó vna mochacha que andaba con ganado y le d[e]sató / lo mesmo le hizieron este día pasado agoado al hijo de la m[erced] d[e]l s[eño]r don luis que vino después d[e]la armada que le tomaron todo lo que traýa asta d[e]xarle sin botas y sonbrero solam[en]te con las calcas y el jubón y así llegó aq[uí] a londres d[e]más d[e] veynte legoas de aq[uí] que le rrobaron muerto d[e] hanbre y d[e] malaventura [...]'.

129 RBME, V-II-4; 'De Cartas venidas de Inglaterra', July 1554, fol. 453^{r}: '[...] es gran estremo quán ásperamente tratan a estra[n]geros porq[ue] a todos sin perdonar a nadie roba[n] a todas oras hasta este punto ay hartos arrepentidos de los q[ue] han venido despaña y mucho más los q[ue] han traýdo las mujeres lo de adelante no se sabe cómo será. / Si es como lo de hasta aquí no creo que avrá español de oy en vn año. y ya se comie[n]can a pasar algunos a fla[n]des'.

Spain's chivalric bestseller, *Amadís de Gaula*, set in Amadís's native England.[130] Alonso de Alguero, servant and chaplain to Antoine Perrenot de Granvelle, bishop of Arras and one of Charles v's closest advisers, complained in a letter to his master that the king's court was dissatisfied with

> [...] this unholy people [...] who know neither God nor the king [...]. They are well armed, so that if over there [Flanders] you are at war with the French, here we are at war with feigned friends. [...] I have been beaten up and almost [...] entirely shaved, for it is true that they are enemies of strangers, especially of men with tonsures and long robes. So much so, that it has been necessary to disguise the habit [...].

The English were more 'ferocious' than the Germans, but Alguero hoped that God would punish them, for 'they hold and fear so little'.[131] Just a few days after the wedding had taken place in Winchester, Ruy Gómez de Silva had also felt compelled to disapprove of the English, complaining that among them there

---

130 Andrés Muñoz, *Svmaria y verdadera relación del buen viaje que el inuictíssimo Príncipe de las Españas don Felipe hizo a Inglaterra, y recebimiento en Vincestre donde casó, y salió para Londres, en el qual se contiene[n] grandes y marauillosas cosas que en este tiempo pasaron. Dedicado a la illustríssima señora doña Luysa Enríquez Girón, condesa de Benauente, por Andrés muñoz criado del sereníssimo Infante don Carlos nuestro señor* (Saragossa: Miguel Zapila, 1554), fol. 37^{v}: 'La vida que allí passan los Españoles no es muy auentajada, ni se hallan tan bien, como se hallaran en Castilla. A esto algunos dizen, que querrían más estar en los rastrojos del reyno de Toledo, que en las florestas de Amadís'. For the relation between England and the Spanish chivalric tradition present in *Amadís de Gaula*, see Edwards, *Mary I*, 182, 185, 192–3, 211–2; Helen Moore, 'The Eastern Mediterranean in the English *Amadis* Cycle, Book v', *The Yearbook of English Studies*, 41, no. 1 (2011), 113–25; Glyn Redworth, '¿Nuevo mundo u otro mundo?: conquistadores, cortesanos, libros de caballerías y el reinado de Felipe el Breve de Inglaterra', in Ralph Penny and Richard Hitchcock, eds., *Actas del Primer Congreso Anglo-Hispano de 1992*, vol. 3 (Madrid: Castalia, 1993), 113–25; Samson, 'The Marriage of Philip of Habsburg and Mary Tudor', 212–4.

131 RBPRM, MSS II-2286-E, fols 55^{r-v}, Alonso de Alguero to Antoine Perrenot de Granvelle, Bishop of Arras; London, 25 October 1554: '[...] esta corte está malcontenta con estas gentes nonsantas porq[ue] al fyn nj conosçen a dios nj al Rei nj temen a las gentes y ansý estará la tierra en especial las posadas agora mandan yr los oficiales. todos traen broqueles saben byen çapear de modo q[ue] si allá tienen guerra contra franceses acá con amjgos fengidos q[ue] es gran trabajo entre ellos tratar dios sabe lo q[ue] acá e pasado que a sydo más trabajo q[ue] el que pasé en alemaña porq[ue] estas gentes son más feroçes porq[ue] como vine algo tenplano e sydo apaleado y avn casi pelado porq[ue] cierto son enemygos destrangeros en especial de onbres de coronas y ropas largas y fue menester andar fengydo el ávito. [...] algunos traydores an prendjdo q[ue] rebolvían estos reynos y componjan çiertos lybros y v[uestra] s[erenida]d cree q[ue] algunos estrangeros azen este mal. suplyco a v[uestra] s[erenida]d p[er]done mj atrevimiento q[ue] djos dará a éstos su castigo pues tan poco tienen ni temen'.

were 'great thieves [...] and they rob in plain sight'. In this, he added, they had an advantage over the Spanish in that the latter robbed 'by stealth and they by force'.[132]

These events make better sense if we remember that Philip and Mary's marriage was one of the greatest international events to take place in the sixteenth century (together with Charles V's abdication ceremony in 1555). As the Tower chronicler indignantly (and exaggeratedly) recorded, during this time there were so many Spaniards in London, 'that a man shoulde have mett in the stretes for one Inglisheman above iiij Spanyerdes, to the great discomfort of the Inglishe nation'.[133] It was not only the Spaniards who felt attracted to London during the celebrations. As Muñoz described, at the marriage there had been 'only but a few nations absent, there being Spaniards, Englishmen, Germans, Hungarians, Bohemians, Poles, Flemings, Italians and Irishmen; and even a lord of the Indies, so that the Indies would be represented', a reference to Martín Cortés, marquis of the Valley of Oaxaca and son of the famous conquistador, Hernán Cortés.[134] The overcrowding of the streets of London facilitated incidents and subsequent comments on the same as those that have already been alluded to. It is unsurprising, therefore, that problems would arise, and there is plenty of evidence that they did.

On 10 August, a gentleman called Gonzalo Salvedra, together with an Englishman, Simon Rouse, assaulted, beat up and robbed the merchant Pedro López Zapato and his wife.[135] Although it has been claimed that Salvedra hoped that the crime would be blamed on the English, this interpretation overlooks not only the fact that it is impossible to know whether Salvedra and López Zapato were Spanish or Portuguese, as it is not specified in the patent rolls, but also the sinister association of Salvedra, whatever his origins, with the Englishman Rouse.[136] Immediately after Philip and Mary's entry on 18 August 1554, Pedro Fernández de Córdoba, *comendador* of Montiel and his

---

132 AGS, Estado 808, leg. 148: Ruy Gómez de Silva to Francisco de Eraso, Winchester, 29 July 1554: '[...] ay grandes ladrones entre ellos y rroban a ojos vistas esta ventaja azen a los españoles q[ue] nosotros lo hazemos con maña y ellos por fuerça [...]'; Loades, *Reign of Mary*, 216.

133 *Chronicle of Jane and Mary*, 81.

134 Muñoz, *Svmaria y verdadera relación*, fol. 36v: 'En otra parte estaua[n] los grandes y caualleros Españoles y ingleses, y se sentaro[n] a comer, Entre los quales faltaua[n] pocas naciones, porque auía Españoles, Ingleses, Alemanes, Vngaros, Bohemios, Polacos, Flamencos, Italianos, y Hibernios, asta vn señor Indiano, porque huuiesse indio'.

135 M. S. Giuseppi, ed., *Calendar of the Patent Rolls Preserved in the Public Record Office. Prepared under the Superintendence of the Deputy Keeper of the Records. Philip and Mary*, vol. 2 (London: Public Record Office, 1936), 97, 159. Henceforth CPR.

136 Loades, *Reign of Mary*, 215–16.

nephew Antonio, lord of Valenzuela, were attacked by a mob who also mocked them on account of the cross of St James on their robes.[137] On 9 September, the tailor Griffin Middleton of London was assaulted by two Spanish yeomen, Alonso Martín and Luis Medina, near the parish of St Clement Danes and his wounds were so severe that he died a few days later.[138] As Henry Machyn, (*c*.1495–1563), a clothier who kept an account of London life, reported, on 15 October a servant of Sir George Gifford was 'shamfully slayne' by a Spaniard outside Temple Bar.[139]

2.4 The Anglo-Spanish Commission of Justice

Such incidents have been variously interpreted as evidence that the Anglo-Spanish co-monarchy was destined to fail. Yet, there can be no doubt that both parties were acutely aware of the existing potential for conflicts, and the joint commission of justice that was set up to prevent them seems in fact to have worked rather well. The idea appears to have come from the Spanish side, which makes perfect sense considering the importance that the Habsburgs placed on national sensibilities. In March 1554, Philip himself had chosen Diego Briviesca de Muñatones, *alcalde de casa y corte* (or justiciar of the household and the court) to exert his judicial representation in order to 'secure peace and agreement between members of the different nations'.[140] Briviesca hailed from a family of lawyers and jurists from Uceda, Guadalajara, and was described by Charles v as being 'accustomed to deal with foreigners'.[141] In this Briviesca followed in the footsteps of his father, Juan Sánchez de Briviesca, who as an *alcalde* (municipal judge) himself had judged over incidents involving different nationalities in Spain.[142] Perhaps sensing the impending waning of his own influence in English affairs, Simon Renard counselled against the coming of

137 CSP Spain, vol. 13, 33.

138 CPR, vol. 2, 243.

139 BL, Cotton Vitellius F. v, fol. 37r.

140 CSP Spain, vol. 12, 147–8.

141 CSP Spain, vol. 12, 160–1.

142 In 1525, for example, Sánchez de Briviesca had ruled in favour of an Italian, Luigi di Campania, against an Englishman, Adrian, who was a servant to Ferdinando d'Aragona, duke of Calabria. In 1527 he had presided over the trial of a monetary issue between the Spaniard Juan de Quincoces and the Florentine Pandolfo Velacci, and in 1533 he had condemned Alonso Rodríguez de Fonseca for some disturbance that had taken place in Salamanca. See AGS, Consejo Real de Castilla, 134, 4; AGS, Consejo Real de Castilla, 137,1; and AGS, Consejo Real de Castilla, 368,1; among many other examples.

Briviesca, claiming that the English would not tolerate his interference.[143] Arras assured him from Brussels, however, that Briviesca would enjoy 'no authority nor exercise jurisdiction over any except foreigners' to England and, even then, he would never 'overstep the limits set by the queen and council'.[144] Briviesca was in Dover on 10 May and on the fifteenth he arrived in London in the company of the lord of Courrières, one of the imperial envoys who had negotiated the marriage treaty.[145] Five days later he had an audience with Queen Mary, the contents of which are mostly unknown to us.[146]

Over the course of the following days, the council deliberated about the powers that Briviesca was to enjoy. Henry Fitzalan, earl of Arundel, as lord steward, granted Briviesca and his English counterpart, Sir Thomas Holcroft, the right to seize and arrest those who would offend around the court.[147] The instructions for the joint commission were drawn up by Briviesca and Arundel, and they confirmed that the former and Holcroft were to be appointed judges for 'all criminal causes' involving 'any of the Spanisshe or other straunge nation amonge themselfes or against any naturall subiecte of the queen or [...] any suche naturall subiecte against any straunger'.[148] This first clause is a remarkable one: contrary to Renard's predictions, it granted joint powers to the Spanish and English judges, who were to 'co[n]fere daylie toggithers'. All offences deserving the capital punishment were to be tried according to the laws of England, but a special caveat was conceded that crimes and offences of a less serious nature were to be tried 'by bothe the [...] co[m]missioners and thoffender to be punished according to the nature [and] qualitie of the faulte'. Punishments were to be carried out by the provost marshals which were to be appointed by Briviesca and Holcroft.[149] The English provost marshal seems to have been Sir Anthony Kingston, appointed as such by Edward VI in 1549, who although a repressor of the Prayer Book rebellion of the same year, had been quick to proclaim Mary during the crisis of July 1553. He must have remained in post until December 1555, when he was put in the Tower for plotting to place Elizabeth on the throne.[150] Kingston's Spanish counterpart was most certainly

143 CSP Spain, vol. 12, 176.
144 CSP Spain, vol. 12, 234.
145 CSP Spain, vol. 12, 260.
146 CSP Spain, vol. 12, 244, 257.
147 CSP Spain, vol. 12, 260.
148 TNA SP 11/4, no. 10.
149 TNA SP 11/4, no. 10.
150 Kingston was pardoned only a few days later, on 23 December. In 1556 he was again arrested for his involvement in the conspiracy of Sir Henry Dudley but died on 14 April at Cirencester while he was on his way to the Tower. See Emily Tennyson Bradley, 'Kingston, Anthony', in Sidney Lee, ed., *Dictionary of National Biography*, vol. 31 (London: Smith,

Francisco de Castilla, himself an *alcalde* and one of the select men who travelled with Philip to England in Martín de Bertendona's ship. Castilla would later be employed in a very similar capacity in Flanders.[151] Minor punishments, the instructions continued, were to be carried out according to the 'vsage of the nation of thoffendar' and the provost marshals and their men were to put all their efforts in the avoiding of 'all occasions of contention betwene nation [and] nation', but they were also severely to punish 'to the terro[u]r [and] example of others' anyone caught trying to destroy peace and amity. The other items of the instructions dealt with other points of substance, such as the procedures to be followed in the event that the offender were a nobleman, an enforcement to circulate Mary's latest proclamation against provoking quarrels with foreigners and the granting to the commissioners of the prerogative to judge over civil causes.[152] In addition, all members of Philip's English household were made to swear an oath that they would 'see good orders kept and offenders punished', and that 'noe Englishman by word or deed should misse vse any stranger'.[153]

The pessimistic views voiced after Philip's arrival by Baraona, Alguero, Ruy Gómez and others have already been noted. In his chronicle, the meticulous Henry Machyn recorded a total of eight serious incidents between 26 September 1554 and 16 December 1556, but none for 1557 and 1558. These incidents included fights, robberies, murders, and executions of offenders. On 26 April 1555, for instance, three Englishmen were hanged for the robbery of a Spaniard. During the execution, one of the offenders railed 'a ganst [the] pope [and] [the] masse', which again raises the issue that anti-Spanish sentiment (if a robbery can be so described) and anti-Catholicism were much more closely related than has been hitherto recognised.[154] This aspect of English opposition to the Spanish

---

Elder & Co., 1892), 185 and David Loades, 'Kingston, Sir Anthony (*c.*1508–1556)', Oxford Dictionary of National Biography www.oxforddnb.com/view/article/15626 [accessed 14 January 2023].

151 Tellechea Idígoras, *Carranza y Pole*, 27; José Ignacio Tellechea Idígoras, 'Bartolomé Carranza en Flandes. El clima religioso en los Países Bajos (1557–1558)', in Erwin Iserloh and Konrad Regpen, eds., *Reformata Reformanda: Festgabe fur Hubert Jedin zum 17. Juni 1965*, vol. 2 (Münster: Verlag Aschendorff, 1965), 317–43.

152 TNA SP 11/4, no. 10. Mary's proclamation was issued at Westminster on 1 March 1554, and it stated that any Spaniard or any other foreigner in Philip's retinue would 'use themselves honestly, friendly, and quietly towards her highness' subjects', and it commanded the same from the English. See TRP, ii, 33–34.

153 TNA, SP 11/4, no. 17; A transcription in modern English to be found in CSP Domestic, 59.

154 BL, Cotton Vitellius F. v. On 26 September 1554 four men were hanged of which one was a Spaniard (fol. 36^{r}); on 15 October a servant of Sir George Gifford was killed by a Spaniard (fol. 37^{r}); on 4 November 'be gane a grett ffray at charyng crosse' between the Spanish and the English (fol. 38^{r}); on 9 January 1555 two Spaniards held an Englishman while a third Spaniard stabbed him to death (in John Gough Nichols, ed., *The Diary of Henry Machyn:*

is related to another incident reported by Giovanni Michieli, the Venetian ambassador, concerning the failed assault in 1555 of a church in which several Spaniards had gathered before going out in procession on Corpus Christi day.[155] Michieli also described a fight in which the improbable number of 500 Englishmen attacked the Spanish and still got the worse part, with four or five dead and twenty-five wounded to the five or six wounded and one dead of the Spanish.[156] Moreover, many of the conflicts recorded were robberies and there is no evidence to suggest that there were any underlying aims other than financial gain. The large amount of silver objects violently extracted by Gregory Baron and others from the count of Fuensalida's home in Fleet Street on 1 October 1555 is typical of this attitude.[157]

In all, the frequency of the conflicts between Englishmen and Spaniards does not support the traditional view that they were a widespread phenomenon stemming from a deeply entrenched enmity. Furthermore, the records are silent about any incidents occurring between 1557 and 1558. In fact, the very same source typically used to reach the conclusion that an understanding between both nations was out of the question, Machyn's chronicle, also presents many occasions of peace and amity between men of both nations.[158] When the Spaniard Carlos de Granado was buried in Westminster Abbey on 6 October 1554, there was 'syngyng boyth english [and] spaneards', and the same happened in the burial of a Spanish gentleman in St Martin-in-the-Fields the following 19 November.[159] The same can be said of the grand funerals held on 17 June 1555 at St Paul's Cathedral for Queen Juana, Philip's grandmother, in which English, Spanish and other foreign mourners did in no way exacerbate

Citizen and Merchant-Taylor of London (1550–1563) (London: The Camden Society, 1848), 79); on 26 April took place the hanging of the three Englishmen referred to in the text (fols 41^{v}, 44^{v}–45^{r}); on 16 December 1556 a Spanish smith, Gregorio, and an Englishman, John Boneard were arrested on account of their association to rob Andrew Alexander, keeper of Newgate (fol. 50^{r}).

155 CSP Venice, vol. 6, 126–7.

156 CSP Venice, vol. 6, 85.

157 Inside the house, between six and eight in the evening, Baron and his accomplices assaulted the count's brother, Luis López de Ayala, and other Spaniards dwelling in the house, and 'wounded and maltreated them so that they despaired of their lives'. For all the brutality of the attack, it is nowhere suggested that it was motivated by anything other than robbery. Baron and his men also stole several silver items which, judging from the detailed description of them contained in the Patent Rolls, seem to have been returned to Fuensalida, which may account for Gregory Baron's pardon on 20 November 1555. See CPR, vol. 3, 112.

158 Loades, *Reign of Mary*, 138, 215, 243.

159 BL Cotton Vitellius, F. v, fols 36^{v}, 39^{r}. I thank Christine Reynolds, Assistant Keeper of the Muniments at Westminster Abbey Library for her kind confirmation of the deceased's name.

ill feelings on the population.[160] There were also tournaments involving both nations – at least four – between 18 December 1554 and 25 March 1555, and during the wedding celebrations of Mary's cousin, Lady Margaret Clifford, to Henry Stanley, Lord Strange, on 7 February 1555, there was 'a grett dener [and] just[e]s [and] aft[er] tornay on horsbake w[i]t[h] sword[e]s [and] aft[er] soper jube [the] cane'; that is, *juego de cañas*, a popular game among the Spanish.[161]

There are several instances in which Spaniards are recorded attending or organising religious processions, sometimes with the king in attendance too, during which no disturbances were documented either before or during the king's absences from the kingdom.[162] The Mass on 30 November 1554 at Westminster Abbey, the day of the reconciliation with Rome, was significantly sang by Spaniards.[163] Apart from tournaments and religious ceremonies, Philip also showed himself to his subjects on a regular basis. On 25 November 1554, dressed in red, the king, without Mary, rode through London in the company of Lord Fitzwalter and some Spanish noblemen.[164] Later the same day, according to an anonymous Italian account, there was a 'most beautiful *juego de cañas*' in which the king, dressed in vermilion, 'moved and manoeuvred in so gentle a fashion that everyone who saw him fell in love with him'. When he ran, the reporter added, 'the people cried "The king! The king!" [...] a most evident proof of how, through the valour shown in all the actions performed by this most serene prince to this day, he has earned this people's favour'.[165]

---

160 BL Cotton Vitellius, F. v, fol. 46ᵛ.

161 BL Cotton Vitellius, F. v, fols 41ʳ–41ᵛ, 42ᵛ, 43ᵛ. For the rules of the *juego de cañas* see Milena Cáceres Valderrama, *La fiesta de moros y cristianos en el Perú* (Lima: Pontificia Universidad Católica del Perú, 2005), 124.

162 BL Cotton Vitellius, F. v. On 18 October 1554, King Philip, accompanied by many Spanish lords and other Spaniards, heard Mass, which was sang by a Spanish bishop, at St Paul's (fol. 37ᵛ). On 2 December the King attended Mass at St Paul's with 400 men of his guard, composed of Englishmen, Germans, Spaniards and Switzers (fol. 40ʳ) and on the 8th both Englishmen and Spaniards went through London together on procession for the Conception of Our Lady (fol. 40ᵛ). On 25 January 1555, a procession for St Paul's day was organised which passed by every parish in London. The king rode to St Paul's with Cardinal Pole, the duke of Savoy and several English and foreign lords and knights. At night there were bonfires and loud ringing of the bells in every church (fol. 42ʳ). The Spaniards were involved in the procession of St Clement Danes on 4 June 1555 (fol. 46ᵛ), and they also organised a more private one in Whitehall on 8 June 1556 (fol. 56ʳ). These are, of course, those recorded by Machyn, but there may have been more.

163 BL Cotton Vitellius, F. v, fol. 40ʳ.

164 BL Cotton Vitellius, F. v, fol. 39ᵛ.

165 Archivio Apostolico Vaticano, Fondo Carpegna, 202, 'Il Felicissimo Ritorno del Regno d'Inghilterra Alla Cattolica vnione, e all'Obedienza della Sede Apost[oli]ca', London, 1 December 1554, ff. 113ʳ–129ʳ, in f. 120ʳ: 'Dirò qui per non lasciar niente in dietro, come la Domenica [Sunday, 25 November 1554] dopo desinare nella Corte d'auanti al Palazzo

Any animosity that may have existed in 1554 seems to have evaporated by 1557. When Philip arrived at Greenwich on 20 March and was approaching the gate, a ship passing by spontaneously shot sixteen times whilst her passengers cried 'god save [the] kyng & [the] quen'.[166] The following day three hoys full of Spaniards arrived in London but the only fight recorded by Machyn between March and July, when Philip left, involved Spaniards only.[167] On 23 March, he rode, this time with the queen, from the Tower wharf through the City in the company of lords, ladies, and the masters, aldermen, sheriffs and all the crafts of London with 'trumpett[e]s blohyng w[i]t[h] odur enstrementt[e]s w[i]t[h] grett joye & plesur & grett shutyng of gones at [the] towre'.[168]

The Spanish sources tend to describe a more amiable situation too. Despite Ruy Gómez's early misgivings, on 12 August 1554 he reported to Charles's secretary, Francisco de Eraso, that things went well in London, and he dismissed 'a few wicked acts' as not uncommon 'given the condition and custom of the land', implying that they were of little concern.[169] On 15 October, Briviesca himself wrote to Arras that affairs in England marched 'from good to better' with God's help. Since he arrived in England he had looked into the nature of the English 'with one eye as much as others would with two', finding them to be 'truly diverse, fickle and inconstant' and learning that they 'detest strangers more than anything'. However, he added, things would calm down thanks to Philip's presence and because the 'private brawls' which had taken place 'will not produce greater fires'. Moreover, he concluded, things were already beginning to 'quieten down'.[170] In his letter to Arras of 28 October, undoubtedly

si fece il gioco delle Canne bellissimo, nel quale fù la persona del Rè. Erano in tutti 60 diuisi in sei Liuree a dieci p[er] ciascuna di vestimenti alla Moresca sopra bellissimi giannetti guarniti all'usanza di Spagna, i colori delle Liuree erano bianco, verde, giallo, azurro, paonazzo, incarnato, e nella Liurea incarnata era il Rè sopra vn legiadrissimo Cauallo di mantello vbero, sopra il quale con si gentil maniera si moueua, e operaua, che innamoraua di se ciascuno, che lo uedeua, e quando correua tutto il Popolo gridaua, Chingh, Chingh, ch'in lingua loro significa il Rè il Rè, segno assaissimo euidente quanto questo Seren[issi]mo Prencipe p[er] il valore, che di lui fin allhora s'è veduto in ogni suo atto s'habbia acquistata la gratia di q[ue]sti Popoli'.

166 BL Cotton Vitellius, F. v, fol. 68^{r}.

167 BL Cotton Vitellius, F. v, fols 68^{r}, 70^{v}.

168 BL Cotton Vitellius, F. v, fol. 68^{r}.

169 AGS, Estado 808, leg. 143; Ruy Gómez de Silva to Francisco de Eraso, Richmond, 12 August 1554: '[…] lo de aquí va bien y en londres avnq[ue] ay algunas vellaq[ue]rías no es cosa nueva avellas sigún la condición y uso de la tierra […]'.

170 RBPRM, MSS II-2286-E, fols 59^{r}–60^{v}; Diego Briviesca de Muñatones to Antoine Perrenot de Granvelle, Bishop of Arras; London, 15 October 1554: '[…] no siento q[ue] las cosas vayan vendito dios sino de bien en mejor y desde el p[rimer]o q[ue] acá passé he stado en esto y como alcalde no dexo de mirar avnq[ue] con vn ojo tanto como otro con dos

dealing with the fate of the murderer of Sir George Gifford's servant mentioned above, Briviesca explained how he – and probably Castilla too – had conferred with the English judges and reached upon the death sentence for the offender. Although some had asked Philip and Mary for a pardon, 'the king's Majesty would not have it', and so the Spaniard had been executed. He continued:

> It was a most convenient thing to do because the king must credit himself as a dispenser of justice before the natives, and in this way take roots [in England]. It has given great satisfaction to the people to understand that justice must be done and is indeed done.[171]

Perhaps one of the most significant pieces of evidence concerning the good functioning of the joint commission and the disappearance of any residual Anglo-Spanish hostility by 1557 comes from a comment made by Machyn about Ruy Gómez in that same year. On 16 September, Ruy Gómez, en route to see Philip at Brussels, stopped in London to pay a visit to Queen Mary and the select council. Whereas in 1554 he had described the English as 'great thieves', in 1557, accompanied by a small retinue 'w[i]t[h] grett cheynes [and] ther hatts sett w[i]t[h] stones [and] perles', Philip's confidant felt comfortable enough to drink at the Horn and Greyhound inns in Fleet Street and to ride through Cheapside at night with a small entourage before leaving for Dover.[172]

---

y darme a conocer estas gentes: q[ue] cierto son varias y mudables y de poca firmeza y q[ue] aborescen extrangeros más q[ue] ottra con todo esto tengo entendido y creído q[ue] el rey a ganado mucho en este reyno porq[ue] según le avían pintado avnq[ue] no lo fuera tanto bueno como lo es en todo ni de tan buen rostro y acogimj[ent]o bastara: gente es mudable pero yo no puedo p[er]suadirme a q[ue] esto no se aquiette cada día más. y no ay renidos ni quistiones de importantia y de las q[ue] ha havido se entiende y así ha parescido q[ue] destas rixas particulares no resulta encenderse mayores fuegos ni pasan más adelante. antes se aquiettan [...]'.

171 RBPRM, MSS II – 2286 – E, fols 143^{r}–144^{r}: Briviesca de Muñatones to Arras; London, 28 October 1554 – '[...] y ansí me confirmo agora q[ue] espero de cada día las cosas de aquí se assentarán mejor aquí suscedió q[ue] vn español mató vn inglés abiéndole dado alg[un]a ocasión porq[ue] abía rescevido vn bofetón del inglés. pero toda vía nos juntamos con los juezes dela tierra y le condenamos a muerte y aunq[ue] hubo p[er]zonas q[ue] tractaron del p[er]dón con la m[ajes]t[ad] de la reina y del rey la m[ajes]t[ad] del rey no dio lugar a ello y assí se executó: y fue cosa muy convenj[ent]e porq[ue] a estos propios se ha de acreditar el rey de justiciero y echar raízes a ssido cosa q[ue] al pueblo ha dado gran satisfactión entender q[ue] se ha de hazer justicia y se haze. y espero todo irá de bien en mejor'.

172 BL Cotton Vitellius, F. v, fol. 79^{v}.

2.5 Conclusion

There are several points to be raised in relation to the dissemination of anti-Spanish sentiment in England in the months preceding and following Philip and Mary's marriage. First, to extrapolate events in London to the rest of the kingdom, claiming that the marriage was unpopular throughout the country is a clear anachronism swayed by the Anglo-Spanish enmity of the 1580s.[173] Moreover, a few violent incidents, perhaps not uncommon but certainly not the norm, do not suffice to prove that the Anglo-Spanish co-monarchy was doomed from the beginning or that the English population widely rejected it. To follow this argument would mean to disregard that popular support for Wyatt in the capital was scant, even though he managed to enter the city and gain the acquiescence of some Londoners. This reading also ignores the fact that Londoners had cheered in support of Philip and Mary's marriage after the queen's famous speech at the Guildhall during the rebellion, an episode which may have been encouraged by the formal proclamation of the marriage treaty earlier in January.[174] It also forgets that at least the merchant community of London had honourably welcomed Philip in August, as evidenced by Elder's descriptions of the pageants set up for the monarchs' entry and that Philip seems to have been rather popular during his visits to England. Arguments in favour of an Anglo-Spanish commercial alliance were self-explanatory and they resonated well into Elizabeth's reign.[175] The possibilities offered not only by Spain and Flanders, but also by the Americas were not lost on the merchant community, but they were echoed in other domains, too, which prompted a steady growth in cultural exchanges, still incipient when Mary died but nevertheless significant.[176] John Wilkinson, for instance, translated Luis de Ávila

173 For this traditional view C. S. L. Davies, *Peace, Print and Protestantism, 1450–1558* (Frogmore: Paladin, 1977), 295–8; Dickens, *English Reformation*, 357–9; Elton, *Reform and Reformation*, 380–2. It has proven to be an extremely resilient perception. For modern examples see Duncan, *Mary I*, 164, McDermott, *England and the Spanish Armada*, 39–46.

174 Whitelock, *Mary Tudor*, 216.

175 Jason Eldred, '"The Just Will Pay for the Sinners": English Merchants, the Trade with Spain, and Elizabethan Foreign Policy, 1563–1585', *Journal for Early Modern Cultural Studies*, 10, no. 1 (2010), 5–28.

176 This subject has been recently explored by Alexander Samson, 'Culture under Mary I and Philip', in Sarah Duncan and Valerie Schutte, eds., *The Birth of a Queen: Essays on the Quincentenary of Mary I* (New York: Palgrave Macmillan, 2016), 155–78. Equally, Christopher Heaney has recently explored the impact that Philip and Mary's marriage and the allure of the riches of America had in the English conceptualisation of Spanish power through the work of Richard Eden and other. See Christopher Heaney, 'Marrying Utopia: Mary and Philip, Richard Eden, and the English Alchemy of Spanish Peru', in

y Zúñiga's (1504–1573) *Comentario de la guerra de Alemaña* (1548) in 1555, and, in his dedicatory epistle to the earl of Derby, he praised Charles v because he had 'spled his ba[n]ners from East vnto the west part of the worlde: and not onely agaynste the Turkes and Mores, but moreouer to subdue the diuersities of sectes'.[177] Richard Eden (*c.*1520–1576), in the preface of his translation of Pietro Martire d'Anghiera's *De orbo nove decades* (1530) on the discovery and conquest of the New World, published the same year, claimed that 'the heroical factes of the Spaniardes of these days' were so deserving of praise that they were 'aboue the famous actes of Hercules and Saturnus and such other which for theyr glorious and virtuous enterpryses were accoumpted as goddes amonge men'.[178]

It is true that there may well have been a residual opposition to the Spanish marriage in London, but this attitude was not reflected in the rest of the kingdom. The immediate failure of three of the rebellions of 1554 has been explained as the result of a lack of preparation on the rebel's side, rather than a lack of support to bring them to fruition. However, the fact that Sir Thomas Dennys was able to protect Exeter from the Carews with the support of the city council, that Suffolk, a great lord, could only raise 140 horsemen and was denied entrance to Coventry, and that Croftes was unable to gain any substantial support in Herefordshire, does suggest that the prospect offered by rebellion was less attractive than that offered by the Spanish marriage. Reports like those sent by John Ridgeway about Totnes and its surrounding areas and by Simon Renard about Wales, the West, the North, Plymouth, and even London,

---

Jorge Cañizares-Esguerra, ed., *Entangled Empires: The Anglo-Iberian Atlantic, 1500–1830* (Philadelphia: University of Pennsylvania Press, 2018), 85–104.

177 Luis de Ávila y Zúñiga, *The Comentaries of Don Lewes de Auela, and Suniga, great Master of Aranter, which treateth of the great vvars in Germany made by Charles the fifth Maximo Emperoure of Rome, King of Spain, against John Frederike Duke of Saxon, and Philip the Lantgraue of Hesson with other great princes and Cities of the Lutherans, wherin you may see how god hath preserued this vvorthie and victorious Emperor, in al his affayres against his enemyes tra[n]slated out of Spanish into English*, tr. John Wilkinson (London: Richard Tottel, 1555).

178 Richard Eden, *The decades of the newe worlde or west India, Conteynyng the nauigations and conquestes of the Spanyardes, with the particular descripcion of the moste ryche and large landes and Ilandes lately founde in the west Ocean perteynyng to the inheritaunce of the kinges of Spayne. In the which the diligent reader may not only consyder what commoditie may hereby chaunce to the hole christian world in tyme to come, but also learne many secreates touchynge the lande, the sea, and the starres, very necessarie to be knowe[n] to al such as shal attempte any nauigations, or otherwise haue delite to beholde the strange and woonderfull woorkes of God and nature. Wrytten in the Latine tongue by Peter Martyr of Angleria, and translated into Englysshe by Rycharde Eden* (London: William Powell 1555), fols a1^{v}–a2^{r}.

as areas which supported Philip's coming should not be dismissed either. It is hardly a coincidence that, once the Spaniards arrived, conflicts were only reported as happening in London and its suburbs.

In any case, these events had been predicted, and the Anglo-Spanish authorities were steadfast in their resolution to crush them. The diminishing number of reported incidents, which disappear altogether after December 1556, lends credence to the notion that the joint-commission under Briviesca and Holcroft served its purpose well. Moreover, the scant details left to us of these incidents are most of the time not indicative of a deeply-rooted anti-Spanish sentiment, but rather of a lucky chance to exploit the opportunity presented by the arrival of rich foreigners by attaining financial gain through robbery. In this there also seems to have been collaboration between both nations, albeit of a sinister tone. Indeed, on 16 December 1556 a Spanish smith named Gregorio was hanged while his accomplice, the Englishman John Boneard was burnt in the hand for their robbery of Andrew Alexander, keeper of Newgate.[179] If Gonzalo Salvedra, who together with an Englishman attacked and robbed a merchant, was indeed Spanish, there would be further proof that some of these attacks were predominantly motivated by a desire to rob, and not by any specific distaste of the Spaniards as a nation. In addition, at times these assaults seem also to have been inspired by religious motivations against the restoration of Catholicism, as has already been noted. This latter aspect of Anglo-Spanish violent incidents seems to justify the view held by the Marian government, John Proctor and others, that heresy was tantamount to sedition, a reading of events that seems to be supported by the unmistakably Protestant religious affiliations of Wyatt and the rest of the rebels.

The year 1554 proved that the Anglo-Spanish alliance would not be free of problems, but there is no evidence to suggest that there was widespread hostility against Philip, the Spaniards, or the reunion with Rome. As we have seen, this animosity was mainly confined to London and, even then, it was quickly outrooted by the Anglo-Spanish authorities. With the joint-commission of justice firmly in place it was now time for King Philip I to take the reins of the government of England.

---

179 BL Cotton Vitellius, F. V, fol. 50r.

CHAPTER 3

In Such Good Concord: The Anglo-Spanish Court of Philip I

While Philip awaited to embark in La Corunna in the summer of 1554, a great number of men and women who were to accompany him were arriving in the city too. Waiting for the winds to be favourable, Andrés Muñoz recorded that it was

> [...] a marvellous thing to hear such noise and voices and the echoes of the same [...] begging wholeheartedly to Christ our Lord to grant them the journey that they all desired and his highness deserved. Others said: 'Oh, Christ our Lord! Save our prince and lord from the fearsome and disastrous fortunes of the sea and make him disembark before the eyes of the most desired and beloved Queen Mary, his wife'. Others said: 'Oh! May the sacred empress of the empire of heaven and earth, with the whole celestial court, take you safely to the new English kingdom for the increase of our holy Catholic faith and the good of Christendom'. Others said: '[...] let France and her flocks come out and they shall see the clemency with which they will be welcomed by the good Philip and his men [...]'. Others said: 'Quiet! We trust in God that the prince our lord shall be knife and sword to all of them and any others who would be rebels against the royal crown'.[1]

1 Andrés Muñoz, *Svmaria y verdadera relación del buen viaje que el inuictíssimo Príncipe de las Españas don Felipe hizo a Inglaterra, y recebimiento en Vincestre donde casó, y salió para Londres, en el qual se contiene[n] grandes y marauillosas cosas que en este tiempo pasaron. Dedicado a la illustríssima señora doña Luysa Enríquez Girón, condesa de Benauente, por Andrés muñoz criado del sereníssimo Infante don Carlos nuestro señor* (Saragossa: Miguel Zapila, 1554), fols 30^{r}–30^{v}: 'Y la gente que en gran cantidad era que en la marina estaua. Cosa marauillosa era ver aquel ruydo y vozes y el echo dellas, entre las quales suplicauan ahincadamente a Christo nuestro señor les diesse aquel viaje que todos deseauan y su Alteza meresçía. Otros, O Christo nuestro señor, al Príncipe y señor nuestro le plega guardar de la temerable y desastrada fortuna del Mar, y desembarques a ojos de su muy deseada y q[ue]rida reyna doña María su muger. Otros, o la sagrada Emperatriz imperio de cielo y tierra, con la corte celestial te lleue con bien y a saluamento al nueuo reyno Inglés para augme[n]to de nuestra santa fe cathólica y bien de la christia[n]dad. Otros, salga, salga Francia y su grey y verá co[n] ña clemencia q[ue] será recebido del bue[n] Felippe y los suyos. Otros, Ya pluguiese a la diuina magestad y tal se le antojasse q[ue] de la saludable fruta q[ue] lleua[n] no les podía faltar

 | DOI:10.1163/9789004536210_005

These themes pervade the history of Philip and Mary's reign. First and foremost, the safeguard of the Catholic faith and the universality of Christianity. Second, the conflict with France that loomed in the background. Finally, Philip's role as a dispenser of justice and the scourge of rebellion. To these three aspects of the English adventure, the Spaniards accompanying the prince in his voyage were fully committed. A considerable number of courtiers and clergymen travelled together with 4,000 soldiers to England from La Corunna on 12 July. The fleet was composed of 125 ships commanded by Álvaro de Bazán, and it was escorted at the rear by thirty warships 'completing', in John Edwards's words, an 'awe-inspiring force'.[2]

As was mentioned in Chapter 1, Diego de Acevedo had arrived in England as Philip's unofficial informant soon after the marriage negotiations began. In May he had been joined by the *alcalde* Diego Briviesca de Muñatones. On 9 June, Pedro Dávila y Zúñiga, marquis of Las Navas and Philip's *mayordomo* (steward), landed in Plymouth, where he was received by Lord William Howard.[3] Navas had come with some fifty men to deliver jewels to Mary on Philip's behalf and was escorted to Wilton, the earl of Pembroke's seat, by the earl's son, Lord Henry Herbert. As one commentator observed, the entertainments at Wilton must have greatly impressed the marquis, as 'hytt was natt a lyttyl marueyle to consyder thatt so greate a preparacyon cowlde be made in so small a warnynge'.[4] Perhaps in the marquis's company were the two other Spaniards who were also in London by June. These were the royal secretary Pedro de Hoyo and the jurist Francisco de Menchaca, who had been a witness to Philip's *ad cautelam* document in January.[5]

---

según son de golosos. Otros, Dexaldos [sic] con sus cantarillos q[ue] algunas vezes dexarán las asas o frentes. Otros, Calla q[ue] nos confiamos en Dios que el Príncipe y señor nuestro, ha de ser cuchillo y espada para todos ellos, y los de más q[ue] rebeldes fueren a la corona real. Y pasando estas razones y motes y otros muchos, se traspuso el armada'.

2 John Edwards and Ronald Truman, eds., *Reforming Catholicism in the England of Mary Tudor: The Achievement of Friar Bartolomé de Carranza* (Aldershot: Ashgate, 2005), 5. Partial lists of those who came to England can be found in Muñoz, *Svmaria y verdadera relación*, fols 1ᵛ–2ʳ; José Ignacio Tellechea Idígoras, *Fray Bartolomé Carranza y el Cardenal Pole: Un navarro en la restauración católica de Inglaterra (1554–1558)* (Pamplona: Diputación Foral de Navarra, Institución Príncipe de Viana and Consejo Superior de Investigaciones Científicas, 1977), 27.

3 TNA, SP 11/4, no. 11; Lord William Howard to the Council, Plymouth, 9 June 1554.

4 TNA, SP 11/4, no. 13; Edward Sutton-Dudley, Lord Dudley to the Council, Basing, 19 June 1554.

5 Menchaca was also the uncle, godfather and mentor of the jurist and humanist Fernando Vázquez de Menchaca, who wrote extensively on natural and civil law. See Víctor Manuel Egío García, 'La pieza que no encaja: reseña crítica a las "Controversias ilustres y de uso frecuente" de Fernando Vázquez de Menchaca', *Biblioteca Saavedra Fajardo de pensamiento político hispánico* (2010), 1–17.

Thus, when Philip landed in Southampton on 20 July, some of his men were already there planting, as was at least Briviesca's case, a Spanish seed in English soil. The great numbers who crossed the Channel that summer were at odds with Philip's earlier wishes to bring his household only; yet the selection of most of them was not arbitrary.[6] Accompanying Philip in Martín de Bertendona's ship were some of his closest associates during his regency in Spain and later on in his reign.[7] The Portuguese Ruy Gómez de Silva had been Philip's close friend since childhood and Gómez Suárez de Figueroa, count of Feria, was also a close friend and confidant. In the same ship also travelled one of Philip's most trusted secretaries, Gonzalo Pérez, a humanist, lawyer, writer, translator and poet from Segovia who had been educated at the College of Oviedo in Salamanca.[8] In 1538 he had been appointed chaplain to Charles V and soon afterwards he had been named archdeacon of Villena by Cardinal Pietro Bembo, who was a member of Cardinal Pole's circle in Italy.[9] Pérez was usually in charge of writing fair copies of Philip's letters and had been close to him since 1543, when he accompanied the prince to receive Maria Manuela of Portugal, his first wife, at the frontier with Castile.[10] With Philip also travelled the councillor Antonio de Toledo, grand prior of the Order of St John of Jerusalem, who would later be – as many of those who travelled to England in 1554 – one of the witnesses in the process against Carranza (in this case a favourable one), as well as the councillor and bookkeeper of the crown of Castile, Gutierre López de Padilla, the latter's wife, María de Bobadilla, Philip's chief quartermaster, Luis Venegas de Figueroa, who would leave England in August 1555 on a

6 AGS, Estado 808, leg. 15; Prince Philip to Simon Renard, Valladolid, 3 February 1554: 'q[ue] solamente llebaré my casa como tengo dicho [...] por q[ue] allá tomaré de los naturales de aq[ue]l reyno [...]'.

7 Tellechea Idígoras, *Carranza y Pole*, 27.

8 For a time after his arrival in England, Gonzalo Pérez lodged with Sir William Cecil. See Peter Marshall, *Heretics and Believers: A History of the English Reformation* (New Haven and London: Yale University Press, 2017), 385. The most complete biography of the Spanish royal secretary, a crucial member of Philip's early court is still that by Antonio González Palencia, *Gonzalo Pérez: Secretario de Felipe Segundo*, 2 vols (Madrid: Instituto Jerónimo Zurita, 1946).

9 On Bembo's friendship with Pole see John Edwards, *Archbishop Pole* (Farnham and Burlington: Ashgate, 2014), 93.

10 Pérez also translated Homer's *Odyssey* into Castilian for the first time, publishing the whole poem in Antwerp in 1556. See Luis Arturo Guichard Romero, 'La *Ulyxea* de Gonzalo Pérez y las traducciones latinas de Homero', in Barry Taylor and Alejandro Coroleu Lletget, eds., *Latin and Vernacular in Renaissance Iberia II: Translations and Adaptations* (Manchester: Manchester University Press, 2006), 49–72.

delicate mission concerning the imperial succession and the dowry of Philip's sister, the Queen of Bohemia, and the *alcalde* (municipal judge) Francisco de Castilla, who was without a doubt the Spaniard who became provost marshal for the Anglo-Spanish commission of justice set up in 1554.[11]

In other ships of the fleet came a large number of courtiers, all prominent in Spain. Among those of the highest rank were the great military leader and noble magnate, Fernando Álvarez de Toledo y Pimentel, duke of Alba, his wife María Enríquez de Toledo and their two adult sons, Fadrique and Diego; Juan de la Cerda y Silva, duke of Medinaceli, who would play a significant part in the English court, and Luis Enríquez y Téllez-Girón, admiral of Castile and duke of Medina de Rioseco, who was accompanied by his son, Luis Enríquez de Cabrera, count of Módica, his daughter-in-law, Ana de Mendoza, and the latter's parents Diego Hurtado de Mendoza, count of Saldaña and María de Mendoza, marchioness del Cenete. Juan de Benavides, son-in-law to the influential councillor Pedro de Navarra, marquis of Cortes, travelled to England in one of his own ships together with his wife, Jerónima de Navarra, Friar Bartolomé de Carranza and other courtiers.[12] Most of these men and women had been recruited on account of their high births, court experience in Spain, and expertise in international affairs.

There was also a significant number of men with a long diplomatic trajectory, such as Hernando de Gamboa, who arrived in England as an ambassador for Maximilian of Austria, and Diego Hurtado de Mendoza (not to be confused with the count of Saldaña), a younger brother of the count of Tendilla who had been educated at the University of Salamanca. Hurtado de Mendoza was a poet and writer of political treatises who had previous experience of

---

11 Antonio de Toledo would be involved years later in the liberation of Miguel de Cervantes from his imprisonment in Algiers. See Pilar Serrano de Menchén, 'Don Antonio de Toledo, gran prior de San Juan y don Francisco de Valencia, caballero de la misma orden, valedores en la liberación de Cervantes del cautiverio de Argel', in Felipe B. Pedraza Jiménez and Rafael González Cañal, eds., *Con los pies en la tierra: Don Quijote en su marco geográfico e histórico: homenaje a José María Casasayas* (Cuenca: Universidad de Castilla-La Mancha, 2008), 195–208. On Gutierre López de Padilla travelling with his wife see CSP Spain, vol. 12, 262. On Venegas's mission to the Empire see AGS, Patronato, leg. 57, no. 143.

12 Pedro de Navarra, marshall of Navarre, came from a family which had been averse to the conquest and integration of the kingdom of Navarre by the crown of Castile, but he quickly became a loyal adviser to Charles V. Elevated to the marquisate of Cortes in 1539, Navarra's career experienced a meteoric rise that culminated in his inclusion in the council of State of Spain in July 1554, an appointment made by Philip as regent. Navarra was poised to become the president of the council when he died unexpectedly, in 1556. His daughter, Jerónima, inherited the marquisate and her husband, who took her surname, exercised the marshallate of Navarre in her name.

England, where he had lived in the late 1530s as a diplomat to discuss the ultimately failed marriage negotiations between Henry VIII and Christina of Denmark and the then Princess Mary and Luis of Portugal.[13] Some noblemen had a mixed background, the result of successive generations establishing collaborative strategies across the different territories of the Spanish Monarchy which had culminated in a number of intermarriages and friendly relations resulting in strong ties with the Spanish nobility. The count of Egmont, who was back in England for the wedding, for instance, had a long history of interactions with the Spanish court. Perhaps more pertinent, however, were the cases of Francesco Fernando d'Avalos d'Aquino d'Aragona, marquis of Pescara, of Spanish-Italian descent, and Pedro Lasso de Castilla, ambassador in the name of Ferdinand, king of the Romans, who was married to a Bohemian lady, Polixena von Ungnand.[14]

Among this large retinue were also the members of Philip's royal chapel. This group was headed by Pedro de Castro Lemos, a native of Orense, Philip's chief chaplain, who had been recently appointed to the see of Cuenca and Lupercio de Quiñones, who was chief almoner, canon of San Isidoro de León and had accompanied Philip in his European tour of 1548–1551, as well as twelve additional chaplains and a further 'twelve cantors of very magnificent voices'.[15] The spiritual well-being of England was a crucial component of the marriage, and Philip had thus taken care to bring a suitable religious entourage. Apart from Castro Lemos, Quiñones and Carranza, several other prelates and theologians were chosen by Philip after having 'heard them preach'.[16] Among them were famous men like Alfonso de Castro, Juan de Villagarcía, and Bernardo de Fresneda, whose roles in England, as subsequent chapters will show, would be as important as they have been strangely neglected.

---

13 Miguel Ángel Ochoa Brun, *Historia de la diplomacia española*, vol. 5 (Madrid: Ministerio de Asuntos Exteriores, 1999), 380.

14 CSP Spain, vol. 13, 9–10; María Dolores Beccaría Lago, *Vida y obra de Cristóbal de Castillejo* (Madrid: Real Academia Española, 1997), 326.

15 Muñoz, *Svmaria y verdadera relación*, fol. 14^{v}. The bishopric of Cuenca bestowed on Castro Lemos would not be confirmed until 5 June 1555. See Pope Paul IV's bull in AGS, Patronato, leg. 62, no. 73. For Quiñones's presence in Philip's entourage in 1548–1551 see Juan Cristóbal Calvete de Estrella, *El felicíssimo viaie del mvy alto y mvy Poderoso Príncipe Don Phelippe, Hijo d'el Emperador Don Carlos Quinto Máximo, desde España a sus tierras de la baxa Alemaña: con la descriptión de todos los Estados de Brabante y Flandes*, (Antwerp: Martín Nucio, 1552), fol. 6^{v}.

16 Muñoz, *Svmaria y verdadera relación*, fol. 14^{v}: 'Son las [sic] que su Alteza ma[n]dó recebir por vnos delos buenos de Castilla, según su Alteza fue informado: au[n]que en particular los oyó predicar […]'.

The composition and spectrum of those who went to England as part of Philip's train was thus considerably varied. Apart from their contribution to the display of power and magnificence expected from the Spanish Monarchy, these courtiers also had the collective aims to collaborate politically with the English and to promote the re-evangelisation of England. The disillusionment of some of these Spaniards has already been noted. There was also the problem of the double household, which brought not only tensions and a certain degree of toxicity in the air, but also a financial problem for the new king of England. Some Spanish gentlemen were in distress due to their not being able to serve the king or the queen and this was true, as well, for the female members of Philip's Spanish court, who had expected to be employed in some capacity in their new queen's household. An unknown observer agreed with María de Mendoza that the Spaniards would never 'be in attendance again, for we are all hanging about with nothing to do'.[17] Another anonymous reporter expressed this feeling of despair in a pessimistic tone claiming that by 17 August, almost a month after the wedding, the ladies Jerónima de Navarra and Francisca de Córdoba had 'not yet seen the queen, and are not going to see her', as they would not join the court because the English ladies were 'of evil conversation'.[18] This may well be more a reflection of the awkwardness produced by linguistic difference and the resentment created by the confusion over Philip's household rather than a true remark about the quality of conversation at the English court, but it is nonetheless telling of how some Spaniards felt.

This initial climate of mistrust and segregation has set the tone for future explorations of Philip and Mary's Anglo-Spanish court. The interpretation of the episode in these terms has caused an enduring impression in the historiography which has contributed to the portrayal of the reign as an unsuccessful one in which Philip was very much powerless, a fact which has been deemed to have influenced his alleged disinterest in English affairs.[19] Philip's role as

---

17 CSP Spain, vol. 13, 9; D. M. Loades, *The Reign of Mary Tudor* (London: Ernest Benn, 1979), 212.

18 CSP Spain, vol. 13, 33.

19 As has been mentioned before, D. M. Loades went so far as to call Philip a 'failure' as king of England in 'Philip II and the government of England', in Claire Cross, David Loades and J. J. Scarisbrick, eds., *Law and Government under the Tudors: Essays Presented to Sir Geoffrey Elton on his retirement* (Cambridge: Cambridge University Press, 1988), 177–94. He later modified his views to allow for a greater integration of Philip within the English power system, but he still judged it modest and considered that the king had had no real power. See David Loades, *Intrigue and Treason: The Tudor Court, 1547–1558* (Harlow: Pearson/Longman, 2004), 178–213; Loades, *Mary Tudor* (The Hill, Stroud: Amberley, 2011), 141–2, 147, 149–50, 156, 175–6, 180. For Philip's alleged 'subordinate role' see Sarah Duncan, *Mary I: Gender, Power and Ceremony in the Reign of England's First Queen* (New York, 2012), 61.

king of England and his position in the English court, it has been claimed, was mainly ceremonial, with all actual power resting in the hands of the queen.[20] There is therefore a glaring need to analyse Philip's actions as king of England and patron at the English court in order to challenge the widely accepted view of him as uninterested in English affairs and out of touch with the machinations of English power. First, I will survey representations of Philip as king of England and this will be followed by a brief exploration of the opportunities that arose for the development of an international elite cooperation strategy. I will then offer an analysis of Philip's pension system and the reconcilement of anti-Spanish dissenters to the new regime. Finally, I will re-evaluate the workings, significance and effectiveness of the select council.

3.1 Conceptualisations and Representations of Philip as King of England

To the novelty of a joint monarchy presided over by a female native queen and a male foreign king, one had to add that for the first year of her reign, Mary had ruled alone and, therefore, she had been represented on her own and, in line with the Act for the Queen's Regal Power, as both female and male depending on the context and the regal attributes that each particular piece of propaganda – coronation, portraits, court ceremonial, etc. – sought to emphasise. After the cession of Naples and the wedding ceremony, a sword of justice would be borne before both Mary and Philip in public ceremonies, but other acts aimed to proclaim Philip's lower status in relation to Mary in England were put in place.[21] At the wedding ceremony and some of the early public events of the joint reign, for instance, Philip appeared at Mary's left, the traditional place reserved for queens consort.[22] On other occasions, Mary sat on a higher chair than Philip to stress her superior status.[23] During their entry into London on 18 August 1554, the City's maze was handed to the queen, rather than the king, and there were other stratagems devised to illustrate that Philip's power and sovereignty in England derived from the queen.[24] It cannot be doubted that the reversal of traditionally gendered placed and spaces was consciously

20 Duncan, *Mary I*, 98–101.
21 The most complete overview of these efforts is to be found in Duncan, *Mary I*, 37–110.
22 Duncan, *Mary I*, 68, 78.
23 Samson, *Mary and Philip*, 110.
24 Duncan, *Mary I*, 86–7.

designed to single out Mary's pre-eminence.[25] As Judith M. Richards has pointed out, these efforts stemmed from the acute anxiety which arose over the precise definition of Philip's authority over Mary, a husband's figure being over that of his wife in common, natural, and divine law.[26]

The unsuccessful attempt to have Philip crowned has been interpreted in this light. The topic was not broached in the parliamentary sessions of November 1554 as the limelight was then taken by the reconciliation with Rome, but a bill for the king's coronation was proposed in January 1555. It was rejected by the House of Commons and neither Mary nor Philip seemed to have had the intention to insist.[27] By way of consolation, in the sessions of 1554, parliament had passed a new Treasons Act which made treason any offences against King Philip, including the denial of his right to the kingly title. The Act also granted Philip the government of England in case Mary died during the minority of their potential heir.[28] That the lack of a coronation, with everything it entailed in England in terms of royal dignity and legitimacy, was a disappointing outcome for Philip is undeniable, but we should not, perhaps, put too much emphasis on the notion that the lack of a coronation seriously undermined Philip's chances of gaining real power in England.[29] Such an approach does not give sufficient credit to Spanish, and more particularly, Castilian constitutional arrangements for monarchs' accessions.

Indeed, medieval Castilian rulers and some of their fellow peninsular monarchs did not have the highly ritualised and sacralised coronation ceremonies of their French and English counterparts. Instead of the crown and the ointments, Castilian kings relied on formal proclamations framed within a legalistic and martial context which was an inheritance of both Roman and Visigothic law and a reflection of the effort of successive medieval rulers to reconquer the lands in Muslim hands which had belonged to the Visigothic kingdom, itself

---

25 Samson, *Mary and Philip*, 110–3.

26 Judith M. Richards, 'Mary Tudor as "Sole Quene"?: Gendering Tudor Monarchy', *The Historical Journal*, 40, no. 4 (1997), 895–924.

27 Loades, *Reign of Mary*, 223–4, 234; Duncan, *Mary I*, 142.

28 Just a few weeks before it had been publicly announced that the queen was with child. As we now know, this was the first of two phantom pregnancies that the queen endured during her reign. For Mary's supposed pregnancies see John Edwards, *Mary I: England's Catholic Queen* (New Haven and London: Yale University Press, 2011), 219, 253, 266–70, 318–20, 332–3, 346, 349.

29 On Philip's disappointment at not being crowned see M.J. Rodríguez-Salgado, *The Changing Face of Empire: Charles V, Philip II and Habsburg Authority, 1551–1559* (Cambridge: Cambridge University Press, 1988), 98–100.

derived from Roman Hispania. This emphasis on legality stressed the king's capacity as a military leader and, at the same time, the favour showed upon him by God, from whom his power derived. Indeed, since Alfonso VII's coronation as emperor in 1135, only five monarchs out of nineteen had gone through some sort of coronation ceremony. Of these, only one had used ointments, the ceremonies had not taken place immediately after their accession but often years later and they had usually served particular political purposes.[30] The *Fuero juzgo* – the Castilian version of the *Liber iudicorum* (654), the compendium of Visigothic law, – emphasised the acceptance of new kings by bishops, lords and commoners and the law of the *Siete Partidas*, the compilation of laws completed by Alfonso X (r. 1252–1284) in 1265, explained that there were four ways through which kings could accede to the throne: through inheritance, through the assent of the community, through marriage and through the authorisation of pope or emperor.[31] From this perspective, Philip's position as king of England was secure, as he was a descendant of Edward III, his title had been accepted and enshrined in law by parliament, he had lawfully married the queen and he had the support of the pope and the emperor.

Besides, although the importance of the coronation in the English context was understood, most of the often-quoted testimonies emphasising Philip's coronation – or lack thereof – were made by Englishmen or foreign diplomats, some whom were not even based in England. Simon Renard's letters,

30 Some of these rulers used their coronations to enhance their rights as pretenders to the imperial crown (Alfonso X, r. 1252–1284), to reassert their power after a long period of regencies and strife (Alfonso XI, r. 1312–1350) or to stress their legitimacy after they had taken the throne from the rightful heir (Sancho IV, r. 1284–1295; Henry II, r. 1369–1379; John I, r. 1379–1390). Of these, only Alfonso XI had been anointed and these kings had either crowned themselves or had been symbolically crowned by St James at Santiago de Compostela, without the mediation of a member of the clergy. See Teófilo F. Ruiz, 'Une royauté sans sacre: la monarchie castillane du Bas Moyen Age', *Annales. Histoire, Sciences Sociales*, 3 (1984), 429–53 and by the same author, *From Heaven to Earth: The Reordering of Castilian Society, 1150–1350* (Princeton: Princeton University Press, 2004), 133–50. Whereas Teófilo F. Ruiz has emphasised that the Castilian monarchs had no use for the sacralisation of power in the ways that their French and English counterparts used ritualised coronation ceremonies, José Manuel Nieto Soria contends that the sacralisation of the Castilian monarchy is evident in the ways in which the kings used sacralised language and symbols. There has been an ongoing and enriching debate on this topic. See José Manuel Nieto Soria, *Fundamentos ideológicos del poder real en Castilla (siglos XIII–XVI)* (Madrid: EUDEMA Universidad, 1988) and his 'La monarquía bajomedieval castellana. ¿Una realeza sagrada?', in Universidad de Murcia, ed., *Homenaje al profesor Juan Torres Fontes* (Murcia: Universidad de Murcia/Academia Alfonso X el Sabio, 1987), 1225–37.

31 Ruiz, 'Royauté sans sacre', 438.

for instance, stressed the importance of the coronation, but his exchange with Charles v confirms that, for the latter, the coronation would give Philip an opportunity to deal with English affairs with 'greater' authority and was, therefore, 'more a matter of satisfaction [...] than of necessity', even if Renard disagreed with his master's views.[32] The Spanish courtiers in England seem to have been, like the emperor, less concerned about the lack of a coronation. In the letters penned by Gonzalo Pérez, Diego Briviesca de Muñatones, Juan de Figueroa and others to the bishop of Arras during the parliamentary sessions of 1554 they discuss different matters raised and debated in parliament, but all three fail to show any anxiety over the lack of a coronation; it is never mentioned.[33] Furthermore, in the instructions to communicate to Charles v drawn up by Philip for Ruy Gómez de Silva in February 1555, after the conclusion of parliament and the rejection of the bill for his coronation, we can only find a passing reference to the coronation among other non-urgent matters, such as how peaceful England was or the images needed for the royal chapel.[34] Philip seems to have been more insistent on the matter in the autumn of 1555, freshly landed in Brussels, but he had given up by April 1556 and we only know of this renewed attempt through Federico Badoero, the Venetian ambassador to the emperor in the Low Countries. In any case, in October 1555 Badoero had reported that Philip had declared that it was Mary who 'desires this result more than he does' and that the king had counselled his wife not to bring up the matter again in parliament unless she could be sure of its success.[35] In other words, Philip, Charles, and the Spaniards do not seem to have been terribly concerned about the lack of a coronation, although had it happened it would have undoubtedly given Philip a boost in prestige.

Moreover, the emphasis on Mary's superior status in England began to wane once the royal couple settled into their new roles as co-monarchs in the first few

32 CSP Spain, vol. 13, 50–1, 95, 102.

33 See several of these letters in RBPRM, MSSII-2286-E, ff. 59r–60v, 129r, 133v, 143r–144r, 194r, 216r–217r, 236r, etc.

34 AGS, Patronato, leg. 55, no 31, fols 162r–163r: Instruction from the king of England and prince of Spain, Philip, to Ruy Gómez, on matters that are to be communicated to the Emperor Charles v, 15 February 1555: 'Lo de la coronación e lo que el embax[ad]or dixo a la R[ei]na acerca desto'.

35 See CSP Venice, vol. 6, 227, 253, 281–2, 299–300, 415–6. It is as problematic to take Badoero's assertions at face value as it is to ignore them. Whether he overemphasised the importance of the coronation in Philip's and the Spanish courtiers' minds between October 1555 and April 1556 or not, Philip seems to have associated the coronation with the capacity to declare war against France without consulting parliament. He seems to have given up on the hope without much of a fight.

months after the wedding, and especially after Charles V's abdication in 1556 made of Philip the partner with an indisputably larger number of proprietary royal titles. This shift could already be perceived in the parliament of 1554–1555, when Philip's activity as king of England intensified as he brokered the reconciliation with Rome – which will be explored in chapter 4 – and he was first recorded standing on the right side of Queen Mary in public.[36] Pictorial representations of the king also stressed this change of attitude. The famous Woburn Abbey panel painting of 1558, for instance, shows Philip on the right-hand side and the king, being the head of the Order of Garter, ostensibly displays his own garter on his left calf.[37] This tendency can also be observed in the monarchs' portraits in the King's Bench rolls preserved in The National Archives. In their first representation together on the rolls dating back to 1554 (see Figure 3.1), each hold an orb to represent *imperium*, and both wear a crown. Mary holds the sceptre (*auctoritas*) whilst Philip holds the sword of justice (*potestas*). The king, in 1554, sits on the left-hand side of the queen, the position traditionally reserved to queens consort. A few months later (see Figure 3.2) the king still sat on the left, but the crown now hovered over both their heads, an unmistakable statement emphasising the union of their crowns. In 1556, however, further changes can be observed (see Figure 3.3). The crown still hovering over both of them, the king and queen are now sat beneath a canopy under the protection of the Holy Spirit with the words *VIVANT REX ET REGINA* (long live the king and queen). They still hold the same regal attributes, but the king now appears on the right side of the portrait, with each monarch flanked by the floral emblems of their respective crowns: the pomegranate for Philip and the *fleur de lis* for Mary.[38] For the remainder of the reign some elements in these depictions might change – in Figure 3.4, for the year 1558, for instance, the motto is replaced by the monarchs' initials, P. R. & M. R. and Mary's emblem is now the Tudor rose – but Philip's position to the right of Mary was retained.

---

36 Samson, *Mary and Philip*, 114.

37 For a survey of Philip's portraits as king of England see P. G. Matthews, 'Portraits of Philip II of Spain as King of England', *The Burlington Magazine*, 142 (2000), 13–19.

38 Although it has been emphasised, especially in studies of Catherine of Aragon's life, that the open pomegranate spilling out seeds was a sign of fertility often linked to feminine attributes, it was also the emblem of the kingdom of Granada and had become part of the Spanish monarchs' coats of arms since the kingdom's conquest in 1492. For the use of the pomegranate by Catherine of Aragon see Hope Johnston, 'Catherine of Aragon's Pomegranate, Revisited', *Transactions of the Cambridge Bibliographical* Society, 13, no. 2 (2005), 153–73.

FIGURE 3.1 The National Archives, King's Bench 27/1172 (1554)
CREDIT TO DR GABRIELLE STOREY

FIGURE 3.2 The National Archives, King's Bench 27/1174 (1554)
CREDIT TO DR GABRIELLE STOREY

FIGURE 3.3 The National Archives, King's Bench 27/1182–1 (1556)
CREDIT TO DR GABRIELLE STOREY

FIGURE 3.4 The National Archives, King's Bench 27/1185–2 (1558)

It is important to note that the royal attributes displayed by Philip and Mary were meant to stress the monarchs' position as partners in their thrones. The bearing of the temporal sword, a symbolic element in legal representations which marked God's granting of temporal power to the monarch, was grounded in Biblical exegesis, especially the analysis of Romans 13:3–7. According to St Paul, the representative of temporal power was 'God's minister: an avenger to execute wrath upon him that doth evil' and he did not bear the sword 'in vain'. This relates to Briviesca's insistence that Philip had to show himself as a dispenser of justice.[39] The sword represented the ruler's *potestas*, their capability to exert power. The sceptre embodied the ruler's *auctoritas* or their ability and legitimacy to convey the exercise of power. Neither, however, were fully functional without *imperium*, the dominion which granted power over life and death and was represented by the orb.[40] That Philip and Mary were represented holding, respectively, the sword and sceptre, both of them with an orb and the crown hovering over their heads signalled that they were both truly and equally monarchs and that their respective powers had been joined to exert *imperium* together.

The reversion to expected gendered positions was apparent in royal seals, too. In an imbricate seal produced in England and now kept at the Museo Nacional de Artes Decorativas in Madrid (see Figures 3.5 and 3.6), Philip and Mary are each mounted bearing their accustomed regal attributes, to the right of their quartered arms, which are crowned and enclosed by the Garter with the Order's motto: *Honi soit qui mal y pense*. The whole scene is encircled by their princely titles (archdukes of Austria, dukes of Burgundy, etc.).[41] On the reverse, the co-monarchs appear both crowned and enthroned, flanking their

39 For the significance of Romans 13 in political and religious thought in early modern England see Steven M. Foster, '"To Take the Sword is to Draw the Sword without the Authority of the Prince": Obedience, Duty and Romans 13 during the 1549 Rebellions in England', *Reformation & Renaissance Review*, 22, no. 1 (2020), 25–47. See also his unpublished thesis, which is currently being turned into a monograph: Steven Michael Foster, 'The Reception of Romans 13:1–7 during the English Reformation' (PhD thesis, University of Leeds, 2017, unpublished).

40 On the evolving relationship between the terms *auctoritas*, *potestas*, and *imperium* in the context of medieval Spain see Adeline Rucquoi, 'Auctoritas, Potestas: Concepts of Power in Medieval Spain', in Flocel Sabaté, ed., *Ideology in the Middle Ages: Approaches from Southwestern Europe* (Leeds: Arc Humanities Press, 2019), 51–72. A crucial exploration of the term *imperium* in the Spanish context can be found in Anthony Pagden, *Lords of All the World: Ideologies of Empire in Spain, Britain and France, c. 1500–c. 1800* (New Haven and London: Yale University Press, 1995), 11–28.

41 More on seal representations of Philip and Mary in José María de Francisco Olmos, 'Las primeras acuñaciones del príncipe Felipe de España (1554–1558): soberano de Milán, Nápoles e Inglaterra', *Documenta &* Instrumenta, 3 (2005), 155–86. I am very grateful for Dr Francisco Olmos's generous sharing of his ideas around this topic with me and his guidance to obtain further information. I would also like to thank Nuria Moreu Toloba

FIGURE 3.5 Philip and Mary. Wax seal obverse
MUSEO NACIONAL DE ARTES DECORATIVAS CE13517

quartered coat of arms, the king being on the right-hand side bearing the sword and the queen on the left bearing the sceptre. Significantly, both rest their hands at the same time over a single orb, a robust representation of their shared rule, their shared *imperium* – it is both Philip and Mary united who bear sword and sceptre over their dominions. This reversion is not to say that Mary had given up her sovereignty to her husband or that she had been in any way demoted. The order of their titles in this English seal amply clarifies this as it is Mary's title which appears first, followed by Spain and the rest of their shared royal nomenclature: *PHILIP[US] ET MARIA D[EI] G[RATIA] REX ET REGINA ANGL[IÆ] HISPANIAR[UM] FRAN[CIÆ] VTRIVSQ[UE] SICILIE IERVSALEM ET HIB[ERNIÆ] FIDEI DEFENSORES* (Philip and Mary, by the grace of God king and queen of England, the Spains, France, the Two Sicilies, Jerusalem and Ireland, Defenders of the Faith). Although undated, it was certainly produced after January 1556, when Charles V had abdicated his patrimonial inheritance.

---

and the rest of her team at the Museo Nacional de Artes Decorativas for their assistance in the identification and analysis of this seal.

FIGURE 3.6 Philip and Mary. Wax seal reverse
MUSEO NACIONAL DE ARTES DECORATIVAS CE13520

A year earlier, before he received his father's estates, Philip had been even bolder in his representation as king of England. On 1 October 1555, a few days after his arrival in Flanders, the king sent a letter to Pope Paul IV (r. 1555–1559) from Brussels in which he requested from him the formal recognition of his titles as king of Naples and Jerusalem, which were papal fiefs but had long belonged to the kings of Aragon. The letter, in which he styled himself 'Philip, by the grace of God king of England, France, Sicily, Jerusalem and Ireland' included a magnificent gold seal (Figures 3.7 and 3.8) which proclaimed Philip's position as king of England in a most assertive manner. On the front side, the king appears enthroned on his own, holding the sword with his right hand and resting his left hand over his crowned coat of arms, significantly without Mary's arms. Surrounding the seal are his royal titles very clearly expressed: *PHILIPPVS DEI GRATIA ANGLIÆ FRANCIÆ CITERORIS SICILIÆ ET HIERVSALEM REX*, leaving Ireland out perhaps for a lack of space. The reverse presents the viewer with Philip as a mounted warrior-king brandishing the sword as if about to strike his enemies. To the king's right is his coat of arms surrounded by the Golden Fleece and to the right is England's coat of arms surrounded by the Garter and its motto: *HONI SOIT QVI MAL Y PENSE*, the whole

FIGURE 3.7 Philip, king of England. Gold seal obverse
ARCHIVIO APOSTOLICO VATICANO A. A., ARM. I–XVIII 522

scene encircled by Philip's princely titles. Far from giving the impression that the king is uninterested in English affairs, suffering from a certain demotion due to the lack of a coronation or an alleged inferiority versus Mary or resentful of his English marriage, this was a confident portrayal of his position as king of England. Perhaps a coronation was not to be had, but Philip certainly had other ways to show his grasp on the English throne in a self-assured manner to his court, to England, and to the world.

FIGURE 3.8 Philip, king of England. Gold seal reverse
ARCHIVIO APOSTOLICO VATICANO A. A., ARM. I–XVIII 522

3.2 Courtly Life and Diplomacy

The Anglo-Spanish court that resulted from the marriage has been described in the past as a space of mutual hostility between Spanish and English courtiers and an environment in which Philip did not exercise the kingly patronage that would be expected from a sovereign.[42] The following section will dispel this myth, focusing on courtly life and the international possibilities opened up by

42 David Loades, 'Philip II and the government of England', 177–94.

Philip and Mary's marriage. It is true that the existence of the two households, as has been mentioned, was initially a major problem for Philip, as he had to bear the expenses of both out of his own pocket. The accounts of Philip's treasurer, Domingo de Orbea, provide a clear picture of the kind of expenditure that the king faced. Concerning the inner chamber of his household, Philip ordered Orbea to pay its members on 23 August 1554, backdating the payment to 1 April, that is, just after the betrothal *per verba de præsenti*, effectively a proxy marriage, had taken place. John, Lord Williams of Thame, Philip's lord chamberlain, was assigned a salary of £100 (94,583 maravedís) per year. Sir John Huddlestone, Philip's vice-chamberlain, was allocated £66/13s/4d per year. The accounts also show the annual wages of Philip's household high officials, the largest of which was that paid to the interpreters 'of the English and Spanish languages' at £25 per year. They were followed by the ushers of the antechamber and the mace-bearers at £20. Next came the *panatiers*, in charge of the king's table service, at £11/10s. Much smaller wages were paid to the grooms, each receiving £2/13s/4d and to the pages at £2.[43] All these payments sum up a total of £480 per year, which add up to a total amount of £2,280 over the four years during which Philip was king of England (see table 3.1). This was a considerable amount, especially if we take into account that this was just the top of the iceberg in a household composed of dozens of men with offices high and low.[44]

43 AGS, Contaduría Mayor de Cuentas, 1ª época, 1184; The master of the grooms is called in the Spanish original 'king of grooms' (*rrey de gromes*) and mentioned only by his first name, Thomas. Although it is not entirely clear, the most likely candidate is Thomas Keyes, who would be serjeant porter under Elizabeth I, and who may have been the person referred to as 'groom of the chamber' in 1558. See TNA, SP 11/12, no. 27. In Queen Elizabeth's reign he was arrested and would remain in the Fleet prison for three years due to his marriage to Lady Mary Grey, which was deemed illicit by the queen. See Leanda de Lisle, *The Sisters Who Would Be Queen: The Tragedy of Mary, Katherine and Lady Jane Grey* (London: Harper Press, 2008), 249–65.

44 D. M. Loades found that in 1559 it was calculated that the king still owed his English pensioners and servants an estimate £11,000. Since the accounts were not complete, he suggested that this must have been just a portion of the kind of expense faced by Philip. See Loades, *Reign of Mary*, 93–4.

TABLE 3.1 Yearly salaries for Philip's household chamber (1554–1558). AGS, Contaduría mayor de cuentas, 1ª época, 1184: Cuentas de Domingo de Orbea

Role	Name	Pounds (£)	Shillings (s)	Pence (d)
Lord chamberlain	John, Lord Williams of Thame	£100	0	0
Vice-chamberlain	Sir John Huddlestone	£66	13	4
Interpreter	Thomas Dennis	£25	0	0
Interpreter	Robert Mofert	£25	0	0
Interpreter	George Everard	£25	0	0
Usher of the antechamber	Lionel Biggins	£20	0	0
Usher of the antechamber	Philip Mannering	£20	0	0
Usher of the antechamber	Francis Everard	£20	0	0
Usher of the antechamber	John Franks	£20	0	0
Mace-bearer	Thomas Enatisforth	£20	0	0
Mace-bearer	John Moore	£20	0	0
Mace-bearer	John Fove	£20	0	0
Panatier	Robert Hugguie	£11	10	0
Panatier	Richard Holford	£11	10	0
Panatier	Reginald Worseley	£11	10	0
Panatier	Thomas Strete	£11	10	0
Panatier	Edward Trevor	£11	10	0
Panatier	Humphrey Brompton	£11	10	0
Master of the grooms	Thomas Keyes	£2	13	4
Groom	George Goldewell	£2	13	4
Groom	John Fonson	£2	13	4
Groom	George Wasted	£2	13	4
Groom	Anthony Greenham	£2	13	4
Groom	Thomas Gaman	£2	13	4
Groom	John Fleming	£2	13	4
Groom	Henry Thorne	£2	13	4
Page	William Henson	£2	0	0
Page	John Scelly	£2	0	0
Page	Randall Hatton	£2	0	0
Page	Peter Palin	£2	0	0
	Total	£471	177	36
	Final yearly amount	£480	0	0
	Amount 1554 with arrears	£360	0	0
	Total paid 1554–1558	£2,280		

Philip's solution was to make the English and the Spanish serve together. Charles v expressed his anxiety in an instruction that he sent over to England with his secretary Francisco de Eraso. Charles had heard about Sir Anthony Browne's 'matter' (*lo de Brun*): he had been dismissed as master of the horse and replaced by Antonio de Toledo, prior of St John of Jerusalem. He then complained that Philip's English servants were not being allowed to serve him and that Thomas Radclyffe, viscount Fitzwalter, one of the few English courtiers proficient in Spanish, had claimed in Brussels that he 'communicated so little with Spaniards that he was soon to forget what he had learnt of the language'.[45] Philip promptly reassured his father through Eraso that Fitzwalter's words were not so 'well-founded'. 'Such treatment is made to him', Philip claimed,

> as well as to the other grandees, that they all give every indication of being very satisfied. Not only are they allowed to come in and out [of his chamber] as many times as they please, but they are also solicited by and have all manner of communication and conversation with the Spanish gentlemen. The ones are in such good concord with the others that your Majesty would rejoice to see it, and the same can be said of the quietness of the people.[46]

Furthermore, although Philip made no mention of it in his instructions, Browne was appeased with his creation as Viscount Montague in the peerage of England

45 AGS, Patronato, leg. 55, no. 27, fol. 125^{v}; Instructions for the secretary Francisco de Eraso from Charles v on what he will have to do in England (undated, summer 1554): 'Tras esto le diréis Que desseando como es razón que sus cosas vayan, e subcedan bien, no he podido escusar de mandaros Le digáis, lo que de allá escriuieron al tiempo que se tractó lo de Brun, e sobre que los que fueron señalados para su cámara, no le siruen, ni entran en ella, e que también Fisbalther, que fue por Embaxador (tractando destas cosas) hauía dicho Que comunicaua tan poco con españoles que presto oluidaría lo q[ue] de aquella lengua hauía aprendido De que entendemos, han tenido, e tienen sentimiento los principales e p[ar]ticulares, e especialmente en Londres, donde han murmurado más dello, publicando que ya se començauan a hazer nouedades [...]'. The last few words are an illuminating reflection of Charles's fears of the potential English reaction to any 'novelties' introduced by his son, undoubtedly a painful memory of the novelties he himself had tried to introduce in Castile early on in his reign and which had caused the Comunero revolt.

46 AGS, Patronato, leg. 55, no. 27, fol. 111^{v}: '[...] y las palabras que dixo, el Vizconde no fueron con tanto fundamento / como allá se han querido entender y / a éste e A, todos los Prinçipales se haze tal tractamiento q[ue] muestran estar muy contentos, porq[ue] no sólo se les permite entrar, e salir las vezes que quieren mas son soliçitados y tienen toda comunicación y conuersaçión con los caualleros Spañoles y están los vnos y los otros en tanta conformidad q[ue] su mag[esta]d olgaría de verlo y también de la quietud deste pueblo [...]'.

on 2 September 1554. Although during the ceremony the lord chamberlain, Sir John Gage, handed the patent to the queen, not the king, it was both Philip and Mary who put on Montague's robe at the pronunciation of *creavimus* and his cap after the words *cape possessionem*. Indeed, having been fully read by the secretary John Bourne, the patent was delivered to the king and queen, who in turn handed it to Montague.[47] New possibilities for patronage and the furthering of international relations were clearly being offered to the English court.

This can be observed at other levels as well. On 8 May 1555, the duchess of Alba wrote directly to Mary from Brussels commending the good services of Thomas Dennis, one of the interpreters in Philip's household, who had accompanied the duchess in her journey from England to Flanders. He had acted with such 'care, discretion and diligence', that the duchess told Mary that she would feel very satisfied if he were to be rewarded 'as befits a good servant of your Majesty's'.[48] Mary became the focus of requests and recommendations, becoming part of the international network of political women in the Habsburg circles.[49] On 6 February 1556, for instance, Queen María of Bohemia, Philip's sister, recommended the services of Ippolito Pallavicino, and requested from Mary all expediency in his mission to confer with Philip as quickly as possible about business concerning Sforza Pallavicino, marquis of Cortemaggiore.[50] In 1557, Princess Christina of Denmark, dowager duchess of Lorraine, possibly still shocked by the accidental death of Sir Jacques Granado during a tournament, which she had witnessed in London in May, felt compelled, on her return to Flanders, to recommend the widow and 'poor

47 TNA, SP 11/4, no. 21: The creation of Sir Anthony Browne as Viscount Montague, 2 September 1554.

48 TNA, SP 69/6, no. 357; María Enríquez de Toledo, duchess of Alba, to Queen Mary, Brussels, 8 May 1555: 'Thomas Dennis [...] ha venido este camino conmigo siruiendo de lengua y ha lo hecho con tanto cuydado, discreción y diligençia que ha mostrado ser persona de mucha virtud y para encomendalle qualquiera cosa de importancia, y a mí me ha puesto en obligación de fauoreçelle en lo q[ue] pudiere, supplico a V[uestra] Ma[jesta]d me haga m[erce]d en mandalle tener por muy encomendado, y hazelle m[erce]d en lo que se offreçiere como a buen criado de V[uestra] Ma[jesta]d q[ue] yo reçebiré en ello muy gran m[erce]d [...]'.

49 This aspect of Mary's position as a Habsburg consort has been studied from the perspective of her efforts to conclude a truce with France, but more work needs to be done to determine her precise role as a female ruler within the House of Habsburg. Indeed, the topic may well deserve a study in its own right. See Loades, *Reign of Mary*, 229–31; Rodríguez-Salgado, *Changing Face of Empire*, 148–9 and Edwards, *Mary I*, 280, 289, 291.

50 TNA SP 69/8, no. 467: María of Austria, queen of Bohemia, to Queen Mary, Vienna, 6 February 1556. Her husband, Maximilian, wrote a letter to Mary in the same terms the following day; see no. 468.

daughter' of the deceased to Queen Mary.[51] Royal marriages were often a point of departure for the reinforcement of family and patronage links among the nobilities of the kingdoms involved. A famous case in point is that of the marriage of the count of Feria. When Feria first arrived in England with Philip in 1554, he was already betrothed to his niece, Catalina Fernández de Córdoba. Whilst in England, however, Feria developed a relationship with one of Mary's favourite ladies of the bedchamber, Jane Dormer, and broke off his betrothal. He arranged to marry Dormer with Philip and Mary's blessing. Once in Spain, the household of the countess – later duchess – of Feria, like those of her grandmother and sister in Flanders, became a refuge for English malcontents and a haven for Catholic conspiracy.[52] The strategy of intermarrying the nobilities of two kingdoms united under one monarch had worked well in the Italian states, and there were also examples of it in the Empire.[53] It would also work to Philip's relative advantage after the unification with Portugal in 1580, profiting from an old custom of intermarriage fostered by the geographical closeness

51 TNA SP 69/10, no. 628; Christina of Denmark, duchess of Lorraine, to Queen Mary, Ghent, 8 June 1557: 'Je supplie très humblement v[ot]re Ma[jes]té me pardonner, si je prens ceste hardiesse que de luy escrire ceste en reco[m]mandation de la vesue de feu Granado, car la compassion que j'ay d'elle et de la poure fille me constraint de ce faire [...]'. A rather graphic account of Sir Jacques Granado's death on 4 May 1557 can be found in Machyn's chronicle. See BL, Cotton Vitellius F. v, fol. 71^{v}: '[and] so he brake ys neke for ys horsse thruw hym aganest the wall [and] hys brauns rane owtt'.

52 There have been no monographic biographies of Jane Dormer since her servant Henry Clifford's 1643 account of her life, which was kept in manuscript by the Dormer family until its first publication in 1887. See Henry Clifford, *The Life of Jane Dormer, Duchess of Feria*, edited by Joseph Stevenson, SJ (London: Burns and Oates, 1887). For the latest research on Dormer see M. J. Rodríguez-Salgado, 'Suárez de Figueroa [Dormer], Jane, duchess of Feria in the Spanish nobility (1538–1612)', ODNB http://www.oxforddnb.com/view/article/7836 [accessed 14 January 2023]; Hannah Leah Crummé, 'Jane Dormer's Recipe for Politics: A Refuge Household in Spain for Mary Tudor's Ladies-in-Waiting', in Nadine Akkerman and Birgit Houben, eds., *The Politics of Female Households: Ladies-in-Waiting across Early Modern Europe* (Leiden and Boston: Brill, 2014), 51–71.

53 Carlos José Hernando Sánchez, *Castilla y Nápoles en el siglo XVI. El virrey Pedro de Toledo. Linaje, estado y cultura (1532–1553)* (Salamanca: Junta de Castilla y León, 1994), 117–50; Bartolomé Yun Casalilla, ed., *Las redes del Imperio. Élites sociales en la articulación de la Monarquía Hispánica, 1492–1714* (Madrid: Marcial Pons Historia/Universidad Pablo de Olavide, 2009), especially Ángeles Redondo Álamo and Bartolomé Yun Casalilla, '«Bem visto tinha». Entre Lisboa y Capodimonte. La aristocracia castellana en perspectiva «trans-nacional» (ss. XVI–XVII)', 39–64. In the Empire, for instance, one of Maximilian II's most trusted advisors, Adam von Dietrichstein married Margarita Folch de Cardona, daughter to the viceroy of Sardinia in 1553 and Wratislaw von Pernstein, future chancellor of Bohemia, married María Maximiliana Manrique de Lara, daughter of the governor of Parma, in 1555. The latter's daughter, Johanna von Pernstein, would go on to marry Fernando de Aragón y Borja, duke of Villahermosa in 1584.

of both kingdoms.[54] There is no reason to reject the idea that, had Mary lived longer, this practice may have been strongly encouraged after Feria set the example.

The relations between the courts of London and Brussels quickly intensified with the sending back and forth of an increasing number of emissaries and envoys. It may be indicative of a reinforcement of the closeness of both nobilities that Henry Fitzalan, Lord Maltravers, the heir to the earl of Arundel, was sent by Mary – not for the first time – to greet and confer with Maximilian and María during their stay in Flanders in the summer of 1556.[55] The emperor had envisaged to send Maltravers back to England with his letters, but a fever took the young nobleman on 30 July. Charles wrote to Mary that the youth's death had caused him 'the regret that you may imagine', not only due to Maltravers's 'virtues and qualities', but also because of the 'service' that he would have been able to perform had he lived.[56] Philip had also favoured Maltravers, who gifted the king his own Latin translation of the rules of the Order of the Garter, a present which King Philip kept for the rest of his life.[57] The king had also attended Maltravers' wedding to Anne Wentworth on 12 April 1555 and had gifted the bride a necklace valued at 1,000 ducats. He was also present at Lord Fitzwalter's wedding to Frances Sidney on 26 April 1555 and had actively participated in the tournaments held to mark the occasion.[58] When the duke of Norfolk's son was christened at Whitehall on 2 July 1557, King Philip, who was then back in England, stood as the child's godfather together with Nicholas Heath, lord chancellor and archbishop of York, and the duke's grandmother, Elizabeth Stafford.[59] The king even honoured the new-born child with his

---

54 Mafalda Soares da Cunha, 'Títulos portugueses y matrimonios mixtos en la Monarquía Católica', in Yun Casalilla, ed., *Las redes del Imperio*, 205–32.

55 CSP Spain, vol. 13, 271. Maltravers had been sent to Flanders on a similar mission at least once before. See TNA, SP 11/6, no. 66; Edward Courtenay, earl of Devon to an unknown recipient, Louvain, 23 November 1554.

56 *Relations politiques*, 44; Charles V to Queen Mary, Brussels, 31 July 1556: 'Madame ma bonne fille et sœur, je pensoye que le s[eigneu]r de Maltravers, par lequel j'avoye receu vostre lettre, fut esté porteur de ma response à icelle; mais il a depuis pleu à Dieu en disposer autrement et l'appeler à sa part, après avoir aucuns jours esté travaillé d'une grande fièvre, dont j'ay eu le desplaisir que povez considérer, tant par les vertus et qualités que treuvoye en luy, que le service que, en suyvant iceulx, il estoit apparent en eussiés reçeu [...]'.

57 Duncan, *Mary I*, 109.

58 CSP Venice, vol. 6, 58; Duncan, *Mary I*, 109.

59 BL, Cotton Vitellius F. V, fol. 74^{v}. Thomas Howard, 4th duke of Norfolk, had inherited the title and estates of his grandfather after the latter's death in August 1554. The child's mother, Lady Mary Fitzalan, was the intellectually gifted teenage daughter of the earl of Arundel, and her *sententiae*, translated into the Latin from Greek and English

name. Decades later, in 1589, Philip Howard, earl of Arundel, was condemned to death (although never executed) for the procuring of Masses to be sung in the Tower – where he was already confined for his attempt to flee England – for the safe arrival of his godfather's Armada.[60] In 1554, the king had also stood as godfather to another boy named Philip, the child of Sir Henry Sidney and Lady Mary Dudley, who would later on become a celebrated Elizabethan author and, contrary to King Philip's other English godson, a militant Protestant who fought against the Spanish in the Netherlands.[61]

Another aspect of international cooperation can be observed in the attitude adopted by the Spanish in the often-quarrelsome issues of precedence that typically arose in diplomatic circles. In July 1555, Sir Edward Carne, England's ambassador in Rome, had an argument with Alonso de Lancastre, the Portuguese ambassador, over who should carry the baldachin's rod during a procession organised by Pope Paul IV. According to Pedro Pacheco, cardinal-bishop of Sigüenza, everyone except the French ambassador seemed to agree that the privilege belonged to Carne, who was supported by Fernando de Castro, marquis of Sarria, the Spanish ambassador in Rome and Lancastre's brother.[62]

---

sources, have been preserved. She died a few weeks after the birth of her only son. See Stephanie Hodgson-Wright, 'Howard, Mary, duchess of Norfolk (1539/40–1557)', ODNB http://www.oxforddnb.com/view/article/47847 [accessed 14 January 2023].

60 Francis Hargrave, ed., *A Complete Collection of State Trials, and Proceedings for High Treason, and Other Crimes and Misdemeanours; Commencing with the Eleventh Year of the Reign of King Richard II. And Ending with the Sixteenth Year of the Reign of King George III*, vol. 1 (Dublin: Graisberry and Campbell, 1793), 181–6.

61 H. R. Woudhuysen, 'Sidney, Sir Philip (1554–1586)', ODNB https://www.oxforddnb.com/view/10.1093/ref:odnb/9780198614128.001.0001/odnb-9780198614128-e-25522?rskey=cXn9OY&result=3 [accessed 14 January 2023].

62 That the Spanish and Portuguese ambassadors to Rome were brothers highlights the importance given by successive Spanish monarchs to the intermarrying of their nobility with those of other kingdoms they had acquired or which they had extreme closeness with, as was the case of Portugal. The entanglement of nobles families would often work to the Spanish Monarchy's advantage. The bishop of Cuenca, Pedro de Castro Lemos, who accompanied Philip to England, was a brother to the Portuguese and Spanish ambassadors in Rome. For Pacheco's account of the dispute between Carne and Lancastre see RBPRM, MSSII – 2286 – E, fol. 99r; Pedro Pacheco Ladrón de Guevara, Cardinal of Sigüenza, to Antoine Perrenot de Granvelle, Bishop of Arras, Rome, 29 July 1555: '[…] no ay cosa de nueuo sino q[ue] su sa[ntida]d hizo ayer gran processión y halláronse allý el enbaxa[d]or de Ingalat[e]rra y el de Portugal y sobre el lleuar la vara del baldaquino huuo differençia sobre la preçedençia enfin su sa[ntida]d mandó a entramos q[ue] se fuessen hasta q[ue] se viesse. Todos dizen que la Razón la tiene el de Ingalat[e]rra y ansí el marqués de Sarria pareçía q[ue] se inclinaua a fauoreçelle aunq[ue] el de Portugal era su her[ma]no. El de Françia [Jean d'Avançon, lord of Saint-Marcel] parece q[ue] se

Although diplomatic quarrels may often seem to be petty incidents, they are revealing metaphors of international relations, and the people involved took them very seriously indeed. In this case, the Spanish ambassador sided with Carne, disregarding not only his own ties of blood and affection with Portugal and his brother, but also the geographical, consanguineous, and traditional ties between the kingdoms of Portugal and Spain and their royal families. The incident indicates that the Spanish were willingly viewing the English as an integral part of the same political entity. On the other hand,the Portuguese, despite kinship and common interests, remained a separate political body. Unlike the English, they were not comprehended within the composite Spanish Monarchy. The goodwill shown by Sarria was not short-lived. A year later, another diplomatic affront involving Carne and Lancastre took place during the anniversary celebrations of Pope Paul's election. Carne arrived at the pontifical court only to find Lancastre standing where Carne believed should have been his place: between the French and Polish ambassadors. Carne first asked politely, but when sweet endeavours did not succeed, he grabbed Lancaster's shoulder and 'removed him out of that place', claiming that it had always been the place of English ambassadors. Before the physicality of the incident escalated, Pope Paul sent both ambassadors home to avoid 'dissenssyon'. As Carne explained in a letter to Queen Mary, however, he eventually had the last word:

> I am moche bounde to the Marques of Saria, he was verey angrie w[i]th the portingall beinge his brother to attempt any suche thinge against your Maiesties Ambassado[u]r and send to me assone as he harde of hyt [...]. I keapt my place from him [Lancastre], sending him to seake his place in suche sorte, that all thambassado[u]rs there thought hit well doone [...]. I wolde not lose a jot of your Ma[jes]tes hono[ur] for no man. for yt is the place for Ambassado[ur]s of England nighe a thowsand yeres before there was any kinge in portingall.[63]

Carne finally won the day due to his persistence and physical pressure on Lancastre, but the episode reflects the level of cooperation that was starting to take place between Spain and England, with the Spanish ambassador siding twice with his English counterpart against his own brother.

---

inclinaua mucho a fauoreçer al de portugal. El neg[oci]o tienen todos por claro, y q[ue] el de Portugal no tiene Razón [...]'.

63 TNA, SP 69/8, no. 508: Sir Edward Carne to Queen Mary, Rome, 9 June 1556.

3.3 King Philip's Pension System

The distribution of Spanish pensions among the English nobles and courtiers played a crucial role in the fostering of relations among both nations and it helped cement Philip's position as king and courtly patron. According to Ruy Gómez, who was writing four days after the wedding, the first step that Philip was to take with views to 'confederate' and 'become friends' with the English was to grant them the pensions that Charles had already envisaged, to present the wives of the English lords with jewels, and to employ some of their sons in Philip's service.[64] The idea of the pensions may have sprung from Charles's mind, but it was Philip who decided whom those pensions would go to. The suggestion to please the ladies was not a negligible one. The official channels of power like council and parliament may have been male-dominated, but as a female ruler, Mary could, and did, lend her ear to the suggestions of the members of her inner household, the privy chamber, who were all appropriately female.[65] Notorious was her intimacy with Susan Clarencieux, and it is important to note that some of her closest ladies of the privy chamber, such as Frideswide Strelley, Frances Waldegrave, Frances Jerningham, Anne Cornwallis, Eleanor Wharton and Anne Petre, were married to privy councillors and could therefore have significant influence in the processes of policy-making.[66] The suggestion to employ the sons of the grandees was also taken on board, and the eldest sons of the earls of Arundel, Derby, Shrewsbury, Pembroke, Sussex and Huntingdon were appointed principal gentlemen of Philip's household.[67] As has been mentioned above, Philip seems to have had particularly close

---

64 AGS, Estado 808, leg. 148: Ruy Gómez de Silva to Francisco de Eraso, Winchester, 29 July 1554: '[...] su alteza va mjrando con q[ué] medio los podrá confederar y azer amjgos y començará esta obra haziéndoles primero la m[erced] de las pensiones q[ue] su m[ajesta]d tiene señaladas q[ue] se den a las personas deste rreyno y dando algunas joyas a las mugeres destos señores q[ue] aquí se han hallado y tomando algunos hijos déstos en su serujçio'.

65 Loades, *Reign of Mary*, 89–90.

66 Dale Hoak, 'Two Revolutions in Tudor Government: The Formation and Organization of Mary I's Privy Council', in Christopher Coleman and David Starkey, eds., *Revolution Reassessed: Revisions in the History of Tudor Government and Administration* (Oxford: Oxford University Press, 1986), 87–115.

67 Loades, *Reign of Mary*, 94. These men were Henry FitzAlan, Lord Maltravers, Henry Stanley, Lord Strange, Lord George Talbot, Lord Henry Herbert, Thomas Radclyffe, Lord Fitzwalter and Lord Henry Hastings.

relationships with the sons of the earls of Arundel and Sussex, the Lords Maltravers and Fitzwalter.

Since the king had received no English patrimony as part of the marriage settlement, the pensions were to come out of his own pocket. He paid for them and, as was the case with his English household, rather generously too. The initial list of pensioners, drawn at some point shortly after Philip's landing, envisaged twenty-one individuals. By the end of 1558, the list had grown to twenty-five after some people had been added and other names initially proposed had been dropped and replaced.[68] The pension system was designed as a means of earning the trust and goodwill of those courtiers perceived as relevant in the process of decision-making or who were seen as influential. This was a common diplomatic practice in the early modern period, but it was especially useful for Philip, given his lack of English patrimony to exert kingly patronage through traditional means, and this becomes apparent in the expenses he was prepared to incur in order to make it work. Unsurprisingly, the initial list as drawn up by Domingo de Orbea was headed by some of the greatest peers of the realm (the earls of Pembroke, Derby, Shrewsbury, Arundel, and Bedford), who were assigned 2,000 crowns per year. Next came Lord Paget, Philip's staunchest English supporter, unique among the pensioners to receive 1,500 crowns. Paget was followed by those with an allocation of 1,000 crowns (the earls of Sussex and Huntingdon, Lord William Howard, Sir Henry Jerningham, Lord Edward Clinton, Sir Robert Rochester, Sir William Petre, Sir Thomas Cheyney and the lord treasurer Paulet). There were some smaller grants of 500 crowns (Lord Edward Hastings, Sir Edward Waldegrave, Sir Francis Englefield and Sir Richard Southwell) and of 300 (Sir John Gage, John Bourne and Thomas, Lord Wharton). All of these men were part of Philip and Mary's privy council and they included a range of great peers, loyal secretaries and some of the Catholic gentlemen who had first rallied to Mary in July 1553. This amounted to a total of 23,400 crowns (£5,850) per year that Philip paid from 1 June 1554 and ordered it to be paid every year in full starting on 1 January 1555 (see Table 3.2).[69]

---

68 Those who had been mentioned but did not eventually get a pension from Philip were the earl of Worcester, Lord William Grey de Wilton, captain of Guînes, Thomas Wentworth, lord deputy of Calais and Lord William Dacre. See CSP Spain, vol. 12, 315–6; Loades, 'Philip II and the government of England', 181–5.

69 AGS, CMC, 1ª época, 1184.

TABLE 3.2 List of King Philip's English pensioners (1554). AGS, Contaduría mayor de cuentas, 1ª época, 1184: Cuentas de Domingo de Orbea (exchange rate stood at 4 crowns to £1)

Name	Title/Role	Pension (crowns)	Pension (£)
William Herbert	Earl of Pembroke	2,000	500
Edward Stanley	Earl of Derby	2,000	500
Francis Talbot	Earl of Shrewsbury	2,000	500
Henry Fitzalan	Earl of Arundel	2,000	500
John Russell	Earl of Bedford	2,000	500
William Paget	Baron Paget	1,500	375
Henry Radclyffe	Earl of Sussex	1,000	250
Francis Hastings	Earl of Huntingdon	1,000	250
William Howard	Lord admiral, baron Howard of Effingham	1,000	250
Sir Henry Jerningham	Vice-chamberlain to Queen Mary	1,000	250
Edward Fiennes de Clinton	Baron Clinton	1,000	250
Sir Robert Rochester	Comptroller of the household	1,000	250
Sir William Petre	Secretary of State	1,000	250
Sir Thomas Cheyney	Lord warden of the Cinque Ports	1,000	250
William Paulet	Lord treasurer, marquess of Winchester	1,000	250
Edward Hastings	Baron Hastings of Loughborough	500	125
Sir Edward Waldegrave	Privy councillor	500	125
Sir Francis Englefield	Privy councillor	500	125
Sir Richard Southwell	Privy councillor	500	125
Sir John Gage	Lord chamberlain	300	75
Sir John Bourne	Secretary of State	300	75
Lord Thomas Wharton	Privy councillor	300	75
	Total	23,400	£5,850

After Mary's death in November 1558, Philip was anxious to make sure that whatever was owed to the pensioners was paid. He entrusted Feria with the task, and the count then drew up a revealing list with his own marginal comments on the character and usefulness of each of the pensioners. To begin with, the initial list of twenty-two men had changed shape and now amounted to twenty-five.[70] Sir John Gage had died in 1556, and the earl of Sussex in 1557, the

70 Lord Williams of Thame, Philip's lord chamberlain, was also included in this list, but only because the king owed him £40. He was not counted in as a pensioner.

latter not having been replaced by his heir, the former Viscount Fitzwalter, who had been sent to Ireland as lord deputy in April 1556.[71] A new addition to the list was the young and pious Viscount Montague, who was assigned a pension of 500 crowns a year (two instalments of which were owing in 1558). Significantly, Philip granted 550 crowns to his gentlemen of the chamber and personal interpreters, the devout Catholics James Bassett and Anthony Kempe, a sign of the king's trust in these men.[72] A new feature of the second list was the inclusion in it of three soldiers. Sir James Croftes, who had unsuccessfully tried to stir rebellion in Herefordshire in 1554, was granted a pension of 400 crowns at least since May 1557. His brother-in-law, captain Edward Randolph, who had transported a group of sappers from Flanders in 1557 for the defence of the English coasts, and Hans Brent, a soldier from Cleves who had also served under Henry VIII and Edward VI, were assigned a pension of 200 crowns each.[73] The replacements and new appointments now amounted to a total 22,400 crowns per year. Therefore, King Philip was spending a total of £5,600 a year exclusively on the payment of his pensioners, to which it should be added the expenses for the running of both his English and Spanish households, the money spent in courtly pursuits such as tournaments, banquets, presents for weddings and other social events, gifts for diplomats and fellow monarchs, etc. Only in terms of the pensions here surveyed, and taking the smaller amount (£5,600) as a guide to estimate, between 1555 and 1558 Philip spent £22,400 which, added to the £3,252/1s/8d paid for the months between June and December 1554, gave a total of £25,652/1s/8d between 1554 and 1558. If comparisons are anything to go by, eleven years before, Henry VIII had bequeathed an annual pension of £3,000 to each of his daughters in his will.[74] It is highly doubtful that Philip would have continued to maintain this large budget had he not considered it beneficial to his position as king of England.

---

71 On the religious ceremonies to mark Fitzwalter's appointment in Dublin see *Carew Manuscripts*, 258–9. On his career in Ireland see Steven G. Ellis, *Ireland in the Age of the Tudors, 1447–1603: English Expansion and the End of Gaelic Rule* (Harlow: Longman, 1998), 271–8.

72 David Loades, *Intrigue and Treason: The Tudor Court, 1547–1558* (Harlow: Pearson/Longman, 2004), 162 (although he calls Bassett Francis, not James). In AGS, Estado leg. 811, fol. 131, Feria incorrectly calls Bassett Antonio, possibly confusing his name with Kempe's.

73 AGS, Estado 811, leg. 131, 'Relación de lo que se da a cada uno de los pensionarios y lo que se les deue hasta en fin del año pasado de 1558'. By the time Feria drew up his list, two of the pensioners had died. Sir Robert Rochester died on 28 November 1557 but was never taken out of the list, hence Feria's comment in it that King Philip could do as he wished with what was owed to deceased pensioners. Sir Thomas Cheyney had died in London just before the end of the year, on 16 December 1558.

74 Robert Hutchinson, *The Last Days of Henry VIII: Conspiracies, Treason and Heresy at the Court of the Dying Tyrant* (London: Weidenfeld and Nicolson, 2005), 214.

TABLE 3.3 List of King Philip's English pensioners (1558). AGS, Estado leg. 811, fol. 131: Relación de lo que se da a cada uno de los pensionarios y lo que se les deue hasta en fin del año pasado de 1558 (exchange rates stood at 4 crowns to £1)

Name	Title/Role	Pension (crowns)	Pension (£)
Edward Stanley	Earl of Derby	2,000	500
Francis Talbot	Earl of Shrewsbury	2,000	500
William Herbert	Earl of Pembroke	2,000	500
Henry Fitzalan	Earl of Arundel	2,000	500
William Paulet	Lord treasurer, marquess of Winchester	1,000	250
Francis Hastings	Earl of Huntingdon	1,000	250
Edward Fiennes de Clinton	Lord admiral, baron Clinton	1,000	250
Sir Thomas Cheyney	Lord warden of the Cinque Ports	1,000	250
Lord William Howard	Lord chamberlain to Queen Mary, baron Howard of Effingham	1,000	250
Sir Henry Jerningham	Vice-chamberlain to Queen Mary	1,000	250
Sir William Petre	Secretary of State	1,000	250
William, Lord Paget	Lord privy seal	1,500	375
Heirs of Sir Robert Rochester	Comptroller of the household	900	225
Anthony Browne	Viscount Montague	500	125
Sir Edward Waldegrave	Privy councillor	500	125
Sir Francis Englefield	Privy councillor	500	125
Sir Richard Southwell	Master-general of the Ordnance	500	125
Lord Thomas Wharton	Warden of the West Marches	300	75
Sir John Bourne	Secretary of State	300	75
Hans Brent	Soldier	200	50
Edward Randolph	Soldier	200	50
Sir James Croftes	Soldier	400	100
Lord Edward Hastings	Master of the horse	500	125
James Bassett	Aid of the chamber and interpreter	550	137.5
Anthony Kempe	Aid of the chamber and interpreter	550	137.5
	Total	22,400	£5,600

Feria's comments at the beginning of Elizabeth's reign shed some light on this. On 21 November 1558, just four days after Mary's death, the count reported that the 'new queen and the men of the kingdom consider themselves to be released from any obligations to your Majesty and will listen to any ambassadors that may come to talk of marriage'.[75] Pessimistically, Feria added that the people were murmuring that Mary had sent Philip vast amounts of money, that Feria himself had taken 200,000 ducats out of the kingdom, and that Philip was to blame for the loss of Calais and the queen's death. According to these rumours, Mary had died of grief because Philip did not come to see her. Feria added that the former lord chamberlain Hastings, 'the greatest enemy of our nation', was spreading these rumours and that former supporters, such as comptroller Cornwallis and secretary John Boxall, were acting as if they 'did not know your Majesty nor ever received any good from your hands'.[76] The 'heretics' were waiting for their chance to persecute the Catholics, and they were also making sure to spread the rumour that 'your Majesty shall have as little place here as if you had never been married in this kingdom', which, despite Feria's indignation, was one of the conditions of the marriage treaty.[77] For all the gloominess of Feria's language, he also warned that the English were 'of an excitable nature' and none at court knew what was to become of them. Thus, they were all in a 'confused' state and therefore, he cautioned, 'we should not judge them so early'.[78]

---

75 AGS, Estado 811, leg. 92; Count of Feria to King Philip, London, 21 November 1558: 'La nueua Reyna y los déste reyno se tienen por sueltos de V[uestra] mag[esta]d y oyrán a qualesquiera embaxadores que les uengan a tratar de Casamiento [...]'.

76 AGS, Estado 811, leg. 92: 'El pueblo se ha soltado mucho a hablar en que la Reyna que aya Gloria embió grandes sumas de dineros a V[uestra] mag[esta]d y q[ue] después q[ue] yo uine he embiado dozientos mil ducados, y que a causa de V[uestra] Mag[esta]d está el reyno con tan gran necessidad, y se perdió Calés, y que por no uenir v[uestra] mag[esta]d a ver a la Reina n[uest]ra señora murió de pena, yo la tengo muy grande de que V[uestra] mag[esta]d permittiesse el honor que se hizo a este ruin del camarero mayor Hastings porq[ue] es el que publica estas cosas y mayor enemigo de n[uest]ra nación y q[ue] más mal dize della /. El contralor [Sir Thomas Cornwallis] y Bóxol [John Boxall] me hazen regalos p[er]o todos está[n] ta[n] desconocidos a V[uestra] mag[esta]d como si nunca huuieran recebido bien de su mano [...]'.

77 AGS, Estado 811, leg. 92: 'El pueblo está más libre que nunca y los Ereges esperando que han de perseguir a los cathólicos [...] Éstos procuran que en toda parte se entienda, que v[uestra] mag[esta]d no terná aquí más cabida de la que tuuiera si no huuiera sido casado en este reyno [...]'.

78 AGS, Estado 811, leg. 92: 'Verdad es que como ellos naturalmente son alterados y no ay nadie que aún sepa lo que ha de ser de él, anda[n] tan desatinados y tan confusos que no se deue hazer juizio dellos tan presto /'.

His cautious approach was vindicated the following month. William Howard, now Elizabeth's lord chamberlain and high in her favour, had regular conversations with Feria, who reported that 'none of them has made as many demonstrations of friendship and willingness to be your Majesty's servant than him – both before the queen died and after'.[79] Paulet, who had retained his position as lord treasurer, was considered by Feria 'a good servant of your Majesty's' and in his list of pensioners he reiterated this and added that he 'always has been'. On the list he also commended Howard's service and added that he had been 'good in religious matters'.[80] The same was said of secretary Petre, although Feria added that he was 'not one of the most favoured' by Elizabeth.[81] Those dismissed from court at the onset of the new regime were Jerningham, Waldegrave, Englefield, Southwell, Wharton and secretary Bourne – the core of Mary's early Catholic supporters – most of whom are described by Feria as good and Christian – i.e. 'Catholic' – men, even if the count felt the need to add that Southwell was 'a great drunkard'.[82] Croftes, the erstwhile rebel, was seen by Feria as 'a man of service'.[83]

The count had no doubts about the effectiveness of the pension system, and he advised Philip that the pensions owed should be paid until the end of 1558, rather than the date of Mary's death. The quantitative difference of the pay was not substantial, but it was a shrewd political move to extend the payment of English courtiers into the new queen's reign. Moreover, the count thought

79 AGS, Estado 811, leg. 99; Count of Feria to Philip, London, 14 December 1558: 'La Reyna ha determinado de embiar a v[uestra] mag[esta]d al Camarero mayor Guillén hauuart [...] de los que ay ninguno ha hecho tantas demonstraciones conmigo de amistad y de querer ser seruy[d]or de v[uestra] mag[esta]d como él, antes que Su M[a]j[esta]d falleciesse y después /'. There is an English translation of the whole dispatch in M. J. Rodríguez-Salgado and Simon Adams, eds., 'The Count of Feria's Dispatch to Philip II of 14 December 1558', *Camden Miscellany*, 28 (London: Royal Historical Society, 1984), 302–344.

80 AGS, Estado 811, leg. 105; Count of Feria to King Philip, London, 29 December 1558: '[...] al Marqués de Winchester han buelto el oficio de Thesorero que el conde [of Arundel] desseava /. [...] A este uiejo [Paulet] tengo por buen seruidor de v[uestra] M[a]j[esta]d y tiénenle respecto estotros, está más moço y mejor que le he visto [...]'; AGS, Estado leg. 811, fol. 131: on Paulet 'éste es buen seruidor de V[uestra] M[a]j[esta]d y siempre lo ha sido'; on Howard 'Ha hecho demostraciones de seruy[d]or de v[uestra] m[ajesta]d y ha estado bien en lo de la religión /'.

81 AGS, Estado 811, leg. 131: 'éste no anda en los muy delanteros, es cuerdo y dizen que seruy[d]or de v[uestra] M[a]j[esta]d /'.

82 AGS, Estado 811, leg. 131: on Jerningham, 'Éste se fue a su casa, es buen hombre y christiano, y seruy[d]or de v[uestra] M[a]j[esta]d'; which applies to Waldegrave and Englefield too; on Southwell: 'Éste no tiene ya el off[ici]o [master general of the ordnance] segú[n] me han dicho, es buen hombre y gran beodo'; on Wharton, 'es buen hombre inocente, vase a su casa'; on Bourne, 'vase a su casa y conózcole muy poco'.

83 AGS, Estado 811, leg. 131 – 'es hombre de seruicio'.

it imperative to grant pensions to Elizabeth's men, including Sir William Cecil, Robert Dudley, Sir Thomas Parry, who had become the new comptroller, and the earl of Bedford, who should receive 1,000 escudos each, although this was never implemented.[84] Furthermore, Feria had secretly offered fresh Spanish pensions to those in the list of 1554–1558 before Elizabeth allowed this, and Admiral Clinton and Lord Paget had accepted them behind the new queen's back.[85] He also suggested that Pembroke's pension be continued, as he was 'one of the best servants' of the king in England, as well as a man of authority.[86] In Feria's eyes, the confusion with which the English courtiers were conducting their affairs was not going to end up well. It was essential that Philip kept his ties with England 'fiercely' (*con las vñas*) to prevent Henry II of France from entering the kingdom and thus avoid 'the destruction of the vine that your Majesty planted here', a sentence charged with as much secular as religious meaning.[87] The fact that many of the English courtiers were considered by Feria to be 'good servants' of the king suggests that this scheme had been successful; the English sources confirm as much. In December 1559, John Middleton of Stamford reported to William Cecil from Antwerp, where Feria and his wife, Jane, were now residing, that

> the county [sic for 'count'] hathe very great intelligens of the affares of inglande: they say here that they [the Spanish] doo knowe the very secret

84 AGS, Estado 811, leg. 99; Feria to Philip, London, 14 December 1558: 'Con los pensionarios entiendo que se ha de tener diferente cuenta, porq[ue] sería razón pagalles hasta el fin deste año, y después dar a los q[ue] fuesse[n] menester, como a Sícel, a quien me parece que se deurían dar mill escudos, al contralor, a Milord Robert, al conde de Bedford otro ta[n]to a cada vno porque destos ay necessidad al presente, en auiendo buena ocasión para podérselo decir se lo diré /'.

85 AGS, Estado 811, leg. 99: '[…] ella [Elizabeth] permittirá que se den dineros a los que se daua[n] q[ue] es muy diferente de lo que me dixo la primera vez, que fue que no lo quería permitir /. A los que hasta aora he dicho que se les darán las pensiones que tenían secretamente y las ha[n] aceptado son el Almirante y preuisel [privy seal], /'.

86 AGS, Estado 811, leg. 99: 'De los que tenían antes pensión v[uestra] mag[esta]d vea a quién manda que se le dé de más de los que arriba he dicho, a mí paréceme que al conde de Pembruch se le deuría dexar, que aunq[ue] no está en muy gran crédito téngole por de los mejores serujdores de v[uestra] mag[esta]d q[ue] aquí ay y es hombre de autoridad y son sus amigos los Almirantes viejo [Howard] y nueuo [Clinton] ha posado siempre en palacio después que la reyna nueua heredó y nunca se aparta della /'.

87 AGS, Estado 811, leg. 105; Count of Feria to King Philip, London, 29 December 1558: 'En effecto estos se gouiernan de manera que han de dar consigo al través, es menester q[ue] v[uestra] mag[esta]d tome el negocio con vñas, y q[ue] desde luego començemos a ver cómo el rey de francia no entre aquí, no se destruya la viña q[ue] v[uestra] mag[esta]d aquí plantó /'.

> bowell[es] of inglande: of the Removing of captaynes from the yle of wyte and portesmothe and placing new in them with theyr names: sayeng that portesmothe ys nothing strong and that a man may gallap hys horse vpp the dyche of all the port[es] and havens he [Feria] dothe knowe them better then I whiche am borne there.[88]

Feria and, therefore, Philip, obviously had informers at the very heart of the English court. In April 1560, Philip still had supporters among Elizabeth's councillors. Lord John Grey, who had miraculously escaped the fate of his brothers the duke of Suffolk and Lord Thomas Grey in 1554, referred to these supporters as the 'Philippians' and suggested to Cecil that Elizabeth should 'ether dyspars them a brode to theer owen howses, or els wype them quit owt of her counsel'. Among these Philippians, Grey counted the earl of Arundel, secretary Petre and Sir John Mason, Philip and Mary's former ambassador in the Low Countries, all of them men averse to religious changes who had been close to Philip either in London or in Brussels throughout his reign as king of England. Grey also mentioned Sir Thomas Parry, but we cannot know exactly what he accused him of, as he refrained from further comment, pointing out that he would rather tell Parry what he thought of him 'to his faes then wryt yt or say yt to anny'. In Grey's view, Elizabeth had to purge her government of Philippians 'becawes yt ys godes cawes, the co[m]mune welthes sauety, and her owen shurete'.[89]

There is evidence to suggest that Philip's influence extended beyond 1560. In 1569 Thomas Percy, earl of Northumberland, and Charles Neville, earl of Westmorland, rose in rebellion in the North, taking Durham, where they celebrated the Latin Mass for the first time since 1559. Their aims were the restoration of Catholicism and the freeing of Mary, queen of Scots, although they failed on both counts and the rebellion was crushed by Elizabethan forces. The rebel earls fled into Scotland, where Northumberland was betrayed, kidnapped and taken to England, where he was beheaded in 1572. Westmorland escaped to Flanders, where he survived on a small pension paid by Philip and confirmed by his son, Philip III (r. 1598–1621), until Westmorland's death in 1601.[90] In the immediate aftermath of the crisis, while the earls were still gathering support in Scotland and there was hope in the Flemish and Spanish courts that the rebellion might prevail after all, George Kempe, brother to Philip's interpreter

88 HHL, Cecil Papers 2/19; John Middleton to Sir William Cecil, Antwerp, 29 December 1559.

89 HHL, Cecil Papers 152/137; Lord John Grey to Sir William Cecil, Pyrgo Palace, 20 April 1560.

90 For the latest reassessment of the rebellion and its implications see K. J. Kesselring, *The Northern Rebellion of 1569: Faith, Politics, and Protest in Elizabethan England* (Basingstoke and New York: Palgrave Macmillan 2007).

while king of England, Anthony Kempe, had been sent from England to the duke and duchess of Feria with information about the earls' whereabouts and their plans to crown Mary Stuart as queen of England. In a letter to the duke of Alba, now governor of the Low Countries, Philip allowed him to receive George Kempe or, if it were not possible, to confer with 'some good English Catholics residing in those estates', the most important of which was none other than Francis Englefield, 'whom', the King added, 'I remember'. In an enterprise like this, or in any other 'touching God's service and the benefit of that kingdom' of England, Philip told Alba that he could count on Englefield's good services 'with much trust', for he was 'a Catholic, a good gentleman and [a man] of good understanding and zeal'.[91] Through Alba's letter of 24 February 1570, describing the failure of the Northern Rebellion, we know with precision who had sent Kempe over from England: none other than Viscount Montague (and some unknown 'English gentlemen').[92] Montague was one of Philip's erstwhile pensioners, a Catholic who had been a lonely voice among his peers in the parliamentary sessions that broke with Rome in 1559, when he openly supported Catholicism, or, as he put it, the religion

91 AGS, Estado 544, leg. 136; King Philip to Fernando Álvarez de Toledo, Duke of Alba, Talavera de la Reina, 22 January 1570: '[…] y que si quisieren y pudieren embiaros al dicho [Jorge] Quempe, lo hagan, con vna carta del mismo Duque [of Feria], que lleua para vos / y si esto les paresciere de dificultad o inconueniente, se entiendan con vos por medio de algunos buenos cath[óli]cos Ingleses que residen en essos estados / El principal y más conoscido de los quales y más confidente a ellos es Francisco Englefild como ya deuéis saber / El qual recuerdo […] a fin que de todo el negocio y de la intención que en él se lleua, tengáis la noticia que conuiene / y con los dichos Condes la buena intelligencia que se requiere para que animados, ayudados, y esforçados por vos / ellos puedan tanto mejor y más presto poner en execución ésta tan justa y sancta empresa / En la buena direction de la qual y de qualquier otro negocio que tocare al seruicio de Dios y al beneficio de aquel Reyno, os podréis preualer y seruir muy confidentemente del dicho Englefild, por ser cath[óli]co y buen cauallero, y de tan buen entendimiento y zelo, como de su trato lo hauréis podido conocer /'. George and William Kempe, Anthony's brother and nephew were both in the service of Spain. See Alan Davidson, 'Kempe, Anthony (by 1529–97), of Slindon, Suss'. In http://www.historyofparliamentonline.org/volume/1509-1558/member/kempe-anthony-1529-97 [accessed 27 April 2020].

92 AGS, Estado 545, leg. 22; Duke of Alba to King Philip, Brussels, 24 February 1570: 'Vltimamente escriuí a v[uestra] M[ajesta]d cómo quedaua oyendo aquel Gentilhombre Inglés [Kempe] q[ue] vino a hablarme de parte de Montagu y de otros caualleros Ingleses / antes que éste viniesse tenían ya concertado los del norte de leuantarse, pero de tal manera que no lo hauían de hazer sin participaçión de otros muchos, antiçipáronse fuera de tiempo, y paró la cosa en lo q[ue] V[uestra] M[ajesta]d haurá visto, como yo lo temí desde la hora q[ue] los vi levantar sin fundamento […]'.

> which I professed in my baptisme, wher I was made a member of Christs misticall bodie, and vowed to beleeve the holy Catholique Churche, as the spowse and only beloved of Christe, by unitie in the which I am to bee saved or damned.[93]

The rebellion ultimately failed, but this Catholic network of malcontents, directly involving two of Philip's former pensioners (Englefield and Montague) and indirectly a third one (Kempe), can only point in the direction of a careful maintenance of the acquaintances made during his brief tenure as king of England.

3.4 The Reconciliation of Dissenters

The pension system established by Philip has been interpreted in the past within the framework of the habitual diplomatic practice of rewarding foreign courtiers with a view to extract information or to unlock particular spheres of influence in a foreign monarch's court.[94] However, the large amounts dispensed, the outcomes envisaged, and the actual consequences of the scheme highlight Philip's heavy involvement in English courtly life and his desire to please and win over his new English courtiers. To the extent that it can be judged considering the reign's brief duration, the system seems to have been largely successful. Had Mary lived longer, the most plausible outcome of the pension system would have been the reinforcement of the relationships made during these few years, as the attitudes of some of the pensioners in Elizabeth's reign seem to suggest, and this would have inevitably led to Philip's greater accruement of power in England.

Other ways of cementing relationships with the English courtiers were implemented, too. Particularly pertinent was the reconcilement of dissenters that Philip and Mary's regime undertook almost as soon as the marriage had taken place. One of the earliest and most well-known episodes was the rehabilitation of the Dudley family. It was apparently through the intercession of the duke of Medinaceli on behalf of the duchess of Northumberland that the latter's four surviving sons John, Ambrose, Henry, and Robert Dudley, were released from the Tower in October 1554. In her will, Jane Dudley rewarded Medinaceli as well as other Spanish noblemen and officials, all close to Philip's inner circle: the duke and duchess of Alba, Ruy Gómez de Silva, Gutierre López de Padilla, Diego Hurtado de Mendoza and Diego de Acevedo, which suggests

93 Edwards, *Archbishop Pole*, 253.

94 Loades, 'Philip II and the Government of England', 182.

that all of them may have played a part.[95] Medinaceli's involvement may account for John Bradford's praise in his 1555 *An Admonicion*. Whereas the 'vilenes which remaineth amongest the best of that nacion [Spain] except the ki[n]gs maiestie' was worse than 'the vileste reporte' that Bradford had ever heard mentioned about an Englishman, there was one other exception to the rule apart from the king. This exception applied only to Medinaceli who was a 'Prince [...] endewed with perfect humilite, trueth, loue, charite and all other princelike vertues'.[96] The eldest of the Dudleys, John, died from an illness a few days after his release, but the other three were formally pardoned on 22 January 1555, just in time to take part in a grand tournament in March which heralded their rehabilitation in courtly society.[97] Robert Dudley made several friends among the Spanish, joined Philip's entourage in Flanders in 1555 and, together with his brothers, volunteered for war against France in 1557.[98] In March 1557, just before Philip visited England for the second and last time, it was Robert Dudley that the king sent over to England from the Continent with letters for Mary, which suggests a high level of trust and familiarity between the king and Elizabeth's future favourite.[99]

The strategy was repeated with some of the rebels of 1554. William Winter, the naval administrator from Bristol, was pardoned on 10 November 1554.[100] In July 1557 he was advising Philip and Mary on naval matters and was entrusted by them to appoint soldiers to ships for the war with France.[101] He was still employed and in favour by the end of the reign. William Pickering, who had been ambassador to France under Edward VI, was pardoned on 4 December 1554 and was employed by Philip in several businesses thereafter.[102] The most important of these was the transportation of 3,000 German soldiers for the defence of the English coasts. Although it never materialised – as Philip decided to keep the

---

95 S. J. Gunn, 'A Letter of Jane, Duchess of Northumberland, in 1553', *The English Historical Review*, 114, no. 459 (1999), 1267–71.

96 Bradford, *An Admonicion*, sig. B1r.

97 CPR, vol. 2, 150–1, 157–8, 158–9.

98 Henry Dudley would die that year at the battle of St Quentin. At the beginning of Elizabeth's reign, Robert Dudley used his presence at the Anglo-Spanish tournaments as a propaganda scheme, refashioning his role as one of English superiority over the foreign Spaniards. See Richard McCoy, 'From the Tower to the Tiltyard: Robert Dudley's Return to Glory', *The Historical Journal*, no. 2 (1984), 425–35. See also Simon Adams, 'The Dudley Clientèle, 1553–1563' in G. W. Bernard, ed., *The Tudor Nobility* (Manchester and New York: Manchester University Press, 1992), 241–65 at 250.

99 BL, Cotton Vitellius F. v, fol. 67v.

100 CPR, vol. 2, 201–2.

101 TNA SP 11/11, no. 20: King Philip and Queen Mary to William Paulet, Lord Treasurer; Dover Castle, 5 July 1557; TNA SP 11/11, no. 29: King Philip and Queen Mary to gentlemen to serve as captains at sea; Richmond, 26 July 1557.

102 CPR, vol. 2, 177.

soldiers in Flemish soil – it was clear that Philip trusted his good services, and Pickering acknowledged in a letter to Mary that the king's treatment of him had been of 'incomparable benignitie and bountifull goodnes'.[103] Peter Carew, who fled to France after the events of 1554, was pardoned on 9 December 1555, although his lands and those of his wife, Margaret, formerly Lady Tailboys, had been forfeited and leased to James Bassett for thirty years.[104] Philip seems to have been very eager to reconcile Carew. With this in mind, he sent Margaret Carew over to Mary to plead for the restitution of their lands, adding, '[m]ay her wishes be carried out'.[105] Carew returned to England in May 1556 and was soon back in favour, the couple's lands being restored to them in September.[106] Having served Philip faithfully at St Quentin in 1557, after Mary's death Carew told Feria that 'he would to God that your Majesty had married the new queen [instead of Mary] so that you would have had children', adding that the English were now much obliged to the king.[107] These remarks may have just been the result of courtly chat, designed to impress Feria in case Philip did marry Elizabeth after all. It should not be forgotten, however, that Carew had been ready to rise up in arms four years before precisely to prevent Philip from having any English children.

Perhaps more telling is the reconcilement of Sir James Croftes, who had been condemned to be hanged, drawn and quartered in 1554. He was pardoned on 16 February 1555, presumably for his great military skill. In addition to the pension he received from Philip, he was employed as a military adviser to the earl of Northumberland in the north and recruited and commanded 100 men from Herefordshire and 200 from London whom he stationed in Berwick to prevent the Scots from attacking the borders in the aftermath of the fall of Calais.[108] His aversion to the Spanish and the Catholic faith seems to have been completely

103 TNA SP 69/13, no. 809; Sir William Pickering to Queen Mary; Brussels, 24 July 1558.

104 For the lease of his lands, including the manors of Mohun's Ottery, Ashwater, Georgeham, Weston Peverell and Monkton in Devon, see CPR, vol. 2, 48; for Carew's pardon see CPR, vol. 3, 45–46.

105 CSP Domestic, 153.

106 He was returned to England as part of a convoluted kidnapping scheme – in which he may have been a willing participant – designed to take Sir John Cheke to England. See J. P. D. Cooper, 'Carew, Sir Peter (1514?–1575)', ODNB http://www.oxforddnb.com/view/article/4634 [accessed 14 January 2023]. For the restoration of the lands see CPR, vol. 3, 551–4.

107 AGS, Estado 811, leg. 105; Feria to Philip; London, 29 December 1558: 'Estuve un vn buen rato hablando con éste [Peter Carew] y díxome que pluguiera a dios q[ue] v[uestra] M[a]j[esta]d se huuiera casado con la nueua reyna porque tuuiera hijos, y grandes cosas de la obligación en que son a v[uestra] mag[esta]d los Ingleses /'.

108 Mary Anne Everett Green, ed., *Calendar of State Papers, Domestic Series, Elizabeth, 1601–1603; with Addenda, 1547–1565* (London: Her Majesty's Stationery Office, 1870), 452, 456, 467.

reversed. In 1566, Diego Guzmán de Silva, Philip's ambassador under Elizabeth, reported that Croftes was 'strongly attached to your Majesty's service', and added that his brother-in-law, captain Randolph, who was a faithful Catholic and also one of Philip's former pensioners, was in his employ as a spy investigating whether there were any links between the Dutch rebels and the English court.[109] In 1570 Guerau de Espés, the new ambassador, described Croftes, who was shortly to be made a privy councillor by Elizabeth, as 'a very honourable Welsh gentleman, who received a pension from your Majesty, and is believed to be Catholic'.[110] He would later refer to him as a 'friend', and one who was 'secretly attached to the Catholic party and your Majesty's service'.[111] Praise for Croftes as a useful man for Spanish interests abounds. In 1581, after accepting a secret Spanish pension of 1,000 crowns from Bernardino de Mendoza, Espés's successor, Croftes went so far as to suggest an invasion of '2,000 men in Ireland under cover of the pope's name' to counter Elizabeth's support for the Flemish rebels.[112] When tensions in Anglo-Spanish relations became dangerous around 1583, Croftes started to limit the information he passed on to the Spanish. The conversion he underwent in 1554, however, suggests that some were indeed enthusiastic about the union of the crowns to the point of reversing their previous principles regarding the Spanish marriage.

3.5 The Select Council

One of the least studied and most misunderstood episodes of the reign of Philip and Mary is the creation of the *consejo escogido*, the select council, in the late summer of 1555.[113] The king had favoured the creation of a new advisory board soon after his arrival and it was not the first he founded in English soil, for in the summer of 1554 he had set up the *junta de Italia*, which would in

109 Martin A. S. Hume (ed.), *Calendar of Letters and State Papers Relating to English Affairs, Preserved Principally in the Archives of Simancas. Elizabeth. 1568–1579*, vol. 2 (London: Her Majesty's Stationery Office, 1894), 540, 599.

110 CSP Spain Elizabeth, vol. 2, 227.

111 CSP Spain Elizabeth, vol. 2, 241, 364.

112 Martin A. S. Hume, ed., *Calendar of Letters and State Papers Relating to English Affairs, Preserved Principally in the Archives of Simancas. Elizabeth. 1580–1586*, vol. 3 (London: Her Majesty's Stationery Office, 1896), 128. For words of praise for Croftes and his dealings with ambassador Mendoza see CSP Spain Elizabeth, vol. 2, 673–4, 681, 683–4, 690, 695–6.

113 I have written on this topic at length in Gonzalo Velasco Berenguer, 'The Select Council of Philip I: A Spanish Institution in Tudor England (1555–1558)', *The English Historical Review*, forthcoming.

time evolve to become the *consejo de Italia*.[114] Although the select council has been interpreted in the past as an ineffectual institution which did nothing but add to the alleged mismanagement of Mary's privy council and which was only sustained to satisfy Philip's ego as king of England, it had a wider significance than hitherto believed.[115] These assumptions, some of which have been challenged in later reassessments, stemmed from the prevailing view that Mary's large council of fifty members was not only quarrelsome and inefficacious in comparison to the smaller councils of Henry VIII (nineteen) and Elizabeth I (thirteen in 1601), but also represented a breach in the traditional composition of privy councils, as its ranks were filled by noblemen and politicians who had served both Henry VIII and Edward VI – men like Paget, Arundel, Pembroke and Petre – as well as by Mary's Catholic friends and early supporters – men such as Rochester, Englefield, Jerningham and Waldegrave.[116] Philip's decision, however, should not be understood as an implicit criticism of the numbers populating Mary's council (its Spanish counterpart, the council of Castile, had

---

114 Antonio Álvarez-Ossorio Alvariño, *Milán y el legado de Felipe II: gobernadores y corte provincial en la Lombardía de los Austrias* (Madrid: Sociedad Estatal para la Conmemoración de los Centenarios de Felipe II y Carlos V, 2001), 28, 37.

115 Traditional interpretations of the alleged inefficacy of Mary's privy can be found in G. R. Elton, *England under the Tudors* [1955] (London: Methuen 1978), 214; Loades 'Philip II and the Government of England', 190–1; John Guy, 'Tudor Monarchy and Political Culture', in John Morrill, ed., *The Oxford Illustrated History of Tudor and Stuart Britain* (Oxford: Oxford University Press, 1996), 219–238; especially 231, 235. As Ann Weikel pointed out in 1980, however, most historiographical accounts of Mary's council stemmed from the letters of the imperial and French ambassadors, rather than through an actual exploration of the functioning of the privy council itself, which she proved was much more effective than had been previously thought. See Ann Weikel, 'The Marian Council Revisited', in Jennifer Loach and Robert Tittler, eds., *The Mid-Tudor Polity, c. 1540–1560* (London: Macmillan, 1980), 52–73. See also M. J. Rodríguez-Salgado, *Changing Face of Empire*, 94–5. Dale Hoak thought that the select council had not only been ineffective but merely an illusion sustained to satisfy Philip's ego. He concluded that '[o]nly the Spanish believed in the separate existence of a "select council"'. See Dale Hoak, 'Two Revolutions in Tudor Government: The Formation and Organization of Mary I's Privy Council' in Christopher Coleman and David Starkey, eds., *Revolution Reassessed: Revisions in the History of Tudor Government and Administration* (Oxford: Oxford University Press, 1986), 87–115.

116 Glyn Redworth strongly argued against previous views on the topic in 1997 and he was the first to suggest convincingly that not only was the select council effective as an advisory board but, also, that it was a 'constitutional innovation' based on the Castilian model. See Glyn Redworth, '"Matters Impertinent to Women": Male and Female Monarchy under Philip and Mary', *English Historical Review*, 112, no. 447 (1997), 597–613. This is a view to which John Edwards has subscribed in his seminal biography of Queen Mary. See Edwards, *Mary I*, 271.

a membership of fifty-three in 1562).[117] Rather, it should be inserted within his strategy to integrate England in the conciliar system of the Spanish Monarchy.

The intricate conciliar structure that Philip inherited had been first developed by Ferdinand and Isabel, who had reinforced the council of Castile already in existence and added the councils of Aragon (1481), Holy Inquisition (1483), Orders (1495) and Crusade (1495). Charles V then created six more stemming from the Council of Castile: Cámara (1518), State (1523–1524), Indies (1524), War (1525), Finance (1525) and the junta of Works and Forests, established in 1545, during Philip's regency.[118] Any council's main role was to discuss matters requiring expertise and to advice the king accordingly. This was accomplished through the memoranda (*consultas*) that each council drew up and presented to the king, who in turn returned these reports with his own annotations and decisions before a draft, and then a final resolution, were written. In order to counter potential misunderstandings and to allow each council to know which business the others were discussing, Philip made some of his principal councillors attend several councils at the same time.[119] Conciliar systems had been a common feature of European monarchies since the Middle Ages, especially from the fourteenth century onwards, and they responded to the Aristotelian notion of 'political friendship' (*politike filia*), which was that exercised by those who advised with a good intention. Although the king was not obliged to take his councillors' advice, he was obliged to listen to it, reciprocating them with the same political friendship that they showed to him.[120]

117 Alfredo Alvar Ezquerra, *Felipe II, la corte y Madrid en 1561* (Madrid: Consejo Superior de Investigaciones Científicas, 1985), 16–21.

118 Geoffrey Parker, *The Grand Strategy of Philip II* (New Haven and London: Yale University Press, 1998), 22; Parker, *Felipe II*, 173; Parker, *Imprudent King*, 65.

119 Parker, *Grand Strategy*, 21–6. Parker surveys the subject again, with little change, in *Felipe II*, 172–9 and *Imprudent King*, 65–7. See also Fernández Álvarez, *Felipe II y su tiempo*, 47–74. For a more detailed discussion of each of the councils and their workings see Jon Arrieta Alberdi, *El consejo supremo de la corona de Aragón (1494–1707)* (Zaragoza: Institución Fernando el Católico, 1994); Carlos J. de Carlos Morales, *El consejo de Hacienda de Castilla, 1523–1602. Patronazgo y clientelismo en el gobierno de las finanzas reales durante el siglo XVI* (Valladolid: Junta de Castilla y León, 1997); Carlos Riba y García, *El Consejo supremo de Aragón en el reinado de Felipe II* (Valencia: Tipografía Moderna for Miguel Gimeno, 1914); José Ramón Rodríguez Besné, *El Consejo de la Suprema Inquisición. Perfil jurídico de una institución* (Madrid: Editorial Complutense, 2000).

120 John Guy, 'The Rhetoric of Counsel in Early Modern England', in Dale Hoak, ed., *Tudor Political Culture* (Cambridge: Cambridge University Press, 1995), 292–310; especially 292–4; John Guy, 'Tudor Monarchy and Political Culture', in John Morrill, ed., *The Oxford Illustrated History of Tudor and Stuart Britain* (Oxford: Oxford University Press, 1996), 219–38; especially 231, 235. For the concept of *politike filia* see Misung Jang, "Aristotle's Political Friendship (*politike philia*) as Solidarity", in Liesbeth Huppes-Cluysenaer and

The new advisory board was created on 29 August 1555, as Philip was readying himself to depart London on his way to Flanders. For 'a better and more expedite deliberation', the king chose several among the privy councillors who were to have 'the special care of all matters of state, [as well as] of financial and other grave matters of the kingdoms'.[121] The council was to be headed by Cardinal Pole 'when he wishes to do so and conveniently can', in a role analogous to that of president in the councils of Spain. Apart from Pole, Philip chose a further eight councillors: Gardiner, lord chancellor and bishop of Winchester (replaced after his death in November 1555 by his successor in the chancellorship, Nicholas Heath, archbishop of York); William Paulet, Lord Treasurer and marquess of Winchester; the earl of Arundel; the earl of Pembroke; Thomas Thirlby, bishop of Ely; Lord Paget, Sir Robert Rochester, comptroller of the household and master secretary Petre.[122] It was no coincidence that this composition mirrored almost exactly that of the Spanish council of state, on which the select council was clearly modelled, as Philip had left it when he embarked in Corunna in July 1554.[123] Philip commanded his select councillors to be 'present together at court' and to transact business relating to 'all matters of state, all financial matters, state possessions, debts and rents' and anything else relating to 'the honour, dignity, and state of the crown'.[124] To the end that they would provide 'the best counsel possible' (*melius consilium*), the king exhorted them

Nuno M. M. S. Coelho, eds., *Aristotle on Emotion in Law and Politics* (Springer: New York, 2018), 417–33.

121 British Library, Cotton Titus B. II, f. 160r: 'Inprimis pro meliori et magis expedita deliberatione, in ijs quæ in Consilio n[ost]ro agenda sunt ex reliquis Consiliarijs n[ost]ris eos quorum nomina seguuntur seligendos putauimus quibus spe[c]ialem cura[m] omniu[m] Causarum status, finantiarum et aliaru[m] Causarum graviorum Regni, co[m]mittendam dvximus et co[m]mitimus'.

122 Presumably, Rochester must have been replaced after his death on 28 November 1557 by his successor as comptroller, Sir Thomas Cornwallis, although I have found no conclusive evidence of this.

123 The king had reorganised its composition whilst waiting to depart from Corunna and its members were two spiritual lords of which one was to be the president (president Antonio de Fonseca, patriarch of the Indies and also president of the royal council of Castile and Fernando Valdés, Grand Inquisitor and archbishop of Seville), four noblemen (Luis Hurtado de Mendoza, marquis of Mondéjar; Pedro de Navarra, marquis of Cortes; Antonio de Rojas and García de Toledo) and one secretary (Juan Vázquez de Molina). For the king's instructions restructuring of the council of State see Evaristo de San Miguel y Valledor, *Historia de Felipe II, rey de España*, vol. 1 (Madrid: Ignacio Boix, 1844), 207–8.

124 BL, Cotton Titus B. II, f. 160r: 'Consiliarij prædicti omnes et singuli erunt presentes in Aula et intelligent et considerabunt omnes Causas status, omnes Causas financiaru[m], statum possessionu[m], Debitoru[m], et quomodo debita cum honore solui possint et generaliter omnes alias causas maioris momenti tangentes honore[m], dignitate[m] et statum Coronæ'.

to quell all discord 'amicably among themselves' and he recommended them an open approach to speaking their minds honestly about those matters that could 'redound in the glory of God as well as in the honour and service of ourselves and of our kingdoms'.[125] There could be no clearer statement of Philip's conception of England and Ireland as integrated members of the Spanish Monarchy than the use of the plural when referring to his kingdoms. The select councillors were now to think about English and Irish affairs from the new perspective of their inclusion in the Spanish composite monarchy.

Conciliar activity began in earnest as soon as Philip left the court and the first memoranda sent by the council, all undated but corresponding to September and October 1555, were written in Latin and annotated by a secretarial hand with Philip's thoughts and decisions on the matters transacted. This was the king's characteristic style when transacting business from all his realms. After the first few weeks, the direct exchanges between monarch and council would be epistolary. If we add to this channel of communication Philip's private correspondence with Mary (the majority of which is now lost), with influential Spanish and English courtiers and with the representatives he sent between 1555 and 1558 (Juan de Figueroa, Christophe d'Assonleville and the count of Feria) and that among the archive he lost at sea in the Channel in 1559 there may well have been more documents related to the select council, we can conclude with all certainty that not only the king and the select council communicated fairly regularly (especially if we remember that England was just one among many realms that Philip ruled *in absentia*) but also that the alleged lack of interest of Philip in English affairs is nothing but a myth.[126]

The select council was an effective vehicle for Philip to intervene directly in English affairs from abroad. The delaying for twelve months of Mason's recall from the Low Countries, the blocking of Gardiner's plan to send Clinton as lord deputy of Ireland, and the sending of Viscount Fitzwalter in his place and Philip's influence in avoiding the position of lord chancellor being granted to the bishop of Ely after Gardiner's death and the same being bestowed upon

125 BL, Cotton Titus B. II, f. 160r: 'Et quo melius Consiliu[m] nobis dare possint hortavimus eos in d[omi]nu[m], q[uod] omne[m] discordia[m] si que inter eos sit mutuo remittentes concorditer, amice, et in timore dei, ea in Consilijs proponant et dicant que dei gloria[m] n[ost]r[u]m et Regni nostri honore[m] et utilitatem promouere possint'.

126 A ship carrying part of Philip's private archive with documents from 1554–1559 as well as chancery minutes sank in the Channel on her way back to Spain in 1559. See Wim de Groot, *The Seventh Window: the King's Window donated by Philip II and Mary Tudor to Sint Janskerk in Gouda (1557)* (Hilversum: Uitgeverij Verloren, 2005), 15. We should also not dismiss the idea that further documentation might emerge in the future in other collections.

Nicholas Heath, are relatively well-known episodes.[127] Apart from Mason's recall, Philip also managed to halt the recall of the English ambassador in France, Nicholas Wotton, in 1556. When the select council wrote to the king asking for Wotton's recall due to his many years of service and advanced age, Philip replied that although the reasons adduced would seem 'to require it', he thought that Wotton's recall should be postponed until he – Philip – was able to go back to England. The king added, however, that if the need was pressing, he wanted to be informed of the decision beforehand, 'so that it is carried out properly'.[128] The hint was taken and the select council did not raise the issue again. Philip clearly needed someone trustworthy to inform from within whilst England remained reluctant to declare war against France. It was only when it had been decided that war would be declared, as it duly was on 7 June 1557, that Philip and Mary sent over instructions for Wotton's recall.[129] The king also intervened in the refurbishment and organisation of the English fleet and when his councillors petitioned insistently that he allow English commercial ventures in the Portuguese enclave of São Jorge da Mina in West Africa, despite the protestations of the Portuguese ambassadors, he disallowed it in an effort to align the kingdom of England with the Treaty of Tordesillas signed between the Spanish and Portuguese crowns in 1494.[130]

During the war with France and the papacy, the select council would demand from Philip a declaration of war against Scotland, as taking advantage of their alliance with France, the Scots had initiated a series of skirmishes on the Berwick area. Philip sent a Flemish envoy, Christophe d'Assonleville, to dissuade them, but the councillors remained obdurate. The conflict also involved Philip's council in the Low Countries, whose members thought that a declaration of war against Scotland would be detrimental to all involved and would open another front in the north of England. It also raised questions around the nature of England's declaration of war against France, which had been in response to the failed taking of Scarborough Castle by Sir Thomas Stafford with French funds rather than to honour the alliance signed between Henry VIII and Charles V in the 1540s. In the end, and using his prerogative as king of England, Philip decided to send D'Assonleville to negotiate a cessation of

127 Edwards, *Mary I*, 271–3.

128 TNA SP 11/9, nos. 31 and 32: Select council to King Philip, Croydon, 16 September 1556; TNA SP 11/9, no. 34: King Philip to the select council, Ghent, 30 September 1556.

129 SP 11/10, no. 64: King Philip and Queen Mary to Edward Fiennes de Clinton, 8th Baron Clinton, Croydon, 29 May 1557.

130 See TNA, SP 11/6, no. 17 for the memorandum dealing with the English fleet. For the episode of São Jorge da Mina, see more in Velasco Berenguer, 'The Select Council', forthcoming.

hostilities directly with Mary of Guise.[131] Although Philip's select councillors might have resented their master's decision, the king's approach reflected his need to accommodate the needs of all the territories of his composite monarchy and not solely those of his English subjects. The select council, nonetheless, was a fully functioning body which placed England and Ireland firmly within the Spanish Monarchy.

3.6 Conclusion

Philip I was king of England for four years and four months and resided among his English subjects for eighteen months in total. In that time, he managed to secure links with some of the English nobles, he devised a new conciliar system for England based on the Castilian experience and he even managed to overcome some of the obstacles offered by his councillors' advice when it did not suit him to follow it. The links between the Spanish and English nobilities were beginning to tighten, and the relationship of the English courtiers as part of the Habsburg political framework had started to blossom. The Catholic network that Philip established in England would later serve to destabilise – even if not as successfully as the king would have wished – Elizabeth's increasingly hostile regime. Philip was not a reluctant ruler of England and, like his father had done before him in Spain, he managed to maintain a power base in the island despite his physical absence and the disagreements in policy-making that he may have had with Mary or their councillors. The fact that he did not always get his way should not be understood as the failure of his methods. Rather, it highlights how his role as an English monarch who had attained the crown by marriage was still being defined. So, too, were the links between England and the Spanish monarchical project. The strategies devised and put in place by the king were effective and consolidated his position as king of England in the brief period during which he held the throne.

131 Velasco Berenguer, 'The Select Council', forthcoming.

CHAPTER 4

Rebuilding the Church: Philip, the Spaniards and the Reconciliation with Rome

The ties of the English crown with Rome had been severed in 1534 by a succession of parliamentary acts passed under Henry VIII culminating in the Act of Supremacy, which recognised the king's position as head of the Church (usurped for centuries by the bishops of Rome) and granted English monarchs the right to intervene in preaching, in the formulation of doctrine, in canon law, in clerical discipline and in the punishment of heretics.[1] The year 1536 saw the beginning of the dissolution of the monasteries, and Convocation, presided over for the first time by a layman, Thomas Cromwell, and receiving input directly from the king, published the Ten Articles, which defined the new system of belief for the Henrician Church in terms which still clung to old Catholic certainties but which dealt only with the sacraments of baptism, Eucharist, and penance.[2] These Articles were followed by the publication, in 1537, of *The Institvtion of a Christen man*, commonly known as the Bishops' Book because it had been produced by an episcopal committee presided over by Thomas Cranmer, archbishop of Canterbury. The Bishops' Book recognised the seven sacraments but stated that, because matrimony, confirmation, holy orders and extreme unction had not been instituted by Christ as sacraments but acknowledged as such by the Church, there was 'a difference in dignitie and necessitie', in comparison to the other three.[3] In 1539, Miles

1 Accounts of the Henrician Reformation can be found in A. G. Dickens, *The English Reformation* [1964] (London and Glasgow: Collins/Fontana, 1972), 169–71; Claire Cross, *Church and People, 1450–1660* (Glasgow: Fontana Paperbacks, 1976), 18–25; G. R. Elton, *Reform and Reformation: England, 1509–1558* (London: Edward Arnold, 1977), 174–92; John Guy, *Tudor England* (Oxford: Oxford University Press, 1988), 116–53; Richard Rex, *Henry VIII and the English Reformation* (Basingstoke and London: Macmillan, 1993), 6–37; G. W. Bernard, *The King's Reformation: Henry VIII and the Remaking of the English Church* (New Haven and London: Yale University Press, 2005), 68–72; Peter Marshall, *Heretics and Believers: A History of the English Reformation* (New Haven and London: Yale University Press, 2017), 203–66.

2 MacCulloch, *Thomas Cranmer: A Life* (New Haven and London: Yale University Press, 1996), 160–66; Elton, *Reform and Reformation*, 256–9; Bernard, *King's Reformation*, 281–92.

3 Episcopate of England, *The Institvtion of a Christen man, conteynynge the exposition or interpretation of the co[m]mune Crede, of the seuen sacramentes, of the x co[m]mandementes, & of the Pater noster, and the Aue Maria, Justificacion and purgatorie* (London: Thomas Berthelet, 1537), fol. 66v. For the discussions which preceded the publication of the Bishops' Book see MacCulloch, *Thomas Cranmer*, 185–97 and Bernard, *King's Reformation*, 175–8.

 | DOI:10.1163/9789004536210_006

Coverdale's vernacular Great Bible was published and, in the same year, parliament passed the Act of the Six Articles which was conservative in tone and asserted the Eucharistic presence.[4] It seemed that Henry's interest in a full-blooded Reformation had been halted, especially after the king commissioned the traditionalist bishops John Salcot of Salisbury, Nicholas Heath of Worcester and Thomas Thirlby of Westminster to revise the Bishop's Book. The resulting product, *The Necessary Doctrine and erudicion of any chrysten man*, known as the King's Book, defended transubstantiation and the indispensable role of good works in the process of justification.[5] Nevertheless, in his last will and testament in December 1546, Henry appointed a council to govern during the minority of his son which was composed mainly of known evangelicals.[6]

The Protestant tendencies of the new government were in line with the devout inclinations of the young Edward VI, a coincidence which soon translated into further changes. In November 1547, parliament repealed Henry VIII's treason and heresy laws together with his Six Articles, which opened the door for further reform.[7] The 1549 Book of Common Prayer, albeit conceived as a moderate solution, gave hints of what was afoot, with the disappearance of any notions of the sacrificial nature of the Eucharist as understood in Catholic theology and the establishment of the English Mass.[8] The Book of Common Prayer that replaced it with the Act of Uniformity in 1552 sought to institute a Eucharistic liturgy, stemming solely from Scripture, which Christopher Haigh has called Calvinist in its inspiration, as it implied the spiritual, rather than corporal, presence of Christ in the sacrament. It represented a complete breach with the past which was meant to be permanent.[9] The Forty-Two Articles, promulgated in June 1553, just a few weeks before Edward's death, were meant to seal this theological drift, and they firmly condemned the doctrines of transubstantiation, purgatory, invocation of the saints and the efficacy of good works.[10]

---

4 MacCulloch, *Thomas Cranmer*, 237–58.

5 Henry VIII, king of England, *A Necessary Doctrine and erudicion for any chrysten man, set furth by the kynges maiestye of Englande, &c.* (London: Thomas Berthelet, 1543), sigs F4v–G2v, S6r–T7r.

6 MacCulloch, *Thomas Cranmer*, 358–67.

7 Peter Marshall, *Reformation England, 1480–1642* [2003] (London: Bloomsbury Academic, 2012), 68–9.

8 Christopher Haigh, *English Reformations: Religion, Politics and Society under the Tudors* (Oxford: Oxford University Press, 1993), 173–6; Marshall, *Reformation England*, 70.

9 Haigh, *English Reformations*, 179–80. Elton thought it was of Zwinglian, rather than Calvinist, inspiration. See Elton, *Reform and Reformation*, 365. See also Marshall, *Reformation England*, 72–3.

10 Haigh, *English Reformations*, 180–1. Although the Continental influences brought to England by Martin Bucer, Bernardino Occhino, Peter Martyr Vermigli and others have given the impression that the Edwardian Church was Calvinist, MacCulloch argues for

The England inherited by Mary was thus one divided by the religious legacy of her predecessors, at least at an institutional level. Despite initial calls for caution, Mary soon moved towards a more traditional position. In September 1553 Thomas Cranmer, archbishop of Canterbury, Hugh Latimer, chaplain to Edward VI, John Hooper, bishop of Worcester, Nicholas Ridley, bishop of London, and other notorious Protestants were arrested and soon afterwards deprived of their sees and benefices. During its autumn sessions, parliament refused to repeal Henry's Act of Supremacy, but it declared Henry's marriage to Catherine of Aragon valid – in agreement with the papal ruling of 1534 – and it passed the Act of Repeal which tore down the whole statutory building of the Edwardian Reformation.[11] The Latin Mass, celebrated spontaneously in many parishes since Mary's accession, was now officially and legally restored.[12] In March 1554, Mary's Royal Injunctions ordered the suppression of heresy by bishops, the deprivation of married clergy, the re-ordination of those who had been ordained as priests under Edward's English Ordinal as well as the restoration of feasts, processions and other religious ceremonies.

Despite this initial progress, Spaniards were not, at first, impressed with the state of religious affairs inherited by Mary from her father and brother. We have already seen how Alonso de Alguero complained that Londoners disliked 'men with tonsures and long robes' and no less than Bartolomé de Carranza himself wrote to Cardinal Pole with alarm on 1 September 1554, after a few weeks of residing in the kingdom. The cardinal had 'no idea', Carranza explained, 'how much animus' the English had against the Spanish and he followed this with a comment on how difficult it was for 'a naturally choleric Spaniard to swallow the insults'. This attitude, he claimed, was a provocation to try King Philip's patience and was tied into a virulent opposition to Catholicism.[13] The alarmist but insightful observer Juan de Baraona, complained that the friars were

---

the originality of Edward's Church. See Diarmaid MacCulloch, *Tudor Church Militant: Edward VI and the Protestant Reformation* (London: Allen Lane/The Penguin Press, 1999), especially 172–9.

11 John Edwards, *Mary I: England's Catholic Queen* (New Haven and London: Yale University Press, 2011), 136–40.

12 On the spontaneous restoration of the Latin Mass see Eamon Duffy, *The Stripping of the Altars: Traditional Religion in England, c.1400–c.1580* (New Haven and London: Yale University Press, 1992), 527–8.

13 Thomas F. Mayer, ed., *The Correspondence of Reginald Pole*, vol. 2 (London and New York: Routledge: Taylor & Francis Group, 2003), 333–4. A transcription of the original Latin letter can be found in José Ignacio Tellechea Idígoras, *Fray Bartolomé Carranza y el Cardenal Pole. Un navarro en la restauración católica de Inglaterra (1554–1558)* (Pamplona: Diputación Foral de Navarra/Institución Príncipe de Viana/Consejo Superior de Investigaciones Científicas, 1977), 184–5.

continuously indoors, not daring 'to go out to say Mass unless they are accompanied by a good number of Spaniards' because the Londoners might otherwise throw stones at them. Consequently, they had determined to say Mass in their lodgings, and confirming Carranza's words, he claimed that the latter and his coreligionist, Friar Juan de Villagarcía, had had experiences which had been 'a strange thing to behold'. Baraona had further reasons to be outraged at the behaviour of the English:

> There are no richer nor more beautiful churches and temples in the world than those built in this land. However, they have suffered the worst ravaging that could be in this world. Within them, saints and crucifixes have been carved up, some have had their noses cut off, others have been defaced and others stabbed. Many of the temples have been torn down. There are no friars or nuns in this land even though they possess [...] the most impressive monasteries in the world. These, however, have been made into pens or simply demolished. [...] The clerics are married, and they go to church to say Mass with their wives by their side. They refuse to believe any of the things that the Holy Father ordains, and they work during feast days, eating meat on Fridays and Saturdays even though the queen has complained about this more than a thousand times, as she is a most Christian woman.[14]

The destruction of truth and religion in England had been accomplished, from Baraona's point of view, not only at a theological and intellectual level but also, quite literally, at a physical level. The erosion of the theological landscape had been effected at the same time as the erosion of the physical landscape, and the ruins of the monasteries stood as testament to the destructive legacy

---

14 RBME, MS V-II-4, f. 425^{r}; Juan de Baraona to Antonio de Baraona, London, 25 October 1554: 'Los frailes que acá pasaron siempre están rrecogidos que no salen d[e] vn colegio a d[e]zir missa no se atreuen a salir si no ban conellos muchos Españoles porque les apedrean y así agora an acordado d[e] decir misa d[e]ntro en su posada El padre frai b[a]r[tolo]mé d[e] miranda y frai J[ua]n de Villag[a]r[cí]a están acá y es vna cosa estrana la vida que pasan // de hedifiçios d[e] yglesias y tenplos no las ay en el mundo tan rricas y tan lindos como los d[e]sta tierra sino que ay vn estragon la mayor d[e]l mundo enellos los santos y crucifixos acuchillados a vnos cortadas las narizes a otros rraspadas las caras y las cruzes acuchilladas y muchos tenplos d[e]rribados / no ay fraile ni monja en toda esta tierra avn que ay monisterios como digo más brauos del m[un]do echos corralacos d[e]rribados [...] / los clérigos son casados yban a la igl[es]ia su muger al lado y dizen luego misa no quieren creer cosa ning[un]a d[e]los que el padre santo manda y todas las fiestas trabajan y comen carne los biernes y sábado avnque las rreyna les haze mil dissabores sobre estas cosas porque ella es muy cristianísima [...]'.

of Henry VIII's and Edward VI's religious changes. There could be no clearer statement, from the point of view of a Catholic commentator, of the consequences of Protestantism and the destruction it brought in its wake. Baraona's comments confirmed what Antonio de Guaras had already advanced in his newsletter surveyed in chapter 1: England had become the earthly city and a rotten member of the Body of Christ. It was imperative to heal the kingdom and bring it back to the Roman fold, a task to which Philip and his courtiers were passionately committed. The Church in England had to be rebuilt, both physically and intellectually.

4.1 Negotiating Ecclesiastical Property

In order to rebuild the English Church and take her back into the confines of Christendom and out of schism and heresy, Queen Mary, her council, and her religious authorities had already taken the first steps: the abandonment of heretical doctrines and the return to Catholic practice. The next crucial and definitive step, however, was the official reconciliation with Rome and the kingdom's renewed oath of obedience to the pope as vicar of Christ. To this end, Pope Julius III (r. 1550–1555) named Cardinal Pole as his legate *ad latere* (a papal ambassador with extensive powers) in August 1553, with powers to represent the papacy in the process of reconciliation.[15] Pole was understandably excited and eager to return to his homeland, where he had had not set foot since 1532. The cardinal, born around 1500, was the child of Sir Richard Pole and Margaret, countess of Salisbury, a first cousin to Henry VIII's mother, Elizabeth of York. Henry had showered his younger cousin with affection and patronage, funding his studies abroad at the university of Padua. Originally on Henry's side in the king's proceedings to divorce Catherine of Aragon, Pole was sent to Paris to obtain favourable opinions from scholars and theologians in the Sorbonne to support his cousin's Great Matter. During the course of his research abroad, however, Pole changed his mind and came to understand the validity of the marriage, therefore counselling Henry to keep Catherine. Deploring the rapid religious changes that were taking place in England, Pole refused to endorse Henry's actions any further and decided not to return to his homeland. His *Pro ecclesiasticae unitatis defensione*, in which he made a

15 John Edwards, *Archbishop Pole* (Farnham: Ashgate, 2014), 122. Pole was also granted a separate legation to broker the peace between the Habsburgs and the Valois. For an account of Pole's second legation (1553–1558; he had already been legate 1537–1539) see Edwards, *Archbishop Pole*, 109–213.

frontal attack on Henry's assault on papal primacy and the royal supremacy, was first sent to the king in manuscript form in 1536 and would later be published in 1539.[16] As a consequence, Pole was declared a traitor and attainted and, together with most of his family, was soon embroiled in charges of conspiracy and treason against the king. As a result of this process, Pole's brother Henry, Lord Montague, their mother, Margaret, and other relatives all went to the block between 1538 and 1541.[17] The cardinal was, therefore, understandably moved by the possibilities that Mary's accession and her desire to return to Catholicism presented.[18]

Despite Pole's expectations and the apparent good progress that Mary was making in England towards the reconciliation, two serious obstacles remained which prevented Pole's prompt return to his homeland. First, on a practical level, Pole's attainder had to be reversed in parliament for, otherwise, he would still be a traitor under English law. Although this could seem to be a mere technicality that could be easily addressed in the next parliament, it was complicated by the second major obstacle to Pole's return: the question of ecclesiastical land and possessions in lay hands as a consequence of the dissolution of the monasteries in Henry VIII's reign.[19] This proved to be a very significant hurdle, for the acquisition of ecclesiastical goods had been so widespread that even lords known for their attachment and loyalty to the old religion were fiercely disinclined to give up their newly acquired possessions. The cardinal's initial position was that, to show true humility and a genuine desire for reconciliation, lands and assets seized and alienated from the Church's patrimony were to be returned by those who had acquired them. Otherwise, the sincerity

16 Reginald Pole, *Reginali Poli ad Henricum octavum Britanniae regem, pro ecclesiasticae unitatis defensione* (Rome: Antonio Blado, 1539). I would like to thank Professor Suzannah Lipscomb for her observations around this topic.

17 For an account of Pole's life in this period and the evolution of his position with regards to Henry, the divorce and religious developments in England see Edwards, *Archbishop Pole*, 11–83. On the alleged conspiracy of the Pole family and the marquess of Exeter see Bernard, *King's Reformation*, 407–32.

18 Pole's emotional turmoil at this time can be discerned in the first letter he exchanged with his niece Catherine Pole, countess of Huntingdon, on 21 June 1554, whilst in Brussels. He explained that although her first letter (he had received two), which described her contentment as a wife and mother, and was the first he had received from any of his relatives in decades, had given him much joy, he could not, however, finish reading it, 'for the sorofull rememberaunce it brought me of the losse of those wych I left in good state at my departing', although he took some comfort 'when I consydere ever what servants of God they were and so dyed'. See F. J. Routledge, ed., 'Six Letters of Cardinal Pole to the Countess of Huntingdon', *The English Historical Review*, 28 (1913), 527–31.

19 On the dissolution of the monasteries and sale of ecclesiastical land under Henry VIII see Bernard, *King's Reformation*, 433–74. See also Marshall, *Heretics and Believers*, 231–3, 244, 259–61, 273–4, 276–7, 281–2, 402.

of their inclination to return to Roman obedience could be put in question. Pope Julius had a more prosaic approach, which matched that of Philip and Mary, and he believed that the key issue was to ensure that England returned to the Catholic fold. If, to achieve this, the Church had to show particular patience to her wayward English children and part with the assets of which she had already been dispossessed, it was a price worth paying if it accomplished the first return to Rome of a schismatic territory since Martin Luther's defiance in the 1520s.[20] A sort of *Paris bien vaut une messe* but on the reverse.

Whilst the cardinal swiftly moved to the Low Countries, hoping to be received in England as soon as possible, Charles V saw an opportunity to delay him in Flanders and thus ensure that the reconciliation would be brokered by Philip in England, a process which the young king had already started. As a consequence, Pole would remain in Flanders for the next few months, a development which the cardinal clearly resented but which could not really be helped until the English parliament reversed his attainder.[21]Although both Charles and Philip had their own political agendas in prolonging this delay, their cautious approach was nonetheless sound, for Pole was vehement in his desire to bring about the reconciliation as quickly as possible, contrary to Philip's intention, which was to negotiate the burning issue of ecclesiastical possessions first. Indeed, the king's English subjects were extremely anxious about this point.[22] On the Spanish side, there also seems to have been a certain level of mistrust towards the English cardinal.

This mistrust stemmed from Pole's early stance that Mary should remain unmarried, a position which was interpreted by some as a specific opposition against the Spanish marriage. On 21 December 1553, Pole's close friend, Cardinal Giovanni Morone, had written to explain that Pope Julius was convinced that Mary ought to marry the prince of Spain. The pope thought that she needed 'a husband in order to rule those ferocious people' and the power that Prince Philip would bring was an exceptional opportunity to re-establish Catholicism. Morone then advanced that the pope 'considers it not only dangerous to obstruct the marriage, but harmful to religion and to the Holy See'. Finally, he cautioned, '[the pope] wishes you to come to the same opinion, and avoid offending the emperor'.[23] A month later Pole wished to counter this version of events and explained to Morone that he had told Pedro de Soto, former

20 Edwards, *Archbishop Pole*, 134–40.
21 Edwards, *Archbishop Pole*, 120–40.
22 M. J. Rodríguez-Salgado, *The Changing Face of Empire: Charles V, Philip II and Habsburg Authority, 1551–1559* (Cambridge: Cambridge University Press, 1988), 96–8; Edwards, *Archbishop Pole*, 133–40.
23 Correspondence Pole, vol. 2, 241.

imperial confessor and professor of Theology at the University of Dillingen, that he had never given Mary any advice about the marriage because she never asked for it and that he had initially thought that she should remain single because of her age. Pole confessed to having had reservations that a foreign marriage might interfere in his mission as legate in England, but he could now clearly see that the marriage would be 'the greatest arm for establishing matters of religion' and he was convinced that '[n]o one will work harder than Philip'.[24] In May 1554 he reiterated these sentiments to Morone, explaining that he had written to Mary that 'a Spanish marriage would fix what another Spanish marriage had broken'. Furthermore, he '[t]old anyone who objected to [a] foreign king that God would fool them, just as he had with Henry than whom no foreign prince could be worse'.[25] As we shall see, Pole and Philip were indeed to work closely together to bring about the reconciliation of England and Rome.

In the meantime, Pole continued to perform his tasks as legate as best he could from Flanders. In February 1554 he sent over his chamberlain, Henry Pyning, with instructions for the confirmation of the bishops so far appointed by Mary. Pole had direct power from the pope in consistory to confirm England's bishops once they were absolved of schism and only if they showed 'sorrow and repentance'.[26] On 8 March, Julius wrote to confirm the expansion of the legatine powers conferred in August 1553, an expansion which gave Pole full powers to absolve any penitents and to deal with the conversion of ecclesiastical property to pious uses. He also granted the cardinal the power to absolve prelates appointed by Henry VIII or Edward VI if he thought it fit. The pope also thought it appropriate to chastise Pole for being 'exaggeratedly scrupulous' in his approach to the reconciliation of English prelates.[27] The cardinal legate promptly began to use his newly expanded powers, and, on 17 March, he absolved and confirmed in his sees seven of Mary's bishops.[28]

As the wedding day approached, Pole's activity intensified. On 21 June he wrote to congratulate Philip on his proxy marriage and to let him know that he hoped for his help in his legation to reunite England with Rome and to

24 Correspondence Pole, vol. 2, 256.

25 Correspondence Pole, vol. 2, 294–5.

26 Correspondence Pole, vol. 2, 267.

27 Correspondence Pole, vol. 2, 269–70.

28 These were Robert Parfew, bishop of Hereford; John White, bishop of Lincoln; Gilbert Bourne, bishop of Bath and Wells; James Brooks, bishop of Gloucester; George Coates, bishop of Chester; Henry Morgan, bishop of St David's and Maurice Griffith, bishop of Rochester. See Correspondence Pole, vol. 2, 275.

establish peace in the kingdom.[29] Over the next few months, Pole would also correspond with Bartolomé de Carranza, then residing in England, wishing for his help in his legatine mission, and with Pedro de Soto, whom he greatly respected and would eventually enlist to teach at Oxford.[30] The thorny issue of ecclesiastical property in lay hands, however, remained. Julius wrote to Pole in late June to stress again that he did 'not wish the question of property to get in the way of saving so many souls' and he reiterated this stance on 1 August.[31] Nine days later, however, Pole tried to pressure Mary into allowing him to return to England immediately, maintaining that he could not give a general or particular dispensation without 'great offence to God and slander to the churches'. In the first place, he needed to establish how the property was held and argued that giving a general grant before paying obedience to Rome was inappropriate. Above all, Pole was adamant that '[o]bedience must come first'.[32]

A couple of months after the marriage had taken place, on 19 September 1554, Philip wrote to Pole from Hampton Court to thank him for the love he had for the queen and his concern for his country and to assure him that he would fulfil the reconciliation expected from his marriage as quickly as he could.[33] A few days earlier, on the ninth, the Franciscan Bernardo de Fresneda, Philip's confessor, had written to Pole to rejoice in his position as legate and to let him know that although he had help in religious matters from Alfonso de Castro and Bartolomé de Carranza, it was imperative that Pole returned quickly. Although the privy council might try to resist his coming, Fresneda added, God would not allow it.[34] Possibly already in possession of this letter, which stressed the urgency of the situation, but not having yet received Philip's, Pole wrote a reprimand to the king (not, significantly, to the queen) on 24 September. The cardinal opened by reminding Philip that it had been a year since he began to knock 'on the doors of this royal house, yet no one has opened them for me'. Pole understood that Mary had been fearful and that, as a consequence, the arrival of Peter's representative had been delayed. However, there was no longer any reason to keep fearing and delaying, and Pole therefore entreated Philip to allay Mary's fears. The king of England, Pole contended, had a great responsibility to admit the papal legate and to redress the ills that had befallen the kingdom. He continued:

29 Correspondence Pole, vol. 2, 318.
30 Correspondence Pole, vol. 2, 330–31.
31 Correspondence Pole, vol. 2, 321–2, 328–9.
32 Correspondence Pole, vol. 2, 331–3.
33 Correspondence Pole, vol. 2, 337.
34 Correspondence Pole, vol. 2, 337.

> But you, Catholic prince, to whom divine providence and benignity has bestowed that other high title of Defender of the Faith which further elevates and adorns the kings of England through Peter's apostolic authority, consider within yourself, how does it serve your piety that all ambassadors sent to you from all princes have had open access to you and have been able to congratulate you on the obtention of such title, yet Peter's successor, who sent to you, sat on your kingdoms' throne, his own legate to this end and to bring forth the peace and grace of Him who excels over all kings, shall not be admitted?

The implication was clear; as the new king of England and Defender of the Faith, it was Philip's task and responsibility to admit the legate back into the kingdom, so that the house could be rebuilt and restored. If this were not accomplished sooner, rather than later, Pole predicted that God, who had so far shown such favour to the English monarchs, would no doubt destroy the house entirely.[35] The legate's letter clarified in unmistakable terms Philip's position as the primary negotiator of the reconciliation with Rome. On 28 September, Pole wrote to Charles V to point out that, since divine providence had given the 'government to your son', it was imperative that he be let into the kingdom to carry out his legatine mission.[36] To exert more pressure, on the same day Pole sent Niccolò Ormanetto to Antoine Perrenot de Granvelle, bishop of Arras, to explain that the inexcusable delay angered the pope and dishonoured Charles, Mary and Philip.[37] On 6 October the cardinal wrote to Fresneda and, in more amiable terms, compared Philip to King Solomon, who succeeded where his father, David, had failed and managed to build the temple of Jerusalem. In the task that lay ahead, Pole urged Fresneda, Castro and Carranza to help him.[38] On the same day he wrote a letter to Carranza, praising his endeavours with 'our most religious king' to pave the way for the reconciliation. It was essential that Philip negotiated the 'obedience to the Church and to the Apostolic See',

35 Bilbiothèque Municipale de Besançon, MS Granvelle, f. 174r–176v; Cardinal Pole to King Philip, Dieleghem, 24 September 1554: 'Tu uero Princeps Catholice, cui nunc diuina prouidentia, et benignitate additum est alterum hoc præclarum fidei defensoris cognomen, quo Reges Angliæ apostolica Petri auctoritate sunt aucti, atq[ue] ornati, tecum nu[n]c considera, quàm id tuæ pietati conueniat, cum omnibus omnium Principum ad te legatis aditus patuerit, ut tibi de hoc ipso cognomine adepto gratularetur, solum successoris Petri, qui hoc dedit, Legatum, qui propterea missus est, ut te in solio regni diuina summi omnium Regis, quam affert, pace, et gratia confirmet, not admitti'. An alternative translation in CSP Spain, vol. 13, 54.

36 Correspondence Pole, vol. 2, 340.

37 Correspondence Pole, vol. 2, 340.

38 Correspondence Pole, vol. 2, 343.

rather than concentrating on other things, just as in order to build, one needs a good foundation first. If the proverb taught, Pole added, that 'the beginning is half the job done, in this case it is indeed the whole thing'.[39]

It is very significant that Pole's exchanges in this period of diplomatic labours to return to his homeland to exercise his legatine mission were with the king and his Spanish clerics rather than with the queen and her English councillors. It placed Philip and his Spaniards at the centre of the efforts to re-Catholicise England. Philip, with the encouragement of his father, had actively sought this role and his authority as king of England and heir of Spain and the impeccable credentials of his theologians had warranted his position as the main negotiator in England's return to the Roman fold. When the matter of ecclesiastical property continued to be a problem, Ormanetto advised Pole's envoy in England, Seth Holland, to convey to Carranza that the cardinal's legatine powers were broader than usual to deal with the restoration of despoiled churches as well as to provide 'peace and tranquillity of conscience and temporal commodity' to holders of ecclesiastical property. Pole had begun to give in. Despite Carranza's concern that the term 'alienation' did not appear expressly in the faculties, which may worry the holders of ecclesiastical property, Ormanetto assured Holland that the faculties amply covered alienated properties. Ormanetto hoped that these reassurances would encourage Carranza to 'work for unity and disabuse interested parties' although he felt it necessary to add that he considered that it was '[l]ess honourable to deal with these matters before obedience' was granted.[40]

4.2 The Reconciliation with Rome

At last, on 14 October 1554, Philip and Mary finally sent for Pole, who was to wait for a verbal communication to be delivered by Seth Holland and for the arrival of Lord Paget and Sir Edward Hastings, who were to escort him back

39 Tellechea Idígoras, *Carranza y Pole*, 187. Pole to Carranza, Dieleghem, 6 October 1554: 'Habes autem exercendi campum latissimum si vel hoc unum pro tua virili parte apud religiosissimum regem nostrum procuraveris, ut obedientia ecclesiæ et sedis apostolicæ primum locum inter regias ejus actiones habeat, et primo quoque tempore restituatur. Quod ni fiat, frustra in caeteris laboratur, perinde ac si quis fundamento non jacto, ædificare se posse putet. Quod si caeteris in rebus illud nos proverbium docet, principium esse totius rei dimidium, in hac quidem est totum'. Calendared in CRP, 2, 343–4.

40 Correspondence Pole, vol. 2, 344; Niccolò Ormanetto to Seth Holland, Dieleghem, 7 October 1554.

to England together with a delegation of prelates and grandees.[41] We know that consent for Pole's return had been brokered by Philip because the cardinal said as much in a letter written to Pope Julius in the middle of the night of 19 October. At two o'clock in the morning, Pole had received an urgent visit from Arras, the nuncio Girolamo Muzzarelli, and the imperial secretary Francisco de Vargas, who told him that they had just received word from Philip explaining that 'he had greatly exerted himself to induce the chief personages interested in the Church property' to consent to Pole's return. The problem that remained, however, was that the papal brief dealing with the concession of property was deemed not to be ample enough. The king had explained that the English wished the words *alienandi cedendi et remittendi* (alienating, ceding, and surrendering) added to the words *componendi et transigendi* (compromising and tolerating) when referring to the cession of ecclesiastical property in the original faculties. Furthermore, they also demanded the cancellation of the clause about having recourse to the Holy See, which they felt opened the door to future disputes over possession, and they wished for the new brief to be dated after the consummation of Philip and Mary's marriage. This latter demand was very convenient to Philip, as it officially sanctioned his role as the main negotiator in the reconciliation, but it was also useful to the possessors of Church property, as it strengthened their own stance to have the king as the one pushing for this change.[42] On the 25th, after a few days to digest the visit he had received a few nights before at ungodly hours, Pole told Julius that he thought that all these demands amounted to nothing more than a purchase of English obedience to the Holy See, but he nonetheless thought the business to be a 'greater and more praiseworthy enterprise than if one should recapture Jerusalem from the infidels'.[43] The extreme urgency of the granting of a new brief before the opening of parliament on 12 November was immediately understood by the pope who, on 6 November, at record speed, informed Pole that after deliberating with twelve cardinals all had agreed that the reconciliation was more important than ecclesiastical property, and he had therefore issued a new brief with the amendments requested by the English through Philip.[44]

Philip's endeavours to allow Pole back into the kingdom are confirmed by an anonymous Spanish source who explained that,

---

41 Correspondence Pole, vol. 2, 347.

42 CSP Venice, vol. 5, 581–2; CRP, 2, 349.

43 CSP Venice, vol. 5, 584–6; CRP, 2, 352–3.

44 Correspondence Pole, vol. 2, 356–7.

> The king-prince, our lord, negotiated with the councillors for eight days before the commencement of parliament (which is what in Castile we call the Cortes Generales), that they would allow Cardinal Pole, a native, a relative of the queen, our lady, and the appointed papal legate to this kingdom, to enter the same, for he had been hindered and stranded in Flanders for more than six months, as they would not let him enter.[45]

That it was Philip the one behind the pressure to obtain securities on the matter of ecclesiastical property was also commented upon by Charles's secretary, Francisco de Eraso, in a letter he addressed to Ruy Gómez from Antwerp at the end of the month, following a brief stay in England. Eraso explained that 'the king had made a decision concerning the [ecclesiastical] goods in communication with the friars and the rest who had assembled' so there was no obstacle for the reconciliation to take place.[46] Philip's prominent role, which confirms his claim that he had been 'the head and main instrument' in the reconciliation mentioned in the introduction, continued once parliament opened on 12 November. As was stated in the previous chapter, on this occasion the positions of king and queen reverted to their traditionally gendered places, with Philip to the right and Mary to the left.[47] The king of England had clearly gained authority and control over the English government, and his status was probably enhanced by the belief that Mary was then pregnant. The anonymous Spanish source described how king, queen and parliament were all dressed in crimson or burgundy and the commentator then proceeded to explain the functioning of the English parliament, with its two houses, one for 'all prelates, bishops and grandees of the kingdom', and another one for 'the representatives of the cities and villages'. Once something had been concluded

---

45 RBME, MS V-II-4, 'Relación de lo que ha sucedido en Inglaterra', f. 456^{r}: 'lo q[ue] en esta tierra ha suçedido es q[ue] el rey prínçipe n[uest]ro señor negoçió ocho días q[ue] se comencase el parlame[n]to q[ue] en castilla llama[n] cortes generales con los del co[n]sejo q[ue] diesen licençia para q[ue] el cardenal polo natural y pariente de la reyna n[uest]ra señora q[ue] venja por legado alatere del papa a este reyno podiese entrar en él porq[ue] avja más de seis meses q[ue] estaua en flandes empedido y detenido q[ue] no lo dexaua[n] entrar'.

46 AGS, Estado 808, leg. 133, Francisco de Eraso to Ruy Gómez de Silva, Antwerp, 29 November 1554: '[...] en este puncto me han querido dar a entender que si no huuieran abierto el despacho que iua p[ar]a Don Juan Manriq[ue] y escripto lo q[ue] aquí se escriuió, que no huuiera hauido tan buen efecto lo de Roma pero yo repliq[ué] la determinación que el Rey tenía tomada e[n]lo de los bienes con comunicación de los frailes y los demás que se juntaron de manera que no hauía peligro [...]'.

47 Alexander Samson, *Mary and Philip: The Marriage of Tudor England and Habsburg Spain* (Manchester: Manchester University Press, 2020), 114.

by the prelates and noblemen, the account continued, the matter passed on to the representatives to determine whether there was consensus or not, because 'if they are not all in agreement about a particular thing or a law made, it is worth nothing'. Significantly, the commentator added that, even if there was agreement, 'it is necessary that this is confirmed by the monarchs, for otherwise it is also worth nothing'.[48] The plural when referring to the monarchs (*los reyes*), suggests Philip's complete integration within the institutional structure of the English monarchy.[49] Without the assent of king and queen, English legislation would not pass in parliament.

The monarchs and the three estates paraded through London and went to hear the Mass of the Holy Spirit at Westminster Abbey, where John White, bishop of Lincoln, delivered a sermon in English and Latin in which, 'among other very good things', he said that,

> Since the king's Majesty has a sword borne before him, he should draw it and begin to punish and cut the throats of heretics and disturbers of the peace and quiet of the republic. And he said with great boldness that he [Philip] should restore the keys of St Peter to the pope, from whom they had been snatched, as Christ had not given them to him. This greatly pleased the king, but it did not please so much all members of parliament.[50]

---

48 RBME, MS V-II-4, f. 456r: 'en el parlame[n]to entra[n] todos los perlados, obispos, y gra[n]des del reyno. estos están todos juntos en vna sala. los procuradores de las çibdades y lugares, está[n] en otra sala. Después q[ue] se ha co[n]cluydo vna cosa por los p[re]lados y gra[n]des aujsan a los procuradores de lo q[ue] tiene[n] concluydo para ver si les paresçe lo mesmo porq[ue] si todos no son conformes en vna cosa e ley q[ue] haga[n] no vale nada. pero au[n]que co[n]forme[n] es menester q[ue] lo co[n]firme[n] los reyes. y sino tampoco vale nada'.

49 It is possible that the plural in 'reyes' makes reference to a generic plural and, therefore, to kings throughout the ages rather than specifically to Philip and Mary. The fact, however, that there was a reigning king and queen suggests that the plural here was used to signify precisely that.

50 RBME, V-II-4, f. 456r: 'vestidos todos así todos juntos vinjero[n] co[n] sus magestades hasta Vsmester q[ue] es vna iglesia collegial donde ay deá[n] y canónigos y allí oyero[n] vna mysa del espíritu sancto y predicó el obispo Linconyense q[ue] es vn muy bue[n] perlado la meitad del sermó[n] fue en inglés y lo demás en latín. tomó por tema ego cogito cogitatumes pacis et non aflictionis q[ue] era el intrato d[e] la mysa de aq[ue]ll[borrón] domynica. en el qual sermó[n] entre otras cosas muy buenas que dixo fue q[ue] pues su mag[es]t[ad] del rey lleuaua vn cochillo delante de sí q[ue] lo sacase y comencase a degollar y castigar a los ereges y perturuadores de la paz y quietud de la república. y díxole co[n] muy buena osadía q[ue] las llaues de san pedro las restituyese al papa a quie[n] las auýa[n] tomado pues christo no se las avía dado de lo qual holgó mucho el rey aunq[ue] no todos los de las cortes'.

After Mass, they all moved to the houses of parliament, 'where the lord chancellor [Gardiner] spoke in the name of the king and conveyed everything that the king wished to convey'.[51] It is crucial to note that, as this source confirms, it was King Philip, not Queen Mary, who delivered the opening address to parliament, even if he did so through Gardiner as an interpreter.[52] Although the original manuscript of the speech seems not to have survived, it was fortunately recorded directly from Spanish state papers by Luis Cabrera de Córdoba (1559–1623) in his 1619 chronicle of the king's life and reign.[53] Philip opened by reminding his English subjects that their forbears had lived and died in the Catholic faith. The Catholic Church, he continued, contained the good and the bad, was made holy through faith and the sacraments, was consolidated through original and apostolic succession, was made one through the union of its members and was of perpetual duration, 'to be governed by him chosen by the Holy Spirit'; that is, the pope. The most pressing issue in the parliamentary agenda was, therefore, the union of the Church, which was to be achieved by professing obedience to her head, the Roman pontiff. Philip, through Gardiner, explained this in unmistakable terms:

> In [the pope] is to be found the maximum authority and the maximum power, as the worthiest of the children of the Church, all of whom are of one mind and constitute a monarchy in which he rules and the rest are Christian and Catholic subjects, even if they are kings, for these only excel in the manner that gold excels among the metals. This pontiff, the successor of St Peter, is truly the vicar of Jesus Christ on earth, [and the latter] lives and reigns in His eternal pontificate. There are not, however, two heads, even if there are two persons, because one is subordinate to the other, like the temporal viceroy is subordinate to his natural king and appointed to govern the kingdom in his absence.[54]

This was a frontal attack against the royal supremacy, which was still, legally, the form of Church headship in England. In this vigorous rejection of the

51 RBME, MS V-II-4, f. 456r: 'oýda su mjsa se fuiro[n] todos juntos a la casa del parlamento donde el gra[n] chançiller habló por el rey todo lo q[ue] su mag[es]t[ad] fue servydo q[ue] les dixese y así aq[ue]l día no vinyero[n] del p[ar]lame[n]to los reyes porq[ue] comyero[n] allá'.

52 It is unclear from the sources whether Philip delivered his speech in Latin first and was then followed by Gardiner in English or whether, like he had done before in Flanders, he said a few words in Latin and then gave the floor to Gardiner on his behalf.

53 Luis Cabrera de Córdoba, *Filipe Segvndo rey de España* (Madrid: Luis Sánchez, 1619), 25–6. See the Appendix at the end for a full transcription and translation of Philip's address to parliament.

54 Cabrera de Córdoba, *Filipe Segvndo*, 25.

powers that Henry VIII had ascribed to the kings of England, King Philip was not only clarifying the pope's position as spiritual head of Christendom as Christ's vicar, but he was also unquestionably including himself and all other monarchs under the pope's spiritual jurisdiction. The king further explained that 'temporal government is not apt for divine matters'. Indeed, it was the upholding of the divine cult and of the 'celestial precepts' that made kings partakers in virtue. The 'being and power of a king' could only partake in the 'being and power of God' by imploring God's favour and obeying 'the vicar of Jesus Christ, the Roman pontiff'. 'The ends of a kingdom's authority and of the office of a king', Philip continued, 'are not solely majesty, riches and dominion, but rather God and His holy Law, and the fulfilment of its precepts, dying for them if necessary'.[55] In order to fulfil God's Law, the Old Testament determined that it should be in the hands of the king, so that he would be the 'fortress and sword of the Church, valiantly repressing the audacity of evildoers, protecting that which is established, restoring peace and rejecting that which is disruptive'.[56] Henry VIII had been obedient to the Roman pontiff and had written against the heretics, his enemies, but through bad counsel and his own sins he became an apostate ('Oh, great misfortune!'), which brought about the 'disdain for and changes in religion which perverted public affairs'. God, in His mercy, now called them to 'return to the flock of Jesus Christ' by repealing all laws against Rome passed under Henry VIII and Edward VI and by accepting Cardinal Pole into the kingdom. The king concluded:

> From your complete surrender, I will receive more happiness, greatness, and contentment than from being, as your lord in such a powerful kingdom together with the queen, my lady and aunt, your supreme head; and I would consider my coming a fortunate event, in such a time of need, if I were to be an instrument to your mending and salvation.[57]

This extraordinary document, in which the king describes himself as an instrument of the salvation of the English, shows Philip taking his role as king-in-parliament very seriously. His vigorous rejection of the royal supremacy to which, by law, he was entitled, set the tone for the rest of the parliamentary sessions, and heralded the symbolic, intellectual, and legal dismantling of the supreme headship of the Church in England and its restoration to the pope. Parliament swiftly repealed Pole's attainder and granted him some of the rents that his mother, the countess of Salisbury, had enjoyed. That day, 'the

55 Cabrera de Córdoba, *Filipe Segvndo*, 26.
56 Cabrera de Córdoba, *Filipe Segvndo*, 26.
57 Cabrera de Córdoba, *Filipe Segvndo*, 26.

king left [parliament] very pleased'.[58] Pole had already landed in England and was making his way to the capital.

The cardinal finally reached London on 24 November and, revealingly, went to visit Philip at Whitehall first. The king was in the middle of lunch, but he left the table hurriedly and went to receive the cardinal. The deference shown by the king to the cardinal-legate 'marvelled' the English gentlemen and prompted William Howard, the lord admiral, to 'mumble' indignantly that the kings of England had never shown such courtesy to their vassals, a comment which elicited Philip's famous icy countenance when displeased, at which point 'the admiral understood that the king was angry'.[59] The anecdote does not only reflect Philip's centrality in the reconciliation with Rome, but it also suggests that his understanding of the English language was not as poor as it has traditionally been assumed. The cardinal took his hat off and Philip corresponded by removing his bonnet and, in a cheerful manner, they proceeded to visit Mary in her ante-chamber, where she knelt before Pole and asked for his hand to kiss, which he refused. The royal couple and their cousin then moved on to the queen's privy rooms 'in good cheer'.[60]

---

58 RBME, MS V-II-4, f. 456r: 'otro día después q[ue] ya el cardenal auja entrado en el reyno tornaro[n] los reyes a parlame[n]to para q[ue] quitase[n] vna ley q[ue] en t[iem]po del rey errique su padre d[e]la reyna se avja hecho contra el cardenal qua[n]do avja salido huyendo en q[ue] dauan licençia a qualquiera del reyno q[ue] lo podiese matar sin pena y lo auja declarado por traydor y co[n]fiscado y tomado su renta veinte y tantos años avía. el parlame[n]to quitó aq[ue]lla ley y declararo[n] no aver sido traydor sino aver hecho como muy bue[n] cauallero y cristiano en lo q[ue] hizo y ma[n]daron restitujrle dos mill ducados de renta de iglesia que él tenja qua[n]do fue huyendo y q[ue] le restituyesen a su casa vn estado de co[n]de q[ue] le auýa[n] quitado el rey enrriq[ue] qua[n]do degolló a su madre del cardenal porq[ue] no co[n]sentía en su opinjó[n] y así se le ma[n]dó ristituir co[n] todos sus frutos y re[n]tas de lo q[ua]l salió el rey muy co[n]tento por auerse hecho también'.

59 RBME, MS V-II-4, f. 456r: 'siete días después de auer comencado el parlame[n]to llegó aquí el cardenal y vino por el agua hasta la casa d[e]l rey. y estando comyendo el rey supo q[ue] llegaua y a media comyda se leva[n]tó con gran priesa y le salió a resçebir hasta la puerta trasera de su casa que sale a donde desembarcaua el cardenal d[e]lo qual se marauyllaro[n] mucho los caualleros ingleses y aun el almyra[n]te deste reyno yua murmura[n]do porq[ue]l rey le hazía tanta cortesía y fauor y dezía q[ue] los reyes desta tierra no acostu[m]braua[n] a hazer aq[ue]llo co[n] sus vasallos. pero n[uest]ro rey como sintió lo q[ue] dezía le myró co[n] vn rostro muy ayrado de manera q[ue] ente[n]dio el amjrante q[ue] el rey estaua enojado'.

60 RBME, MS V-II-4, f. 456r: 'Luego como se viero[n] quitando su gorra y bonete se saludaro[n] muy graciosame[n]te. y el rey se rogaua co[n] el cardenal sobre la mano derecha pero el cardenal no la quiso. y reyé[n]dose fueron anbos muy gra[n] rato desbonetados. La reyna le salió a resçebir hasta la sala de presençia que es dos salas antes de su aposento y muy regozijada hincadas las rodillas le pidió la mano como a legado del papa

Three days later, on the 27th, Philip took a barge up the Thames to visit Pole at Lambeth without Mary and it was believed that he purposely visited Pole himself, rather than wait for the cardinal to visit him, to emphasise the respect that ought to be paid to the legate as a representative of the papacy. Pole was not a mere vassal of the English crown and it was imperative that the English understood this to be the case. As the anonymous Spanish commentator observed, the stratagem worked, as 'from then onwards, both Catholics and non-Catholics went to visit [Pole]'.[61] In the afternoon of the same day there were public celebrations and a *juego de cañas* during which Philip was cheerfully acclaimed by the populace, as recorded by an unknown Italian source.[62] The following day, Monday, 28 November, according to the same source, Pole 'privately' visited Philip's chambers 'to commence the negotiations appertaining to his legation', but before he reached Philip's rooms, the king came out to meet him with letters from the pope confirming the amendment of the faculties regarding ecclesiastical property, which he had just received.[63] On the 29th, it was Philip who paid a visit to Pole in his chambers,

> where they remained together for a good while, discussing, and negotiating the business of the subduing [of the English], in which discussion his Majesty displayed a truly religious disposition and a most inclined and firm intention to conclude successfully that which was being discussed and hoped.

---

aunq[ue] él no se la dio. y así muy regozijados se entraro[n] los tres al aposento de la reyna d[e]lo qual quedaro[n] todos los ingleses muy admyrados. pero no sin mysterio se le hizo aq[ue]l fauor para que los de más viendo lo q[ue] los reyes hazía[n] aprendiese[n] a serujr y honrrar al cardenal y a las cosas d[e]l papa'. Pole wrote to Cardinal Innocenzo Ciocchi del Monte on to recount his meeting with Philip and Mary. See CRP, 2, 363–4.

61 RBME, MS V-II-4, f. 456^r: 'Dende a tres días fue el rey en vn barco por agua a su posada del cardenal y créese q[ue] lo hizo para q[ue] los demás come[n]case[n] a entender la dignidad que era ser legado del papa y q[ue] quie[n] a su legado hazía aq[ue]llo mejor lo haría con el papa q[ue] lo e[n]biaua ha parescido esto muy bie[n] a todos los católicos y de aý adelante católicos y no católicos le fuero[n] a visetar'.

62 AAV, Fondo Carpegna, 202, 'Il felicissimo ritorno del regno d'Inghilterra alla cattolica vnione, e all'obedienza della Sede Apost[oli]ca', f. 120^r.

63 AAV, Fondo Carpegna, 202, ff. 120^r–v: 'Il Lunedì [Monday, 28 November 1554] seguente il Legato andò priuatamente alla Maestà dei Rè per cominciare a negotiare circa il bisogno della sua Legatione, e appressandosi alla Camera del Rè, [f. 120v] S[ua] M[aes]tà gli uenne incontro con un piego di lettere in mano, poco prima portato da un Corriero uenuto di Roma dalla santità di N[ost]ro Signore con l'ampliatione delle facoltà del Legato mandato da Sua B[eatitudi]ne et egli disse uegga V[ostra] S[erenità] R[everendissi]ma quanto Iddio fauorisca questo santo negotio, che ha fatto venire così in tempo questo spaccio, che tanto si desideraua, e poi per la medesima via se ne ritornò alla sua stanza [...]'.

When Pole handed him the papal brief, 'his Majesty showed much respect to the queen, stating that he would not open it, because it was addressed to her as well as to him'.[64] The gesture again points out that Philip and Mary understood their reign to be a co-monarchy, modelled after that of their ancestors, Ferdinand and Isabel, but the documents here explored clearly show that it was Philip who had negotiated the cardinal's return and parliament's acquiescence and that it was he who was negotiating with Pole the main item of his legatine mission. On 28 November, parliament agreed to repeal the Henrician legislation, and it became clear that the kingdom was to give its obedience to Rome. Out of 440 votes, only two had not been in favour of the reconciliation, 'one by abstaining and another one by alleging that he had scruples over the oath he had previously sworn to the contrary; that is, that he would never be under the obedience of the pope'. They were soon convinced to give in.[65]

On 30 November, St Andrew's day, Pole came to Westminster and presented his legatine powers. The king and queen knelt and, in the name of the kingdom, asked for absolution, which Pole granted. The legate then asked Philip for permission to address parliament in English and proceeded to deliver an address to the prelates, nobles and MPs gathered there. Thanking them for the reversal of his attainder, he then reminded them of the glorious past of England as one of the Church's most noble daughters, so successfully converted in times of Pope Gregory the Great (r. 590–604). This nobility and greatness were lost when a king repudiated his wife out of lust for Anne Boleyn, an 'evil woman' who had lain with her own brother. The whole kingdom then decided to follow the king in his path to perdition. However, God had shown his mercy by preserving a woman, who despite being 'considered the weaker sex', had turned out to be, in fact, the 'sole candle' of the faith. In her quest she was aided by the two greatest powers. One was Philip, the emperor's son, who came to England to rebuild, as a new King David. He came unarmed, a 'man of peace and sincerity' and the harbinger of 'temporal peace'. The other power was Pole himself,

64 AAV, Fondo Carpegna, 202, f. 121r: 'Dopo desinare venne il Rè anch'egli a Visitare priuatam[en]te il Legato alla stanza sua, doue stettero insieme vn buon spatio, ragionando, e trattando il negotio della ridutione, nel qual ragionamento Sua Maestà mostrò veramente vn animo religioso, e un proposito inclinatissimo, e fermo a condurre a buon porto quanto si desideraua, e trattaua. E dandoli il Legato il Breue della Santità del Papa S[ua] Maestà mostrò uerso la Regina questo rispetto, che non volse aprire; perciò che era indrizzato a lei insieme con lui, partendosi il Rè, il Legato l'accompagnò infino alla barca, facendo S[ua] M[aes]tà molte volte resistenza, che non passasse più oltre, e dicend[o]li nel montare in barca, che tornarebbe altre volte a visitarlo'.

65 AAV, Fondo Carpegna, 202, f. 123r: '[...] l'uno tacendo, e l'altro dicendo hauer scrupolo del giuram[en]to altra volta preso in contrario di non esser mai sotto l'obedienza del Papa [...]'.

representing the pope, who brought 'spiritual peace'. He had come not to menace, but to show love and to act 'like a good shepherd and a gracious father' to restore the English to their 'ancient spiritual nobility'. But, before he could do that, they had to return to God.[66] Following the delivery of his speech, Pole proceeded to absolve the prelates, nobles and MPs and, with them, the entire kingdom, 'which truly was a great display of devotion to have witnessed, for many of them had flows of tears running down their faces, remembering the evil state in which they had been and thanking God for the mercy He had presently granted them'.[67]

Pole wrote to Pope Julius immediately after the emotional ceremony, to commend Philip and Mary's piety and to praise their marriage as the consolation of the human race.[68] Philip also wrote to the pope on the same day, and recounted the news in exultating terms:

> Our Lord has been pleased to allow [...] that today, St Andrew's day, in the afternoon, the whole kingdom, with unanimous agreement from those who represent it (who displayed great repentance for the past and showed much happiness for that which they were about to do) have given their obedience to your Holiness and to that Holy See and through the queen's intercession and mine, the legate has absolved them. [...] I will not say much else, but only that the queen and I, like true and devout children of your Holiness, have received the greatest contentment that one can express in words, knowing that not only does this redound in the service of our Lord but, also, that a kingdom such as this one has returned, in the time of your Holiness, to the union of His holy and universal Church [...]. I hope in Him, that your Holiness will know that that Holy See has never

66 A summary and comparison of the different versions of the speech and its many drafts can be found in Correspondence Pole, vol. 2, 368–9. A narrated version of the speech in Spanish which was not recorded by Mayer can be found in RBME, MS V-II-4, f. 456^{r}, where can be found the reference to Anne Boleyn: 'díxoles q[ue] myrasen como avía degollado a Ana bolén por cuyos amores auja dexado a su verdadera muger la reyna doña catalina madre de n[uest]ra reyna y se avía casado con ella la qual como mala se echaua co[n] su herma[n]o por lo q[ua]l los co[n]denó a ellos y a todos los q[ue] entendía[n] y sabía[n] aq[ue]llo y no lo avía[n] avi[sado?] a q[ue] los degollasen en pública plaça y así se hizo'. Owing to a letter written by Pole on 27 November, it has been assumed that the oration took place on the 28th, but the account in El Escorial leaves no doubt that it took place on the day of the reconciliation.

67 RBME, MS V-II-R, f. 456^{r}: 'y cierto ver esto fue cosa de gra[n] deuoción porq[ue] a muchos les corría[n] las lágrimas de hilo en hilo por el rostro acordándose del mal estado en q[ue] auýa[n] estado dando gracias a dios por la merçed q[ue] al pr[esen]te les auja hecho'.

68 Correspondence Pole, vol. 2, 369–74.

> had a more obedient son than I, nor one more desirous to preserve and increase her authority.[69]

London erupted in celebrations and *Te Deum* Masses, and St Andrew's day was consecrated as a holiday.[70] Spaniards in England and abroad rejoiced at the developments in the country and wrote reports charged with optimism for the religious future of the kingdom. Gonzalo Pérez, Philip's chief secretary, wrote on 1 December that it was the 'most admirable event' that had been heard of for many years, and he added that 'the people are happier [...] than it would have been thought'; in this, God had 'shown His power'.[71] Five days later, Pérez enthusiastically explained that for the first time since the feast had been abolished, St Paul's Cathedral had celebrated St Nicholas's day following the tradition of the Boy Bishop, a feast that had been carried out with much 'pomp, banqueting and celebrating both among the clerics and the lay people'.[72] It

69 AAV, Fondo Carpegna, 202, ff. 130r–v; King Philip to Pope Julius III, London, 30 November 1554: 'E stato seruito N[ost]ro Signore / alla cui bontà sola si deue attribuire, e a V[ostra] S[anti]tà che ha tenuta tanta cura di guadagnar queste anime / che hoggi il giorno di Sant'Andrea su'l tardi tutto questo Regno vnanimi, e conformi quelli che lo rappresentano, e con gran pentimento del passato, e contentamento di quello che ueniuano per fare, han data l'obedienza a V[ostra] S[anti]tà, e a cotesta S[an]ta Sede, e a intercessione della Regina, e mia, il Legato li ha'assoluti. [...] io non dirò altro, se non che la Regina, e io come tanti veri, e deuoti figli di V[ostra] S[anti]tà hauemo riceuuto il maggior contentamento, che si potess'esprimere con parole, conoscendo che oltre al concorrere in questo il seruitio di Nostro Signore torna nel tempo di V[ostra] S[anti]tà a mettersi nel gremio della Sua Santa, e vniuersal Chiesa un Regno, come questo, e similmente non mi satio di [f. 130v] render le gratie per quello, che hoggi si è fatto. E spero in Lui, che la Santità Vostra conoscerà sempre che cotesta Santa Sede non ha hauuto figliolo più obediente che io, ne più desideroso di conseruare, e augumentare la sua autorità'.

70 Eamon Duffy, 'Cardinal Pole Preaching: St Andrew's Day, 1557' in Eamon Duffy and David Loades, eds., *The Church of Mary Tudor* (Aldershot: Ashgate, 2006), 176–200.

71 RBPRM, MS II-2286-E, fol. 265r; Gonzalo Pérez to Antoine Perrenot de Granvelle, bishop of Arras, London, 1 December 1554: 'Anoche quando se despachó el correo a su Mag[esta]d: con la buena nueua de la obedie[n]cia q[ue] ha dado este reyno a su S[antida]d y a la Santa iglesia romana no tuue lugar de scriuir a V[uestra] S[erenidad] R[everendísi]ma como quisiera y era razó[n] agora [...] me he querido alegrar con v[uestra] s[erenida]d del buen successo deste negocio que ha sido el más admirable q[ue] nun[n]ca se ha oýdo y el aucto más de ver q[ue] en muchos años se ha visto sea dios Loado por ello / creo tal se ha de hazer mañana en Londres en la yglesia mayor y sola vna cosa quiero añadir a lo q[ue] se ha scripto q[ue] los del pueblo está[n] más contentos y mejor de lo q[ue] se pensaua que es cosa en q[ue] dios ha mostrado su poder / él sea alabado por ello [...]'. On the propaganda efforts to publicise the reconciliation with Rome in England and abroad see Corinna Streckfuss, 'England's Reconciliation with Rome: A News Event in Early Modern Europe'. *Historical Research*, 82, no. 215 (2009), 62–73.

72 This was a medieval tradition that involved the election, on 6 December, St Nicholas day, of a boy from among the choristers or altar boys of a cathedral to serve as bishop until the

was obvious, he concluded, that this had been God's work, emphasising 'how bloodlessly this kingdom has been subdued'.[73] Ten days later he also reported positive developments since the reconciliation, pointing out again that it had been God's work.[74] When he heard the news, Pedro Pacheco, cardinal-bishop of Sigüenza and viceroy of Naples, sang the praises of the reconciliation in a most effusive manner, stating,

> I, for one, have never read about anything of the sort at least since the times of Constantine. To see a kingdom as big, powerful, and even indomitable as that of England, subdued in the manner in which it has been subdued – with no resort to force of arms or the convening of a general council! [...] I have pondered that a king to gain a kingdom by force has been done many times before and it is well-thought of, but to win a kingdom for God *a seculo non est auditum* [...]. Who would have said a year ago, that the prince of Spain was to become king of England? For it was possible but plagued by difficulties. But if someone had said that [the kingdom] would have been subdued to the obedience of the Church, and in such a manner, it would have been taken for a frivolity. Anyway, for everything we ought to be thankful to God *quia sic visitavit plebem suam*.[75]

day of the Holy Innocents (28 December). It involved feasts and celebrations and was very popular across Europe. It is still celebrated in many cathedral cities in Catholic countries to this day. In England it had been abolished by Henry VIII in 1542. Restored by Mary in 1554, it would be abolished again by Elizabeth I after the renewed break with Rome in 1559. On Henry's abolition of the tradition see Peter Marshall, *Heretics and Believers: A History of the English Reformation* (New Haven and London: Yale University Press, 2017), 284.

73 RBPRM, MS II-2286-E, fol. 265r; Pérez to Arras, London, 6 December 1554: '[...] las cosas d[e]la religió[n] después q[ue] se dio la obediencia al papa va[n] muy bien y siempre en crescimyento y ayer se hizo vna cosa en la yglesia de Londres que no se ha visto ha muchos años y fue vn obispillo de Sanct Nicolás q[ue] hizieron y le truxero[n] co[n] mucha pompa y huuo vanquetes y mucha fiesta así entre los de la yglesia como entre los legos sea dios alabado por todos que bie[n] [aresce q[ue] ha sido esta obra de su mano pues tan sin sangre se ha reduzido este rey[n]o'.

74 RBPRM, MS II-2286-E, fol. 297r; Pérez to Arras, London, 16 December 1554: 'Razón tiene V[uestra] s[erenidad] de estar tan contento como lo muestra del buen successo q[ue] ha tenido lo de la redución de los deste Rey[n]o porque cierto se ha hecho harto más cumplidamente q[ue] se pudiera humaname[n]te dezir ni dessear, bien se conosce lo mucho q[ue] en ello ha querido obrar n[uest]ro s[eño]r como se deuía sperar siendo suya la causa / la cosa va de bien en mejor cada día y se assentará como conuenga / q[ue] el zelo destos bien auenturados Reyes es tal que no se desuelan en otra cosa [...]'.

75 RBPRM, MS II-2286-E, fols 327v–328v; Pedro Pacheco Ladrón de Guevara, cardinal-bishop of Sigüenza to Arras, Naples, 22 December 1554: 'Yo no sé por dónde me començasse encareçer esta Reduçión de Ingalat[e]rra a la obediencia de la igl[es]ia y creo q[ue] su

As the words of Philip, the cardinal-bishop of Sigüenza and others make clear, the episode was conceived as a 'subduing' of the kingdom and, therefore, literally understood as a spiritual conquest. One that, thankfully, had been achieved bloodlessly. The return to Rome had been brought about by God's grace and mercy, the pope's patience, and Philip and Mary's piety. England was once again part of Christendom and her peaceful path to obedience was a miraculous deliverance from heresy and sin. Spain itself exploded in processions and thankful prayers to mark and celebrate the event, which were still being offered to God as late as February 1555.[76] The reconciliation was, however, only the first step towards full reintegration with Catholic Christianity but to aid in the process of religious revitalisation Philip had brought a team of experienced Spanish prelates and theologians who, in collaboration with their English counterparts, were expected to bring intellectual lustre and religious discipline to the reconstructed English Church. It is to them that we must now turn our attention.

---

mag[esta]d çes[áre]a y la mag[esta]d del Rey se pueden tener por los más bienauenturados hombres q[ue] ha hauido grandes tiempos ver en su tiempo y guiada por su mano vna cosa la mayor q[ue] aora podía acaecer, a lo menos yo de Constantino acá no he leýdo cosa semejante que vn Reino tan grande como el de Ingalat[e]rra y tan potente y aun indómito velle reduzido de la manera q[ue] se a reduzido sin fuerca de armas y sin hauerse juntado conçilio g[e]n[er]al que se aya reduzido desta manera. no podemos decir sino que es mutatio dextere exçelsi. yo para mí consideraua vna cosa, que ganar vn Rey por fuerça otro reino muchas vezes se a hecho y en mucho se tiene. pero ganar vn reino para dios a seculo non est auditum, en fin la obra toda es de dios, pero los ministros que en ello han entendido en este mundo lo sentirán bien. y en el otro mucho mejor. en fin la co[n]stançia y la paçiençia y la fee de la reina algo hauían de poder con dios. y dios paga muy differentemente q[ue] pagan los hombres del mundo. quién dixera aora ha vn año q[ue] el Prín[cip]e despaña auía de [ser] Rey de Ingalat[e]rra y aunque era cosa hazedera pero tenía en sí hartas difficultades. Pero quien dixera q[ue] hauía de estar reduzido a la obedien[ci]a de la igl[es]ia y de la manera q[ue] se a hecho creo q[ue] se tuuieran por algo liuiano. en fin por todo sean dadas muchas gr[aci]as a n[uest]ro señor. quia sic uisitauit plebem suam'.

76 AGS, Estado leg. 809, fol. 36; King Philip to Princess Juana, London, 27 February 1555: '[…] yo sé bien el contentamiento que os avrá dado aver entendido el buen subçesso que en este reino tuuo lo de la religión, lo qual como en esotra carta digo va cada día de bien en mejor a dios gracias / y regraçioos mucho todo lo que çerca desto dezís / y el cuidado que tuuistes de mandar que aý se hiziesse tan solene proçessión / y de scriuir a las ciudades grandes y prelados del reino advirtiéndoles dello / e a los prelados e iglesias catedrales y provinciales de las órdenes que hiziessen hazer proçessiones y oraciones dando gracias a n[uest]ro señor por lo hecho / y porque le plega lleuarlo adelante / él lo tenga así por bien […]'.

4.3 Aiding in the Reconstruction of the Church: Spanish Theologians in England

The team of religious men that King Philip brought with him to England in July 1554 was composed of prelates, friars, chaplains, and theologians. Heading these was Philip's chief chaplain, Pedro de Castro Lemos (*c.*1506–1561), recently transferred as bishop from the see of Salamanca to that of Cuenca, an alumnus of Alcalá de Henares and former lecturer on St Thomas Aquinas there between 1540 and 1542.[77] Also in the Chapel Royal was Lupercio de Quiñones, chief almoner and sommelier of the oratory.[78] There were also twelve choir boys, four chaplain pages and two porters, and the Chapel Royal was rounded up with twelve chaplains: Cristóbal de Becerra, Melchor de Vozmediano (1514–1587), future bishop of Guadix, a doctor in Philosophy and Theology who had studied at the University of Paris and had been in Trent, where he delivered a speech on the sacraments in 1547; Friar Alonso de Hazaña, prior of Alcañiz of the Order of Calatrava and nine others whose names have not come down to us.[79]

Apart from Vozmediano, with the king also travelled a strong body of Spanish theologians. The best known of these is perhaps the Dominican Friar Bartolomé de Carranza (1503–1576), a native of Miranda de Arga, in Navarre, who brought with him two servants, Jorge Gómez and Friar Antonio de Utrilla, OP, who would faithfully defend him during his inquisitorial process. Carranza had received his education at the hands of his uncle, the humanist Sancho de Carranza, at Alcalá de Henares, and he had later transferred to the College of San Gregorio, in Valladolid. In San Gregorio he lectured on St Thomas's *Summa Theologiae* and on Scripture until, in 1545, Charles V ordered him to attend the Council of Trent, where he was praised for his sermons and interventions, particularly those touching upon Scripture, justification and the Eucharist.[80]

---

77 He was the son of an old Hispanic-Portuguese noble family, brother to the ambassadors of Spain and Portugal in Rome who we met in the preceding chapter. See Vicente Beltrán de Heredia, *Cartulario de la Universidad de Salamanca (1218–1600)*, vol. 4 (Salamanca: Universidad de Salamanca, 1972), 536.

78 Calvete de Estrella, *El felicíssimo viaie*, fol. 6v.

79 Muñoz, *Svmmaria y verdadera relación*, fol. 14v. Vozmediano intervened in Trent as an appointed theologian for Francisco de Navarra, bishop of Badajoz, on 25 January 1547, and in the following weeks, giving speeches on baptism, confirmation, and the Eucharist. See his trajectory at Trent and his career as bishop of Guadix in Constancio Gutiérrez, SJ, *Españoles en Trento* (Valladolid: Consejo Superior de Investigaciones Históricas/Instituto Jerónimo Zurita, 1951), 9, 804–15.

80 Outlines on Carranza's family, education and early career can be found in Marcelino Menéndez Pelayo, *Historia de los heterodoxos españoles*, vol. 2. [1882] (Madrid: Biblioteca

Between 1550 and 1551 he attended the famous Valladolid debates, where he contributed to the discussions on the rights of the native peoples of America led by Bartolomé de las Casas and Juan Ginés de Sepúlveda, lending his support to the former, who argued for a fair treatment of the Indians as fellow human beings.[81] Carranza was an inquisitorial agent, with a special permission to read heretical books and had been appointed regent of San Gregorio in 1553, a few months before Philip decided to take him to England as part of his team of theologians. With Carranza came his bright and promising disciple, Friar Juan de Villagarcía OP (*c*.1529–1564), a remarkable student who, although just twenty-five years old, had already held some lectureships in the College of San Gregorio.[82]

The Franciscan Alfonso de Castro (1495–1558), born in Zamora, had studied in Alcalá, and taught as professor of Law and Theology alongside the Franciscan Luis de Carvajal (*c*.1500–50) and the Dominican Francisco de Vitoria at the University of Salamanca. He was already a theologian of renown, whose two most famous works against heresy, *Adversus omnes haereses* (Paris, 1534) and *De iusta haereticorum punitione* (Salamanca, 1547), had already been through several editions. Like Carranza, he had attended Trent's two first sessions.[83] Others in Philip's theological entourage were the Franciscan Bernardo de Fresneda (1495–1577), Philip's confessor; Juan Salazar de Burgos (†1555), bishop of Lanciano in Naples, who had contributed to the drafting of the Tridentine decree on

---

de Autores Cristianos, 1967), 5–12; José Ignacio Tellechea Idígoras, *Fray Bartolomé Carranza de Miranda (Investigaciones históricas)* (Pamplona: Gobierno de Navarra/Departamento de Educación y Cultura, 2002), 463–76; John Edwards, 'Introduction: Carranza in England', in John Edwards and Ronald Truman, eds., *Reforming Catholicism in the England of Mary Tudor: The Achievement of Friar Bartolomé de Carranza* (Aldershot: Ashgate, 2005), 1–20; John Edwards, 'Fray Bartolomé Carranza's Blueprint for a Reformed Catholic Church in England', in Thomas F. Mayer, ed., *Reforming Reformation* (Farnham and Burlington: Ashgate, 2012), 141–60 in 142–44.

81 José Ignacio Tellechea Idígoras, 'Bartolomé de Las Casas y Bartolomé Carranza. Una página amistosa olvidada'. *Scriptorium victoriense*, 6, no. 1 (1959), 7–34.

82 Doris Moreno, '*Cadena de oro para atraer a los herejes*. Argumentos de persuasión y estrategias de supervivencia en fray Juan de Villagarcía, O. P., discípulo de fray Bartolomé de Carranza', *Hispania Sacra*, 65, no. 131 (2013), 29–71.

83 Little research has been done into Alfonso de Castro's life and legal, philosophical, and theological writings since the 1950s. Apparently, there was a biography published in the 1940s, which I have been unable to retrieve: Teodoro Olarte, *Alfonso de Castro (1495–1558). Su vida, su tiempo y sus ideas filosóficas jurídicas* (San José, Costa Rica, 1946). See a biographical sketch in Manuel Castro, OFM, 'Fray Alfonso de Castro, O. F. M. (1495–1558), consejero de Carlos V y de Felipe II'. *Salmanticensis*, 5, no. 2 (1958), 281–322. On the ways in which he used Scripture in his writings, especially in his juridical works, see Claudio Gancho, O. F. M., 'La Biblia en Alfonso de Castro, O. F. M.', *Salmanticensis*, vol. 5, no. 2 (1958), 323–49.

justification and died in London in September 1555; Dr Antonio Corrionero (1476–1570), a disciple of Domingo de Soto and Francisco de Vitoria at Salamanca who would end his days as bishop of Almería, proud of his experiences in England, as attested by his epitaph; Dr Bartolomé de Torres (1512–1568), an expert in Thomism who would throw himself into the reform of the diocese of Canarias as its bishop years later; and, finally, Dr Carlos de Motiloa, a familiar of the bishop of Cuenca for whom Carranza requested a permission to read heretical books soon after their arrival in England.[84]

A later incorporation was the Dominican Pedro de Soto (1493–1563). A native of Alcalá de Henares, Soto studied at the University of Salamanca, later becoming prior of Ocaña (twice) and of Talavera de la Reina.[85] Having become a Master of Theology at the same time as his famous coreligionist, Melchor Cano (1509–60), in 1541, Soto became Charles V's confessor in 1542 and accompanied the emperor through the Holy Roman Empire, where he became vicar general of the Order of Preachers.[86] In Germany, Soto fought heresy through his published writings, his preaching and personal encounters with Protestants in an effort to convert them. One such meeting was that in 1543 with the Spanish Protestant exile Francisco de Encinas (1518–52), known as Dryander, who sought Charles V's approval of his Spanish translation of the Bible. Soto advised him to desist, warning him of the danger that he was putting himself in due to his 'erroneous ideas'. Indeed, Dryander would be arrested shortly thereafter at Soto's instigation, although he would manage to flee to Wittenberg in 1545.[87] In 1546, the Dominican obtained a papal licence to imprison the Protestant archbishop of Cologne, Hermann von Wied (1477–1552), and even though Wied managed to escape, Soto encouraged the election of his orthodoxly Catholic successor, Adolf von Schauenburg (1511–56), with whom he would keep an

84 On the bishop of Lanciano see Gutiérrez, *Españoles en Trento*, 702–7. Corrionero's epitaph, commissioned by his nephew after his death in 1570, remembered his English sojourn among other accomplishments: '*ANGLICA QUE COMITE VIDERUNT REGNA PHILIPI*'. See Juan López Martín, *La Iglesia de Almería y sus obispos*, vol. II (Almería: Instituto de Estudios Almerienses, Caja Rural de Almería y Unicaja, 1999), 235–271. On Bartolomé de Torres's life see Enrique Llamas Martínez, OCD., *Bartolomé de Torres. Teólogo y obispo de Canarias* (Madrid: CSIC, 1979), 171–83; Carranza's petition for Motiloa's permission to read heretical books in CRP, 3, 39.

85 Venancio D. Carro, *El maestro fr. Pedro de Soto, O. P. (Confesor de Carlos V) y las controversias político-teológicas en el siglo XVI*, vol. 2 (Salamanca: Convento de Dominicos, 1950), 853–855.

86 Venancio D. Carro, *El maestro fr. Pedro de Soto, O. P. (Confesor de Carlos V) y las controversias político-teológicas en el siglo XVI*, vol. 2 (Salamanca: Convento de San Esteban, 1931), 9–10, 19–21, 24–5, 29–33.

87 Carro, *Pedro de Soto*, vol. 1, 115–120.

epistolary exchange for the rest of the latter's life.[88] In 1548, Soto contributed to the writing of the Interim decree during the Diet of Augsburg, where he championed the idea of waging war against the German Protestants if they could not be brought to conformity.[89] In the same year he moved to Dillingen an der Donau, where he established a fertile friendship with Otto Truchsess von Waldburg (1514–73), cardinal-bishop of Augsburg, with whom he co-founded the University of Dilingen, one of the future centres of Tridentine Reformation, where Soto lectured in Theology until his departure for England on 23 March 1555.[90]

As has been mentioned, Cardinal Pole strongly desired the presence of Soto, whom he had met in Dilingen in October 1553 whilst on his way to the Low Countries, and in January 1555 he requested from Truchsess his transfer to the University of Oxford.[91] After a stay in Flanders close to Charles, Soto arrived in Oxford in May 1555 and lectured there from his arrival. He was inscribed as Doctor of Divinity on 24 October 1555, at the same time as his fellow Dominican, Juan de Villagarcía.[92] Soto taught at Oxford for over a year, during which time he also participated in the English Synod convened by Pole, leaving England in the summer of 1556, and reaching Brussels by 2 September of that year.[93] In Spain by 1558, Soto was briefly accused of heresy during the upheaval following Carranza's arrest. The charges were soon dropped, and Pope Pius IV (r. 1559–1565) invited him to take part in the third and final phase of the Council of Trent. Despite Philip's attempts to prevent his departure due to his Carranzan sympathies, Soto defied royal orders and was able to contribute to the final sessions at Trent, where he died after a short illness in 1563, before the Council was officially concluded.

Despite the Spanish clerics' early misgivings due to attacks against some of them in the streets of London, it seems that they were openly active in their reforming activities in many ways. Due to Carranza's long and tortuous inquisitorial process after 1559, we have some glimpses of his involvement in

---

88 Carro, *Pedro de Soto*, vol. 1, 116–19.

89 Carro, *Pedro de Soto*, vol. 1, 127–31, 177–206.

90 Carro, *Pedro de Soto*, vol. 1, 36, 220–235.

91 On Pole's desire for Soto to aid in the re-Catholicisation of England see Correspondence Pole, vol. 3 22. For more examples and to follow the process whereby Soto moved to England see Edwards, *Archbishop Pole*, 181–2 and Carro, *Pedro de Soto*, I, 237–44.

92 Joseph Foster, ed., *Alumni Oxonienses: The Members of the University of Oxford, 1500–1714*, vol. 1 (Oxford: Parker and Co., 1891), 229. See also Carro, *Pedro de Soto*, I, 246–7.

93 CSP Venice, vol. 6, 589. An overview of Soto's and Villagarcía's activities at Oxford is given in Andrew Hegarty, 'Carranza and the English Universities', in Edwards and Truman, eds., *Reforming Catholicism*, 153–72; Claire Cross, 'The English Universities, 1553–8', in Duffy and Loades, eds., *Church of Mary*, 57–76.

the religious affairs of England, which makes his activity the most well-known out of all the Spaniards.[94] Alonso de Aguilar, a Spanish courtier, would later declare that Carranza had 'treated religious matters' whilst in England 'both within and without the pulpit' and that he had counselled the king 'to attend first to God's affairs through the punishment of heretics' that God would then attend to the king's.[95] Despite his master, the bishop of Cuenca's enmity towards Carranza, Dr Motiloa declared that the prelate 'had been fruitful in matters of faith [...] because he preached with great fervour and was very privy with the queen'.[96] Later on in his deposition, Motiloa reiterated the same belief, pointing out that,

> it was said that [Carranza] spent two or three hours almost daily with the king on their own. Besides this, this witness also heard more particularly that when the king left for Flanders, he had entrusted the kingdom to Cardinal Pole and to [...] Friar Bartolomé de Miranda.[97]

Carranza was heavily involved in the revival of the monasteries and in the English Synod. He preached several times, usually in front of the court, and he also organised two processions: the first one in Fulham at the request of Edmund Bonner, bishop of London, and the second one in Kingston upon

---

94 Tellechea Idígoras, *Carranza y Pole*, 25–76.

95 BAV, Vat. Lat. 13138, fol. 52r; Deposition of Alonso de Aguilar, Montilla, 8 November 1562 – Q. 64: 'dixo q[ue] sabe q[ue] el d[ic]ho arcob[is]po estubo en inglaterra aquel t[iem]po y trataua de las cosas de la Religión como allí dize y así en púlpito como fuera dél le parece q[ue] entendía q[ue] aconsejaua al Rey q[ue] hiziese primero los neg[oci]os de dios castigando los herejes q[ue] después dios haría los suyos y otra cosa particular dello no sabe'. Henceforth BAV.

96 BAV, Vat. Lat. 13138, fol. 87v; Deposition of Carlos de Motiloa, Cuenca, 21 November 1562 – Q. 42: 'Dixo que porq[ue] lo vio estando este t[estig]o en ynglaterra con el ob[is]po de Cuenca don pedro de castro y por q[ue] se yban a comer a casa del d[ic]ho ob[is]po muchas vezes el d[ic]ho Frai b[a]r[tolo]mé de myranda y Fresneda confesor y frai Alonso de castro y sus conpañeros y q[ue] le paresçe q[ue] hizo fructo [en] las cosas de la fee el d[ic]ho frai b[a]r[tolo]mé por que predicaua con mucho heruor y hera muy priuado de la rreyna [et] por esto piensa este t[estig]o que deviera de hazer mucho fruto'.

97 BAV, Vat. Lat. 13138, fol. 88r; Deposition of Carlos de Motiloa – Q. 43: '[...] para sí tiene q[ue] hizo mucho fruto y trauajó mucho [en] lo que toca a la rreligión porq[ue] dezían q[ue] Casi todos los días estaua con el rrey dos o tres oras solos y que después desto oyó dezir este testigo p[articu]larmente q[ue] partiéndose el rrey para flandes avía dexado encargado el rreyno al cardenal polo y al d[ic]ho Frai b[a]r[tolo]mé de myranda y q[ue] lo demás que tiene d[ic]ho q[ue] lo saue es porquestaua en ynglaterra con el d[ic]ho ob[is]po de Cuenca y lo vio'.

Thames.[98] The chaplain Cristóbal de Becerra was present at the Kingston procession and, according to the transcripts,

> the costs for this procession were covered by the said most reverend [Carranza] and by this witness. And [Becerra] saw many Englishmen who came to see the procession with haste and vehemence. And when the most reverend elevated the most Blessed Sacrament in his hands, he saw many Englishmen kneeling down, and crying, thanking God for all the goodness they had witnessed and asking for blessings for those who had been the cause of such goodness.[99]

Many other depositions bore witness to Carranza's involvement in the affairs of Church and state in England.[100] In a second set of interrogations, during which Carranza hoped to prove that his accusers' allegations were void due to their personal animosity towards him, we catch further glimpses of the life of the Spaniards in England. Carranza claimed that of his accusers, Philip's confessor, Fresneda, and the bishop of Cuenca, had engendered a particular dislike for his person due to their disagreement about the sale of *encomiendas* in the Indies, which Carranza disapproved of.[101] Motiloa explained that

---

98 José Ignacio Tellechea Idígoras, 'Fray Bartolomé Carranza: a Spanish Dominican in the England of Mary Tudor', in Edwards and Truman, *Reforming Catholicism*, 21–31; John Edwards, 'Corpus Christi at Kingston upon Thames: Bartolomé Carranza and the Eucharist in Marian England', in Edwards and Truman, *Reforming Catholicism*, 139–51.

99 BAV, Vat. Lat. 13138, fols 98v–99r; Deposition of Cristóbal de Becerra, Audiencia of the Holy Inquisition of Toledo, 14 November 1562 – Q. 56: 'A las çinq[uen]ta y seis preg[unt]as dixo q[ue] no se halló prese[n]te a la p[ri]mera proçessió[n] q[ue] [dice] la preg[unt]a mas de q[ue] vio q[ue] fuero[n] el d[ic]ho R[everendísi]mo y toda la Cap[ill]a del Rey [...] y q[ue] a la seg[un]da q[ue] se hizo [en] Londres se halló prese[n]te este t[estig]o y q[ue] la costa q[ue] se hizo [en] la d[ic]ha processió[n] fue a costa del R[everendísi]mo y deste t[estig]o e que vio muchos Ingleses q[ue] con gran priessa e furia viniero[n] a verla d[ic]ha p[ro]cessió[n] y eleuando el d[ic]ho R[everendísi]mo el sanct[ísi]mo sacra[men]to [en] las ma[n]os vio a muchos ingleses hincados de rrodillas llora[n]do dando gr[aci]as a dios por ver tanto bie[n] e bendiz[ien]do a los q[ue] ovieren sido causa de aq[ue]llo'.

100 For the questions relating to Carranza's activities to England see BAV, Vat. Lat. 13138, fols 6r–9v. A transcription of the same and of relevant answers can be found in Tellechea Idígoras, *Carranza y Pole*, 92–118.

101 The *encomienda* system, although stemming from late medieval Castilian experience, developed its own peculiarities in the New World. *Encomiendas* were a grant from the crown to a specific individual of a number of natives attached to a territory who would exchange their labour in return for instruction in the Christian faith and in the Spanish language as well as protection and the building and upkeeping of infrastructure. Among other things relating to the treatment of American natives which were hotly debated in the 1550s was the question of whether *encomiendas* could be granted in perpetuity or at

in a three-day long meeting in London chaired by Cuenca in 1554, there had been a quarrel between Carranza and Fresneda over the *encomiendas* and, although he could not confirm whether this meeting had been the spark of the animosity between the two, he claimed that Carranza and Fresneda had very little love for each other – 'even the stones were aware of this'.[102] Concerning Cuenca, Motiloa recounted that the latter was envious of Carranza's appointment as archbishop of Toledo in 1557 and he also blamed the Dominican for his early recall to Spain in late 1554. Motiloa remembered a conversation he allegedly had with Carranza during which the Navarrese showed astonishment at Cuenca's presence in England, as 'he would better be in his bishopric tending to his sheep', expressing the view that a way had to be found to make him leave.[103] The expression certainly rings true to what we know about

all. For the origins and development of the *encomienda* system see Esteban Mira Caballos, *Las Antillas Mayores, 1492–1550. Ensayos y documentos* (Madrid: Iberoamericana-Vervuert, 2000), 13–30. See also J. H. Elliott, *Empires of the Atlantic World: Britain and Spain in America, 1492–1830* (New Haven and London: Yale University Press, 2006), 39–41. For a focussed exploration of the subject see, for instance, the classic work by Silvio A. Zavala, *La encomienda indiana* (Madrid: Centro de Estudios Históricos, 1935); and, also, Robert Himmerich y Valencia, *The Encomenderos of New Spain, 1521–1555* (Austin: University of Texas Press, 1991); José de la Puente Brunke, *Encomienda y encomenderos en el Perú (estudio social y político de una institución colonial)* (Seville: Diputación Provincial de Sevilla, 1992).

102 BAV, Vat. Lat. 13138, fols 432^{r}–432^{v}; Deposition of Carlos de Motiloa, Cuenca, 21 November 1562 – Q. 1: '[…] desde bruselas enbió [Charles V] a Fran[cis]co de heraso su secretario a londres en Ingalat[e]rra y con él [en]bió vna çédula a Don pedro de castro ob[is]po de Cuenca q[ue] entonçes hera p[ar]a q[ue] presidiese [en] la disputa q[ue] se auja de hazer sobre si sería bien vender los yndios los questauan En encomyenda en perpetuidad o no. Se juntaron tres días a la disputa el d[ic]ho ob[is]po en su posada y el licen[cia]do menchaca el liçen[cia]do muñatones heraso frai bar[tolom]é de myranda frai alonso de castro fresneda confesor el dotor corrionero el dotor Vozmediano el dotor andrés pérez del consejo de inq[uisici]ón el primero día. el dotor arnedo y otros y q[ue] en toda la disputaçión que duró tres días como d[ic]ho tiene sienp[re] fueron de contrario paresçer frai b[a]r[tolo]mé de myranda y fresneda confesor y q[ue] lo demás q[ue] no lo saue s[i] [hu]bo enojo o si armaron Enemystad más de q[ue] no se querían vien [et] así lo entendían las piedras pero que no saue por qué [et] questo saue desta preg[un]ta'.

103 BAV, Vat. Lat. 13138, fols 433^{r-v}; Deposition of Carlos de Motiloa – Q. 13: '[…] saue q[ue]l d[ic]ho ob[is]po de Cuenca no le tenía buena voluntad Al d[ic]ho frai b[a]r[tolo]mé de myranda espeçialm[en]te después q[ue] le bio Arçob[is]po y este t[estig]o lo saue por q[ue]l d[ic]ho ob[is]po lo comunycó con él muchas vezes deziendo q[ue] le corría vn poco de pasión et ynbidia por uerlo arçob[is]po e tanbién por q[ue] tuuo entendido el d[ic]ho ob[is]po de Cuenca que frai b[a]r[tolo]mé de myranda fue Causa q[ue]l rrey con tan buena voluntad le diese licençia para q[ue] se benyese de yngalaterra por q[ue] tratando este testigo con el d[ic]ho frai b[a]r[tolo]mé de myranda en londres en […] su aposento el d[ic]ho frai b[a]r[tolo]mé de myranda le dixo qué haze aquí el ob[is]po mejor estaría en su ob[is]pado rregiendo sus obejas pues en verdad q[ue] hemos de hazer que se

Carranza's approach to episcopal residency and pastoral care.[104] Through the count of Feria's deposition we know that the Spanish did not only meet among themselves to discuss Spanish matters but they apparently met regularly with Cardinal Pole too, which is very significant and clarifies that the Spanish were seriously involved in English affairs.[105]

Most of the men surveyed in the preceding pages left England with Philip in September 1555, but others, namely Carranza, Soto and Villagarcía, stayed behind. Soto, as has been mentioned, left in September 1556 and during his stay, he had not only taught in Oxford, but he had also written a confutation against the German reformer Johannes Brenz, *Defensio catholicae fidei*, which he published in Antwerp in 1557. In the summer of the same year Carranza left after he was appointed as archbishop of Toledo, eager to fulfil his pastoral duties in the archdiocese. His letters to Villagarcía are full of praise for England and the friends he had made there. He remembered warmly not only Pole and his associates, Alvise Priuli and Donato Rullo, but also John Fuller, master of Jesus College, Cambridge and chancellor of Ely, where he had been involved in the suppression of heresy; John Rastell, who had graduated with an MA from Oxford in 1555 and who would flee to Louvain in 1560 to become a Jesuit in 1568; John Feckenham, chaplain and confessor to Mary and, from 1556, abbot of the revived Benedictine community of Westminster; William Peryn, theologian, prior of St Bartholomew's in Smithfield, author of the Loyolan-influenced *Spirituall exercyses and goostly meditacions* (1557), and successor of Carranza as vicar general of the Dominican Order in England; Nicholas Sanders, the famous theologian and future *bête noire* of the Elizabethan regime, and

---

baya y este t[estig]o se lo dixo al d[ic]ho ob[is]po et se yndinó mucho et conçibió grande enojo dello [...]'.

104 José Ignacio Tellechea Idígoras, 'El formulario de visita pastoral de fray Bartolomé de Carranza, Arzobispo de Toledo', *Anthologica Annua*, 4 (1946), 385–437; José Ignacio Tellechea Idígoras, *Bartolome Carranza, Arzobispo Prelado evangélico en la silla de Toledo (1557–1558): Discurso inaugural del año académico 1958–1959 en el Seminario de San Sebastián* (San Sebastián: Izarra, 1958).

105 BAV, Vat. Lat. 13138, fols 408^{r}–408^{v}; Deposition of Gómez Suárez de Figueroa, Count of Feria, Madrid, 19 October 1562 – Q. 1: Feria reported that many of the Spaniards in England were envious that the king listened more to Carranza than to the others and that Fresneda had been told that Carranza was a Judaizer. Then he added that, 'cada vez q[ue] yvan a Juntarse con el car[dena]l polo legado le hallaua [Feria found Carranza] allá antes q[ue] fuesen los demás le avía puesto sospecha del d[ic]ho ar[zobis]po y q[ue] el d[ic]ho fray ber[nard]o dezía lo del d[ic]ho q[ue] avía contra el d[ic]ho ar[zobis]po [that he was a Judaizer] a este t[estig]o para q[ue] este t[estig]o se refrenase y templase de la amistad y afiçión q[ue] tenía al d[ic]ho fray bar[tolom]é de miranda y esto sabe desta preg[un]ta'.

others.[106] In these letters Carranza discussed the future of the Dominican order in England, advised not to include lectures on Duns Scotus in Cambridge, for he considered the university not yet sufficiently purged, and sent over from Flanders a Spanish Dominican, Bernardo de Celada, to help Villagarcía at Oxford, later changing his mind and allocating him to the revived priory of St Bartholomew's, where he judged his stay would be more profitable.[107]

The single most important consequence of Carranza's sojourn in England was his authorship of a monumental catechism, the *Comentarios sobre el catechismo christiano* (Antwerp, 1558), commissioned to him by the English Synod of 1556 and anticipating that of the Council of Trent by a decade, which was to be written in Spanish and translated into English. There was no time for the translation, as Mary died shortly after the catechism's publication in 1558, but the creation of this work was of momentous importance. This was a catechism written in Spanish, published in Antwerp, and intended to be used in a re-Catholicised England. There could be no clearer statement of the universalist aspirations of Philip's monarchical project than this religious manual, which was intended to be used across his Monarchy. This, however, was not to be, as Carranza was accused of making heretical assertions in his catechism and arrested by the Inquisition in 1559. As a result, the archbishop of Toledo became entangled in a lengthy inquisitorial process that would eventually be transferred to Rome in 1567, as Carranza argued with relative success that his accusers had acted out of personal animosity. Although he was never officially deprived of his archbishopric, this most pastorally inclined of prelates never really had the chance to put in practice his innovative plans for pastoral care in his archdiocese. He would finally be exonerated in 1576, having been made to recant sixteen of the propositions present in the catechism. Carranza died a few weeks later, a broken man, in his seventies.[108] His catechism, however, did not fall into oblivion. Banned in Spain by the Inquisition but declared to be orthodox by the Council of Trent in 1563 – thanks, in part, to Pedro de Soto's efforts – it had a very strong influence on the Roman catechism published by Pope Pius v (r. 1566–1572) in 1566. This meant that, paradoxically, Catholic Spain would ban the Roman catechism until the eighteenth century whilst the

106 Tellechea Idígoras, *Carranza y Pole*, pp. 257–82. On Peryn see Wizeman, *Theology and Spirituality*, 210–7.

107 Tellechea Idígoras, *Carranza y Pole*, 258, 261–2, 265, 268, 270, 272.

108 The best studies of Carranza's life, work and inquisitorial process are still those by Tellechea. Apart from his *Carranza y Pole* and *Fray Bartolomé Carranza*, cited above, see his *El proceso romano del Arzobispo Carranza (1567–1576)* (Rome, 1988).

rest of the Catholic world indirectly enjoyed the fruits of Carranza's theology through his influence in such a fundamental Catholic work.[109]

Villagarcía remained in Oxford after Mary's death and did not relinquish his lectureship until the early spring of 1559, when the new break with Rome was effected in Parliament. Still, Villagarcía delayed his departure until June, when he arrived in Flanders and had an interview with Philip about the state of affairs in England. Arrested on 24 August, two days after Carranza was intercepted by the Inquisition in Torrelaguna, Villagarcía was transported to Spain, where he spent the next four years in the prisons of the Inquisition, accused of sharing heretical ideas with his friend and mentor. During his imprisonment, he wrote a treatise on how to attract heretics to the true faith which he was never to publish, as he died shortly after his exoneration, in March 1564.[110]

4.4 Conclusion

When Philip married Mary in July 1554, the English realm was ailing from years of religious conflict and policy changes. The Spaniards who accompanied Philip in his journey to England were impressed by the kingdom's religious material heritage but were appalled and concerned by the current state of affairs. Their impressions may have been coloured by their experience in London, where there were large pockets of Protestants, but what they witnessed nevertheless indicated that there was still some work to do to bring England back to the Catholic fold. Mary's regime had already started to re-establish some elements of Catholicism as soon as the queen had ascended the throne in July 1553: the Latin Mass was restored, some religious festivities were reinstated, images were rescued and returned to churches, etc. However, for full reintegration, the kingdom had to be reunited with Rome first.

The first hurdle to achieve this was to allow back into the country the queen's cousin, Cardinal Reginald Pole, Pope Julius III's legate, who had been attainted for treason by Henry VIII in the 1530s. The situation was exacerbated by the thorny question of ecclesiastical property in lay hands, which caused a high degree of anxiety among those who had acquired it during the dismantling of religious houses in the reign of Henry VIII. Even men known for their Catholic religiosity were determined to hold on to their newly acquired lands and assets. Pole was, therefore, made to wait in Flanders, in what was a shrewd political

109 On Spanish objections to the Roman catechism see Pedro Rodríguez, *El Catecismo Romano ante Felipe II y la Inquisición española* (Madrid: Rialp, 1998), 38–47.

110 Moreno, 'Cadena de oro', 30, 41–42.

manoeuvre engineered by Charles V and Philip, whilst the issue was resolved. From the correspondence surveyed in this chapter, it becomes apparent that it was Philip who negotiated Pole's return to England, a negotiation which is confirmed by English, Spanish, and Italian sources. Not only that, Pole also wrote directly to Philip's Spanish religious advisers in his quest to be allowed back in England, rather than to English prelates and theologians. Whether he did so because he thought the Spaniards closer to power or because he thought they were untainted by years of schism like the English, or both, is difficult to determine, but that he sought their intercession is remarkably revealing. Philip's objectives in becoming the main negotiator were twofold. First, his role solidified his position as king of England and Ireland with impeccable Catholic credentials and, second, his intervention sought to ensure that his English subjects retained their ecclesiastical property. This was an important point because it encouraged the English elite to view their interests tied with those of their king but, also, because it may be an indication that Philip may have envisaged an arrangement for the English Church similar to that enjoyed by the Spanish Church. Indeed, since the Alexandrine Bulls of 1493, the Spanish crown had enjoyed a *Patronato Real* (royal patronage), which allowed the kings of Spain extensive powers in ecclesiastical appointments, in the uses given to tenths and other religious taxes, and in the allocation of lands and revenue for evangelisation purposes.[111] It is impossible to know whether a similar arrangement with Rome was in Philip's mind when he brokered the agreement over ecclesiastical property, but he was definitely exerting his kingly patronage in religious matters. Despite the cardinal's reprimand that Philip, as king of England and Defender of the Faith, ought to restore the union with Rome immediately, the king insisted on ensuring his subjects' rights to Church assets first.

Philip's preeminent position in the reconciliation and in the government of England is evidenced again in his conduct once Pole arrived in the kingdom. The king was the one meeting with Pole to iron out the details of the reconciliation and it was he, and not Mary, who gave the opening address to parliament when it commenced on 12 November 1554. Philip's address was a frontal attack on the royal supremacy and a robust defence of the primacy of the pope, and it lay the foundations for the official reconciliation of the realm with Rome on 30 November and the full reestablishment of Catholic doctrine that ensued.

---

111 For the importance of the Patronato Real in Spain and Portugal and appraisals of its history see Antonio de Bethéncourt Massieu, 'El Real Patronato', *Anuario de Estudios Atlánticos*, 1, no. 48 (2002), 155–214; Paulina Numhauser, 'El Real Patronato en Indias y la Compañía de Jesús durante el período filipino (1580–1640). Un análisis inicial', *Boletín Americanista*, 67 (2013), 85–103.

The king's behaviour and actions throughout the entire process amply confirm his later claims in 1561 and 1570, surveyed in the introduction, that he had been the main instrument in the revitalisation of Catholicism in England.

To enable this process, the king brought to England several Spanish theologians. Besides the members of his royal chapel, which always accompanied Philip wherever he went, the king also purposely chose some of the top thinkers that Spanish universities had to offer. Men such as Bartolomé de Carranza, Alfonso de Castro, Pedro de Soto, and Juan de Villagarcía were to be, in one way or another, active in religious activity in England. Whether organising religious processions, being involved in visitations, teaching at Oxford, or writing about the identification and punishment of heresy, these men were picked to be integral parts of the reestablishment of Catholicism in England. That they met regularly with Cardinal Pole, as the records of Carranza's future inquisitorial process show, only evidences their centrality in the monarchical project of Philip and Mary. This centrality raises the question of the sort of theology that they brought to England and how it fit with English theological approaches. To understand their role and the theology that these men fostered and developed and how it helped in the reintegration of England into the universality claimed by the Catholic faith it is to their writings and those of their English counterparts that we must now turn our attention.

CHAPTER 5

A Communion of the Faithful: Anglo-Spanish Theological Concerns

The weeks and months following Mary's accession in July 1553 saw the spontaneous resumption of the Latin Mass and the celebration of the Eucharist according to traditional Catholic rites in many parishes. In 1554, as we have seen, Cardinal Pole began to absolve the English prelates appointed by Mary (or re-confirmed if they had recanted their Protestantism) as part of his legatine mission. There followed, as we explored in the previous chapter, a period of intense negotiations between the cardinal and King Philip once he arrived in England which culminated in the reconciliation of the kingdom with Rome on 30 November 1554. These developments towards full doctrinal and institutional reintegration were joined with concerted efforts to restore the state of the Church to its pre-Henrician material outlook and vibrancy which began as soon as Mary came to the throne. New images were commissioned, and old ones were recovered. Roods and stone altars were re-erected, furnishings were renovated, and hundreds of candles once again lit the interior of churches and the faces and silhouettes of saints and virgins. In the process, the Marian regime was aided by some enthusiastic subjects, supporters of the old religion, who had hidden religious images and symbols during the iconoclasm of Edward VI's reign and now proudly displayed them again in their local churches.[1]

The full restoration of Church lands that Pole would have hoped for, however, never materialised. Philip and Mary ceded some of the lands acquired by the crown during the dissolution of the monasteries hoping to set an example for their subjects, but progress done in this respect by the time Mary died in November 1558 was negligible.[2] Although slow, there was more progress in the restoration of the religious orders in England, Wales and Ireland, especially after the prompt provided by Pope Paul IV in his bull *Præclara charissimi* of 21 June 1555.[3] The Observant Franciscan friary attached to Greenwich Palace, where Mary had been baptised in 1516, was restored even before Pole arrived

---

1 Eamon Duffy, *The Stripping of the Altars: Traditional Religion in England, 1400–1580* (New Haven and London: Yale University Press, 2005), 527–8.

2 D. M. Loades, *The Reign of Mary Tudor: Politics, Government, and Religion in England, 1553–1558* (London: Ernest Benn, 1979), 313–4.

3 Edwards, *Archbishop Pole*, 189.

 | DOI:10.1163/9789004536210_007

in England, and the community was welcomed in their new house on Palm Sunday 1555. An attempt was made to restore the Observant house of the London Greyfriars, off Newgate Street, which had been turned into Christ's Hospital under Edward. However, after a visitation by the Franciscan Alfonso de Castro and the Dominican Juan de Villagarcía, they were so impressed by the hospital and school that they advocated for the preservation of the new foundation.[4] Other attempts were more successful. In 1556, Westminster Abbey was restored as a Benedictine monastery, and John Feckenham, Mary's confessor and the man who had debated with and comforted Lady Jane Grey on her last days, was chosen as its abbot.[5] In 1557, a Franciscan friary was renewed in Southampton and, in the same year, Bartolomé de Carranza was involved in the restoration of two Dominican houses: the Blackfriars in Littlegate for males and a convent for Dominican nuns in an unknown location. By the end of the reign, Carranza had been involved in the reestablishment of four other Dominican houses: one in London and one in Oxford for males and one in King's Langley, Hertfordshire, and another one in Oxford for females. Also restored were the Carthusian house at Sheen, near Richmond Palace and the Bridgettine convent at Syon, near London. Great care was also taken to revive the Order of St John of Jerusalem – which included the restoration of their house of St John at Clerkenwell – a process in which Antonio de Toledo, the order's commander for the kingdom of León, was involved.[6] Although, famously, no formal invitation was extended to the Society of Jesus, a number of their fathers accompanied the count of Feria in his visit to England of March 1558. One of them, Pedro de Ribadeneyra (1527–1611), was present at Mary's deathbed and would later on recount his memories of the queen's death in his *Hystoria ecclesiástica del scisma* [...] *de Inglaterra* (1588), a negative history of the English Reformation and hagiography of English Catholic martyrs.[7] Although far from its former glory when Elizabeth I broke with Rome

4 Keith Duncan Brown, 'The Franciscan Observants in England, 1482–1559' (PhD thesis, University of Oxford, unpublished, 1986), 222–233.

5 C. S. Knighton, 'Westminster Abbey Restored', in Eamon Duffy and David Loades, eds., *The Church of Mary Tudor* (Aldershot: Ashgate, 2006), 77–123; J. F. Merritt, *The Social World of Early Modern Westminster: Abbey, Court and Community, 1525–1640* (Manchester: Manchester University Press, 2005), 54.

6 A superb overiview of the restoration of orders and monastic houses in England is provided in Edwards, *Archbishop Pole*, 189–201.

7 Ribadeneyra's work was based on Nicholas Sanders' *De origine ac progressu schismatis Anglicani* (1585) but included a great deal of his own original material. For him Mary had been the epitome of a good Christian ruler and he dispelled the rumours that she had died from poison. See Pedro de Ribadeneyra, SJ, *Hystoria ecclesiástica del scisma del Reyno de Inglaterra. En la qual se trata*[*n*] *las cosas más notables q*[*ue*] *han sucedido en aquel Reyno*

in the spring of 1559, there had been good progress in the restoration of English monasticism.

More swift and resoundingly successful was the reconstruction of Catholic theology and learning at the English universities. To this success contributed the fact that Protestantism had not managed to take deep roots at Oxford under Peter Martyr Vermigli (1499–1562), who found his students recalcitrant. Even at Cambridge, where Martin Bucer (1491–1551) had been more popular than his Italian colleague at Oxford, the German theologian still complained that many of his students suspected him and other new lecturers of heresy. Once Mary came to the throne, the programme of reform of the universities commenced right from the offset. Sir John Mason, chancellor of Oxford, was happy with the changes and was therefore allowed to continue in post and, at Cambridge, the chancellorship was taken away from the duke of Northumberland and restored to Stephen Gardiner, who had been deprived of it by the duke of Somerset in 1547. At Cambridge, Gardiner was enthusiastic about the university's return to orthodoxy, and he also contributed to the reform of Oxford as visitor. There, although he found New College and Corpus Christi College generally safe from heresy, he thought it fit to purge Magdalen College through several expulsions in 1553 and 1554. A few heads of houses had to be replaced at Oxford, and most at Cambridge, but the regime otherwise found fertile ground for the re-Catholisation of the universities.[8]

Spanish theologians were equally eager to contribute to the revitalisation of Catholicism in the English universities. Pedro de Soto, as has been mentioned, arrived at Oxford in May 1555 and would remain there until August 1556. He immediately observed that Oxford was in need of solid scholastic theology and proposed a course on the Sentences of Peter Lombard, for which he put

---

toca[n]tes a nuestra sancta Religión, desde que començó hasta la muerte de la Reyna de Escocia (Lisbon: Antonio Alvares, 1588), ff. 134^r–157^v.

8 The best assessments of Oxford and Cambridge under Philip and Mary are to be found in Elizabeth Russell, 'Marian Oxford and the Counter-Reformation' in Caroline M. Barron and Christopher Harper-Bill, eds., *The Church in pre-Reformation Society: Essays in Honour of F. R. H. Du Boulay* (Woodbridge: The Boydell Press, 1985), 212–7; James McConica, 'The Catholic Experience in Tudor Oxford', in Thomas M. McCoog, ed., *The Reckoned Expense: Edmund Campion and the Early English Jesuits* (Woodbridge: Boydell, 1996), 39–63; Andrew Hegarty, 'Carranza and the English Universities', in John Edwards and Ronald Truman, eds., *Reforming Catholicism in the England of Mary Tudor: The Achievement of Friar Bartolomé de Carranza* (Aldershot: Ashgate, 2005), 153–72; Claire Cross, 'The English Universities, 1553–1558', in Eamon Duffy and David Loades, eds., *The Church of Mary Tudor* (Aldesrhot: Ashgate, 2007), 57–76; Edwards, *Archbishop Pole*, 121–2, 178–81; Ceri Law, 'The 1557 Visitation of the University of Cambridge', in Elizabeth Evenden and Vivienne Westbrook, eds., *Catholic Renewal and Protestant Resistance in Marian England* (Farnham: Aldershot, 2015), 65–91.

himself forward. The regius professorship of Hebrew, which had few takers, was reconverted to this purpose. Juan de Villagarcía, Carranza's protégé, was incorporated as Bachelor of Divinity on 14 November 1555 and became reader in Theology at Magdalen College. He was later appointed regius professor of Theology in 1556, when Dr Richard Smyth resigned. Villagarcía became a Doctor of Divinity at Oxford on 11 July 1558 and, as has been mentioned, did not relinquish his professorship and leave Oxford and the kingdom until June 1559, when Elizabeth had renewed the break with Rome. The efforts of theologians and intellectuals at the universities were reinforced by some of the decrees of the English Synod of 1556, in which Carranza had been involved, aimed directly at the revitalisation of Catholicism in educational institutions and the visitations that were subsequently put in place to implement the decrees.[9]

The intellectual impetus of the programme of university regeneration undertaken by Philip and Mary was perceived to have been disastrous to the Protestant cause by the supporters of the latter. On 20 March 1559, John Jewel, who was about to be appointed bishop of Salisbury by Elizabeth, complained to Peter Martyr that since his departure from Oxford, 'ignorance and obstinacy' had increased and that at the university 'religion, and all hope of good learning and talent is altogether abandoned'. On 22 May he lamented again, this time to Heinrich Bullinger, that:

> Our universities are so depressed and ruined, that at Oxford there are scarcely two individuals who think with us, and even they are so dejected and broken in spirit, that they can do nothing. That despicable friar, Soto, and another Spanish monk [Villagarcía] [...] have so torn up by the roots all that Peter Martyr had so prosperously planted that they have reduced the vineyard of the Lord to a wilderness. You could scarcely believe so much desolation could have been effected in so short a time.[10]

Less attention has been given, however, to the theological framework upon which these men worked and, although the proactive approach of Spanish theologians in England is regularly acknowledged in the literature, no comprehensive attempt has been made to ascertain what it was that these men were

9 On Carranza's involvement see J. Ignacio Tellechea Idígoras, *Fray Bartolomé Carranza y el Cardenal Pole. Un navarro en la restauración católica de Inglaterra (1554–1558)* (Pamplona, 1977), 61–3. On the development of the English Synod see Edwards, *Archbishop Pole*, 169–79.

10 Hegarty, 'Carranza and the English Universities', 159–60; Eamon Duffy, *Fires of Faith: Catholic England under Mary Tudor* (New Haven and London: Yale University Press, 2009), 200.

teaching and disseminating. What was it, exactly, that Spanish and English theologians were discussing and teaching that was so detrimental to those whose thought aligned with that of Bullinger and his fellow English Protestants? The debate over Spanish influence in the revival of Catholicism in England has suffered from a historiographical paradox for, even though some historians have linked the regime's alleged failure to its association with Spain and the strand of Catholicism that these men brought, there have been no attempts to integrate the theologies of English and Spanish authors to discern whether the Spanish religious thought of the 1550s was actually so odious and incompatible to that of the English.[11] Some of the most comprehensive studies revolving around theology in Marian England have stressed the Englishness of theological works during Philip and Mary's reign.[12] Ellen A. Macek surveyed English 'traditionalist' theology and found it solid and coherent, but she did not even explore the possibility that Spanish theological developments may have played any part in the revitalisation of Catholicism. On the contrary, she concluded that the Marian project ultimately failed because English theologians 'offered merely an automatic reversion to Catholic belief and practice', and because Catholicism had been hindered by the Spanish marriage, religious persecution, and fear of Church-land repossession.[13] Lucy E. C. Wooding rightly pointed out that the humanism present in many Marian works provided common ground for both Catholic and Protestant writers of the period, but she concluded that the Marian Church did not import 'foreign ideas', and that the theology displayed during the reign was one with its own 'distinctive approach' to Scripture

---

11 Dickens, *English Reformation*, 384–5; Elton, *Reform and Reformation*, 395; Loades, *Mary Tudor*, 261–2. All these interpretations, which have lingered heavily in most readings of the joint reign, assume that Spaniards were universally hated for their insularity, arrogance and, of course, the cruel Inquisition, but these tropes had not yet become commonplace to create the negative vision of Spain that was to be circulated during the Dutch Revolt and afterwards. A negative vision which was, in any case, not universally accepted. According to these historiographical understandings of the episode, the actions and behaviour of the Spanish in England associated irredeemably the reputation of the Catholic Church with 'foreign tyranny'. This is a teleological reading of historical events, which as Alexander Samson has aptly put it, equates English Protestantism with a 'movement of national liberation'. See Samson, *Mary and Philip*, 222. For a recent survey of current historiographical trends on the topic of Marian religiosity which argues that studies should focus on the dynamism of Marian Catholicism, rather than on its 'failure' or 'success', see Frederick E. Smith, 'Reinventing the Counter-Reformation in Marian England', *The Historical Journal*, 64, no. 4 (2021), 1105–27.

12 Ellen A. Macek, *The Loyal Opposition: Tudor Traditionalist Polemics, 1535–1558* (New York: Peter Lang, 1996); Lucy E. C. Wooding, *Rethinking Catholicism in Reformation England* (Oxford: Oxford University Press, 2000).

13 Macek, *Loyal Opposition*, 163–84.

and authority which was 'a perpetuation of [...] Henrician Catholicism'.[14] No attempt has been made, however, to put the theory of the Englishness of Marian theology to the test by comparing it to foreign works. There have been, however, some attempts at setting the record straight. As has been mentioned, Duffy has explored Alfonso de Castro's contribution briefly, and the works of Wizeman and Edwards have dealt with Carranza's influence during Philip and Mary's reign, but the subject remains grossly underexplored.[15]

In the previous chapter we already established that the Spanish had been actively involved in religious activities in England and that they even met regularly with Pole. This chapter focuses on the theology that was written and promoted by Spaniards in the period. I will look mainly at the works of those who accompanied Philip to England in 1554 or arrived later on (whether they were still in England by the end of the reign or not), but also of those theologians who were writing in Spain. The three most crucial issues in religious debates of the sixteenth century were justification, the Eucharist and papal primacy, and they are therefore the themes which have been mainly explored in this chapter. By comparing the theological approaches and preoccupations of Spanish theologians with those of their English theologians, whose works are better known in the context of Marian religiosity, I will prove that these men were promoting a very similar religiosity, one which proudly shared the universalist aspirations of Roman Catholicism, was in line with what Trent had so far decreed and would have only intensified had it been given the chance to continue.

5.1 Justification

Despite his indecisiveness during the reign of Edward VI, under Philip and Mary the theologian Dr Richard Smyth (*c.*1500–1563) wrote a compendium of Catholic doctrine in two parts called *A bouclier of the catholyke faith* (1555). In it Smyth traced a genealogy of the errors contained in Peter Martyr's theology, a fight in which he had been involved since the Edwardian period. Smyth explained Vermigli's two main ideas on justification; that is, that man's salvation depended only on the election and mercy of God and that salvation was only founded in God's grace, a claim he made referring to Romans 9. These ideas appeared on the Protestant theologian's commentaries on 1 Corinthians

14 Wooding, *Rethinking Catholicism*, 150–1, 179–80.

15 Duffy, *Fires of Faith*, 113–4, 149; Wizeman, *Theology and Spirituality*, passim; Edwards, 'Corpus Christi', 139–51; Edwards, 'Carranza's Blueprint', 141–60.

and Smyth associated them to William Tyndale's preface to his translation of the Epistle to the Romans and to the works of the Italian reformer Bernardino Ochino, translated into English by a gentlewoman whom Smyth does not name but who we know to have been Anne Cooke.[16] In a sarcastic remark, Smyth exposed what he believed to be Vermigli's error by enumerating precisely the elements that justified humans in Catholic theology:

> This opinion is not onelye agaynste mans free wyll, but also against manye euidente places of the scripture. For if oure saluation standeth onelye in Gods election, Gods promise, mercye, and grace: than it consisteth not in the hearing of Goddes worde, not in his faieth, not in hys repentaunce, or penaunce, not in hys praying to God for the pourchasinge of it, not in geuinge of almes, not in fasting, not in his fiaunce to God or hope of saluation, not in the receauing of baptisme, not in the dreade of God, not in charitee, finallie not in good works, whiche all together are manistly [sic] against Gods holy worde.[17]

Soteriological questions of justification had been among the most contested in the polemics following the rise of Protestantism. They led to a highly intellectual debate that flourished both at the universities and at the printing presses. Due to the complexity of the subject, these exchanges were usually framed in an academic context.[18] However, explaining how Christ justified humanity was of the utmost importance to theologians on either side of the religious divide. Marian authors were concerned with similar themes when it came to debunking the *sola fides* position, a theological stance that they took on the basis of a humanist tradition.[19] The debate on justification had been central – and acrimonious – during the first sessions of the Council of Trent and its defining decree had been one of the first to be agreed.[20] Cardinal Pole himself had left Trent to avoid discussing his delicate beliefs in justification by

---

16 Richard Smyth, *The seconde parte of the booke called a Bucklar of the Catholyke fayeth, conteyninge seuen chapiters: Made by Rychard Smyth doctoure of diuinitie of Oxforde, & reader of the same there* (London: Robert Caly, 1555), sig. B8^r–B8^v.

17 Smyth, *Seconde parte of a Bucklar*, sig. C1^r.

18 Wizeman, *Theology and Spirituality*, 96–7; Euan Cameron, *The European Reformation* (Oxford: Oxford University Press, 1991), 121–8; C. Scott Dixon, *Contesting the Reformation* (Chichester: Wiley-Blackwell, 2012), 50–56.

19 Wooding, *Rethinking Catholicism*, 154–66; Wizeman, *Theology and Spirituality*, 97–107.

20 John W. O'Malley, SJ, *Trent: What Happened at the Council* (Cambridge, Massachusetts and London: The Belknap Press of Harvard University Press, 2013), 107–16.

faith alone.[21] The Council defined justification, first, by explaining that even though Christ had died for all, not all were saved. Men were made just through the free gift of prevenient grace by the merits of Christ's passion. Through the laver of regeneration, or baptism, men were born again in Christ. No longer the children of Adam, Christians were clean from sin and became the adopted children of God and co-heirs to the Kingdom with Christ. However, human frailty required the cooperating or helping grace of God to achieve conversion by freely accepting that grace. It was human free will that accepted the gift of grace, but this was only possible through inner conversion by the special illumination of the Holy Spirit.[22] Grace was, therefore, God's communication of His own self to humanity, a gift of salvation.[23]

The crux of the debate lay in the different interpretations surrounding the origins and development of sin. Reformers such as Zwingli, Calvin and Cranmer had followed Martin Luther's initial analysis which equated sin to concupiscence, emphasising the depravity of human beings, who were tainted by sin from conception.[24] English Marian authors, however, viewed sin as an evil that humans chose to follow freely. Concupiscence did remain after baptism, but it was not sin in itself, rather an inclination to sin which was naturally present in humanity. This position was clearly expounded by Smyth, who claimed that that 'whiche Adams synne had infected or defiled' was completely cleansed through baptism, leaving 'no spotte of original synne nor of actuall'. In the margin he summarised that, therefore, 'the co[n]cupiscence remaining in the chylde baptised is no synne'.[25] Edmund Bonner (*c.*1500–1569), bishop of London, in his *A profitable and necessarye doctrine*, explained that, despite baptism's 'great efficacy' in the removing of all sins, 'there remayneth in vs [...] a certayne infirmitie, or inclination, to synne, called concupiscence'.[26]

---

21 Dermot Fenlon, *Heresy and Obedience in Tridentine Italy* (Cambridge: Cambridge University Press, 1972), 118–36; Mayer, *Reginald Pole*, 148–63; Edwards, *Archbishop Pole*, 98–101, 105–8.

22 H. J. Schroeder, OP, ed., *Canons and Decrees of the Council of Trent* (Rockford, Illinois: Tan Books and Publishers, INC., 1978), 30–42. Henceforth *Canons and Decrees*. For an account of the evolution of the theology of grace see Cornelius Ernst, OP, *The Theology of Grace* (Butler, Wisconsin: Clergy Book Service, 1974), 52–61.

23 Roger Haight has defined it as 'an offer of personal encounter' in 'Sin and Grace', in Francis Schüssler Fiorenza and John P. Galvin, eds., *Systematic Theology: Roman Catholic Perspectives*, vol. 2 (Minneapolis: Fortress Press, 1991), 75–141, in 114–26.

24 Cameron, *European Reformation*, 116–7; Roger du Barry, 'Cranmer's Doctrine of the Lord's Supper in its Gospel Context', *Churchman*, 120, no. 4 (2006), 285–320, in 296–301.

25 Smyth, *Seconde parte of a Bucklar*, sigs. G4^{v}–G5^{r}.

26 Edmund Bonner, *A profitable and necessarye doctrine, with certayne homelyes adioyned thervnto set forth by the reuerend father in God, Edmunde Byshop of London, for the*

The position taken in this matter by some of the Spanish theologians who came to England was equally clear on this distinction. Castro, in his *Adversus omnes haereses* used Romans 6, Galatians 3 and Titus 3 to explain that salvation had been granted to men not through the justice of men's works, but through God's mercy. Through Christ's justifying grace, men were made heirs in hope of eternal life by the regeneration of the cleansing infused by the Holy Spirit. 'Therefore',, he concluded, 'it is clearly manifest by these testimonies from Scripture, that baptism has the force and power of wiping sin and conferring grace'.[27] Further on in his work, Castro went on to claim that it was on this identification of concupiscence with sin that the foundations of Lutheran errors lay; against Luther's idea that 'all our works are sin', Castro referred to several scriptural passages that disprove him.[28] Carranza was of the same mind, explaining in his *Comentarios sobre el catechismo christiano* that baptism operated through the Holy Spirit not only to clean original and actual sin, but also to infuse the virtues to fight against the 'sensible capabilities which are engrained in the flesh'; the 'concupiscible and irascible part' of the 'sensible appetite'.[29]

---

instruction and enformation of the people being within his diocesse of London, & of hys cure and charge (London: John Cawood, 1555), sig. N3^{r-v}.

27 Alfonso de Castro, OFM, *Aduersus omnes haereses libri quatuordecim* [1534] (Cologne: Joannis Novesiani, 1558), fol. 66^{r}: 'Et in epist[ola] ad Titum iteru[m] Paulus eande[m] co[n]firmat sentential[m], dicens: Cùm aut[em] benignitas & humanitas apparuit saluatoris nostril Dei, no[n] ex operibus iustitię, quæ tecimus nos, sed secundum sua[m] misericordiam saluos nos fecit, per lauacrum regeneratonis & renovationis spiritus sancti, quem effudit in nos abunde per Iesum Christum saluatorem nostrum, vt iustificati gratia ipsius, hęredes simus secundu[m] spem vitae æternę. Haec ibi Paulus: Nihil aut[em] his verbis expressius quicq[uam] dici potuit: quoniam dicit nos saluos fecisse per lauacrum regenerationis: lauisse aut[em], vt iustificati gratia ipsius, haeredes efficeremus vitae aeternae. His ergo tam claris scripture testimonijs manifestum est, baptismum habere vim & potestatem peccata delendi, & gratiam conferendi'.

28 Castro, *Adversus omnes haereses*, fols 222^{v}–223^{r}; where he uses Genesis 22, Galatians 3, Job 1, 1 Corinthians 7, 2 Peter 1, 1 John 3, 1 John 4, etc.

29 Bartolomé de Carranza, OP, *Comentarios sobre el catecismo christiano* (Antwerp: 1558), vol. I, José Ignacio Tellechea Idígoras, ed., (Madrid: Biblioteca de Autores Cristianos, 1972), 138–9: 'Así, cuando el segundo hombre, que es Jesucristo, vino a reparar los daños que se habían hecho en la caída del primer hombre, reparó no solamente lo principal, que es el alma, pero todos los instrumentos, que son las potencias por donde ella obra. Y así en la primera justificación del hombre que se hace en el baptismo, no solamente pone Dios su gracia y su espíritu en el alma del justo, que éstos asientan en la substancia de la misma alma; pero pone, como es nevesario, en el entendimiento, fe que remedie los daños que allí se hicieron, y en la voluntad, caridad y otras virtudes con otros dones del Espíritu Santo que reparen los males y daños que hizo en ella el pecado; y en otras potencias sensibles que tienen asiento en la carne, que llamamos partes y potencias del apetito

Pedro de Soto published his *Assertio catholicae fidei* against the Württemberg Confession in Cologne in 1555, when he was already lecturing at Oxford. In it, the Dominican theologian declared that baptism was necessary for the 'true and wholesome remission and abolition of all sins', which was effected 'not only by faith' and he condemned what the 'adversaries of the Church contend today' – that is, that the concupiscence that remained after baptism was sin – as 'a manifest error, contrary to the sense that is to be found in Scripture and the Fathers'. To support his claim, Soto employed an exegetical analysis of examples from the Old Testament (Ezekiel 36), as well as from the New, sharing Romans 6 and 1 Timothy 3 with Castro and expanding his claims with 2 Corinthians 11 whilst referencing three of St Augustine's works and a sermon by Pope Leo I.[30] In Soto's voluminous *Institutione sacerdotum*, a collection of his Dilingen lectures first published in 1558 at the behest of Cardinal Otto von Truchsess, Soto expounded that the first effect of baptism was the 'full and perfect remission of all sins' as proclaimed in Ezekiel 36, confirmed by St Paul in Colossians 3 and Romans 6 and explained by St Augustine in his *Enchiridion*, where he had claimed that when the 'grace of regeneration' reached humans their sins would be forgiven and their guilt removed by their 'being reborn', and in *De peccatorum meritis et remissione*, where Augustine affirmed that baptism cleansed humans from sin, but that concupiscence remained.[31] He then accused Luther and his followers of twisting the Pauline perspective on

---

sensible, que son la parte concupicible y iracible, hasta en éstas pone Cristo unas virtudes infusas, a manera de las virtudes naturales, aunque son muy más excelentes, y con esto no queda parte en el hombre a la cual no le den su remedio, como no quedó parte alguna en la cual no hubiese hecho algún daño el pecado de los primeros hombres'.

30 Pedro de Soto, OP, *Assertio Catholicae fidei circa articulos confessionis nomine illustrissimi Dvcis Wittenbergensis oblatae per legatos eius Concilio Tridentino, XXIII Ianuarij Anni M. D. LII* (Cologne: Joannes Novesianus, 1555), fols R3r–L1r: 'CREDIT Catholica Ecclesia, per Baptismum, qui adultis & parulis necessaries est, veraciter & plenè omnium peccatorum remissionem ac abolitionem fieri, non per fidem solum, vel tradentis vel suscipientis, & cuiuscunque denique, quanquam in adultis ad hoc sit necessaria, sed per ipsam virtutem sacramenti diuinamq[ue] promissionem.

Quòd vero contentiosissime hodie aduersarij Ecclesiae co[n]tendunt, concupiscentiam quae post baptismum manet, verè ese peccatum, manifestissimus est error, contra scripturam & partum sensum [...]'.

31 Pedro de Soto, OP, *Tractatus de institvtione sacerdotvm, qvi sub episcopis animarum curam gerunt* (Dilingen an der Donau: Sebaldum Mayer, 1558), fols 39r–v. Compiled by Truchsess for their popularity, the volume was used as a textbook at the University of Dilingen and it went through eleven editions between 1558 and 1586, being published in Germany, Flanders and Venice. It would be a sound conjecture to think that Soto must have used similar material whilst he lectured at Oxford in the period 1555–1556. For Augustine see St Augustine of Hippo, *Enchiridion ad Laurentium sive de fide, spe et charitate* (420), ch. XXXI, no. 119; St Augustine of Hippo, *De peccatorum meritis et remissione et de baptismo parvulorum*, book II, ch. XXVII, nos 43, 46.

the frailty of human flesh and Augustine's views on this to assert that baptism did not fully cleanse original sin. On the contrary, Soto argued employing both Pauline and Augustinian quotations, baptism conferred an infusion of grace in the receiver – whether an adult or a child although emphasising the role of baptism in the latter – which operated a 'true and inner mutation' that most certainly remitted sin.[32] Here was a strong emphasis on the rebirth of baptised humanity in Christ with a washing away of all sins despite the permanence of concupiscence. This concurred with the Marian authors, but also with Spanish theologians who were writing in Spain in the same period such as Carranza's fellow Dominicans and staunch supporters during his process, Diego Jiménez (1490–*c.*1578) and Felipe de Meneses (1515–*c.*1572), the Riojan cleric resident in Salamanca Alonso Martínez de Laguna († *c.*1555) or the prolific Sevillian humanist, mathematician, geographer, cartographer and historian Pedro de Medina (1493–1567).[33] The same idea was reiterated in the translation of the Dutch theologian Peter Canisius's (1521–1597) *Summa doctrinae christianae*, first published in 1555 and edited in Spanish in 1558 by the young Valencian humanist Juan Martín Cordero (1531–1600), who had been in England between July and November 1554 and had become, by the time that his translation was published, a student in the University of Louvain.[34]

---

32 Soto, *Institvtione sacerdotvm*, fols 41^{r}–43^{v}: [f. 43r] 'Sicut igitur de peccatorum remissione dictum est, ita de hace iustificatione & renouatione nu[n]c dicimus, inchoatur cùm baptizamur, & virtute ipsius baptismatis in ea proficimus, vsq[ue] quo tandem ad perfectam renouationemvirtute ipsius baptismatis perueniamus: Quod Paulus apertè dicit [...]. Igitur credenda est vera & interior mutation per occultissimam gratiam infusam per baptismuum paruulis [...]'.

33 Diego Jiménez, OP, *Enchiridión o Manual de Doctrina Christiana (que también puede seruir de Confessionario) diuidido en cinco partes: en que por vía de preguntas y respuestas se enseña al Christiano todo lo q[ue] deue creer, y no creer: dessear, y aborrecer: hazer, y no hazer: saber, y no saber. Hecho y copilado de muchos libros de sana doctrina por el R. P. fray Diego Ximénez, de la orden de los Predicadores. Dirigido al Rey de Portugal* (Lisbon: Germán Gallarde, 1552), f. 142v; Felipe de Meneses, OP, *Lvz del alma Christiana contra la ceguedad y ygnorancia en lo que pertenece a la fe y ley de Dios, y de la yglesia: y los remedios y ayuda que él nos dio para guardar su ley. En el qual tractado se da tambié[n] luz assí a los confessores, como a los penite[n]tes, para administrar deuidamente el sacramento ta[n] necessario de la penitencia* (Seville: Martín de Montesdoca, 1555), fols 108^{r}, 109^{r}; Alonso Martínez de Laguna, *Svmma de doctrina christiana, compuesta por el Bachiller Alonso Martínez de Laguna de los Cameros, para prouecho de los Christianos* (Salamanca: Juan de Cánova, 1555), fols 90^{r}–92^{r}; Pedro de Medina, *Libro de la Verdad. Donde se contiene[n] dozientos Diálogos, que entre la Uerdad y el hombre se tractan sobre la conuersión del peccador. Dirigido al muy Illustre y reuere[n]díssimo señor do[n] Pedro Gasca Obispo de Palencia, Conde de Pernía, Del consejo de su Magestad, &c.* (Valladolid: Francisco Fernández de Córdoba, 1555), fols 87^{v}–88^{r}; 159^{r-v}.

34 St Peter Canisius, SJ, *Svmma de la doctrina christiana. Compuesta por Preguntas y Respuestas, para prouecho y vtilidad de la Re Christiana: agora nueuamente traduzida*

Marian theologians did not neglect the role of grace in the process of justification, following the definition of justification enunciated by John Fisher which was later to match that decreed by the Council of Trent in 1547 during its first sessions under Paul III (r. 1534–1549) and supported by Spanish theologians such as Domingo de Soto (1494–1560).[35] According to the Tridentine decree, those cut off from God for their sins 'may be disposed through His quickening and helping grace to convert themselves to their own justification by freely assenting and cooperating with that grace'.[36] Mary's English theologians were in full agreement with Trent.[37] It was Christ's redemption through His merits that provided the free gift of prevenient grace, which had to be consented unto by men.[38] Thomas Watson (1515–84), who was to become Bishop of Lincoln in 1557, had published in 1554 his *Holsome and Catholyke Doctryne*, in which he followed Paul in Titus 3:5–7 to state that through God's mercy, humans were given a gift of regeneration by the pouring of the Holy Spirit into them through Christ, so 'that we being justified by his grace, might be heyres by hope of eternal lyfe'.[39] John Harpsfield (1516–78), in a homily on the redemption of man, affirmed that salvation was offered amorously by Christ,

---

en Romance Castellano por I. M. C. Por mandamiento y avthoridad d'el Sereníssimo Rey d'España, d'Inglatierra, Francia, y Nápoles, Don Phelipe nuestro Señor, tr. Juan Martín Cordero (Anwerp: Guillermo Simón, 1558), fols 34ᵛ–35ᵛ. On Cordero and his trajectory in Flanders after his brief spell in England see Josep Lluís Martos Sánchez, 'Juan Martín Cordero en Flandes: Humanismo, mecenazgo e imprenta', *Revista de Filología Española*, 95, no. 1 (2015), 75–96.

35 Richard Rex, *The Theology of John Fisher* (Cambridge: Cambridge University Press, 1991), 128; Venancio D. Carro, 'El Maestro Domingo de Soto y las controversias sobre la justificación dentro y fuera del Concilio de Trento', *Ciencia Tomista*, 87 (1960), 423–65; Sixto Sánchez-Lauro, 'Itinerario vital y doctrinal de Domingo de Soto: implicación político-social desde la ortodoxia', *Revista europea de historia de las ideas políticas y de las instituciones públicas*, 1, no. 2 (2011), 113–36, in 123–5. For Soto's views on justification in 1547 in the wake of the Council see Domingo de Soto, OP, *Fratris Dominci Soto, Segobiensis, theologi, ordinis praedicatorum, & Caesarea maiestatis Caroli quinti Imperatoris à sacris co[n]fessionibus, ad sanctum concilium Tridentinum De natura & gratia. Quod opus ab ipso authore denuo recognitu[m] est, nonnullisque in locis emendatum, & Apologia contra reuerendu[m] Episcopum Catharinum auctum* [1547] (Paris: Jean Foucher, 1549), fols 132ʳ–99ʳ.

36 *Canons and Decrees*, 31–2.

37 Wizeman, *Theology and Spirituality*, 98–101.

38 Thomas Watson, *Twoo notable Sermons, made the thirde and fyfte Fridayes in Lent last past, before the Quenes highnes, concernynge the reall presence of Christes body and bloude in the blessed Sacrament: & also the Masse, which is the sacrifice of the newe Testament* (London: John Cawood, 1554), sigs N6ʳ–N7ᵛ, X5ᵛ–X8ʳ; Thomas Watson, *Holsome and Catholyke doctryne concerninge the seuen Sacramentes of Chrystes Church, expedient to be knowen of all men, set forth in maner of shorte Sermons to bee made to the people, by the reuerend father in God Thomas byshop of Lincolne* (London: Robert Caly, 1558), fols 76ʳ–77ᵛ; Bonner, *Profitable and Necessarye Doctrine*, sigs Q3ʳ–R1ʳ.

39 Watson, *Holsome and Catholyke Doctrine*, fols 9ᵛ–11ᵛ.

but that humans should 'condignely receaue the merites thereof', as 'God requyreth in vs certayne thynges, to be accomplished by our owne wyll and consent'. Otherwise, he concluded, salvation was not possible.[40] For Bonner, grace made men 'more strong, and able to resist, and withstand' the concupiscence that remained after baptism; and for Miles Huggarde, a hosier who was one of the most prolific religious pamphleteers of the Marian period, grace was God's offering '[w]hich by the fre wyll, thou mayest leue or take' and only through the second option could anyone be justified.[41] When the prevenient grace first offered by Christ through his merits and passion was freely accepted, humans grew in cooperating grace, which, coupled with faith, the first step towards salvation, put men towards the path of justification.

In 1548, following the Augsburg Synod, Cardinal Truchsess had commissioned from Pedro de Soto a treatise for the instruction of the people which was published the same year under the title of *Institvtiones christianae*. The volume turned out to be very popular in the period, going through six different editions in Latin, Flemish and German between 1548 and 1554.[42] In this work, the views expounded by some of the English theologians were firmly defended. Christ's merits and satisfaction were communicated to humans through the grace acquired in the sacraments. This grace was described as being both justifying and sanctifying, but it had to be maintained with good works. Human cooperation thus increased grace, and it was only through this increase that the true Christian life under the presence and authority of God could be achieved.[43] Soto followed in this vein even more forcefully in his *Assertio*, where he explained that prevenient grace, offered through Christ's

---

40 In Edmund Bonner, *Homelies sette forthe by the righte reuerende father in God, Edmunde Byshop of London, not onely promysed before in his booke intituled, A necessarye doctrine, but also now of late adioyned, and added therevunto, to be reade within his diocesse of London, of all persons, vycars, and curates, vnto theyr parishioners, vpon sondayes, & holydayes* (London: John Cawood, 1555), fols 16v–17v.

41 Bonner, *Profitable and Necessarye Doctrine*, sigs N3r–v; Miles Huggarde, *A new treatyse in maner of a Dialoge / whiche sheweth the excellency of ma[n]nes nature / in that he is made to the Image of God, and wherin it restyth / and by howe many wayes a man dothe blotte, and defyle the same Image* (London: Robert Wyer, 1555), sig. D1r.

42 Carro, *Pedro de Soto*, vol. 2, 64–5, 80–2.

43 Pedro de Soto, OP, *Institvtionis Christianae libri tres priores: Ivssv Reverendissimi Domini D. Othonis Cardinalis & Episcopi Augustani a doctis theologis lecti & probati, ac illius authoritate editi* (Augsburg: Valentin Othmar, 1548), sigs C2v–C3r: 'Verum nihilhominus sic semper manet homo liberi arbitrii, ut ad pecandum nunquam aut cogatur, aut cogi possit, nec unq[uam] non possit no[n] paenitere peccati, sive post remissum peccatum, ad bona operanda, & ad perseuerandum in ipsis auxilio gratiae semper egeat: iuxta illud Christi: sine me nihil potestis facere [Jn 15:5]. Quae tria, libertatem arbitrii, infirmitatem eius, & necessitate gratiae, firmissime credere debet fidelis quilibet: quantumuis non intelligat. [...]

merits and not by those of human beings, was followed by the infusion of faith, hope and charity, in which men persevered by cooperating with grace through free will, through true penance following a sincere conversion to God and through the sacraments, in which grace was 'continued', leading to men's justification. Soto supported this view by quoting patristic sources (St Hilary of Poitiers and St Ambrose) but, especially, an array of scriptural citations mainly drawn from the New Testament in which James 2 had special prominence.[44] In *Institvtione sacerdotvm*, he described the process of justification as comprising four phases. The infusion of divine grace, with which men ought to cooperate, was followed by men's acceptance of it through free will, which effected a true conversion to God that necessarily participated of faith and charity. The fourth step was the detestation of sin, which kept men safe from losing the grace acquired and increased. Following these steps, any sins committed could be remitted through penance and, therefore, the true penitent could be justified. Soto claimed that this was the doctrine held by St Thomas Aquinas, St Bonaventure and St Alexander of Hales, but he also provided numerous scriptural sources, his arguments displaying a strongly Pauline outlook.[45]

[…] Quam conuersionem deus ipse nos iustificans, nobiscum, ut agens principale, operatur: ut in hoc opere praecipue illud Pauli sit uerum: non est uolentis, nec currentis, sed dei miserentis [Rom. 9:16].

Tum meritis Christi & satisfactione communicare hominibus hanc gratiam per sacramenta re, uel uoto suscepta: perquam etiam in ha cuita iusti & sancti esse possumus, atq[ue] in iustitia & sanctitate proficere: quod per bona opera gratiam sequentia, & ab ea emanantia consequimur coram deo, iuxta illud: qui sanctus est, sanctificetur ad huc: qui iustus est, iustificetur adhuc [Rev. 22:12]'.

44 Soto, *Assertio catholicae fidei*, sigs E2^{r}–F2^{r}: 'Credit Catholica Ecclesia, quod iustificatio impij, qua scilicet ex peccatore fit iustus, sola Dei gratia per Christum, nullo nostro merito fiat. Idque occulta inspiratione & infusion fidei, spei & charitatis, cooperante in ratione vtentibus libero arbitrio, per veram poenitentiam vel conuersionem in Deum & sacramenta, vt a CHRISTO praeceptum est, re vel voto suscepta. Propter has igitur virtutes intrepide Catholica fides, homine[m] justum esse coram Deo confitetur, & earum meritis sibi esse fidendum.

Sentit etiam vera fides Catholica, hominem ita iustificatum, non reputatione tantum, sed veritate etiam coram Deo iustum esse, & gratia Dei continuo egere, ad exercendam pietatem, implemendamque iustitiam. Qua simul cum libero arbitrio opera fidei spei & charitatis exercet, quibus coram Deo proficit in iustitia, & his meritis in iudicio. […] Etsi enim propter nos iustificari à peccatis, & iustificatos proficere, non tamen propterea, & virtutes, & earum opera, quae eius meritis, & gratia Dei, per ipsum in nobis sunt, sunt excludenda.

Id circo maiores nostril rectè dixerunt: Nos non sola fide iustificari'. Soto's other biblical material to counter the Württemberg Confession was: Ezekiel. 18, Luke 7, Acts of the Apostles 2, Romans 2 and 4.

45 Soto, *Institvtione sacerdotvm*, fols 2^{v}–5^{v}.

The infusion of the theological virtues, faith, hope and charity, effected by the Holy Spirit, was essential, but the latter two could only grow if the first one existed. As Smyth concluded, supporting his arguments with scriptural and Augustinian citations, 'fayth is first of al geue[n] to ma[n], that other thynges necessarie for his saluation, maybe gotte[n] through it'.[46] His English peers were in agreement.[47] But men could only cooperate with Christ's salvific grace through lively or formed faith. This kind of faith was differentiated from dead or unformed faith, which was the mere belief in Christ's commandments, without human cooperation with grace through the virtues infused by the regeneration of baptism. This was a special preoccupation of Bonner's, who strongly distinguished between the two meanings of faith.[48] Faith was God's gift and

> a perswasion and belief, wrought by god in mans harte, whereby man assenteth, graunteth and taketh for true, not onely that God is [...] but also that all the wordes and sayinges of God [...] are of most certayne trueth, and infallible veritie.

To Bonner, this faith was 'an entrye [...] verye necessarye for the begynnyng of all ryghtousnes' but without it being joined with 'hope and charitie', it was 'a deade faythe, because it is voyde and destitute of lyfe'.[49] However, if hope and charity were conjoined with faith, then this faith showed an absolute hope in God's promises through Christ and an immense love for God and his commandments. This was a 'lyuely' and 'effectual' faith. Although not always expressed in the same terms, the idea that faith, to be efficacious and to help men cooperate with Christ's salvific grace, required humans freely embracing hope and charity was similarly expounded by other Marian theologians following a tradition that was in line with Fisher's theology.[50]

---

46 Smyth, *Seconde parte of a Bucklar*, sigs C3^{v}–D8^{r}.

47 John Harpsfield in Bonner, *Homelies*, fols 16^{v}–17^{r}; Watson, *Holsome and Catholyke doctrine*, fols 95^{v}; Miles Huggarde, *A treatise entitled the Path waye to the towre of perfection* (London: Robert Caly, 1554), sig. E1^{r}; Miles Huggarde, *A mirrour of loue, which such light doth giue, That all men may learne, howe to loue and liue* (London: Robert Caly, 1555), sigs C3^{v}–4^{v}; Miles Huggarde, *The displaying of the Protestantes, & sondry their practises, with a description of diuers their abuses of late frequented. Newly imprinted agayne, and augmented, with a table in the ende, of all suche matters as is specially contained within this volume* (London: Robert Caly, 1556), fols 112^{v}–115^{r}.

48 Wizeman, *Theology and Spirituality*, 103–7.

49 Bonner, *Profitable and Necessarye Doctrine*, sigs B1^{r}–B2^{r}.

50 St John Fisher, *A Sermon very notable, fruicteful, and Godlie, made at Paules Crosse in London. Anno domini 1521* (London: Robert Caly, 1554), sigs C2^{v}–3v, D2^{r}; Wizeman, *Theology and Spirituality*, 103–7.

Through formed faith, humans cooperated with Christ's grace as a consequence of their good works. This was a prominent perspective in the theology of Carranza's *Comentarios*. The Navarrese explained that the Christian faith was one whether men were 'good or bad', unless a bad person became so through heresy, in which case faith would be lost. Nevertheless, faith had two states. In one of them faith was not accompanied by the other Christian virtues and this faith, Carranza explained, was an 'unformed faith', as theologians called it, although it could also be termed a 'dead faith', as St James stated: 'Faith without works is dead' (James 2:17, 26). However, faith accompanied by the virtues of hope and charity; that is, a faith that quickened good works, was a 'formed faith, made lively and animated by God's Spirit, who assists and presides the heart in which it resides'. This was supported by Christ's saying in Matthew 7:17 that the bad tree (unformed faith) gave bad fruits, whereas the good tree (formed faith) gave good fruits, which was in line with Fisher's theology too.[51] Soto agreed in his *Institvtiones christianae* when he argued against the doctrine of *sola fides* that justice before God could not be found 'without faith, charity or any other virtues'.[52] Also resorting to James 2:15–17, Soto explained that 'faith, if not accompanied by works, is dead in itself'. He then quoted Luke 12:47 to emphasise that men ought to know God's will and act accordingly by following His commandments and concluded that 'true faith can be without charity and works, but it is dead'.[53] Castro quoted James 2:17

51 Carranza, *Comentarios sobre el Catechismo*, I, 136–7: 'En la fe principalmente has de considerar dos estados: el primero es cuando está sola sin las otras virtudes cristianas, esperanza y caridad. [...] En este estado llaman los teólogos fe informe, porque falta el Espíritu Santo, que forma y anima todas las cosas de la vida espiritual, y así propiamente le ponen este nombre de informe, y con la misma y mayor propiedad la llama el apóstol Santiago fe muerta diciendo: *La fe sin obras muerta es*; no porque las obras den vida a la fe, sino porque son señal y testimonio de que la fe está viva, como, en el árbol, las hojas verdes y el fruto dado a su tiempo son cierto testimonio que el árbol vive, y si no las tiene en su tiempo, es cierto testimonio que está muerto. [...] El segundo estado es cuando está la fe acompañada de las otras virtudes cristianas: en este estado dícese la fe ya formada, y fe viva y animada por el espíritu de Dios, que asiste y preside en el corazón donde está. En este estado no sufre malas obras; sino las buenas obras se dicen la flor, y la hoja y los frutos de la fe. El corazón del hombre, cuando tiene la fe en este estado, llama Cristo buen árbol; en el primer estado le llama mal árbol'. See Fisher, *Sermon very notable*, sig. C2^{v}.

52 Soto, *Institvtiones christianae*, sig. M2^{r}: 'Vere enim sine fide, nec charitas, nec ulla alia uirtus, aut iusticia potest apud deum ese, aut inueniri'.

53 Soto, *Institvtiones christianae*, sig. M2^{r}–M2^{v}: 'Iacobus etia[m] ratione apertissima, & exemplo probat fide[m], quae opera non habet, mortua[m] esse: Si autem (scribens) frater, aut soror nudi sunt, & indigea[n]t uictu quotidiano, dicat autem aliquis ex uobis, illis: Ite in pace, calefacimini, & saturamini: non dederitis autem eis, quae necessaria sunt corpori, quid proderit: Sic & fides, si non habeat opera, mortua est in semetipsa. [...] Vnde scribitur in euangelio: Seruus qui cognouit uoluntatem domini sui, & non se praeparauit,

too and posed a rhetorical question to debunk the doctrine of *sola fides*, affirming that the sense about 'dead faith' was perfectly clear in James. Luther, he claimed, 'appealing to that common refuge of all heretics' affirmed that the Epistle of James had not been written by the Apostle nor was it 'worthy of the Apostolic Spirit'. However, Castro counter-argued, confirmation of James's conception of 'dead faith' could be found in Revelation 14:13.[54]

Villagarcía, in his 'Diálogo llamado cadena de oro', the unpublished treatise he wrote while in prison, explained that *sola fides* stemmed from an erroneous understanding of Paul and that it was an assault on the Scriptural text, concluding that,

> It is one thing to say that I write with a pen and a different one to say that I write only with a pen. The first assertion is a great truth, the second one is a great lie, for I also write with my hand, and without the hand the pen would be of little importance. It is one thing to say that a man has a body, and a different one to say that he only has a body. The first assertion is well said, but the second one cannot be uttered truly, because he also has a soul which gives life to and animates the body. In the same manner, faith justifies, but much more so charity, without which no one is just no matter how much faith they may have.[55]

& non fecit secundum oluntatem eius, uapulabit multis [Luke 12:47]. Itaq[ue] vera fides esse potest sine charitate, & operibus: sed mortua ea est: quia quamuis tunc etiam dei opus in nobis sit: nostra tamen culpa id non reddit nos deo gratos'.

54 Castro, *Adversus omnes haereses*, fol. 169^{r}: 'Et rursus: Sicut enim corpus sine spiritu mortuu[m] est, ita fide sine operibus mortua est [James 2:17]. Vides q[uam] apertè, q[uam] sine vllis inuolucris hanc sententiam docet beatus Iacobus? Tam clara certè sunt haec pro nostra, hoc est, catholica doctrina testimonia, vt Lutherus eorum claritate[m] & efficaciam perspiciens, nesciens quò se diuerteret, ad commune omnibus haereticis asylum co[n]fugiat, dicens talem epistola[m] no[n] esse Iacobi apostoli, neq[ue] apostolico spiritu dignam'.

55 Biblioteca Nacional de España, MSS 010547; Juan de Villagarcía, OP, 'Diálogo llamado cadena de oro. Compuesto por el muy R[everen]do religioso y doctíssimo padre maestro F. Joan de Villagarçía Regente del insigne Collegio de S. Greg[ori]o de Vall[adoli]d entre dos [crist]ianos, Conuiene a saber. Ioan y Antonio: Y sirue para dar a entender aquellas cosas conq[ue] vn herege se pueda y deua voluer a la sancta fee cathólica de Iesu[crist]o' (*c.*1559–1563), fols 28^{r-v}: 'Dize S[an] Pab[lo] que [Christ] dixo antes del Abachuc, que el justo viue por fee. En estas palabras no ay sino verdad, pues las dixo dios que ni quiere ni puede me[n]tir. Dize Luthero y sus consortes, que sola la fee justifica al peccador. Este error viene del mal entendimj[ent]o quedan ala scriptura, laqual no dize que sola la fee justifica y que el justo viue por fee solame[n]te esto que añade Luthero destruye el texto porque le es contrario: pues es, otra cosa dezir yo scribo con pluma o scribo con sola la pluma. Lo primero es / gran verdad: Lo segundo es gran mentira / que tanbién scribo con la mano: que sin la mano poco importa la pluma./ Otra cosa es dezir el hombre tiene

Spanish contemporary theologians such as the Dominicans Agustín de Esbarroya (*c.*1495–1554), Bernardo de Nieva and Domingo de Baltanás (1488–1568), the latter of whom was associated to the Sevillian *alumbrados* and would later be accused of heresy by the Inquisition, concurred, and in Cordero's translation of Peter Canisius's *Summa* the distinction between dead and lively faith was emphasised too.[56] In these tracts it can be observed that the English and Spanish theologians were very much in agreement over many of the issues surrounding the debate on justification by faith and they were all pursuing the agenda set out by the Council of Trent.

5.2 The Eucharist

The Eucharist or sacrament of the altar was key to the religious discourses of the sixteenth century. The Mass was one of the central elements of the theology and devotional impetus of the Church of Philip and Mary in England. It had been one of the first elements of traditional religion to be restored after Mary's accession and because the Protestant 'assault' on the Eucharist was perceived as an attack of some of the most defining aspects of Catholic doctrine – denying, as Catholic theologians saw it, the centrality of Christ's role in the Eucharist – the responses it elicited were vigorous.[57] As the sacrament which sustained the grace conferred upon the believer by Christ through baptism, which was the gateway, the Eucharist was seen as one of the most important

---

cuerpo o tiene sólo cuerpo. Lo primero es bien dicho, lo segundo no se puede dezir con verdad, pues tanbién tiene alma: Y ésta da ser y vida al cuerpo y le anima. Pues assí la fee justifica, pero mucho más la Char[ida]d: sin la qual nadie es justo por más fee q[ue] tenga'.

56 Agustín de Esbarroya, OP, *Libro Intitulado purificador dela consciencia: en el qual se co[n]tienen dos tractados, En el primero se tracta dela contrición y atrición: por lo qual el ánima se dispone para ser purificada del peccado, y rescebir la gracia. En el otro se contienen reglas para conoscer de qualquier pensamiento palabra o obra, quándo es peccado mortal o no. Compuesto por el maestro fray Augustín de Esbarroya* (Seville: Juan Canalla, 1550), fols a3^{r-v}; Bernardo de Nieva, OP, *Svmmario manval de información de la Christiana conscie[n]cia. Compuesto, y corregido por el presentado fray Bernardo de Nieua, de la orde[n] de los predicadores. Dirigido a la muy Illustre Señora Marquesa de las Navas, &c.* (Medina del Campo: Francisco del Canto, 1556), fol. 154^{v}; Domingo de Baltanás, OP, *Doctrina Christiana: en que se tracta de lo que deue cada vno creer, huyr, tener, obrar, dessear, y qué cosa es Dios: co[n] otras cosas dignas de saber* (Seville: Martín de Montesdoca, 1555), fols 12^{r-v}, 17^{r}; Peter Canisius, *Svmma de la doctrina christiana*, fols 84^{v}–85^{r}.

57 Duffy, *Stripping of the Altars*, 464–74; Haigh, *English Reformations*, 206–7; Ronald Hutton, *The Rise and Fall of Merry England: The Ritual Year, 1400–1700* (Oxford: Oxford University Press, 1994), 98; Peter Marshall, *The Catholic Priesthood and the English Reformation* (Oxford: Clarendon Press, 1994), 76–8; Wizeman, *Theology and Spirituality*, 162.

of the seven sacraments. It was the first doctrinal point discussed at Trent in its second phase under Julius III (1551–1552). The Tridentine decrees stressed the real and substantial presence of Christ in the sensible forms of bread and wine, confirmed the definition of transubstantiation as expounded by the Fourth Lateran Council (1215) and emphasised its sacrificial character to be perpetually offered in remembrance of Christ's passion, uniting all Christians as members of Christ's mystical body.[58] All of these elements were prominent in the works of Marian theologians.[59] Paul Bush (1490–1558), former bishop of Bristol, who had been deprived for being married but who had turned to Catholicism, explored scriptural sources to declare that 'Chryst hym selfe, affyrmeth that his moste holy and blessed bodi bothe fleshe & blud was really, corporally, naturally and substancially present at this worthy Maundy vnder the accedental fourmes of bred and wyne'.[60] In 1554 the Welsh vicar of Luton in Bedfordshire, John Gwynneth († 1557), re-printed one of his works, which he had written against John Frith (1503–1533), an evangelical who had rejected transubstantiation and had been burnt for heresy under Henry VIII. In his work, Gwynneth presented a dialogue between Hereticus and Catholicus, in which the former put forward Frith's arguments, which were then countered by Catholicus. The matters debated were still of paramount importance in the 1550s. To Hereticus's doubts about how Christ's body could be present in the Eucharist, being in heaven at the same time, Catholicus replied,

> First whether thou put the case of his blessed body, in heauen, or els in the holy Sacrament, all that is one to me. For I put no difference betwene them in the verite therof, but that it is the very same in the one place, that it is in the other. [...] If thou put it [the meaning] also to that substance, and call it corporall, meanynge it to be corporall, by reason of a supernatual [sic] connection of that substance, and suche supernaturall quantitee and qualitees together, as are beyond al thexperience and reche of any mortall mans wit, reason, or vnderstanding, I holde so well with that to.

However, if the implication was that Christ was corporally present in the sacrament in a physical, corruptible manner, the ideas of Hereticus were erroneous.

58 *Canons and Decrees*, 73–8.

59 Wooding, *Reforming Catholicism*, 123–5; Wizeman, *Theology and Spirituality*, 162–80.

60 Paul Bush, *A brefe exhortation set fourthe by the vnprofitable seruant of Jesu christ, Paule Bushe, late bishop of Brystowe, to one Margarete Burges wyfe of Jhon Burges, clothear of kyngeswode in the Countie of Wilshere* (London: John Cawood, 1556), sigs B2^{r-v}.

The body of Christ was present supernaturally and super-corporally, in ways that the human reason was not able to comprehend entirely.[61] English theologians affirmed Christ's real presence mainly through the accounts of the Last Supper, the Pauline narrative to be found in 1 Corinthians 11 and in the literal interpretation of John 6.[62]

In Carranza's theology, the sacrament of baptism communicated to Christians the spiritual life that God offered to humanity through the death of Jesus Christ, and the sacrament of confirmation provided strength and increment in such a life. The sacrament of communion, the Eucharist, had been offered by God to ensure that humans were able to 'sustain and preserve the spiritual life received in baptism'. This was so because,

> this sacrament, which is administered at the altar, contains really and truly the true body and the true blood of Jesus Christ under the figures of material bread and wine that we see with our corporeal eyes. And this body of Jesus Christ contained under the same is the same in substance as that which was born of the Virgin Mary, His Mother, and the same which suffered for our redemption at the Cross and resurrected on the third day, ascended to heaven forty days later and is now at the right side of God the Father. [...] And as natural bread and wine are the nourishment which sustain and preserve the natural life of the body, so the body and blood of Jesus Christ, who is in this sacrament, is the nourishment that sustains and preserves the spiritual life of the soul.[63]

---

61 John Gwynneth, *A Manifeste Detection of the notable falshed of that part of John Frithes boke, which he calleth his foundacion, And bosteth it to be inuincible: newly set foorthe by John Gwinneth Clerke* (London: Thomas Berthelet, 1554), fols 60^{r}–67^{v}.

62 Wizeman, *Theology and Spirituality*, 163–5; see examples of this perspective in the works of Marian theologians in Bonner, *Homelies*, fols 57^{r-v}, 69^{r-v}; John Gwynneth, *A Playne Demonstration of Iohn Frithes lacke of witte and learnynge in his vnderstandynge of holie Scripture, and of the olde holy doctours, in the blessed Sacrament of the Aulter, Newly set foorthe by John Gwynneth, Clerke* (London: Thomas Powell, 1557), fols 61^{v}–62^{r}; Miles Huggarde, *The assault of the sacrame[n]t of the Altar containyng aswell sixe seuerall assaultes made from tyme to tyme against the sayd blessed sacrament: as also the names & opinions of all the heretical captaines of the same asaultes: Written in the yere of oure Lorde 1549. by Myles Huggarde, and dedicated to the Quenes moste excellent maiestie, beyng then ladie Marie: in whiche tyme (heresie then raigning) it could take no place. Now newly imprynted this present yere. 1554.* (London: Robert Caly, 1554), sig. B2^{v}; Cuthbert Tunstall, *De ueritate Corporis et sangvinis domini nostri Iesu Christi in Eucharistia, Authore Cutheberto Tonstallo Dunelmensi Episcopo* (Paris: Michaëlis Vascosani, 1554), fols 19^{v}, 35^{r}, 69r; Watson, *Holsome and Catholyke doctryne*, fols 40^{v}–41^{v}; Watson, *Twoo Sermons*, sigs C8^{v}–D1^{r}.

63 Bartolomé de Carranza, OP, *Comentarios sobre el catecismo christiano* (Antwerp: 1558), vol. 1, José Ignacio Tellechea Idígoras, ed., (Madrid: Biblioteca de Autores Cristianos, 1972),

This emphasis on the species of bread and wine containing the whole body and blood of Christ were also to be found in Carranza's treatment of the effects of this sacrament in his 1546 *Summa omnium conciliorum*, which he had re-edited in Antwerp in 1556, while he was still in England.[64] In similar vein, Alfonso de Castro launched an attack in *Adversus omnes haereses* against Oecolampadius's (1482–1531) theological stance that the words *hoc est corpus meum* (Luke 22:19) were in fact a metaphor to signify Christ's body, an error that Castro linked to the heresy of Berengar of Tours in the eleventh century. Referring to previous scriptural citations (1 Corinthians 10, Matthew 26) and to patristic sources (Augustine, John Chrysostom, Ambrose, and Theophylact), Castro asserted that Christ's words, when speaking about his body and blood, far from being 'a trope or figurative locution', clearly demonstrated that,

> it truly is the body of Christ, who was born of a Virgin, hanged for us from the Cross, and was laid in the sepulchre, wherefrom he resurrected and ascended to heaven. All of this is confirmed in the sixth chapter of John in which this sentence, that He frequently repeats, leaves no room for us to doubt. '*Ego sum*', says Christ, '*panis vivus, qui de coelo descendi, siquis manducaverit ex hoc pane, vivet in aeternum. Et panis quem ego dabo, caro mea est, quam ego dabo pro mundi vita*'.

If Christ's passion was to be communicated to humanity, then the verb *dabo* (I give), certainly referred to Christ actually offering humanity the gift of His body as spiritual food to reach eternal life and the verb *est* (is), should not be

202–3: 'Porque este sacramento, que se administra en el altar, contiene real y verdaderamente el cuerpo verdadero y la sangre verdadera de Jesucristo debajo de aquellas figuras de pan material y vino que vemos con los ojos corporales. Y el cuerpo de Jesucristo contenido debajo de ellas es el mismo en sustancia que nació de la Virgen María, su madre, y el mismo que padeció por nuestra redención en la cruz y resucitó al tercero día, y después a los cuarenta días subió a los cielos, y agora está a la diestra de Dios Padre. [...] Y como el pan y vino natural son el mantenimiento que sustenta y conserva la vida natural del cuerpo, así el cuerpo y sangre de Jesucristo, que está en este sacramento, son el mantenimiento que sustenta y conserva la vida espiritual de la alma'. A similar emphasis on the sustenance of the soul to be found in 211.

64 Bartolomé de Carranza, OP, *Svmma omnivm conciliorvm, a Sancto Petro vsque ad Iulium quartum* [sic] *Pontificem, omnibus sacrae scripturae studiosis vtilissima* (Antwerp: Ioannes Steelsii, 1556), fol. 363r: 'Forma huius Sacramenti sunt verba saluatoris quibus hoc conficitur Sacramentum. Sacerdos enim in persona Christi loquens, hoc confici sacramentum. Nam ipsorum verborum virtute substa[n]tia panis in corpus Christi, et substantia vini in sanguinem coruentuntur, ita tamen quod totus Christus continetur sub specie panis, & totus sub specie vini, sus qualibet quoque parte hostiae consecratae, & vini consecrati, separation facta totus es Christus'.

understood as *significat* (signifies), for Christ had not said: 'The bread that I will give signifies my flesh or is a figure of my body'.[65] Castro further backed his claims with two additional scriptural citations, an assortment of Fathers and early Church theologians in agreement and the authority of two councils.[66]

In his brief *Compendium doctrinae catholicae* (1550), Pedro de Soto offered a very similar definition of the Eucharist.[67] This was further developed in his *Institvtione sacerdotvm*, where Soto described the institution of the sacrament as he perceived it to be contained in Matthew 26, Mark 14, Luke 22 and 1 Corinthians 11. From his point of view, the words of consecration *hoc est corpus meum* and *hic est calix* contained two truths held by the Church:

> First, these words do signify the true presence of Christ's body and blood, and thus of Christ himself wholly. Their other meaning is that the substance of bread and wine is not there. Thus, true faith holds these two

---

65 Castro, *Aduersus omnes haereses*, fols 142ᵛ–146ᵛ: 'Primò ergo illa verba Christi expressa sunt quibus ait: Hoc est corpus meu[m] [Luke 22:19]. Nil certe expressius quicquam dici potuit: nec in re tanti momento, qualis est ista, credendum est Christum tropo aliquo aut figurata loquutione vsum fuisse, ne ansam erra[n]di hac occasione nobis praeberet. Verùm quum de hac re iam satis dixerimus, opus est vt ex alijs testimonijs ostendamus nullum ibi esse tropu[m], verumq[ue] ibi esse corpus Christi, quod natum est de virgine, & pro nobis in cruce pependit, iacuit in sepluchro, ac deinde reuixit, ad coelosq[ue] ascendit. Hoc aut[em] totum illud Ioannis sextum caput confirmat, in quo saepissime hanc sentential[m] repetit, vt nulla nobis dubitation maneret. Ego sum (inquit Christus) panis vius, qui de coelo descendi, siquis manducauerit ex hoc pane, viuet in aeternum. Et panis quem ego dabo, caro mea est, quam ego dabo pro mundi vita. Ecce hic bispositum hoc verbum dabo, vt semel referas ad donationem in modu[m] cibi, iterum autem referas ad passionem, in qua seipsum morti tradidit pro nostra omnium vita: ac si parum expressius dixisset: Panis quem vobis daturus sum ad comede[n]dum, caro mea est, caro inqua[m] illa quam dabo pro vestra omnium vita. Verùm fortè vt iam coepisti, etiam hic interpretaberis verbum est, per significat, vt dicas sic esse intelligendu[m]: Panis quem ego dabo, carne[m] mea[m] significat, aut figura quaeda[m] est corporis mei'.

66 Matthew 4 and John 8, Theophylact, Cyril, Chrysostom, Augustine, Cassiodorus, Gregory the Great, Ambrose, Hilary of Poitiers, Cyprian, Origen, Leo I, Juvencus, Arnobius, Irenaeus, Polycarp, Ignatius and the Councils of Ephesus (431) and Constance (1414–1418).

67 Pedro de Soto, OP, *Compendium doctrinae Catholicae, in usum plebis Christianae recte instituendae R. F. Petri de Soto, Dominicani Theologi, Confessoris Caesaree Maiest. collectum, additi cuique loco aptis precatiunculis, & adiuncta breui explicatione Ecclesiastici cultus, maxime Sacrae Missae eodem Authore* (Ingoldstadt: Alexander Weissenhorn, 1550), sig. B1ᵛ: 'Eucharistia est, in qua nutrimur, conseruaturq[ue] in nobis gratia per Christi uerum corpus, & sanguinem, in quae co[n]secrationis verbis, panis & uinum conuertuntur, manentibus solis accidentibus, sub quorum qualibet specie totus Christus sumitur, offerturq[ue] patri in ritu[m] sacrae Missae, prout in Catholica Ecclesia celebrator, atq[ue] adoratur etiam sub qualibet praedictarum specierum'.

> things, namely that Christ's body is present truly and substantially, but the substance of the bread in no way [remains].[68]

If Christ's own words were not enough, Soto contended, especially as transmitted in John 6 and 1 Corinthians 10 and 11, the heretics – from Berengar all the way down to Oecolampadius and Zwingli – also erred against the 'authority and agreed sense' that the Fathers had ascribed to these words. Augustine had interpreted them in this way in his *De doctrina christiana*, and as such they had been conveyed by Peter Lombard in his *Sententiarum* in the eleventh century and by the canon lawyer Gratian in his *Decretum* in the twelfth. They had been thus understood by the 'whole Church from the Apostles until now' and this, Soto continued, had been amply corroborated by 'John, bishop of Rochester, a most pious Englishman and glorious martyr of our times'.[69] Placing great emphasis on the historical authority of tradition, Soto followed Fisher's *De veritate* (1527) to explore the patristic lineage of the definition of the real presence, based upon scriptural exegesis, as presented by Ambrose, Chrysostom, Augustine, Cyril and others to which he added his own examples extracted from Dionysius the Areopagite, Origen, Jerome, Cyprian and Gregory the Great. Retaking a scholastic dialectic, Soto challenged the claims of the heretics that Scripture did not 'satisfactorily prove' the real presence by replying that 'much less does Scripture prove the contrary'.[70] Therefore, to avoid doubts arising, to ascertain the non-figurative meaning of Christ's words, Soto advocated fidelity to the historical tradition of the Fathers. Any other attitude would amount to a denial of the 'efficacy' operated by Christ's own words.[71]

---

68 Soto, *Institvtione sacerdotvm*, fols 67ᵛ–72ᵛ: 'Duo igitur sunt, quae Ecclesia circa hoc certissima habet. Primum, his verbis significari veram praesentiam carnis Christi & sanguinis, atq[ue] adeò totius ipsius Christi. Alterum, significari etiam, non esse ibi substantiam panil vel vini, atq[ue] ideo duo ista effici credit vera fides, vt scilicet corpus Christi sit praesens veraciter & substantialiter, panis verò substantia nullo modo'.

69 Soto, *Institvtione sacerdotvm*, fols 72ᵛ–73ʳ: 'De hoc ergò vt certissimum habeatur, omnem Ecclesiam ab Apostolis vsq[ue] nunc, ita veritatem huius sacramenti tenuisse & docuisse: vt quàmprimum aliquis aliter docuisse fuerit deprehensus, mox ipsum damnauerit. Itaq[ue] non verbis tantùm, sed re ipsa etiam constare, hanc semper fuisse veram fidem Ecclesię. Deducit hoc latius Ioannes Roffensis Episcopus magnae pietatis Anglus, & gloriosus nostril temporis martyr, in libris 5. Quos de hoc aedidit contra Oecolampadium, maximè in proemijs trium posteriorum libroru[m]'.

70 Pseudo-Dionysius the Aeropagite (who lived in the fifth or sixth centuries) was an influential figure in the history of Christianity. Although by the sixteenth century some theologians (including Erasmus) had accepted that he was not the same person as the Athenian convert in Acts 17:34 – a confusion which stemmed from Pseudo-Dionysius's own misleading assertions – the fact had not yet been officially acknowledged.

71 Soto, *Institvtione sacerdotvm*, fols 72ᵛ–75ᵛ.

Other Spanish authors expressed very similar views, in concordance with their countrymen who went to England with Philip as well as with the Marian theologians and the decrees promulgated at Trent. Diego Jiménez described the Eucharist in very similar terms to those employed by his friend Carranza.[72] According to Pedro de Medina, 'Christ, God and Man' was wholly contained in the sacrament of the altar.[73] Felipe de Meneses also analysed John 6 to describe the sacrament as the sustenance for 'the life of the soul', as the body and blood of Christ were contained in it.[74] In his manual for confessors, another friend of Carranza and a fellow Navarrese, Martín de Azpilcueta (1491–1586), advised spiritual directors to ask their penitents whether they had any doubts about the presence of the 'true body and blood' of Christ under the visible forms of bread and wine.[75] Bernardo de Nieva was in agreement with the preceding views and in Cordero's translation of Canisius's *Summa* there is a succinct but clearly delivered discussion of the same theme, in which the Dutch Jesuit offered many of the same scriptural and patristic sources to defend the real presence.[76]

With regards to the doctrine of transubstantiation, there has been a long-standing view in the historiography that has had English Catholic theologians (or traditionalists, in earlier historiographical parlance) 'abandon' the defence of the sacrament and the precise doctrine of transubstantiation. Their defence of the latter had been ambivalent and, at best, lukewarm.[77] William Wizeman found that, on the contrary, the portrayal of transubstantiation offered by English authors was solid and coherent and followed the arguments of earlier theologians such as Fisher, Thomas More or Johann Cochlaeus.[78] Only four of the Marian theologians failed to use the term 'transubstantiation' (Roger Edgeworth, George Marshall, Paul Bush and John Gwynneth), yet they all

72 Jiménez, *Enchiridión*, fol. 143^{r}.

73 Medina, *Libro de la Verdad*, fols 133^{v}–134^{r}.

74 Meneses, *Lvz del alma*, fol. 119^{r}.

75 Martín de Azpilcueta, *Manval de confessores, y penitentes, qve clara y breuemente contiene, La vniuersal y particular decisión de quasi todas las dudas, que en las confessiones suelen ocurrir de los pecados, absoluciones, restituciones, censuras, & irregularidades* (Antwerp: Ioannes Steelsii, 1557), 426.

76 Canisius, *Svmma de la doctrina christiana*, fols 39^{v}–40^{r}.

77 This traditional overview was inaugarated by J. W. Martin, 'The Marian Regime's Failure to Understand the Importance of Printing', *Huntington Library Quarterly*, 44, no. 4 (1981), 231–47 and Edward J. Baskerville, *A Chronological Bibliography of Propaganda and Polemic Published in English between 1553 and 1558, from the death of Edward VI to the death of Mary I* (Philadelphia: American Philosophical Society, 1979), 1–30 and further developed by Macek, *Loyal Opposition*, 70–1.

78 Wizeman, *Theology and Spirituality*, 162–9.

described the transformation of bread and wine into the body and blood of Christ in a manner much like that of the doctrine as defined by Lateran IV and confirmed in 1551 by Trent.[79]

Thomas Watson, for instance, provided a definition of transubstantiation based on Matthew 26, 1 Corinthians 10, Ignatius, Chrysostom, and Eusebius of Emesa. After the words of consecration were uttered,

> the holy churche and all true christen men her members dooe grounde theyr faithe concernynge the change whiche the holye ghoste by his vnspeakable power worketh in this sacrament, where the inward substaunce of breade and wyne is changed into the substaunce of the bodye and bloude of Chryste, the outwarde forms [...], with the quantitie and qualities of the same, styll remaining vnchaunged, whiche maner of change because it is singuler and hathe none lyke it, eyther in nature or otherwise, therefore the holy Churche dothe cal it by the name of Transubstantiatio[n], the which woorde was inuented by the holy churche in the greatest generall counsell that euer was, [...] the counsel of Lateranense.[80]

Openly admitting that the word itself had been 'inuented', Watson did not hesitate to mention the number of prelates that attended Lateran IV ('seuenty Archebyshoppes and foure hundred Byshops') to underline the foundations of the doctrine as being within the assent of the whole Church gathered together under the authority of a general council.[81] This, Watson continued, did not mean that the change itself was new, but it had been given a name to avoid impairing and raising doubts about 'the olde knowen trueth reueled to the Churche by the holye ghoste', a truth that 'the Churche learneth of Christes owne wordes'. These were crucial for the effects of the consecration, through which the inner substance of the bread and wine was changed into that of the body and blood of Christ, whilst 'the outward apparaunce', the accidents

79 Wizeman, *Theology and Spirituality*, 168.

80 Watson, *Holsome and Catholyke Doctrine*, fols 42^{v}–43^{r}.

81 Watson, *Holsome and Catholyke Doctrine*, fols 43^{r}. The same idea was also expressed by Dr Alban Langdale, archdeacon of Chichester, in his work written during the disputations with Nicholas Ridley at Cambridge about the Eucharist held under the reign of Edward VI and printed in the reign of Philip and Mary in Paris. See Alban Langdale, *Catholica confutatio impiae cvivsdam determinationis D. Nicolai Ridlęi, eo tempore sedem Episcopalem apud Roffam occupantis, post disputationem de Eucharistia in Academia Cantabrigie[n]si, habitae, in tres libros diuisa* (Paris: Michaëlis Vascosani, 1556), fols 60^{r}–61^{v}: 'Non erubescit transsubstantiationis nomen cum re affirmare, & eam non à scholasticis inuenta[m], sed ab Ecclesia definita[m] apertè asserit'.

of bread and wine, remained. It was the omnipotent power of Christ's words which, through faith, enabled transubstantiation.

> And as in the person of Chryste, his humanitie was sene and his diuinitie was secret vnsene, euen so in this sacrament the outward forme of bread appeareth to mans sight, and the inward substance of Christ god and ma[n] appeareth not to a mans corporall eyes, but to the eye of his soule, whiche is faith [...]. For he that can create all thynges of nought with his woorde, can also change things that be created with his word.[82]

This defence of the doctrine, supported by an array of patristic and scriptural sources, was repeated by Watson more succinctly in his collection of sermons, where he claimed that the change in substance was propitiated by God's 'omnipotente power and wyll' with the assistance of 'the due administration of the Priest'.[83] Bonner, too, used Scripture and the Fathers to describe transubstantiation, affirming that the change took place 'daylye, by the mynysterye of the preistes in consecration[n]'.[84] Equivalent ways of explicating the doctrine were taken by most Marian theologians.[85]

In his *Comentarios*, Carranza offered a similar definition, based on Matthew 26: 26–28, Mark 14:22–24 and Luke 22:19–20, a reference to the Corpus Christi hymn *Pange lingua* to underline the importance of faith in the validation of the sacrament, and a reference to the Fathers of the Church to explain the origins of the term.

---

82 Watson, *Holsome and Catholyke Doctrine*, fols 43^{r-v}.

83 Watson, *Twoo Sermons*, sig. A8^{r}.

84 Bonner, *Profitable and Necessarye Doctrine*, sigs V1^{r}–X2^{r}.

85 Bonner and Harpsfield in Bonner, *Homelies*, fols 6^{r}, 56^{r}–58^{v}, 59^{r-v}, 65^{r-v}; Bush, *Brefe Exhortation*, sigs B1^{r}–B8^{r}; George Marshall, *A compendious treatise in metre declaring the firste originall of the Sacrifice, and of the building of Aultares and Churches, and of the firste receauinge of the Christen fayth here in Englande by G. M.* (London: John Cawood, 1554), sig. B3^{r}; Huggarde, *Assault of the sacrame[n]t of the*, sigs B2^{r}–B4^{r}; James Brooks, *A Sermon very notable, fruictefull, and Godlie, made at Paules crosse the .xii. daie of Noue[m]bre, in the first yere of the gracious reigne of our Souereigne ladie Quene Marie her moste excellent highnesse, by James Brokis Doctor of Diuinitie, & Master of Bailye College in Oxforth, with certain additions, whiche he at the tyme of vttering, for auoidyng of tediousness, was faine to omitte* (London: Robert Caly, 1553), sigs E1^{r}–F7^{v}; Leonard Pollard, *Fyve Homiles of late, made by a ryght good and vertuous clerke, called master Leonarde Pollarde, prebendary of the Cathdrall Churche of Woster, directed and dedicated to the ryght reuerende Father in God Rychard by the permissyon of God byshoppe of Woster his specyall good Lorde* (London: William Griffith, 1556), sigs A7^{v}–B2^{v}.

> Following the consecration made by the priest by those divine words with which Jesus Christ our Lord consecrated the Supper, the bread transforms into the body of Jesus Christ and the wine into His blood. This transformation is now called by the Fathers of the Church transubstantiation because the substance of one turns into that of the other and thus of the bread and wine that were there before nothing remains but the accidents of the outward appearance. This is what Christ said to his disciples when he gave them communion at the Supper [...]. It was thus rendered by St Matthew, St Mark and St Luke, the three evangelists, and this is how the Church has declared it since her foundation. Everything in this sacrament is miraculous and performed by God's omnipotence which is why the Church sings [at the *Pange lingua*] that, to confirm the heart in the truth of this sacrament, faith alone is sufficient, our senses lacking [for that purpose].[86]

Soto concurred in ascribing such an importance to the agreement of the Fathers, a stance designed to signal the long lineage of the doctrine despite the fact that the term had been coined relatively recently – the same strategy followed by their English counterparts. The tenet of the faith surrounding transubstantiation, Soto expounded in his *Institvtione sacerdotvm*, was that after the conversion effected by the words of consecration, Christ's body was truly there and that what remained was not bread. The transformation of the substance of bread into the substance of Christ's body had been manifestly understood by all the Fathers in the words *hoc est corpus meum* and *hic est calix novum testamentum in sanguine meo*. This was supported by Ambrose, who had highlighted the 'efficacious' nature of Christ's words, by John Damascene, by Eusebius of Emesa, and by other Fathers quoted previously, including the testimony of John Fisher. Contrary to the 'present heretics' who 'mocked' the term and called it a 'human invention', Soto explained how the Church,

---

86 Carranza, *Comentarios sobre el catechismo christiano*, II, 211: 'Después de la consagración que el sacerdote hace con aquellas palabras divinas que Jesucristo N. S. consagró en la cena, se convierte el pan en el cuerpo de Jesucristo, y el vino en la sangre suya. Esta conversión llaman agora los Padres de la Iglesia transubstanciación, porque la sustancia de lo uno se convierte en lo otro, y del pan que antes había y del vino no queda nada, sino sólo los accidentes que parecen por de fuera. Esto es lo que Cristo dijo a sus discípulos cuando los comulgó en la cena. [...] Así los refieren los tres evangelistas, S. Mateo, S. Marcos y S. Lucas, y así lo tiene declarado la Iglesia desde su fundación. En este sacramento todas las cosas son milagrosas y hechas por la omnipotencia de Dios, y por esto lo canta la Iglesia que, para confirmar el corazón en la verdad de este sacramento, basta la fe sola, pues que falta el sentido'.

following the agreed 'sense of all the Fathers', had defined the doctrine in Lateran IV under Innocent III (r. 1198–1216) just as the name *homousius* had been accepted by the Council of Nicaea (325) to describe the consubstantiality of the three persons of the Trinity. Following the same logic, the term transubstantiation emerged from faith, Scripture and tradition and was accepted by the Church.[87] In Soto's theology there is a strong emphasis in the fact that it was God's omnipotence, his 'divine virtue', that effected the transmutation of substances. The miraculous nature of transubstantiation exceeded human reason and judgement, like many other 'miracles in Scripture', and the only way truly to attain the benefits of the sacrament was to come to it with faith, as had been amply explained by St Thomas Aquinas, Chrysostom, John Damascene and Hilary.[88]

For the Franciscan Castro, Berengar's errors had been revived by John Wycliffe (*c.*1328–1384) and more recently by Luther. Accusing the latter of distorting the true sense of the words *hoc est corpus meum* and *hic est calix*, Castro exposed what he perceived to be Lutheran subterfuge by examining the function of pronouns, articles and gender in those passages and how Luther had used them with the intention to confound.[89] Like his Spanish and English colleagues, he explored the same passages in the Synoptic Gospels (Matthew 26, Mark 14 and Luke 22) to conclude that, '[f]rom all the words of the evangelists it appears that in no place it is said "bread" or "wine" after the consecration of the sacrament has been performed, but only "body" or "blood"'.[90] From Castro's perspective, what was truly important was the meaning of the doctrine itself, rather than the word used to define it, although he acknowledged its validity as a definition inspired by the Spirit and approved in a general council. Castro proceeded to ridicule Luther's mocking and his claims that 'transubstantiation is a recent invention, [...] it being but three hundred years old'. What Lateran IV had defined in 1215, the Council of Constance had confirmed in

87 Soto, *Institvtione sacerdotvm*, fols 81^{r}–81^{v}: 'Quod sanè considerandum est etia[m] contra praesentes haereticos, qui nomen hoc conuersionis & transsubstantiationis omnino irrident, & humanu[m] inuentum dicunt: cùm tamen Ecclesia ex patrum omnium sensu hoc definierit, conuerti videlicet totam substantiam panis, materiam scilicet & formam, in totum corpus Christi iam praexistens. Ita Innocentius tertius in co[n]cilio Lateranensi, vt habetur ca Firmiter. de summa Trinitate et fide Catholica. Vocabulum igitur transsubsta[n]tiationis ita ex ipsa fide & scriptura atq[ue] traditione intulerunt, sicut nomen homusion in concilio nicaeno receptum fuit'.

88 Soto, *Institvtione sacerdotvm*, fols 80^{v}–81^{r}, 81^{v}–82^{r}, 84^{r-v}.

89 Castro, *Adversus omnes haereses*, fols 147^{v}–148^{r}.

90 Castro, *Adversus omnes haereses*, fol. 148^{r}: 'Ex omnibus Euangelistorum verbis patet nullum esse locum in quo post factam consecrationem sacramentum vocetur panis aut vinum, sed tantum corpus aut sanguis'.

1415 in its condemnation of Wycliffe's theology as heresy. The insistence on the name was, Castro concluded, ultimately irrelevant.

> Whether this translation is called transubstantiation, transmutation, or conversion, it makes no difference, provided it is professed that the bread does not remain after consecration, as it has translated into the body of Christ.[91]

Therefore, the doctrine was not the 'invention of recent scholastic theologians', nor one merely three hundred years old, but one that had been held by many of the Fathers until its confirmation by the Council of Constance, and he proceeded to quote examples from Theophylact, John Damascene, Gregory of Nyssa, Cyprian and Irenaeus.[92]

In strongly Thomist terms, the humanist Pedro de Medina emphasised the same role ascribed to God's omnipotence in the process of transubstantiation. If the prophet Elijah had prompted fire to descend from heaven through his prayers [1 Kings 18:38], and nature turned nourishment into flesh in a man's body, it was obvious that Christ's words could 'mutate the bread and wine into his body and blood'. After all, it was a greater thing 'to create something from nought, than to transmutate something into another'.[93] Using the same

---

91 Castro, *Adversus omnes haereses*, fol. 149^{r}: 'Verùm etsi hoc sufficienter ostendat panem non manere, non tamen ostendit pane[m] transubsta[n]tiara in corpus Christi, quod Lutherus negat, irridetq[ue] dicens hanc transsubstantiationem esse recens inuentam, nec vetustiorem quam trecentenariam. Si de vocabulo solo est dissidium, indigna prorsus res est vt pro ea digla diemur, modò conueniat inter nos de re. Res autem est, panem non manere post consecrationem, ipsumq[ue] conuerti in corpus Christi. Siue autem illam versionem appellet transsubstantiationem, siue transmutationem, siue conuersionem, non multum curabo, dummodo fateatur panem non manere post consecrationem, ipsumq[ue] verti in corpus Christi'.

92 Castro, *Adversus omnes haereses*, fols 149^{r}–150^{r}: 'Horum primum iam oste[n]dimus cum ex aliijs, tum ex concilij Constantiensis definitione. Alterum ostendere superest, panem scilicet verti in corpus Christi, idq[ue] non esse recens theologorum scholasticorum inuentum, nempe tricentenarium, vt Lutherus ait. Pro qua re plurima sanctorum patrum citabo testimonia: quae omnia si bene consideres lector, videbis etiam aduersus praedictam Berengarij & Oecolampadij haeresim manifestè pugnare'.

93 Medina, *Libro de la Verdad*, fols 138^{r-v}: 'Mira hombre guarda te mucho de escudriñar ynútil y curiosamente, este profundíssimo sacramento, si no quieres ser sumido en el abismo de las dubdas. No seas escudriñador de la magestad d[e]l señor. Mira que más puede dios obrar, que el hombre entender ni pensar. [...] Y si por la palabra de Elías descendió fuego del cielo, porqué? por la palabra de Jesu christo dios todo poderoso no se mudara el pa[n] y el vino en carne, y sangre suya, y mira que no es mucho esto para dios, pues que natura haze que lo que el hombre come y beue se buelua en carne, y sangre, y cierto es que más fuerça tiene dios que natura, pues ella crió. Luego mejor puede de pan conuertir

sources as the English theologians and Carranza, Soto and Castro, the Dutch Peter Canisius also emphasised the role of faith in God's omnipotence when it came to explaining the 'transubstantial mutation' of the bread and wine.[94]

English Catholic theologians were also in unison concerning the description and defence of other aspects of the Eucharist such as the role that the Mass had as an offering of Christ's perpetual sacrifice as a means for Christians to participate in their own redemption by placing their own works alongisde Christ's sacrifice for humanity at the Cross.[95] Furthermore, these theologians agreed that one of the greatest effects of the sacrament, such as the sustenance of divine grace and the preparation of the soul for eternal life through the spiritual food offered at the Mass, was the union with Christ that it achieved.[96] This union in the mystical body of Christ had strong Erasmian undertones, and it signalled a way of understanding the Church as a communion of saints.[97] This idea had greatly influenced Spanish writers since the early sixteenth century, both those with an orthodox outlook as well as those who had tendencies towards or had openly embraced Protestantism.[98] It was an understanding of man's relationship with Christ rooted in humanist ideas of biblicism and a strong emphasis on a Pauline christology. It placed Christ at the centre of a relationship uniting all Christians in a communion of believers. The clergyman Leonard Pollard († 1556) expressed this in clear terms:

> For lyke as the headde and the bodye maketh but one thynge, so the body of our sauyour Chryste, wherewith the Church is dayly fedde, being heade of the Church, and the Churche that eateth the same bodye beinge

en cuerpo suyo, y del vino en sangre. Pues más es de nada criar algo, que de lo que es algo trasmudar en otra cosa'. For St Thomas Aquinas see his 'Lectio sexta' on the feast of Corpus Christi: 'Quod si tantum valuit sermo Heliae ut ignem de caelo praeponeret, non valebit sermo Christi ut species mutet elementorum?'

94 Canisius, *Svmma de la doctrina christiana*, fol. 40v.

95 Wooding, *Rethinking Catholicism*, 170; Wizeman, *Theology and Spirituality*, 169–72.

96 Wooding, *Rethinking Catholicism*, 174–5; Wizeman, *Theology and Spirituality*, 176–8.

97 Wooding, *Rethinking Catholicism*, 174; M. A. Screech, *Erasmus: Ecstasy and The Praise of Folly* (London: Duckworth, 1980), 117–29.

98 For the implication of Christ's mystical body in Erasmus's *Enchiridion militis Christiani* (1501) and how it influenced Spanish orthodox theologians, *alumbrados*, and Protestants see Marcel Bataillon, *Erasmo y España, estudios sobre la historia espiritual del siglo XVI*, tr. Antonio Alatorre [1937] (Mexico City: Fondo de Cultura Económica, 1950), 206–9, 565–6. Stefania Pastore has posited that the upsurge in works treating this theme was due to the influence of Calvin's *Institutio Christianae religionis* (1536), reflected in the anonymous *Beneficio di Cristo* published in Venice in 1543 and in Carranza's *Comentarios*. See Stefania Pastore, *Una herejía española. Conversos, alumbrados e Inquisición (1449–1559)*, tr. Clara Álvarez Alonso [2004] (Madrid: Marcial Pons Historia, 2010), 307.

> so made one with Chryst, that it is his body, so whan the Church doth offer his body in the sacrame[n]t, the Church doth offer her selfe, for she offereth her heade. For [...] as the thynge that is eaten, and the thynge that eateth, are by eatynge made one, so by eatynge Chrystes blessed body we be made (as sayth Ciryll) really and corporally one with him [...] and thereupon are we called members of Chryste, and he indede is our heade.[99]

The anonymous author of *A plaine and godlye treatise, concernynge the Masse* concurred, quoting St Paul, in that by receiving Christ's body and blood at the sacrament, 'the whole Churche of Chryst is made one mysticall bodye of Chryste'.[100] The union of the worthy receivers in Christ's mystical body was a recurring theme in the works of Watson and Cuthbert Tunstall, bishop of Durham, and it was mentioned, with varying degrees of emphasis by Bonner and Alban Langdale too.[101]

Carranza, in his *Comentarios*, believed that the divine substance of Christ entered the worthy receiver by eating the body and drinking the blood of Christ and thus, he argued, 'we become members of the Christian body, this being a testimony to charity and ecclesiastical union', as St Paul had proclaimed in 1 Cor 10:17, a view that he had already summarised in his *Svmma omnium conciliorum*.[102] Pedro de Soto wholeheartedly agreed. The Eucharist was

---

99 Pollard, *Fyve homiles*, fols C3^{v}–C4^{r}.

100 Anon., *A plaine and godlye treatise, concernynge the Masse & the blessed Sacrament of the Aulter, for the instruccion of the symple and vnlerned people* (London: John Wayland?, 1556), sigs B7^{v}–B8^{v}.

101 Watson, *Holsome and Catholyke Doctrine*, fols 39^{r}, 53^{r-v}; Watson, *Twoo Notable Sermons*, sigs F2^{v}–F8^{r}; Tunstall, *De ueritate*, fols 22^{r-v}, 80r, 81^{r}–87^{v}; Bonner, *Profitable and Necessarye Doctrine*, sigs Z8^{v}–Aa1^{r}; Bonner, *Homelies*, fols 66^{v}–67^{r}, 90^{v}–92^{v}; Langdale, *Catholica confutatio*, fols 66^{v}–67^{v}: 'Quasi diceret, An adhuc ignoratis, aut non meministis potius, quòd hic panis quem frangimus, sit communicatio corporis Christi, quòdque calix similiter cui benedicimus, sit ipsius sanguinis co[m]municatio? quotquot enim hunc calicem, & hunc panem dignè sumitis, arctissima coniuctione (ueluti unus panis) Christo coniungimini'. 'Hoc argume[n]tum demo[n]strat Paulus, quid nobis praecipuè in hoc sacramentum quaerendum, uidelicet, qua totus homo toti Christi coniungitur'. 'Co[m]municatio autem corporis, quid aliud est, qua[m] corporu[m] nostrorum, cum corpore eius, & spirituu[m] nostroru[m] cu[m] spiritu eius, no[n] dico participatio aut annexio, sed magis membrorum ad caput unio, qua, non fide & charitate solùm, sed re ipsa unum corpus multi sumus?'

102 Carranza, *Comentarios sobre el catechismo christiano*, vol. 2, 213–4: '[...] recibiendo este sacramento dignamente, recibimos al Hijo de Dios, y nos incorporamos con él y nos hacemos miembros suyos; y recibiendo a Cristo, recibimos el Tesoro con el cual se pagaron todos los pecados y se destruyó la muerte y se ganó la vida eterna. [...] Otro efecto principal se sigue de éste, y es que comiendo el cuerpo y bebiendo la sangre de Cristo, nos

necessary for the preservation and increase of the spiritual life; it was medicine for the soul.[103] The foundational scriptural passages for this effect of the sacrament, he explained, were to be found in John 6:51 and Genesis 49:11, which 'signified [...] the mystical body of the Church, that is, the unity of all the faithful, who convene in this unity not unlike diverse wheat grains and grapes unite in one bread and in one wine'.[104] This was confirmed by Augustine in *Tractatus in Evangelium Joannes*, and it meant that worthy receivers were members of Christ in the unity of the Church.[105] The Pauline passage in 1 Corinthians 10:17 (*unus panis et unum corpus multi sumus, omnes qui de uno pane et calice participamus*) and Galatians 2:20 (*vivo autem iam non ego, vivit vero in me Christus*) plainly explained this and, Soto added,

> [t]his is the special effect of this sacrament which is suggested to us by the bread and wine, the matter of this sacrament; namely, that if we wish to be members of Christ's body and to belong to the unity of the Church, let us allow ourselves to be broken like the grains of wheat and depart from our own will. Thus we become of one heart and of one soul with the others.[106]

hacemos miembros del cuerpo cristiano, siendo este un testimonio de la caridad y de la unión eclesiástica, como lo declara S. Pablo escribiendo a los de Corinto, diciendo: *Todos los que participamos de un pan y de un cáliz* en la mesa de Cristo, *siendo muchos, somos un pan y un cuerpo*'.; Carranza, *Svmma omnivm conciliorvm*, fol. 363^{r-v}: 'Huius sacramenti effectus, quem in anima operatur dignè sumentis, est adunatio hominis ad Christum. Et quia per gratiam homo Christo incorporatur, & membris eius vnitur, sequitur quod per hoc sacramentum in sumentibus digne gratia augeatur: omnemque effectum, quem materialis cibus & potus quo ad vitam agunt corporalem, hoc idem quo ad vitam spiritualem & hoc sacramentum operator'.

103 Soto, *Institvtione sacerdotvm*, fols 98^{r-v}.

104 Soto, *Institvtione sacerdotvm*, fol. 107^{r}: 'Sed significant etiam corpus ipsum mysticum Ecclesiae, hoc est, vnitatem fidelium ómnium, qui in hanc vnitatem conueniunt no[n] aliter quàm diuersa grana tritici et votri in vnum panem & vinum'.

105 Soto, *Institvtione sacerdotvm*, fol. 107^{r-v}: 'Ita enim Augustinus inquit in sextum cap. Ioannis: quòd propterea dominus corpus suum & sanguinem nobis comme[n]dauerit in iijs rebus, quae ex multis in vnum aliquid rediguntur, vt significetur haec Ecclesiae vnitas. Igitur & hoc efficit istud sacramentum sicut significat: vnit omnes sumentes: & primò quidem in ipsum Christum illos transformat: deinde coaptat caeteris omnibus membris Christi [...]'.

106 Soto, *Institvtione sacerdotvm*, fols 107^{v}–108^{r}: 'Hic est huius sacramenti proprius effectus: hoc ipsum admonet nos panis & vinum, quae materia sunt huius sacramenti: vt videlicet, si volumus membra esse corporis Christi, & ad Ecclesiasticam vnitatem pertinere, permittamus nos sicut grana tritici frangi, & à propria volu[n]tate discedamus: vt sic simus cor vnum & anima vna cum alijs'.

The crucial position that the Eucharist possessed in relation to the body of Christ was also common to other Spanish authors still residing in Spain. For Martínez de Laguna, 'Through communion, / We become one body and one union, / With the redeemer, / If with honour and cleanliness, / It is taken by the receiver, / As in glorious St Paul's prayer'.[107] Through the Eucharist, Martínez de Laguna explained, Christians were 'incorporated into Christ', and Felipe de Meneses agreed that communion meant to be joined with Christ and that those who received Him 'participated of His virtue and divinity' united in 'faith and religion', as St Paul expounded in 1 Corinthians 10.[108] In Cordero's translation of Canisius, the efficacy of the sacrament of the altar as the vehicle for a union 'of all the faithful Christians as members of one body' presided by Jesus Christ as head was also emphatically presented.[109]

5.3 Papal Primacy

The unity of believers in the same body was of paramount importance to one of the most thorny issues of the English Reformations: the visibility and authority of the Church under the primacy of the bishop of Rome. It had been almost twenty years since papal jurisdiction had been abolished in England when Mary I came to the throne in 1553. In the context of Philip and Mary's joint reign, besides the parliamentary sessions which allowed the reunion with Rome in November 1554, little has been said about how the pope's figure fitted in the regime's intellectual and theological mindset. A. G. Dickens treated the reconciliation as an almost purely secular procedure and concluded that there were probably no 'passionate feelings in either direction' among the English populace. Admittedly, through the lenses of foreign residents in England, he viewed the restoration of papal jurisdiction as an event which stirred little interest.[110] Christopher Haigh perceived that not much was done to strengthen loyalty to Rome besides the commemorative sermons by John Harpsfield and Cardinal Pole in 1556 and 1557 respectively and the former's homilies printed in Bonner's collection.[111] Wooding understood the papacy to have been 'conspicuously absent' in the preoccupations of Marian theologians, who 'failed to ascribe any

107 Martínez de Laguna, *Svmma de doctrina christiana*, fols 90^{r-v}: 'Por la comunión / nos hazemos vn cuerpo, y vna mesma vnión / con el redemptor, /si la rescibimos con aquel honor, / y vera limpieza. / que aquel glorioso sant Pablo nos reza [...]'.

108 Martínez de Laguna, *Svmma de doctrina christiana*, fol. 91^{v}; Meneses, *Lvz del alma*, fol. 89^{v}.

109 Canisius, *Svmma de la doctrina christiana*, fols 45^{v}–46^{r}.

110 Dickens, *English Reformation*, 360–1.

111 Haigh, *English Reformations*, 223–4.

decisive role to the papacy'.[112] This consensus has been recently contested, but the place of Spanish theologians in this debate remains unexplored.[113]

Marian theologians did present a coherent theory of papal authority. The Catholic Church was the communion of saints as expressed in the Symbol of the Apostles and, Bonner expounded,

> as al the lyuing parts and members of the naturall body of man, do naturally communicate and be participante of one spirit or soule which gouerne the sayde bodye, and euerye lyuelye parte therof, euen so doe all good Chrysten men, participate of one holy ghost, whyche alwayes gouerneth the catholyke churche, and al lyuely membres of the same.[114]

In Bonner's pespective, the communion of the faithful was therefore imbued with the Holy Spirit, who ruled the Church. Papal primacy had been instituted by Christ to maintain unity and order, and He had appointed a 'chief vycar, and substitute of Chryst' – the first of whom had been Peter – entrusted, together 'with other ministers vnder him', with 'the good order, and rule of the [...] militant churche'.[115] John Standish (*c.*1509–1570), a deprived married prebendary who reconciled to Catholicism and repudiated his wife, wrote that all those who truly professed the Christian religion were 'membres of Christes ecclesiastical body vnder hym as head, whether they be priestes or lay men, Emperours Kinges, or byshoppes'. However, anyone who broke Christ's order that 'Peter should be lafte as head vnder him ouer all hys flocke', could not be counted to be under Christ's headship.[116] John Harpsfield, in his 1556 commemorative sermon of the reunion with Rome, followed St Augustine as well as Luke 22 and Matthew 21 to explain that papal primacy had indeed been instituted by Christ in Peter and his successors.

112 Wooding, *Rethinking Catholicism*, 127–35.

113 Marshall, *Reformation England*, 99; Wizeman, *Theology and Spirituality*, 127–36; Duffy, *Fires of Faith*, 45–50. Loades conceded that the efforts to present papal primacy as a symbol of the unity of the Church, as Wizeman had argued, had been indeed more powerful than previously acknowledged, but he still considered the ideology behind them little more than an 'over-simplified view' of conciliarist overtones. See Loades, *Religious Culture*, 43–4.

114 Bonner, *Profitable and Necessarye Doctrine*, sig. K1^{v}.

115 Bonner, *Profitable and Necessarye Doctrine*, sig. J8^{v}.

116 John Standish, *The triall of the supremacy wherein is set fourth* [*the*] *vnitie of christes church milita*[*n*]*t geue*[*n*] *to S. Peter and his successours by Christe: And that there ought to be one head Bishop in earth Christes Vicar generall ouer all hys churche militant: wyth answeres to the blasphemous objections made agaynste the same in the late miserable yeres now paste* (London: Thomas Marshe, 1556), sig. C6^{v}.

> Christe did not pray for James and John and for the rest of his Apostles, but for Peter, in whome the rest are co[n]tained. In the .xxi. of Mathew we finde how our sauiour sayed vnto Peter in most speciall and earnest maner, *pasce agnos, pasce agnos, pasce oues*, fede my lambes fede my lambes, fede my shepe. And though certe[n] of the other apostles, & thei also the most notablest, were then present, Yet he gaue the charge onely to Peter.[117]

There was a notable tendency to view this account of the institutionalisation of papal primacy as the means through which to hold the Church together. Standish claimed that England's recent example showed that nothing was to be feared more than 'to be deuided from the vnity of christes churche' by forsaking 'the head therof'.[118] This was also Pollard's view, which he explained alluding to Romans 12 and 1 Corinthians 12.[119] Watson expounded that, 'the greatest authoritie that euer Chryste lefte in his Churche', was the 'iudgement of the successour of sainct Peter in the chayre of Chryste', but this authority was inextricably coupled to the 'Byshops and pastours of Chrystes flocke' in a general council.[120] It was under the universality of the Church presided by the pope that true Christians were to find salvation, which was impossible outside the Catholic Church. There was a strong emphasis, however, in the fact that it was Christ who was the head of the Church, but that He had appointed Peter and his long line of successors as 'vicars' so that His visible body, the Church, could be better governed and kept in unity. Peter was the rock, *tu es Petrus* (Matthew 16:18), upon which Christ had laid the foundation of the visible Church.[121]

The Spanish theologians who accompanied Philip to England shared many of the concerns expressed by their English counterparts. In his analysis of the Symbol of the Apostles in his *Comentarios*, Carranza did not even mention the pope, ascribing the headship of the Church solely to Christ.

---

117 John Harpsfield, *A notable and learned Sermon or Homilie, made vpon saint Andrewes daye last past 1556 in the Cathedral churche of S. Paule in London, by Mayster Jhon Harpesfeild doctour of diuinitie and Canon residenciary of the sayd churche, Set furth by the bishop of London* (London: Robert Caly, 1556), sigs B2^{v}–B3^{r}.

118 Standish, *Triall of the Supremacy*, sig. T3^{r}.

119 Pollard, *Fyve Homiles*, sig. F1^{r}.

120 Watson, *Holsome and Catholyke Doctrine*, fol. 47^{r}.

121 Harpsfield, *Notable and Learned Sermon*, sigs B4^{v}–B5^{v}; Standish, *Triall of the Supremacy*, sigs D4^{v}–D5^{r}.

> The Church is a congregation of human beings who are joined in a mystical body, formed and governed by one spirit, which is the Holy Spirit. They are called to this republic in hope of a reward, which is eternal life in heaven. They all have one Lord and one head, who is Christ, and they all profess one faith and the same sacraments. To believe that there is a republic on earth which conforms a body in the manner that we have said and that St Paul says [Ephesians 4:4–5] is an article of faith. This is the Christian republic, which is the one, holy and Catholic Church, founded by Christ and then expanded and completed by the preaching of the Apostles.[122]

Carranza qualified this statement later on in his discussion, adding that the Church 'has one head in heaven, who is Christ, and a vicar on earth'. The first vicar had been St Peter, followed by his Roman successors and that lineage was to be 'until the end of the world'.[123] The Dominican elaborated on this in his treatment of the ecclesiastical hierarchy of priests, who 'are called shepherds of Christ's sheep in Holy Scripture' [Acts 20:28; 1 Peter 5:2–3]. Carranza divided this hierarchy into five degrees, the first four being, in ascending order, priests, bishops, archbishops, and patriarchs. The 'fifth and supreme degree' was reserved to 'the patriarch of Rome' presiding over all other degrees and peoples of the Church.

> In this place Christ put St Peter when, after the resurrection, he ordered him to feed and govern his sheep and he was succeeded by the bishops of the Church of Rome [John 21:15–17]. This has been observed since the death of St Peter, who was the first pope in the Church. He is above all others in office, dignity and jurisdiction, although in the priestly order he is equal to the rest. […] Only him who is in this place is the successor of St Peter and, after Christ our Lord, he is the head of the whole Church

122 Carranza, *Comentarios sobre el catechismo christiano*, vol. 1, 373: 'Iglesia es una congregación de hombres que hacen un cuerpo místico, formado y gobernado por un espíritu, que es el Espíritu Santo, llamados a esta república para esperar todos un premio, que es la vida eterna en el cielo. Tienen todos un Señor y una cabeza, que es Jesucristo; profesan todos una fe y unos sacramentos. Creer que hay en la tierra una república que hace un cuerpo de la manera que habemos dicho y dice S. Pablo, esto es un artículo de fe. Esta es la república cristiana, que es una, santa, católica Iglesia, fundada por Cristo y después extendida y acabada por la predicación de los Apóstoles'.

123 Carranza, *Comentarios sobre el catechismo christiano*, vol. 1, 389: 'Ésta [the Church] es una y católica; toda ella tiene una cabeza en el cielo, que es Cristo, y un vicario en la tierra. El primero fue S. Pedro, y después los sucesores suyos en la Iglesia de Roma; y así lo es agora, y lo será hasta la fin del mundo el obispo que por tiempo fuere de Roma'.

> and of spiritual and all matters pertaining to the eternal salvation of our souls; a father and prelate over all those who live within the Church.[124]

The similiarities between Carranza's theology and that of the Marian authors are not that striking if we consider that his Catechism had been ordered by the English Synod (1555–1556) to cater for the particular needs of the English Church.[125] The pope's role was emphasised to be that of Christ's vicar and he possessed the maximum degree of jurisdiction because he had been appointed as primate of the whole Church by Christ himself. Notwithstanding the special character of Carranza's Catechism as an English commission, the same arguments can be found in other Spanish theologians in England.

The term 'congregation', identified by Wooding as one which suggested reformed connotations in some English works, was nonetheless the word used by Carranza, and Alfonso de Castro also defined the Church as 'the congregation of all the faithful' as described by St Paul in Romans 12 and 1 Corinthians 13.[126] To Castro, all the baptised were one body 'whether Jews or Gentiles, whether bond or free', with Christ, the head. Employing sources from both the Old and New Testaments which he confirmed with Bede, Castro created an analogy with Christ's transfiguration to explain why the Church needed visibility so that Christ, her head, would be forever visible too. The whole body, therefore, became visible and that was, Castro claimed, what Christ had intended when he commanded Peter *pascite qui in vobis est gregem* [1 Peter 5:2] and *pasce oves meas* [John 21:17] for, he asked, how could a sheperd tend to his flock if he were invisible?[127]

---

124 Carranza, *Comentarios sobre el catechismo christiano*, vol. 2, 304: 'El quinto y supremo grado tiene el patriarca de Roma, el cual preside sobre todos los otros grados y órdenes y personas de la Iglesia. En este lugar puso Cristo a S. Pedro cuando, después de su resurrección, le mandó apacentar y gobernar sus ovejas; y a él suceden los obispos de la Iglesia de Roma. Y así se ha guardado desde la muerte de S. Pedro, que fue el primer papa en la Iglesia. Éste es sobre todos en oficio, y en dignidad y jurisdicción, aunque en la orden sacerdotal es igual con los otros. Llámase por especial nombre papa, que en griego quiere decir padre, porque, dado que los otros obispos sean padres espirituales, el romano lo es por excelencia. Sólo el que en este lugar está es sucesor de S. Pedro. Y debajo de Cristo N. S., es cabeza de toda la Iglesia; y en las cosas espirituales y concernientes a la salvación eterna de nuestras almas, padre y perlado sobre todos los moradores de la Iglesia'.

125 On the English Synod see Mayer, *Reginald Pole*, 235–45. For a comparison between the English Synod's dispositions and Carranza's plan for an episcopal visitation of the archdiocese of Toledo see Tellechea Idígoras, *Carranza y Pole*, 305–39.

126 Wooding, *Rethinking Catholicism*, 117.

127 Castro, *Adversus omnes haereses*, fols 11^{r}–12^{r}: 'Et ergo caput Ecclesiae Christus omni tempore vissibile: & quum de alijs Ecclesiae membris non sit qui dubitet ea esse vissibile. Adde quòd eadem Ecclesia aliquando vocatur grex, iuxta iuxta illud Petri: Pascite qui in vobis est gregem. Huius autem gregis oues singulae sunt singuli fideles, quos eidem Petro

In a different section of *Adversus omnes haereses*, Castro described Christ's appointment of Peter as vicar mainly relying on the *tu es Petrus* passage [Matthew 16:18] and incorporating other citations from Matthew, Mark and Luke as well as 1 Corinthians which were further backed with the testimony of several of the Fathers.[128] Nevertheless, Castro decisively pointed out to whom the headship of the Church truly belonged.

> However, it does not follow that the body of the Church is a bicephalous monster (as Luther objects), for we do not say that Peter is an equal head to Christ, but a head under Christ. Truly we say that Christ is the first and supreme head of the Church. However, we do not say that Peter is the first head of the whole body which is the Church, but rather the vicar of the head; that is, the substitute head in Christ's place and the second head after Christ; the head of all others apart from Christ.[129]

The pope was the head of all human beings united in Christ's mystical body, the visible expression of which was the Church. To stress the administrative role of the papacy, Castro then offered a secular analogy. The Roman pontiff's office was like that of a proconsul with respect to a consul or that of a viceroy with respect to a king. They were all heads of a partial body, but it was the emperor who was the first head, integral to the whole secular body. Therefore, in the same manner, Peter did not constitute the sole foundation of the Church, for that role was reserved to Christ only.[130] A similar analogy, as we saw in the

---

ut verbo & doctrina pasceret, co[m]missit dominus dicens: Pasce oues meas. At quomodo erit grex inuisibilis, cuius omnes oues conspicuae sunt? Aut quomodo pastor pascet gregem quem non videt, nec eum vllo modo cognoscere potest?'

128 Castro, *Adversus omnes haereses*, fols 229^{r-v}. He supported his claims with Jerome, Hilary, Augustine, Chrysostome, Leo I, Gregory the Great, Tertullian and Origen.

129 Castro, *Adversus omnes haereses*, fol. 231^{r}: 'Nec tamen inde sequitur Ecclesiae corpus esse monstrum biceps (vt Lutherus nobis objicit) quoniam Petrum non dicimus esse caput aequale Christo, sed caput sub Christo. Christum enim dicimus esse primum & supremum Ecclesiae caput: Petrum autem non dicimus esse primum caput totius corporis quod est Ecclesia, sed vicariu[m] caput, hoc est caput Christi loco subrogatum, & caput secundum post Christum, id est, caput aliorum omnium à Christo'.

130 Castro, *Adversus omnes haereses*, fol. 231^{r}: 'Corporis vero mystici, quod ex alijs hominibus à Christo coalescit, Petrus est caput: & ita non est caput totius corporis integri: quoniam non est caput Christi qui ad hanc Ecclesiam pertinet. Simillimum est huic quod in alijs rebus publicis videmus. Nam Proconsul caput est illius prouinciae quam administrat, quamuis Consul sit illo superior, & primum omnium prouinciarum caput. Prorex caput est illius regni cuius cura[m] gerit: rex tamen est illo superior, & primum omnium suorum regnorum caput. Prorex enim aut Proconcul est caput partialis corporis, videlicet talis regni, aut talis prouinciae: Imperator autem est caput primum totius integri corporis. Sic Petrus & Christus. Ad hunc modum etiam oportet intelligere id quod suprà diximus,

previous chapter, had been employed by King Philip in his address to parliament in November 1554.

Villagarcía would later express in his 'Diálogo' a similar idea through an anatomical metaphor of the mystical body in which each member had, just like in the human natural body, an essential role to play, a perspective that he based on passages from Paul. An infringement of any of the jurisdictions belonging to each of the members would be fatal to the whole body. In this metaphor prelates were the eyes, preachers were the mouth, those who 'maintain' and 'defend' the Church – knights, soldiers, farmers and officers – were the hands and feet, and the people as a whole were the ears to be instructed in the Word of God. The head, of course, was Christ 'and the pope who is his tenant on earth'.[131] Later on he elaborated on this, throwing back at the Protestants the common accusation of the bicephalous nature of the papacy in a passage which reveals the impression that his time in England had caused in him:

> If there were not a supreme prelate, a supreme head, how would it be a Church? If all archbishops were supreme and would not depend on the pope, there would be as many churches as archbishoprics. If all kings were supreme heads in matters spiritual as Henry VIII, king of England, devised (and some heretics have claimed after him) what a wondrous monster we would have, with as many heads as kingdoms there would be! Never did Ovid nor Virgil know of any such chimerical monster even though they invented [...] hydras with many heads and eyes.[132]

Petrum videlicet esse petram & fundamentum Ecclesiae: fundamentum in quam non primu[m], cui scilicet totius Ecclesię structure innititur, quoniam tale fundamentum est solus Christus: de quo Paulus ait: Fundamentum aliud nemo potest ponere praeter id quod positum est, videlicet Christus Deus noster [1 Corinthians 3:11]'.

131 Villagarcía, 'Diálogo llamado cadena de oro', fols 43^{r-v}: 'S. Pab[lo] Apóstol bien claro enseña en la Ep[ísto]la ad Rom[anos] en el cap[ítul]o 12 y en el mesmo cap[ítul]o de la primera ad corinto que no todos los miembros dela Yglesia son vn miembro, sino que ay diuersidad de offiçios y ministerios, como lo ay en el cuerpo natural como ay cabeza, ojos: oýdos: boca manos pies, en el cuerpo del hombre natural: // Así en el cuerpo místico ay vna cabeza que es [Crist]o y el papa que tiene sus veçes en la tierra. Ay ojos que son los perlados: boca / los predicadores: pies y ma[n]os que son los que con su sudor y trauajo ma[n]tienen la Yglesia y la defienden como los caualleros los soldados, los labradores y offiçiales. Ay oýdos para oýr. ge[n]til cosa sería que los oýdos quisiesen ver como los ojos: y los pies y manos se quisiesen enseñar el camino por donde han de caminar y obrar. Los ojos veen y guían a los oýdos y a los pies y a las manos. Así en la Ygl[es]ia de dios el pueblo tenga oýdos para oýr y no quiera ser ojos: Los pies y las manos déxense guiar; de la vista de los ojos, que de otra manera, ningú[n] miembro hará su offi[ci]o'.

132 Villagarcía, 'Diálogo llamado cadena de oro', fol. 115^{r}: '[...] si no vuiera vn supremo perlado, vna suprema cabeza, Cómo fuera una Yg[lesi]a? si Todos los Arzob[is]pos fueran supremos que no dependieran del Papa, vuiera tantas Ygl[esi]as como Arzob[is]pados: Si todos

Villagarcía then recounted the story of an anonymous 'saintly' Englishman – perhaps he had Thomas More in mind – who had been 'martyred' for refusing to sign Henry VIII's oath of Supremacy. When a 'heretic' told him how disgusted he was that this man, 'being so learned', would support the pope's authority when there should only be one head of the Church, the 'saintly martyr' had defiantly replied:

> More marvelled am I at you all who put a hundred heads, for you make all kings supreme heads. We only put one [head], which is Jesus Christ, and the pope as his vicar in the same manner as we have but one king, even though in his absence he may leave a governor or viceroy. Thus, for this mystical body of Christ not to be a monster, but beautiful, it must have a single visible head who is the pope, vicar of Jesus Christ, who is the head, even though an invisible one.[133]

This was confirmed by Augustine and Cyprian, and Villagarcía concluded that the papacy was the only possible guarantee for just rulings in ecclesiastical disagreements over religion and faith.[134] It is certainly noteworthy that, as we saw in chapter 4, the very same analogy comparing the pope's role to that of a viceroy had been made by Philip in his address to parliament in November 1554.

Pedro de Soto, Villagarcía's fellow lecturer at Oxford, wrote copiously about the role of the papacy. In his *Assertio catholicae fidei*, he wrote how Christ had left the Church as a Christian republic and 'Peter as his vicar […] to be a visible head in His place'. The Roman pontiffs had been entrusted with the 'care

---

los Reyes fueran supremos cabezas en lo sp[irit]ual como inuentó En[rr]ico 8º Rey de Inglat[e]rra y después han dicho algunos Hereges, gentil Monstruo tuuiéramos de tantas cabezas como Reynos vuiera? Nunca Ouidio, ni Virgilio supieron de tal monstruo chimera avnque inuentaron algunos Ydras con muchas cabezas y ojos'.

133 Villagarcía, 'Diálogo llamado cadena de oro', fol 115^{r-v}: 'Estando para martyrizar vn sancto hombre en Inglat[e]rra, Porque no quiso firmar los errores que En[rr]ico 8º Rey della ordenó. Díxole vn Herege […] spantado estoy de ti / siendo tan docto que tengas y creas la authoridad del papa viendo que no ha de auer sino vna cabeza en la Ygl[esi]a; Y tú pones dos. Respondiole el Mártyr sancto, Más me marauillo yo de vosotros que ponéis cient cabezas pues hazéis a todos los Reyes supremas cabezas. Nosotros solamente ponemos vna que es a Jesu [Crist]o y al Papa por viccario suyo que tiene sus vezes, como no ponemos sino vn Rey, avnque en ausençia suya deje vn Gobernador o bi[rr]ey. De manera que como este cu[e]rpo místico de la Ygl[esi]a no sea monstruo sino hermoso, ha de tener sola vna cabeza Visible que es el Papa el qual es viccario de Jesu christo que es cabeza avnq[ue] inuisible […]'.

134 Villagarcía, 'Diálogo llamado cadena de oro', fols 115^{v}–116^{r}.

of the universal Church' and the power to govern the same and to 'direct the faithful towards what pertains to piety and salvation'.[135] In his *Institvtiones christianae*, Soto presented the familiar claim that, even though the Protestant assertion that Christ convened the Church through His Spirit and virtue as head of the same was true, no less true was it that Christ had wanted a visible head and had instituted the primacy of the papacy for that purpose as expounded in John 21:15–17, Luke 22:32 and Matthew 16:18. To make his point, he provided several examples from papal letters and conciliar resolutions to show the governing role of the popes as streaming from the unbroken succession to Peter's See.[136] A vigorous defence of the papacy is to be found in a book which Soto composed precisely during his time in Oxford. The work, entitled *Defensio catholicae confessionis* and published in Antwerp in 1557, was specifically designed as a challenge to the Württemberg Confession and the reformer Johannes Brenz's 'Prolegomena'. In his treatment of the succession of ministers from the times of the Apostles, Soto analysed the places where references were made to Peter's special status in the same passages that he had used in his *Institvtiones christianae*, and he then provided a commentary on tradition as represented by the Fathers and the authority of the councils.[137] What is most significant is that Soto brought forth the testimony of Thomas More and John Fisher, 'glorious martyrs' of England to prove that the pope was the cornerstone of the Church, planted by Christ to govern the Christian republic. Fisher had confirmed More in his orthodoxy among the differences of opinion in Henry's times, and both had provided an example to each other and the rest of the world.[138] If the Spaniard had been summoned to England to re-Catholicise the kingdom through his teaching, it was also clear that England had influenced his theology through two of her most egregious and recent martyrs.

---

135 Soto, *Assertio catholicae fidei*, sigs r2ʳ–r3ʳ: 'Agnoscit vera & Catholica fides, certa scripturae autoritate, & patrum omnium consensu, atque conuenientissima ratione, quòd Christus Dominus, qui Ecclesiam suam vnice dilexit, & firmissime vsque ad finem seculi duraturam fundauit, nec quicquam quod ad bene institutam Rempublicam pertinere potest non concessit, eidem Petru[m] vicarium[m] suum, atque visibile caput loco sui, vt curam vniuersalis Ecclesiae incorpore hic peregrinantis gereret, constituit, ita vt hoc in perpetuu[m] in Ecclesia permaneret. Quare in Petro etiam eius successores Romani scilicet Pontifices hoc ipsum acceperunt, vt capus sint vniuersalis Ecclesiae, & summam habeant potestatem in iijs quae ad gubernandam Ecclesiam, & fideles ad pietatem & salutem dirigendos, pertinent'.

136 Soto, *Institvtiones christianae*, fols Z3ᵛ–Aa4ʳ.

137 Pedro de Soto, OP, *Defensio catholicę confessionis, et scholiorvm circa confessionem, illvstrissimi Ducis Vvirtenbergensis nomine editam, aduersus Prolegomena Brentij* (Antwerp: Martín Nucio, 1557), fols 69ʳ–76ʳ, 80ʳ–84ᵛ, 88ʳ–96ᵛ.

138 Soto, *Defensio catholicę confessionis*, fols 79ʳ–80ʳ.

It is clear that the Marian authors and their Spanish companions in England treated the primacy of the pope on numerous occasions, sometimes in passionate language; but this was no infallible, ultramontane version of the papacy. Their main concern, and the one which they took most diligent care to emphasise, was the pastoral role of the pope as deputy head of the visible Church to govern the communion of the faithful and keep it together. To put their point across, they mainly used scriptural sources, supported by a strong body of patristic and conciliar references. In this, they all concurred with other Spanish theologians writing in Spain whose preoccupations, in a kingdom that had not undergone a schism as England had, were very much the same. Nieva and Baltanás, for instance, painted an identical picture of the pope's role as shepherd of Christ's sheep.[139] Others described Christ's position as head of the Church without mentioning the pope at all.[140] The acknowledgement of the pope as vicar of Christ was crucial to avoid disension and schism. It fulfilled, as Catholics understood it, Christ's desire for the building of a solid Church upon Peter as the principal shepherd of the Christian flock. This was not an exalted view of the papacy after a monarchical fashion – although the secular similarities were certainly acknowledged by these authors – but a secure guarantee of unity for the universality of the Catholic Church in the face of Protestant assaults against what they believed to be true doctrine.

5.4 Conclusion

The defence of some of the most hotly disputed tenets of the Catholic faith during the Reformations, such as human cooperation in the process of justification, Christ's real presence and transmutation in the Eucharist and its effect on the union of the faithful, and the primacy of the popes as guarantors of the cure of souls in a communion of saints, was treated by English and Spanish theologians with comparable coherence and vigour. Drawing on humanist sources, these men all employed a mixture of Scripture, tradition and the authority of the Church, always giving preeminence to the former, to vindicate very similar positions. Rather than stressing the insularity and uniqueness of the English Church inherited by Philip and Mary, the theology that Marian authors produced was very similar in aims, sources, themes and preoccupations – even if employing particular and sometimes idiosincratic styles – to that produced by their Spanish counterparts – both of those who

139 Nieva, *Svmmario manval*, f. 36v; Baltanás, *Doctrina christiana*, f. 107r.

140 Jiménez, *Enchiridión*, f. 46v; Meneses, *Lvz del alma*, ff. 58v–59v.

had come to England to contribute to the revitalisation of Catholicism and of those who had stayed back home. Their theologies were also aligned to what the Council of Trent had already decreed on these issues and their treatment of papal primacy mirrored that of Trent, for the Council did not produce any specific decrees on the matter, but asserted the same in other resolutions. The authority of the pope was only crucial in the sense that it allowed for the sustenance of Christ's authority on earth through the Church as Catholic authors perceived it. In only five years, English Catholic writers had managed to build a solid and consistent theological apparatus which had much in common with that being written and discussed in the Spanish kingdoms, with which England was now united.

Although these debates were launched in a particular intellectual milieu, the expectation was that they would be transmitted to the people at large. The purpose of most of these works was a pastoral one: homilies designed to be pronounced at parishes across England, catechisms and devotional works in English to be read and used by parish priests with their flocks and others in Latin for priests to adapt according to the needs of their parishioners, and a concerted effort to eradicate heresy and schism which would redound to the benefit, as they saw it, of the English population. It was the same strategy used in Spain. With all of these points in common, it is difficult to see how a longer reign would not have succeeded in implementing a solid base for the reforming Catholicism implicit in all these works. The cooperation between Anglo-Spanish theologians could have very plausibly resulted in a very strong strand of Catholicism that emphasised the universality of Christianity. It would have served not only the theological concerns present in these men's works, but also the political aims pursued by Philip throughout the Catholic Monarchy. Richard Pate, bishop of Worcester, in a letter to Queen Mary in which he advised her not to allow Pole to go to Rome to answer for heresy charges, explained how crucial it was that the queen, 'our most soueraigne lord the kyng', and Pole should remain united, 'neuer to be seuerallED, as in sprite, so in bodely presence *et hac trinitate foeliciter, et pie viuamus in hoc regno* (and thus, under this trinity, may we live happily and piously in this kingdom)'.[141] In practice, the most difficult task of Philip and Mary's Church was to crush the divisions that had grown as a result of the changing religious policies of Henry VIII and Edward VI. Indeed, heresy was prominent in the regime's agenda, as it has been in the historiography, and it is to this subject that we must now turn our attention.

141 TNA SP 11/11, no. 41; Richard Pate, Bishop of Worcester, to Queen Mary, Hatlebury, 16 August 1557.

CHAPTER 6

Obedience to God and Prince: Religious Prosecutions in England and Spain

> The vehement zeale of Queene Mary, which was like to haue set vp the Pope here againe in England for euer, if it had so much pleased the Lord God as it pleased her self: or if it had ben so godly as it was bloudy, no doubt but Gods blessing would haue gone withall. But when was the realme of England more barren of al Gods blessings? what prince euer raigned here more shorter tyme, or lesse to his owne hartes ease then dyd Queene Mary?[1]

In this paragraph, inserted in one of his concluding chapters dealing with the providentially unprosperous ends of the 'enemies of the Gospel', John Foxe encapsulated what was to be the prevailing view of later historians concerning the reign of Philip and Mary as a whole, placing the fierce persecution of Protestants, which resulted in the death of 284 men and women, at the centre of their narrative. The largely accepted historiographical account of this episode rests upon a quantitative approach to the seemingly unparalleled number of victims that the reign produced. In agreement with Foxe, it concludes that this was a disastrous means of social and religious disciplining; it could only stem from the vindictiveness of a monarch – Mary – intent on stamping out, through blind force, what was by then already taking deep roots in English society. It was therefore a cruel, clumsy, misguided, and ultimately ineffectual strategy.[2] Since the 1970s, the historiography has started to

1 John Foxe, *The First Volume of the Ecclesiasticall History, contayning the Actes & Monumentes of thinges passed in euery Kinges time, in this Realme, especially in the Churche of England principally to be noted with a full discourse of such persecutions* (…) (London: John Day, 1576), 2003. Henceforth *A&M*, 1576.

2 A. G. Dickens, *The English Reformation* [1964] (London and Glasgow: Collins/Fontana, 1972), 362-385; Owen Chadwick, *The Reformation* [1964] (London: Penguin Books, 1990), 125-9; G. R. Elton, *Reform and Reformation: England, 1509-1558* (London: Edward Arnold, 1977), 382-89; D. M. Loades, *The Reign of Mary Tudor: Politics, Government, and Religion in England, 1553–1558* (London: Ernest Benn, 1979), 273–79; David Loades, *Mary Tudor* (The Hill, Stroud: Amberley,

 | DOI:10.1163/9789004536210_008

move on, but even assessments like that of Ellen A. Macek, who argued for the solidity of Marian theology, concluded that the regime's religious programme was strongly undermined by the Spanish marriage, the perceived threat of repossession of Church property and, of course, the persecution of heretics.[3] Edmund Bonner, bishop of London became, in Foxe's account and in the nascent English national collective imagination, a 'bloody butcher', a monstrous and wholly uncharitable man who revelled in the sending of meek lambs to the slaughterhouse of the fires of Smithfield. Gina Alexander, in a perceptive and well-researched text, found that not only had he been strongly directed by the queen and the privy council but, also, that he did as much as he could to convert imprisoned heretics rather than summarily sending them to the flames. However, she too concluded that the burnings were the 'wrong weapons' in the revitalisation of Catholicism in England and that they turned what she assumed to be a 'wavering majority' against Mary and her religion.[4]

This narrative line is problematic for two reasons. In the first instance, it assumes that the persecution of heresy and the condemnation of other human beings to die at the stake was as repugnant to those inhabiting the early modern period as it is to us in the twenty-first century. This is patently wrong, as some sections of the chapter that follows will show. The second problem is that this perspective is so imbued with John Foxe's narrative account and the English Protestant national sentiment that it produced, that it clouds the investigation of the actual persecution – its justification, its aims, its effects – to such an extent that most accounts have read the events surrounding this topic backwards. Indeed, the taking for granted of the narrative lines adopted by Foxe and subsequent Protestant apologists, has produced a lack of concern for the actual development and significance of the persecution, and a historiography that has been characterised, instead, by a concerted effort to condemn it. Eamon Duffy has convincingly argued that this approach is wrong and misleading, not because the burning of religious dissenters is not an appalling act, but because it was not to religious and secular authorities back then. In *Fires of Faith*, which persuasively places the Marian campaigns in a context where religious tolerance would have been unthinkable, Duffy has highlighted that the campaign against heresy was carefully planned and that this effort

2011), 202-3, 227-28; David Loades, 'The English Church During the Reign of Mary', in John Edwards and Ronald Truman, eds., *Reforming Catholicism in the England of Mary Tudor: The Achievement of Friar Bartolomé de Carranza* (Aldershot: Ashgate, 2005), 33–48; Andrew Pettegree, *Marian Protestantism: Six Studies* (Aldershot: Scholar Press, 1996), 161–63.

3 Ellen A. Macek, *The Loyal Opposition: Tudor Traditionalist Polemics, 1535–1558* (New York: Peter Lang, 1996), 146, 164, 174-78.

4 Gina Alexander, 'Bonner and the Marian Persecution', in Christopher Haigh, ed., *The English Reformation Revised* (Cambridge: Cambridge University Press, 1987), 157–75, especially 171, 175.

turned it into a success by the end of the reign. The fact that there were fewer burnings in the last few months of Mary's life was not due, as had been traditionally believed, to the inertia following the regime's realisation that their efforts were yielding no fruit and antagonising the population. It was rather the result of a determined method of enforcement which was finally achieving its desired effects.[5] This tendency to present the last months of the campaign as lukewarm and almost admitting defeat can also be shown to derive from Foxe. In his account of John Lithall's 'deliverance', he explains that the latter's neighbours provided bonds to ensure that he would be set at liberty, which Dr Thomas Derbyshire, the bishop of London's chancellor, did. According to Foxe, however, Derbyshire had not been moved to release Lithall out of 'any zeale of charitie',

> but onely feare of the tyme, vnderstandyng the daungerous and vnrecouerable sickenesse of Queene Mary, which then began somewhat to asswage the cruell proceedynges of these persecutours, whereby they durst not do that they would: for els Lithall was not lyke to haue escaped so easily.[6]

These lines are pure conjecture, a narrative plot devised by Foxe to show at once the futility of persecution against the righteous, as well as the hypocrisy and godlessness of anyone involved in it. It is his own interpretation – with a very particular intent and audience – of events and conversations which he did not witness directly. In other historical topics, scholars would be cautious not to take assertions of this nature at face value, yet the flavour of his conclusions in this matter still permeates most accounts of the Marian persecution.

Another important aspect of the campaign against heresy which has been consistently misunderstood in the historiography is the role played by the Spanish in it, which has traditionally been downplayed or overlooked. This is partly due to a relative lack of sources and partly to the impression encouraged by Foxe himself in his influential account, where the Spaniards are almost completely obliterated from the picture. This sits uncomfortably with some claims

---

5 Eamon Duffy, *Fires of Faith: Catholic England under Mary Tudor* (New Haven and London: Yale University Press, 2009), especially 75–101. In similar vein, William Wizeman emphasised that English persecutors saw no alternative if they were to crush what they understood as recalcitrant heresy. See William Wizeman, SJ, *The Theology and Spirituality of Mary Tudor's Church* (Aldershot and Burlington: Ashgate, 2006), 153–57. A similar perspective is to be found in Thomas S. Freeman, 'Burning Zeal: Mary Tudor and the Marian Persecution', in Susan Doran and Thomas S. Freeman, eds., *Mary Tudor: Old and New Perspectives* (New York: Palgrave Macmillan, 2011), 171–205.

6 *A&M* [1576], 1985.

that Catholicism's alleged decline in popularity arose from it being tainted by its association with Spain and the persecution. Foxe had indeed very little to say about Spanish activity in England; although he referred several times to his intention to deal with the Spanish Inquisition and its practices, he disappointingly failed to include this in the *Acts and Monuments*. This was no doubt due to the fact that, after 1558, he had a different axe to grind. With Mary dead and the threat of further Spanish influence apparently neutralised, his main targets became exclusively the persecuting Catholics, thoroughly English, who had to be denigrated to support Elizabeth's new religious settlement.[7]

Furthermore, what Foxe did say has distorted perceptions about Spanish involvement in the repression of heresy. On 10 February 1555, when the campaign against heresy had just begun, six men having been burnt at Smithfield the day before, the Franciscan Alfonso de Castro preached a sermon at court in which, according to Foxe, he scolded the bishops 'for burnyng of men, saying plainly that they learned it not in scripture to burne any for his conscience: but the contrary, that they should liue, and be conuerted'.[8] This remark, coupled with the alarming reports of the volatile Simon Renard and the partial Giovanni Michieli, the imperial and Venetian ambassadors in England, about popular malaise at the burnings, have prompted historians to dismiss Spanish influence as negligible, even though Spaniards were blamed for the persecution.[9] Duffy detected that something was amiss in this interpretation, as Castro was the author of some of the most famous early modern manuals against heresy, and suggestively put forward that Castro's preaching may have been a political move by Philip to cover his back in case the burnings were unpopular and, also, that the sermon may have just reflected Castro's own personal preferences to show benignity rather than harshness.[10]

The point can be taken further, especially when we remember that persecution was not peculiar to England but was taking place throughout Europe and cannot, therefore, be adequately understood in isolation. The Spanish case is especially pertinent, given that the two realms now shared their monarchs, and that it was under Philip and Mary's parliament of 1554–1555, the one that reconciled the kingdom to Rome, that the heresy laws of Richard II (1382), Henry IV (1401), and Henry V (1414), abolished by Edward VI, were re-enacted with the specific aim of

7 I am indebted to Dr Elizabeth Evenden-Kenyon for her very insightful observations on this topic.

8 *A&M* [1576], 1456.

9 Chadwick, *Reformation*, 127–8; Loades, *Reign of Mary*, 334; Loades, 'English Church During the Reign of Mary', 46–8; Alexander, 'Bonner and the Persecution', 160–2.

10 Duffy, *Fires of Faith*, 82–3.

> eschewing and avoiding of errors and heresies which of late have risen, grown and much increased within this realm, for that the ordinaries have wanted authority to proceed against those that were infected therewith.[11]

That the Spanish theologians and religious men present in England were involved in the persecution is undeniable. Through Bartolomé de Carranza's process we know that he was actively involved in the confiscating of English Bibles in London and in the burning of heretical books. He also played a part in the burning of the bones of Catherine Dammartin (Peter Martyr Vermigli's deceased wife, who had died in 1553) and their re-burial in unconsecrated ground in Oxford. It is possible that he was involved in the burning of Martin Bucer's remains in Cambridge, too. Carranza also intervened personally to ensure that Archbishop Cranmer and William Flower, who stabbed a priest while he was giving communion at St Margaret's, Westminster, were burned.[12] Foxe himself recounts that the Dominicans Pedro de Soto and Juan de Villagarcía were involved in the examinations and recantations of Cranmer, and the Franciscans Castro and Bernardo de Fresneda, Philip's confessor, in those of John Bradford, prebendary of St Paul's.[13] The first question that Fresneda – who according to the account was mostly silent for the rest of the examination – posed to Bradford was 'whether he hadde not seene nor heard of one Alphonsus that had written against heresies?'[14] When Bradford claimed not to know who he was, Fresneda introduced him to Castro, but the question certainly implies that Castro was famous enough to be widely read, despite

11 G. R. Elton, ed., *The Tudor Constitution: Documents and Commentary* (Cambridge: Cambridge University Press, 1965), 400–1.

12 BAV, Vat. Lat. 13138, fols 7^r, 8^r, 8^v, 9^r, 99^r, 138^v, 139^r. See also Tellechea Idígoras, *Carranza y Pole*, 92–118. John Edwards has approached this subject incisively, exploring particularly the commonalities shared in the burning of the bones of deceased heretics in England and Spain. See his, 'The Spanish Inquisition Refashioned: The Experience of Mary I's England and the Valladolid Tribunal, 1559', *Hispanic Research Journal* vol. 13, no. 1 (2012), 41–54. See also, Elizabeth Evenden, 'Spanish Involvement in the Restoration of Catholicism during the Reign of Philip and Mary', in Elizabeth Evenden and Vivienne Westbrook, eds., *Catholic Renewal and Protestant Resistance in Marian England* (Farnham: Aldershot, 2015), 45–64 and Ceri Law, 'The 1557 Visitation of the University of Cambridge', in the same volume, 65–91.

13 Cranmer's first recantation was witnessed by Villagarcía. See Thomas Cranmer, *All the svbmyssyons, and recantations of Thomas Cranmer, late Archebyshop of Canterburye, truely set forth both in Latyn and Englysh, agreable to the Originalles, wrytten and subscribed with his owne hande* (London: John Cawood, 1556) and *A&M* [1576], 1804. See also Diarmaid MacCulloch, *Thomas Cranmer: A Life* (New Haven and London: Yale University Press, 1996), 581–82, 586–89, 595–96. For Castro and Fresneda's examination of Bradford see *A&M* [1576], 1560–62.

14 *A&M* [1576], 1560.

Bradford's dismissiveness. In fact, we know that Castro's works were certainly being used by the English inquisitors. In Foxe's account, George Marsh, a farmer-turned-minister who was to be burned at Chester on 24 April 1555, recounted that one of his examiners,

> brought vnto me a booke of one alphonsus a Spanish Frier, of all heresies wherewith the Churche of Rome, which hee called Christes true Church, had bene troubled since Christes tyme, willing me to read and take counsell of that booke: and appoynted me a place, where this authour did write agaynst them that say, the lay people ought to receiue vnder both kyndes.[15]

Another piece of evidence comes from John Barrett's career. Barrett, an ex-Carmelite who had become a prominent reformed divinity lecturer and preacher in Norwich, returned to Catholicism after Mary's accession and became a keen examiner in the diocese under its bishop, John Hopton, and the latter's chancellor, Michael Dunning, securing the recantations of two of his old evangelical companions. Although Barrett would later accommodate to Elizabeth's settlement, at his death in 1563, his library was composed solely of orthodoxly Catholic works, including titles by John Fisher, Martín Pérez de Ayala, archbishop of Valencia, and, more significantly in this context, by Alfonso de Castro.[16] It is necessary, therefore, to explore the ideological justifications devised by Spanish and English authors to ascertain the extent to which they coincided if we are to understand the motivation for the campaign against heresy.

Another crucial episode to be explored in this chapter which is consistently ignored in most accounts of the Marian persecution is that there was a parallel campaign against heresy taking place in Spain. Indeed, in 1557 two distinct communities of alleged Lutherans were discovered in Seville and Valladolid, and arrests promptly began that year. It had taken some time for Fernando Valdés, the Inquisitor General, to assemble all the evidence he needed to request from King Philip a full-scale persecution of Protestantism in Seville and Valladolid. Tangible proof finally came through the apprehension of Julián Hernández, known as Julianillo, who was smuggling Bibles translated in Spanish by Juan Pérez de Pineda, exiled in Geneva, as well as other unorthodox

15 *A&M* [1576], 1506.

16 Ralph Houlbrooke, 'The Clergy, the Church Courts and the Marian Restoration in Norwich', in Eamon Duffy and David Loades, eds., *The Church of Mary Tudor* (Aldershot: Ashgate, 2006), 124–46, especially 145.

theological writings and personal letters into Spain.[17] Although the *autos de fe*, in which eighty-one people were to meet their deaths at the stake, took place in 1559, 1560 and 1562, the examination of suspects began after Hernández's arrest in 1557 and continued throughout 1558, making the English and Spanish campaigns exactly contemporary. To understand the Spanish persecution in the English context and to explore the extent to which this process was part of a bigger-scale attempt to enforce the universality of Catholicism which transcended English borders, some attention needs to be given to the ideological and theological standpoint upon which the campaign was built. I will do this, first, through an examination of the works of English and Spanish theologians, with particular attention to Castro, to determine their similarities, and, second, through a comparison of some of the specific heresies that were being persecuted in England and Spain to determine whether both kingdoms were fighting a similar 'enemy'. Only then will it be possible to assess the outcomes of the campaigns and to determine whether they were indeed 'wrong weapons' or an instrument to ensure, in Duffy's words, the 'effective containment of dissent'.[18]

6.1 Heresy: An Infection of the Body of Christ and a Rebellion against the Prince

In his work *The displaying of the Protestantes*, the hosier Miles Huggarde defined heresy as 'any false or wrong opinion, whiche any man choseth to him selfe to defende against the catholike fayth of the vniuersall church'.[19] The Dominican Felipe de Meneses, writing in Spain, explained that a heretic was someone who, having previously received the faith, later rejected it partly, 'ceasing to believe an article of faith or a truth found in holy Scripture or determined by the Church'.[20] Alfonso de Castro, in *De iusta hæreticorum punitione*, defined it

17 Marcelino Menéndez Pelayo, *Historia de los heterodoxos españoles*, vol. 2. [1880–82] (Madrid: Biblioteca de Autores Cristianos, 1967), 74–75; José Luis González Novalín, *El inquisidor general Fernando de Valdés (1483–1568). Su vida y su obra* (Oviedo: Universidad de Oviedo, 1968), 303; Stefania Pastore, *Una herejía española. Conversos, alumbrados e Inquisición* (1449–1559), trans. by Clara Álvarez Alonso [2004] (Madrid: Marcial Pons Historia, 2010), 311–12; Tomás López Muñoz, *La reforma en la Sevilla del XVI*, vol. 1 (Seville: CIMPE/Eduforma, 2011), 109–114.

18 Alexander, 'Bonner and the Persecution', 175; Duffy, *Fires of Faith*, 79.

19 Miles Huggarde, *The displaying of the Protestantes, & sondry their practises, with a description of diuers their abuses of late frequented. Newly imprinted agayne, and augmented, with a table in the ende, of all suche matters as is specially contained within this volume* (London: Robert Caly, 1556), fols 11^{v}–12^{r}.

20 Felipe de Meneses, OP, *Lvz del alma Christiana contra la ceguedad y ygnorancia en lo que pertenece a la fe y ley de Dios, y de la yglesia: y los remedios y ayuda que él nos dio*

as a 'false enunciation or proposition, and therefore repugnant to the Catholic faith, with which it cannot exist at the same time'.[21] It was not so much, Castro continued, the external acts that constituted heresy, as the intellectual intention or meaning behind them.[22] Heresy was, furthermore, a dangerous element against stability. As such it was a lethal threat against the mystical body of Christ and, consequently, against the body politic of the monarchy. Castro lamented that,

> If rigorous discipline, rather than moderate, had been used in Germany against the heretics, the damage to the Catholic faith would not have been such as has been experienced, nor would we have endured such a grievous and dangerous infestation of heretics as we now do endure.

If those heretics in Germany who would not be corrected had been punished more harshly, Castro continued,

> they would not have dared to vomit upon the people their heretical venom, devised of their own minds, and therefore not as many of the same people would have been affected by this pestiferous infection.[23]

---

para guardar su ley. En el qual tractado se da también luz assí a los confessores, como a los penitentes, para administrar deuidamente el sacramento tan necessario de la penitencia (Seville: Martín de Montesdoca, 1555), fol. 66^{v}: 'Hereges se dize[n] aq[ue]llos q[ue] rescibida vna vez la fe, la dexa[n] no e[n] todo, sino en p[ar]te, dexa[n]do de creer algú[n] artículo de fe o alguna verdad dela escriptura sagrada, o determinada por la yglesia'.

21 Alfonso de Castro, OFM, *De ivsta haeretocorum punitione, libri III* (Lyon: Heirs of Jacques Giunta, 1556), 10: 'Haeresis est enunciatio, siue propositio falsa fidei Catholicę ita repugnans, vt cum illa simul esse non possit'.

22 Castro, *De ivsta haereticorum punitione*, 10: 'Cum diximus haeresim esse enunciationem, siue propositionem falsam, aperte satis oste[n]dimus factum aliquid, aut quamlibet rem gestam non esse haeresim: quoniam haeresis no[n] respicit opus exterius, neque ex illo pendet, vt haeresis dici possit: sed ex intellectu. Non est enim haeresis in opere: sed in errore intellectus, hoc aut illud iudicantis'.

23 Castro, *De ivsta haereticorum punitione*, 260: 'Si vel mediocri aliquo disciplinae rigore aduersus haereticos vsa fuisset Germania, nec tantum fidei catholicae detrimentum fuisset experta, nec tam molestam, & tam periculosam hęreticorum infestationem pateretur, sicut nunc patitur. Quia illorum effrontem, & nimis effraenatam audaciam timor durae punitionis repressisset. Quibus timore perterritis, si illi correcti, & emendati non fuissent, hoc saltem non spernendum commodum inde hausisset Germania, quòd suae haereseos virus, quod mente conceperant, non fuissent ausi in populum euomere, & sic non tantus populous fuisset illorum pestifera infectus'.

Paul Bush, former bishop of Bristol, in his explication of St Vincent of Lérins's interpretations of St Paul's sentences of anathema in Galatians 1:8–9, concluded that being anathemised meant to

> be seperated, segregated, and excluded as one accursed, leaste the dangerous infection[n] of one corrupte shepe, may poison and infect to [sic] whole sound flocke of Chryst with his venenous permyxtion.

Therefore, Bush exhorted the addressee of his work, Margaret Burges, that it was 'not laufull for you, nor for anye other priuate personne', to follow any doctrines outside such as the Catholic Church believed.[24] Doctrine was not something to be devised or believed by oneself, as it needed the interpretation of the Church. By holding to their erroneous opinions, heretics placed themselves outside the Christian body, having no respect for Scripture, the universal assent of the Church or the tradition of the Fathers. Becoming a heretic was, therefore, a conscious and individual decision.

Error and heresy were born of ignorance and vanity and were a danger to the unity of the Church. Pedro de Soto explained that among men there was 'a Church which is to be called a city, a kingdom, a family, and a true and single body'. It was a kingdom of which Christ was the king, composed of cities which were the people. Catholics formed a family of which Christ was the 'father and Lord', who was served by ministers who were the Apostles and their successors. Finally, the Church was a living body of which Christ was the head and all the rest were its members. This conceptualisation of Christ's Body was no mere metaphor but was instead understood to be a living, organic entity. As Paul admonished in 1 Corinthians 12, God had created such a perfect body so 'that there might be no schism in the body, but its members might mutually care for one another'. 'And if one member were to suffer', Soto continued quoting from Paul, 'all members are to suffer with him; and if one member were to receive glory, all members are to rejoice with him'. This was, he concluded, a 'perfect communion of saints'.[25]

24 Paul Bush, *A brefe exhortation set fourthe by the vnprofitable seruant of Jesu christ, Paule Bushe, late bishop of Brystowe, to one Margarete Burges wyfe of Jhon Burges, clothear of kyngeswode in the Countie of Wilshere* (London: John Cawood, 1556), sig. C2^{r}.

25 Pedro de Soto, OP, *Institvtionis Christianae libri tres priores: Ivssv Reverendissimi Domini D. Othonis Cardinalis & Episcopi Augustani a doctis theologis lecti & probati, ac illius authoritate editi* (Augsburg: Valentin Othmar, 1548), sig. Y4^{v}–Z1^{r}: 'Ex quibus hominibus existit una ecclesia: quae una ciuitas, unum regnum, una familia, & uerissime unum corpus esse dicitur. Etenim regnum unum est: in quo rex est Christus [...]. Plebs uero & omnes reliqui, ciues sunt: iuxta suum gradum obtinens quilibet proprium locum. Item domus una ac familia dicitur: in qua pater & dominus est Christus: serui ac ministri sunt apostoli & eorum successores [...]. Deniq[ue] corpus etiam unum uocatur: cuius caput

Against this perfect unity of the Church were those whom an anonymous author called the 'lying maysters & pseudoprophetes'.[26] Leonard Pollard reminded his readers that St Peter had warned in 2 Peter 2:1 'that as there were false prophetes in the tyme of the lawe: that so there shulde be teachers of false and damnable sectes in the tyme of the Gospell'. Thousands of these pseudo-prophets had arisen since this warning was first uttered, and many had 'most damnably fallen into heresy and blasphemous vanities'.[27] Pollard perceived the Protestants as promoters of dissension and accused them of devising their own personal interpretations of the Bible. Paraphrasing St Augustine's *Contra fundamentum*, for instance, Pollard asserted that the only way to discern between the canonical and the apocryphal Gospels was through the authority of the Church, which 'was neuer caste yet downe' and was 'the house that is buylt as Christ sayth vpon the rocke'. This house was characterised by its 'greatnesse and largenesse' and, unlike the 'lyttle pretty feate houses' built by Protestants in England and Germany, God's true house was so large 'that it reacheth frome the rysynge of the sonne to the goynge downe of the same', a comment which is unquestionably imbued with the universalist aspirations of Catholicism.[28] John Angell and Felipe de Meneses made very similar descriptions of the threat posed to the unity of the Church by false prophets.[29]

est Christus: a quo omnis gratia, omnis motus, atque gubernatio est in ecclesia. [...] Nos autem huius corporis membra sumus: ut abunde Paulus declarant: sicut in uno corpore (scribens) multa membra habemus: omnia autem non eundem actum habent: ita multi unum corpus sumus in Christo: singuli autem alter alterius membra, habentes donationes secundum gratiam, quae data est nobis, differentes [Romans 12:4–6]. [...] nos etiam Paulus admonet: ut non sit (inquiens) scisma in corpore, sed in id ipsum pro inuice[m] solicita sunt membra. Et si quid patitur unum membrum: compatiuntur omnia membra: siue gloriatur unum membrum, congaudent omnia membra [1 Corinthians 12:25–26]. Quanqua[m] sunt enim sunt Parochiae, dioeceses, prouinciae diuersae, atq[ue] in harum qualibet diuersa instituta, societalesq[ue], & animae, quae Christo domino militant, eiq[ue] placent: una tamen est ex his omnib[us] ecclesia [...]'.

26 Anon., *A plaine and godlye treatise, concernynge the Masse & the blessed Sacrament of the Aulter, for the instruccion of the symple and vnlerned people* (London: John Wayland?, 1556), sig. G2r.

27 Leonard Pollard, *Fyve Homiles of late, made by a ryght good and vertuous clerke, called master Leonarde Pollarde, prebendary of the Cathdrall Churche of Woster, directed and dedicated to the ryght reuerende Father in God Rychard by the permissyon of God byshoppe of Woster his specyall good Lorde* (London: William Griffith, 1556), sig. E2r.

28 Pollard, *Fyve homiles*, sigs E3v–E4r. Pollard's references were based on Psalms 18 and 106.

29 John Angell, *A collection or gatherynge together, of certayne scriptures, both of the holy scripture, and also of the auncient and Catholyke doctours of Christes church, co[n]cernyng the most holy and blessed body and blode of Christ to be royally present in the Sacrament of the Aulter* (London: Robert Wyer, c.1554), sigs C2r–v; Meneses, *Lvz del alma*, fols 58v–59v.

In line with this insistence on the common assent of the Church, Thomas Watson pointed out that, to avoid diverging interpretations, there were three safe ways: Scripture, the Fathers, and the consent of the universal Church. The most secure way for Christians to hold their faith was to follow all three simultaneously. Scripture was the first step, but without the consent of the Church it could be used against the faith, as Arius and Nestorius had first done in a long line of heresiarchs. Scripture, Watson cautioned, 'is not the bare letter, as it lieth to be taken of every man, but [the] true sense, as it is delyuered by the vniuersal consent of Christes churche'. The writings of the Fathers had to be contextualised with each other to create a theological body of assent, rather than to understand them (and support or reject them) as individual opinions on Scripture. Consequently, the surest way not to err was to follow the consent of the Church.[30] In his letter to the 'pious readers' at the beginning of his *Comentarios*, Carranza explained that the translation of Bibles into the vernacular had been one of the roots of diversity in doctrine. In Spain, under Ferdinand and Isabel, Bibles in the vernacular had been allowed and published. However, after it was discovered that Judaisers were using them to teach their children the Jewish faith, they had been banned. One of the first subterfuges used by the 'demon's ministers' in Germany had been,

> to write their false doctrines in vernacular languages, translating the sacred Scripture into German and French, and then into Italian and English, so that the people could judge for themselves and see on which foundations lay their opinions. This caused infinite harm and brought enmity to houses and families, so that not two can be found that are of the same opinion, for each understands Scripture as they see fit and interprets it as they think best to set up their own opinions, as by experience has been seen in the province of Germany and in the kingdom of England.

Acknowledging this danger, one of the first things that 'the Catholic Monarchs, Philip and Mary', – had done after 'restoring the old and true religion', had been to confiscate the 'vernacular Bibles that the heretics had made'.[31] It is

30 Thomas Watson, *Twoo notable Sermons, made the thirde and fyfte Fridayes in Lent last past, before the Quenes highnes, concernynge the reall presence of Christes body and bloude in the blessed Sacrament: & also the Masse, which is the sacrifice of the newe Testament* (London: John Cawood, 1554), sigs B7ʳ–B8ʳ.

31 Bartolomé de Carranza, OP, *Comentarios sobre el catecismo christiano* (Antwerp: 1558), vol. 1, José Ignacio Tellechea Idígoras, ed. (Madrid: Biblioteca de Autores Cristianos, 1972), 109-11: 'Después de las herejías de Alemaña, se entendió que una de las astucias que tuvieron los ministros que he dicho del demonio fue escribir sus falsas doctrinas en lenguas

important to note that Carranza was referring to them by the title first granted by Pope Alexander VI to Ferdinand and Isabel (*reyes católicos*), which again emphasises not only Philip and Mary's position as joint monarchs – rather than mere consorts – but, also, their duty towards the universality of Catholicism. Juan Villagarcía concurred with his mentor in the matter of the Bibles, arguing that he had 'tried this recipe and medicine in England' (the confiscation of vernacular Bibles), 'and found it to be very good'. During the reign of Philip and 'the queen of good memory', the prohibition to use vernacular Bibles was so profitable that 'the illnesses to be found there before had started to weaken and perish'.[32] Heresy is again described as an infectious illness which threatens to destroy the whole Body of Christ unless remedies against its spread are put in place. The interpretation that to divulge the Scripture in the vulgar tongue was dangerous and a potential source of disunity since John Wycliffe's time was also common in the writings of some English authors, especially John Standish, who was rather vehement when it came to this topic.[33]

In *The Assault of the Sacrament of the Altar*, Miles Huggarde reviewed the history of attacks against the Eucharist as a war between the forces of evil and the armies of true doctrine. The attacks of Berengar of Tours in France, of Jerome of Prague and Jan Hus in Bohemia, of Luther, Oecolampadius and Andreas Karlstadt in Germany, and those of Cranmer, Hooper, Holgate, Ridley and others in England were seen as stemming from the same root. They all belonged to a single heretical family; and not one that got on particularly well.

vulgares, y trasladaron la Santa Escritura en tudesco y francés, y después en italiano y en inglés, para que el pueblo fuese juez y viese cómo fundaban sus opiniones. Esto causó infinito daño y puso enemistades en las casas y familias, que no hay dos de una opinión, porque entienden la Escritura como a cada uno se le antoja y porque cada uno la saca como le parece que está mejor para fundar sus opiniones, como por experiencia se ha visto en la provincia de Alemaña y en el reino de Inglaterra. […] En Inglaterra, cuando los reyes católicos don Felipe y doña María restituyeron la antigua y verdadera religión, de las primeras cosas que hicieron fue la una quitar las biblias vulgares que habían hecho los herejes'.

32 Biblioteca Nacional de España, MSS 010547; Juan de Villagarcía, OP, 'Diálogo llamado cadena de oro. Compuesto por el muy R[everen]do religioso y doctíssimo padre maestro F. Joan de Villagarçía Regente del insigne Collegio de S. Greg[ori]o de Vall[adoli]d entre dos [crist]ianos, Conuiene a saber. Ioan y Antonio: Y sirue para dar a entender aquellas cosas conq[ue] vn herege se pueda y deua voluer a la sancta fee cathólica de Iesu[crist]o' (*c*.1559–1563), fols 33^{v}–34^{r}: 'Yo he p[ro]bado esta reçeuta y medisçina en Ynglat[e]rra por muy Buena do[n]de en t[iem]po que allá Reynó N[uestro] Rey y la Reyna de Buena memoria su muger se hizo tanto p[ro]uecho con p[ro]hibir estas Byblias vulgares que ya se yuan gastando y acauando las enfermedades que antes auía'.

33 John Standish, *A discourse wherin is debated whether it be expedient that the scripture should be in English for al men to reade that wyll* (London: Robert Caly, 1554), sigs A2^{r}, A7^{r-v}.

> But then because into sectes, they did fall,
> Hauing amonge them no kinde of agrement,
> Conserning the right faieth in the sacrament,
> Eche against the other his fancye did defende,
> Thus brauling with the[m] selues this assaulte did ende.[34]

Heretical opinions brought nothing but division and strife and they were a direct attack against the mystical body of Christ through the rejection of its vicar, the pope, but also by sowing rebellion against the prince. In the anonymous *Oratio pia, & erudita*, written to commemorate the marriage of Philip and Mary, the author praised God's 'non-human providence' for delivering England from the enemies of His Gospel, of His spouse the Church and of the Spanish marriage. Philip and Mary, God's 'faithful champions and the Holy Church's most constant defenders' were to cleanse the kingdom from that infection that were rebels, murmurers, heretics and schismatics.[35] The ramifications of Protestantism in Wyatt's rebellion have already been studied in chapter two. In the theological framework of English and Spanish authors, heresy was forcefully described as a rebellion in itself, an idea which was inseparable from the conceptualisation of heresy as an infection attacking the whole body. Before the reconciliation with Rome, in the aftermath of Wyatt's rebellion, John Christopherson, who was to become bishop of Chichester, wrote:

> Lyke as there be manye and sondrye diseases [...] which chaunsing to a mans body, so sore manye times trouble and vexe the same, that they [...] at lengthe kill and destroye it altogether: So in a realme or commonwealth (whiche maye well be compared to a mans bodye) there are

34 Miles Huggarde, *The assault of the sacrament of the Altar containyng aswell sixe seuerall assaultes made from tyme to tyme against the sayd blessed sacrament: as also the names & opinions of all the heretical captaines of the same asaultes: Written in the yere of oure Lorde 1549. by Myles Huggarde, and dedicated to the Quenes moste excellent maiestie, beyng then ladie Marie: in whiche tyme (heresie then raigning) it could take no place. Now newly imprynted this present yere. 1554* (London: Robert Caly, 1554), sigs C3^{r}–E3^{r}.

35 Anon., *Oratio pia, & erudite pro statu illustrissimorum Principum Philippi & Mariae, Regis & Reginae Angliae Franciae, etc. ut deus eos in multos annos conseruet, & illustrissimam Reginam faciat pulchra prole letam matrem* (London: John Cawood, *c.*1554), unnumbered: 'Tu scis domine quoniam testamenti tui sancti, & ecclesiae sponse tue, inimici, contra Philippum, non humana sed tua prouidentia Regem nostru[m] et Mariam ancillam tuam, traque ordinatione Reginam nostram, tui testamenti, tuque fidei assertores, & sanctae ecclesiae defensores constantissimos, rebelles sunt infestissimi, ac murmuratores queruli, iuxta concupiscentias suas ambulantes, quorum os loquitur tumida, ut haereticoru[m], scismaticoru[m]que regnu[m] stauant, robore manuum suarum uolunt tua mutare promissa, & tuam haereditatem disperdere et delere, & claudere ora laudantium et, & extinguere gloriam ecclesiae tue catholicae, & altaris'.

> manye sore sicknesses, that oftentimes so greuously noye the same, that yf remedye be not founde out betime, they [...] worke the vtter ruine and destruction thereof.[36]

Christopherson followed Aristotle's distinction of causes for rebellion as expounded in the fifth book of his *Politics* to explain that these were 'lucre, losse of goods, honoure, welth[,] feare, contempt, and diuersite of maners or contreys'. Significantly, however, he added a final cause, religion, and warned that although many were the causes that could excite hatred among men, 'yet nothing is there, that bredeth so deadly hatred, as diuersitie of myndes, touching religion'.[37] It made no difference how good a ruler was – if a number of his subjects were of a different religion they would travail 'to withdrawe the heartes of all men from him' and 'openly rebell agaynst him' as soon as occasion arose.[38] From Pollard's point of view, heretics were part of the devil's army. Since the devil was weak, he had to fight against the 'army of Chryst' in small parts of 'Chrystes dominion' following a *divide et impera* logic even if, as rebels, the heretics' machinations were doomed. Pollard further denounced what he saw as irrefutable proof of their hypocrisy and perfidy:

> as rebellions in theyr rebellion, pretende some tytle of reformation, myndinge in dede ruine and destruction: so doth his [the devil's] rebels pretende that they be moued by the gospell, which is the lawe of the Church, but as it is vayne to alege the law ageynst rebels: so it is in vayne to aleage the scripture and to dispute with heretyckes.[39]

Heretics were, therefore, deceitful false prophets who claimed to aim at reform, when what they actually aimed at was at the Church's destruction. Against this objective, he contended, no argument could win them back, for it was not their intention to argue or to dispute but to rebel. If Pollard alleged ulterior motives behind the heretics' pretence to reform religion, Meneses explained that heresy had its origins in 'corruption of manners' and a 'lack of knowledge

---

36 John Christopherson, *An exhortation to all menne to take hede and beware of rebellion: wherein are set forth the causes, that commonlye moue men to rebellion, and that no cause is there, that ought to moue any man therevnto, with a discourse of the miserable effectes, that ensue thereof, and of the wretched ende, that all rebelles comme to, moste necessary to be redde in this seditiouse & troublesome tyme, made by John Christoferson. At the ende whereof are ioyned two godlye Prayers, one for the Quenes highnes, verye conuenient to be sayd dayly of all her louing and faythfull subiectes, and an other for the good & quiete state of the whole realme* (London: John Cawood, 1554), sig. A2^{r}.

37 Christopherson, *An Exhortation*, sigs B7^{v}, C4^{r}.

38 Christopherson, *An Exhortation*, sig. C4^{v}.

39 Pollard, *Fyve homiles*, sig. E4^{v}.

or ignorance of God'. These were the perfect ferment for heresy to thrive, as the example of Germany proved. In Spain, Meneses warned, the same symptoms were starting to show, although the Inquisition, a 'wall of fire' set up by God Himself, had managed to contain it so far. Ignorance was, therefore, the main root of heresy, from which stemmed the 'bait' that 'this new Muhammad that Luther is', had used to entrap Germany: liberty. This misunderstood liberty, Meneses expounded, was extremely dangerous, as it implied that Christians could find 'freedom and exemption from many of God's laws and from all those of the Church'. The 'Spanish nation' was, Meneses claimed, 'of more worth than others', but this very same quality presented a trap too, as it was sometimes accompanied by an inclination to 'pride and sedition', both of which were fertile ground for the sounds of the 'drum of Lutheran liberty'.[40] Heretics, just as overtly political rebels did, perverted the true sense of liberty and law to their own ends. These ends were at odds with those of the commonwealth and by pursuing them, heretics were breaking the divinely ordained social order. From the point of view of the authorities, through the rejection of the links that bound them to the Catholic faith, heretics severed themselves from their political and social obligations.[41]

Through their attack against the body politic, they assaulted Christ's body by repudiating the authority of God's anointed, the monarch. The tension present in some of those accused concerning their obedience to God and prince was clearly exemplified in the examination of John Newman, a pewterer from Maidstone burned at Saffron Walden on 31 August 1555. Newman claimed during his examination to have been converted to the 'true faith' by the preachers who 'were commanded by the king and laws of the realm' to divulge the doctrine that was 'agreeable' to God's Word. This preaching had been set forth by Edward VI with the consent of the whole council and by the authority of

40 Meneses, *Lvz del alma*, fols 18^r–19^r: 'Dos principios [...] tuuo Alemania en su perdición. El vno fue la corrupción de las costumbres, y ésta vemos en España muy crescida y puesta en la cumbre quanto a todo lo que es de mundo [...]. El otro principio fue la falta del conoscimiento de Dios y la ignorancia, lo qual tampoco falta [...]. La segunda conjectura q[ue] en esto tengo y me pone harto pauor, es el effecto que se ha seguido de la ignorancia, y es q[ue] el mesmo ceuo co[n] que este nueuo mahoma, q[ue] es Luthero, pescó a Alemania hallo en España. El primero con q[ue] los ganó y que les echó fue libertad y esención de muchas leyes de Dios, y de todas las de la yglesia, porq[ue] éste es su apellido, libertad Que como la nació[n] Española sea de valor más q[ue] otras, y los bienes deste mundo ordinariamente no sean puros, sino mezclados de mucha escoria: este valor trae consigo soberuia y leuantamie[n]to: y la soberuia, amor y apetito de libertad y esenció[n]. Pues si auiendo este aparejo en España, sonasse el atambor de la libertad lutherana, temo q[ue] haría ta[n]ta gente como en Alemania hizo'.

41 Ricardo García Cárcel and Doris Moreno Martínez, *Inquisición. Historia crítica* (Madrid: Temas de Hoy, 2000), 360–1.

parliament. However, immediately after declaring this strong emphasis on the legal framework upon which the Edwardian Reformation had been built, Newman denied Mary's authority to coerce her subjects into conformity by violence since faith, the gift of God, 'co[m]meth not of man, neither of mans lawes'.[42] This selective interpretation of the crown's right to impose a particular strand of Christianity was a dangerous one which was at odds with the ideas of the authors, both English and Spanish, studied in this chapter. In every man's struggle for salvation, Christopherson explained, it was sometimes natural to doubt, but a man should 'not sticke onlye to hys owne iudgement', but follow that of men 'whose doctrine hath euer [...] bene by the whole churche of God well liked & allowed'. If the spirit of a man who tried his faith was inspired by God, he argued, 'it will not resist the authorite of the churche [...] but will always submytte it selfe thervnto'.[43] Heresy was, therefore, a dangerous infection which threatened to affect all members and it was a rebellion against God, the Church and the prince or, in other words, against the body politic of the realm and the mystical body of Christ. As such, it had to be crushed.

6.2 Punishing Heresy in English and Spanish Intellectual and Theological Thought

It is in this context that we ought to understand the language of war employed in some theological works. Thomas Watson, employing Job 7, 1 Timothy 1 and 2 Corinthians 10 as ammunition, likened man's life to a war in which, Christ, the king, had true Christians serve as 'soldiours against the deuill' whose faith was established, confirmed, nurtured and increased through the seven sacraments.[44] Heretics were 'rauenouse wolfes' disguised as sheep and through the teaching of 'olde rotten heresyes', they intended the maintenance of vice, disobedience, sacrilege, 'and open conspiracye, to the subuersion of them selfes, & of that state vnder whiche they lyue'.[45] Warfare and repression were inexorably linked in Castro's work. The Franciscan recalled that, during the wars in Germany and at the Council of Trent, some had reproached Charles V for waging war against fellow Christians. It was illicit, they had claimed, quoting

42 *A&M* [1576], 1870.

43 Christopherson, *An Exhortation*, sigs I5^{r-v}.

44 Thomas Watson, *Holsome and Catholyke doctryne concerninge the seuen Sacramentes of Chrystes Church, expedient to be knowen of all men, set forth in maner of shorte Sermons to bee made to the people, by the reuerend father in God Thomas byshop of Lincolne* (London: Robert Caly, 1558), fols 1^{v}–5^{v}.

45 Watson, *Twoo Sermons*, sig. G7^{r}.

John the Baptist in Luke 3:12–14, when he told the soldiers not to exert violence upon anyone and to be content with their pay. Castro, however, argued that the Baptist's exhortation did not apply to just wars. Not only did Jesus command men to pay tribute to Caesar in Matthew 22:17–21 but Paul, in Romans 13:3–7, reminded us that tribute ought to be paid to the prince, who was God's minister.[46] The prince, as well as God, had to be obeyed.

Castro extracted from Scripture ten different reasons for which war could be justified and concluded that two of them certainly applied to heretics. The most obvious of these causes was a 'decline in the true worship of God' – not believing in God, in His spouse the Church, or in the tenets of the faith was a manifest just cause for war. The other one was to oppose 'those who rebel against their superior, to whom they owe complete reverence'.[47] All heretics, therefore, were 'manifest rebels against the Holy Catholic Church', whose doctrine all believers ought to receive, and yet they chose to oppose it, preferring their own opinions and condemning the Church's precepts.[48] This was the interpretation that was to be given to Job 24:13 (*ipsi fuerunt rebelles luminis nescierunt vias eius nec reversi sunt per semitas illius*) and thus it had been interpreted by St Gregory I in *Moralia, siue expositio in Job*.[49] The implications of Castro's arguments were conducive to the only outcome possible for those who rejected the prince's authority:

> It is just […] that the prince to whose authority they are subject to, can undertake a war against them. […] If it is just to condemn pertinacious heretics to death, whether this death be inflicted by, namely, sword, fire, water or any other means, it follows that, as is just, war may be waged

46 Castro, *De iusta haereticorum punitione*, 369–70.

47 Castro, *De iusta haereticorum punitione*, 383: 'Iustam belli causam secundo loco supra collocauimus: recessum à vero Dei cultu. At haeretici, qui de Deo, aut sponsa illius ecclesia non credunt, quae credenda sunt, Deum vere, & vt oportet, non colunt. Iusta igitur belli causa est haeresis, quam qui deserere noluerint, iuste de bellari possunt. Altera iusti belli cause, quam octauo loco rece[n]suimus, est, si quis rebellet aduersus superiore[m], cui reuerentiam integra[m] praestare tenentur'.

48 Castro, *De iusta haereticorum punitione*, 383: 'Et certe ex hac etia[m] ratione apertissime conuincitur, iustum esse bellum, quod aduersus pertinaces haereticos geritur. Nam haeretici omnes sunt aperte rebelles ecclesiae sanctae catholicę, cuius doctrina[m] omnes fideles suscipere tenentur. Haeretici autem superbia excaecati propria[m] sententiam preaferunt doctrinae sanctae matris ecclesiae, & ideo vt suam sententia[m] tueantur, non dubita[n]t doctrinae ecclesiae catholicae contradicere, & illius praecepta contemnere'.

49 Castro, *De iusta haereticorum punitione*, 383–4.

> against pertinacious heretics and rebels to their destruction, and that the prince may impose death upon those who deserve it.[50]

Even if heretics were counted as rebels against God, Church, and prince, and therefore liable to be condemned to death, there were also caveats to this position. Heresy may have been the most repugnant of offences in early modern Europe, yet it was one of the very few from which one could escape alive. In fact, the ultimate goal of heresy examinations or inquisitions was the conversion of the accused, not their death.[51] This is evident in many of the examples provided by Foxe in which the examiners gave the accused several opportunities to recant, do penance and be set free. In John Rogers's examination, for instance, Foxe recounted how Gardiner claimed that they had wished to follow Christ's example to convert him so that he would live, but since Rogers refused to be converted, 'w[it]h sorrow of mynde & bitternes of hart',, he condemned him to prevent his wickedness from infecting 'the lords flocke'.[52] A few of those mentioned by Foxe did indeed conform and others recanted only to relapse and end at the stake. In these efforts, the use of high-profile recantations to be used as effective propaganda for the Catholic cause was undoubtedly in the examiners' minds, but we should not brush aside the notion that many did have a genuine desire for heretics to be converted for the salvation of their souls and the preservation of their bodies. Richard Woodman, an ironworker from Sussex who was examined a startling thirty-two times, is a case in point.[53] After his first examination in early 1556 by George Day, bishop of Chichester, Woodman and four others were released,

> out of the butchers handes, requiring nothing els of vs but that we should be honest men, & members of the true catholike Church, that was builded vpon the Prophets & Apostles, Christ being the head of the true church:

50 Castro, *De iusta haereticorum punitione*, 384: 'Et inde apertissime sequitur, vt si illi huic iustae punitioni resistere velint: Princeps cuius ditioni subduntur, iuste ob hoc possit bellum aduersus illos mouere. Nam qui poena[m] iustam ex Principis mandato decretam subire recusat, & ne illam patiatur Principi resistit, rebellis est. [...] Rursum, si haereticus pertinax, iuste est ad mortem damnandus, nec refert [...] qua morte, gladio videlicet, aut igne, aut aqua, aut quouis alio modo mors illi inferatur: conseque[n]s est, vt iustum sit, haereticos pertinaces, & rebelles bello oppugnare, vt pereant, & sic illos, ut erant meriti, Princeps morte mulctare possit'.

51 Susan Brigden, *London and the Reformation* (Oxford: Clarendon Press, 1989), 607; Brad S. Gregory, *Salvation at Stake: Christian Martyrdom in Early Modern Europe* (Cambridge, Massachusetts and London: Harvard University Press, 1999), 80–2.

52 *A&M* [1576], 1444.

53 For his final six examinations before being condemned see *A&M* [1576], 1902–21. The reference to his being examined for heresy thirty-two times in 1902.

> the which all we affirmed, that we wer me[m]bers of the true church, & purposed by Gods helpe therin to dye.[54]

Although Woodman – and Foxe – framed it to suggest a hypocritical intent in the formulation of this bond, there was nothing in it that contradicted the theological foundations of Philip and Mary's Church, as we saw in the previous chapter.[55] However, relapsed heretics, considered to be stubborn traitors by the authorities, deserved death. Christopherson, writing about rebellion in general, explained that resisting the authority of the prince was to make war 'agaynst God, forasmuch as the prince is [...] appointed by God'. Furthermore, he concluded, 'excepte he repente betime, he shall receaue the rewarde of a traytour in hell'.[56] The key concept was that of repentance, for a timely offer to recant and return to the Church marked the difference between the reconciled convict who was prescribed to do penance (what the Spanish Inquisition called *penitenciados* or *reconciliados*, depending on the degree of their offence), and the pertinacious heretic who deserved death (those who were *relajados*, 'relaxed', or handed over to the secular arm for execution).

In August 1558, upon his return to Spain as archbishop of Toledo, Carranza preached a sermon in Valladolid about the manner in which repentant and unrepentant heretics were to be treated; a sermon that was to give him grief during his inquisitorial process.[57] The sermon caused scandal because some thought that Carranza was proposing leniency towards heresy.[58] Friar Francisco de Tordesillas, OP, explained that whoever had thought so did not understand what Carranza actually meant. Tordesillas pointed out that Carranza had compared the treatment that the Church should dispense to heretics to the treatment that a wall receives in wartime. If the wall were to be broken, it could be put together again,

---

54 *A&M* [1576], 1902.

55 Richard Woodman would eventually be burnt at Lewes, Sussex, together with nine other men and women on 22 June 1557.

56 Christopherson, *An Exhortation*, sigs $I6^{v}$–$I7^{r}$.

57 BAV, Vat. Lat. 13138, fols 226^{r}–233^{r} for the questions in the 'Interrogatorio de indirectas'. The question explored here is number thirty, in fol. 230^{r-v}, where Carranza asked if they had been present at the sermon in San Pablo of Valladolid in August 1558 where he had explained '[...] La manera y forma que la yglesia cathólica tiene con los herejes que se conuierten a ella, y con Los que no se quieren reducir [...]'.

58 See, for instance, BAV, Vat. Lat. 13138, fol. 320^{r}: Deposition of Juana de Austria, princess of Portugal, before Gaspar de Zúñiga y Avellaneda, archbishop of Santiago de Compostela and Pedro de Tapia, notary of the Inquisition, Madrid, 26 October 1562. In her typically stern manner, Philip's sister explained that she had not felt 'scandalised' by the sermon, but that she had felt that Carranza had treated the matter too 'mildly', and that she had later learnt that Fernando Valdés and others had indeed been scandalised by the sermon.

> with the same stones if they remained intact but, if not, then they would put new ones in. From this some inferred that he wanted to persuade them that heretics were to be pardoned. However, this witness understood that [he meant] only those who truly wanted to be subdued [...] and these he called 'the stones that were left intact'. Those who would not convert he called 'unprofitable stones' and others, as he said, 'were to be put in their place'. That is, those who did not convert were to be cast out of the Church.[59]

In one of his Canterbury sermons, Cardinal Pole also employed an architectural metaphor to justify Thomas Cranmer's condemnation. In the ladder of Catholic truth that the archbishops of Canterbury embodied, Cranmer was 'a broken steppe, which is now taken awaye, a new one of that same matter that your fathers steppes were made of putt in his place'.[60] These men, who were at the forefront of Catholic revitalisation in England, agreed, through the use of architectural tropes, that the reformation plan envisaged for the Catholic Church included the prosecution of pertinacious heretics, condemning them if necessary. The rebuilding of the Church in England and her reinforcement in Spain were crucial matters, but the materials used to build and reinforce the Church had to be solid.

However, if, as their architectural metaphors suggested, heretics preferred to be intact stones or unbroken steps, death would not be required. In the same vein, Castro analysed the genealogy of the concept of pertinacity, tracing it back to Marcus Terentius Varro, Seneca, Livy and Cicero, and concluding that '[p]ertinacious is he who persists in error and, as such, is held accountable under his crime'. This applied to both those who persisted in making

59 BAV, Vat. Lat. 13138, fols 374r–384r. Deposition of Friar Francisco de Tordesillas, OP, before the inquisitors Dr Riego and Licenciado Diego González and Loreña, notary of the Inquisition, Valladolid, 4 July 1564, fol. 378v: 'A las treynta preguntas dixo q[ue]ste t[estig]o se halló presente al d[ic]ho s[er]món e tres cos[a]s prençipales de que algunos se escandaliçaron son éstas la primera dezir que [en] la forma q[ue] se avía de auer con estos hereges le parezía que avía de s[er] como sean los çercados [en] vn combate que si les rrompen el muro p[ro]cura[n] de çerrar el portillo con las mysmas piedras si quedan enteras y sino ponen ot[ra]s de nuevo de lo qual alg[un]os entendieron q[ué]l quería p[er]suadir que p[er]donasen estos herejes pero este t[estig]o no entendió sino los q[ue] se quisiesen rreduçir v[er]daderam[en]te porq[ue] ansí lo declaró dizi[en]do con las piedras que quedasen enteras y a los q[ue] no se conv[ir]tiesen llamáuales piedras q[ue] ya no heran de p[ro]becho en cuyo lugar dezía que avían de poner otras lo qual es dezir estos que no se convierten échenlos fuera de la igl[es]ia [...]'.

60 AAV, Vat. Lat. 5868, fol. 467r. Eamon Duffy has made an exploration of Pole's sermons in Eamon Duffy, *Saints, Sacrilege and Sedition: Religion and Conflict in the Tudor Reformations* (London: Bloomsbury, 2012), 179–94. I am grateful to Prof. Duffy for bringing to my attention the existence of this sermon.

false assertions and those who persisted in doubting the truth.[61] The Church, however, was willing to receive back those who truly repented, following the lead of Christ himself, who wanted everyone to be saved, leaving no one out, as expounded in 1 Timothy 2:4 and John 6:37 and promised in Jeremiah 3:1.[62] Founding his arguments upon Ambrose's reading of Leviticus 19 and Jerome's interpretation of Ezekiel 22, Castro concluded that those 'Jews, Saracens or heretics' who abandoned their errors and converted to the Catholic faith were to be 'benignly' received and 'sweetly' treated.[63] However, those heretics and relapsed infidels who chose not to repent, could only expect one outcome. Contrary to what some Protestants and others claimed, Castro explained, failing to fulfil the duty to punish heresy was 'manifestly repugnant to natural law'. No man, 'however demented he might be', could believe the contrary, for there was not and there never had been 'so barbaric a people that would not stoutly punish robbers, thieves and murderers, for otherwise neither goods nor lives would be safe, nor would any republic last for long but everything would quickly perish'.[64] There were several examples of malefactors being

61 Castro, *De iusta haereticorum punitione*, 85: '[Following an exploration of the classical writers mentioned] Hac igitur vocis significatione praemissa, rei definitionem statuere oportet, iuxta quam sit quilibet de pertinacia examinandus. Pertinax est, qui persistit in errore, quem sub reatu culpae deserere tenetur. Ex prima huius definitionis parte colligitur non solum illum esse pertinacem dicendum, qui falsum asserit: sed qui de veritate dubitat'.

62 Castro, *De iusta haereticorum punitione*, 204: 'Haereticum hominem si resipuerit, solet pia mater ecclesia, quae sponsi sui dulcissimi vestigia sequitur, extensis (vt aiunt) vlnis recipere. Imitatur siquidem sponsum suum, qui (vt ait Paulus) vult omnes homines saluos fieri, & ad agnitionem veritatis venire [1 Timothy 2:4]. Eum, qui venerit ad me, inquit Saluator noster, non eiiciam foras [John 6:37]. Iustum est ergo, vt ecclesia illius sponsa non eiiciat foras eos, qui ad Christum redire voluerint. Deus per Hieremia[m] prophetam Iudeaorum synagogue, quae cum amatoribus multis per varias idolorum culturas fuerat fornicata, promisit se illam recepturum, si ad illam reuerteretur [Jeremiah 3:1]: ergo oportet, vt ecclesia filios, qui ab eius gremio per haeresim recesserant, recipiat, cum ad illam reuertuntur'.

63 Castro, *De iusta haereticorum punitione*, 206: '[Following his exploration of Ambrose and Jerome] Iustius est ergo, vt qui à Iudaeis, siue Sarracenis, siue haereticis, eorum erroribus desertis, ad fidem ecclesiae catholicae conuertuntur, benigne recipiantur, dulciter tractentur, ne nimia austeritate deterriti, à coepta fide recedant: sed potius benignitate, & blanditiis sanctis allecti, in fide, quam semel susceperu[n]t alacriter perseuerent'.

64 Castro, *De ivsta haereticorum punitione*, 253–254: 'Vt autem hanc doctrinam falsam procul, & longissimi ab ecclesia relegemus, oportet, vt multis vrgentissimisque rationibus conuincamus, iustam esse & necessariam haereticorum punitionem. Primo igitur eos, qui haec docent percontor, an id quod de haereticis docent, ad omnes sceleratos homines etiam pertinere censeant, ita vt nullum malefactorem hominem quamlibet scelestum puniendum esse credant: sed omnem talem diuino iudicio relinquendum potent. Non credo hominem aliquem: nisi demens ille sit, taliter sentire: quoniam hoc naturali legi apertissime repugnat. Nulla enim est, aut nunquam fuit tam barbara gens, quae latrones,

punished in the New Testament and both Horace in the sixteenth epistle of his *Epistularum liber primus* and Augustine in his exposition of Psalm 127 had argued that the punishment of offenders was 'in the public and common interests of all republics'.[65] As Paul expounded in 1 Timothy 5:20, it was also convenient to deter potential sinners through fear by punishing those who did sin.[66] In fact, Castro reiterated, if Germany had been treated with more rigour, the 'dangerous heretical infection' would not have advanced much.[67] If those who sinned against the republic deserved punishment, then heretics ought to be punished, as they sinned against the republic too. As the Emperor Theodosius (r. 379–395) had declared against the Manicheans, 'that which is committed against divine religion, is committed against all'. If kings, bishops, and other public powers punished those who sinned against their neighbours and the republic, it followed that 'it was necessary and much more worthy to punish those who sin against God and the Church'.[68]

Against those who adduced God's commandment not to kill, Castro affirmed that there were many instances in the Old Testament in which it was just to kill particularly wicked offenders. He then recounted the story of Ananias and his wife Sapphira in Acts 5:1–10. The couple had sold their lands to give the profits to the community, as was the practice in the Early Church, but they had lied and kept part of the money. When Peter confronted them, they dropped dead. Furthermore, Christ himself had warned that 'all that take the sword shall perish by the sword' (Matthew 26:52) and, in this context, to embrace heresy as a rebellious act was tantamount to taking the sword. Getting rid of unrepentant heretics was, therefore, essential for the upkeep of the republic's safety and the quietude and peace of the people.[69] Huggarde followed a very similar narrative line and asked, 'if Emperours do punishe theft, murder, rape, adulterie,

---

fures, homicidas, non acerrime puniat, quoniam alias nullius esset tuta supellex, nullios vita secura, nulláq[ue] respubl[ica] diu persisteret: sed omnes citissime perirent'.

65 Castro, *De ivsta haereticorum punitione*, 254–8.

66 Castro, *De ivsta haereticorum punitione*, 259.

67 Castro, *De ivsta haereticorum punitione*, 260.

68 Castro, *De ivsta haereticorum punitione*, 260–1: 'Si is qui in rempublicam peccat, merito punire potest, consequens est vt haereticus etiam iustissime puniatur: quia haereticos etiam in rempublicam peccat. Vnde piisimus Imperator Theodosius in l. Manicheos .C. de haereticis. ait: Quod in religionem diuinam committitur, in omnium fertur iniuriam. Praeterea si Rex, aut Episcopus, aut quaeuis alia publica potestas valet punire peccantes in proximum & in rempublicam, consequens est & necessarium, vt multo magis punier valeat eos qui peccant in Deum & in ecclesiam'.

69 Castro, *De ivsta haereticorum punitione*, 344–5: 'Deinde si propter nullam causam licet hominem quamlibet sceleratu[m] occidere, nulla poterit respublica salua consistere: quoniam nisi sceleratissimi occida[n]tur, nulla erit in populo quies, nulla pax permanebit in illo'.

and periurie, why shuld thei not as well punyshe heresie and sacrilege?'[70] To the Protestants who claimed that no men were to die for their conscience, Huggarde replied by asking why Joan Bocher and George van Parris had been burnt at the stake under Edward VI. If anyone could believe as they pleased, he argued, then it made no sense not to allow the Turks to follow Muhammad's law among the English. Significantly, the hosier then used the same example of Ananias and Sapphira, concluding that their death had been a condemnation for their lies.[71]

Huggarde then brought into the debate the parable of the wheat and the tares (Matthew 3:24–30) to counter those who alleged that it had been commanded by Jesus to 'suffre the Cockell too growe with the good corne tyll the haruest come', as it was the 'lorde of the haruest' who was to 'cast the cockle into the fyre'. Again with a line of argument which ran parallel to that of Castro, Huggarde explained that it would be difficult for a king 'to gouerne his common wealth', if those who committed 'treason, murder, or felony should liue'.[72] Interpreting the parable and other places in the New Testament in this sense, Huggarde concluded that Scripture itself 'perswaded' that 'rotte[n] branches' were to be burnt and that this was done out of charity, to avoid heretics falling deeper into damnation. Borrowing from Augustine's *Contra Cresconium* (V. 4), Huggarde postulated that heresy was like the dead flesh in a wound which had to be cut off lest it 'fester and ranckle the other membres'. Now that the 'good corne' had a 'stronge roote', the tares could be easily identified and 'roted out' without the action posing any risks to the good corn.[73]

In the same vein, Castro argued that in the parable of the wheat and the tares, the lord of the harvest had not forbidden the 'eradication' of the tares per se, but only when they could not be discerned from the wheat. Ceasing the cause for which the precept had been established, and this was accomplished by adhering to the laws of the Church, it followed that the prohibition ceased too, although here he introduced a caveat. If inquisitors and lay powers were to proceed against someone without the heretical character of the accused's propositions fully proven, they would be acting unfairly, as they risked eradicating the wheat together with the tares. If, on the contrary, a person was known to be a heretic and would not receive the Catholic Church after being admonished, their death would be licit.[74] This interpretation of the parable was not exclusive of Catholic authors. As Brad S. Gregory has found,

---

70 Huggarde, *Displaying of the Protestantes*, fol. 44^{r}.

71 Huggarde, *Displaying of the Protestantes*, fols 57^{r-v}.

72 Huggarde, *Displaying of the Protestantes*, fols 57^{v}–58^{r}.

73 Huggarde, *Displaying of the Protestantes*, fols 59^{r}–60^{r}.

74 Castro, *De ivsta haereticorum punitione*, 366–369.

Calvin drew from it the same conclusion. The story of Ananias and Sapphira, employed by the scholastic Johann Eck with the same purpose as Castro and Huggarde, was used by Calvin and Heinrich Bullinger too.[75] That the examples put forward to justify the execution of heretics by an English hosier and a Spanish renowned theologian were the same was not a fortuitous coincidence. It clearly exemplifies that they were both part of a wider, Catholic understanding of the world and it also suggests that Spanish works (Castro's *De iusta punitione* had been first published in 1547) may have influenced English authors of the Marian period. English Marian Catholicism was in every way integrated with Continental Catholic thought.

6.3 Anglo-Spanish Heresies

In terms of the punishment of religious dissent, English and Spanish authors seem to have been strongly in agreement and it will be crucial to determine whether they were persecuting the same ideas and attitudes, too. Whilst in England the persecution of Protestants began as soon as the heresy laws were reintroduced in 1555, in Spain, arrests of Protestants began in Seville in 1557 under the close scrutiny of Fernando Valdés.[76] At the beginning the Inquisition was lenient, releasing prisoners soon enough, as the Inquisitor General thought that a light-touch approach at the beginning might encourage people to talk. Much emphasis has been given to the political motivations behind Valdés's implacable move against the suspected heretics (called *luteranos* in the documentation almost invariably, whatever the nuances of the doctrines they defended may have been), not least because his political influence was rapidly waning and he sought to kill two birds with one stone by entangling his rival, Carranza, in the process.[77] When the Inquisition's investigations bore fruit after Julianillo's examinations, the arrests that followed caused a sensation. The 'Lutheran' group in Seville was believed to have developed around the Hieronymite Monastery of San Isidoro del Campo in the outskirts of the city and its germ was attributed to Dr Juan Gil, better known by his Latinised

75 Gregory, *Salvation at Stake*, 89.

76 The Inquisition, of course, did not just concern itself with Protestants. It also persecuted the real or imagined unorthodox opinions and attitudes of conversos, bigamy, blasphemy, sodomy, bestiality and other acts considered to go against Catholic doctrine. In this work, however, we will be focusing on the persecution of those accused of having Protestant leanings.

77 For an account of the events which led to the denunciation of *luteranos* and Carranza, which tends to be sympathetic to Valdés, see González Novalín, *Fernando de Valdés*, vol. 1, 290–99, 310–329.

name, Dr Egidio (*c.*1495–1555). The latter, from a religiosity deeply rooted in Erasmus and Juan de Valdés, had developed a reformed perspective on justification which he had instilled in many of the monks at San Isidoro, namely men like Antonio del Corro (1527–1591), Casiodoro de Reina (*c.*1520–1594) and Cipriano de Valera (1531–1602). Dr Constantino de la Fuente (1502–1560), commonly known as Dr Constantino, was also believed to have become a Protestant either through Egidio's influence or at the same time.[78] A canon of Seville Cathedral and former royal preacher and chaplain to both Charles V and Philip, he had accompanied the latter to England and departed with him in the summer of 1555 for Flanders, from where he returned to Seville. Already notorious for his theological works, in Seville he became widely famous for his ardent preaching.[79] From this group of sophisticated theologians, heresy had spread to all sorts of men and women, including nobles, members of the city's elites, embroiderers, weavers and other artisans as well as foreigners.[80]

The Valladolid group seems to have been more aristocratic, but its reach proved equally alarming given the speed at which it grew. One of the two key figures in the movement was Carlos de Seso (*c.*1515–1559), an Italian who had served Charles V in the wars in Germany and had settled in Logroño, where he married a member of a bastard branch of the Castilian royal family.[81] At the time of his arrest he resided in Toro, where he had been appointed *corregidor*.[82] The other leader was Dr Agustín Cazalla (1510–1559), one of ten siblings from

78 Menéndez Pelayo, *Heterodoxos españoles*, vol. 2, 54–8; José C. Nieto, *El Renacimiento y la otra España. Visión cultural socioespiritual* (Geneva: Librairie Droz, 1997), 189–213; Pastore, *Una herejía española*, 287–302; López Muñoz, *Reforma en Sevilla*, vol. 1, 72–80, 90–6. Although traditionally called Constantino Ponce de la Fuente, Salvador Fernández Cava has been the first to notice that there is no documented evidence for 'Ponce' being his surname, as in the contemporary evidence he is always called 'Fuente', 'de la Fuente', 'Fontius', or 'Phonti', where the mistake probably stems from. See Salvador Fernández Cava, *Constantino Ponce de la Fuente (1505–1559): el camino de la verdad* (Ciudad Real: Almud and Ediciones de Castilla-La Mancha, 2007), 9.

79 Bataillon saw in Constantino an Erasmian, an idea which was later repeated in the historiography. Nieto, however, has strongly argued that Constantino's theology had a Protestant outlook with influences which were both Lutheran and Calvinist. See Marcel Bataillon, *Erasmo y España, estudios sobre la historia espiritual del siglo XVI*, tr. Antonio Alatorre [1937] (Mexico City: Fondo de Cultura Económica, 1950), 525–45 and Nieto, *Renacimiento y la otra España*, 349–62.

80 González Novalín, *Fernando de Valdés*, vol. 1, 260, etc. For a full account of the persecution in Seville see López Muñoz, *Reforma en Sevilla*, vol. 1, 209–52.

81 Isabel de Castilla, his wife, was a descendant of King Peter I of Castile (r. 1350–1369) through an illegitimate line. Accused of heresy with her husband, she saved her life as a *reconciliada* in the *auto de fe* of 8 October 1559. Her uncle, Alonso de Castilla y Zúñiga, had been bishop of Calahorra (1523–1541).

82 A judicial officer who acted as a representative of royal jurisdiction in a certain city, town or district.

a very powerful Valladolid family of converso origins.[83] Like Constantino, Cazalla had been an imperial preacher and chaplain and had accompanied the emperor around Europe, from where, according to one source, 'he came back already a heretic', although he always maintained that it had been Seso, in Spain, who converted him.[84] Upon his return to Valladolid in 1552, Dr Cazalla was in permanent communication with Seso, and their doctrines soon spread to several Castilian cities and localities (Valladolid, Zamora, Toro, Palencia, Pedrosa del Rey, etc.) thanks to the proselytising ventures of several of the group's members. Particularly active were three of Dr Cazalla's siblings: Pedro de Cazalla, parish priest of Pedrosa; Francisco de Vivero, a cleric; and Beatriz de Vivero, who visited friends and family tirelessly in her evangelising zeal.[85] In Pedrosa, the group recruited Juan Sánchez, Pedro de Cazalla's servant, and Isabel de Estrada, of lowly extraction, who disseminated reformed ideas through the village and the neighbouring city of Valladolid. The most prominent member of the group was Friar Domingo de Rojas, OP, an old disciple and friend of Carranza and the son of Elvira de Rojas, marchioness of Alcañices, a prominent Castilian lady who also had close ties with the archbishop of Toledo. The doctrines of this group spread mainly to members of their own families, but they were also proving attractive to many others from all echelons of society. The example of the Cistercian Monastery of Belén in Valladolid, from where four nuns were 'relaxed' to the secular arm for their heresies is particularly poignant. But the network also included gentlemen, ploughmen, *beatas*, and a silversmith.[86]

---

83 The Cazalla-Vivero siblings were born to Pedro de Cazalla, a royal bookkeeper already deceased by 1557, and Leonor de Vivero, both of converso origin. Pedro's siblings Juan de Cazalla, titular bishop of Berissa, and, María de Cazalla, both underwent inquisitorial processes due to their *iluminismo*, which stemmed from an appreciation of Erasmus and Juan de Valdés and advocated an intimate and introspective faith. See Nieto, *Renacimiento y la otra España*, 111 and, for a full account, Milagros Ortega Costa, *Proceso de la Inquisición contra María de Cazalla* (Madrid: Fundación Universitaria Española, 1978).

84 Menéndez Pelayo, *Heterodoxos españoles*, vol. 1, 932–40.

85 Following the custom prevalent at the time in some Spanish regions and among certain social classes, parents and children could choose which family name they were to carry. These names could be inherited from both male and female ancestors. Hence the difference in the Cazalla-Vivero siblings' surnames.

86 Menéndez Pelayo, *Heterodoxos españoles*, vol. 1, 950–66; Jesús Alonso Burgos, *El luteranismo en Castilla durante el siglo XVI. Autos de fe de Valladolid de 21 de mayo y de 8 de octubre de 1559* (San Lorenzo de El Escorial: Swan, Avantos & Hakeldama, 1983), 59–85. The *beatas* were pious lay women who lived apart from society on their own or on small female communities called *beateríos* and enjoyed a certain reputation for sanctity although they often got in trouble with the Inquisition. See Adelina Sarrión Mora, *Beatas y endemoniadas: Mujeres heterodoxas ante la Inquisición, siglos XVI a XIX* (Madrid: Alianza Editorial, 2003).

The Protestant credentials of Reina, Valera and Corro after they fled Seville in 1557 are irrefutable and have been explored elsewhere.[87] It is significant that all three resided at some point in England under Queen Elizabeth, Valera and Corro both dying there during her reign. Constantino had published his famous *Summa de doctrina christiana* in 1543 and it went through several editions until its inclusion in the *Index librorum prohibitorum* compiled by Fernando Valdés in 1559. Constantino's *Summa* did not openly reject the Catholic Church, but it did have a reformed flavour. In Constantino's colloquium, his characters avoided the discussion of the sacraments of confirmation, extreme unction, order, and marriage. In his treatment of confession, Constantino made remarks that could be – and were – interpreted as unorthodox. He stated that the true 'medicine' against mortal sin was 'to consider in my heart who it was against whom I had erred and whose commandment I had held in little esteem'. Only after acknowledging one's sin before God was it useful to confess to the priest.[88] This was a perfectly orthodox opinion, but the insistence on heartfelt contrition and private supplications to God could easily be deemed to come close to the mental confession advocated by some Protestant reformers. In his treatment of the Eucharist, Constantino put a lot of emphasis on the character of the Mass as a 'memorial and representation' of Christ's death and passion and, although he did say that the Mass put the believer in remembrance of Christ's sacrifice, he did not call the Mass a sacrifice in itself.[89] Furthermore, he had nothing to say about the adoration of the Blessed Sacrament, made no explicit or implicit mention of the real presence or transubstantiation, referring only to the 'receiving' of Christ's body and blood, and he recommended to read the gospel and epistle of the day in the vernacular before hearing Latin Mass.[90]

Juan Pérez de Pineda (*c.*1500–1567), rector of the Colegio de la Doctrina in Seville, who fled to Geneva after Egidio had been in trouble with the Inquisition in the early 1550s, published in 1557 a letter to King Philip in which he launched a vigorous attack against the papacy which shared much with the English

87 Bataillon ascribed their religious evolution to *alumbrado*, Erasmian and Valdesian influences rather than to a properly Protestant reformed theology. See Bataillon, *Erasmo y España*, 704–7. Other authors, acknowledging these influences, have more convincingly advocated for a Protestant theology which was perceived by the Roman Church in Spain as a threat. See Nieto, *Renacimiento y la otra España*, 396–403, 480–91; Pastore, *Una herejía española*, 317–42; López Muñoz, *Reforma en Sevilla*, 143–75.

88 Constantino de la Fuente, *Summa de doctrina Christiana, Compuesta por el Doctor Constantino. Item, El sermón de Christo nuestro redemptor enel monte, Traduzido en Castellano por el mismo Author. Puso se también ala fin vna dotrina, que muestra cómo cada vno deue regir y gouernar su casa, ordenada por sant Bernardo* (Antwerp: Martín Nucio, *c.*1549), fols 121^r–124^r.

89 Constantino, *Summa de doctrina christiana*, fol. 129^v.

90 Constantino, *Summa de doctrina christiana*, fols 126^v–129^v.

foundations of the royal supremacy. To begin with, he explained, Pope Paul IV hated the king, the emperor and, more generally, all 'Spanish blood'.[91] Pérez de Pineda accused the pope of forgetting his obedience to God's laws by placing kings 'under his foot, daring to kick and stamp on their royal dignity', which had been instituted by God.[92] By usurping God's authority, the pope attributed to himself the same authority that God had over Christian kings, using inquisitors to take away true faith and life from 'the hearts of Christians', and to 'destroy and extinguish the charity that comes from it', condemning as heretics those who, unlike the popes, could see the 'pure truth of the Gospel'.[93] Pérez de Pineda argued that Philip's power over his kingdoms did not 'depend on any superior power here on earth, but from that of the God of heaven who established it and governs it through His providence'.[94] Here was a complete rejection of the notion of papal primacy in unmistakable terms from a Spaniard in an attempt to convince King Philip to take back the powers that the popes had usurped from him. The book was addressed to Philip as king of Spain and England and it would have been lost on no one that Philip and Mary's immediate predecessors in the English throne had done just that.

From the inquisitorial processes against the Valladolid circle which are still extant we can get a clearer picture of the kind of heresy that was being persecuted there. The full processes of the brothers Pedro de Cazalla and Francisco de Vivero and that of Marina de Guevara, a nun from Belén, have survived intact and the accusation's final report for the condemnation of Domingo de Rojas is available too. It was frequent practice to include fragments of other prisoners' processes to aid in the accused's cross-examination which provides us with glimpses of others' views on the doctrines and events examined. A comparison of their activities and beliefs with those of the English victims will

---

91 Juan Pérez de Pineda, *Carta embiada a nvestro avgvstíssimo senor príncipe don Philippe, Rey de España, de Inglaterra, de Nápoles, y delas Indias del Perú, &c. en que se declaran las causas delas guerras y calamidades prese[n]tes, y se descubre[n] los medios y artes co[n] que son robados los Españoles, y las más vezes muertos quanto al cuerpo, y quanto al ánima: y contra estos daños se ponen juntamente algunos remedios que son proprios y efficazes, delos quales puede vsar su Majestad para conseruación de sus Repúblicas, y cada vno de sus vasallos en particular para poder los euitar, y ser preseruados en vida, y enrriquecidos de todo bien temporal y eterno* (c.1557), 7–8.

92 Pérez de Pineda, *Carta embiada a don Philippe*, 11: 'No es de marauillar que pues los Reyes tienen tan poca estima de su propria dignidad, que contra Dios se abaxan hasta besalle el çapato en señal de subjeçión, que él los tenga debaxo del pie, y que se atreua a acoçear y pisar su dignidad real, cosa que Dios aprueua, y en quien quiso que se manifestasse su Majestad, y poder'.

93 Pérez de Pineda, *Carta embiada a don Philippe*, 26, 51–52.

94 Pérez de Pineda, *Carta embiada a don Philippe*, 77–8: 'La potestad que vuestra Majestad tiene en sus Reynos, no depende de otra potestad superior sobre la tierra, sino dela de Dios del cielo que la estableció, y la gouierna por su prouidencia'.

help to discern any patterns in these Anglo-Spanish inquisitions. The main difference that stands out between the two groups was that whereas the articles put forward against English Protestants tended to emphasise heterodox beliefs in the sacrament of the altar, those against the Spanish *luteranos* were more typically centred around the doctrine of justification and the denial of purgatory. However, this should not divert attention from the fact that the heretical propositions of which they were accused were very similar: the assertion that there were only two sacraments, baptism and the Lord's Supper, the rejection of transubstantiation and of the adoration of the host and, at best, an ambiguous attitude towards the real presence; the understanding that auricular confession was unprofitable and unnecessary and that priests did not have any power to absolve sins, the abhorrence of the cult of the saints and the perspective that Catholic ceremonies were idolatrous, the staunch support for the marriage of priests, monks and nuns, the denunciation of the Roman Church as a false sect and of the pope as Antichrist, the illegal gathering of conventicles and reading of forbidden books and a general admiration for other heretics and martyrs.

In his examinations, John Bradford explained that all who truly believed in Christ were 'partakers of Christe and all his merites'. Jesus had been 'a Mediatour, paying the raunsome and price of redemption for Adame and his whole posteritie that refuse it not finally'. No Catholic would have disagreed with those assertions. However, Bradford explained that these profits of Christ's merits were given to those whom 'God the Father before the beginnyng of the worlde hath predestinate in Christe vnto eternal life', an election which stemmed from 'the free mercy and grace of God in hys owne wyl, through faith in Christ his sonne, chusing and preferryng to life, such as pleaseth hym'. Faith was the 'immediate cause' that 'worketh our iustification', and works of charity were 'hie gifts in man, and not of man, geuen of God to man', and none of them were required for salvation. Indeed, in the doctrine of election first, 'all woorkes of the law and merites of deseruing, whether they goe before faith, or come after', were excluded.[95] Robert Samuel followed the same argument, claiming that the remission of sins came 'by the onely meanes and merites of Christes death and passion'.[96] Similarly, Dr Cazalla confessed that he believed 'that only through Christ are we justified, and that works were not necessary for [justification], but a consequence and sign of gratitude for the benefit received

95 *A&M* [1576], 1601–3.
96 *A&M* [1576], 1638.

from Christ'.[97] Cristóbal de Padilla, a gentleman from Zamora, claimed that Pedro de Cazalla, Domingo de Rojas and others had taught him,

> this doctrine of justification, which is that Jesus Christ our Lord came to this world to save all sinners, and that His death and passion had been sufficient to pay for all the sins of all the elect and predestined by God, who enjoyed the remission of sins.

Christ's satisfaction was obtained only through 'lively faith' that worked through love and the forgiveness of sins did not require any exterior works of penance.[98] Pedro de Cazalla confessed that he understood justification in these terms and that from this understanding he had one day come to the conclusion that purgatory, therefore, did not exist. The three reasons he adduced were, first, that the 'mercy' received from God through Christ was abundant for the remission of sins. Second, that neither the Gospels, nor St Paul ever mentioned purgatory, whereas they did mention heaven and hell. Finally, that after Seso had confided in him such beliefs before he himself embraced them, he had consulted Carranza when he was about to set sail for England in 1554 and the future archbishop had advised him not to denounce Seso and had not given much credit to the doctrine of purgatory.[99] Elizabeth Young,

---

97 AHN, Consejo de Inquisición, leg. 5353, no. 8, Marina de Guevara (1559), unnumbered: 'En la materia de la Justificaçión q[ue] por sólo Jesu[crist]o somos justificados / et que las obras no eran neçessarias para ella / sino en consequençia et agradesçimy[ent]o del benefiçio Reçebido de [Crist]o. / et que desta rraíz naçía no aver purgatorio /'.

98 AHN, Consejo de Inquisición, leg. 1864, no. 2, Pedro de Cazalla (1558), fol. 38^{r-v}: 'Al segundo capítulo q[ue] le fue leýdo dixo qve de año y medio a esta parte poco más o menos [Padilla's confession dates from 30 July 1558] comunicando este confesante con frai Domingo de rrojas y con p[edr]o de cazalla cura de pedrosa y con el bachiller herrecuelo v[ecin]o de toro e con Jhoan Sánchez criado q[ue] hera a la sazón de P[edr]o de cazalla entendió este confes[an]te y le dixeron los suso d[ic]hos esta Doctrina de la Justificaçión q[ue] es que Jesu[crist]o n[uest]ro senor vino a este mundo a salbar los peccadores e q[ue] su muerte y pasión fue bastante para pagar todos los peccados de los escoxidos y predestinados de dios los q[ua]les gozauan de la rremysión de los peccados y de esta Satisfaçión de Jesu [Crist]o n[uest]ro señor tenyendo fee viua que obra por Amor creyendo particularmente y acetando la muerte de Jesu[crist]o n[uest]ro señor y su pasión por suyas y ofreçiéndola como tal suya al padre Eterno por sus peccados e q[ue] p[ar]a el perdón dellos no hera necesario penitencias exteriores de azotes e seliçios e ayunos ni Jubileos ny bullas ny purg[atori]o porque queriendo Satisfazer con esto no creýa la satisfaçión de Jesu[crist]o n[uest]ro señor q[ue] obiese sido entera pues el hombre quería satisfazer por sus peccados por otra parte [...]'.

99 AHN, Inquisición, leg. 1864, no. 2, fols 85^{v}–86^{r}: 'acaesçió que vn día estando yo solo junto a la puerta de mj iglesia, pensando en el benefi[ci]o de Jesu[crist]o, y su muerte, se me ofreció, que no auí [sic] porqué parar en el negar el purgatorio. Y p[ar]a esto se

who was arrested for smuggling forbidden books into England and would be released after nine examinations, significantly used the same argument as Cazalla to reject purgatory, stating that she had 'neuer heard in the scriptures of Purgatory, but in the scripture I haue heard of heauen and hel'.[100] Francisco de Vivero confessed that he held the same beliefs concerning justification and purgatory and explained that neither St Paul nor St Peter ever mentioned the existence of purgatory, which had been invented by humans concerned with their own interests.[101] Consequently, prayers for the souls of the departed were of no use. Similarly, John Lithall, who was finally released on bond and was free when Mary died, expressed the deeply held view that 'our iustification, righteousnesse, and saluation, commeth onely and freely by the merites of our Sauiour Iesus Christ, and all the inuentions and workes of men, be they neuer so glorious, be altogether vayne'.[102]

Except for Cristóbal de Padilla, who seems to have believed that there were three sacraments – baptism, penance and communion – it appears that the Valladolid heretics, like the Marian martyrs, were united in the Protestant reformed belief that Christ had instituted two sacraments: baptism and the Lord's Supper. The large number of those persecuted who expressed such views about the number of sacraments instituted by Christ both in England and in Spain suggests, not only that they were being influenced by the same or similar theological works and attitudes but, also, that the inquisitorial systems in both kingdoms were aware of this and were very efficient in detecting this particular belief.[103] In Valladolid, the Inquisition was very concerned with the

me ofrecieron algu[n]as Raçones. La p[ri]m[er]a que creyedo [sic] no le auer, confésauamos de dios auer Resçebido mayor misericordia, y p[or] la pasión de Jesu[crist]o abundante p[ar]a toda Remisión,. la 2ª raçón que seme ofreçió fue, no allar enel euangelio, ni en san pablo no[m]brado espresame[n]te este lugar del purgatorio, como en muchos lugares está no[m]brado espresame[n]te, el çielo, y el ynfierno. lo 3º que seme ofreció fue, acordárseme del poco, o ningún escrúpulo q[ue]l s[eñ]or arçobispo auía hecho, del caso que con su s[erenísim]a comuniq[ué] ni ponerme obli[gaci]ón a denunciar del dicho don Carlos, sauiendo su s[erenísim]a que auía yo entendido, no quedar el dicho don Carlos Reduçido en aq[uel] caso, de la plática q[ue] allí pasó. lo q[ua]l todo junto digo, q[ue] me vençió p[ar]a q[ue] yo creyase no auer el dicho purga[tori]o'.

100 *A&M* [1576], 1988.

101 AHN, Consejo de Inquisición, leg. 5353, no. 9, Francisco de Vivero (1559), fols 128v, 136v, 141v.

102 *A&M* [1576], 1984.

103 For Spanish examples see AHN, Consejo de Inquisición, leg. 1864, no. 2, fols 16r, 24r, 37v–38r, 41r, 85r–86v, 90r–93r; Archivo Histórico Nacional, Consejo de Inquisición, leg. 5353, no. 16, Friar Domingo de Rojas (1559), fols 1r–5v. Some of the English Protestants who alluded specifically to the existence of only two sacraments were John Launder, Thomas Iveson, John Denley, George Tankerfield and Robert Smith, among a great many others. See *A&M* [1576], 1619, 1621, 1623, 1627.

way in which the Protestant circle had taken communion. Isabel de Estrada, a woman from Pedrosa of farmer stock, described one such service. Several of Pedro de Cazalla's relatives and some of Pedrosa's inhabitants gathered together after lunch in Cazalla's home there, and Domingo de Rojas had a table set up with bread and wine. After he had preached some passages from the Lord's Supper he told them that he would give them communion as Christ had to His disciples, for which they all knelt.

> And then Friar Domingo took the bread, blessed it, and broke a piece which he blessed. From that bread, he took a little and gave it to each of them, saying 'this is my body, receive it truly'. And then he took a cup with wine in it and, blessing it, he gave each of them a sip, saying, 'this is my blood, receive it truly', and thus they all received it. He then said [...] 'this is my body and my blood, take it as a memorial of me'.[104]

Therefore, there was no altar, no consecration, no adoration, no representation of the sacrificial nature of the Mass, the service was conducted in Spanish and those present received communion in both kinds with no previous fasting; indeed, after lunch. In his own confession, Rojas explained that he believed Christ to be neither 'truly nor sacramentally' in the host as the consecration used by the Roman Church was not such and, therefore, the host was nothing but bread, and adoring it was idolatry.[105] Furthermore, he acknowledged

---

104 AHN, Inquisición, leg. 1864, no. 2, fols 30^{v}–31^{r}: '[...] sentose frai domingo a la caueza de la mesa [en] vna sylla y todos los demás alrreedor [en] vnas arcas y en lo que avía y comenzó luego a predicar el d[ic]ho fray domingo el Euangelio del Jueues de la çena y después de predicado les dixo a todos q[ue] les quería comulgar como [Crist]o a sus Disçípulos e que se llegasen a la mesa. E yncados todos de rodillas al rrededor de la mesa y los hombres syn caperuzas no se acuerda su les dixo que dixesen la confesión general más q[ue] vio que estauan con deuoçión y llorauan todos [...]. Entonçes tomó el pan el d[ic]ho fray domyngo e vendíxolo y partió vn pedazo de aquel pan lo qual vendixo y de aquel pan tomaua vn poquito y daua a cada vno y dezía éste es mi cuerpo verdaderamente reçiuildo y luego tomó vn vasso y vino [ené]l y tomole e vendíxolo y dio a cada vno vn trago diciendo ésta es my sangre verdaderam[en]te reciuildo y así lo reçiuyeron todos y luego les dixo tornó a d[ecir] que quando les daua el pan y el vino éste es mi cuerpo y mi sangre reçiuildo y así: lo resçiuieron Todos y luego éste es mi cuerpo y mi sangre reçiuildo [en] mi memoria'.

105 AHN, Consejo de Inquisición, leg. 5353, no. 16, fols 4^{r-v}: '[...] auía tenido y creído y así lo abía ensenado y dogmatizado a otras p[er]sonas que [ene]l santísimo sacramento del Altar e ostia consagrada no estaba ny asistía verdadera ny sacramental mente Jesu[crist]o nuestro dios y Redemptor e q[ue] la ostia consagrada no hera sino pan ny se abía de adorar porq[ue] hera ydolatrar e que los clérigos nj saçerdotes no consagrauan avnque dixesen las palabras de la consagración de que la ygl[es]ia rromana vsa y q[ue] hera gran maldad decir misa e alçar la ostia porq[ue] hazían idolatrar a los [crist]ianos e q[ue] la mayor ofensa q[ue] se hazía a Dios hera dezir mysa ^{v} yten dixo quel d[ic]ho frai

having administered communion in both kinds as he had read in Calvin.[106] This was in line, not only with some of Cranmer's and other English and Continental reformers' teachings on communion, but also with the doctrine upheld by many of the English victims.[107]

In their rejection of the Church of Rome and the papacy, English and Spanish heretics also held very similar positions. Rojas himself confessed to teaching that 'Lutherans held the true Church', affirming that neither the Roman Church nor the pope, councils or priests had any 'power or authority to bind any Christians to their precepts'. The ministers of the Catholic Church 'made war' against the Gospel and the truth, contradicting both for their own purposes with 'a thousand superstitions, misdeeds and superfluous ceremonies'. In conclusion, he asserted, the 'visible Church' was nothing but 'mockery and lies' and the pope was the Antichrist for persecuting the Protestants.[108] In

---

domingo de rrojas avía d[ic]ho y creído que no hera pecado dezir misa después de auer comido y Rez[i]bir el santísimo sacramento y hera ansí que con este herror el d[ic]ho frai domingo muchas e Diuersas vezes antes antes [sic] que dixese misa abía comido y bebido y después se hiba a celebrar y dezir misa e que ansimjsmo abía aconsejado e ynduzido a otras p[er]sonas que comiesen y bebiesen antes dela comunión diziéndoles que no hera pecado y después de aber comido les admjnistraba el santísimo sacramento y con este herror diciendo misa vna vez abía dexado de alçar la ostia y el cáliz porque no le adorasen [...]'.

106 AHN, Inquisición, leg. 5353, no. 16, fol. 3r: '[...] confesó otros herrores entre los quales dixo que en comemoraçión de la çena del señor avía dado pan e vino consangrándolo primero a çiertas p[er]sonas y ellos lo avían tomado e rreçebido con aquella yntençión que él les dezía e q[ue] algunas de las d[ic]has p[er]sonas le dixeron que avía de comulgar devaxo de ambas especies de pan e vino e que así lo abía leído en calbino y abía concedido con ellos y así comfesaua que meresçía mayor castigo por conçeder con todos [...]'.

107 Euan Cameron, *The European Reformation* (Oxford: Oxford University Press, 1991), 161–66; MacCulloch, *Thomas Cranmer*, 379–80, 403–9. Some of the English Protestants who specifically referred to communion in both kinds were John Philpot, Bartlet Green and Steven Gratwick. See *A&M* [1576], 1734, 1739, 1772, 1895.

108 AHN, Inquisición, 5353, 16, fols 4v–5r: '[...] q[ue] los Luteranos tenían la verdadera Ygl[es]ia diziendo e afirmando quel papa nj la ygl[es]ia católica rromana nj sacros conçilios ni ningún sacerdote de la ygl[es]ia no tenýan poder ny autoridad de obligar a ningún [crist]iano con sus preçebtos ny mandamientos e que la iglesia ny el papa no podían ynponer ayunos nj prohiuir manjares nj mandar q[ue] se guarden fiestas ny vigilias nj q[ue] se prohíba la carne en quaresma ny viernes ny otros días ny los [crist]ianos heran obligados a guardar estos preçebtos ny pecaba en q[ue]brantarlos [...] e que el sumo pontífize nj la ygl[es]ia católica no tenían poder ni autoridad de conçeder bulas ny yndulgençias nj perdones ni Jubileos e q[ue] todo hera burla e mentira e quell papa e los cardenales y ob[is]pos e todos los sacerdotes e ministros de la ygl[es]ia católica heran los que más guerra y contradiçión hazían al hebangelio e a la verdad porque avían cargado la iglesia de myll superstiçiones e maldades e çerimonjas superfluas por sus intereses particulares e que la iglesia bisible de los [crist]ianos que no hera ygl[es]ia sino burla e mentira. llamando al papa ante [Crist]o porque contradecía y perseguía a los luteranos y a su maldita seta [...]'.

one of his numerous confessions, Francisco de Vivero gave a vividly detailed account of what he understood to be the true Church:

> I understand the holy and Catholic Church to be the congregation of faithful Christians who know and believe to be justified by the death and passion of Jesus Christ. [...] This is the true spouse of Jesus Christ and [...] not the Roman and visible one. One and the other [...] are clearly depicted in the holy Book of the Apocalypse, where one follows the lamb which is in front of God's throne amidst tribulations, travails, infamy, death, and persecution because she follows the dead lamb wherever it may go. The other one, visible and hideous, shows to us that Jezebel who, sat upon the great beast, inebriates the powerful on earth with the wine of fornication, causing them to follow and fear her [Revelation 2:20–23, 5:6–14, 17:1–18].[109]

The same passages from the Book of Revelation, and similar ones, were employed by the English victims to express their rejection of Rome. Bradford claimed the papists to be 'caste into Iezabels bed of securitye, which of all plages is the greuousest plage that can be'.[110] Margaret Mearing said that the Mass was 'the plaine cup of fornication, and the whore of Babilon', rejecting the pope as Antichrist and the religion held in his Church with him.[111] Alice Driver, who in Foxe's words defied 'the Pope with all his papisticall trashe', was very much expressing the same political implications in Vivero's tirade on Jezebel's hold on the powerful when she likened Queen Mary to Jezebel, a comment for which Sir Clement Highman, the chief judge, ordered Driver's ears to be cut off.[112]

---

109 AHN, Inquisición, leg. 5353, no. 9, fol. 146v: '[...] digo y declaro que por la igl[es]ia sancta y chathólica entiendo la congregaçión delos fieles christianos. que conocen y creen [ser] justificados / por la muerte y pasió[n] de Jesú christo n[uest]ro señor y le son fieles y ésta es la esposa de Jesú chr[ist]o y ésta creo. y no la Romana y visible. la vna y la otra si dios nos abriese los ojos tenemos claram[en]te pintadas en el libro sancto del Apocalipse por q[ue] la vna sigue al cordero q[ue] estádelante del trono de dios con tribulaçiones y trabajos con infamja y muerte y persecución, por q[ue] sigue al cordero muerto do qujera que fuese y la otra visible y espantosa nos muestra aq[ue]lla Jezabel. que está sentada sobre aq[ue]lla bestia grande. q[ue] con el vino de su fornjcaçión embriaga a todos los poderosos de la tierra y los haze q[ue] la sigan y la tema[n]'.

110 *A&M* [1576], 1574.

111 *A&M* [1576], 1950.

112 *A&M* [1576], 1968. Vivero was mixing up the Book of Revelation's Jezebel with the whore of Babylon, and Driver may have referred to Queen Jezebel instead [1 Kings 16:31], but the point being made still followed the same, seditious, argument.

If we have plenty of examples in Foxe's account of English Protestants embracing – and even seeking – their death as martyrs, the documentary *lacunae* in the Spanish archives may have prevented us from learning more about how the Valladolid Protestants felt about facing death at the stake. In the end, all the condemned save Carlos de Seso, Domingo de Rojas, Antonio Herrezuelo, a lawyer from Toro, and Juan Sánchez, Pedro de Cazalla's proselytising servant, reconciled to Catholicism *in extremis* to avoid being burned alive and were instead garrotted before their bodies were cast into the fire. However, the *fiscal* (prosecutor), basing his accusation on the deposition of witnesses, claimed that the nun Marina de Guevara had participated in secret gatherings in her convent with other nuns and lay women – among which was Isabel de Estrada – as well as Juan Sánchez, in which they 'praised the damned and condemned heresiarch Luther', desiring 'to be burned in the defence and belief of this sect'.[113] There is evidence that these conversations did happen.[114] Francisco de Vivero signed and retracted several recantations during his imprisonment. On one occasion he asked the inquisitors 'to cut off the tongue with which he had confessed and the hand with which he wrote and signed his confession', for it was all dissimulation and he wished to be burned, for he 'repents of having repented his errors', an episode reminiscent of Cranmer's decision to burn the hand which had signed his recantation before being consumed by the fire in 1556.[115] In his final confession Vivero confirmed himself in this position, stating: 'I say that it is true that I have wished to die for the faith

113 AHN, Inquisición, leg. 5353, no. 8, fol. 46^{r}: 'item digo q[ue] demás de lo susodicho la dicha doña marjna de guebara se a hallado en muchas juntas e ajuntamjentos particulares en los quales juntamente con otras p[er]sonas nombrando e alabando al maldito y conde[m]nado heresiarcha lutero aprobando su doctrjna y seta e diziendo q[ue] deseauan ser quemadas por la defensa y creencia desta maldita seta'. Among those people were Juan Sánchez, former servant to Pedro de Cazalla, now serving one Catalina de Ortega, who was also there; Isabel de Estrada and the nuns Catalina de Reinoso, Margarita de Santisteban, Francisca de Zúñiga, Felipa de Heredia, Catalina de Alcaraz and María de Miranda. Of this group, only Zúñiga, Heredia and Alcaraz were reconciled and released as *penitenciadas* from the *auto de fe* on 8 October 1559; the rest all met the flames.

114 AHN, Inquisición, leg. 5353, no. 8, fols 4^{v}, 32^{r}.

115 AHN, Inquisición, leg. 5353, no. 9, fol. 137^{r}: '[...] e como fue pres[en]te le fue d[ic]ho que qué ha pensado más [ene]ste su negocio Dijo después de averle hablado y amonestado muchas vezes dijo q[ue] le saquen la lengua con q[ue] confesó su prim[er]a e segunda confisión e la mano con que escribió e firmó su confisión e luego le quemen por que todo lo dijo con cautela / e fingido / e se a[rr]epiente de av[er]se a[rr]epentido de sus herrores/'. For Cranmer see *A&M* [1576], 1808 and MacCulloch, *Thomas Cranmer*, 598–605.

of Jesus Christ and for his truth and love and thus I now confess that I will die and embrace this martyrdom as an act of gratitude'.[116]

The authorities were steadfast in their persecution of these heresies. Just as the English government was vigorous and resolute in its discovery and crushing of conventicles and secret congregations, the Spanish authorities were also concerned about these private reunions, charged with what they perceived to be strong subversive connotations.[117] In these reunions, conversations took place in which religion was discussed from an unorthodox perspective and illicit books were distributed and read. In 1555 Philip and Mary issued a proclamation against Protestant books by Luther, Oecolampadius, Zwingli, Calvin, Bernardino Ochino, Bucer, Cranmer and several other English and Continental reformers and the privy council actively sought to apprehend those who smuggled forbidden books into England.[118] The Spanish Inquisition discovered that the Spanish heretics were reading works by Calvin, Wolfgang Musculus, Brenz, Luther, Ochino, Juan de Valdés and Constantino, some of which had been smuggled by Carlos de Seso.[119] The potential for dissent in secret conventicles

116 AHN, Inquisición, leg. 5353, no. 9, fol. 148r: 'Al 42 Digo que es verdad q[ue] he deseado morir por la fe de Jesuchristo y por su verdad y amor y que ansí confieso agora morir y abraçar este martirio con hazimj[ent]o de graçias /'.

117 Many of those prosecuted by Philip and Mary's regime had been either travelling ministers, heavily involved in secret congregations or were accused of spreading false doctrines seditiously. Such is the case of Julins Palmer, John Rough, William Mount, his wife Alice, and stepdaughter Rose Allin, among many others. See *A&M* [1576], 1857, 1924, 1948; AHN, Inquisición, leg. 1864, no. 2, fol. 30v, 92v; AHN, Inquisición, leg. 5353, no. 8, fols 16v, 46r; AHN, Inquisición, leg. 5353, no. 9, fols 131r–132v.

118 Philip and Mary, king and queen of England, *Proclamation by the Kinge and the Quene* (London: John Cawood, 1555). Other forbidden authors and works were Johannes Bugenhagen, Doctor Pomeranus; Jan Łaski, Heinrich Bullinger, Philipp Melanchthon, Erasmus Sarcerius, Peter Martyr Vermigli, Hugh Latimer, Robert Barnes, John Bale, Justus Jonas, John Hooper, Miles Coverdale, William Tyndale, William Turner, Thomas Becon, John Frith, William Roy, *Hall's Chronicle*, and any of the former published in Latin, Dutch, English, Italian or French. See APC, vol. 6, 124, 346. Another royal commission of February 1556 issued in the name of Philip and Mary to halt secret reunions in *A&M* [1576], 1888–9 and the full text in *A&M* [1563], 1642–4.

119 AHN, Inquisición, leg. 1864, no. 2, fol. 116r: '[…] este [co]n[fesan]te [Pedro de Cazalla] los vio todos e delos que se acuerda son los siguj[en]tes / La instituçión de calbino [en] latín musculo sobre s[an]t matheo y s[an]t Joan en latín brençio sobre s[an]t Joan e s[an]t lucas [en] latín / calbino sobre muchas epístolas de s[an]t pablo luthero sobre el canticum gradum [en] latín postila de el mismo / sobre todos los ebangeljos de fiestas e domingos del año quatro o çinco libros pequeños de el capuchino [Bernardino Ochino] […] y que todo era de sermones e co[n]sideraciones de valdés [en] toscano / e otros muchos libros [en] toscano que no se acuerda de ellos e otros papeles escriptos de mano que no se acuerda dellos […]'. AHN, Inquisición, leg. 5353, no. 8, fol. 4v: '[From Margarita de Santisteban's deposition] y esto entendía y con esto me holgaba y desto [the doctrine of

in which forbidden books were read was anxiously acknowledged by both English and Spanish authorities. One of the most serious accusations against Marina de Guevara and the nuns of Belén was that they had read from heretical books to each other. Especially damning was the knowledge that Francisca de Zúñiga had taken to the task of translating into Spanish 'a very good book about the epistles of St Paul', which may have been by Calvin, and these translations had begun to be read 'publicly'. The nuns had also sent the book to be translated by someone else outside the convent.[120] What this example clarifies is that this was no isolated event, but the creation of a movement of religious dissent based on Protestant propositions which was beginning to expand. As it increased in numbers and intensity – both in Valladolid and in Seville – the authorities began to feel more nervous about the potential these groupings had to infect the disease of heresy, threatening to bring illness, decay and, ultimately, destruction to the body politic and the mystical body of Christ. The persecutions in England and Spain in the 1550s were not mere indiscriminate assaults, but instead responded to an acute awareness of the heresies and

justification] trataba con las señoras doña marina de guebara e otras monjas que nonbro. y estas pláticas tenjamos muchas vezes y p[ar]a hablar en ellas y en cosas semejantes y p[ar]a leer en constantino y en los Evangelios nos juntábamos muchas vezes […]', and f. 35r: [From Marina de Guevara's confession] 'muchas veçes nos ju[n]távamos y las q[ue] an venydo a my cella comygo a tratar de cosas de dyos y del alma y anymá[n]donos vnas a otras y dyçyendo de n[uest]ros aprovechamientos y otras veçes leyendo la dotryna crystyana de constantyno y como otras demás monjas les pareçýa novedad esta manera de tratar y conv[er]sar quando estábamos ju[n]tas y pasava algunas dellas callávamos por q[ue] no nos q[ue]rýamos vender por santas […]'.

120 AHN, Inquisición, leg. 5353, no. 8, fol. 34r: '[From Marina de Guevara's confession] Yten este mismo [Juan Sánchez] vn día tratando de cosas de dios dixo q[ue] tenía vn muy buen libro q[ue] trataua delas epístolas de sanct pablo y díxele yo y otras delas susodichas q[ue] nos le diese y él me le dio vn día desta quaresma pasada y yo le di a doña margarita [de Santisteban] y aquella noche me leyó la dicha doña margarita algunos capítulos dél estando yo en mj çella en vn estrado y me pareçió muy bien todo lo q[ue] dél se leyó y después la dicha doña margarita lleuó el dicho libro y no le vj más hasta el día q[ue] se traxo q[ue] lo tomó n[uest]ro reformador para lleuar lo a v[uestra] m[erced] he oýdo decir q[ue] se leyero[n] algunos capítulos dél pública mente y se començó a trasladar en la çelda de doña fran[cis]ca de çúñiga – esto porque no lo vi lo Remito a quien lo vja q[ue] sé que lo djrán /' and fol. 32r: '[From Catalina de Reinoso's deposition] vn día díxonos Ju[an] Sánchez que tenía vn libro muy bueno q[ue] le auía hecho vn muy gran cristiano y Rogámosle mucho que nos le diese y él nos le dio con grande ymportunaçión q[ue] le deboluiésemos muy presto y quixímosle trasladar y porq[ue] le hiziese presto diole maría de myranda a fran[cis]co de coca porq[ue] le trasladase más presto porq[ue] le daua mucha prisa por el d[ic]ho Ju[an] Sánchez y en casa quedaron sacados dos o tres capítulos q[ue] sacaron entre doña f[rancis]ca mi her[ma]na e doña cat[alin]a de alcaraz yo leý [ene]l libro dos o tres capítulos y bi leher [ene]l vna noche sola a Doña margarita De Santisteban y estauan presentes quando leýa Doña marina de gueuara yo no me acuerdo si abía más […]'.

attitudes that subjects of Philip and Mary were disseminating, and which were perceived to be extremely dangerous by their joint regime. The Protestants that were prosecuted in these years were seen as criminals, and of the worst sort, for they attacked, at the same time, God and the prince. This double act of rebellion was dealt with swiftly and sternly in both kingdoms with the impulse and assent of both monarchs.

Indeed, it has already been established that, in England, Mary, Pole and the privy council were instrumental in the ferocity of the persecution and that the latter was not the unplanned and random result of the murderous inclinations of English Catholic clerics, as Foxe and other Protestant apologists had claimed – even if horrendous excesses did occur – but instead the result of a methodical approach to a well-known and tested recipe against religious dissent and rebellion[121] The question of Philip's position has been more elusive until now, but there is evidence that he wholeheartedly supported both campaigns against heresy. Whatever the nature and intentions of Castro's sermon of 10 February 1555 and despite Renard's protestations about malaise at the burnings, the truth is that King Philip wrote a letter to his sister Juana soon after the re-enactment of the heresy laws in 1555 in unequivocal terms.

> I and [...] the queen have, with the intercession of [...] parliament, made a law in which it is declared the way that heretics [...] are to be punished, renewing the old laws that existed in this kingdom to that effect, which are very purposeful, [...] and adding forces for the punishment and execution of everything.[122]

The king's attitude remained the same three years later, when Protestant groups were discovered in Valladolid and Seville. On 6 September 1558, the king wrote a letter to Fernando Valdés expressing his sadness at the taking root of heresy in the Spanish kingdoms which had so far shown 'such cleanliness'. Philip clearly felt that, in the service of God, Valdés had to 'proceed against the accused with all rigour, because you can see how important this is at the

---

121 Alexander, 'Bonner and the Persecution', 157–75; Duffy, *Fires of Faith*, 93–4, 186–7.

122 Printed in Pedro de Ribadeneyra, SJ, *Hystoria ecclesiástica del scisma del Reyno de Inglaterra. En la qual se tratan las cosas más notables que han sucedido en aquel Reyno tocantes a nuestra sancta Religión, desde que començó hasta la muerte de la Reyna de Escocia* (Lisbon: Antonio Alvares, 1588), fols 144^{r-v}; King Philip to Princess Juana, 15 January 1555: 'Después yo y la Sereníssima Reyna, con intercessión del dicho Parlamento, auemos hecho ley, en que se declara la orden que han de tener en el castigo de los hereges, y de los que contrauiniessen a lo que la Sa[n]ta Madre Yglesia manda: renouando las leyes, que antiguamente auía sobre ello en este Reyno, que son muy a propósito, y mandando de nueuo que aquellas se obseruen, añadiendo fuerças para el castigo y execución de todo'.

beginning, and it is just and necessary to do so to curtail such a great evil'.[123] It is hard to imagine that this would have been his conclusion if he felt that the campaign against heresy in England which he had contributed to bring forward in the parliament of 1555 was being unsuccessful in the last months of Mary's life. On the contrary, it seems to have convinced him that the most expedient route against religious dissent was the stamping out of the same. This was, in any case, the solution proposed by the English and Spanish authors who dealt with the topic when recalcitrant heretics could not be brought to conformity.

6.4 Conclusion

The first *auto de fe* in Valladolid took place on 22 May 1559, presided over by Princess Juana and Prince Carlos, as Philip was still in Flanders. In it, fourteen men and women were 'relaxed to the secular arm', including Dr Agustín Cazalla and his siblings Beatriz and Francisco de Vivero, the latter of whom, despite his earlier protestations to embrace martyrdom, showed some repentance on the day and was garrotted before his corpse was cast into the flames. Only the lawyer Antonio Herrezuelo was burned alive and with all of them the remains of Leonor de Vivero, the mother of the Cazalla-Vivero siblings, who had died before the process concluded.[124] This *auto* was followed on 24 September by the first of the *autos* in Seville, in which twenty-two Protestants perished, and by another one in Valladolid on 8 October in which Philip presided, and swore an oath before Valdés to favour the Holy Office and to 'force' his subjects to 'obey and keep' all ecclesiastical constitutions in defence of the 'holy Catholic faith against the heretics and those who would believe, receive or favour them'.[125] In this *auto* twelve *luteranos* were executed, including Carlos de Seso, Domingo de Rojas, Pedro de Cazalla and Marina de Guevara. Seso

123 José Luis González Novalín, ed., *El inquisidor general Fernando de Valdés. Cartas y documentos*, vol. 2 (Oviedo: Universidad de Oviedo, 1971), 210; King Philip to Fernando Valdés, 6 September 1558: '[…] mi hermana, me había avisado de lo que escrebís, así vos particularmente como los del consejo; y he sentido, cuanto se puede encarecer, que haya subcedido en esos reinos, en quien ha habido tanta limpieza, cosa desta calidad y que hayan caído en ella tales personas y estoviese tan cundido como decís. Y, bendito nuestro Señor, que se descubrió y divulgó en tiempo que se pudiese atajar y remediar. […] os encargo cuanto puedo que […] proveáis todo lo que conviniere para la breve expedición, procediendo contra los culpados con todo rigor, porque ya véis lo que importa al principio, y es muy justo y necesario hacerlo por excusar tan gran mal […]'.

124 Menéndez Pelayo, *Heterodoxos españoles*, vol. 1, 950–60; González Novalín, *El inquisidor general*, vol. 2, 239–48.

125 Menéndez Pelayo, *Heterodoxos españoles*, vol. 1, 963–4.

and Rojas were burned alive and the rest were garrotted first.[126] There were three more *autos* in Seville dealing with those processed in the late 1550s on 22 December 1560, 26 April 1562 and 28 October 1562, with 33 more people put to death, including three Englishmen.[127] In all, eighty-one men and women were burnt in the years 1559–1562 accused of Protestant affiliations. Philip's staunch support of this fierce campaign clearly suggests that he considered the English persecution to have been successful. It certainly was in Spain, where the apprehension and condemnation of Protestant heretics was marginal after 1562 and often involved foreigners.[128] Some of those involved seemed to have believed as much. Dr John Story, chancellor of the dioceses of London and Oxford, a very eager examiner of heresy and one of Foxe's 'bloody butchers', wrote to the earl of Devon in June 1555 that in London the situation was appeasing and God's cause increasing 'partly for love and partly for fear'. Even if some of the heretics had been stout in their executions, 'and seemed to glory in their malignity', 'the sharpness of the sword, and other corrections', were now starting to turn their 'stony hearts'. He was hopeful that severity would be beneficial to 'universal unity in religion' and concluded that heretics, 'shall shortly so be weeded, that these choke not the corn [...]'.[129] If we are to believe Juan de Villagarcía's impressions in his 'Diálogo', the English campaign against heresy had been very successful:

> When I left England, for every heretic that could be counted, one would find ten Catholics; and in Spain, by God's mercy, I do not think one true heretic can be found. This is because when this weed first appears, it is immediately rooted out, as lately has been done here [in Valladolid].[130]

His comments are all the more insightful given that Villagarcía himself was in the prisons of the Inquisition accused of heresy when he wrote those lines. This confirms that, to understand how these English and Spanish inquisitions

126 Menéndez Pelayo, *Heterodoxos españoles*, vol. 1, 964–5.

127 Tomás López Muñoz, ed., *La Reforma en la Sevilla del XVI. Corpus documental* (Seville: CIMPE/Eduforma, 2011), 209–30, 257–63, 270–8. The three Englishmen executed were William Brook, a sailor from Shoreham-by-Sea (212), Nicholas *Bertoum*, from Newcastle upon Tyne (212), and Robert *Cleofot* (perhaps Clifford), a naval carpenter from *Folsam* (perhaps Folkestone) (271).

128 Alonso Burgos, *Luteranismo en Castilla*, 119–21; García Cárcel and Moreno Martínez, *Inquisición*, 273–5.

129 CSP Venice, vol. 6, 111.

130 Villagarcía, 'Diálogo llamado cadena de oro', fol. 74^{r}: 'En Ynglat[e]rra quando de allá salí, por buena cuenta se hallauan por vn herege diez cathólicos y en España por la misericordia de dios creo no ay vn Herege fino: Porque en asomando esta malayerba, luego la arrancan de Raíz: como los días pasados aquí se hizo'.

worked, it is more useful to approach the subject from a qualitative rather than a quantitative point of view. The fact that there were 284 victims in England and 81 in Spain does not necessarily suggest an extraordinary cruelty on the part of the persecutors, particularly when compared to other judiciary institutions. Rather, it suggests that the system that they had put in place to detect and eradicate heretical and, therefore, seditious elements within the commonwealth worked well. The key did not lie in the precise nuances of the accused's theological stances – in ascertaining whether they were more or less Lutheran, Calvinist, *iluminado* or Edwardian – but in how dangerous their positions concerning justification, the Eucharist or papal primacy, and exterior acts such as secret conventicles and the reading of forbidden books, were to the crown and to the unity of Catholicism. The people apprehended, condemned, and executed were uttering words and acting in ways which were expressly branded as heretical and, therefore, traitorous, by both English and Spanish religious authorities. As the development of events in Spain after 1558 suggests, the persecution in England helped shape events in Spain after Philip's return, and there is evidence that Spanish expertise in the eradication of religious dissent had been felt in England too.

There was an ideology founded upon scriptural interpretations and rooted in a solid legal framework that understood heretics as the worst enemies of Church and State. The English and Spanish authors we have examined were certainly in agreement about the causes, implications and solutions which existed to fight what was, for them, an infection that threatened the whole fabric upon which the mystical body of Christ and the body politic of the prince rested. Burning recalcitrant heretics was an effective instrument of repression even for those monarchs less inclined to persecute religious deviation by this means, as attested by Joan Bocher and George van Parris under Edward VI and by the six radical Protestants burned by Elizabeth I between 1575 and 1589.[131] Elizabeth, in fact, eventually solved the problem of her own Catholic heretics, who threatened to destroy her conception of the body politic and of the body of Christ, by cleverly extricating the heretical nomenclature from the equation and prosecuting them solely as traitors and rebels instead.[132] This shift did

131 On Bocher and Van Parris see MacCulloch, *Thomas Cranmer*, 474–8. On those burned under Elizabeth see Daniel Neal, *The History of the Puritans, or Protestant Nonconformists; from the Reformation in 1517 to the Revolution in 1688*, vol. 2 (New York: Harper & Brothers, 1855), 360–1; Matthew Reynolds, *Godly Reformers and their Opponents in Early Modern England: Religion in Norwich, c.1560–1643* (Woodbridge: The Boydell Press, 2005), 86–7.

132 Elizabeth repealed the heresy laws revived by Philip and Mary in 1555, but new laws were approved in parliament which sought to persecute – with varying degrees of intensity – those who defied the Elizabethan settlement, who were to be treated as traitors and rebels only, rather than heretics. For these laws see *Tudor Constitution*, 73–7, 422–4, 424–7,

not subtract anything from the condition of Catholics as religious dissenters within the Elizabethan settlement, but it still ensured that they would be prosecuted, fined and, if deemed necessary, killed by her authorities in manners no less cruel and horrific than dying at the stake.

Furthermore, in the context of Philip and Mary's reign, the association of heresy with rebellion was incompatible with the aspiration to *monarchia universalis* based on universal Catholicism which was the cornerstone of Philip's political project. One could not be a subject of the Catholic Monarch and a heretic at the same time. As Philip famously put it in 1566 in a letter to his ambassador in Rome, Pope Pius V (r. 1566–72) could rest assured that there would be no 'fissure' in his defence of the Catholic religion. The king would rather 'lose all my estates and a hundred lives if I had them, for I do not intend nor want to be a lord to heretics'.[133] Rebellion under the pretence of religion, as the Marian and Philippine regimes viewed heresy, was extremely dangerous to the Spanish Monarchy, as events in the Low Countries and in the Alpujarras were to prove.[134] Those who supported heresy, if not conformable, had to be 'rooted out'. Only politically unstable or isolated governments like those of Catherine de Medici in France under the minorities of her sons, of Mary of Guise and Mary Stuart in Scotland or of Elizabeth in her early years as queen, tried to compromise with religious divisions, but this was done more out of necessity than genuine conviction. In the context of the sixteenth century, religious persecutions cannot be understood merely as the result of oppression and tyranny. However much we may sympathise with the victims from a twenty-first century perspective, for most contemporaries, heretics were rebels against God and prince and, as such, they had to choose between conversion and death. From a historical point of view, therefore, it makes sense to consider these cases as episodes of prosecution for offences which were grounded in a theological framework and enshrined in law. In this respect, the 284 victims of Philip and Mary's heresy campaign in England are no different

427–32. For the polemics that ensued between Catholics and Protestants on whether the reasons why the government persecuted English Catholics were religious or political see Peter Lake, *Bad Queen Bess? Libels, Secret Histories, and the Politics of Publicity in the Reign of Queen Elizabeth I* (Oxford: Oxford University Press, 2016).

133 Quintín Aldea Navarro, 'Felipe II. Política y religión', in Felipe Ruiz Martín, ed., *La Monarquía de Felipe II* (Madrid: Real Academia de la Historia, 2003), 69–110 in 80–1; Doris Moreno Martínez, *La invención de la Inquisición* (Madrid: Fundación Carolina. Centro de Estudios Hispánicos e Iberoamericanos, 2004), 296: '[…] Antes que sufrir la menor quiebra del mundo en lo de la religión y del servicio de Dios, perderé todos mis estados y cien vidas que tuviese, por que yo ni pienso ni quiero ser señor de herejes […]'.

134 Martin van Gelderen, *The Political Thought of the Dutch Revolt* (Cambridge: Cambridge University Press, 1992), 62–109; Geoffrey Parker, *Imprudent King: A New Life of Philip II* (New Haven and London: Yale University Press, 2014), 201–3.

from the 216 executed by Henry VIII after the Pilgrimage of Grace, the more than 4,000 killed by Edward VI's government during the Prayer Book rebellion or the 450 to 600 put to death by Elizabeth I in 1570 in the aftermath of the Northern rebellion.[135]

With the successful uprooting of heresy in both England and Spain, most Protestant leaders and theologians either dead or in exile and, – had Mary survived – a tight control of the Low Countries through England, the entrance of Protestant evangelising missions akin to those of the Jesuits and other Catholics after the 1570s would have been extremely difficult. It is entirely plausible that, if not completely eradicated, Protestantism may have become a negligible minority destined to disappear, as Villagarcía thought. For all their brutality, the Anglo-Spanish inquisitions, sharing a common ideology and a common enemy, were powerful and effective tools at the service of both Church and State.

135 Madeleine Hope Dodds and Ruth Dodds, *The Pilgrimage of Grace, 1536–1537 and the Exeter Conspiracy, 1538*, vol. 2 (Cambridge: Cambridge University Press, 1915), 226; Anthony Fletcher and Diarmaid MacCulloch, *Tudor Rebellions* [1968] (Abingdon and New York: Routledge, 2016), 59–60, 107–8; K. J. Kesserling, *The Northern Rebellion of 1569: Faith, Politics, and Protest in Elizabethan England* (Basingstoke and New York: Palgrave Macmillan, 2007), 119–43.

Conclusion: Bound to Each Other

Between five and six in the morning of 17 November 1558, during Mass and after having experienced pleasant visions of choirs of angelic children who invited her to follow them, Mary I, queen of England, Ireland, and Spain departed this world at the age of forty-two. The news was momentarily concealed from Reginald Pole, who lay ill in his bed himself, to protect him from such a devastating blow in his delicate state. It was to no avail, and the cardinal died at seven in the evening of the same day.[1] From that day onwards, the dispatches that the count of Feria sent to Philip were of an increasingly sombre tenor. Feria now wrote not as the representative of the absentee king of England, but as the ambassador of the foreign king of Spain. Thenceforth, most accounts of Philip and Mary's reign presented it as a tale of failure and regret – it became the history of two monarchs intent on bringing back a world which had long ceased to exist. This was not, of course, the prevailing view at the time. The eventual success of the long and tortuous process of the Elizabethan Reformation was by no means a foregone conclusion.

On 14 December 1558, at Mary's exequies in Westminster Abbey, John White, bishop of Winchester, gave an oration in which he unfeignedly extolled the deceased queen's virtues. Quoting from Ecclesiastes 9:4, 'better a live dog than a dead lion', White advocated for things to remain as they were, although the new queen understood it as a personal slight – which it may well have been – and placed him under arrest after the ceremony concluded. To White, the departed queen, Mary, had more fear of God than 'the poorest creature' in London:

> She had the love, commendation, and admiration of al [sic] the world [...]. She used singular mercy toward offenders. She used much pity and compassion towards the poor and oppressed [...]. She restored to the church such ornaments as in the time of schism were taken away and spoiled. She found the realm poisoned with heresy, and purged it; and remembering herself to be a member of Christ's Church, refused to write herself *head* thereof.[2]

1 John Edwards, *Mary I: England's Catholic Queen* (New Haven and London: Yale University Press, 2011), 332; Thomas F. Mayer, *Reginald Pole: Prince & Prophet* (Cambridge: Cambridge University Press, 2000), 344.

2 John Strype, *Ecclesiastical Memorials, Relating Chiefly to Religion, and the Reformation of It, and the Emergencies of the Church of England, under King Henry VIII, King Edward VI and*

 | DOI:10.1163/9789004536210_009

White's was not a lonely voice. The Burgundian Augustinian François Richardot, titular bishop of Nicopolis and one of Philip's preachers in Flanders, delivered the funeral oration for Mary before the duke of Savoy and the king's court at Brussels on 2 January 1559.[3] Of the three perfect states of human beings – civil, Christian, and heavenly – Mary had attained the first two through her prudence, strength, and continence, and Richardot was quite certain that this had led to her obtaining the third state too. Mary's Christian faith had been, contrary to that of most who called themselves Christians, a 'lively, fruitful, and obliging' one. This faith had been, Richardot continued,

> not only whole, without it being embellished or corrupted by the false paradoxes of the heretics; not only ardent in charity and replenished with good works; not only stable and unflinching, as it had God's true Word as safe support and firm foundation, but also – and what is more – [her faith had been] great, admirable, and heroic.

With King David as her example, Mary had demolished the 'forts of the infidels', restoring 'the honour of God and His Church' in England, re-introducing 'Christian doctrine and discipline' against the devices of the 'seditious'. Her actions had been driven by the 'virtue of her faith' like those of Joshua, Gideon, Barak, Samson, Daniel, and many other biblical characters.[4]

Queen Mary I, with Large Appendixes, Containing Original Papers, Records, &c, vol. 3 [1721] (Oxford: Clarendon Press, 1822), 546. For White's entire sermon see 536–50.

3 Philip was not present because he had been mourning in the monastery of Grunendal since he received the news of his father's death in October 1558. This spiritual retreat was a practice that Philip would repeat in later years on the deaths of spouses and children. On this occasion, apart from a period of mourning for his father, he also mourned for his aunt Mary of Hungary, who died on 18 October, and his wife Mary of England, who died on 17 November. The king stayed in Grunendal, conducting business from the monastery, until April 1559.

4 François Richardot, OSA., *Le sermon fvnebre, fait devant le Roy, par Messire Francois Richardot, Euesque de Nicople, & Suffragant d'Arras: Aus Obseques & Funerailles du Tresgrand, & Tresuictorieus Empereur Charles Cinquième. Celebrées à Bruxelles en la grande Église ditte Sainte Gudle* (...) (Antwerp: Christophe Plantin, 1559), fol. 23v: 'Ce que facilement se peut voir, si nous considerons en premier lieu, que sa foy, n'a esté, ny morte, ny sterile, ny oiseuse; comme elle est vulgairement en la plus part de ceus qui font profession du nom Chrestien: mais, viue, fructueuse, & officieuse, comme elle s'est monstrée en ceus, à qui les saintes Lettres donnent tesmoinage, que la foy leur a esté reputée à justice. Laquelle foy, en ceste vertueuse Princesse, a esté non seulement entière, sans estre farcie, ny, des faus paradoxes des heretiques: non seulement ardente de charité; & abondanté de bonnes oeuures: non seulement stable, & immobile; aiant la certaine parolle de Dieu, pour seur appuy, & ferme fondement: mais, que plus est, grande, admirable, & heroique. [...] Et pour, à l'exemple de Dauid, abattre le fort des infidèles; & restituer en ce Roiaume, l'honneur de Dieu, & de l'Église: pour dompter tant de tumultes; appaiser tant de seditions; & remettre sus, la doctrine & discipline

In the triple funerals held in Augsburg in the spring of 1559 by Emperor Ferdinand for Charles v, Mary of Hungary and Mary of England, the oration to commemorate the latter's life was pronounced by the Flemish Jesuit Nicholas de Lannoy, who presented his audience with a biography of the English Queen extolling her virtues, among which he gave special attention to the sophisticated education she had received at the hands of Thomas Linacre (*c*.1460–1524) – an education encouraged and maintained by the virtuous Catherine of Aragon, who had instilled in her daughter the 'notable piety' that she had in turn inherited from Ferdinand and Isabel.[5] For her constancy, it seemed that God had always protected the 'heir and future liberator of the kingdom of the English'. Through her faith and confidence in God, Mary had survived the reign of her brother, she had overcome the duke of Northumberland and Thomas Wyatt and had emerged victorious from all adversities.[6] Once destined to be Charles v's bride, she had instead found in him a loving father, a bond which had been strengthened by her marriage to Philip. This alliance had been divinely inspired and it had been a 'righteous' and 'most useful' event for the 'Christian republic'. Philip and Mary's 'perpetual bond' had merged 'the two kingdoms of the Spanish and the British, and their most fierce peoples, to restore the English republic from the troublesome damages which had afflicted it'. Mary's 'lamentable' death without issue of her body was God's doing and was not to be questioned, for she had been 'freed from the tribulations of the temporal kingdom and carried to the tranquillity of the eternal one'.[7]

Chrestienne. Ce qu'elle a fait, par la vertu de sa foy: comme feirent, Iosué, Gédéon, Barac, Samson, Daniel, & tant d'autres grands personnages illustres, par les saintes Escritures'.

5 Friedrich Staphylus, ed., *De exeqviis Caroli v, maximi, imperatoris, qvas Ferdinandvs avgvstissimvs imperator germano fratri suo charissimo, Augustae Vindelicorum fecit fieri. Item de exeqviis Mariae Vngariae, & Mariae Angliae reginarum, per eundem Imperatorem nostrum, aliquot diebus post celebratis* (Augsburg: Philippus Ulhardus, 1559), sigs f2^r–f4^v.

6 Staphylus, *De exeqviis*, sig. g2^v–g3^r: 'Pari etiam misericordiae priuilegio Deus castitatis, & in se confide[n]tium amator & protector, Mariam regni Anglicani haeredem ac futura[m] liberatrice[m], semper dignatus est p[ro]tegere, quemadmodum narration sequentiu[m], adhuc manifestius edocebit'.

7 Staphylus, *De exeqviis*, sigs g3^v–g4^v: 'Porrò ut vires additę viribus, statu[m] reflorescente[m] Britannici regni, firmioribus vinculis confirmarent, ac sancti conatus huius p[re]clarissimae generosissimaeq[ue] foeminae, melioribus p[ro]sperentur successibus, sapientissimè nec sine diuino fauore cogitatum est, vt Philippu[m] Hispaniar[um] principe[m] pote[n]tissimu[m], Maritum acciperet, et quae olim Carolo patri sponsa destinabatur, filius nunc haberet vxorem. Et sanè hęc foedera co[n]iugalia nulla, nisi causa honestissima, et reip[ublica] Christianae vtilissima iniri suasit, haec solum spectabant tam ipsoru[m] coniugu[m] vota, q[uam] eoru[m] confilia, qui huiusmodi copulae authores extiterant, ut scilicet coaelescentibus perpetuo foedere, duorum regnoru[m] Hispanici atq[ue] Britannici, bellicosissimis populis, redintegraret Anglicana resp[ublica] tot damnis grauissimus attrita. [...] Sed omnino

The Dutch painter and chronicler Hubert Goltzius closed his 1560 edition of his volume on the lives and portraits of the Roman emperors with a few words of grateful remembrance for King Philip's second wife. Goltzius affirmed that Queen Mary had 'ascended to heaven, having left on earth an eternal memory of herself for her doings and wonderful works'. He then launched an enthusiastic panegyric which broke the barriers of sixteenth-century gender expectations. In the Dutch painter's words, Mary had been,

> not only equal to as many brave matrons and queens as there have been, but she exceeds them all, and her feats are equal to those of the best king that the world ever had. This is so because, having been held for nothing and utterly despised during the time when her brother, King Edward, reigned, she stood up so powerful after his death, trusting only in God and in Emperor Charles's help, that only this sufficed to put the most powerful princes of her kingdom under her foot and to take their lives, for they had wickedly risen against her and the Catholic Church.[8]

In all these accounts, praise for the deceased queen of England was high, and if the failure to secure a Catholic succession was explained as a divine mystery by Lannoy, it was altogether obliterated, together with the loss of Calais and the bad harvests and illnesses which had plagued England, from all other orations and narrations dealing with Mary's life. Constant in her faith, unassailable to

ęquanimiter ferendu[m], quòd diuinae complacuit Maiestati, boniq[ue] co[n]sulendum, quod ipsa iam corporeis solute uinculis, seme[n] carnis suę non reliquerit, à Deo factum est istud, cui nemo dicere potest, Cur ita facis? Iam nostril causa quide[m] lugenda mors, Defunctae vero potius congratulandu[m], quod temporalis regni turbinibus libera, ad ęterni regni tra[n]quillitatem sit euecta'.

8 Hubert Goltzius, *Los vivos retratos de todos los Emperadores, desde Iulio César hasta el Emperador Carlos V y Don Fernando su hermano: sacados de las más antiguas monedas, no como fueron sacadas por otros, sino pintadas muy fiel y verdaderamente, y las vidas y hechos, costumbres, virtudes, y vicios, pintados con sus colores, y puestos por historia. Al poderosíssimo Príncipe Don Phelipe Cathólico Rey de España* (Antwerp: Gillis Coppens van Diest, 1560), sig. Gg2^{r}: 'Y poco después murió el Cardenal Polo en Inglaterra: y la Sereníssima y Christianíssima María Reyna de Inglaterra se subió al cielo, auiendo dexado en la tierra eterna memoria de sí por sus hechos y obras marauillosas [...] no se yguala solame[n]te con quantas matronas y Reynas vuo valerosas, pero que las excede à todas, y se ygualan sus hechos con los d'el mejor Rey que el mundo tuuo: porque siendo tenida en nada y muy menospreciada en el tiempo que reynó su hermano el Rey Eduardo, luego después de muerto, se leuantó tan poderosa, confiada en Dios solamente, y en la ayuda d'el Emperador Carlos, que bastó con esto à poner debaxo de sus pies los más poderosos Príncipes de todo su Reyno, y à todos quitó la vida, porque se auían leuantado malamente contra ella, y contra la yglesia Cathólica'.

misfortune, the queen had 'liberated' her kingdoms from the yoke of heresy and she had reinstated the Church, allying herself to the king of Spain, the most powerful monarch of her time. The men who produced these portrayals – an Englishman, a Burgundian, a Fleming, and a Dutchman – had more in common with one another than the hagiographic undertones of their pieces: they had all been the English queen's subjects and, as such, they had set out to honour the memory of their mistress in their accounts. The so-called Spanish marriage meant much more for England than a union with Spain. It placed both the English and Irish crowns in a global political entity which included all the territories under the control of King Philip, and it made of Mary the queen of peoples as far apart as the Neapolitans and the subjects of New Spain and Peru. The significance of this aspect of the marriage is revealed in a curious incident which took place during the peace negotiations at Cercamp between the English, the Spanish, and the French that would lead in 1559 to the peace of Cateau-Cambrésis. When Mary was still alive, the commissioners selected to represent English interests had been Thomas Thirlby, bishop of Ely, Nicholas Wotton, erstwhile ambassador to France, and Henry Fitzalan, earl of Arundel. During the last months of Mary's life, they had formed part of a single team with Philip's representatives – Ruy Gómez de Silva, William of Orange, the duke of Alba, the bishop of Arras and Viglius, president of the council of the Low Countries. On 1 December 1558, the English commissioners reported back home to Queen Elizabeth (unknowingly, for they did not have firm confirmation of Mary's demise) an argument they had witnessed between Philip's commissioners and those of King Henry II of France concerning the settlement of Calais.[9] When Philip's men, eager, as their master was, to secure the return of the stronghold to English hands, complained that English matters had not yet been agreed, the Frenchmen replied that this was not incumbent on them anymore, since Queen Mary had died, to which Philip's commissioners replied that they were not aware of that and did not believe it to be true. Even if it were, they continued, they were bound to the English not only because of Philip and Mary's marriage, but also because of the treaties made by Charles V and Henry VIII in 1543 and 1546.

> Why? what do you meane? quod the Frenche, ar yow the Englishemennes slaves? – 'Yea of truthe, quod the Kings Commissioners, yn this point we ar the Englishemens slaves, and they our maisters. And so, in the like

---

9 The French commissioners for Henry II were Charles de Guise, cardinal of Lorraine, Anne de Montmorency, constable of France, and Jacques Dalbon, lord of Saint-André and marshal of France.

> pointe, they ar our slaves, and we their maisters; for we ar so straytelye bownde to eche other that we can make no peace, nor truce without theim, nor they without us'.[10]

Thirlby, Wotton and Arundel then concluded that the King's commissioners had 'usid theim selfes honnorably and accordinge to their promesse' and that Philip's reply to their letter showed him to be 'constant in this mynde to conclude nothinge' unless it had first been agreed with the English.[11]

Eventually Elizabeth commenced secret negotiations with Henry II which left Philip out of the agreement leaving Calais in French hands.[12] However, the protestations of Philip's Spanish, Flemish and Dutch commissioners, and the praise they received from their English counterparts for them reflect the ideological ferment upon which their relationship had been built over the previous four years. The plenipotentiaries representing the King's patrimonial inheritance proclaimed themselves to be 'straytelye bownde' to those representing his kingdoms by marriage. The implications of this episode suggest that the machinery in favour of the notion of *monarchia universalis* was at play here, and the fact that Elizabeth chose to follow a different path should not distract us from the accomplishments of Philip as king of England and Ireland. Mary's inheritance, as Antonio de Guaras had hoped, had 'become one' with that of Philip. This had not happened in the tyrannical fashion imagined by Thomas Wyatt, John Bradford, or the author of *A Supplicachon to the quenes maiestie*, but through the punctilious observance of legality which Philip had been keen to maintain, undoubtedly influenced by his father's experience in Castile during the Comunero crisis of 1520–21 and the experience of joint-monarchy provided by the example of Ferdinand and Isabel. Philip did not contravene a single article of the marriage treaty, and he relinquished his English and Irish kingly titles as soon as he had confirmation of Mary's death, without pretending any rights to the crowns that Elizabeth had inherited. The veiled accusation implicit in many accounts of the reign that Philip did not respect the point on war present in the treaty by drawing England into the Habsburg war with France is not accurate. First, the treaty stipulated that Philip 'as much as he can, shall see peace observed between France and England, and give no cause of breach, but may assist his father in defence of his lands'.[13] This

10 *Relations politiques*, 319–20.

11 *Relations politiques*, 322.

12 M. J. Rodríguez-Salgado, *The Changing Face of Empire: Charles V, Philip II and Habsburg Authority, 1551–1559* (Cambridge: Cambridge University Press, 1988), 310–8.

13 CSP Domestic, 14.

ambiguity gave the king and the queen leverage to frame the declaration of war as a defensive response to French aggression. Furthermore, when England declared war against France in a proclamation issued by Mary on 7 June 1557, it did so in her own terms. Henry II, it was claimed, had not only given support to Northumberland, Wyatt, Sir Henry Dudley, and other conspirators, and ignored all of Mary's entreaties to peace and amity, but he had also provided Sir Thomas Stafford with ships and ammunition for his aborted attempt at taking Scarborough Castle and had engaged in 'ugly endeavours to take Calais'. In the long list of affronts against England which rendered Henry II a public enemy to the queen and to the 'nation', there was only a brief reference to the obligation to defend the Low Countries, but the treaties signed by Charles V and Henry VIII in the 1540s were not alluded to specifically.[14]

Resistance to the marriage, prompted by the fear of foreign domination fuelled by a female succession to the throne, became inseparable from anti-Catholic sentiment, and crystallised in the disastrous fourfold rebellion of 1554, but it never took a decisive shape, and it was soon disarmed once Philip set foot in England. The exchange of invectives and physical attacks did occur between the English and the Spanish, but they do not seem to have been a widespread reaction. Anglo-Spanish enmity was confined to London and was propitiated by the extraordinarily large number of foreigners that had come to the city in Philip's train rather than by any specific and ubiquitous distaste of the Spanish. On the contrary, the dramatic fights, robberies and murders that occurred after July 1554 in the capital must be weighed against the considerable amount of evidence which shows that there was also plenty of room for friendship and peace and that Philip was, in general, a popular king. Furthermore, clashes had been foreseen and an intense collaboration between English and Spanish authorities through a joint commission of justice produced a resolute response to conflicts between nations. No incidents of notice seem to have occurred after December 1556, not even when Philip and a large retinue of Spanish and Flemish courtiers resided again in England between March and

14 AGS, Estado, leg. 810, fol. 1; Relación del pregón q[ue] se izo en londres a 7 de Junio en el ronpimiento de la Guerra con francia: '[...] harmó este otro día / a hestaforde con naos y municiones p[ar]a q[ue] tomase el n[uest]ro castillo de starboro. no contento de aber tanto tienpo andado en tratados muy feos. por tomar a calés. y otras piezas nuestras allende el mar / [...] y porq[ue] con exército a entrado en las tierras bajas de Flandes. – Las q[ua]les somos obligados a defender – nos a parecido de pregonar a nuestros basallos que hantes tengan al dicho Rey. por su público enemigo nuestro y de la nación / q[ue] no sufrirá so color de amistad q[ue] nos engañen más/'. See the English version in TRP, vol. 2, 77–9.

July 1557 and put pressure on the English government to declare war against France.

This degree of collaboration was reflected in other areas of the reign too. The ties between the nobilities of both crowns were becoming progressively strengthened, and patterns for association were starting to flourish. Philip and Mary were wise enough to reconcile malcontents to the idea of being ruled by a Spanish king and some of the connections made during this period would last for the rest of Philip's long reign. The loyalty of some men towards Philip has been surveyed in the preceding pages; men like James Crofts, Viscount Montague, the Kempe brothers or Sir Francis Englefield. The latter's case is particularly important because, as we have seen, he established himself in the Low Countries and became the main point of contact for English Catholics in the region. Later on he would settle in Spain, where he received a pension from Philip until his death in Valladolid in 1596. He lies buried in the Real Colegio de San Albano, founded by the Jesuit Robert Persons in 1590 under Philip II's patronage.[15] The king also reached a political understanding with many other of his English courtiers, a relationship cemented with pecuniary rewards that he disbursed from his own pockets, exerting an influence which went beyond the channels initially provided by his marriage to Mary. Philip also developed an institutional innovation, the select council, composed of trusted English advisers, which was built upon the conciliar experience in Spain, and which placed England firmly in the context of the Spanish Monarchy as one of its integral members.

This universality was also clearly expressed in the religious ideology developed in England and Spain during Philip and Mary's reign. The return to Rome, as has been proven in this book, was mainly brokered by King Philip, who secured for his English subjects the ecclesiastical property that they had acquired during the Henrician schism whilst, at the same time, strongly rejecting the royal supremacy in his address to parliament during the reconciliation sessions of November 1554. In this vein, and far from displaying the insular Catholicism often ascribed to English authors of the period, the sources, methods, inspirations, and conclusions present in the works of English and Spanish theologians denote a common theological frame which was also linked to the latest developments on the Continent. Their treatment of justification was

15 On Englefield's career in Spain see Albert J. Loomie, *The Spanish Elizabethans: The English Exiles at the Court of Philip II* (New York: Fordham University Press, 1963), 14–51. In the book, Loomie meticulously dissects the lives of four other Spanish Elizabethans: the spy Hugh Owen (1538–1618), the duchess of Feria, Jane Dormer (1538–1612), the soldier Sir William Stanley (1548–1630) and the seminarian Joseph Creswell, SJ (1556–1623). Of them all, only Englefield and Dormer had been part of Philip and Mary's court.

rooted in the conclusions that the Council of Trent had already reached, therefore endorsing the determinations of the Roman Church. That the authority of Trent was not always specifically acknowledged, at a time when the Council had not yet concluded, should not obscure the fact that these authors were following the same line to present this Catholic doctrine. The real presence of Christ in the Eucharist and the doctrine of transubstantiation were expounded with outstanding vigour and coherence, reflecting once again the Tridentine understanding of the sacrament of the altar. Their defence of the role of the pope as an administrator of the Church in his capacity as its head under Christ, and not instead of Christ, was consistent and based on Scripture and it provided the human structure upon which the mystical body of Christ was constituted. A testament to the strength of the theological agenda pursued is the fact that, for the first time since Henry VIII's break with Rome, the whole episcopate of England except for two men, refused to acknowledge the new religious settlement, for which they were deprived of their sees and imprisoned for life. The other two were the eighty-eight-year-old Anthony Kitchin, bishop of Llandaff, and Thomas Stanley, absentee bishop of Sodor and Man.[16]

The religious persecutions – or prosecutions – of the 1550s are to be understood, in this context, as the response of the regimes of Philip and Mary, both in England and in Spain, against what the authorities perceived as an attack against the mystical body of Christ. Heresy was understood as a breach of the social order, a manifestation of disobedience to crown and Church and, therefore, to Christ Himself who had instituted them. It was the ultimate act of opprobrium, a rebellion which had to be punished according to the offender's inclination, or lack thereof, to be corrected. Religious deviation, deemed a subversive element by Catholic and Protestant regimes alike, did not only put in jeopardy the ruler's authority, but it was also a direct threat to the foundations of the Catholic Monarchy which sought unity across its many and diverse members through a steadfast – albeit often acrimonious – loyalty to Rome which underpinned notions of identity from Lima to Catania.

In this respect, Philip and Mary's co-monarchy represents a shift in perspectives regarding the construction of nationhood in the sixteenth century. During Charles V's reign, the emperor, charged with the responsibilities of evangelising the Indies, suppressing the Protestant Reformation, and halting Ottoman advances into the West, had never wavered in his association with Rome despite his turbulent relationships with most of the incumbents of the See of St Peter

16 Eamon Duffy, *Fires of Faith: Catholic England under Mary Tudor* (New Haven and London: Yale University Press, 2009), 195 and Peter Marshall, *Heretics and Believers: A History of the English Reformation* (New Haven and London: Yale University Press, 2017), 436.

and the tragic affairs which contributed to worsen it, notably the sack of Rome in 1527. For the undertaking that the emperor faced, the universality claimed by the Catholic faith became a unique tool that could glue together the disparate territories and peoples of Charles's sprawling empire. Catholicism was understood as a gateway to transnationalism and a strong remedy – even if not one devoid of problems of its own – against the lethal disagreements that thinkers like Alfonso de Castro, Juan de Villagarcía, John Christopherson or Miles Huggarde ascribed to the rise of the Protestant Reformations. Philip pursued this ideology with determination both out of political expediency and sincere religious devotion. From this point of view, the links to Rome were necessary to cement relationships between Christian peoples and this was true even when papal interests did not coincide with those of the Spanish Monarchy. John Edwards has rightly pointed out that, when Queen Mary died, the English crown was proving itself as defiant of papal mandates as Henry VIII had been in the 1530s.[17] Mary obdurately ignored Paul IV's demands that Cardinal Pole be sent to Rome to be tried for heresy, and Philip and his father were both at one point excommunicated by the pope, with whom Philip was at that moment at war.[18] However, the possibility of breaking with Rome was never invoked. The alliance with the pontifical throne prevailed even though Philip's relations with the papacy were never easy, even after Paul IV's death in 1559. Bartolomé de Carranza's inquisitorial process became a thorn in the side of Spanish-Roman relations and the conflict escalated when Pius V published the Catechism of the Council of Trent in 1566. Compiled by four prominent theologians (three Italians and a Portuguese) and supervised by Charles Borromeo – who, as a Milanese, was Philip's subject – and three other Italian cardinals, the Catechism was heavily influenced by the archbishop of Toledo's *Comentarios al catechismo christiano*, a work intended for England which had been written in Spanish and published in Flanders. Since the Spanish Inquisition had placed the *Comentarios* in the Index of forbidden works, Philip simply refused to allow the Tridentine Catechism to be published in his territories, despite his self-fashioning as the champion of the Roman Church. As a result of such refusal, the Catholic Monarchy would not see this decision overturned and the

17 John Edwards, *Mary I. The Daughter of Time* (London: Allen Lane, 2016), 75.

18 José Ignacio Tellechea Idígoras, 'Lo que el Emperador no supo. Proceso de Paulo IV a Carlos V y Felipe II', in José Martínez Millán, ed., *Carlos V y la quiebra del humanismo político en Europa (1530–1558)*, vol. 4 (Madrid: Sociedad Estatal para la Conmemoración de los Centenarios de Felipe II y Carlos V, 2001), 181–96.

Catechism published legally in any of its territories until 1780, during the reign of Charles III (1759–1788).[19]

The identification of the Spanish Monarchy with Catholicism, however, would continue to strengthen, and the prohibition to print the Tridentine Catechism was circumvented by theologians who based their works on the canons and decrees of the Council of Trent, whose determinations were swiftly implemented – and carefully supervised – by King Philip in the 1560s.[20] The implications of this association would continue to evolve into what was to become known as *política española* (Spanish politics) in the seventeenth century, a concept which acknowledged religion to be historically, as Friar Juan de Salazar, OSB stated in 1619, 'the foundation and pedestal of [...] this great Monarchy'.[21] Religion transcended the realm of politics but it also determined its course, producing a tendency to consider oneself aligned to others with the same religious beliefs inhabiting the domains of the Catholic Monarch; a sort of Catholic Hispanic confessionalisation which influenced the perceptions of peoples living in Europe, Africa, the Americas and, after the conquest of the Philippines in 1564 and the incorporation of Portugal and its territories to the crown in 1580, in Asia too. In the smooth understanding of the theologians explored in this book, there is a sense that they were Catholic, or Christian, before being English or Spanish, a transnational sentiment of identity which shaped the political and religious agendas of the reign. This has been explored for a later period of the history of the Spanish Monarchy by Pablo Fernández Albaladejo, but the shift from Charles's initial idea that reconciliation with the Protestants was possible to Philip's realisation that only a steadfast – albeit negotiable – alliance with Rome and the crushing of religious dissent could bind the Catholic Monarchy together had already happened by 1558, and the king's achievements in England open a new window from which to tackle the questions of nationhood and confessionalisation in the sixteenth century.[22] Philip's absenteeism in the Low Countries after he returned to Spain in 1559

19 Pedro Rodríguez, *El Catecismo Romano ante Felipe II y la Inquisición española. Los problemas de la introducción en España del Catecismo del Concilio de Trento* (Madrid: Ediciones Rialp, 1998), 17–8.

20 Geoffrey Parker, *Felipe II. La biografía definitiva* (Barcelona: Planeta, 2010), 226–40.

21 Juan de Salazar, OSB, *Política española. Contiene vn discurso cerca de su Monarquía, materias de Estado, aumento, i perpetuidad* (Logroño: Diego Mares, 1619), 45–7.

22 Pablo Fernández Albaladejo, 'Católicos antes que ciudadanos: Gestación de una «política española» en los comienzos de la Edad Moderna' in José Ignacio Fortea Pérez, ed., *Imágenes de la diversidad: El mundo urbano en la Corona de Castilla (s. XVI–XVII)* (Santander: Universidad de Cantabria. Asamblea Regional de Cantabria, 1997), 103–27.

contributed to alienate some sectors of the Flemish and Netherlandish populations, Protestant and Catholic alike. However, control of the Low Countries depended greatly on relations with England, as events were to prove, and a prolonged hold on the kingdom after 1558 would have made the success of the Dutch rebellion very unlikely and it would have probably forced Philip to ensure that there was a stronger representation of the Spanish Monarchy in Northern Europe. The co-monarchy of Philip and Mary cannot be brushed aside as an unwelcome anomaly or a brutal tyranny; it was a strong alliance which culminated the centuries-old ties existing within the triangle formed by England, Flanders, and Castile. It was grounded in common and coherent ideological and theological systems and aims, and it gave England a central relevance in international affairs which the kingdom struggled to re-gain in decades to come. In that respect, it was the insularity of Elizabeth's regime that was an anomaly, not Philip and Mary's bet for a union of their crowns. Between 1554 and 1558, the English and Spanish monarchies had indeed been 'straytelye bownde to eche other'.

Appendix

King Philip's Address to Parliament, 12 November 1554. In Luis Cabrera de Córdoba, *Filipe Segvndo rey de España* (Madrid: Luis Sánchez, 1619), 25–6

Spanish Original

Vuestros Mayores (i en saber i poder) vivieron i muriero[n] en la profesión de la Religión Católica, i en la obediencia de la Iglesia Romana, Cristiana hermandad en multitud junta profesora del nombre de Iesu Christo en vnidad de fe, i legítimamente ordenada, que haze el Pueblo vnido al Sacerdote, como el rebaño a su pastor. Ésta según el estado del Nuevo Testame[n]to es nuestra Iglesia Católica, que tuvo principio en Ierusalén, i esparcida por el vniverso creció ilustre i manifiesta, mista de buenos i malos, santa por Fe i Sacramentos, de origen i sucesión Apostólica, con anplitud Católica, por vnión de los mienbros vna, con duración perpetua, gobernada por elegido por el Espíritu Santo. En él está la Suma autoridad i sumo poder, como en el más digno de los hijos de la Iglesia que sienten de vna manera i constituyen Monarquía él Imperante i súbditos Cristianos Católicos, aunque sean Reyes, si bien con la ecelencia del oro entre los metales. Este Pontífice sucesor de san Pedro es verdaderamente Vicario de Iesu Christo en la tierra, viviendo él i reynando eternamente en su Pontificado, sin aver dos cabeças, aunque sean dos personas vna subordinada a la otra, como el Virrey tenporal a su Rey natural nonbrado para que gobierne en su ausencia el Reyno. Por esto en la ley antigua se mandó a los Hebreos poner en el fre[n]te del sumo sacerdote el nonbre inefable de Dios esculpido en lámina. Es la Iglesia Militante divinamente traslado de la Triunfante; i vio san Iuan decender del cielo a Ierusalén nueva i santa. Como en ella ai vn Príncipe Dios, debaxo de cuya obediencia está sujeta perfetísimamente, en la Militante ai vn Romano Pontífice Príncipe espiritual, que precede a todos i ecede como mayor en dignidad, potestad, institución, autoridad: i anima el cuerpo, por razón del sujeto de mayoria más noble, i con más ecelencia por mejores i mayores súbditos. El obedecerle i a sus decretos es necesario para la salud de las almas. Este Príncipe soberano eligen los Cardenales colunas de la Iglesia que tienen las vezes de los Apóstoles, por cuyo consejo gobierna la Religión buen sentir i reverencia de Dios, veneración de su conocida deidad, que con ciertas leyes i ceremonias en el alma obliga interna i esterna sumo bien nuestro. Su conocimiento don sobrenatural guía con la Fe a conocer a Dios, levanta los humildes, enriquece los pobres, fortalece los débiles, haze los ignorantes sabios. El gobierno tenporal no es ábil para la divinidad, como el culto divino i guardia de los preceptos celestiales, que hazen partícipes de su virtud i vna participación el ser i poder del Rey del ser i poder de Dios, i el sustentarle dignamente pide favor del cielo, i para tener le obedecer al Vicario de Iesu Christo el Romano Pontífice. De la potestad

 | DOI:10.1163/9789004536210_010

de Reyno i oficio de Rey no es sólo su fin la Magestad, riqueza, señorío; Dios i su ley santa fue, i el cunplimiento de sus preceptos, muriendo por ello si conviniere. Por esto mandó en el Viejo Testamento tuviese el Rey en sus manos la ley, i ponérsela en la cabeça los Sacerdotes coronándole; porque sobre todo se a de estimar i defender, i ser antemural i espada de la Iglesia, reprimiendo valerosamente la audacia de los malos, anparando lo establecido, restituyendo la paz, apartando lo que perturba. El señor Rey don Enrique obediente al Romano Pontífice contra los ereges sus enemigos escrivió; i después apóstata (desgracia grande) mal aconsejado perdió el temor de Dios, i la inpiedad el de pecar, i los consejos inpíos truxeron el menosprecio i mudança de religión que pervirtió las cosas públicas. La misericordia de Dios os llama, para que obedeciendo al Romano Pontífice bolváis al rebaño de Iesu Christo incorporándoos en su Iglesia Católica. I assí anulando las leyes contra los decretos Pontificales i entradas de los ministros Apostólicos por los señores Reyes Enrique i Eduardo establecidas, conviene admitir al Cardenal Polo natural de la Isla Legado del sumo Pontífice, i como le avéis çertificado a vuestra Reyna deseáis darle la obediencia, ser hijos verdaderos de la Iglesia Católica. Votad este punto, i alunbre Dios vuestro e[n]tendimie[n]to, i mueva vuestros coraçones, para cuyo servicio i provecho vuestro se propone i encamina. Del reduziros enterame[n]te me resultará mayor felicidad, grandeza i contento, que por ser en tan poderoso Reyno señor con la Reyna mi señora i tía, vuestra cabeça suprema, i tendría por bienave[n]turada mi venida en tienpo tan necesario para ser instrumento de vuestro reparo y salvación.

English Translation

Your forebears (who were great in wisdom and power) lived and died professing the Catholic religion and in obedience to the Roman Church, a Christian confraternity in which a multitude, joined together, professes the name of Jesus Christ in a unity of faith which is legitimately ordained, and which joins the people to the priest like the flock is joined to its shepherd. This is, according to the New Testament, our Catholic Church, which had its beginnings in Jerusalem and – spread through the universe – grew illustrious and visible, mixed with the good and the bad, made holy through faith and the sacraments, of apostolic origin and succession, possessor of a catholic amplitude [i.e. universal], made one through the union of its members, of perpetual duration and governed by him chosen by the Holy Spirit. In him is to be found the maximum authority and the maximum power, as the worthiest of the children of the Church, all of whom are of one mind and constitute a monarchy in which he rules and the rest are Christian and Catholic subjects, even if they are kings, for these only excel in the manner that gold excels among the metals. This pontiff, the successor of St Peter, truly is the vicar of Jesus Christ on earth, who[1] lives and reigns in His eternal pontificate. There

1 Jesus.

are not, however, two heads, even if there are two persons, because one is subordinate to the other, like the temporal viceroy is subordinate to his natural king and appointed to govern the kingdom in his absence. It is for this reason that in the Old Law it was ordered that the Hebrews should place upon the high priest the Ineffable Name of God engraved on a plate. The Church Militant is a divine translation of the Triumphant, which St John saw descend from heaven as a new and holy Jerusalem. Since in her there is a Prince-God, under whose obedience she is perfectly subdued, in the Militant one there is a Roman pontiff, a spiritual prince who precedes and exceeds everyone else as the greatest dignity, power, institution and authority, and animates the whole Body,[2] the reason being that in him is contained the greatest nobility and excellency among the best and greatest subjects. To obey him and his decrees is necessary for the salvation of souls. This sovereign prince is elected by the cardinals, pillars of the Church and representatives of the Apostles, through whose counsel he governs religion, the good understanding and reverence of God, and the veneration of His known divinity, which together with certain laws and ceremonies move our souls internally and externally towards things which are most benign for us. His knowledge is a supernatural gift which, together with faith, guides us to know God, exalts the humble, enriches the poor, strengthens the weak, and makes sages out of ignorant people. Temporal government is not apt for divine matters, such as the divine cult and the guardianship of celestial precepts, which allow us to partake in His virtue. For the being and power of a king to partake in the being and power of God and to have the capacity to sustain the same with dignity, it is required to gain heaven's favour, and to obtain it one must obey the vicar of Jesus Christ, the Roman pontiff. The ends of a kingdom's authority and of the office of a king are not solely majesty, riches, and dominion, but rather God and His Holy Law, and the fulfilment of its precepts, dying for them if necessary. This is why the Old Testament ordained that the Law should be in the hands of the king, and that it should be placed upon his head by the priests at his coronation, because he is to esteem and defend it above all, and be the fortress and sword of the Church, valiantly repressing the audacity of evildoers, protecting that which is established, restoring peace and rejecting that which is disruptive. King Henry was obedient to the Roman pontiff and wrote against the heretics, his enemies. Then he became an apostate (oh, great misfortune!) and lost, through bad counsel, the fear of God and, through impiety, the fear of sin. This impious advice brought forward the disdain for and changes in religion which perverted public affairs. God's mercy now calls you, so that in obeying the Roman pontiff, you may return to the flock of Jesus Christ, joining His Catholic Church. And thus, after repealing the laws against pontifical decrees and the entry of apostolic ministers that were established by your lords, Kings Henry and Edward, it will be convenient to admit Cardinal Pole, a native of the island and the legate of the supreme

2 The Body of Christ.

pontiff, and, as you have assured your queen that you wish to give him your obedience, in this way become true children of the Catholic Church. Vote on this matter, and may God guide your discernment and move your hearts, for it is in His service and in your benefit that it has been proposed and designed. From your complete surrender, I will receive more happiness, greatness, and contentment than from being, as your lord in such a powerful kingdom together with the queen, my lady and aunt, your supreme head; and I would consider my coming a fortunate event, in such a time of need, if I were to be an instrument to your mending and salvation.

Bibliography

Manuscripts

Besançon

Bilbiothèque Municipale de Besançon

MS Granvelle.

Hatfield

Hatfield House Library

Cecil Papers 2/19, 152/137.

Kew

The National Archives

King's Bench 8/29, 9/587, 27/1172, 27/1174, 27/1182, 27/1185.

State Papers 10/18 (19), 11/2 (5, 6, 8, 13, 15, 33), 11/4 (10, 11, 13, 17, 21), 11/6 (17, 66), 11/9 (31, 32, 34), 11/10 (64), 11/11 (20, 29, 41), 11/12 (27), 11/13 (10, 20), 69/8 (467, 468), 69/4 (189, 197), 69/5 (246, 249, 251), 69/6 (354), 69/9 (542), 69/8 (508), 69/10 (628), 69/13 (809).

London

British Library

Add MS 25425.

Cotton Titus B. II.

Cotton Vitellius F. V.

Madrid

Archivo Histórico Nacional

Consejo de Inquisición, 1864 (2), 5353 (8, 9, 16).

Biblioteca Nacional de España

MSS 9937.

MSS 010547.

Real Biblioteca del Palacio Real de Madrid

MSS II-2286-E.

Rome

Archivio Apostolico Vaticano

Fondo Carpegna 202.

A. A., Arm. I–XVIII 522.

Biblioteca Apostolica Vaticana

Vat. Lat. 13138.

San Lorenzo de El Escorial

Real Biblioteca del Monasterio de San Lorenzo de El Escorial

MS V-II-4.

Seville

Archivo General de Indias

Indiferente 427/30.

Simancas

Archivo General de Simancas

Contaduría Mayor de Cuentas 1ª época, 1184.

Consejo Real de Castilla 134/4, 137/1, 368/1.

Estado 516/86, 544/21, 544/136, 545/22, 808/6, 808/7, 808/15, 808/24, 808/38–1, 808/133, 808/141, 808/143, 808/147, 808/148, 808/174, 809/36, 810/1, 811/56, 811/92, 811/99, 811/105, 811/131.

Patronato Real 3/17, 3/137, 55/27, 55/31, 55/32, 57/143, 62/73.

Vienna

Österreichisches Staatsarchiv

Großbritannien Diplomatische Korrespondenz 15, Konv. 1553.

Printed Calendars of Sources

A Complete Collection of State Trials and Proceedings for High Treason and Other Crimes and Misdemeanors from the Earliest Period to the Year 1789, vol. 1. Edited by T. B. Howell. London: T. C. Hansard, 1816.

A Complete Collection of State Trials, and Proceedings for High Treason, and Other Crimes and Misdemeanours; Commencing with the Eleventh Year of the Reign of King Richard II. And Ending with the Sixteenth Year of the Reign of King George III, vol. 1. Edited by Francis Hargrave. Dublin: Graisberry and Campbell, 1793.

A London Provisioner's Chronicle, 1550–1563, by Henry Machyn: Manuscript, Transcription, and Modernization. Edited by Richard W. Bailey, Marilyn Miller, and Colette Moore. University of Michigan. Available from http://quod.lib.umich.edu/m/machyn. Accessed 27 March 2020.

Acts of the Privy Council of England, vols 4–6. Edited by John Roche Dasent. London: Her Majesty's Stationery Office, 1892–1893.

Alumni Oxonienses: The Members of the University of Oxford, 1500–1714, vol. 1. Edited by Joseph Foster. Oxford: Parker and Co., 1891.

Calendar of Letters and State Papers Relating to English Affairs, Preserved Principally in the Archives of Simancas, 2 vols. Edited by Martin. A. S. Hume. London: Her Majesty's Stationery Office, 1894–96.

Calendar of Letters, Despatches and State Papers Relating to the Negotiations Between England and Spain Preserved in the Archives at Vienna, Simancas, Besançon, Brussels, Madrid and Lille (vols. 10, 12 and 13). Edited by Royall Tyler. London: Her Majesty's Stationery Office, 1914–54.

Calendar of State Papers and Manuscripts Existing in the Archives and Collections of Venice, and in Other Libraries of Northern Italy, (vols. 5 and 6). Edited by Rawdon Brown. London: Her Majesty's Stationery Office, 1873–77.

Calendar of State Papers, Domestic Series of the reign of Mary I, 1553–1558. Edited by C. S. Knighton. London: Public Record Office, 1998.

Calendar of State Papers, Domestic Series, Elizabeth, 1601–1603; with Addenda, 1547–1565. Edited by Mary Anne Everett Green. London: Her Majesty's Stationery Office, 1870.

Calendar of the Carew Manuscripts, Preserved in the Archiepiscopal Library at Lambeth, 1515–1574. Edited by J. S. Brewer and William Bullen. London: Public Record Office, 1867.

Calendar of the Patent Rolls Preserved in the Public Record Office. Prepared under the Superintendence of the Deputy Keeper of the Records. Philip and Mary, 2 vols. Edited by M. S. Giuseppi. London: Public Record Office, 1936.

Camden Miscellany, vol. 28. Edited by the Royal Historical Society. London: Royal Historical Society, 1984.

Canons and Decrees of the Council of Trent. Edited by H. J. Schroeder, OP. Rockford, Illinois: Tan Books and Publishers, INC., 1978.

Colección de documentos inéditos para la Historia de España, vol. 1 and 3. Edited by Martín Fernández Navarrete, Miguel Salvá and Pedro Sáinz de Baranda. Madrid: Viuda de Calero, 1842–3.

Epistolario de la emperatriz María de Austria: Textos inéditos del Archivo de la Casa de Alba. Edited by Juan Carlos Galende Díaz and Manuel Salamanca López. Madrid: Nuevos Escritores, 2004.

Relations politiques des Pays-Bas et de l'Angleterre, sous le règne de Philippe II, vol. 1. Edited by Joseph, Baron Kervyn de Lettenhove. Brussels: F. Hayez/Académie Royale de Belgique, 1882.

Strype, John, *Ecclesiastical Memorials, Relating Chiefly to Religion, and the Reformation of It, and the Emergencies of the Church of England, under King Henry VIII, King Edward VI and Queen Mary I, with Large Appendixes, Containing Original Papers, Records, &c*, vol. 3 [1721]. Oxford: Clarendon Press, 1822.

The Correspondence of Reginald Pole, 3 vols. Edited by Thomas F. Mayer. London and New York: Routledge: Taylor & Francis Group, 2003.

The Papers of George Wyatt, Esquire of Boxley Abbey in the County of Kent, Son and Heir of Sir Thomas Wyatt the Younger. Camden Fourth Series, vol. 5. Edited by D. M. Loades. London: Royal Historical Society, 1968.

The Tudor Constitution: Documents and Commentary. Edited by G. R. Elton. Cambridge: Cambridge University Press, 1965.

Tudor Royal Proclamations, vol. 2, The Later Tudors, 1553–1587. Edited by Paul L. Hughes and James F. Larkin, eds. New Haven: Yale University Press, 1969.

Printed Sources

'Six Letters of Cardinal Pole to the Countess of Huntingdon'. Edited by F. J. Routledge. *The English Historical Review*, 28 (1913): 527–31.

'The Count of Feria's Dispatch to Philip II of 14 December 1558'. Edited by M. J. Rodríguez-Salgado and Simon Adams. *Camden Miscellany*, 28, 302–44. London: Royal Historical Society, 1984.

Angell, John. *A collection or gatherynge together, of certayne scriptures, both of the holy scripture, and also of the auncient and Catholyke doctours of Christes church, concernyng the most holy and blessed body and blode of Christ to be royally present in the Sacrament of the Aulter*. London: Robert Wyer, c.1554.

Anon. *La coronaçión de la ínclita y sereníssima reyna doña María de Inglaterra que oy reyna bienauenturadamente en aquel reyno con todos los autos solenidades y cerimonias que se hizieron el día de su coronación: y la manera como fue jurada y alçada por reyna en primero de octubre: Año de mil y quinientos y cinquenta y tres Años*. 1553.

Anon. *The Lamentacion of England*. 1557.

Anon., *A plaine and godlye treatise, concernynge the Masse & the blessed Sacrament of the Aulter, for the instruccion of the symple and vnlerned people*. London: John Wayland?, 1556.

Anon., *A Supplicachon to the quenes maiestie*. 1555.

Anon., *Oratio pia, & erudite pro statu illustrissimorum Principum Philippi & Mariae, Regis & Reginae Angliae Franciae, etc. ut deus eos in multos annos conseruet, & illustrissimam Reginam faciat pulchra prole letam matrem*. London: John Cawood, c.1554.

Arredondo y Alvarado, Gonzalo de. *Castillo inexpugnable defensorio d[e] la fee y concionatorio admirable para vencer a todos enemigos espirituales y corporales, y verdadera relació[n] de las cosas marauillosas antiguas y modernas, y exortación para yr contra el turco y le vencer y anichilar la seta de mahoma y toda infidelidad y ganar la tierra sancta con famoso y bienauenturado triumpho*. Burgos: Juan de Junta, 1528.

Ávila y Zúñiga, Luis de. *The Comentaries of Don Lewes de Auela, and Suniga, great Master of Aranter, which treateth of the great vvars in Germany made by Charles the fifth Maximo Emperoure of Rome, King of Spain, against John Frederike Duke of Saxon, and Philip the Lantgraue of Hesson with other great princes and Cities of the Lutherans, wherin you may see how god hath preserued this vvorthie and victorious Emperor, in al his affayres against his enemyes translated out of Spanish into English.* Translated by John Wilkinson. London: Richard Tottel, 1555.

Azpilcueta, Martín de. *Manval de confessores, y penitentes, qve clara y breuemente contiene, La vniuersal y particular decisión de quasi todas las dudas, que en las confessiones suelen ocurrir de los pecados, absoluciones, restituciones, censuras, & irregularidades.* Antwerp: Ioannes Steelsii, 1557.

Baltanás, Domingo de, OP. *Doctrina Christiana: en que se tracta de lo que deue cada vno creer, huyr, tener, obrar, dessear, y qué cosa es Dios: con otras cosas dignas de saber.* Seville: Martín de Montesdoca, 1555.

Beeard, Richard. *A godly psalme of Marye Queene which brought us comfort al, through God, whom wee of dewtye prayse, that gives her foes a fal.* London: John Kingston for William Griffith, 1553.

Beuter, Pere Antoni. *Segunda parte De la Corónica general de España, y especialmente de Aragón, Cathaluña y Valencia. Donde se tratan las cobranças destas tierras de poder de Moros: por los ínclytos Reyes de Aragón, y Condes de Barcelona. Y pónese en particular la conquista de la ciudad y reyno de Valencia, y Murcia, con las yslas Mallorca, Menorca, Euiça, y las otras: con muchas cosas de notar, como por las tablas se podrá ver.* Valencia: Joan de Mey, 1551.

Billingsley, Nicholas. *Kosmobrephia, or the Infancy of the World: With and Appendix of Gods Resting Day, Eden Garden; Mans Happiness Before, Misery After, his Fall.* London: Robert Crofts, 1658.

Bonner, Edmund. *A profitable and necessarye doctrine, with certayne homelyes adioyned thervnto set forth by the reuerend father in God, Edmunde Byshop of London, for the instruction and enformation of the people being within his diocesse of London, & of hys cure and charge.* London: John Cawood, 1555.

Bonner, Edmund. *Homelies sette forthe by the righte reuerende father in God, Edmunde Byshop of London, not onely promysed before in his booke intituled, A necessarye doctrine, but also now of late adioyned, and added therevunto, to be reade within his diocesse of London, of all persons, vycars, and curates, vnto theyr parishioners, vpon sondayes, & holydayes.* London: John Cawood, 1555.

Bradford, John. *An Admonicion to all Englishe men. To the right honorable lords &c. the erles of Arundell, Darby, Shreusbury & Penbrok, their true and faythfull seruant wisheth, as to al other of our nobilitie increase of grace in gods fauour, with perfect honor, and the preseruacyon of their most honorable states and country. Thoughe ye reioyce not in readyng my foolyshe reasons, yet geue God thankes, that I haue discouered suche detestable treasons.* 1555.

Brooks, James. *A Sermon very notable, fruictefull, and Godlie, made at Paules crosse the .xii. daie of Nouembre, in the first yere of the gracious reigne of our Souereigne ladie Quene Marie her moste excellent highnesse, by James Brokis Doctor of Diuinitie, & Master of Bailye College in Oxforth, with certain additions, whiche he at the tyme of vttering, for auoidyng of tediousness, was faine to omitte.* London: Robert Caly, 1553.

Burnet, Gilbert. *The History of the Reformation of the Church of England. In Two Parts*, part II. London: T. H. for Richard Chiswell, 1683.

Bush, Paul. *A brefe exhortation set fourthe by the vnprofitable seruant of Jesu christ, Paule Bushe, late bishop of Brystowe, to one Margarete Burges wyfe of Jhon Burges, clothear of kyngeswode in the Countie of Wilshere.* London: John Cawood, 1556.

Cabrera de Córdoba, Luis. *Filipe Segvndo rey de España.* Madrid: Luis Sánchez, 1619.

Calvete de Estrella, Juan Cristóbal. *El felicíssimo viaie del mvy alto y mvy Poderoso Príncipe Don Phelippe, Hijo d'el Emperador Don Carlos Quinto Máximo, desde España a sus tierras dela baxa Alemaña: con la descripción de todos los Estados de Brabante y Flandes.* Antwerp: Martín Nucio, 1552.

Canisius, St Peter, SJ. *Svmma de la doctrina christiana. Compuesta por Preguntas y Respuestas, para prouecho y vtilidad de la Re Christiana: agora nueuamente traduzida en Romance Castellano por I. M. C. Por mandamiento y avthoridad d'el Sereníssimo Rey d'España, d'Inglatierra, Francia, y Nápoles, Don Phelipe nuestro Señor.* Translated by Juan Martín Cordero. Anwerp: Guillermo Simón, 1558.

Carion, Johann and Francisco de Támara. *Suma y compendio de todas las chrónicas del mundo, desde su principio hasta el año presente, traduzida por el bachiller Fra[n]cisco Thámara, Cathedrático en Cádiz. Es la Chrónica de Iuan Carion, con diligencia del traductor quitado todo lo superfluo, y añadidas muchas cosas notables de España.* Medina del Campo: Guillermo de Millis, 1553.

Carranza, Bartolomé de, OP. *Comentarios sobre el catecismo christiano* (Antwerp: 1558), 2 vols. Edited by José Ignacio Tellechea Idígoras. Madrid: Biblioteca de Autores Cristianos, 1972.

Carranza, Bartolomé de, OP. *Svmma omnivm conciliorvm, a Sancto Petro vsque ad Iulium quartum* [sic] *Pontificem, omnibus sacrae scripturae studiosis vtilissima.* Antwerp: Ioannes Steelsii, 1556.

Castro, Alfonso de, OFM. *Aduersus omnes haereses libri quatuordecim* [1534]. Cologne: Joannis Novesiani, 1558.

Castro, Alfonso de, OFM. *De ivsta haeretocorum punitione, libri III.* Lyon: Heirs of Jacques Giunta, 1556.

Christopherson, John. *An exhortation to all menne to take hede and beware of rebellion: wherein are set forth the causes, that commonlye moue men to rebellion, and that no cause is there, that ought to moue any man therevnto, with a discourse of the miserable effectes, that ensue thereof, and of the wretched ende, that all rebelles comme to, moste necessary to be redde in this seditiouse & troublesome tyme, made by John Christoferson. At the ende whereof are ioyned two godlye Prayers, one for the Quenes highnes, verye conuenient to be sayd dayly of all her louing and faythfull subiectes, and an other for the good & quiete state of the whole realme.* London: John Cawood, 1554.

Clifford, Henry. *The Life of Jane Dormer, Duchess of Feria.* Edited by Joseph Stevenson, SJ. London: Burns and Oates, 1887.

Cranmer, Thomas. *All the svbmyssyons, and recantations of Thomas Cranmer, late Archebyshop of Canterburye, truely set forth both in Latyn and Englysh, agreable to the Originalles, wrytten and subscribed with his owne hande.* London: John Cawood, 1556.

Eden, Richard. *The decades of the newe worlde or west India, Conteynyng the nauigations and conquestes of the Spanyardes, with the particular descripcion of the moste ryche and large landes and Ilandes lately founde in the west Ocean perteynyng to the inheritaunce of the kinges of Spayne. In the which the diligent reader may not only consyder what commoditie may hereby chaunce to the hole christian world in tyme to come, but also learne many secreates touchynge the lande, the sea, and the starres, very necessarie to be knowen to al such as shal attempte any nauigations, or otherwise haue delite to beholde the strange and woonderfull woorkes of God and nature. Wrytten in the Latine tongue by Peter Martyr of Angleria, and translated into Englysshe by Rycharde Eden.* London: William Powell, 1555.

Elder, John. *Copie of a letter sent into Scotlande, of the ariuall and landynge, and moste noble marryage of the moste Illustre Prynce Philippe, Prynce of Spaine, to the most excellente Princes Marye Quene of England, solemnisated in the Citie of Winchester: and howe he was receyued and installed at Windsore, and of his triumphyng entries in the noble Citie of London. Wherunto, is added a brefe ouerture or openyng of the legacion of the most reuerende father in God Lorde Cardinall Poole, from the Sea Apostolyke of Rome with the substaunce of his oracyon to the kyng and Quenes Magestie, for the reconcilement of the Realme of Englande to the vnitie of the Catholyke churche. With the very copye also of the Supplycacion exhibited to their highnesses by the three Estates assembled in the parlamente. Wherin they representing the whole body of the Realme and dominions of the same, haue submitted the[m]selues to the Popes Holynesse.* London: John Wayland, 1555.

Episcopate of England. *The Institvtion of a Christen man, conteynynge the exposition or interpretation of the co[m]mune Crede, of the seuen sacramentes, of the x commandementes, & of the Pater noster, and the Aue Maria, Justificacion and purgatorie.* London: Thomas Berthelet, 1537.

Esbarroya, Agustín de, OP. *Libro Intitulado purificador dela consciencia: en el qual se contienen dos tractados, En el primero se tracta dela contrición y atrición: por lo qual el ánima se dispone para ser purificada del peccado, y rescebir la gracia. En el otro se contienen reglas para conoscer de qualquier pensamiento palabra o obra, quándo es peccado mortal o no. Compuesto por el maestro fray Augustín de Esbarroya.* Seville: Juan Canalla, 1550.

Fisher, St John. *A Sermon very notable, fruicteful, and Godlie, made at Paules Crosse in London. Anno domini 1521.* London: Robert Caly, 1554.

Foxe, John, *The First Volume of the Ecclesiasticall history contaynyng the Actes and Monumentes of thynges passed in eyery kynges tyme in this Realme, especially in the Church of England principally to be noted:with a full discourse of such persecutions, horrible troubles, the sufferyng of martyrs.* London: John Day, 1570.

Foxe, John. *The First Volume of the Ecclesiasticall History Contayning the Actes and Monumentes of Thinges Passed in Every Kinges Time, in This Realme, Especially in the Churche of England Principally to be Noted. With a Full Discourse of Such Persecutions, Horrible Troubles, the Suffring of Martirs, the* Severe *Punishment of Persecutors.* London: John Day, 1576.

Fuente, Constantino de la. *Summa de doctrina Christiana, Compuesta por el Doctor Constantino. Item, El sermón de Christo nuestro redemptor enel monte, Traduzido en Castellano por el mismo Author. Puso se también ala fin vna dotrina, que muestra cómo cada vno deue regir y gouernar su casa, ordenada por sant Bernardo.* Antwerp: Martín Nucio, *c.*1549.

Gardiner, Stephen (attributed). *A Machiavellian Treatise by Stephen Gardiner.* Edited by Peter Samuel Donaldson. Cambridge: Cambridge University Press, 1975.

Goltzius, Hubert. *Los vivos retratos de todos los Emperadores, desde Iulio César hasta el Emperador Carlos v y Don Fernando su hermano: sacados de las más antiguas monedas, no como fueron sacadas por otros, sino pintadas muy fiel y verdaderamente, y las vidas y hechos, costumbres, virtudes, y vicios, pintados con sus colores, y puestos por historia. Al poderosíssimo Príncipe Don Phelipe Cathólico Rey de España.* Antwerp: Gillis Coppens van Diest, 1560.

Goodman, Christopher. *How svperior powers oght to be obeyd of their subiects: and wherin they may lawfully by Gods worde be disobeyed and resisted. Wherin also is declared the cause of all this present miserie in England, and the onely way to remedy the same.* Geneva: John Crispin, 1558.

Guaras, Antonio de. *Carta de nueuas de Antonio de Guaras criado de la Sereníssima y Cathólica Reyna de Inglaterra, al Ilustre Señor Duque de Alburquerque: Visorrey y Capitán general del Reyno de Nauarra etc. En la qual se trata en qué miserias y calamidades ha estado el Reyno tantos años ha: y de las passiones y muertes que ha huuido. Cómo Doña María fue proclamada por Reyna: y de todos obedescida. Un Razonamiento que hizo el Duque de Northumberland antes de morir: amonestando al pueblo que dexassen la secta en que viuían: y se abraçassen con la Sancta Fe Cathólica: y que en todo obedesciessen a la Magestad de la Reyna María.* 1553.

Gutiérrez de Torres, Álvaro. *El sumario de las marauillosas: y espantables cosas que en el mundo han acontescido*. Toledo: Ramón de Petras, 1524.

Gwynneth, John. *A briefe declaration of the notable victory given of God to our Soveraygne Ladye Quene Marye made in the church of Luton the 23 July in the first yere of her gracious reign*. London: John Cawood, 1553.

Gwynneth, John. *A Manifeste Detection of the notable falshed of that part of John Frithes boke, which he calleth his foundacion, And bosteth it to be inuincible: newly set foorthe by John Gwinneth Clerke*. London: Thomas Berthelet, 1554.

Gwynneth, John. *A Playne Demonstration of Iohn Frithes lacke of witte and learnynge in his vnderstandynge of holie Scripture, and of the olde holy doctours, in the blessed Sacrament of the Aulter, Newly set foorthe by John Gwynneth, Clerke*. London: Thomas Powell, 1557.

Harpsfield, John. *A notable and learned Sermon or Homilie, made vpon saint Andrewes daye last past 1556 in the Cathedral churche of S. Paule in London, by Mayster Jhon Harpesfeild doctour of diuinitie and Canon residenciary of the sayd churche, Set furth by the bishop of London*. London: Robert Caly, 1556.

Henry VIII, king of England. *A Necessary Doctrine and erudicion for any chrysten man, set furth by the kynges maiestye of Englande, &c.* London: Thomas Berthelet, 1543.

Hooker, John. 'Life of Sir Peter Carew'. In *Calendar of the Carew Manuscripts, Preserved in the Archiepiscopal Library at Lambeth, 1515–1574*, lxvii–cxviii. Edited by J. S. Brewer and William Bullen. London: Public Record Office, 1867.

Huggarde, Miles. *A mirrour of loue, which such light doth giue, That all men may learne, howe to loue and liue*. London: Robert Caly, 1555.

Huggarde, Miles. *A new treatyse in maner of a Dialoge / whiche sheweth the excellency of mannes nature / in that he is made to the Image of God, and wherin it restyth / and by howe many wayes a man dothe blotte, and defyle the same Image*. London: Robert Wyer, 1555.

Huggarde, Miles. *A treatise entitled the Path waye to the towre of perfection*. London: Robert Caly, 1554.

Huggarde, Miles. *The assault of the sacrament of the Altar containyng aswell sixe seuerall assaultes made from tyme to tyme against the sayd blessed sacrament: as also the names & opinions of all the heretical captaines of the same asaultes: Written in the yere of oure Lorde 1549. by Myles Huggarde, and dedicated to the Quenes moste excellent maiestie, beyng then ladie Marie: in whiche tyme (heresie then raigning) it could take no place. Now newly imprynted this present yere. 1554*. London: Robert Caly, 1554.

Huggarde, Miles. *The displaying of the Protestantes, & sondry their practises, with a description of diuers their abuses of late frequented. Newly imprinted agayne, and augmented, with a table in the ende, of all suche matters as is specially contained within this volume*. London: Robert Caly, 1556.

Jiménez, Diego, OP. *Enchiridión o Manual de Doctrina Christiana (que también puede seruir de Confessionario) diuidido en cinco partes: en que por vía de preguntas y respuestas se enseña al Christiano todo lo que deue creer, y no creer: dessear, y aborrecer: hazer, y no hazer: saber, y no saber. Hecho y copilado de muchos libros de sana doctrina por el R. P. fray Diego Ximénez, de la orden de los Predicadores. Dirigido al Rey de Portugal.* Lisbon: Germán Gallarde, 1552.

Knox, John, *The First Blast of the Trumpet Against the Monstrvovs Regiment of Women.* 1558.

Langdale, Alban. *Catholica confutatio impiae cvivsdam determinationis D. Nicolai Ridlęi, eo tempore sedem Episcopalem apud Roffam occupantis, post disputationem de Eucharistia in Academia Cantabrigiensi, habitae, in tres libros diuisa.* Paris: Michaëlis Vascosani, 1556.

Machyn, Henry. *The Diary of Henry Machyn: Citizen and Merchant-Taylor of London (1550–1563).* Edited by John Gough Nichols. London: The Camden Society, 1848.

Malfatti, C. V. ed. *The Accession, Coronation and Marriage of Mary Tudor as Related by Four Manuscripts of the Escorial.* Barcelona: Sociedad Alianza de Artes Gráficas and Ricardo Fontá, 1956.

Marshall, George. *A compendious treatise in metre declaring the firste originall of the Sacrifice, and of the building of Aultares and Churches, and of the firste receauinge of the Christen fayth here in Englande by G. M.* London: John Cawood, 1554.

Martínez de Laguna, Alonso. *Svmma de doctrina christiana, compuesta por el Bachiller Alonso Martínez de Laguna de los Cameros, para prouecho de los Christianos.* Salamanca: Juan de Cánova, 1555.

Medina, Pedro de. *Libro de la Verdad. Donde se contienen dozientos Diálogos, que entre la Uerdad y el hombre se tractan sobre la conuersión del peccador. Dirigido al muy Illustre y reuerendíssimo señor don Pedro Gasca Obispo de Palencia, Conde de Pernía, Del consejo de su Magestad, &c.* Valladolid: Francisco Fernández de Córdoba, 1555.

Mejía, Pedro. *Historia Imperial y Cesárea, en la qval en svmma se contienen las vidas y hechos de todos los césares Emperadores de Roma, desde Iulio César hasta el Emperador Maximiliano: la qual compuso el Magnífico Caualllero Pero Mexía, vezino de Seuilla. Agora nueuamente impressa con tres tablas muy copiosas* [1545]. Antwerp: Martín Nucio, 1552.

Meneses, Felipe de, OP. *Lvz del alma Christiana contra la ceguedad y ygnorancia en lo que pertenece a la fe y ley de Dios, y de la yglesia: y los remedios y ayuda que él nos dio para guardar su ley. En el qual tractado se da también luz assí a los confessores, como a los penitentes, para administrar deuidamente el sacramento tan necessario de la penitencia.* Seville: Martín de Montesdoca, 1555.

Muñoz, Andrés. *Svmaria y verdadera relación del buen viaje que el inuictíssimo Príncipe de las Españas don Felipe hizo a Inglaterra, y recebimiento en Vincestre donde casó, y salió para Londres, en el qual se contiene[n] grandes y marauillosas cosas que en este tiempo pasaron. Dedicado a la illustríssima señora doña Luysa Enríquez Girón, condesa de Benauente, por Andrés muñoz criado del sereníssimo Infante don Carlos nuestro señor.* Saragossa: Miguel Zapila, 1554.

Nebrija, Antonio de. *Arte de la lengua castellana.* Salamanca, 1492.

Nieva, Bernardo de, OP. *Svmmario manval de información de la Christiana consciencia. Compuesto, y corregido por el presentado fray Bernardo de Nieua, de la orde[n] de los predicadores. Dirigido a la muy Illustre Señora Marquesa de las Navas, &c.* Medina del Campo: Francisco del Canto, 1556.

Ocampo, Florián de. *Los cinco libros primeros de la Crónica general de España, que recopila el maestro Florián de Ocampo, Cronista del Rey nuestro señor, por mandado de su Magestad, en Çamora.* Medina del Campo: Guillermo de Millis, 1553.

Pérez de Pineda, Juan. *Carta embiada a nvestro avgvstíssimo senor príncipe don Philippe, Rey de España, de Inglaterra, de Nápoles, y delas Indias del Perú, &c. en que se declaran las causas delas guerras y calamidades presentes, y se descubren los medios y artes con que son robados los Españoles, y las más vezes muertos quanto al cuerpo, y quanto al ánima: y contra estos daños se ponen juntamente algunos remedios que son proprios y efficazes, delos quales puede vsar su Majestad para conseruación de sus Repúblicas, y cada vno de sus vasallos en particular para poder los euitar, y ser preseruados en vida, y enrriquecidos de todo bien temporal y eterno.* c.1557.

Philip and Mary, king and queen of England. *Proclamation by the Kinge and the Quene.* London: John Cawood, 1555.

Pole, Reginald. *Reginali Poli ad Henricum octavum Britanniae regem, pro ecclesiasticae unitatis defensione.* Rome: Antonio Blado, 1539.

Pollard, Leonard. *Fyve Homiles of late, made by a ryght good and vertuous clerke, called master Leonarde Pollarde, prebendary of the Cathdrall Churche of Woster, directed and dedicated to the ryght reuerende Father in God Rychard by the permissyon of God byshoppe of Woster his specyall good Lorde.* London: William Griffith, 1556.

Ponet, John. *A Shorte Treatise of politike pouuer, and of the true Obedience which subiectes owe to kynges and other ciuile Gouernours, with an Exhortacion to all true naturall Englishe men.* 1556.

Proctor, John. *The historie of wyates rebellion, with the order and maner of resisting the same, wherinto in the ende is added an earnest conference with the degenerate and sedicious rebelles for the serche of the cause of their daily disorder.* London: Robert Caly, 1554.

Pulgar, Hernando del. *Chrónica. De los muy altos y esclarecidos reyes Cathólicos don Fernando y doña Ysabel de gloriosa memoria. Dirigida a la Cathólica Real Magestad del Rey don Philipe nuestro Señor.* Valladolid: Sebastián Martínez, 1565.

Reynolds, John, *Vox Cœli, or Newes from Heaven, of a consvltation there held by the high and mighty Princes King Hen.8. King Edw.6. Prince Henry. Queene Mary. Queene Elizabeth, and Queene Anne; wherein Spaines ambition and treacheries to most*

Kingdomes and free Estates of Evrope, are vnmask'd and truly represented, but more particularly towards England, and now more especially vnder the pretended match of Prince Charles with the Infanta Dona Maria. VVherunto is annexed two letters written by Queene Mary from heauen, the one to Count Gondomar, the ambassadour of Spaine, the other to all the Romane Catholiques of England. London: William Jones, 1624.

Ribadeneyra, Pedro de, SJ. *Hystoria ecclesiástica del scisma del Reyno de Inglaterra. En la qual se tratan las cosas más notables que han sucedido en aquel Reyno tocantes a nuestra sancta Religión, desde que començó hasta la muerte de la Reyna de Escocia.* Lisbon: Antonio Alvares, 1588.

Richardot, François, OSA. *Le sermon fvnebre, fait devant le Roy, par Messire Francois Richardot, Euesque de Nicople, & Suffragant d'Arras: Aus Obseques & Funerailles du Tresgrand, & Tresuictorieus Empereur Charles Cinquième. Celebrées à Bruxelles en la grande Église ditte Sainte Gudle. Par lequel est faite, non moins eloquemment, que pieusement, & doctement, ample, & vraie deduction des grandes vertus, magnanimitez, hautes entreprinses, faits heroiques, viue foy Catholique, Chrestienne vie, & sainte fin dudit Seigneur Empereur. Avtre sermon fvnebre fait devant le Roy, par icellvy Richardot, avs obseques de la Serenissime Royne Douairière de Hongrie, Bohème, &c. Celebrées audit Bruxelles en la Chappelle du Palais. Encores, vn avtre sermon, fait par le svsdit Richardot, devant Monseigneur le Duc de Sauoye: Aus Obseques de la Royne Marie d'Angleterre. Celebrées audit Bruxelles en ladite Église Sainte Gudle.* Antwerp: Christophe Plantin, 1559.

Ridley, Nicholas. *The Works of Nicholas Ridley, Sometime Bishop of London, Martyr, 1555.* Edited by H. Christmas. Cambridge: Parker Society, 1841.

Salazar, Juan de, OSB. *Política española. Contiene vn discurso cerca de su Monarquía, materias de Estado, aumento, i perpetuidad.* Logroño: Diego Mares, 1619.

Sepúlveda, Juan Ginés de. *De regno et regis oficio* [1571]. In Real Academia de la Historia, ed. *Joannis Genesii Sepulvedæ cordubensis. Opera, cum edita, cum inedita,* vol. 4. Madrid: Tipografía regia de la Gaceta, 1780.

Seton, John. *Panegyrici in victoriam illvstrissimae D. Mariae, Angliae, Franciae, & Hiberniae Reginae, &c. Item In Coronationem eiusdem Serenis. Reginae, congratulation. Ad haec De sacrosanta Eucharistia Carmen.* London: Reginald Wolfe, 1553.

Smith, Richard. *The Life of the Most Honovrable and Vertvovs Lady the Lady Magdalen Viscovntesse Montagve,* trans. By C. F. [1609]. Saint-Omer: English College Press, 1627.

Smyth, Richard. *The seconde parte of the booke called a Bucklar of the Catholyke fayeth, conteyninge seuen chapiters: Made by Rychard Smyth doctoure of diuinitie of Oxforde, & reader of the same there.* London: Robert Caly, 1555.

Soto, Domingo de, OP. *De iustitia e iure.* Salamanca: Andrea de Portonaris, 1553.

Soto, Domingo de, OP. *Fratris Dominci Soto, Segobiensis, theologi, ordinis praedicatorum, & Caesarea maiestatis Caroli quinti Imperatoris à sacris confessionibus, ad sanctum concilium Tridentinum De natura & gratia. Quod opus ab ipso authore denuo recognitum est, nonnullisque in locis emendatum, & Apologia contra reuerendum Episcopum Catharinum auctum* [1547]. Paris: Jean Foucher, 1549.

Soto, Pedro de, OP. *Assertio Catholicae fidei circa articulos confessionis nomine illustrissimi Dvcis Wittenbergensis oblatae per legatos eius Concilio Tridentino, XXIII Ianuarij Anni M. D. LII*. Cologne: Joannes Novesianus, 1555.

Soto, Pedro de, OP. *Compendium doctrinae Catholicae, in usum plebis Christianae recte instituendae R. F. Petri de Soto, Dominicani Theologi, Confessoris Caesaree Maiest. collectum, additi cuique loco aptis precatiunculis, & adiuncta breui explicatione Ecclesiastici cultus, maxime Sacrae Missae eodem Authore*. Ingoldstadt: Alexander Weissenhorn, 1550.

Soto, Pedro de, OP. *Defensio catholicę confessionis, et scholiorvm circa confessionem, illvstrissimi Ducis Vvirtenbergensis nomine editam, aduersus Prolegomena Brentij*. Antwerp: Martín Nucio, 1557.

Soto, Pedro de, OP. *Institvtionis Christianae libri tres priores: Ivssv Reverendissimi Domini D. Othonis Cardinalis & Episcopi Augustani a doctis theologis lecti & probati, ac illius authoritate editi*. Augsburg: Valentin Othmar, 1548.

Soto, Pedro de, OP. *Tractatus de institvtione sacerdotvm, qvi sub episcopis animarum curam gerunt*. Dilingen an der Donau: Sebaldum Mayer, 1558.

St Augustine. *Concerning the City of God against the Pagans*. Trans. by Henry Bettenson. London: Penguin Books, 2003.

St Thomas Aquinas, *Commentary on Aristotle's* Politics (*In libros Politicorum expositio*).

Standish, John. *A discourse wherin is debated whether it be expedient that the scripture should be in English for al men to reade that wyll*. London: Robert Caly, 1554.

Standish, John. *The triall of the supremacy wherein is set fourth the vnitie of christes church militant geuen to S. Peter and his successours by Christe: And that there ought to be one head Bishop in earth Christes Vicar generall ouer all hys churche militant: wyth answeres to the blasphemous objections made agaynste the same in the late miserable yeres now paste*. London: Thomas Marshe, 1556.

Staphylus, Friedrich ed. *De exeqviis Caroli V, maximi, imperatoris, qvas Ferdinandvs avgvstissimvs imperator germano fratri suo charissimo, Augustae Vindelicorum fecit fieri. Item de exeqviis Mariae Vngariae, & Mariae Angliae reginarum, per eundem Imperatorem nostrum, aliquot diebus post celebratis*. Augsburg: Philippus Ulhardus, 1559.

Stopes, Leonard. *An Ave Maria in commendation of our most virtuous queene*. London: Richard Lant, 1553.

Taverner, Richard. *An oration gratulatory made upon the joyfull proclayming of the moste noble princes Quene Mary Quene of Englande*. London: John Day, 1553.

The Chronicle of Queen Jane, Two Years of Queen Mary, and Especially of the Rebellion of Sir Thomas Wyatt. By a Resident in the Tower of London. Edited by John Gough Nichols. London: The Camden Society, 1850.

Thomas, William. *Il pellegrino inglese ne'l quale si difende l'innocente, et la sincera vita de'l pio, et religioso re d'Inghilterra Henrico ottavo, bugiardamente calonniato da Clemente VII et da gl'altri adulatori de la Sedia Antichristiana*. Zürich: Andreas Gessner and Rudolf Wyssenbach, 1552.

Tunstall, Cuthbert. *De ueritate Corporis et sangvinis domini nostri Iesu Christi in Eucharistia, Authore Cutheberto Tonstallo Dunelmensi Episcopo*. Paris: Michaëlis Vascosani, 1554.

Ulzurrun, Miguel de. *Catholicum opus imperiale regiminis mundi*. Zaragoza: Jorge Coci, 1525.

Vitoria, Francisco de, OP. *Reverendis patri F. Francisci de Victoria, ordinis Praedicatorum, sacrae Theologiae in Salmanticensi Academia quondam primarij Professoris, Relectiones Theologicae XII in duos Tomos diuisae*, vol. 1. Lyon: Jacques Boyer, 1557.

Watson, Thomas. *Holsome and Catholyke doctryne concerninge the seuen Sacramentes of Chrystes Church, expedient to be knowen of all men, set forth in maner of shorte Sermons to bee made to the people, by the reuerend father in God Thomas byshop of Lincolne*. London: Robert Caly, 1558.

Watson, Thomas. *Twoo notable Sermons, made the thirde and fyfte Fridayes in Lent last past, before the Quenes highnes, concernynge the reall presence of Christes body and bloude in the blessed Sacrament: & also the Masse, which is the sacrifice of the newe Testament*. London: John Cawood, 1554.

Wingfield, Robert, 'The "Vita Mariae Angliae Reginae" of Robert Wingfield'. Edited by Diarmaid MacCulloch. In *Camden Miscellany*, vol. 28, 181–301. London: Royal Historical Society, 1984.

Secondary Sources

Adair, E. R. 'William Thomas: A Forgotten Clerk of the Privy Council'. In R. W. Seton-Watson, ed. *Tudor Studies Presented by the Board of Studies in History in the University of London to Albert Frederick Pollard: Being the Work of Twelve of His Colleagues and Pupils*, 133–60. London: Longmans, Green & Co, 1924.

Adams, Simon. 'The Dudley Clientèle, 1553–1563'. In G. W. Bernard, ed. *The Tudor Nobility*, 241–65. Manchester and New York: Manchester University Press, 1992.

Akkerman, Nadine and Birgit Houben, eds. *The Politics of Female Households: Ladies-in-Waiting across Early Modern Europe*. Leiden and Boston: Brill, 2014.

Aldea Navarro, Quintín. 'Felipe II. Política y religión'. In Felipe Ruiz Martín, ed. *La Monarquía de Felipe II*, 69–110. Madrid: Real Academia de la Historia, 2003.

Alexander, Gina. 'Bonner and the Marian Persecution'. In Christopher Haigh, ed. *The English Reformation Revised*, 157–75. Cambridge: Cambridge University Press, 1987.

Alonso Burgos, Jesús. *El luteranismo en Castilla durante el siglo XVI. Autos de fe de Valladolid de 21 de mayo y de 8 de octubre de 1559*. San Lorenzo de El Escorial: Swan, Avantos & Hakeldama, 1983.

Alsop, J. D. 'The Act for the Queen's Regal Power, 1554'. *Parliamentary History*, 13, no. 3 (1994): 261–76.

Alvar Ezquerra, Alfredo. *Felipe II, la corte y Madrid en 1561*. Madrid: Consejo Superior de Investigaciones Científicas, 1985.

Álvarez-Ossorio Alvariño, Antonio. *Milán y el legado de Felipe II: gobernadores y corte provincial en la Lombardía de los Austrias*. Madrid: Sociedad Estatal para la Conmemoración de los Centenarios de Felipe II y Carlos V, 2001.

Anon. *An Address to Electors, on Their Duty as Englishmen, or the Triumph of British Right over Infidel & Papal Tyranny*. Whitby: R. Rodgers, 1826.

Arrieta Alberdi, Jon. *El consejo supremo de la corona de Aragón (1494–1707)*. Zaragoza: Institución Fernando el Católico, 1994.

Barron, Caroline M. and Christopher Harper-Bill, eds. *The Church in pre-Reformation Society: Essays in Honour of F. R. H. Du Boulay*. Woodbridge: The Boydell Press, 1985.

Baskerville, Edward J. *A Chronological Bibliography of Propaganda and Polemic Published in English between 1553 and 1558, from the death of Edward VI to the death of Mary I*. Philadelphia: American Philosophical Society, 1979.

Bataillon, Marcel. *Erasmo y España, estudios sobre la historia espiritual del siglo XVI*. Translated by Antonio Alatorre [1937]. Mexico City: Fondo de Cultura Económica, 1950.

Beccaría Lago, María Dolores. *Vida y obra de Cristóbal de Castillejo*. Madrid: Real Academia Española, 1997.

Beem, Charles. *The Lioness Roared: The Problems of Female Rule in English History*. New York: Palgrave Macmillan, 2006.

Beltrán de Heredia, Vicente. *Cartulario de la Universidad de Salamanca (1218–1600)*, vol. 5. Salamanca: Universidad de Salamanca, 1972.

Bernard, G. W. ed. *The Tudor Nobility*. Manchester and New York: Manchester University Press, 1992.

Bernard, G. W. *The King's Reformation: Henry VIII and the Remaking of the English Church*. New Haven and London: Yale University Press, 2005.

Bertoméu Masiá, María José. 'Relaciones de sucesos italianas sobre la boda de Felipe II con María Tudor'. *Cartaphilus*, 5 (2009): 6–17.

Bethéncourt Massieu, Antonio de. 'El Real Patronato'. *Anuario de Estudios Atlánticos*, 1, no. 48 (2002): 155–214.

Bindoff, S. T. *Tudor England*. London: Penguin, 1950.

Bosbach, Franz. *Monarchia universalis: Storia di un concetto cardine della politica europea (secoli XVI–XVIII)*. Trans. by Cesare De Marchi [1988]. Milan: Vita e Pensiero, 1998.

Botella-Ordinas, Eva. '"Exempt from Time and from its Fatal Change": Spanish Imperial Ideology, 1450–1700'. *Renaissance Studies*, 26, no. 4 (2012): 580–604.

Bradley, Emily Tennyson. 'Kingston, Anthony'. In Sidney Lee, ed. *Dictionary of National Biography*, vol. 31. London: Smith, Elder & Co., 1892.

Brigden, Susan. *London and the Reformation*. Oxford: Clarendon Press, 1989.

Brown, Keith Duncan. 'The Franciscan Observants in England, 1482–1559'. PhD thesis, University of Oxford, unpublished, 1986.

Burdiel, Isabel. *Isabel II. Una biografía*. Madrid: Taurus, 2010.

Cáceres Valderrama, Milena. *La fiesta de moros y cristianos en el Perú*. Lima: Pontificia Universidad Católica del Perú, 2005.

Cameron, Euan. *The European Reformation*. Oxford: Oxford University Press, 1991.

Cañizares-Esguerra, Jorge, ed. *Entangled Empires: The Anglo-Iberian Atlantic, 1500–1830*. Philadelphia: University of Pennsylvania Press, 2018.

Cardim, Pedro and Joan-Lluís Palos, eds. *El mundo de los virreyes en las monarquías de España y Portugal*. Madrid and Frankfurt am Main: Iberoamericana-Vervuert, 2012.

Carlos Morales, Carlos J. de. *El consejo de Hacienda de Castilla, 1523–1602. Patronazgo y clientelismo en el gobierno de las finanzas reales durante el siglo XVI*. Valladolid: Junta de Castilla y León, 1997.

Carro, Venancio D. 'El Maestro Domingo de Soto y las controversias sobre la justificación dentro y fuera del Concilio de Trento'. *Ciencia Tomista*, 87 (1960): 423–65.

Carro, Venancio D. *El maestro fr. Pedro de Soto, O. P. (Confesor de Carlos V) y las controversias político-teológicas en el siglo XVI*, 2 vols. Salamanca: Convento de Dominicos, 1931–50.

Castro, Manuel, OFM. 'Fray Alfonso de Castro, O. F. M. (1495–1558), consejero de Carlos V y de Felipe II'. *Salmanticensis*, 5, no. 2 (1958): 281–322.

Cervantes, Fernando. *The Hispanic World in the Historical Imagination: The John Coffin Memorial Lecture in the History of Ideas (28 January 2005)*. London: Institute for the Study of the Americas, 2006.

Chadwick, Owen. *The Reformation* [1964]. London: Penguin Books, 1990.

Clark, Peter. *English Provincial Society from the Reformation to the Revolution: Religion, Politics, and Society in Kent, 1500–1640*. Hassocks: The Harvester Press, 1977.

Clemencín, Diego. *Elogio de la reina Católica doña Isabel, al que siguen varias ilustraciones sobre su reinado*. Madrid: J. Sancha for Academia de la Historia, 1821.

Coleman, Christopher and David Starkey, eds. *Revolution Reassessed: Revisions in the History of Tudor Government and Administration*. Oxford: Oxford University Press, 1986.

Cooper, J. P. D. 'Carew, Sir Peter (1514?–1575)'. *Oxford Dictionary of National Biography*. Oxford: Oxford University Press, 2004. Available from http://www.oxforddnb.com/view/article/4634. Accessed 27 April 2020.

Criado Mainar, Jesús. *El palacio de la familia Guaras en Tarazona*. Tarazona: Centro de Estudios Turiasonenses and Fundación Tarazona Monumental, 2009.

Croft, Ryan J. 'Sanctified Tyrannicide: Tyranny and Theology in John Ponet's *Shorte Treatise of Politike Power* and Edmund Spenser's *The Faerie Queene*'. *Studies in Philology*, 108, no. 4 (2011): 538–571.

Cross, Claire David Loades and J. J. Scarisbrick, eds. *Law and Government under the Tudors: Essays Presented to Sir Geoffrey Elton on his retirement.* Cambridge: Cambridge University Press, 1988.

Cross, Claire. 'The English Universities, 1553–8'. In Eamon Duffy and David Loades, eds. *The Church of Mary Tudor*, 57–76. Aldershot: Ashgate, 2006.

Cross, Claire. *Church and People, 1450–1660*. Glasgow: Fontana Paperbacks, 1976.

Crummé, Hannah Leah. 'Jane Dormer's Recipe for Politics: A Refuge Household in Spain for Mary Tudor's Ladies-in-Waiting'. In Nadine Akkerman and Birgit Houben, eds. *The Politics of Female Households: Ladies-in-Waiting across Early Modern Europe*, 51–71. Leiden and Boston: Brill, 2014.

Danvila y Collado, Manuel. *Historia crítica y documentada de las Comunidades de Castilla* 6 vols. Madrid: Viuda e hijos de M. Tello, 1897–1900.

Davidson, Alan. 'Kempe, Anthony (by 1529–97), of Slindon, Suss'. *History of Parliament Online.* Available from http://www.historyofparliamentonline.org/volume/1509-1558/member/kempe-anthony-1529-97. Accessed 27 April 2020.

Davies, C. S. L. 'England and the French War, 1557–1559'. In Jennifer and Robert Tittler, eds. *The Mid-Tudor Polity, c. 1540–1560*, 159–85. London: Macmillan, 1980.

Davies, C. S. L. *Peace, Print and Protestantism, 1450–1558*. Frogmore: Paladin, 1977.

De Groot, Wim. *The Seventh Window: the King's Window donated by Philip II and Mary Tudor to Sint Janskerk in Gouda (1557)*. Hilversum: Uitgeverij Verloren, 2005.

De Iongh, Jane. *Margaret of Austria: Regent of the Netherlands.* New York: W. W. Norton, 1953.

De Lisle, Leanda. *The Sisters Who Would Be Queen: The Tragedy of Mary, Katherine and Lady Jane Grey.* London: Harper Press, 2008.

Dickens, A. G. *The English Reformation* [1964]. London and Glasgow: Collins/Fontana, 1972.

Dixon, C. Scott. *Contesting the Reformation*. Chichester: Wiley-Blackwell, 2012.

Dodds, Madeleine Hope and Ruth Dodds. *The Pilgrimage of Grace, 1536–1537 and the Exeter Conspiracy, 1538*, vol. II. Cambridge: Cambridge University Press, 1915.

Dongil y Sánchez, Miguel. 'Margarita de Austria (1480–1530): Regente de los Países Bajos y tutora de Carlos I de España'. *Iberian*, 2 (2011): 6–17.

Doran, Susan and Thomas S. Freeman, eds. *Mary Tudor: Old and New Perspectives*. New York: Palgrave Macmillan, 2011.

Du Barry, Roger. 'Cranmer's Doctrine of the Lord's Supper in its Gospel Context'. *Churchman*, 120, no. 4 (2006): 285–320.

Duffy, Eamon and David Loades, eds. *The Church of Mary Tudor*. Aldershot: Ashgate, 2006.

Duffy, Eamon. 'Cardinal Pole Preaching: St Andrew's Day, 1557'. In Eamon Duffy and David Loades, eds. *The Church of Mary Tudor*, 176–200. Aldershot: Ashgate, 2006.

Duffy, Eamon. *Fires of Faith: Catholic England under Mary Tudor*. New Haven and London: Yale University Press, 2009.

Duffy, Eamon. *Saints, Sacrilege and Sedition: Religion and Conflict in the Tudor Reformations*. London: Bloomsbury, 2012.

Duffy, Eamon. *The Stripping of the Altars: Traditional Religion in England, c.1400–c.1580*. New Haven and London: Yale University Press, 1992.

Duncan, Sarah and Valerie Schutte, eds. *The Birth of a Queen: Essays on the Quincentenary of Mary I*. New York: Palgrave Macmillan, 2016.

Duncan, Sarah. *Mary I: Gender, Power, and Ceremony in the Reign of England's First Queen*. New York: Palgrave Macmillan, 2012.

Edwards, John and Ronald Truman, eds. *Reforming Catholicism in the England of Mary Tudor: The Achievement of Friar Bartolomé de Carranza*. Aldershot: Ashgate, 2005.

Edwards, John. 'Corpus Christi at Kingston upon Thames: Bartolomé Carranza and the Eucharist in Marian England'. In John Edwards and Ronald Truman, eds. *Reforming Catholicism in the England of Mary Tudor: The Achievement of Friar Bartolomé de Carranza*, 139–51. Aldershot: Ashgate, 2005.

Edwards, John. 'Fray Bartolomé Carranza's Blueprint for a Reformed Catholic Church in England'. In Thomas F. Mayer, ed. *Reforming Reformation*. Farnham: Ashgate, 2012.

Edwards, John. 'Introduction: Carranza in England'. in John Edwards and Ronald Truman, eds. *Reforming Catholicism in the England of Mary Tudor: The Achievement of Friar Bartolomé de Carranza*, 1–20. Aldershot: Ashgate, 2005.

Edwards, John. 'The Spanish Inquisition Refashioned: the Experience of Mary I's England and the Valladolid Tribunal, 1559'. *Hispanic Research Journal*, 13, no. 1 (2012): 41–54.

Edwards, John. *Archbishop Pole*. Farnham: Ashgate, 2014.

Edwards, John. *Mary I: England's Catholic Queen*. New Haven and London: Yale University Press, 2011.

Edwards, John. *Mary I: The Daughter of Time*. London: Allen Lane, 2016.

Egío García, Víctor Manuel. 'La pieza que no encaja: reseña crítica a las "Controversias ilustres y de uso frecuente" de Fernando Vázquez de Menchaca'. *Biblioteca Saavedra Fajardo de pensamiento político hispánico*. (2010): 1–17.

Eldred, Jason. '"The Just Will Pay for the Sinners": English Merchants, the Trade with Spain, and Elizabethan Foreign Policy, 1563–1585'. *Journal for Early Modern Cultural Studies*, 10, no. 1 (2010): 5–28.

Elliott, J. H. *Empires of the Atlantic World: Britain and Spain in America, 1492–1830*. New Haven and London: Yale University Press, 2006.

Elliott, John H. *Spain, Europe & the Wider World, 1500–1800*. New Haven and London: Yale University Press, 2009.

Ellis, Steven G. 'Croft, Sir James (*c*.1518–1590)'. *Oxford Dictionary of National Biography*. Oxford: Oxford University Press, 2004. Available from http://www.oxforddnb.com/view/article/6719. Accessed 27 March 2020.

Ellis, Steven G. *Ireland in the Age of the Tudors, 1447–1603: English Expansion and the End of Gaelic Rule*. Harlow: Longman, 1998.

Ellis, Steven G. *Tudor Ireland: Crown, Community and the Conflict of Cultures, 1470–1603*. London and New York: Longman, 1985.

Elton, G. R. *England under the Tudors* [1955]. London: Methuen, 1974.

Elton, G. R. *Reform and Reformation: England, 1509–1558*. London: Edward Arnold, 1977.

Erickson, Carolly. *Bloody Mary*. Garden City, N.Y.: Doubleday, 1978.

Ernst, Cornelius, OP. *The Theology of Grace*. Butler, Wisconsin: Clergy Book Service, 1974.

Evenden, Elizabeth and Vivienne Westbrook, eds. *Catholic Renewal and Protestant Resistance in Marian England*. Farnham: Aldershot, 2015.

Evenden, Elizabeth. 'Spanish Involvement in the Restoration of Catholicism during the Reign of Philip and Mary'. In Elizabeth Evenden and Vivienne Westbrook, eds. *Catholic Renewal and Protestant Resistance in Marian England*, 45–64. Farnham: Aldershot, 2015.

Fenlon, Dermot. *Heresy and Obedience in Tridentine Italy*. Cambridge: Cambridge University Press, 1972.

Fernandes, Isabelle. *Marie Tudor. La souffrance du pouvoir*. Paris: Tallandier, 2012.

Fernández Albaladejo, Pablo. 'Católicos antes que ciudadanos: Gestación de una «política española» en los comienzos de la Edad Moderna'. In José Ignacio Fortea Pérez, ed. *Imágenes de la diversidad: El mundo urbano en la Corona de Castilla* (s. XVI–XVII), 103–27. Santander: Universidad de Cantabria. Asamblea Regional de Cantabria, 1997.

Fernández Álvarez, Manuel. *Carlos V. El César y el hombre* [1999]. Barcelona: Planeta DeAsgostini, 2007.

Fernández Álvarez, Manuel. *Felipe II y su tiempo* [1998]. Pozuelo de Alarcón: Espasa, 2006.

Fernández Cava, Salvador. *Constantino Ponce de la Fuente (1505–1559): el camino de la verdad*. Ciudad Real: Almud and Ediciones de Castilla-La Mancha, 2007.

Fernández, Manuel F., Carlos Alberto González and Natalia Maillard, eds. *Testigo del tiempo, memoria del unvierso. Cultura escrita y sociedad en el mundo ibérico (siglos XV–XVIII)*. Málaga: Ediciones Rubeo, 2009.

Fiorenza, Francis Schüssler and John P. Galvin, eds. *Systematic Theology: Roman Catholic Perspectives*, 2 vols. Minneapolis: Fortress Press, 1991.

Fleming, Gillian B. *Juana I: Legitimacy and Conflict in Sixteenth-Century Castile.* London: Palgrave Macmillan, 2018.

Fletcher, Anthony and Diarmaid MacCulloch. *Tudor Rebellions* [1968]. Abingdon and New York: Routledge, 2016.

Fortea Pérez, José Ignacio, ed. *Imágenes de la diversidad: El mundo urbano en la Corona de Castilla* (*s. XVI–XVII*). Santander: Universidad de Cantabria. Asamblea Regional de Cantabria, 1997.

Foster, Steven M. '"To Take the Sword is to Draw the Sword without the Authority of the Prince": Obedience, Duty and Romans 13 during the 1549 Rebellions in England'. *Reformation & Renaissance Review*, 22, no. 1 (2020): 25–47.

Foster, Steven Michael. 'The Reception of Romans 13:1–7 during the English Reformation'. PhD thesis, University of Leeds, 2017, unpublished.

Francisco Olmos, José María de. 'Las primeras acuñaciones del príncipe Felipe de España (1554–1556): Soberano de Milán, Nápoles e Inglaterra'. *Documenta & Instrumenta*, 3 (2005): 155–86.

Freeman, Thomas S. 'Burning Zeal: Mary Tudor and the Marian Persecution'. In Susan Doran and Thomas S. Freeman, eds., *Mary Tudor: Old and New Perspectives*, 171–205. New York: Palgrave Macmillan, 2011.

Freeman, Thomas S. 'Inventing Bloody Mary: Perceptions of Mary Tudor from the Restoration to the Twentieth Century'. In Susan Doran and Thomas S. Freeman, eds., *Mary Tudor: Old and New Perspectives*, 78–100. New York: Palgrave Macmillan, 2011.

Froude, James Anthony. *History of England: From the Fall of Wolsey to the Death of Elizabeth*, vol. 6. New York: Scribner, Armstrong, and Co., 1875.

Galende Díaz, Juan Carlos, ed. *III Jornadas Científicas sobre Documentación de la época de los Reyes Católicos*, 273–301. Madrid: Universidad Complutense de Madrid, 2004.

Gancho, Claudio, OFM. 'La Biblia en Alfonso de Castro, O. F. M.'. *Salmanticensis*, 5, no. 2 (1958): 323–49.

García Cárcel, Ricardo and Doris Moreno Martínez. *Inquisición. Historia crítica.* Madrid: Temas de Hoy, 2000.

García Hernán, Enrique. *Irlanda y el Rey Prudente.* Madrid: Ediciones del Laberinto, 2000.

García Hernán, Enrique. *Vives y Moro. La amistad en tiempos difíciles.* Madrid: Cátedra, 2016.

González Novalín, José Luis. *El inquisidor general Fernando de Valdés (1483–1568). Su vida y su obra.* Oviedo: Universidad de Oviedo, 1968–71.

González Palencia, Antonio. *Gonzalo Pérez: Secretario de Felipe Segundo*, 2 vols. Madrid: Instituto Jerónimo Zurita, 1946.

Granger, James. *A Biographical History of England, from Egbert the Great to the Revolution*, vol. 1 [1769]. London: William Baynes and Son, 1824.

Gregory, Brad S. *Salvation at Stake: Christian Martyrdom in Early Modern Europe*. Cambridge, Massachusetts and London: Harvard University Press, 1999.

Guichard Romero, Luis Arturo. 'La *Ulyxea* de Gonzalo Pérez y las traducciones latinas de Homero'. In Barry Taylor and Alejandro Coroleu Lletget, eds. *Latin and Vernacular in Renaissance Iberia II: Translations and Adaptations*, 49–72. Manchester: Manchester University Press, 2006.

Gunn, S. J. 'A Letter of Jane, Duchess of Northumberland, in 1553'. *The English Historical Review*, 114, no. 459 (1999): 1267–71.

Gutiérrez, Constancio, SJ. *Españoles en Trento*. Valladolid: Consejo Superior de Investigaciones Históricas/Instituto Jerónimo Zurita, 1951.

Guy, John. 'The Rhetoric of Counsel in Early Modern England'. In Dale Hoak, ed. *Tudor Political Culture*, 292–310. Cambridge: Cambridge University Press, 1995.

Guy, John. 'Tudor Monarchy and Political Culture'. In John Morrill, ed. *The Oxford Illustrated History of Tudor and Stuart Britain*, 219–38. Oxford: Oxford University Press, 1996.

Guy, John. 'Tudor Monarchy and Political Culture'. In John Morrill, ed. *The Oxford Illustrated History of Tudor and Stuart Britain*, 219–38. Oxford: Oxford University Press, 1996.

Guy, John. *Tudor England*. Oxford: Oxford University Press, 1988.

Haar, Christoph Philipp. *Natural and Political Conceptions of Community: The Role of the Household in Early Modern Jesuit Thought, c. 1590–1650*. Leiden and Boston: Brill, 2019.

Haigh, Christopher, ed. *The English Reformation Revised*. Cambridge: Cambridge University Press, 1987.

Haigh, Christopher. *English Reformations: Religion, Politics and Society under the Tudors*. Oxford: Oxford University Press, 1993.

Haight, Roger. 'Sin and Grace'. In Francis Schüssler Fiorenza and John Galvin, eds. *Systematic Theology: Roman Catholic Perspectives*, vol. 2, 75–141. Minneapolis: Fortress Press, 1991.

Haliczer, Stephen. *The Comuneros of Castile: The Forging of a Revolution, 1475–1521*. Madison, Wisconsin: Univeristy of Wisconsin Press, 1981.

Harbison, E. Harris. 'French Intrigue at the Court of Queen Mary'. *The American Historical Review*, 40, no. 3 (1940): 533–51.

Heaney, Christopher. 'Marrying Utopia: Mary and Philip, Richard Eden, and the English Alchemy of Spanish Peru'. In Jorge Cañizares-Esguerra, ed. *Entangled Empires: The Anglo-Iberian Atlantic, 1500–1830*, 85–104. Philadelphia: University of Pennsylvania Press, 2018.

Hegarty, Andrew. 'Carranza and the English Universities'. In John Edwards and Ronald Truman, eds. *Reforming Catholicism in the England of Mary Tudor: The Achievement of Friar Bartolomé de Carranza*, 153–72. Aldershot: Ashgate, 2005.

Hernando Sánchez, Carlos José. *Castilla y Nápoles en el siglo XVI. El virrey Pedro de Toledo. Linaje, estado y cultura (1532–1553)*. Salamanca: Junta de Castilla y León, 1994.

Himmerich y Valencia, Robert. *The Encomenderos of New Spain, 1521–1555*. Austin: University of Texas Press, 1991.

Hoak, Dale, ed. *Tudor Political Culture*. Cambridge: Cambridge University Press, 1995.

Hoak, Dale. 'Two Revolutions in Tudor Government: The Formation and Organization of Mary I's Privy Council'. In Christopher Coleman and David Starkey, eds. *Revolution Reassessed: Revisions in the History of Tudor Government and Administration*, 87–115.

Hoak, Dale. 'Two Revolutions in Tudor Government: The Formation and Organization of Mary I's Privy Council'. In Christopher Coleman and David Starkey, eds. *Revolution Reassessed: Revisions in the History of Tudor Government and Administration*, 87–115. Oxford: Oxford University Press, 1986.

Hodgson-Wright, Stephanie. 'Howard, Mary, duchess of Norfolk (1539/40–1557)'. *Oxford Dictionary of National Biography*. Oxford: Oxford University Press, 2004. Available from http://www.oxforddnb.com/view/article/47847. Accessed 26 April 2020.

Hood, Edwin Paxton. *The Dark Days of Queen Mary*. London: Partridge & Oakey, 1851.

Hoskins, W. G. *A New Survey of England: Devon*. London: Collins, 1959.

Houlbrooke, Ralph. 'The Clergy, the Church Courts and the Marian Restoration in Norwich'. In Eamon Duffy and David Loades, eds. *The Church of Mary Tudor*, 124–46. Aldershot: Ashgate, 2006.

Houlbrooke, Ralph. 'What Happened to Mary's Councillors?'. In Alice Hunt and Anna Whitelock, eds. *Tudor Queenship: The Reigns of Mary and Elizabeth*, 209–24. New York: Palgrave Macmillan, 2010.

Hume, Martin A. S. 'The Visit of Philip II'. *The English Historical Review*, 7, no. 26 (1892): 253–80.

Hunt, Alice and Anna Whitelock, eds. *Tudor Queenship: The Reigns of Mary and Elizabeth*. New York: Palgrave Macmillan, 2010.

Hutchinson, Robert. *The Last Days of Henry VIII: Conspiracies, Treason and Heresy at the Court of the Dying Tyrant*. London: Weidenfeld and Nicolson, 2005.

Hutton, Ronald. *The Rise and Fall of Merry England: The Ritual Year, 1400–1700*. Oxford: Oxford University Press, 1994.

Ives, Eric. *Lady Jane Grey: A Tudor Mystery*. Oxford: Wiley-Blackwell, 2009.

Jang, Misung. "Aristotle's Political Friendship (*politike philia*) as Solidarity". In Liesbeth Huppes-Cluysenaer and Nuno M. M. S. Coelho, eds. *Aristotle on Emotion in Law and Politics*, 417–33. Springer: New York, 2018.

Jerez, José Joaquín. *Pensamiento político y reforma constitucional durante la guerra de las Comunidades de Castilla (1520–1521)*. Madrid, Barcelona, and Buenos Aires: Marcial Pons, 2007.

Johnston, Hope. 'Catherine of Aragon's Pomegranate, Revisited'. *Transactions of the Cambridge Bibliographical Society*, 13, no. 2 (2005): 153–73.

Juderías, Julián. *La Leyenda Negra de España* [1914]. Madrid: La Esfera de los Libros, 2014.

Kamen, Henry. *Philip of Spain*. New Haven and London: Yale University Press, 1997.

Kamen, Henry. *Spain, 1469–1714: A Society of Conflict* [1983]. Harlow: Longman, 2005.

Kelsey, Harry. *Philip of Spain, King of England: The Forgotten Sovereign*. London and New York: I. B. Tauris, 2012.

Kesselring, K. J. *The Northern Rebellion of 1569: Faith, Politics, and Protest in Elizabethan England*. Basingstoke and New York: Palgrave Macmillan, 2007.

Kewes, Paulina. 'Godly Queens: The Royal Iconographies of Mary and Elizabeth'. In Alice Hunt and Anna Whitelock, eds. *Tudor Queenship: The Reigns of Mary and Elizabeth*, 47–62. New York: Palgrave Macmillan, 2010.

Kewes, Paulina. 'Two Queens, One Inventory: The Lives of Mary and Elizabeth Tudor'. In Kevin Sharpe and Steven Zwicker, eds., *Writing Lives: Biography and Textuality, Identity and Representation in Early Modern England*, 187–207. Oxford: Oxford University Press, 2008.

Knighton, C. S. 'Westminster Abbey Restored'. In Eamon Duffy and David Loades, eds. *The Church of Mary Tudor*, 77–123. Aldershot: Ashgate, 2006.

Koenigsberger, H. G. *Politicians and Virtuosi: Essays in Early Modern History*. London: A & C Black, 1986.

Lake, Peter. *Bad Queen Bess? Libels, Secret Histories, and the Politics of Publicity in the Reign of Queen Elizabeth I*. Oxford: Oxford University Press, 2016.

Law, Ceri. 'The 1557 Visitation of the University of Cambridge'. In Elizabeth Evenden and Vivienne Westbrook, eds. *Catholic Renewal and Protestant Resistance in Marian England*, 65–91. Farnham: Aldershot, 2015.

Lehmberg, Stanford. 'Throckmorton, Sir Nicholas (1515/16–1571)'. *Oxford Dictionary of National Biography*. Oxford: Oxford University Press, 2004. Available from http://www.oxforddnb.com/view/article/27394. Accessed 28 March 2020.

Llamas Martínez, Enrique, OCD. *Bartolomé de Torres. Teólogo y obispo de Canarias*. Madrid: CSIC, 1979.

Llanos y Torriglia, Félix de. *María I de Inglaterra ¿la Sanguinaria?, reina de España*. Madrid: Espasa-Calpe, 1945.

Loach, Jennifer and Robert Tittler, eds. *The Mid-Tudor Polity, c. 1540–1560*. London: Macmillan, 1980.

Loach, Jennifer. *Edward VI*. New Haven and London: Yale University Press, 1999.

Loach, Jennifer. *Parliament and the Crown in the Reign of Mary Tudor*. Oxford: Oxford University Press, 1986.

Loades, D. M. 'The Authorship and Publication of "The Copye of a Letter Sent by John Bradforth to the Right Honorable Lordes the Erles of Arundel, Darbie, Shrewsbury and Penbroke" (S.T.C. 3480)', *Transactions of the Cambridge Bibliographical Society*, vol. 3 no. 2 (1960), 155–60.

Loades, D. M. *Politics and the Nation, 1450–1660*. Glasgow: Collins/Fontana, 1974.

Loades, D. M. *The Oxford Martyrs*. London: R. T. Batsford, 1970.

Loades, D. M. *The Reign of Mary Tudor: Politics, Government, and Religion in England, 1553–1558*. London: Ernest Benn, 1979.

Loades, D. M. *Two Tudor Conspiracies*. Cambridge: Cambridge University Press, 1965.

Loades, David. 'Kingston, Sir Anthony (c. 1508–1556)'. *Oxford Dictionary of National Biography*. Oxford: Oxford University Press, 2004. Available from www.oxforddnb.com/view/article/15626. Accessed 29 March 2020.

Loades, David. 'Philip II and the government of England'. In Claire Cross, David Loades and J. J. Scarisbrick, eds. *Law and Government under the Tudors: Essays Presented to Sir Geoffrey Elton on his retirement*, 177–94. Cambridge: Cambridge University Press, 1988.

Loades, David. 'The English Church During the Reign of Mary'. In John Edwards and Ronald Truman, eds. *Reforming Catholicism in the England of Mary Tudor: The Achievement of Friar Bartolomé de Carranza*, 33–48. Aldershot: Ashgate, 2005.

Loades, David. 'The Reign of Mary Tudor: Historiography and Research'. *Albion: A Quarterly Journal Concerned with British Studies* 21, no. 4 (1989): 547–58.

Loades, David. 'Winter, Sir William (c.1525–1589)'. *Oxford Dictionary of National Biography*, Oxford: Oxford University Press, 2004. Available from http://www.oxforddnb.com/view/article/29769. Accessed 28 March 2020.

Loades, David. *Intrigue and Treason: The Tudor Court, 1547–1558*. Harlow: Pearson/Longman, 2004.

Loades, David. *Mary Tudor*. The Hill, Stroud: Amberley, 2011.

Loades, David. *Mary Tudor: A Life*. Oxford: Oxford University Press, 1989.

Loades, David. *The Religious Culture of Marian England*. London: Pickering & Chatto, 2010.

Longford, Elizabeth. *The Oxford Book of Royal Anecdotes*. Oxford: Oxford University Press, 1989.

Loomie, Albert J. *The Spanish Elizabethans: The English Exiles at the Court of Philip II*. New York: Fordham University Press, 1963.

López Martín, Juan. *La Iglesia de Almería y sus obispos*, vol. 2. Almería: Instituto de Estudios Almerienses, Caja Rural de Almería y Unicaja, 1999.

López Muñoz, Tomás. *La reforma en la Sevilla del XVI*, 2 vols. Seville: CIMPE/Eduforma, 2011.

MacCaffrey, Wallace T. *The Shaping of the Elizabethan Regime*. Princeton: Princeton University Press, 1968.

MacCulloch, Diarmaid. *Reformation: Europe's House Divided, 1490–1700*. London: Penguin Books, 2004.

MacCulloch, Diarmaid. *Thomas Cranmer: A Life*. New Haven and London: Yale University Press, 1996.

MacCulloch, Diarmaid. *Tudor Church Militant: Edward VI and the Protestant Reformation.* London: Allen Lane/The Penguin Press, 1999.

Macek, Ellen A. *The Loyal Opposition: Tudor Traditionalist Polemics, 1535–1558.* New York: Peter Lang, 1996.

Madden, Frederick. *Privy Purse Expenses of the Princess Mary, Daughter of King Henry the Eighth, Afterwards Queen Mary: with a Memoir of the Princess, and Notes.* London: William Pickering, 1831.

Maltby, W. S. *The Black Legend in England: the Development of anti-Spanish Sentiment, 1558–1660.* Durham, North Carolina: Duke University Press, 1971.

Maravall, José Antonio. *Las comunidades de Castilla: Una primera revolución moderna.* Madrid: Revista de Occidente, 1963.

Marshall, Peter. *Heretics and Believers: A History of the English Reformation.* New Haven and London: Yale University Press, 2017.

Marshall, Peter. *Reformation England, 1480–1642* [2003]. London: Bloomsbury Academic, 2012.

Marshall, Peter. *The Catholic Priesthood and the English Reformation.* Oxford: Clarendon Press, 1994.

Martin, J. W. 'The Marian Regime's Failure to Understand the Importance of Printing'. *Huntington Library Quarterly*, 44, no. 4 (1981): 231–47.

Martínez Millán, José, ed. *Carlos V y la quiebra del humanismo político en Europa (1530–1558)*, vol. 4. Madrid: Sociedad Estatal para la Conmemoración de los Centenarios de Felipe II y Carlos V, 2001.

Martínez, Miguel. *Comuneros. El rayo y la semilla (1520–1521).* Gijón: Hoja de Lata, 2021.

Martos Sánchez, Josep Lluís. 'Juan Martín Cordero en Flandes: Humanismo, mecenazgo e imprenta'. *Revista de Filología Española*, 95, no. 1 (2015): 75–96.

Matthews, P. G. 'Portraits of Philip II of Spain as King of England'. *The Burlington Magazine*, 142, no. 1162 (2000): 13–19.

Mayer, Thomas F. *Reginald Pole: Prince & Prophet.* Cambridge: Cambridge University Press, 2000.

Mayer, Thomas F., ed. *Reforming Reformation.* Farnham: Ashgate, 2012.

McConica, James. 'The Catholic Experience in Tudor Oxford'. in Thomas M. McCoog, ed. *The Reckoned Expense: Edmund Campion and the Early English Jesuits*, 39–63. Woodbridge: Boydell, 1996.

McCoog, Thomas M., ed. *The Reckoned Expense: Edmund Campion and the Early English Jesuits.* Woodbridge: Boydell, 1996.

McCoy, Richard. 'From the Tower to the Tiltyard: Robert Dudley's Return to Glory'. *The Historical Journal*, 27, no. 2 (1984): 425–35.

McDermott, James. *England and the Spanish Armada: The Necessary Quarrel.* New Haven and London: Yale University Press, 2005.

Menéndez Pelayo, Marcelino. *Historia de los heterodoxos españoles*, vol. 2. [1880–82]. Madrid: Biblioteca de Autores Cristianos, 1967.

Merritt, J. F. *The Social World of Early Modern Westminster: Abbey, Court and Community, 1525–1640*. Manchester: Manchester University Press, 2005.

Mignet, François. *Histoire de Marie Stuart*, vol. 1. Paris: Bonaventure et Ducessois, 1852.

Miller, Helen. 'George Harper (1503–1558)'. *History of Parliament Online*. Available from http://www.historyofparliamentonline.org/volume/1509-1558/member/harper-george-1503-58. Accessed 28 March 2020.

Mira Caballos, Esteban. *Las Antillas Mayores, 1492–1550. Ensayos y documentos*. Madrid: Iberoamericana-Vervuert, 2000.

Molas i Ribalta, Pere. 'La administración real en la Corona de Aragón'. *Chronica nova: Revista de historia moderna de la Universidad de Granada*, 21 (1993–1994): 427–40.

Moore, Helen. 'The Eastern Mediterranean in the English *Amadis* Cycle, Book v'. *The Yearbook of English Studies*, 41, no. 1 (2011): 113–25.

Moreno Martínez, Doris. *La invención de la Inquisición*. Madrid: Fundación Carolina. Centro de Estudios Hispánicos e Iberoamericanos, 2004.

Moreno, Doris. '*Cadena de oro para atraer a los herejes*. Argumentos de persuasión y estrategias de supervivencia en fray Juan de Villagarcía, O. P., discípulo de fray Bartolomé de Carranza'. *Hispania Sacra*, 65, no. 131 (2013): 29–71.

Morrill, John, ed. *The Oxford Illustrated History of Tudor and Stuart Britain*. Oxford: Oxford University Press, 1996.

Muller, Aislinn. *The Excommunication of Elizabeth I: Faith, Politics, and Resistance in Post-Reformation England, 1570–1603*. Leiden: Brill, 2020.

Murray, James. *Enforcing the English Reformation in Ireland: Clerical Resistance and Political Conflict in the Diocese of Dublin*. Cambridge: Cambridge University Press, 2009.

Neal, Daniel. *The History of the Puritans, or Protestant Nonconformists; from the Reformation in 1517 to the Revolution in 1688*, vol. 2. New York: Harper & Brothers, 1855.

Nieto Soria, José Manuel. 'La monarquía bajomedieval castellana. ¿Una realeza sagrada?'. In Universidad de Murcia, ed. *Homenaje al profesor Juan Torres Fontes*, 1225–37. Murcia: Universidad de Murcia/Academia Alfonso X el Sabio, 1987.

Nieto Soria, José Manuel. *Fundamentos ideológicos del poder real en Castilla (siglos XIII–XVI)*. Madrid: EUDEMA Universidad, 1988.

Nieto, José C. *El Renacimiento y la otra España. Visión cultural socioespiritual*. Geneva: Librairie Droz, 1997.

Numhauser, Paulina. 'El Real Patronato en Indias y la Compañía de Jesús durante el período filipino (1580–1640). Un análisis inicial'. *Boletín Americanista*, 67 (2013): 85–103.

O'Malley, John W. SJ. *Trent: What Happened at the Council*. Cambridge, Massachusetts and London: The Belknap Press of Harvard University Press, 2013.

Ochoa Brun, Miguel Ángel. *Historia de la diplomacia española*, vol. 5. Madrid: Ministerio de Asuntos Exteriores, 1999.

Ortega Costa, Milagros. *Proceso de la Inquisición contra María de Cazalla*. Madrid: Fundación Universitaria Española, 1978.

Pagden, Anthony. *Lords of all the World: Ideologies of Empire in Spain, Britain and France, c. 1500–c. 1800*. New Haven and London: Yale University Press, 1995.

Pallarés Méndez, María del Carmen and Ermelindo Portela Silva, *La reina Urraca*. San Sebastián: Editorial Nerea, 2006.

Panateri, Daniel. 'Las Siete Partidas: entropía, control y variación. Un itinerario histórico-político de su existencia'. *Conceptos Históricos*, 2, no. 2 (2016): 154–87.

Parker, Geoffrey. *Emperor: A New Life of Charles V*. New Haven and London: Yale University Press, 2019.

Parker, Geoffrey. *Felipe II. La biografía definitiva*. Translated by Victoria E. Gordo del Rey. Barcelona: Planeta, 2010.

Parker, Geoffrey. *Imprudent King: A New Life of Philip II*. New Haven and London: Yale University Press, 2014.

Parker, Geoffrey. *The Grand Strategy of Philip II*. New Haven and London: Yale University Press, 1998.

Pastore, Stefania. *Una herejía española. Conversos, alumbrados e Inquisición (1449–1559)*. Translated by Clara Álvarez Alonso [2004]. Madrid: Marcial Pons Historia, 2010.

Peardon, Barbara. 'The Politics of Polemic: John Ponet's *Short Treatise of Politic Power* and Contemporary Circumstance, 1553–1556'. *Journal of British Studies*, 22, no. 1 (1982): 35–49.

Pedraza Jiménez, Felipe B. and Rafael González Cañal, eds. *Con los pies en la tierra: Don Quijote en su marco geográfico e histórico: homenaje a José María Casasayas*. Cuenca: Universidad de Castilla-La Mancha, 2008.

Penny, Ralph and Richard Hitchcock, eds. *Actas del Primer Congreso Anglo-Hispano de 1992*, vol. 3. Madrid: Castalia, 1993.

Pérez Martín, María Jesús. *María Tudor. La gran reina desconocida*. Madrid: Rialp, 2008.

Pérez, Joseph. *La revolución de las Comunidades de Castilla (1520–1521)*. Translated by Juan José Faci Lacasta. Barcelona: Siglo XXI de España, 2005.

Pérez, Joseph. *Los comuneros*. Madrid: La Esfera de los Libros, 2001.

Pérez-Prendes Muñoz-Arraco, José Manuel. '*De regno*: Introducción jurídica'. *Interpretatio: revista de historia del derecho*, 10 (2004): 497–508.

Pettegree, Andrew. *Marian Protestantism: Six Studies*. Aldershot: Scholar Press, 1996.

Pinilla Pérez de Tudela, Regina. *Valencia y doña Germana: castigo de agermanados y problemas religiosos*. Valencia: Consell Valencià de Cultura, 1994.

Pogson, Rex. 'Revival and reform in Mary Tudor's church: A question of money'. *Journal of Ecclesiastical History*, 25 (1974): 249–65.

Pollard, A. F. *The History of England from the accession of Edward VI to the death of Elizabeth*. London: Longmans/Greens, 1910.

Porter, Linda. *Mary Tudor: The First Queen*. London: Piaktus, 2009.

Prescott, H. F. M. *Mary Tudor: The Spanish Tudor* [1940]. London: Phoenix, 2003.

Puente Brunke, José de la. *Encomienda y encomenderos en el Perú (estudio social y politico de una institución colonial)*. Seville: Diputación Provincial de Sevilla, 1992.

Redondo Álamo, Ángeles and Bartolomé Yun Casalilla. '«Bem visto tinha». Entre Lisboa y Capodimonte. La aristocracia castellana en perspectiva «trans-nacional» (ss. XVI–XVII). In Yun Casalilla, Bartolomé ed. *Las redes del Imperio. Élites sociales en la articulación de la Monarquía Hispánica, 1492–1714*, 39–64. Madrid: Marcial Pons Historia/Universidad Pablo de Olavide, 2009.

Redworth, Glyn. '¿Nuevo mundo u otro mundo?: conquistadores, cortesanos, libros de caballerías y el reinado de Felipe el Breve de Inglaterra'. In Ralph Penny and Richard Hitchcock, eds. *Actas del Primer Congreso Anglo-Hispano de 1992*, vol. 3, 113–25. Madrid: Castalia, 1993.

Redworth, Glyn. '"Matters Impertinent to Women": Male and Female Monarchy under Philip and Mary'. *English Historical Review*, 112, no. 447 (1997): 597–613.

Redworth, Glyn. 'Where Were the English? Antoon van den Wijngaerde, the Evidence of Visual Culture, and the 1557 Siege of Saint-Quentin'. In Ana Sáez-Hidalgo and Berta Cano-Echevarría, eds., *Exile, Diplomacy and Texts: Exchanges between Iberia and the British Isles, 1500–1767*, 15–31. Leiden: Brill, 2021.

Rex, Richard. *Henry VIII and the English Reformation*. Basingstoke and London: Macmillan, 1993.

Rex, Richard. *The Theology of John Fisher*. Cambridge: Cambridge University Press, 1991.

Reynolds, Matthew. *Godly Reformers and their Opponents in Early Modern England: Religion in Norwich, c.1560–1643*. Woodbridge: The Boydell Press, 2005.

Riba y García, Carlos. *El Consejo supremo de Aragón en el reinado de Felipe II*. Valencia: Tipografía Moderna for Miguel Gimeno, 1914.

Richards, Judith M. 'Mary Tudor as "Sole Quene"?: Gendering Tudor Monarchy'. *The Historical Journal*, 40, no. 4 (1997): 895–924.

Richards, Judith. 'Examples and Admonitions: What Mary Demonstrated for Elizabeth'. In Alice Hunt and Anna Whitelock, eds., *Tudor Queenship: The Reigns of Mary and Elizabeth*, 31–45. New York: Palgrave Macmillan, 2010.

Ridley, Jasper. *Elizabeth I*. London: Constable, 1987.

Rivero Rodríguez, Manuel. *La edad de oro de los virreyes. El virreinato en la Monarquía Hispánica durante los siglos XVI y XVII*. Madrid: Akal, 2011.

Robison, William B. 'The National and Local Significance of Wyatt's Rebellion in Surrey'. *The Historical Journal*, 30, no. 4 (1987): 769–90.

Rodríguez Besné, José Ramón. *El Consejo de la Suprema Inquisición. Perfil jurídico de una institución*. Madrid: Editorial Complutense, 2000.

Rodríguez, Pedro. *El Catecismo Romano ante Felipe II y la Inquisición española*. Madrid: Rialp, 1998.

Rodríguez-Salgado, M. J. 'Suárez de Figueroa [Dormer], Jane, duchess of Feria in the Spanish nobility (1538–1612)'. *Oxford Dictionary of National Biography*. Oxford: Oxford University Press, 2004. Available from http://www.oxforddnb.com/view/article/7836. Accessed 26 April 2020.

Rodríguez-Salgado, M. J. *The Changing Face of Empire: Charles V, Philip II and Habsburg Authority, 1551–1559*. Cambridge: Cambridge University Press, 1988.

Rossi, Sergio. 'Un «italianista» nel Cinquecento inglese: William Thomas'. *Aevum*, 40 (1966): 281–314.

Rucquoi, Adeline. 'Auctoritas, Potestas: Concepts of Power in Medieval Spain'. In Flocel Sabaté, ed. *Ideology in the Middle Ages: Approaches from Southwestern Europe*, 51–72. Leeds: Arc Humanities Press, 2019.

Ruiz Martín, Felipe ed. *La Monarquía de Felipe II*. Madrid: Real Academia de la Historia, 2003.

Ruiz, Teófilo F. 'Une royauté sans sacre: la monarchie castillane du Bas Moyen Age'. *Annales. Histoire, Sciences Sociales*, 3 (1984), 429–53.

Ruiz, Teófilo F. *From Heaven to Earth: The Reordering of Castilian Society, 1150–1350*. Princeton: Princeton University Press, 2004.

Russell, Conrad. *The Crisis of Parliaments: English History, 1509–1660*. London and New York: Oxford University Press, 1971.

Russell, Elizabeth. 'Marian Oxford and the Counter-Reformation'. In Caroline M. Barron and Christopher Harper-Bill, eds. *The Church in pre-Reformation Society: Essays in Honour of F. R. H. Du Boulay*, 212–17. Woodbridge: The Boydell Press, 1985.

Sabaté, Flocel, ed. *Ideology in the Middle Ages: Approaches from Southwestern Europe*. Leeds: Arc Humanities Press, 2019.

Sáez-Hidalgo, Ana and Berta Cano-Echevarría, eds. *Exile, Diplomacy and Texts: Exchanges between Iberia and the British Isles, 1500–1767*. Leiden: Brill, 2021.

Samson, Alexander Winton Seton. 'The Marriage of Philip of Habsburg and Mary Tudor and Anti-Spanish Sentiment in England: Political Economies and Culture, 1553–1557'. PhD thesis, Queen Mary and Westfield College, unpublished, 1999.

Samson, Alexander. 'Culture under Mary I and Philip'. In Sarah Duncan and Valerie Schutte, eds. *The Birth of a Queen: Essays on the Quincentenary of Mary I*, 155–78. New York: Palgrave Macmillan, 2016.

Samson, Alexander. 'Power Sharing: The Co-Monarchy of Philip and Mary'. In Alice Hunt and Anna Whitelock, eds. *Tudor Queenship: The Reigns of Mary and Elizabeth*, 159–72. New York: Palgrave Macmillan, 2010.

Samson, Alexander. *Mary and Philip: The Marriage of Tudor England and Habsburg Spain*. Manchester: Manchester University Press, 2020.

San Miguel y Valledor, Evaristo. *Historia de Felipe II, rey de España*, vol. 1. Madrid: Ignacio Boix, 1844.

Sanchez, Mark G. 'Anti-Spanish sentiment in English literary and political writing 1553–1603'. PhD thesis, University of Leeds, unpublished, 2004.

Sánchez Prieto, Ana Belén. 'La intitulación diplomática de los Reyes Católicos: un programa político y una lección de historia', in Juan Carlos Galende Díaz, ed., *III Jornadas Científicas sobre Documentación de la época de los Reyes Católicos*, 273–301. Madrid: Universidad Complutense de Madrid, 2004.

Sánchez-Lauro, Sixto. 'Itinerario vital y doctrinal de Domingo de Soto: implicación político-social desde la ortodoxia'. *Revista europea de historia de las ideas políticas y de las instituciones públicas*, 1, no. 2 (2011): 113–36.

Sanz Camañes, Porfirio. *Los ecos de la Armada: España, Inglaterra y la estabilidad del Norte (1585–1660)*. Madrid: Sílex, 2012.

Sarrión Mora, Adelina. *Beatas y endemoniadas: Mujeres heterodoxas ante la Inquisición, siglos XVI a XIX*. Madrid: Alianza Editorial, 2003.

Scard, Margaret. *Tudor Survivor: The Life and Times of William Paulet*. Stroud: The History Press, 2011.

Screech, M. A. *Erasmus: Ecstasy and The Praise of Folly*. London: Duckworth, 1980.

Serrano de Menchén, Pilar. 'Don Antonio de Toledo, gran prior de San Juan y don Francisco de Valencia, caballero de la misma orden, valedores en la liberación de Cervantes del cautiverio de Argel'. In Seton-Watson, R. W., ed. *Tudor Studies Presented by the Board of Studies in History in the University of London to Albert Frederick Pollard: Being the Work of Twelve of His Colleagues and Pupils*. London: Longmans, Green & Co, 1924.

Sharpe, Kevin and Steven Zwicker, eds. *Writing Lives: Biography and Textuality, Identity and Representation in Early Modern England*. Oxford: Oxford University Press, 2008.

Skidmore, Chris. *Edward VI: The Lost King of England*. London: Phoenix, 2007.

Skinner, Quentin. *The Foundations of Modern Political Thought*, 2 vols. Cambridge: Cambridge University Press, 1978.

Smith, Frederick E. 'Reinventing the Counter-Reformation in Marian England'. *The Historical Journal*, 64, no. 4 (2021): 1105–27.

Soares da Cunha, Mafalda. 'Títulos portugueses y matrimonios mixtos en la Monarquía Católica'. In Yun Casalilla, Bartolomé ed. *Las redes del Imperio. Élites sociales en la articulación de la Monarquía Hispánica, 1492–1714*, 205–32. Madrid: Marcial Pons Historia/Universidad Pablo de Olavide, 2009.

Solís de los Santos, José. 'Relaciones de sucesos de Inglaterra en el reinado de Carlos V'. in Manuel F. Fernández, Carlos Alberto González and Natalia Maillard, eds. *Testigo del tiempo, memoria del unvierso. Cultura escrita y sociedad en el mundo ibérico (siglos XV–XVIII)*, 640–98. Málaga: Ediciones Rubeo, 2009.

Stone, J. M. *Mary I, Queen of England. As Found in the Public Records, Despatches of Ambassadors in Original Private Letters, and Other Contemporary Documents.* London: Sands & Co., 1901.

Strayer, Joseph. *On the Medieval Origins of the Modern State.* Princeton: Princeton Univerisy Press, 1970.

Streckfuss, Corinna. '"Spes maxima nostra": European Propaganda and the Spanish Match'. In Alice Hunt and Anna Whitelock, eds. *Tudor Queenship: The Reigns of Mary and Elizabeth*, 145–57. New York: Palgrave Macmillan, 2010.

Streckfuss, Corinna. 'England's Reconciliation with Rome: A News Event in Early Modern Europe'. *Historical Research*, 82, no. 215 (2009): 62–73.

Strickland, Agnes. *Lives of the Queens of England, from the Norman Conquest; with Anecdotes of Their Courts, Now First Published from Official Records and other Authentic Documents, Private as Well as Public*, vol. 5. London: Henry Colburn, 1842.

Suárez, Luis. *Isabel I, Reina.* Barcelona: Ariel, 2010.

Taylor, Barry and Alejandro Coroleu Lletget, eds. *Latin and Vernacular in Renaissance Iberia II: Translations and Adaptations.* Manchester: Manchester University Press, 2006.

Taylor, James D. *Sir Thomas Wyatt the Younger, c. 1521–1554 and Wyatt's Rebellion.* New York: Algora Publishing, 2013.

Tellechea Idígoras, J. Ignacio. *Fray Bartolomé Carranza y el Cardenal Pole. Un navarro en la restauración católica de Inglaterra (1554–1558).* Pamplona: Diputación Foral de Navarra/Institución Príncipe de Viana/Consejo Superior de Investigaciones Científicas, 1977.

Tellechea Idígoras, José Ignacio. 'Bartolomé Carranza en Flandes. El clima religioso en los Países Bajos (1557–1558)'. In Erwin Iserloh and Konrad Regpen, eds. *Reformata Reformanda: Festgabe fur Hubert Jedin zum 17. Juni 1965*, vol. 2, 317–43. Münster: Verlag Aschendorff, 1965.

Tellechea Idígoras, José Ignacio. 'Bartolomé de Las Casas y Bartolomé Carranza. Una página amistosa olvidada'. *Scriptorium victoriense*, 6, no. 1 (1959): 7–34.

Tellechea Idígoras, José Ignacio. 'El formulario de visita pastoral de fray Bartolomé de Carranza, Arzobispo de Toledo'. *Anthologica Annua*, 4 (1946): 385–437.

Tellechea Idígoras, José Ignacio. 'Fray Bartolomé Carranza: a Spanish Dominican in the England of Mary Tudor'. In John Edwards and Ronald Truman, eds. *Reforming Catholicism in the England of Mary Tudor: The Achievement of Friar Bartolomé de Carranza*, 21–31. Aldershot: Ashgate, 2005.

Tellechea Idígoras, José Ignacio. 'Lo que el Emperador no supo. Proceso de Paulo IV a Carlos V y Felipe II'. In José Martínez Millán, ed. *Carlos V y la quiebra del humanismo político en Europa (1530–1558)*, vol. 4, 181–96. Madrid: Sociedad Estatal para la Conmemoración de los Centenarios de Felipe II y Carlos V, 2001.

Tellechea Idígoras, José Ignacio. *Bartolome Carranza, Arzobispo Prelado evangélico en la silla de Toledo (1557–1558): Discurso inaugural del año académico 1958–1959 en el Seminario de San Sebastián*. San Sebastián: Izarra, 1958.

Tellechea Idígoras, José Ignacio. *El proceso romano del Arzobispo Carranza (1567–1576)*. Rome: Iglesia Nacional Española, 1988.

Tellechea Idígoras, José Ignacio. *Fray Bartolomé Carranza de Miranda (Investigaciones históricas)*. Pamplona: Gobierno de Navarra/Departamento de Educación y Cultura, 2002.

Thorp, Malcolm R. 'Religion and the Wyatt Rebellion of 1554'. *American Society of Church History*, 47, no. 4 (1978): 363–80.

Tittler, Robert. *The Reign of Mary I*. London: Longman, 1983.

Torres de Castilla, Alfonso (pseudonym of Fernando Garrido Tortosa). *Historia de las persecuciones políticas y religiosas, ocurridas en Europa desde la Edad Media hasta nuestros días*, vol. 4. Barcelona: Salvador Manero, 1865.

Tytler, Patrick Fraser. *England under the Reigns of Edward VI, and Mary, with the Contemporary History of Europe, Illustrated in a Series of Original Letters Never Before Printed. With Historical Introductions and Biographical and Critical Notes*, vol. 1. London: Richard Bentley, 1839.

Universidad de Murcia, ed. *Homenaje al profesor Juan Torres Fonte*. Murcia: Universidad de Murcia/Academia Alfonso X el Sabio, 1987.

Valdeón Baruque, Julio. 'Alfonso X y el Imperio'. *Alcanate: Revista de estudios Alfonsíes*, 4 (2004–5): 243–55.

Van Gelderen, Martin. *The Political Thought of the Dutch Revolt*. Cambridge: Cambridge University Press, 1992.

Velasco Berenguer, Gonzalo. 'Reigning in the Highest Places: The Excommunication of Queen Elizabeth I in Its Roman and Spanish Contexts'. *Sixteenth Century Journal*, 51, no. 3 (2020): 763–90.

Velasco Berenguer, Gonzalo. 'The Select Council of Philip I: A Spanish Institution in Tudor England (1555–1558)'. *The English Historical Review*, forthcoming.

Villacorta Baños, Antonio. *La jesuita: Juana de Austria*. Barcelona: Ariel, 2005.

Virgoe, Roger. 'Sir Edward Rogers (1498/1502–1568), of Cannington, Som'. *History of Parliament Online*. Available from http://www.historyofparliamentonline.org/volume/1509-1558/member/rogers-sir-edward-14981502-68. Accessed 28 March 2020.

Viso, Alberto, 'Historiografía reciente sobre el reinado de María Tudor', *Espacio, Tiempo y Forma*, 27 (2014), 327–51.

Waller, Maureen. *Sovereign Ladies: The Six Reigning Queens of England*. New York: John Murray, 2006.

Warton, Thomas. *The Life of Sir Thomas Pope, Founder of Trinity College Oxford* [1772]. London: Thomas Cadell, 1780.

Weikel, Ann. 'The Marian Council Revisited'. In Jennifer Loach and Robert Tittler, eds. *The Mid-Tudor Polity, c. 1540–1560*, 52–73. London: Macmillan, 1980.

Weir, Alison. *Children of England: The Heirs of King Henry VIII, 1547–1558*. London: Jonathan Cape, 1996.

White, Beatrice. *Mary Tudor*. London: Macmillan, 1935.

Whitelock, Anna and Diarmaid MacCulloch. 'Princess Mary's Household and the Succession Crisis, July 1553'. *The Historical Journal*, 50, no. 2 (2007): 265–87.

Whitelock, Anna. *Mary Tudor: England's First Queen*. London: Bloomsbury, 2009.

Willen, Diane. 'Lord Russell and the Western Counties, 1539–1555'. *Journal of British Studies*, 15, no. 1 (1975): 26–45.

Wizeman, William, SJ. 'The Religious Policy of Mary I'. In Susan Doran and Thomas S. Freeman, eds., *Mary Tudor: Old and New Perspectives*, 153–70. New York: Palgrave Macmillan, 2011.

Wizeman, William, SJ. *The Theology and Spirituality of Mary Tudor's Church*. Aldershot and Burlington: Ashgate, 2006.

Wooding, Lucy E. C. *Rethinking Catholicism in Reformation England*. Oxford: Oxford University Press, 2000.

Woudhuysen, H. R. 'Sidney, Sir Philip (1554–1586)'. *Oxford Dictionary of National Biography*. Oxford: Oxford University Press, 2004. Available from https://www.oxforddnb.com/view/10.1093/ref:odnb/9780198614128.001.0001/odnb-9780198614128-e-25522?rskey=cXn9OY&result=3. Accessed 24 March 2021.

Yates, Frances A. *Astraea: The Imperial Theme in the Sixteenth Century*. London and Boston: Routledge and Kegan Paul, 1975.

Yun Casalilla, Bartolomé ed. *Las redes del Imperio. Élites sociales en la articulación de la Monarquía Hispánica, 1492–1714*. Madrid: Marcial Pons Historia/Universidad Pablo de Olavide, 2009.

Zavala, Silvio A. *La encomienda indiana*. Madrid: Centro de Estudios Históricos, 1935.

Index